CAMBRIDGE LIBRARY COLLECTION

Books of enduring scholarly value

Literary studies

This series provides a high-quality selection of early printings of literary works, textual editions, anthologies and literary criticism which are of lasting scholarly interest. Ranging from Old English to Shakespeare to early twentieth-century work from around the world, these books offer a valuable resource for scholars in reception history, textual editing, and literary studies.

The Works of John Ruskin

The influence of John Ruskin (1819–1900), both on his own time and on artistic and social developments in the twentieth century, cannot be over-stated. He changed Victorian perceptions of art, and was the main influence behind 'Gothic revival' architecture. As a social critic, he argued for the improvement of the condition of the poor, and against the increasing mechanisation of work in factories, which he believed was dull and soul-destroying. The thirty-nine volumes of the Library Edition of his works, published between 1903 and 1912, are themselves a remarkable achievement, in which his books and essays – almost all highly illustrated – are given a biographical and critical context in extended introductory essays and in the 'Minor Ruskiniana' – extracts from letters, articles and reminiscences both by and about Ruskin. This twelfth volume contains Ruskin's lectures on architecture and painting.

D1213850

Cambridge University Press has long been a pioneer in the reissuing of out-of-print titles from its own backlist, producing digital reprints of books that are still sought after by scholars and students but could not be reprinted economically using traditional technology. The Cambridge Library Collection extends this activity to a wider range of books which are still of importance to researchers and professionals, either for the source material they contain, or as landmarks in the history of their academic discipline.

Drawing from the world-renowned collections in the Cambridge University Library, and guided by the advice of experts in each subject area, Cambridge University Press is using state-of-the-art scanning machines in its own Printing House to capture the content of each book selected for inclusion. The files are processed to give a consistently clear, crisp image, and the books finished to the high quality standard for which the Press is recognised around the world. The latest print-on-demand technology ensures that the books will remain available indefinitely, and that orders for single or multiple copies can quickly be supplied.

The Cambridge Library Collection will bring back to life books of enduring scholarly value (including out-of-copyright works originally issued by other publishers) across a wide range of disciplines in the humanities and social sciences and in science and technology.

The Works of
John Ruskin

Volume 12: Lectures on Architecture and Painting

John Ruskin
Edited by Edward Tyas Cook
and Alexander Wedderburn

CAMBRIDGE
UNIVERSITY PRESS

CAMBRIDGE UNIVERSITY PRESS

Cambridge, New York, Melbourne, Madrid, Cape Town, Singapore,
São Paolo, Delhi, Dubai, Tokyo

Published in the United States of America by Cambridge University Press, New York

www.cambridge.org
Information on this title: www.cambridge.org/9781108008600

© in this compilation Cambridge University Press 2010

This edition first published 1903
This digitally printed version 2010

ISBN 978-1-108-00860-0 Paperback

Additional resources for this publication at www.cambridge.org/9781108008600

THE COMPLETE
WORKS OF
JOHN RUSKIN

Two thousand and sixty-two copies of this edition—of which two thousand are for sale in England and America—have been printed at the Ballantyne Press, Edinburgh, and the type has been distributed.

J.E. Millais.

Allen & Co.Sc.

John Ruskin, 1853.

(From the picture in the possession of Rear-Admiral Sir William A.Dyke Acland, Bart.)

MINOR RUSKINIANA : *Continued :—*

comparison and contrast which Ruskin drew at the time between Millais and Turner: see *Pre-Raphaelitism*, §§ 21–24. Ruskin perhaps wished to settle the points at variance by convincing Millais that he was a Turnerian without knowing it.[1] Millais did not go to Switzerland in 1851; the Ruskins were accompanied, as we have seen, by other friends.[2] During 1852 Ruskin was hard at work, and so was Millais also, but by the middle of 1853 both were in need of a holiday, and Ruskin renewed his proposal for a joint expedition. He had, as many a passage in this volume will show, a profound admiration for Millais's genius, and a firm belief in the great works it might accomplish. He was essentially a missionary and a preacher. As was the case with Rossetti a year or two later, so with Millais; he wanted to keep his eye, as it were, on the young artist, to mould the ripening genius into accord with his own ideals, to instruct him in the way he should go.

The holiday party consisted of five persons: Ruskin and his wife, Miss M'Kenzie, who was a friend of the latter, Millais and his brother. They went first to Wallington, on a visit to Ruskin's friends, Sir Walter and Lady Trevelyan. This was his first visit to a house where he was often afterwards to stay. Ruskin in after years had "no memory, and no notion when he first *saw* Pauline, Lady Trevelyan;"[3] already in 1851 they were fast friends. "I enclose a letter for Lady Trevelyan," he writes to his father from Venice (Sept. 22, 1851), "which after reading please seal and send. Her letter is enclosed also, which I am sure you will like—you will see she is clever; if you knew how good and useful she was also, you would be flattered by her signature to me—'your own dutiful and affectionate scholar.'" His first impressions of Lady Trevelyan's home were recorded in the usual letters to his father:—

"WALLINGTON, 23 *June*, 1853.—This is the most beautiful place possible—a large old seventeenth-century stone house in an old English terraced garden, beautifully kept, all the hawthorns still in full blossom; terrace opening on a sloping, wild park, down to the brook, about the half a mile fair slope; and woods on the other side, and undulating country with a peculiar *Northumberlandishness* about it—a faraway look which Millais enjoys intensely. We are all very happy, and going this afternoon over the moors to a little tarn where the sea-gulls come to breed."

[1] But see further on this subject, p. li., below.
[2] See Vol. X. p. xxiii.
[3] *Præterita,* ii. ch. xii. § 226.

And later, after he had left:—

> "BRIG OF TURK, 5 *July* [1853].—. . . The pleasantness of these people
> consists in very different qualities: in Lady Trevelyan in her wit and
> playfulness, together with very profound feeling; in Sir Walter in
> general kindness, accurate information on almost every subject, and
> the tone of mind resulting from a steady effort to do as much good
> as he can to the people on a large estate, I suppose not less than
> twenty square miles of field and moor. He has a museum at the
> top of the house containing a very valuable collection of minerals,
> birds, and shells, which was very delightful to me, as the days were
> generally wet."

It was at Wallington also that Ruskin first met a man who became
one of his dearest friends, Dr. John Brown.[1]   On the same occasion he visited Sir John Swinburne at Capheaton in order to see his
Turners.

After a stay of some days at Wallington, the party set out for the
Trossachs, travelling by stage-coaches.   They took the journey leisurely,
and visited many picturesque romantic places on the way, such as
Melrose, Stirling, and Dunblane.   Ruskin used his sketches at the latter
place to illustrate his lectures, and wrote enthusiastically of it to his
father:—

> "DOUNE [2 *July*, 1853].—We have just dined at Stirling; drove
> on to Dunblane and saw the most lovely abbey there—far the finest
> thing I have seen in Scotland. . . . Dunblane is exquisitely beautiful
> in its simplicity: grand concentric arches, and the oval window in
> the centre of the west end set with two leaves alternately sloping
> as in the margin [sketch], and the proportion of the whole quite
> heavenly.[2]   It is a lovely afternoon, and William Millais is half
> beside himself with delight, and all of us very happy."

At Callander the two brothers found apartments in the New Trossachs
Hotel, but took most of their meals with the Ruskins, who were accommodated in the schoolmaster's house, at Brig o' Turk, a few hundred yards
away.   "We are in a Highland cottage," Ruskin wrote to his parents,
July 13, "just under Ben Ledi, established in the most delightful way
possible, and you could be within four hundred yards of us, in a clean
and comfortable inn.   I wish you would come."   The Highland scenery,
however, by no means satisfied him:—

---

[1] See *Præterita*, ii. § 227.
[2] This is the window shown in Plate IV., and described in the text, p. 31.

"Scotland," he writes (July 17), "is immeasurably inferior to Switzerland in her sponginess. The hills here are *never* dry; in places here and there, yes, but never for more than a hundred square yards; it is always squash, splash, plash, at every little indentation where morass can form itself."

And so again in a letter (August 28) referring to Chamouni :—

"There is nothing like it; there is no sensation of mountains here which in the least degree is comparable to or connectable with it. I don't care the least for the hills here; they are totally without effect upon me. I like the heather and rocks and little lapping pools of lakes, but there is always a sense of smallness and desolation, comfortless diminutiveness, which I cannot get over. Switzerland is so rich as well as so vast, so warm in its majesty, so homely and happy in its sublimity; I never expect to see anything to come near it on the face of the earth."

But in the end the scenery around Glenfinlas conquered him :—

"*October 23.*—I am sorry to leave this place. I have grown fonder and fonder of it; the hills seem more beautiful than ever. I was in fact over-tired when I came down, in mind. I find even scenery and other objects, which are quite the mind's medicine, are not properly enjoyed till it *is* medicined. I felt the gloom of the wild moorland country oppressive at first; now I begin to look on it with the childish feeling of delight again that I used to have in crossing Shap fells with you and mama in the post-chaise from Kendal. What *intense* happiness that was! This Scotch scenery has always a powerful effect on me from its association with my strong childish feeling at Glenfarg, and the hills of Moncrieff, never to be forgotten. There is a hill just above the place where Millais is painting me, with pines on it, always putting me in mind of my baby verses :

'Those trees stand firm upon the rock,
    And seem as if they all did lock
    Into each other. Tall they stand,
    Towering above the whitened land.'[1]

---

[1] The lines are from the "Poetry Discriptive" of 1827 to 1829 (see Vol. II. p. 530). The piece, which is headed "Wales," consists of nine lines, and is as follows :—

"That rock with waving billows on its side,
    That hill with beauteous forests on its top,
    That stream that with its rippling waves doth glide,
    And oh, what beauties has that mountain got ;
    That rock stands high against the sky,
    Those trees," etc.

I recollect you and my mother wondering why I didn't say *darkened* land. I suppose I meant the rocks looked whiter by contrast with the pines—a very artistical observation for a child."

For the cottage, too, Ruskin had conceived a great affection :—

> "*October* 9.—We shall be very sorry to leave our cottage, and I shall especially regret a grassy walk, some twenty yards long, which I walk up and down whenever I want exercise, without going far from home ; but it is very beautiful, with a few clusters of brambles twining among the rocks at the side of it, and itself quite smooth sward, a group of ash-trees at the bottom overhanging a rocky stream, and the open hills above it."

They were a merry party, and in spite of constant rain the days passed cheerily. "Both Millais and I," wrote Ruskin to Miss Mitford (August 17), "came down here to rest; he having painted, and I corrected press, quite as much as was good for either of us; but he is painting a little among the rocks, and I am making some drawings which may be useful to me; and when either of us are tired we go and build bridges over the stream, or piers into the lake, or engage in the more laborious and scientific operation of digging a canal to change the course of the stream, where it is encroaching on the meadows." "I had a long letter to-day," wrote Miss Mitford to a friend, "from John Ruskin, who is in the Highlands with two young friends—the Pre-Raphaelite painter and his brother, and his own beautiful wife. They are living in a hut on the borders of Loch Achray, playing at cottagers, as rich people like to do." Millais was in the same holiday mood. "This year," he wrote to Mr. Combe, "I am giving myself a holiday, as I have worked five years hard. . . . Ruskin comes and works with us, and we dine on the rocks all together. . . . We have in fine weather immense enjoyment painting out on the rocks, and having our dinner brought to us there, and in the evening climbing up the steep mountains for exercise, Mrs. Ruskin accompanying us." Among other pursuits Millais was able to indulge his passion for fishing, and Ruskin sent some of the spoils to Denmark Hill :—

> "I am so very glad," he writes (September 21), "the salmon came well and tasted well. I don't like any *killing* sports, but there was great interest in seeing the fish brought up through the dark water, looking like a serpent at the end of a lance, and thrust into the shallow current among the rocks, his scales flashing through the amber water and white foam."

On wet days and in the evenings there were discussions on art or Scottish history. Millais would make fun of the old masters, or draw sketches for a comic history of Scotland. Several of his sketches are given in the Life of him by his son. One of them shows a game of battledore and shuttlecock; Ruskin does not figure in it, but Dr. Acland, who was on a visit to Ruskin, is taking a hand. Of the party in a more serious mood, we get a glimpse in letters from Dr. Acland. He was impressed by the intensity of Millais. "The point is in his work, and not in his words. He is a man with powers and perception granted to very few; not more imagination, not more feeling, but a finer feeling and more intuitive and instantaneous imagination than other men. Of this his nonsense affords the most striking proof." On Ruskin, Millais had made the same impression:—

> "Millais is a very interesting study," he writes to his father (July 24), "but I don't know how to manage him; his mind is so *terribly* active, so full of invention that he can hardly stay quiet a moment without sketching either ideas or reminiscences; and keeps himself awake all night with planning pictures. He cannot go on this way; I must get Acland to lecture him."

By Ruskin's own earnestness and enthusiasm Acland was profoundly struck. "Ruskin," he writes, "has knocked off my sketching for ever, having quite convinced me that the paltry drawings I have been in the habit of doing are most injurious to the doer in his moral nature. What I can try to do is to draw something really well. I hope to be well enough to try to-morrow a bit of rock and water." And again: "Ruskin I understand more than I have before; truth and earnestness of purpose are his great guides, and no labour of thought or work is wearisome to him;" and again, "I ought to say, as a key to Ruskin, I had no idea of the intensity of his religious feeling before now."[1]

Though both Ruskin and Millais went to Scotland for relaxation, they stayed to work. Millais's principal work was the portrait of Ruskin, which is reproduced as frontispiece to this volume. It was at Acland's suggestion that this portrait of Ruskin standing on the rocks, with the torrent thundering beside him, was undertaken. Ruskin was rejoiced, seeing in this work the promise of such

---

[1] *Sir Henry Wentworth Acland, Bart., K.C.B., F.R.S.: A Memoir*, by J. B. Atlay, 1903, pp. 173–174.

a loving and faithful study of wild nature as had never yet been accomplished :—

> "Millais," he writes (July 6), "has fixed on his place, a lovely piece of worn rock, with foaming water and weeds and moss, and a noble overhanging bank of dark crag; and I am to be standing looking quietly down the stream; just the sort of thing I used to do for hours together. He is very happy at the idea of doing it, and I think you will be proud of the picture, and we shall have the two most wonderful torrents in the world, Turner's 'St. Gothard' and Millais' 'Glenfinlas.' He is going to take the utmost possible pains with it, and says he can paint rocks and water better than anything else. I am sure the foam of the torrent will be something quite new in art."

In a similar strain is a letter to Dr. Furnivall :—

"GLENFINLAS, *October 16th.*

"MY DEAR FURNIVALL,—I have been living so idle a life for the last month or two that the laziness has become quite inveterate, and I can't so much as write you a letter—except to answer your kind questions.

"We have been since *5th July* living in this kind of house, with a little garden, about eighteen feet long by ten wide, sloping down the bank in front, and part of Ben Ledi sloping up (among the writing) behind.[1] A bog in front—a wonderful rocky dingle in the distance at A—where Millais is painting a picture of a torrent among rocks, which will make a revolution in landscape painting if he can only get it finished. It is not nearly done yet, and the cold is coming fast.

"I am to lecture at Edinburgh, *1st November* to *11th.* I hope to be home before Christmas, but shall linger on the road, though it is too late to Turner-hunt. I have stopped all this time to keep Millais company—to keep him up to the Pre-Raphaelite degree of finish—which I have done with a vengeance, as he has taken three months to do half a background two feet over, and perhaps won't finish it now. But I have got maps of all the lichens on the rocks, and the *bubbles* painted in the foam.

"I am glad you like my education bit [2]—but before you give all the people a share in the government, hadn't you better make

[1] See the *facsimile* of a portion of this letter, containing Ruskin's slight pen sketch of the house.

[2] This refers to Appendix 7 ("Modern Education") in the third volume of *The Stones of Venice*, then just issued.

FACSIMILE OF A PAGE OF RUSKIN'S LETTER TO DR. FURNIVALL, FROM GLENFINLAS, OCTOBER 16, 1853

p. xxiv

them all lawyers and physicians? It is much easier to write out deeds, and raise difficulties about them—and to make pills, and prescribe them—than to govern a country.

> " Effie's best regards,
>
> " Ever affectionately yours,
>
> " J. Ruskin." [1]

Ruskin's diary is also full of Millais's picture :—

> " Glenfinlas, *July* 20, 1853.—Yesterday drawing on the rocks by the stream; Everett ill with headache. The skies all turquoise and violet, and melted in dew, and heavenly bars of delicate cloud behind Ben Venue in evening.
>
> " Millais's picture of Glenfinlas was begun on Wednesday; outlined at once, Henry Acland holding the canvas, and a piece laid in that afternoon. None done on Thursday—about an hour's work on Friday."

Then Ruskin keeps a sort of time-table of the number of hours' work put into the picture each week—in the first week, four days of from 11 or 12 to 5 or 6; next week, three days 11–5, two 4–7; third week, four days 1–5; one 4–7; fourth week, three days 12–6; fifth week, three days, "a good forenoon"; sixth week, a "good three hours," on four days; seventh week, "good days, about three hours each"; eighth week, only two "good days"; ninth, three "good forenoons"; on two other days, an hour each; the tenth and last week recorded showed three "excellent days." The portrait was not completed till the following winter, for on January 12 and 19, 1854, there are entries in Ruskin's diary of sittings to Millais.

During the progress of the work in Scotland Ruskin sometimes very literally stood over Millais, and an entry in the diary shows us what thoughts we may read in his eyes as he stands contemplatively in the picture :—

> " *August* 2.—Out with Millais at six, holding the umbrella over him as he worked, and watching the stream, looking down it, due south; the sun of course on my left. It is curious how unconscious the eye is of colour, under any circumstances which render the forms to which it belongs altogether vague. Thus if we stand by a Highland stream in sunlight, we shall probably at first be struck merely by its marked gradations of one colour, from the pale golden where it glides in shallow ripples over the white pebbles, deepening

---

[1] This is Letter V. in a volume (privately printed in 1897) of *Letters from John Ruskin to Frederick J. Furnivall*, edited by T. J. Wise. The word "sloping" is there (p. 16) misprinted "slipping."

gradually into clear, glowing brown—into the black space of eddying
pool, streaked with foam. But presently, as we look more carefully,
we shall see there is a cold and gloomy colour mingled among this
golden brown (which we shall feel has a strange power in giving
the stream its . . . .[1])—at least we shall think it gloomy in contrast
with the gold—but when we examine it carefully, we shall find it is
reflection of pure blue sky, deepened and dulled a little by the
brown of the water, but still visibly and sweetly blue, and in
reality of infinite beauty as it breaks among the brown waves.
Looking a little longer, we shall find that the deep brown, which
at first we thought was one colour, owes its appearance of lustre
to the mingling of two; and on watching these, we shall find that
instead of brown, one half of this part of the water is deep green—
being the reflection of the trees on the bank, and the rest a brown
which in its various gradations expresses all the shadows and lights
of the rocks on the bank, and that there *is no blackness* without
such a reflection. Finally, we shall find part of the water in a kind
of light which quite keeps us from seeing the bottom even in shallow
places, or white playing unintelligible light, which will puzzle us
at first considerably, but at last we shall find it to be the reflection
of pieces of white cloud."

Ruskin himself made many drawings at Glenfinlas, one of which is
here given as a companion to the picture of Millais, done at the same
time and place. But his chief work at this time was the preparation
of the lectures to be given under the auspices of the Philosophical
Institution at Edinburgh, in the autumn, on Architecture and Painting.
The suggestion that he should give these lectures came from his friend
J. F. Lewis, the painter, and it pleased him—both as a sign that his
work was beginning to make an impression, and as an opportunity
for widening his circle of influence. But his father and mother did
not like the idea. They seem to have thought that there was something
derogatory in appearing on a platform as a public lecturer; or perhaps,
though they put it in that way, they were afraid of their son over-
straining his powers; and Ruskin's father, who was already beginning
to wonder whether *Modern Painters* would ever be resumed and finished,
saw in this new departure a fresh danger of dissipation of energies. In
his replies to such remonstrances, Ruskin tried to reassure his parents on
all points:—

"(*August* 18.)—I do not mean at *any* time to take up the trade
of a lecturer; all my real efforts will be made in writing, and all
that I intend to do is merely, as if in conversation, to say to these

[1] The space here is left blank in the MS. diary.

I

J.Ruskin.   W.L.Colls.

Gneiss rock: Glenfinlas;
1853

people, who are ready to listen to me, some of the simple truths about architecture and painting which may perhaps be better put in conversational than literary form. I shall however write the lectures first that I may be sure of what I have to say, and send them you to look over."

"(*August* 19.)— . . . I cannot now get off without a great fuss, as I have sent a synopsis of the four lectures to be regularly printed with the others published at the commencement of the season. I rather liked the idea of giving my first lecture in your native city; and therefore met the request more immediately and unhesitatingly than I should have done had it come from any other quarter; besides that, I have many friends and admirers in Edinburgh, and am in some respects far better understood there than in London. The Edinburgh artists—Harvey, D. O. Hill, Noel Paton,[1] etc., are all eager to meet me, while the London ones are all too happy to get out of my way, and the only letter you have yet got, showing true appreciation of my book, except George Richmond's, is from the Edinburgh Dr. Brown. If I succeed *at all*, I shall do my cause more *immediate* good than by twenty volumes (although I consider that for ultimate purposes writing is best); and I cannot fail altogether because I shall assuredly have plenty to say, and shall say it in a gentlemanly way, if not fluently. I have given plenty of lectures with only one or two people to listen to me, and I don't see why it should be a great condescension to spend the same words on the cleverest people in Edinburgh. Every one of my friends whom I have mentioned my purpose to—and I spoke of it to many in London when I first got Lewis's letter—strongly urged me to lecture: there was not one dissentient voice. I hope, as you think over the matter more, it may not seem so objectionable to you; it seems to me a matter of very little consequence one way or the other; for, however well I may succeed, I shall not lecture much; and if I should fail, people will only say I can write but not talk, which has been the case with many men before me."

"(*October* 2).—The lectures have not delayed *Modern Painters*, as I did not intend to write any more till I had a rest. The lectures have been quite by the way. I will promise you the first chapter of *Modern Painters* as a New Year's gift, if I remain in good health."

Having decided, then, to give the lectures, Ruskin occupied himself at Glenfinlas in preparing both the discourses themselves and the

---

[1] Sir George Harvey (1806–1876), an original member and afterwards President of the Royal Scottish Academy; David Octavius Hill (1802–1870), landscape and portrait painter, secretary to the Scottish Society of Arts; Sir Noel Paton we shall meet again in a later volume.

drawings with which he meant to illustrate them. He went over some of the ground with Millais, who took up the subject of architecture with avidity. He had already mastered *The Stones of Venice.* " If you have leisure to read," he wrote to Mr. Combe, " get Ruskin's two last volumes, which surpass all he has written." [1] In a later letter he says:—

" Ruskin and myself are pitching into architecture; you will hear shortly to what purpose. I think now I was intended for a Master Mason. All this day I have been working at a window, which I hope you will see carried out very shortly in stone. In my evening hours I mean to make many designs for church and other architecture, as I find myself quite familiar with constructions, Ruskin having given me lessons regarding foundations and the building of cathedrals, etc., etc. This is no loss of time—rather a real relaxation from everyday painting—and it is immensely necessary that something new and good should be done in the place of the old ornamentations. . . . Do, if you can, come and hear Ruskin's lectures." [2]

Ruskin, it will thus be seen, had made a convert by his lectures before they were delivered; and one catches in Millais's words a reflection of that spirit of eager zeal and fervid enthusiasm of which Ruskin when he lectured seemed, in later years at any rate, a living embodiment. Millais's help, however, was not limited to the rôle of sympathetic listener at rehearsals. " We are busy making drawings for the lectures," he writes in a later letter; the artist's drawing of a tiger (Plate IX.), which was shown at the first lecture, was given as the frontispiece to the original edition of the lectures.

The following letter addressed to the Secretary of the Philosophical Institution gives Ruskin's synopsis:—

" *Monday,* Glenfinlas, *8th August.*

" My dear Sir,—I can hardly tell what I shall say in November at present, as I am down here tired, and cannot at present set myself to arranging a plan of lectures properly; but I believe the following sketch will not be much departed from :—

" *1st Lecture. General Construction of Domestic Buildings.*

" General aspect of Edinburgh. Dependent on its position more than its architecture, and on its houses more than its public buildings. Interest of its citizens in domestic architecture. Fault of modern

---

[1] *Life of Millais,* vol. i. p. 203.

[2] *Ibid.,* p. 204; on which page there is also a reproduction of a design made by Millais for a Gothic window. It is added that Millais made a large number of other designs at this time for architectural decoration. That for the window

houses. General laws of construction, with respect to exterior appearance. Roofs. Windows. Doors and Porches. The generosity of external rather than internal decoration.

" 2nd Lecture.   General Decoration of Domestic Buildings.

" Means of colour at the disposal of the British designer. Methods of employing it. Mosaic and inlaying. Sculpture, as exhibited in Scotland. Ancient domestic architecture of Scotland. Examples of possible decoration of windows and doors, with ornamentation derived from Highland flowers. Future prospects of architecture.

" 3rd Lecture.   Turner and his Works.

" Progress of landscape art from the 13th to the 19th century. Its peculiar position in the modern mind. Early training of Turner. Disadvantages to which he was exposed. Mistaken ideas respecting his works. Their true character and probable future effect. Character of the painter.

" 4th Lecture.   Pre-Raphaelitism.

" Meaning of the word Pre-Raphaelitism. Character of art before and after Raphael. Causes of decline after Raphael's time. State of modern historical painting. Nature of the reaction which is taking place. Merits and faults of the works of Hunt and Millais. Probable effect of the movement. Objects now principally to be kept in view by the modern artist and his patrons.

" I should be grateful to you also to mention to any person who asks any questions about these lectures, that I cannot take much pains in preparing them, as I came down here entirely for rest. I mean to *write*, but not to read them. I shall write them as fast as I can, and deliver them just as I should speak in private conversation; but as I am both slow and hesitating in talking, I am very sure that I shall not lecture well, and that those who expect *fluent* lectures will be disappointed; but I believe the substance will be interesting, and I shall prepare the illustrations with care on a large scale. Could you be so good as to tell me the size and shape of the lecture-room, and position of seats in it?

" Yours very truly,

" J. Ruskin." [1]

" represented angels saluting one another, the light being admitted through ovals, round which the arms of each figure clasped and met." Ruskin is said (p. 206) to have exhibited this at Edinburgh, but it is not mentioned in the reports.

[1] This letter has been kindly communicated by the present secretary of the Institution, Mr. W. Addis Miller. The synopsis as afterwards printed shows some slight alterations from Ruskin's first draft of it. The outline of each lecture, as given in the printed synopsis, will be found below, see pp. 13, 53, 102, 134. It was thus headed :—" I. Two Lectures on Architecture, chiefly Domestic (Illustrated by Drawings). By John Ruskin, Esq., Author of 'Modern Painters,' 'The Stones of

The lectures were fixed for the beginning of November, and on October 26 the Ruskins left Glenfinlas. They paid a visit on the way to Sir John Maxwell, uncle of the historian of the artists of Spain, at Keir, reaching Edinburgh—"arrived safe," Ruskin writes, "diagrams and all"—on October 29 :—

> "I really have hardly ever seen anything so lovely," he writes to his father (Oct. 29), "as the view from Keir in the morning: a great park sloping towards the valley of the Teith, the Ochils against the sunrise, exquisite in form, and covered with pines like the Jura —Stirling rising like an island out of the mist, and the broken crags about the Bridge of Allan and the farther hills beyond Stirling appearing and disappearing as the mist melted or formed."

The first of the four lectures—that on Domestic Architecture—was delivered on the evening of November 1. Friends and admirers had travelled to Edinburgh to hear and see the author of *Modern Painters* and *The Stones of Venice*. His father and mother, however—either as still disapproving, or from nervousness—had remained at home, and Ruskin's letters to them give full accounts of it all :—

> "*Wednesday morning* [2 *Nov.*, 1853].—Everything went off capitally, and I was heard very well without any exertion. I found myself quite at my ease, and that people thought so, and they are all very much pleased."
>
> "*Wednesday evening.*—Dr. Guthrie, Sir W. and Lady Trevelyan, and Mr. Jameson, formed our dinner party to-day. Dr. Guthrie just as delightful out of pulpit as in it—a Scottish Mr. Melvill;[1] much interesting conversation about ragged schools.[2] He paid me many

Venice,'" etc. [Then the synopsis of Lectures i. and ii.] "II. Two Lectures on Painting : with Reference to the Prospects and Objects of Modern Schools (Illustrated by Drawings). By John Ruskin, Esq." [Then the synopsis of Lectures iii. and iv.]

[1] See Vol. I. p. 490.

[2] Dr. Guthrie was minister of the St. John's Free Church. A few days after meeting Ruskin, he received the following letter, accompanying a copy of *The Stones of Venice* :—

> "I found a little difficulty in writing the words on the front page, wondering whether you would think the 'affectionate' misused or insincere. But I made up my mind at last to write what I felt—believing that you must be accustomed to people's getting very seriously and truly attached to you, almost at first sight, and therefore would believe me.
>
> "You asked me, the other evening, some kind questions about my father. He was an Edinburgh boy; and in answer to some account by me of the pleasure I had had in hearing you, and in the privilege of knowing you, as also of your exertions in the cause of the Edinburgh poor, he desires me to send you the enclosed—to be applied by you in such

most kind compliments on my lecture, but begged me to give them a passage or two of the highly-worked kind, so I must write a little bit for them. I find them all so inclined to hear what I have to say that I must really work up the lectures to a little higher mark, and am going to bed to meditate over a passage or two. Guthrie asked me to tell him whether I worked up my writing or not; I told him, of course, the truth in a moment, that whenever I thought a piece worth working out, I wrote it over four or five times. He said 'he was *sure* of it, but as people had disputed it with him he wanted to have it from my own mouth; that Macaulay did the same, and that, in fact, it *couldn't* be done in any other way.' He thanked me also earnestly for the tone of my lecture, and for its closing application, which he said every one agreed was magnificent. You had not seen this : I enclose it, but it was made a good deal better in delivering than it can possibly read."

The remark that Ruskin here makes about his " working up " and polishing has been already illustrated abundantly by the notes and fac-similes in this edition. But in the case of these Edinburgh lectures he trusted a good deal to extempore delivery, though in this respect (as the letter indicated) the later lectures were more fully written out than the earlier. This fact is noted in a contemporary critique of the lectures, which is further interesting as giving an account of the lecturer's appearance and manner :—

"The door by the side of the platform opens, and a thin gentleman with light hair, a stiff white cravat, dark overcoat with velvet collar, walk-ing, too, with a slight stoop, goes up to the desk, and looking round with a self-possessed and somewhat formal air, proceeds to take off his great-coat, revealing thereby, in addition to the orthodox white cravat, the most ortho-dox of white waistcoats. . . . 'Dark hair, pale face, and massive marble brow—that is my ideal of Mr. Ruskin,' said a young lady near us. This proved to be quite a fancy portrait, as unlike the reality as could well be imagined. Mr. Ruskin has light sand-coloured hair; his face is more red than pale ; the mouth well cut, with a good deal of decision in its curve, though somewhat wanting in sustained dignity and strength ; an aquiline nose ; his forehead by no means broad or massive, but the brows full and

manner as you may think fittest for the good of his native city. I have added slightly to my father's trust. I wish I could have done so more largely, but my profession of fault-finding with the world in general is not a lucrative one.—Always respectfully and affectionately yours,
"J. Ruskin."

This letter is reprinted from *John Ruskin: A Study*, by the Rev. R. P. Downes, 1890, pp. 22–23.

well bound together; the eye we could not see in consequence of the shadows that fell upon his countenance from the lights overhead, but we are sure it must be soft and luminous, and that the poetry and passion we looked for almost in vain in other features are concentrated there. . . .

"And now for the style of the lecture, you say; what was it? Properly speaking, there were in the lectures two styles essentially distinct, and not well blended,—a speaking and a writing style; the former colloquial and spoken off-hand; the latter rhetorical and carefully read in quite a different voice,—we had almost said intoned. When speaking of the sketches on the wall, or employing local illustrations,—such as the buildings of the city,—he talked in an apt, easy, and often humorous manner; but in treating the general relations of the subject, he had recourse to the manuscript leaves on the desk, written in a totally different style, and, naturally enough, read in a very different tone of voice. The effect of this transition was often strange; the audience, too, evidently sometimes had a difficulty in following the rapid change, and did not always keep up with the movement. It would on all accounts have been better had one style been observed throughout. This was plainly seen in the lectures on Turner and the Pre-Raphaelites, which were almost entirely read, and certainly had far more unity and compactness than either of the previous ones. Mr. Ruskin's elocution is peculiar; he has a difficulty in sounding the letter 'r'; but it is not this we now refer to, it is to the peculiar tone in the rising and falling of his voice at measured intervals, in a way scarcely ever heard except in the public lection of the service appointed to be read in churches. These are the two things with which, perhaps, you are most surprised,—his dress and his manner of speaking,—both of which (the white waistcoat notwithstanding) are eminently clerical. You naturally expect, in one so independent, a manner free from conventional restraint, and an utterance, whatever may be the power of voice, at least expressive of a strong individuality; and you find instead a Christ Church man of ten years' standing, who has not yet taken orders; his dress and manner derived from his college tutor, and his elocution from the chapel reader. At first you altogether refuse to identify the lecturer with the author of *Modern Painters* and the *Seven Lamps;* he sometimes reminds you of that individual, but is still not the same. By degrees, however, you get over this feeling; you see more points of resemblance, and begin to understand that they are really one. This, for the most part, is the effect of the more solemn and earnest passages, whether of exhortation, warning, denunciation, or entreaty, which are, more than anything beside, characteristic of both lecturer and writer" (*Edinburgh Guardian*, November 19, 1853).

One gathers from this description that Ruskin did not attain at the first attempt the freedom and mastery which he afterwards displayed in the lecture-room; but those who have heard his later lectures will recognise some familiar traits. The contrast, of which the reporter seems to complain, between more rhetorical and more familiar parts of the lecture, was maintained by Ruskin in most of his Oxford discourses. In the lecture-room, again, he cultivated and developed the manner which the reporter well describes as " apt, easy, and often humorous." In the preparation and display of his diagrams and drawings Ruskin was often studious of humorous effect. The reader will notice that two of the Plates in this volume are furnished with covering flaps; a feature reproduced here from the first edition of the *Lectures*. The flaps are provided so that the reader may in each case examine the figure at the top before seeing the one at the bottom. Ruskin adopted some similar device when showing the original illustrations, and the humorous effect of incongruity was thus enhanced.

The description of his lectures, just cited, appeared at the conclusion of the course; we must return to Ruskin's letters for particulars of them. The second lecture (Nov. 4) was equally successful :—

> " (*November* 5.)—I got on capitally again last night; at least everybody says so. I was not so well satisfied myself, for the lecture was longer, and I had not a thorough command of it, and had to read a good deal; and I had a sense of *sham* in speaking the fine bits learned by heart, which kept me from being at my ease. The odd thing is that everybody tells me I seemed more at my ease than in my first lecture, and spoke far better. The lobbies were filled with people standing."

The old people at home thirsted, however, for further and more detailed accounts :—

> " EDINBURGH, *Sunday*, 6*th November*.— . . . I should have given you more explicit accounts of time of lectures, etc., had I considered the thing of any importance. . . . But from the beginning I looked on this as merely a bye-way sort of thing, being quite sure, as far as I could be sure of anything, that I should not prove quite 'Stickit'; but not intending to make any effort at eloquence or effect—but merely to say plain things plainly. I did not think a *lecture* at all like a *sermon*. I did not consider its delivery as a critical period in my life, but merely as a compliance with John Lewis's request; a compliment to him, and a thing likely certainly to do some good to my cause in general. When, however, I heard that Lady Trevelyan and others of my friends were coming hundreds of miles to hear me, and found how much importance the Edinburgh people attached to the thing themselves, I saw that I must do more than I at first intended; and now when I find that I have to address a thousand people

each night, besides crowded passagefulls, just as if I were Mr. Melvill himself, there is nothing for it but doing as well as I possibly can; and, as I explained to you before, it has forced me to write you such miserable letters, wanting all the *quiet* time I ever get for retouching."

Ruskin was suffering at the time from a slight affection of the throat, as well as from nervous headaches; and owing to his indisposition the two remaining lectures had to be postponed from the 8th and 11th of November to the 15th and 18th :—

" *Wednesday morning, 16th November.*— . . . I think last night was the most successful of all the three lectures. . . . I never coughed once during the lecture of an hour and twenty minutes, speaking louder and clearer, people said, than before my cold; an awful crowd in the room; doors open at half-past seven, and the place filled instantly; people waiting patiently their hour, and standing right out into the street. I had worked up my lecture a good deal since you saw it, and have reason to think everybody thought themselves very well rewarded for their trouble."

" *Thursday evening, 17th November.*— . . . I don't think they are generally of opinion here that I am a *gentle* lecturer or a *cloudy* one. They think me rather *violent* and *clear*, more of the mountain stream than of the mist. Lady Trevelyan says everybody was alike delighted with the last, and that she heard a man whose time was very valuable, muttering, near here, at being obliged to wait for an hour in order to get a place, but saying afterwards that he would have waited *two* hours rather than have missed it. She and I got into some divinity discussions, until she got very angry, and declared that when she read me, and heard me, at a distance, she thought me so wise that anybody might make an idol of me, and worship me to any extent, but when she got to talk to me, I turned out only a *rag doll* after all."

The last lecture, that on Pre-Raphaelitism, was delivered on Friday, November 18 :—

" *Saturday morning, 19th November.*—. . . I got through excellently, though I was not altogether in such good trim as the evening before. . . . I felt a little weak and nervous before the lecture, and not so much at my ease *in* it, but people say I spoke it very vigorously and was heard all over the house; and I am agreeably surprised at the *lasting* power of my voice, as I was not in the least fatigued."

Even yet his parents were not satisfied. He had told them what he

said, how he said it, and how he was received; he had not mentioned how he was dressed:—

> "My dress at lectures," wrote Ruskin to his father (Dec. 1), " was
> my usual dinner dress, just what you and my mother like me best
> in; coat by Stulz.[1] It only produced *an effect* here, because their
> lecturers seem usually to address them, and they come to hear, in
> frock coats and dirty boots."

Ruskin seems to have been much lionised on the occasion of this
visit to Edinburgh (during which he lodged in Albyn Place), and in
a lively letter (November 27) to his father, he gives a long list of the
various people, small and great, who had paid him attention and whose
calls or other civilities he had been backward in returning. In most
cases the names are accompanied by little character-sketches—sometimes caustic but never ill-humoured—of most of the leaders of Edinburgh society in that day, including Lord Cockburn, Hugh Miller (the
geologist), Sir George and Lady Home, Mr. Dennistoun (author of *The
Dukes of Urbino*), and Sir William Hamilton. The friends made on
this occasion whom he most valued were Dr. John Brown—" called by
his friends the ' beloved physician '—and Professor John Stuart Blackie."
Here is Ruskin's first impression of the latter:—

> " Professor and Mrs. Blackie. Professor very funny, very clever;
> wife very nice, a great admirer of mine; Professor (of Greek) a
> great adversary, but all above board; has been ill. I have had to
> inquire for, and contend with him. I have quarrelled him well
> again."

The more he saw of the Professor the more he liked him :—

> " (*December* 4.)— . . . I have made some agreeable and valuable
> friends, most especially Professor Blackie, a thoroughly original, dar-
> ing, enthusiastic, amiable, eccentric, masterly fellow. . . . He has
> taught me more Greek in an hour than I learnt at Oxford in six
> months, having studied the *living* language. I am in a great state
> of delight at knowing for the first time in my life that it is a living
> one. The Professor gave me to-day a Greek *newspaper*, about a week
> old, printed at Athens, and in good old Attic Greek hardly differing
> in a syllable from the language of Alcibiades, except in its subject-
> matter."

---

[1] Compare Vol. III. p. 380 *n.* Stulz is named as the typical tailor in Carlyle's
Past and Present, book iii. ch. xiii.

After leaving Edinburgh Ruskin went on some visits, including one to Hamilton, where the Duke had invited him to see the MSS.[1]

Ruskin returned home at the end of the year, resumed his sittings to Millais, and prepared the Lectures for publication. This involved a good deal of work. As we have seen, he did not write out the whole of the earlier lectures, and accordingly, as he explains in the Preface (see p. 7), he had to fill up these blanks in his manuscript. The *manuscript* of the book as printed is in Mr. Allen's possession, written on about 210 leaves of various sizes; in large part it seems to embody the original MS. for the lectures as delivered—consisting partly of passages wholly written out, and partly of notes and memoranda. Some passages in the lectures as delivered were omitted in the book; but the MS. does not enable the editors to supply them, as it contains at these places a few memoranda only; nor are the reports in the local press full enough to be of any assistance. A few passages which occur in the MS. in a completed form are, however, added (see pp. 22, 62, 73–74, 76–77, 122).

In addition to revising and completing the Lectures, Ruskin wrote, as "Addenda to Lectures i. and ii.," a reply to his critics and a re-statement of his main propositions. These will already be familiar to readers of *The Seven Lamps* and *The Stones of Venice*. Indeed it may be said generally of these *Lectures on Architecture and Painting* that they break little new ground; they are rather a re-statement, on a smaller scale and in a more popular and direct form, of the leading ideas and doctrines contained in his previous works. This will appear from the references to parallel passages supplied in the footnotes.

The Lectures had been reported in several journals at the time of their delivery, and were widely noticed in the press upon their publication in book-form in April 1854.[2] This was a period of crisis in Ruskin's

---

[1] See below, p. lxvii.

[2] The Lectures were reported (among other places) in the *Edinburgh Courant* and the *Edinburgh Guardian*, and criticised upon their conclusion in that paper (November 19) and in the *Edinburgh Advertiser* (November 22). They were also reported (except the last one) in the *Builder* (November 12, 26, December 3); and criticised in that paper (December 31), the article being signed "W. M. B." The book was reviewed in the *Athenæum*, May 20 and 27, 1854 (No. 1386, pp. 611–612, No. 1387, pp. 650–652); *Spectator*, May 27; *Builder*, June 10, 1854 (and in the same periodical in 1856—March 22, 29, April 12, 26, and May 10—a series of articles on "Revolutionary Architectural Principles," signed "Leny," criticising the Edinburgh Lectures, etc.); the *Leader*, June 10; *Blackwood's Magazine*, June 1854 (vol. 75, pp. 740–756); the *New Quarterly Review*, July 1854 (vol. 3, pp. 374–378); the *Prospective Review*, August 1854 (vol. 10, pp. 352–368); the *New Monthly Review*, edited by W. H. Ainsworth, August 1854, vol. 101, pp. 413–418; *Putnam's Monthly*, August 1854; the *Rambler*, August and September 1854, vol. 2 (N. S.), pp. 155–162, 247–258; the *British Quarterly*, October 1854, vol. 20, pp. 301–334 (an article headed "Fine Art in the Crystal Palace," noticing, among other books, the Edinburgh Lectures and *Stones of Venice*, vol. iii.); the

private fortunes, to which only a brief reference need here be made. His wife left him in April 1854; returned to her parents, and immediately instituted a suit. Ruskin declined to put in any answer, and went abroad with his parents in May. The marriage (which in many respects had not been happy) was annulled on July 15, and a year later, on July 3, 1855, Millais was married at Bowerswell to Euphemia Chalmers Gray.[1]

Ruskin and his parents returned from abroad early in October 1854, and resumed their old life together at Denmark Hill. The summer tour is noticed in another volume, in connexion with other tours which also were seed-time, as it were, for the later volumes of *Modern Painters*. His feelings and attitude at this time are best expressed in a letter to Miss Mitford :—

> "DENMARK HILL,
> "Tuesday afternoon,
> "*3rd October,* '54.

"DEAR MISS MITFORD,—Four hours ago we arrived happily at home, by God's blessing well, all of us—after five months' wandering. Two letters were put into my hand when I arrived, and the first I opened was yours, and the first words my eye fell upon : "'The only fear is, lest I should do too much!'

"Could any happier, kinder, sweeter welcome have been given me?

"Indeed, among the many causes of gratitude which I have to number before God to-night, it is not one of the least that He permits me to look forward still to the pleasure of your friendship, to

---

Ecclesiastic and Theologian, October 1854, No. 22 (N. S.), pp. 473–481 (a review of Lectures 1 and 2); January 1855, No. 25, pp. 1–5 (a review of *Pre-Raphaelitism* and the Edinburgh Lectures 3 and 4); the *Christian Reformer*, February 1855, vol. 11 (N. S.), pp. 69–80 (a review of the Edinburgh Lectures and the *Stones of Venice*); the *Eclectic*, January 1856, vol. 11 (N. S.), pp. 1–20; and the *London Quarterly*, January 1857, vol. 7, pp. 478–501 (an article, entitled "Gothic Art," containing a review of the Lectures). Most of these reviews were favourable. It is interesting to note that one of them (*The New Monthly*, p. 418) questioned "whether Mr. Ruskin judged well in aiding and abetting the current craze for public lectures." *Blackwood* was even more bitter than usual. The book was "the keystone in the arch of Mr. Ruskin's absurdities." "We can only be sorry for him." "We confess that the excessive puppyism and calm pretension of this book has considerably raised our bile." The writer seems to have been present at the Lectures, and says (p. 740) : "He is by no means qualified by nature for a public appearance on a rostrum, and he committed an egregious error in attempting to act as his own rhapsodist." He had "a bad delivery, a pedantic manner, and a monotonous voice."

[1] It will thus be seen that Mr. Frederic Harrison is altogether wrong in stating that the time of the Edinburgh Lectures "was ill-chosen for a public appearance, whilst he was a party to a matrimonial suit" (*John Ruskin*, English Men of Letters Series, 1902, p. 83). He is also wrong in stating that the suit was brought "in the Scotch court" (p. 57).

rejoice with you in your recovering strength, and to learn from
you how to enjoy, and how to love.

"God willing, I will come to see you about the middle of next
week, writing again to tell you the day. I cannot come sooner,
because it is necessary that I should now show myself for a few
days in London, in order to convince my friends, and some, who
are otherwise than friends, that I am the same person I used to
be. You will perhaps not easily believe that of all my friends *you*
are the only one whose tact—whose sympathy and feeling, I ought
rather to say—have been unerring, during the trial I have had
lately to go through. Some wrote to me asking questions which
very little common sense might have told them *never* could be
answered; others wrote in useless and inappropriate condolence;
some in the style of Eliphaz and Zophar; and the rest kept a
terrified silence, depriving me of the pleasure I might have had
in hearing from them about 'their own affairs. *You only* knew
what to do.

"I have a great deal to talk to you about when I come, so
that I shall stay for a day or two at Reading, and come each day
at the time when you are able to see me, and therefore I must
engage my days at once. Can you give me a little bit of Wednesday, Thursday, and Friday, next week? Do not trouble to write
if you can, but if you have any other appointments made for
Wednesday or Thursday, would you just send me the merest line?
If the appointment be for *Friday*, do not write, as I will come on
Wednesday, and then arrange with you. My father and mother
are most *thoroughly* happy to hear you are better, and send their
sincere love.

"Ever, dear Miss Mitford,
"Most affectionately yours,
"J. RUSKIN."

On settling down to a new life, which was yet the old, Ruskin threw
himself with fervour into various activities of unselfish beneficence. It
was at this time that he began to cultivate a friendship with Dante
Rossetti and his fiancée, Miss Siddal, for whose benefit he devised one
of those unnumbered acts of generosity by which (says Rossetti's brother)
"he will be remembered hardly less than long by his vivid insight into
many things, and his heroic prose."[1] Ruskin's relations with Rossetti
are disclosed in numerous letters which will be found in a later volume
of this edition. So also will several further letters to Miss Mitford.

[1] *Dante Gabriel Rossetti: his Family Letters*, with a Memoir by William Michael
Rossetti, 1895, i. 184.

She was wisely sympathetic to him, and Ruskin on his side did much by kindness and thoughtful generosity to cheer her closing years. He threw himself also into work of a more public character. His acquaintance with F. D. Maurice, which will presently be referred to (p. lxxv.), gave one opportunity for this in connexion with the Working Men's College. Other work of a similar kind was that which he did in lecturing in the late autumn of this year at the Architectural Museum. A full report of these lectures is given below (pp. 474–508); they form the latest in date of the Papers collected in the present volume. At this point, therefore, we break off the biographical thread, and turn back to notice in their order the contents of the volume which follow the Edinburgh Lectures.

II

The Second Part of the volume contains various Papers on Art, written by Ruskin between the years 1847 and 1854. The first is a Review of Lord Lindsay's *Sketches of the History of Christian Art.*[1] The circumstances in which this work was undertaken for the *Quarterly* (June 1847) have been already noticed (Vol. VIII. p. xxiv.). Ruskin was wont to refer to Lord Lindsay as his "first master in Italian art."[2]

---

[1] In connexion with this Review of Lord Lindsay, Ruskin's other references to the author and his book may usefully be collected. The author was Alexander William Crawford, Baron Lindsay, 25th Earl of Crawford and 8th Earl of Balcarres. His *Sketches of the History of Christian Art* was published in 1847. Ruskin says in *Præterita*, and in the Epilogue to the second volume of *Modern Painters*, that this book had prepared him for his study of early Christian Art in 1845, but (as already noted, Vol. IV. p. xxiii. *n.*) in looking back he ante-dated Lord Lindsay's influence. The earliest reference to the book, other than the Review, is in *The Seven Lamps* (1849), where he refers to Lord Lindsay's observations on finish in art (Vol. VIII. p. 197, and see below, p. 232). Later on, in a note to the 1880 edition, Ruskin again refers to Lord Lindsay's estimate of Byzantine architecture as anticipating his own (Vol. VIII. p. 121). In the first volume of *The Stones of Venice* (1851) he makes a passing criticism on the metaphysical distinctions in Lord Lindsay's "noble book," and refers to the author as "a man from whom I have learned much" (Vol. IX. p. 67, and *cf.* p. 445); later in the same volume, Lord Lindsay's "opposition of good and evil, the antagonism of the entire human system" is cited with approval (*ibid.*, p. 306). In *Stones of Venice*, vol. ii., there are references to Lord Lindsay's remarks on Basilicas (Vol. X. p. 22 *n.*) and on St. Mark's (*ibid.*, p. 138 *n.*), and several to his notes on Giotto's frescoes at Assisi (*ibid.*, pp. 384, 392, 400). In the *Lectures on Architecture and Painting*, a passage from the book is cited as the best "preface to an essay on civil architecture" (below, p. 8). When he came to write on *Giotto and his Works in Padua*, Ruskin had repeated occasion to refer to Lord Lindsay (see that work, *passim*). In later books Ruskin often reverted to Lindsay's work as a pioneer in the explanation of Christian art and Christian mythology; see *Modern Painters*, vol. v. pt. ix. ch. ii. § 4, *The Eagle's Nest*, § 46, *The Art of England*, § 47; while in *Mornings in Florence*, Lindsay is again frequently cited.

[2] *Val d'Arno*, § 264; and compare *The Eagle's Nest*, § 46.

But this very fact made the pupil shy of laying hands on his father Parmenides, "being well aware," as he says, "that Lord Lindsay knew much more about Italian painting than I did." This is a form of compunction which, if admitted, would make short work of the reviewer's trade, and Ruskin put it aside with the further reflection—which, let us hope, other reviewers may with equal justice entertain—that "no one else was likely to do it better." But Ruskin was by no means satisfied with his experience as a contributor to anonymous periodicals. He moved uneasily in the restraints imposed by the form, and his MS. was "laboured." Then Lockhart, the editor, asked him to "cut out all his best bits," and for prudential reasons excised a critical reference of some severity to Gally Knight, one of John Murray's authors.[1] On the whole Ruskin was not greatly satisfied with this exercise; which, however, in some respects must have been thoroughly congenial. Lord Lindsay's book, in its descriptive passages, went over ground with which Ruskin was thoroughly familiar. The Review gave him occasion (as the footnotes to it in this edition will show) to use many of the entries in his diaries, and to re-inforce many of the points already made in the second volume of *Modern Painters*. And although the Review is not in all respects one of his most characteristic pieces, yet here and there the real man flashes out through the constrained disguise of the impersonal reviewer. He is severe upon Lord Lindsay, it will be seen, for his system-mongering. He had tried the thing himself, in the first and second volumes of *Modern Painters*, and was already beginning to find it irksome. "Much time is wasted by human beings," he afterwards wrote, "on establishment of systems; and it often takes more labour to master the intricacies of an artificial connection, than to remember the separate facts which are so carefully connected."[2] It is worth noticing that Ruskin's early admiration of Michael Angelo finds full and eloquent expression in this essay (see especially § 61), which indeed throughout reflects the temper and the point of view of the second volume of *Modern Painters*.

The Review of Eastlake's *History of Oil-Painting*, which comes next in this volume, appeared in the *Quarterly* of March 1848. It is of particular interest as showing the study which Ruskin had given to the

---

[1] See *Præterita*, ii. ch. x. § 193; and compare the Preface to *Academy Notes*, 1856. Ruskin there refers to the two Reviews for the *Quarterly* here reprinted as if they were his only anonymous articles. He forgot the paper on Prout (see below, p. xlii.). Another anonymous review, of a very slight character, was contributed to *The Morning Chronicle*, January 20, 1855 (see *Arrows of the Chace*, 1880, ii. 250, and a later volume of this edition).

[2] Preface to *Modern Painters*, vol. iii.; and see also Vol. III. pp. xlvii., 93 *n*.

technique of oil-painting. The reader will remember his emphatic statement in one of the Oxford lectures, that "oil-painting is the Art of arts; that it is sculpture, drawing, and music, all in one, involving the technical dexterities of those three several arts."[1] And so, again, in an earlier passage, "Colour, ground with oil, and laid on a solid opaque ground, furnishes to the human hand the most exquisite means of expression which the human sight or expression can find or require."[2] This essay illustrates how carefully Ruskin had considered and analysed the processes and methods of manipulation by which mastery in this "art of arts" had been obtained, and the illustration is re-inforced in this volume by the "Notes in the Louvre"—largely, as will be seen, of a technical character.[3] Ruskin, as already noted,[4] made some early essays in oil-painting, but did not take kindly to them. Later in life, he perceived that to become an accomplished painter in this medium demanded the whole and the best energies of a strenuous life; but his critical study of oil-painting and its methods was long and careful, and the study was also so far experimental that he was constantly copying the works which he criticised and appraised.[5]

Ruskin's Review naturally followed closely the scope of the book to which it was devoted, but the paper contains many passages in which the individuality of the reviewer makes itself heard. It begins characteristically with a description of a favourite spot at Florence, where he had spent happy hours in 1845 (see p. 251). The criticism on the management of the National Gallery, which he was presently to publish with emphasis, is hinted a little later in the Review (p. 256). His indifference to mere technicalities, in which he thought that Eastlake too much indulged, is clearly expressed (p. 255); the passages in which he gives the subject a wider scope, and connects technical processes with artistic aims and the characteristics of several schools, are among the most interesting in the Review (§§ 16, 27, 28). To point out these and other illustrations of doctrines new and old in the body of Ruskin's teaching is a principal object of the footnotes to the text.

The essay on Prout, which stands next in this collection,[6] is among

---

[1] "The Relation between Michael Angelo and Tintoret" (*Aratra Pentelici*, § 227).
[2] *The Stones of Venice*, vol. ii., App. 12 (Vol. X. p. 456).
[3] Compare in this connexion the Epilogue to *The Stones of Venice* (Vol. XI. p. 237).
[4] See Vol. I. p. xxxii.
[5] See Vol. IV. p. li.
[6] At Vol. VIII. pp. xxxiii.-xxxiv. it was stated that this essay would be included in the volume containing Ruskin's later "Notes on Prout" (1879). On further

the most charming of Ruskin's earlier pieces. It appeared in *The Art Journal* of March 1849, and was published anonymously; though, indeed, it was signed all over by the author of *Modern Painters*. To the friendship of Ruskin and his father with Prout, reference has already been made;[1] both at Herne Hill and Denmark Hill they had him for a neighbour. The biographical details given in this essay were doubtless derived from the artist himself, and it is therefore the standard authority in that connexion. For Prout's drawing, Ruskin had from very early years a great admiration; it served as the model for his own first exercises in sketching.[2] In the first volume of *Modern Painters* he bore his testimony—somewhat cautious in the original edition, larger and more emphatic in the third—to Prout's high qualities as an artist.[3] The more Ruskin studied mediæval architecture, the higher became his appreciation of Prout's rendering of it. In the first volume of *The Stones of Venice* he coined the word "Proutism,"[4] to denote the system of treatment whereby that artist reproduced with signal fidelity the spirit of the architecture he loved. Further study confirmed his judgment:—

> "Please tell Mr. Prout when you happen to see him," Ruskin wrote to his father from Venice (October 14, 1851), "that I have constant occasion to refer to him, as the only modern parallel of Lombardic sculptors, that I find my word 'Proutism' the most useful I have yet coined, and that I enjoy and admire his works more than ever. Only this morning I have been looking all the while I was dressing at that sketch of the Hotel de Ville at Ulm, which you must recollect our going hunting for (*i.e.* not the sketch, but the subject of it), ages ago, in the town itself; and I am quite amazed at the skill and science of little bits of drawing which I used to think mere manner and accident, and that I should be able in time to do like them myself. But I find Prout is inimitable—in his way—as even Turner. And the poor shallow coxcombs of artists that pretend to look down upon him!"

The constant occasion thus to refer to Prout's work was taken in several pages of the second and third volumes of *The Stones of Venice*.[5]

consideration, it has been thought more convenient to give the earlier paper in this place, in order to complete the collection of Ruskin's occasional pieces during the present period. For the one exception still admitted, see above, p. xvii.

[1] Vol. I. pp. xlii., 216 *n.*, 662.
[2] See Vol. II. pp. xl., xli.
[3] See Vol. I., comparing pp. 216–220 with p. 256.
[4] See Vol. IX. pp. 300, 303; and compare p. 320.
[5] See Vol. X. p. 301, Vol. XI. pp. 24 *n.*, 58, 160.

In the present paper Ruskin does justice to Prout's unerring eye for the picturesque, and his dexterity in rendering it. But he emphasises chiefly another point—namely, the unique value of this artist as an *historian*. Ruskin's mind was much occupied at this time with the neglect and wanton destruction, and (no less disastrous) the well-meaning restoration, of ancient buildings.[1] It had been Prout's mission to make records of these historical monuments, while they were still comparatively untouched; his work in this sort was valuable, and would be more than ever recognised at its true worth "when the pillars of Venice shall lie mouldering in the salt shallows of her sea, and the stones of the goodly tower of Rouen have become ballast for the barges of the Seine."[2] Some of Ruskin's Oxford students discovered this paper in the files of *The Art Journal*, and reprinted it in 1870 for private circulation: the bibliographical particulars are given below (p. 304).

The next pieces in this volume—dealing with "The Pre-Raphaelite Brotherhood"—introduce us to an interesting episode in Ruskin's literary career. It has already been briefly referred to in its chronological place (Vol. IX. p. xlvii.), but a fuller account of it is here necessary, both in order to explain the circumstances in which these pieces were composed, and to correct erroneous ideas which are sometimes circulated on the subject. It was supposed at the time, and has often been repeated since, that Ruskin was the inspirer of the Pre-Raphaelites.[3] On the other hand, by reaction from this view, it is sometimes asserted that Ruskin had nothing to do with the movement. The truth lies between the two statements; Ruskin himself, in a preface to a collection of his notes on pictures by Millais, explains that "the painters were entirely original in their thoughts, and independent in their practice;" but, on the other hand, one at least of them owed something to Ruskin's books, and they were all much indebted to his encouragement and advocacy.

The Pre-Raphaelite Brotherhood was formed in 1848, its members being Dante Rossetti, Millais, Holman Hunt, William Rossetti, Thomas Woolner, F. G. Stephens, and James Collinson. Other artists who, though not members of the Brotherhood, were working on the same lines, were Arthur Hughes, Frederic Sandys, Noel Paton,

[1] See Vol. VIII. p. 20.
[2] See below, p. 315. The same aspect of Prout's work is emphasised in the pamphlet on *Pre-Raphaelitism*, § 26, below, p. 362.
[3] As, *e.g.*, by Max Nordau in his *Degeneration*, 1895, p. 77. Millais, on being shown this passage, characteristically remarked upon it as "twaddling rubbish on a subject of which he knows absolutely nothing" (*Life of Millais*, i. 62).

Charles Collins, and Walter Deverell. Holman Hunt and Millais were fellow-students at the Royal Academy schools, and a friendship sprung up between them. Dante Gabriel Rossetti was a student there also, and he greatly admired the picture of "The Eve of St. Agnes," which Hunt had painted in 1848, and the two young artists took a studio together at 7 Gower Street; Millais was living with his parents at 87 in the same street. At Millais's house the three were one night assembled, when they found a book of engravings of the frescoes in the Campo Santo at Pisa — the very frescoes which to Ruskin three years before had opened "a veritable Palestine" (Vol. IV. p. xxx.). "It was the finding of this book at this special time," says Holman Hunt, "which caused the establishment of the Pre-Raphaelite Brotherhood. Millais, Rossetti, and myself were all seeking for some sure ground, some starting-point for our art which would be secure, if it were ever so humble. As we searched through this book of engravings, we found in them, or thought we found, that freedom from corruption, pride, and disease for which we sought. . . . 'Pre-Raphaelite' was adopted, after some discussion, as a distinctive prefix, though the word had first been used as a term of contempt by our enemies. And as we bound ourselves together, the word 'Brother-hood' was suggested by Rossetti as preferable to clique or associa-tion. It was in a little spirit of fun that we thus agreed that Raphael, the Prince of Painters, was the inspiring influence of the art of the day; for we saw that the practice of contemporary painters was as different from that of the master whose example they quoted, as estab-lished interest or indifference had ever made the conduct of disciples. It was instinctive prudence, however, which suggested to us that we should use the letters P. R. B., unexplained, on our pictures (after the signature), as the one mark of our union." [1] In the following year's Academy, 1849, the first pictures with the mystic initials were exhibited —Millais's "Lozenzo and Isabella" (now in the Liverpool Gallery) and Hunt's "Rienzi." In the same year's Rossetti's "Girlhood of Mary Virgin" was exhibited at the Hyde Park Gallery. In 1850 Millais had at the Academy "Christ in the House of his Parents" and "Ferdinand lured by Ariel," and Hunt, "Claudio and Isabella," and "A Converted British Family sheltering a Missionary." In January 1850 had appeared the first number of *The Germ*, the organ of the Brotherhood, its principle being declared in the preface—"to encourage and enforce an entire adherence to the simplicity of nature."

---

[1] "The Pre-Raphaelite Brotherhood : a Fight for Art," *Contemporary Review*, April 1886, pp. 480, 481.

The Brotherhood had thus found and proclaimed its faith, and brought forth works illustrative of it, before Ruskin took up the cudgels on their behalf, and at the time when he did so he had no personal knowledge of any of them. Nor was the merit of their work at that time his own discovery. He had observed Millais's picture in the Academy of 1850, and had not been very favourably impressed by it (see below, p. 320). William Dyce, R.A., he says, " dragged me, literally, up to the Millais picture of ' The Carpenter's Shop,'[1] which I had passed disdainfully, and forced me to look for its merits."[2] It is therefore clear that Ruskin was not directly the inspirer of the Pre-Raphaelites.

They were, however, glad of his help, and it was at the instance of one of their number that this was invoked. The attacks of the critics on the Pre-Raphaelite pictures of 1850 had been very severe; they were penned with the express object, it would seem, of deterring purchasers. " We have great difficulty," wrote *Blackwood's Magazine* of " The Carpenter's Shop," by Millais, " in believing a report that this unpleasing and atrociously affected picture has found a purchaser at a high price. Another specimen from the same brush inspires rather laughter than disgust."[3] Such attacks were renewed in the notices of the following year's Academy, when Millais showed his " Mariana," " Return of the Dove to the Ark," and " Woodman's Daughter." The *Times* led the way in a violent article quoted below (p. 319), declaring that such work " deserved no quarter at the hands of the public." " Our strongest enemy," writes Holman Hunt, " advised that the Academy, having shown our works so far, to prove how atrocious they were, could now, with the approval of the public, depart from their usual rule of leaving each picture on the walls until the end of the season, and take ours down and return them to us." Officials of the Academy itself fanned the flame. " In the schools (as we were told) a professor referred to our works in such terms that the wavering students resorted to the very extreme course of hissing us."[4] Other newspapers and magazines afterwards took up the hue and cry, and such attacks were calculated to be very damaging to young artists who had as yet no powerful

---

[1] *Notes on Some of the Principal Pictures of Sir John Everett Millais*, 1886, edited by A. Gordon Crawford (pseudonym for A. G. Wise). Ruskin's contributions to the pamphlet are reprinted in a later volume of this edition.
[2] See a letter to Ernest Chesneau, of December 28, 1882, in a later volume of this edition. And compare, also in a later volume, *The Three Colours of Pre-Raphaelitism*, § 16.
[3] July 1850; vol. 68, p. 82. For other notices, see below, p. 320 *n.*
[4] *Contemporary Review*, April 1886.

patrons, and whose means were very narrow. The article in the *Times* filled Millais with alarm and indignation, and he bethought himself of some move to parry the blow. He was acquainted with Coventry Patmore; he had painted a portrait of the poet's first wife, and the subject of one of the pictures in the Academy, denounced by the *Times*— " The Woodman's Daughter "—had been taken from Patmore's piece, so entitled, in his volume of *Poems* (1844). Millais knew that Ruskin was a friend of Patmore, and turned in his anger and vexation to the author of *Modern Painters* for help. Patmore himself has recounted the tale :—

"The day when the *Times* made its furious attack on Millais's picture of Christ in the Carpenter's Shop, Millais came to me in great agitation and anger, and begged me to ask Ruskin to take the matter up. I went at once to Ruskin, and the next day after there appeared in the *Times* a letter of great length and amazing quality, considering how short a time Ruskin had to examine the picture and make up his mind about it." [1]

This is the first of the letters here printed (below, pp. 319–323). It was written quickly, as Patmore says, but it was not immediately printed. Letters from Ruskin to Patmore continue the story :—

"DENMARK HILL,
"*10th May* [1851].

"DEAR PATMORE,—I wrote to the *Times* yesterday; but the letter is not in it to-day; it went late, and might have been too late; but if it is not in in Monday's, the letter shall go to the *Chronicle*, in a somewhat less polite form. My father has written to ask if the Ark picture be unsold, and what is its price. I wish Hunt would also let me know his price for Valentine. I may perhaps be of service to him."

"Yours ever faithfully,
"J. RUSKIN.

"COVENTRY K. PATMORE, Esq." [2]

Ruskin did not do things by halves. Not content with writing a defence of the picture in the press, he offered to buy one of those by Millais and made inquiries with regard to Hunt's. These inquiries were apparently made on behalf of Mr. M'Cracken of Belfast, or with

---

[1] *Memoirs and Correspondence of Coventry Patmore*, by Basil Champneys, 1900, i. 85.
[2] This and the letter on p. xlviii. are reprinted from the *Memoirs and Correspondence* of Patmore, ii. 288–289.

a view of suggesting the purchase to him. Mr. Hunt afterwards sent the picture to Liverpool Exhibition, where it obtained a £50 prize; and on the strength of this, and of Ruskin's praise, it was purchased, says Hunt, by "a correspondent in Belfast—*who* had never seen the work, but was interested from what he had read of it—made me an offer of the sum I asked for the picture, 150 or 200 guineas (I forget which), to be paid £10 at the time monthly, with sixty guineas of the sum to be represented by a picture of Danby's." A letter from Ruskin to his father written at the time records the same transaction :—

> "VENICE, *January* 19 [1852].—I got yesterday a letter from M'Cracken of Belfast, saying that he hoped in a week to have Hunt's Proteus and Valentine, for which he has given 100 guineas and a picture of *young Danby's*. I pity poor Hunt for the bargain; but there was enclosed in the letter a very interesting critique on Hunt's picture from a Liverpool paper, and an extract of a letter from himself, all excellent."

To Hunt, Ruskin's intervention was a godsend. His artistic prospects at the time were almost desperate. He had written a letter, but could not tell, he says, "where to find a penny for the stamp." "In the midst of this came thunder out of a clear sky. It was a letter from Ruskin in the *Times* in our defence. The critic had, amongst other charges, accused our pictures of being false in linear perspective. This was open to demonstration. Ruskin challenged him to establish his case, and the cowardly creature skulked away, and was heard of no more."[1]

Ruskin's offer to buy Millais's "Dove" was made immediately, and before the letter appeared in the *Times*. The picture had, however, already been bought by his friend and first patron, Mr. Combe of Oxford,[2] to whom he wrote in great glee, describing Ruskin's offer: "No doubt you have seen the violent abuse of my pictures in the *Times*, which I believe has sold itself to destroy us. That, however, is quite an absurd mistake of theirs, for, in spite of their denouncing my pictures as unworthy to hang on any walls, the famous critic, Mr. Ruskin, has written offering to purchase your picture."[3]

---

[1] *Contemporary Review*, May 1886, pp. 747, 749.
[2] Thomas Combe (1797–1872), printer, connected with the Clarendon Press. On the death of his widow his collection of Pre-Raphaelite pictures went by his bequest to the Oxford University Galleries.
[3] *Life of Millais*, i. 101.

The Pre-Raphaelites sent their thanks to Ruskin through Patmore, as appears from the following letter, which is undated :—

"DEAR PATMORE,—I am very glad your friends were pleased with the letter. I wrote a continuation of it, which I have not sent, because to people who did not know that there are not ten pictures in the Academy which I would turn my head to look at, it might have read carping; but I wish, *entre nous*, you would ask Millais whether it would have been quite impossible for him to have got a bit of olive branch out of some of our conservatories, instead of painting one on Speculation, or, at least, ascertained to some approximation what an olive leaf was like; and also whether he has ever in his life seen a bit of old painted glass, near; and what modern stuff it was that he studied from?

"Pray tell Hunt how happy I shall be to be allowed to see his picture.

"Yours ever faithfully,
"J. RUSKIN."

The "continuation" here referred to was afterwards sent to the *Times* (May 30), with the edge of the "carping" turned, however, by further praises. This second letter is given below, at pp. 324–327; it will be seen that some of the points mentioned in the letter to Patmore are therein dealt with.

Ruskin's intervention was a turning-point in the fortunes of the Pre-Raphaelites. It encouraged the painters themselves, confirmed the wavering opinions of patrons and picture-dealers, and caused many of the critics to reconsider their opinions. With Millais, as we have seen, Ruskin speedily formed a friendship; and to Rossetti, with whom also he presently became intimate, he was able to render much assistance. It seems, too, that Ruskin moved his father to cast about for some way of befriending Deverell, another member of the Brotherhood.

Three years later Ruskin again wrote to the *Times* in praise of Pre-Raphaelite work. In the interval he had lost no opportunity of calling attention to their pictures in other places. Thus, in revising the first volume of *Modern Painters* for the fifth edition (1851), he alluded to their works as "in finish of drawing and in splendour of colour the best in the Academy;" then came the pamphlet upon *Pre-Raphaelitism*, next to be noticed; while in *The Stones of Venice* he introduced frequent references to Millais, Rossetti, and Hunt.[1]

---

[1] The references are Vol. III. pp. 599, 621 ; Vol. X. p. 219 ; XI. pp. 36, 109, 198, 205, 217, 220, 229.

The lecture at Edinburgh followed in 1853. In the following year's Academy Hunt exhibited one of his greatest works, "The Light of the World." Ruskin had for some time been his friend, and had taken a lively interest in this picture, for which, during its inception, he had suggested the title of "The Watchman."[1] On its completion Hunt had started on a journey to the East, and Ruskin came forward as interpreter of a work which, he felt, needed for its right understanding thought as deep and serious as had gone to its production.

In the letter to the *Times*, as first written, Ruskin had included also some commendatory notices of other pictures by C. R. Leslie, R.A., and J. W. Inchbold respectively. The letter, however, was not inserted; and Ruskin, supposing that its length was the objection, withdrew it and substituted a shorter one, as printed below (pp. 328–332), dealing with Hunt's picture only.[2] In a further letter (pp. 333–335), published three weeks later, he discussed Hunt's other picture of the year, "The Awakening Conscience." And in later years, he returned to a general consideration of Hunt's work, with particular reference to "The Triumph of the Innocents."[3]

In considering Ruskin's relations with the Pre-Raphaelites we must remember further that though he had not directly inspired them, yet their practice and their theories were in accord with his teaching, and were in some sort the outcome of a general tendency to which his writings had contributed. We have seen already how Holman Hunt, during his student days at the Academy, had come across the first volumes of *Modern Painters*, and "felt that it was written expressly for him" (Vol. III. p. xli.). In the spring of 1851 Ruskin was revising that volume for a fifth edition, and, as he read, he came upon a passage which he felt had been written, though he knew it not, expressly for the whole Pre-Raphaelite school. It was the famous passage—often quoted and oftener misquoted[4]—about the young artist "going to nature in all singleness of heart . . . rejecting nothing, selecting nothing, and scorning nothing." As he studied the works of the young Pre-Raphaelites, he saw that they had carried out this advice to the letter, and, for their reward, had been assailed with the most scurrilous abuse. He was, therefore, doubly called upon to defend them—for their sake and for his own. This work he set himself in the piece which follows the

---

[1] *William Holman Hunt*, by F. W. Farrar, *Art Annual* publication, p. 10.
[2] Ruskin stated these facts in the Supplement to *Academy Notes*, 1855.
[3] *The Art of England*, Lecture i.
[4] See Vol. III. p. 624 *n*.

Letters to the *Times* in this collection—the well-known pamphlet entitled *Pre-Raphaelitism*, published on August 13, 1851.

In this pamphlet (§ 19) Ruskin mentions as an instance of the violent hostility entertained towards the new school, an anonymous letter which he received the day after his second letter appeared; he defends once more their pictures against the specific attacks made upon them; and hints not obscurely his regret at the Academy's attitude towards the most promising of its students. Then taking broader scope, he seeks a harmony of his conclusions in admiring both Turner, with his imaginative sweep, and the Pre-Raphaelites, with their minuteness of detail. Taking Millais as the typical representative of the school, he draws out a contrast between the natural powers and aptitudes of the two artists. The element that he finds common to both is their sincerity in the study of nature.

The turn thus given to the pamphlet was no doubt due in part to the criticisms made on the previous Letters. To the second Letter of 1851 the *Times* made an editorial reply which is printed below[1] as necessary to the sequence of the story. The reply, it will be seen, sought

---

[1] "We should find it no difficult task to destroy the web which the paradoxical ingenuity of our correspondent, the 'Author of *Modern Painters*,' has spun, but we must confine our reply within narrower limits than the letters with which he has favoured us. If we spoke with severity of the productions of the young artists to which this correspondence relates, it was with a sincere desire to induce them, if possible, to relinquish what is absurd, morbid, and offensive in their works, and to cultivate whatever higher and better qualities they possess; but at present these qualities are wholly overlaid by the vices of a style which has probably answered its purpose by obtaining for these young gentlemen a notoriety less hard to bear, even in the shape of ridicule, than public indifference. This perversion of talent—if talent they have—we take to be fairly obnoxious to criticism; and we trust the authority of the 'Author of *Modern Painters*' will not have the opposite effect of perpetuating or increasing the defects of a style which, in spite of his assertions, we hold to be a flagrant violation of nature and truth. In fact, Mr. Ruskin's own works might prove the best antidote to any such false theory; for (if we remember rightly) he has laid it down, in his defence of Mr. Turner's landscapes, that truth in painting is not the mere imitative reproduction of this or that object, as they *are*, but the reproduction or image of the general effect given by an assemblage of objects as they *appear* to the sight. Mr. Millais and his friends have taken refuge in the opposite extreme of exaggeration from Mr. Turner; but, as extremes meet, they both find an apologist in the same critic. Aërial perspective, powerful contrasts of light and shade, with form and colour fused in the radiance of the atmosphere, are characteristic of Mr. Turner. The P. R. B.s, to whom the 'Author of *Modern Painters*' has transferred his affections, combine a repulsive precision of ugly shapes, with monotony of tone in such works as 'Sylvia' or 'Convent Thoughts,' or distorted expression, as in 'Mariana' or the 'Dove in the Ark.' Mere truth of imitation in the details of a flower, of a lock of hair, ceases to be truth in combination with the laws of effect. Nobody compares the pimples on a face by Denner with the broad flesh of Titian. Many of our correspondent's assertions may be more summarily disposed of by a reference to the pictures in question than by discussion in this place; but though he has carried the rights of defence to their utmost limits, we submit that enough

by reference to his praise of Turner to convict Ruskin of inconsistency in supporting the Pre-Raphaelites. In preparing his later pamphlet Ruskin met this criticism boldly by placing Turner, as it were, among the Pre-Raphaelites, and Millais, the chief of the Brotherhood, as a Turnerian *in posse.* "I am very glad," he wrote to his father (Les Rousses, August 11, 1851), "you are satisfied with the little pamphlet, and the *de trop* of Turner is a good fault, as people have been accusing me of changing my mind." The critics were not, however, convinced. Thus the *Daily News* objected that it was inconsistent to admire both Turner and the Pre-Raphaelites, between whose methods there were "striking dissimilarities," and on this review Ruskin wrote:—

> "Sunday, *September* 21 [1851].—I rather wonder at *Daily News* attacking *Pre-Raphaelitism* unless they have committed themselves by first attacking the pictures. They talk of my inconsistency because they cannot see two sides at once: all people are apparently inconsistent who have a wide range of thought, and can look alternately from opposite points. The most inconsistent of all books is the Bible—to people who cannot penetrate it.[1] Nevertheless, I should have thought the *Daily News* people had wit enough to get at the thread of the story in *P.-R.;* it is not so profound as all that."

Other critics made the same objections, and it was no doubt with these in his mind that Ruskin in revising his *Lectures on Architecture and Painting* once more claimed Turner as "the first and greatest of the Pre-Raphaelites," (see below, p. 159), and emphasised as the characteristic common to them all a love of sincerity as opposed to conventional ideas of a spurious beauty (§ 133, p. 158). To the same subject Ruskin returned in the third and fourth volumes of *Modern Painters* (1856), and the reader who desires, in connexion with the letters and pamphlets in the present volume, to have the point further elucidated, may be advised to refer to the passages of that book.[2]

remains, even on his own admissions, to condemn these unfortunate attempts, and that the mere expression of a difference of taste does not suffice to shake any of those established rules of art and criticism upon which such works have been tried and found wanting. It will give us great pleasure if we find next year that these young painters are able to throw off the monkish disguise in which they have been fooling, and stand forth as the founders of the illustrious school which our correspondent announces to the world."

[1] For some remarks of Ruskin's developing this idea, see Introduction to Vol. V.

[2] See especially *Modern Painters*, vol. iii. ch. x. § 5, comparing with it vol. iv. ch. iv. § 8. It may be useful to add some further references to the Pre-Raphaelites in other passages of Ruskin's writings. For general references, see *Modern Painters*,

The pamphlet on *Pre-Raphaelitism* created some stir in artistic circles, and produced in the same year a reply by E. V. Rippingille, to whose magazine Ruskin had been a contributor (see Vol. III. p. 645).[1] A little later came a lecture by the Rev. Edward Young, to which Ruskin refers in this volume (below, p. 163 *n.*). Ruskin himself was well pleased with his own production, which (as he says in a letter) had given him much trouble to compose. " I have the pamphlet *Pre-Raphaelitism*," he wrote to his father from Venice (September 11, 1851), " and think it reads excellently." That was not the opinion of his old enemy in the *Athenæum*, which made merry over the alleged inconsistencies in the argument, and waxed especially wroth over the " vaingloriousness" of the author's Preface.[2] Ruskin's father duly passed on this critical chastening to his son.

> " It is quite true," wrote Ruskin in reply (September 9), " that preface reads haughty enough ; but, as you say, I cannot write with a modesty I do not feel. In speaking of art I shall never be modest any more. I see more and more every day that all over Europe people are utterly ignorant of its first principles, and more

vol. iii. ch. iii. § 9 ; ch. iv. § 23 ; ch. vi. § 8 *n.* ; ch. x. § 21 ; ch. xvi. § 10 *n.*, § 26 ; Appendix i. ; vol. iv. ch. ii. § 5 (on their morbid choice of subjects) ; ch. iv. § 2 ; vol. v. pt. vi. ch. v. § 2, § 5 (on their leaf painting) ; ch. x. § 8 ; pt. viii. ch. iii. § 5. The gradual advance of the school and its influence on the whole range of contemporary art are traced in successive issues of *Academy Notes*. The *Letters* to *Chesneau* (in a later volume of this edition) contain many references to the Brotherhood ; and in his later period, Ruskin devoted some passages to them—Lecture i. in *The Art of England*, and *The Three Colours of Pre-Raphaelitism*.

[1] See Bibliographical Note on p. 338, below. The following reviews, among others, of *Pre-Raphaelitism* appeared in the press : The *Daily News*, August 13, 1851 ; *Builder*, September 23, 1851 ; *Economist*, August 23, 1851 (pp. 933–934) ; *Athenæum*, August 23, 1851, No. 1243, p. 908 ; *Leader*, August 23, 1851 (pp. 803–804) ; *Spectator*, October 4, 1851 (a note to an article on Pre-Raphaelitism) ; *Art Journal*, November 1851 (pp. 285–286) ; very bitter on the " conceit or craft" of the Pre-Raphaelite Brethren, and characterising Ruskin's pamphlet as a " maundering medley" ; *Irish Quarterly Review*, December 1851, vol. 1, pp. 740–762 ; *Scotsman*, January 3, 1852 ; *Art Journal*, September 1, 1854 (referred to in *Modern Painters*, vol. iii. ch. x. § 5 *n.*) ; *Fraser's Magazine*, June 1856, vol. 53, pp. 686–693 (an article entitled " Pre-Raphaelitism from Different Points of View," " reviewing Ruskin's pamphlet, and *What is Pre-Raphaelitism*, by John Ballantyne, A.R.S.A., 1856 ; the article is signed ' A. Y.—R. S.' ")

[2] The following are passages from the review in the *Athenæum* (pp. 908–909) : The author, it said, has " betaken himself to satisfy us that hot and cold are one, that licence and formality are alike to be reverenced, and that with Turner-*olatry* as strongly professed by him as ever, the canonization of *St.* Millais and other Pre-Raphaelites is entirely compatible, and on every ground to be defended." With regard to the Preface, the reviewer said : " Rarely has any oracle's *ego* been stretched farther in the demand for blind faith and acquiescence than in this pamphlet ;—rarely has *ego* been more vainglorious. . . . The cool and unhesitating assumption in all this of a commission ' to bind and to loose' is something to turn the authority, whatever it might otherwise have been worth, into ridicule."

especially the upper classes; that the perception of it is limited to a
few unheard-of artists and amateurs; that it has been the same for
three centuries; and that it will need a century more, with hard
work from all the men who know anything about the matter, merely
to make the people of Europe understand their position, and begin
properly. I don't know if the world is to last so long, but I shall
work and write as if it were."

In a later letter Ruskin launched out at his critics more angrily :—

> "*September* 28.—. . . When I read those reviews of *Pre-Raphael-
> itism*, I was so disgusted by their sheer broad-faced, sheepish, swinish
> stupidity, that I began to feel, as I wrote in the morning, that I was
> really rather an ass myself to string pearls for them. It is not the
> malice of them—*that*, when it is clever, is to be met boldly and with
> some sense of its being worth conquering. But these poor wretches
> of reviewers do, in their very inmost and most honest heart, Misunder-
> stand every word I write, and I never could teach them any better."

The reader of Ruskin's books will admit, however, that the author
did not weary in instructing a perverse generation, and was very well
able to give, as well as to receive, hard blows. Meanwhile a private
appreciation of the pamphlet came from a distinguished artist and an
old friend of his father, and gave Ruskin much pleasure :—

> "VEVAY, *August* 20, 1851.—I am deeply grateful for George Rich-
> mond's letter, both to himself and to you for copying it. Such a
> letter is indeed enough reward for much labour; but I am at a loss
> to understand the *depth* of the feeling he expresses, for there is
> nothing in the pamphlet but common sense, and he, of all men,
> has no reason to wish that his genius had been otherwise employed.
> To how many human souls has he given comfort, companionship,
> memory; of how many noble intellects has he preserved the image!
> What could [he] have done better and have looked back to with
> greater delight?"

Pre-Raphaelitism had even more to say about Turner than about
the Pre-Raphaelites, and its history from this point of view remains
to be noticed. It may, indeed, apart from its title, be called the first
of Ruskin's many pamphlets on that painter. It was written after a
visit to Farnley. Mr. Walter Fawkes, of Farnley Hall, had been one
of the oldest and staunchest of Turner's friends, a warm admirer of his

genius, and a constant purchaser of his works. Turner repeatedly visited him between 1803 and 1820, and after his death in 1825 "could not speak of the shore of Wharfe," on which Farnley Hall looks down, "but his voice faltered." At Farnley were preserved, and in large part are preserved still, numerous studies of the Hall and its grounds by the painter, a splendid series of drawings and a few oil-pictures. Ruskin had become acquainted with Mr. Francis Hawksworth Fawkes, the son of Turner's friend, and in April 1851, he and his wife went to Farnley on a visit, that he might study there its art treasures. On the occasion of a later visit in 1884 Ruskin spoke the following words, which were entered by his hostess in the Visitors' Book :—

> "Farnley is a perfectly unique place. There is nothing like it anywhere ; a place where a great genius had been loved and appreciated, who did all his best work for that place, where it is treasured up like a monument in a shrine." [1]

To Ruskin at the time of his earlier visit the shrine was still instinct with the spirit of the great genius. The master of the house, the eldest son of Turner's old friend, knew the painter well, and had many reminiscences of him ; it is to Mr. Hawksworth Fawkes that some of the not very numerous extant letters of Turner are addressed, and it was he who made from life the well-known caricature-sketch of the little great man. He was able to show Ruskin where Turner had painted this effect or that ; to take him on Turner's favourite walks ; and to tell him many an anecdote of the drawings and pictures on the walls. Ruskin stayed for several days, and every night he used to take one of Turner's water-colours up to his bedroom, to look at it the first thing in the morning.[2] Ruskin wrote as usual to his father, giving his first impressions of the Hall and his host :—

> "MY DEAREST FATHER,—I have your line of yesterday. I am not doing much, but just because I give a great deal of time to do very little, I appear in a hurry. I am quite resting, and more enjoying the pictures than working at them — making notes of dates, etc. Mr. Fawkes is exactly like one of the Aclands, without their Puseyism, but a Whig and a free trader—only perfectly honest in both, and antagonist to all railroads. I wish you could have heard him

---

[1] *The Nineteenth Century*, April 1900, p. 622. The words are also printed (with some slight variations) in an article on "Farnley Hall," by S. A. Byles, in *The Magazine of Art*, July 1887, p. 295.
[2] See the article by Mrs. Ayscough Fawkes, on "Mr. Ruskin at Farnley," in *The Nineteenth Century*, April 1900, p. 617.

describing the way he obstructed the surveyors on his estate: first turning them all out of his grounds, and then, when they tried to survey on the roads, watching them all day, and getting between the surveyor and his assistant—sitting on his pony in their line of sight—and enjoying it as much as a schoolboy all the time.

"I wish you could see the room we have prayers in, in the morning; the furniture—veritable old oak; the oriel window with its small and delicate crests; Cromwell's hat, the one he wore at Marston, and sword, on the wall among the deers' heads and antlers; Fairfax's sword, and Cromwell's watch; and much strange old plate and indescribable antiquities in venerable order. I have several other letters to write to-day, so must be short.

"Dearest love to my mother,

"Ever, my dearest father,

"Your most affectionate son,

"J. RUSKIN."

Ruskin made brief memoranda of the Farnley pictures and drawings and occasional references occur in his books, but it is in this pamphlet on *Pre-Raphaelitism* that his principal notice of them occurs. The pamphlet became indeed an account of Turner, written round the Farnley collection. To Mr. Fawkes, therefore, it was dedicated, and Ruskin afterwards wrote from Venice, hoping that the acknowledgment was not unwelcome:—

"VENICE,

"8th February, 1852.

"DEAR MR. FAWKES,—I have long been wishing to write to you, and more to hear from you; but since I left London I have been far from well, and able to write only few letters; but I cannot stay longer without knowing, first how you are, and secondly, that you were not offended at my inscribing my pamphlet to you, of which, not having heard from you since, I have been in some little fear. There was so much in it about your collection that I did not like it to appear without some special acknowledgment of your kindness, but if you do not wish your name to be associated with the opinions expressed in other parts of the pamphlet, I will withdraw it in future editions. But I want, first of all, to know how you are; for you must have felt very deeply what has occurred since last I saw you. For myself, I had been expecting it, and yet it has cast more shadow than I thought over these lagoons which he painted so often —what must it over your secret walks and glens?

"I have heard nothing definite of what he has done—probably you have heard more than I. I was in hopes at first, from a vague report of the will, that all the pictures, sketches, and drawings, had been left to form a grand gallery; now, they tell me, it is the finished pictures only. Alas! these are finished in a double sense— nothing but chilled fragments of paint on rotten canvas. The Claudites will have a triumph when they get into the National Gallery.[1]

"I am longing to get home to see what has been found in his cellars and drawers, but I have a great deal to do here yet; perhaps I shall have to run home and return. Are you thinking of coming to town this season, or were you discouraged by the unfortunate result of last year?—nay, I am sure you will be up if only to see the Queen Anne Street pictures once more on the old walls, and I should be grieved if I did not meet you there.

"I was very sorry that I did not see Lady Barnes when she came to town. We were just leaving when she arrived. I was, besides, in much confusion, not only leaving for the Continent, but leaving the town house—I hope the last, as it was the first town house in which I shall ever live. The man who breakfasts with a brick wall opposite to him when he may have a green field, deserves to be bricked up in it.

"You will not be much interested in anything that I can tell you about Venice; you have enough to entertain you at home— the brave doings of our clever Ministry. I think, however, I shall make Effie write you an account of one of Marshal Radetzky's balls, which I broke through my vows of retirement to take her to the other day at Verona. There was much of interest in it, but chiefly seeing the old Marshal and his intense solicitude that every one, and especially the ladies, should have enough to eat; standing behind their chairs at the supper table, reconnoitring the table as if it had been a field of battle, and running every now and then himself to the kitchen to order up the reserves.[2] I think, also, I must get you to write to Effie, in order to remind her that she has some friends in England; also, I do not know how I am to get her away from here, the Austrians have made such a pet of her that she declares if she ever leaves Venice it must be to go to Vienna. But, at any rate, pray write a single line either to Effie or me, saying how you all are—a letter will always find me, sent to the *Poste Restante* here; I have a direction, but it is a troublesome and long one, and the letter will be quite as safe at the Post Office. I must do the Austrians justice in this respect. My father writes to me twice a week, and I to him every day. I have been five months in Venice and never a letter has missed. I hope this will not be the first to be lost, for I am really getting very anxious to hear from you.

[1] For the reference here, see below, p. 408.
[2] See the letter from Ruskin given in Vol. X. pp. xxxi.–xxxii.

"Have you done anything to the drawings of birds yet? I am terrified lest any harm happen to them in framing.[1] Pray tell me they are safe, and if the large pictures are still down, and you continue to like them so. Effie sends her best love, and says (which my letter above will confirm), first, 'that she is as wild as ever; secondly, which is rather inconsistent with my statements, 'that she hopes to come and have some more walks at Farnley,' which I am exceedingly glad to hear; and lastly, that she hopes 'to come to be kept in order by you again some day,' which is the most sensible thing I have heard her say for a long time. Our best regards to Mrs. Fawkes.

"Ever, my dear Mr. Fawkes,

"Most sincerely yours,

"J. RUSKIN."[2]

The pamphlet was not reprinted till 1862, and the dedication, above referred to, was then withdrawn, for in the interval Ruskin's relations with Farnley had been broken off. In 1884, on the invitation of the next generation of its masters, he visited the Hall again; some letters and reminiscences referring to that visit will be found in a later volume of this edition.

The *manuscript* of the latter portion of the pamphlet (§ 40 to the end) is in Mr. Allen's possession, written on seventeen leaves of blue foolscap. A *facsimile* of a page of it is given between pp. 392 and 393. A few variations in the printed text are noted in their place. Bibliographical particulars are given on p. 338.

With the next pieces in this collection—consisting of Letters to the *Times* on the National Gallery—we come to another of Ruskin's interests during the years now under discussion—an interest which, later on, was to become more direct in connexion with Turner's bequest

---

[1] This allusion is thus explained by Mrs. Ayscough Fawkes: "There is a book of birds' feathers, compiled by a member of the Fawkes family early in the century, in the library at Farnley; on one side the feathers from the head, back, breast, etc., fastened down; on the other side of the page, drawings of the bird by various hands; of these some twelve are by Turner, some of them said to be shot by him. Mr. Ruskin was of opinion that the fact of rubbing against the feathers was injurious to these works of art, which were very badly mounted, so they were placed in a book, and many years later we had them window-mounted with great care."

[2] This letter is reprinted from the article in the *Nineteenth Century* already cited. The following postscript was there added: "Dear Mr. Fawkes,—Pray don't mind what Mr. Ruskin says about me on the opposite page. I love you and dear Mrs. Fawkes and Farnley as much as ever, and no Austrians or anybody else will make me forget you or your kindness to me. Mr. Ruskin and I often talk of you and Mrs. Fawkes.—Ever, believe me, sincerely yours, EFFIE."

to the nation. Some knowledge of the early history of the Gallery is necessary to understand the circumstances in which Ruskin's letters were written.

The present organisation of the National Gallery (with some modifications which need not concern us) dates back to 1855, and was in part brought about by the controversies in which Ruskin here takes part. The executive authority has since that date been vested in a Director; in some matters he can only act with the concurrence of the Trustees, but the real responsibility is his. Before 1855, however, the executive officer held a more subordinate position; he was called "Keeper"; and responsibility for the purchase and care of pictures was divided, in an undefined way, between him, the Trustees, and the Treasury. In 1843, Mr. (afterwards Sir) C. L. Eastlake was appointed Keeper. Ruskin, as we have already seen from a private letter (Vol. III. p. 670), was "put into a desperate rage" by some of the first purchases under Eastlake's régime. These had been of Guidos and Rubenses, whereas Ruskin wanted to see the collection strengthened by the accession of works by the early Italians and the great Venetians. These came in later years—in large measure, we may fairly conclude, owing to the interest created by Ruskin's writings. In the autumn of 1846 a correspondence was opened in the columns of the *Times*, attacking the administration of the Gallery generally. During the previous vacation many of the pictures had been cleaned and restored. Eastlake was blamed not only for thus damaging (as it was alleged) good pictures, but also for buying bad ones. The attack was led by the picture-dealer, and at one time artist, Mr. Morris Moore, writing at first under the pseudonym of "Verax," and afterwards in his own name. Eastlake resigned office in 1847, and was succeeded by Thomas Uwins, R.A., who held the office of Keeper till 1855, when Eastlake was appointed Director with enlarged power. Mr. Moore, however, continued his opposition through several years, especially during 1850 and 1852. He also published some pamphlets on the subject, amongst them one entitled *The Revival of Vandalism at the National Gallery: A Reply to John Ruskin and Others* (London, Ollivier, 1853). The whole discussion may be gathered in all its details from the Parliamentary Report of the Select Committee on the National Gallery in 1853. Such references to this Report as are necessary to explain passages in Ruskin's letters, are given in footnotes to the text: the particulars in at least one instance are somewhat curious (see p. 400 *n.*). His first letter (pp. 397–406) was written on January 6, 1847, when the first campaign of "Verax" was in full vigour. It touches on some of the particular cases of restoration in controversy, and then passes to the subject already mentioned—namely, the neglect to purchase good Italian pictures. " Let agents be sent to all the cities of Italy," said Ruskin in conclusion, " let the noble pictures which are perishing there be rescued." In after years his advice was taken; successive directors made annual tours of investigation in Italy, and many noble pictures were thus secured for the national collection.

Five years later the administration of the Gallery under Mr. Uwins, R.A., was criticised even more severely than that under his predecessor. Eastlake was then a Trustee, and there was internal dissension regarding the extent to which the Keeper should be allowed to carry out his " cleaning" operations. Some of the Trustees (Eastlake among them) desired to restrict the renovation to removing the old varnish; others were prepared to authorise the Keeper " to improve or repair the surface of the pictures below."[1] The dispute found its way, as such things do, into the newspapers; there was a loud outcry, which in the following year led to the appointment of a Select Committee. To this second discussion Ruskin contributed another letter (pp. 407–414) to the *Times* (December 29, 1852). In this he laid special stress on the desirability of protecting the pictures by glass. Here, again, his advice was taken; the process of glazing the pictures was continued from year to year as the funds provided by the Treasury allowed, and has now for some time been completed. Ruskin went on to explain his views about the proper arrangement and display of a Picture Gallery generally. This was a subject to which he had been giving much attention during 1852, in connexion with hopes and plans for the Turner bequest; he returned to the subject in 1856, in his pamphlet on the oil-pictures included in that bequest; such illustrative matter from his letters and diaries of the time as pertains to this topic is reserved for the next volume, in which that pamphlet is reprinted.

At a later date Ruskin bore testimony to the great improvement of the Gallery, especially under the directorship of his friend the late Sir Frederick Burton.[2] In a preface to a book on the Gallery first published in 1888 Ruskin declared, of a collection which in 1852 he had stigmatised as a " European jest" (below, p. 398), that it was " without question now the most important collection of paintings in Europe, for the purposes of the general student."[3] The improvement of the

[1] *Report of the Select Committee* of 1853, p. ix.
[2] See *The Laws of Fésole*, ch. iv.
[3] Preface (reprinted in a later volume of this edition) to E. T. Cook's *Popular Handbook to the National Gallery*.

Gallery, and especially its acquisition of Italian pictures, were due in large measure to the taste and enthusiasm which his own writings had stimulated.

In connexion with one of the principal topics in these letters, it is interesting to know that Ruskin tried to practise what he preached. He wanted the National Gallery to be enriched, as we have seen, with pictures of the great Venetians. When he was at Venice in 1851–1852, he saw a chance of securing for the Gallery two first-rate pictures by Tintoret; one of these, the "Crucifixion" in St. Cassiano, was in his opinion "among the finest in Europe;"[1] the other was the great "Marriage in Cana," of the Salute.[2] Among the Trustees of the National Gallery was Lord Lansdowne, with whom Ruskin had some acquaintance. He opened the subject to the Trustees in March 1852, as appears from the following letter to his father:—

"VENICE, *March* 1852.— . . . Now that Lord Lansdowne is at leisure, I am going to write to him to ask him if there is no way of getting some of these pictures to England. It is a piteous thing to see the marks and channels made down them by the currents of rain, like those of a portmanteau after a wet journey of twelve hours; and to see the rents, when the bombshells came through them, still unstopped—indeed better so, for if they were to patch them up, they would assuredly begin to retouch them, and so farewell Tintoret."

Through his friend Mr. Cowper-Temple, Ruskin enlisted also the support of Lord Palmerston, and he was in correspondence further with Sir Charles Eastlake, who was then President of the Royal Academy as well as a Trustee of the Gallery. The first answers seem to have been encouraging, though Ruskin chafed—as who has not?—at the dilatoriness of official ways. "I have a letter from Sir Charles Eastlake," he writes to his father, on May 16, ". . . with some important report of progress respecting National Gallery and Tintoret. I will enclose you his letter on Tuesday, but must show it to some people to-morrow. I fear nothing can be done—they are too slow, but I am glad to find that I have *some* power, even with such immoveable people as Trustees for [the] National Gallery." The Trustees, meanwhile, were consulting Edward Cheney, who, as Ruskin afterwards believed, "put a spoke in

---

[1] See Venetian Index in Vol. XI. p. 366.
[2] *Ibid.*, p. 429.

the wheel for pure spite."[1] At the time, however, he thought that Cheney's co-operation in the matter had been secured :—

> "*May* 17.— . . . I enclose Sir C. Eastlake's letter, which has given me a good deal to do in talking over Mr. Cheney, so as not to make him jealous. A word that piqued him might have spoiled all; however it is all right, only they ought to have told me this a fortnight ago. I fear it is now too late. I shall be at Verona when the Trustees give me their final answer, and can only set the thing in train, if *anything* can be done at all."

But it was not "all right," as will be seen by the following extract from the minutes of a meeting of the Trustees on June 7, 1852 :—

> "*Read*—A letter from Mr. Ruskin, at Venice, of the 19th May, addressed to Sir Charles Eastlake, and enclosing one from Mr. Cheney, in the former of which Mr. Ruskin stated that he is willing to undertake to procure for this Gallery two pictures by Tintoretto, the "Marriage at Cana" in the Madonna della Salute, and the "Crucifixion" in St. Cassiano; the former valued by him at £5000, the latter at £7000. But although he would use his endeavours to procure them at a less cost, he is unwilling to move in the matter, unless the Government will ultimately sanction the expenditure of £12,000 for the two pictures.
>
> "*Resolved*—That the Trustees do not find themselves in a position to ask from the Government so considerable a sum as that required by Mr. Ruskin as the basis of his negotiation for the pictures in question, especially as Mr. Cheney does not entirely concur with him in his valuation of the works, and as the Trustees have not sufficient means of arriving at their true value; they therefore request that Sir Charles Eastlake will be so obliging as to communicate to Mr. Ruskin their unwillingness that he should proceed further in this matter."[2]

So ended Ruskin's attempt to procure for this country two of Tintoretto's finest works. It was his first disappointment, in matters where he was personally concerned, in connexion with the National Gallery. The Turner Bequest was to be attended with other disappointments, yet more poignant—as we shall see hereafter.

In the summer of 1854, as has been stated above (p. xxxvii.), Ruskin went abroad with his parents, and in Switzerland he wrote the piece

---

[1] *Præterita*, iii. ch. ii. § 29, where Ruskin by a slip of memory dates the transaction in 1845. Cheney was an Englishman of antiquarian tastes resident in Venice : see the appendix to Ruskin's *Guide to the Academy at Venice*.

[2] *National Gallery Return*, 1847–1852 : House of Commons Papers, 1853, No. 104, p. 47.

which comes in this volume next after the National Gallery Letters. As is not uncommonly the case with Ruskin's works, the title—*The Opening of the Crystal Palace*—gives no very immediate or obvious indication of its contents. The real subject is a plea for the Preservation of Ancient Monuments; the title tells us only of the occasion which suggested the piece. In June 1854 the newspapers had been full of the new Palace at Sydenham. The Crystal Palace, it may be well to remind the reader, was a later birth of the enthusiasm and ideals which had produced the Great Exhibition of 1851—ideals which Tennyson expressed in a verse which once stood part of his poem " To the Queen " :—

> " She brought a vast design to pass,
> When Empire and the scattered ends
> Of our fierce world did meet as friends
> And brethren in her halls of glass."

To readers of the present day there is perhaps a touch of bathos here; at the time when the lines were written, they appealed to ideas which, originating with the Prince Consort, had penetrated from the Court throughout the country, and taken firm hold of men's minds. It was thought intolerable that the Great Exhibition should pass away as though it had never been. It was decided therefore to construct out of its materials a permanent Hall of Glass which should continue and extend the educational and artistic influence of the Exhibition. The Palace was designed by Sir Joseph Paxton, and was opened by the Queen and the Prince Consort in state on June 10, 1854. Ruskin, as appears from this pamphlet, and from passages in his other writings, shared to the full the high and generous hopes with which the Palace was started upon its chequered career. " It is impossible," he says, " to estimate the influence of such an institution on the minds of the working classes " (p. 418); and, as we have already seen, he took particular interest in a collection of casts of sculpture and architecture which had been made for exhibition in the Palace (Vol. X. pp. 114, 416). But in the pæans of popular enthusiasm which saw, in the Exhibition and the Palace, the birth of a new Order of Architecture, as well as the dawn of a New Era, Ruskin could have no sympathy whatever. We have seen already, in an appendix to the first volume of *The Stones of Venice*, his protest against the notion that the construction of a greenhouse " larger than ever greenhouse was built before " had any artistic significance, however great its mechanical ingenuity might be (Vol. IX. pp. 455–456). We shall meet with the same protest in a later work, where this so-called "edifice of Fairyland " is faithfully dealt with (*Aratra Pentelici*, §§ 53, 54; and *On the Old Road*, 1899, vol. ii. § 195). It was to this same point that his pamphlet on *The Opening of the Crystal Palace* was primarily directed (p. 419); but the event suggested further thoughts on a subject which had for some years past been much in his mind. While the British public was congratulating itself on having achieved, in its halls of glass, "an entirely novel order of architecture," the old architecture of the world was perishing every day by fire, war, revolution, and neglect; and by a foe, even more destructive than any of these—namely, "restoration." This is the main theme of the pamphlet, which thus carries a stage further the plea for the preservation of ancient buildings already advanced in *The Seven Lamps of Architecture*, and repeated in scattered passages of later writings. The pamphlet should especially be compared with the chapter on "The Lamp of Memory" in the earlier work (Vol. VIII. pp. 242-247); but here Ruskin adds a practical suggestion. "An association," he says, "might be formed, thoroughly organised so as to maintain active watchers and agents in every town of importance, who, in the first place, should furnish the society with a *perfect* account of every monument of interest in its neighbourhood, and then with a yearly or half-yearly report of the state of such monuments, and of the changes proposed to be made upon them" (p. 431). The reader will see from this passage, and the further suggestions which follow it, that Ruskin's scheme was precisely that which William Morris carried out twenty-three years later in the formation of "The Society for Protection of Ancient Buildings"—a title altered by Morris for popular usage into "The Anti-Scrape."[1] Of this Society both Ruskin and Carlyle were original members. With the Society's efforts in connexion with Venice, we shall be concerned in a later volume including *St. Mark's Rest*. In the meanwhile Ruskin's appeals must have confirmed and encouraged other individuals who were working on the same lines, and he himself was ever ready to intervene in particular cases; of such intervention, the volume containing *The Arrows of the Chace* bears record.

The pamphlet is of further interest as containing—like most of Ruskin's writings on architecture—an incidental passage which is eloquent of his strong and growing social sympathies. In this passage (§ 18, p. 430), he describes the "few feet of ground (how few!) which

---

[1] Mr. Mackail says in *The Life of William Morris* (i. 339), that until Morris moved no "clear statement of principle" had been enunciated in the matter. To Ruskin belongs the credit of the suggestion; to Morris, that of embodying it in an organised shape. Ruskin suggested, further, that the Association should in cases of need save ancient monuments from destruction by purchase—an object partly aimed at by the recently formed "National Trust."

are indeed all that separate the merriment from the misery." The time was presently to come, when in words of yet more poignant appeal he was to call upon his generation to "raise the veil boldly" and "face the light";[1] and when, having made his appeal to others, he was himself to embark on direct schemes of social amelioration.

The pamphlet on *The Opening of the Crystal Palace*, was written, as might be concluded from its tone of burning enthusiasm, quickly and under strong emotion. His diary enables us to fix the middle of June as the time at which the first suggestion occurred to him as he was journeying from Vevay to the Simmenthal (below, p. 417); he must have written it at his next stopping-places, and sent the MS. immediately to England—trusting, no doubt, to his old friend W. H. Harrison to see it through the press, for it was published on July 22.[2] But though written quickly, it was composed carefully. The *manuscript* of the greater part of it is in Pierpont Morgan's possession, having been bound up by Ruskin together with the MSS. of *Modern Painters* (Vol. III. p. 682). It shows once more how carefully Ruskin "worked up" his writings (above, p. xxxi.). The *facsimile* of a page of it will enable the reader to note the process (p. 429).

In an Appendix to Part II. of this volume, some minor notes on Art are given. First comes a series of Letters written by Ruskin in 1844 to his friend, Mr. Edmund Oldfield, on the subject of Painted Glass. They refer primarily to a stained-glass window which was erected at the east end of St. Giles' Church, Camberwell, from designs by Oldfield and Ruskin. Oldfield had been a fellow pupil with Ruskin at Mr. Dale's (Vol. I. p. xlix.), and his family and the Ruskins were neighbours at Denmark Hill. The artistic tastes of the two young men were known in the parish, and they were commissioned to prepare designs for a window in the new church, erected (1841–1843) in the Early Decorated Style, from designs by Gilbert Scott.[3] "They seem to desire," writes Ruskin in his diary for 1844 (May 3), "to put in my design for the window; hope they may like it if they do, but it will make me very anxious." In the first instance designs for the window-head only were to be submitted. These were prepared by Ruskin, and approved by the Committee, but a fresh design by Oldfield was substituted

[1] *Unto this Last*, § 85.
[2] Reviews of the pamphlet appeared in the *Athenæum*, August 12, 1854, No. 1398, pp. 998–999 (very hostile, praising the architecture of the Palace and ridiculing Ruskin's ideas about restoration); *Builder*, August 12, vol. 12, p. 421 (leading article); *New Quarterly Review*, 1854, vol. 3, p. 515.
[3] A description of the church is given in C. L. Eastlake's *History of the Gothic Revival*, pp. 220–223.

for the central light, Ruskin perceiving—as explained in *Præterita* (ii. ch. viii. § 153)—that his own "figures adopted from Michael Angelo" were "not exactly adapted to thirteenth-century practice." The window-head was liked, and it was decided to fill the five vertical lights in the same manner. These, however, Ruskin left entirely to Oldfield, who attained, he says, "a delicate brilliancy, purer than anything I had before seen in modern glass." The letters given in this volume (pp. 435–447) show Ruskin absorbed in studying the old glass of Rouen and Chartres, with a view to the window which he and his friend were to design for Camberwell. Like those to a College Friend (in Vol. I.) they are written in the lighter vein of familiar correspondence; the date of them is 1844. The illustration of the window here given (p. 440) will enable the reader to follow many of Ruskin's allusions.

The letters show once more the zeal with which Ruskin threw himself into a new and congenial study. It is interesting also to learn from them that the remarks on painted glass, which occur in various places in his books, were founded on studies thus commenced in 1844. The most important of those passages are, first, Appendix 12 in *Stones of Venice*, vol. ii. (Vol. X. pp. 456–457), where he shows how the essential qualities of the material—its transparency and susceptibility of the most brilliant colours—forbid "the attempt to turn painted windows into pretty pictures"; the standards of perfection in this art, he adds, are the French windows of the twelfth and thirteenth centuries. So, again, secondly, in *The Two Paths*, he says that "no man who knows what painting means, can endure a painted glass window which emulates painters' work," and refers, in illustration, to Reynolds' disappointment at the result of his designs for the window in the ante-chapel of New College, Oxford.[1]

The next Appendix contains a series of Notes on the Louvre. Of all the foreign galleries, the Louvre was at this period the best known to Ruskin, and it is to pictures there that in his earlier writings he refers most often (after perhaps the Dulwich Gallery, which was almost at his own door). "To enter a room in the Louvre," he says elsewhere, "is an education in itself."[2] It has been thought well to print, here for the first time, some of the notes and impressions he recorded in the

---

[1] *Two Paths*, § 78 and Appendix ii. ; see also §§ 82, 161. Among minor references to the subject, the more interesting are : *Seven Lamps* (Vol. VIII. p. 180), good figure-drawing impossible in a good painted window, with which passage compare *Stones of Venice*, App. 17 (Vol. IX. p. 455); *Stones of Venice*, vol. ii. (Vol. X. pp. iii., 174); *Giotto and his Works in Padua*, § 11 ; *Modern Painters*, vol. iv. ch. xx. § 23; *Eagle's Nest*, § 226 ; and in this volume, Review of Lord Lindsay, § 22, p. 192.

[2] A letter reprinted from the *Art Journal* in *On the Old Road*, 1899, vol. ii. § 195.

Louvre, both for their intrinsic interest, and in order to illustrate further the careful and elaborate nature of his studies in this sort. For this purpose he gave in the Epilogue to *The Stones of Venice*, as " a *pièce justificative*," some extracts from his notes on the galleries of Genoa, but those which are here put together from his diaries relating to the Louvre are both fuller and of more permanent interest.

The earliest of these Notes on the Louvre belong to 1844; the most elaborate, and the most carefully written, to 1849. The notes of that year are prefaced by a general passage in enthusiastic praise of the art of painting (p. 456). Similar Notes from a later diary (1854) follow. References to passages in his works where the same pictures are noticed are supplied in the footnotes. The references to the pictures have been altered to fit the present numbering of the Gallery. These written memoranda were supplemented, it should be remembered, by sketches, and sometimes by more elaborate studies from or copies of the pictures. An example of a study of this kind is Plate No. XII., in the *Lectures on Architecture and Painting* (see below, p. 112).

The next Appendix (p. 474) introduces us to a further artistic interest which had occupied much of Ruskin's time and thought, as well as to a new form of activity. This Appendix contains reports of three Addresses on Decorative Colour as applicable to Architectural Purposes, given by Ruskin in November 1854. The addresses were never printed by him; and it seems doubtful if he had written them out; they seem to have been, as he says (p. 474), informal talks. The only manuscript referring to the lectures, which has been found among his papers, are a few rough notes in his diary of 1854. They were, however, reported at the time in the public press. The lectures, which were delivered on Saturday afternoons, excited a good deal of curiosity, and attracted large audiences. At the first, a vote of thanks was moved by Mr. Beresford Hope, and the reporters noticed that few working-men were present. The second and third lectures, on the other hand, were largely attended by artisans, and Ruskin was heartily cheered. The present reports are here reprinted for the most part from a version put together in a privately-printed volume of *Ruskiniana* issued in 1892. (For bibliographical particulars, see below, p. 474 n.) Quotations have been verified; some passages amended; and others added from Ruskin's notes. Several drawings have been found at Brantwood which seem to have been used at these lectures, and from these, illustrations are now introduced. A few words are here necessary, first on the contents of these lectures, and secondly on the occasion of their delivery, in order to bring them into their place in Ruskin's life.

The third of the lectures—on General Principles of Colour—needs no introduction; it contains doctrines with which we are already familiar in Ruskin's earlier works, and which we meet again in the third volume of *Modern Painters*. The first two lectures, which are mainly concerned with the art of Illumination, introduce us to a new interest which first, during the years now under consideration, entered into Ruskin's artistic ken. He has described in his autobiography "the new worlds" which were opened to him in 1850 or 1851, when he "chanced at a bookseller's in a back alley on a little fourteenth-century Hours of the Virgin."[1] The collection and study of illuminated manuscripts henceforth became one of the greatest of his pleasures and the most constant of his pursuits. His work at Venice in 1851–1852, and then his absorption in completing *The Stones*, left him little time for his new hobby; but in 1853, when the pressure of that book was removed, the acquisition and study of illuminated manuscripts became a principal pre-occupation, filling many pages of his diaries, and often figuring in his letters. Wherever he went he used any opportunities that offered to look at treasures of this kind. He notes in his diaries the points of a MS. Bible in the Library at Edinburgh,[2] and of a Psalter at Glasgow. He went also, as already briefly mentioned (above, p. xxxvi.), to Hamilton, at the tenth Duke's invitation, to study the famous collection there. His first glimpse seems to have been disappointing:—

"HAMILTON, *Thursday evening* [*December* 22, 1853].—After some meditation I have determined not to stay in Glasgow, which is an *awful* place, but to go on Saturday to Durham. . . . The seeing the Cathedral there has long been an object with me; besides that I may perhaps see St. Cuthbert's prayer-book.

"I have been all the evening looking over the MSS. with the Duke and another missal admirer, Mr. Sneed, . . . nobody but the Duke and Duchess and we two bibliomanists at dinner. House much too stately for my mind, though perfectly warm and comfortable, but five servants waiting on four people are a nuisance.

"The MSS. are of course magnificent, but I would not give my £180 one for *any* one I have yet seen. There is not *one* of the time, and out of some thirty books I have examined, there are only three that would have been great temptations to me, even if I had seen them in a bookseller's shop. He seems to take good care of them, which rejoices me. I am promised great things for to-morrow morning."

[1] *Præterita*, iii. ch. i. §§ 18, 19.
[2] See also some passages in the *Lectures on Architecture and Painting*, §§ 121 n., 122, 123 n.

The Duke, it will be seen, had kept his best books for the last. Ruskin in his diary noted some of the most beautiful of them, and made drawings from them. How highly he valued the collection was to appear thirty years later when the manuscripts came into the market. He then issued an appeal for funds in the hope of securing some of them for public collections;[1] but the story of that effort belongs to a later volume. On returning to London, Ruskin entered at the British Museum upon a systematic study of the illuminated manuscripts in that opulent collection; on his visits to the Museum (1853–1854) he was often accompanied by Millais. Page after page in his diaries contains notes upon the MSS. The notes are hardly intelligible or significant to any one else, but it is at any rate possible, and it is interesting, to follow his method of study. He went all through the collection, noting dates and styles. Then he threw them into groups, according to subjects or styles or arrangements of colours. He made careful notes on the manuscripts in his own possession, indexing their initial letters and subjects. The studies thus indicated in his diaries were often utilised for incidental illustration in his books, but he never published anything dealing exclusively with the subject. The report of these Lectures of 1854, though not complete, is for this reason of special interest.

The intense delight which Ruskin experienced in these "fairy cathedrals," as he called them, "full of painted windows,"[2] was attended, however, by some qualms of conscience. The artistic and the moral sides of his nature were then as often at strife, and it was only gradually that a reconciliation was reached. The mood is seen very clearly in some letters to his father:—

"*Sunday, 23rd* [*October*, 1853].— . . . My love of art has been a terrible temptation to me, and I feel that I have been sadly self-indulgent lately — what with casts, *Liber Studiorum*, missals, and Tintorets. I think I must cut the whole passion short off at the root, or I shall get to be a mere collector, like old Mr. Wells of Redleaf,[3] or Sir W. Scott, or worst of all Beckford or Horace Walpole. I am sure I ought to take that text to heart, "covetousness which is idolatry," for I do idolize my Turners and missals, and I can't conceive anybody being ever tried with a heavier temptation than I

---

[1] See *General Statement Explaining the Nature of and Purpose of St. George's Guild*, dated February 21, 1882.

[2] *Præterita*, iii. ch. i. § 19.

[3] Mr. Wells, of Redleaf, Penshurst, for many years a sea-captain in the East India Company's service, formed a large collection of modern works of art. Notices of him may be found in many books of artists' reminiscences; see, *e.g.*, Frith's *Autobiography*, i. 319, and J. C. Horsley's *Recollections of a Royal Academician*, p. 55.

am to save every farthing I can to collect a rich shelf of thirteenth-century manuscripts. There would be no stop to it, for I should always find the new ones illustrating all the rest. I believe I shall have to give up all idea of farther collection, and to rest satisfied with my treasures."

Later letters confirm these good resolutions, if such they were, and one of them is further interesting as premonitory of feelings which were soon to grow in intensity :—

" *Wednesday morning, 16th Nov.*— . . . My next birthday is the keystone of my arch of life—my 35th—and up to this time I cannot say that I have in any way 'taken up my cross' or 'denied myself'; neither have I visited the poor nor fed them, but have spent my money and time on my own pleasure or instruction. I find I cannot be easy in doing this any more, for I feel that, if I were to die at present, God might most justly say to me, 'Thou in thy lifetime receivedst thy good things, and likewise Lazarus evil things.' I find myself always doing what I like, and that is certainly not the way to heaven. I feel no call to part with anything that I have, but I am going to preach some most *severe* doctrines in my next book, and I *must* act up to them in not going on spending in works of art."

The letter goes on to propound a scheme for ending and revising his collection, but a little loophole is allowed; "I won't make a vow that if, by any chance, I should hear of some exquisite thirteenth-century work being in the market, I may not consider whether I should be justified in buying it to take care of it."

The chance was soon to occur, and the temptation (or opportunity) was not allowed to pass. In his diary for 1854 is the following entry :—

" *February* 26.—On Friday the 24th I got the greatest treasure I have yet obtained in all my life—St. Louis's Psalter."

This exquisite Psalter was an unfailing delight to Ruskin. It was used to illustrate the Lectures here reported, and many references to it occur in his books.

Whatever Ruskin possessed, he desired to share. This desire, and the free scope he gave to it, saved him effectually from "getting to be a mere collector." His books, he used to say, were "for use and not for curiosities." He treated them in a way which can hardly be recommended for general practice. He annotated some of his most valuable manuscripts not merely in pencil, but in ink. He cut them to pieces, re-arranged them to his own desire, and of the St. Louis Psalter he dispersed many of the pages. Some were given to his school at Oxford; others found their way to the Bodleian Library; and others were given to his friend, Professor Norton. Some entries in his diary may well cause "a mere collector" to despair:—"*Dec.* 30, 1853.—Cut out some leaves from large missal." "*Jan.* 1, *Sunday.*—Put two pages of missal in frames." "*Jan.* 3. —Cut missal up in evening; hard work." Dean Kitchin relates an anecdote in this connexion: "One day at Brantwood, I was looking through these lovely specimens of monastic skill, and finding the St. Louis missal in complete disorder, I turned to Mr. Ruskin, who was sitting in his wonted chair in his library, and said, 'This MS. is in an awful state; could you not do something to get the pages right again?' and he replied, with a sad smile, 'Oh yes; these old books have in them an evil spirit, which is always throwing them into disorder'—as if it were through envy against anything so beautiful: the fact was that he had played the 'evil spirit' with them himself."[1] But his ripping up of such treasures was at any rate done, as Mr. Collingwood observes,[2] "not for wanton mischief, or in vulgar carelessness, but to show to his classes at lectures," or to give to friends of that which he valued most. Other valuables he treated in the same way, and sometimes, it must be admitted, with less praiseworthy reason. If a book would not fit a particular shelf, he had no compunction in sending for a tool and chopping not the shelf, but the book. Several of the books in his library received this summary execution.

The Lectures on Colour and Illumination are of interest in Ruskin's biography from another point of view than that of illustrating one of his favourite studies. They were among the first-fruits of the resolution recorded in the letter given above to spend himself in some measure on work, done otherwise than by the pen, for the pleasure and instruction of others. The Working Men's College was one sphere of such work at this time, as we shall see presently under the next head of this Introduction; the Architectural Museum, where these lectures were delivered, was another. The foundation of this Museum in 1851 has been already briefly noted. A principal aim of the institution was to render possible the training of workmen in the arts of their

---

[1] *Ruskin in Oxford and Other Studies,* 1904, p. 39 *n.* The St. Louis Psalter has now passed into the collection of Mr. Henry Yates Thompson. Mrs. Arthur Severn succeeded in replacing all the pages in their proper places.
[2] *Ruskin Relics,* 1903, p. 184.

crafts. "Singularly enough among all the antiquarian collections in London, accessible to the public, there were none which included a good assortment of casts from decorative sculpture, and the few which did exist were almost exclusively taken from classic and Italian examples. The advisability of securing such objects for the inspection and study, not only of young architects, but of art-workmen, became apparent to all who knew how much the success of modern Gothic depends on the spirit and vigour of its details."[1] The Architectural Museum was founded by a few architects and amateurs to supply the deficiency, and Ruskin, as soon as he was free from the pressure of immediate literary work, threw himself heartily into assisting a scheme which fell in so entirely with the ideas and aspirations expressed by him in *The Seven Lamps of Architecture* and in the chapter on "The Nature of Gothic." His presentation of casts of Venetian architecture has been already noticed, and in the preface to the second edition of *The Seven Lamps* (1855), he urged others to add to the collections of the Museum.[2] The Curator's Report for 1854 mentions other services and benefactions rendered by Ruskin:—

"A complete set of panels from the North doorway of Rouen Cathedral presented by Mr. Ruskin.

"A complete series of the Royal Seals of England from William I. to William IV., also presented by Mr. Ruskin. And Mr. Ruskin has besides kindly secured a set of casts of the sculptured panels on the sides of the great door of the cathedral of Notre Dame at Paris. He has also placed in the rooms of the Museum some drawings executed by himself of foreign architecture, and has promised still further aid to the students, by the loan of any casts and drawings in his possession that may be useful to them.

"The following three lectures were given by Mr. Ruskin. The first on the distinction between illumination and painting, the second on the general principles of outline, the third on the general principles of colour.

"Mr. Ruskin has, since these lectures, kindly attended at the Museum to direct the students in the study and practice of the Art of Illumination."

The pleasures of acquisition, in the case of illuminated manuscripts, were thus combined with the fulfilment of service to others.

---

[1] C. L. Eastlake's *History of the Gothic Revival*, p. 299. The Museum was successively housed in Cannon Street, in Bowling Street, and in Tufton Street, Westminster.

[2] See Vol. VIII. p. 13, Vol. X. p. 467.

III

The next Part of this volume takes us to a different thread in the web of Ruskin's life, though this, too, was destined indirectly to work out in the direction of social service. The *Notes on the Construction of Sheepfolds* was, as we have already learnt, an excursus on *The Stones of Venice* (Vol. IX. p. 437). The Gothic Revival in England was, it will be remembered,[1] largely associated with a Catholic revival, Roman and Anglican. Ruskin, on the other hand, was at this time a strong and even a bigoted Protestant. It was essential from his point of view to dissociate the two movements; the more so because Pugin, with whose works Ruskin's architectural writings had some superficial kinship, was a convert to Roman Catholicism, and made it his object to "lure" men "into the Romanist Church by the glitter of it."[2]   It was as a protest against this movement that Ruskin gave an aggressively anti-Romanist tone to many passages in *The Seven Lamps* and *The Stones of Venice*. But, again: his historical references to the Venetian State, and its hostility to the Papal power, had led him to remark on the proper functions of Church and State, a subject to which Catholic Emancipation, at this time bitterly opposed by Ruskin, had given additional cogency. The first line of thought led him to examine in a spirit of critical hostility the basis of Priestly claims; the second, to examine the basis of anti-Episcopalian doctrines. The result was a treatise on the principles of Church organisation—or, as we may call it with reference to its drift, an essay towards Protestant re-union. The architectural title was a natural play on words, suggested by the circumstances in which the essay originated; it was an appendix to *The Stones of Venice*, printed separately "for the convenience of readers interested in other architecture than that of Venetian palaces."[3]   Those Border farmers, however, who, having bought the pamphlet under the idea that it was a manual of husbandry, cried out that they had been deceived, were not perhaps entirely without excuse.[4]

Although this pamphlet on Church organisation was thus written in a particular connexion, the subject had long been in Ruskin's mind. He refers at the outset (§ 1) to pages in his private diary, and examination shows that the questions discussed in the pamphlet had

---

[1] See Vol. VIII. p. xlvi. ; Vol. X. p. lv.

[2] See Vol. IX. p. 437.

[3] Vol. IX. p. 437 n.

[4] "It is a very capital joke indeed," writes Ruskin to his father (Oct. 20, 1853), "Archie's sending my pamphlet to the farmer. I hope it may do him good." And see p. lxxiv. n.

often been in his mind during preceding years. Thus in his diary for March 18, 1849, we find the following entry on Episcopacy :—

> " Reading to-day part of Hooker's seventh book, it seems to me that the question is very conclusively settled by the two passages quoted from Jerome ; showing it to be a thing of custom only, but that ancient. And if on either side prejudice might be dismissed, it could not but seem reasonable that, granting the administration of the Church to be in the hands of Presbyters, yet as in less important affairs bodies of men naturally appoint over themselves for their better regulation one who—either for convenience' sake has a regulative office, as a chairman of a committee, or else, being thought wiser and more prudent and learned than the rest, has some superior authority put in his hands, or at least has a tacit weight, and is asked counsel at, by the rest ; so in the most important matter of Church government : for it is in this manner only that the greatest profit may be reaped from the mind and labours of the better men, whose authority to enlarge is to provide more largely for the well-being of the Church and of all ; for in all things the secret of good success is to place that which works best where it will work most, and to increase the power of the things which have healthiest operation. Doubtless the difficulties are great in the matter of appointment ; only it would be well if the prime question were first settled : whether or no Episcopacy, with good bishops, be not a good and desirable thing (we admitting it not to be a thing commanded) ; and thereafter to consider how far it is in our power to secure goodness in bishops, and what dangers attend on our failure so to do, or what collateral inconveniences even on the event of our success. . . ."

He then goes on to collate all the texts in the Bible in which the word "Church" is mentioned, and several pages follow of notes on Hooker and collateral authorities. The method of Ruskin's argument in the pamphlet is very characteristic. He was essentially a Bible Christian. He was a constant student of the Bible ; he knew it by heart, and the literal text of it was the test to which he brought all statements. The reader will already have noticed this in all Ruskin's writings from his essay in Volume I.—"Was there death before Adam fell ?"—down to the time of the present volume. The Catholic theory of the Church as the repository of truths not contained in, or at any rate not obviously deducible from, the text of the Bible, was repugnant alike to the Protestant traditions in which Ruskin had been reared, and to the daily practice of his own Scriptural exercises.

The conclusion at which Ruskin arrived by the application of his Bible test to principles of Church government was that on a Protestant basis the re-union of the Churches was perfectly possible. The High Anglicans had only to renounce their pretensions to "Priesthood," and the Presbyterians to waive their objections to Episcopacy, and then would the text be fulfilled—"And there shall be one fold and one Shepherd." There was a difficulty still in the way—that of Baptismal Regeneration. But apart from this, it was soon made apparent that he had asked more than the rival Churches were willing to grant; but in after years it was to be borne in upon him that his error lay not in too much comprehension but in too much exclusion. "It amazes me to find," he wrote in the Preface to the edition of 1875, "that, so late as 1851, I had only got the length of perceiving the schisms between sects of Protestants to be criminal and ridiculous, while I still supposed the schism between Protestants and Catholics to be virtuous and sublime."

But this was a lesson still to come. For the moment Ruskin had enough to do to defend even his modest measure of comprehension. The publication of the pamphlet inundated him with correspondence, as he states in the preface to the Second Edition (p. 519); some of it, commendatory; but more of it, controversial. There were also published replies to his pamphlet (see p. 514)—among them one by his friend, William Dyce, the Royal Academician. The "Notes" had to be reprinted almost immediately. Reviews in the newspapers were numerous, and "letters to the editor" followed as is usual on the track of any religious or ecclesiastical controversy. To these letters and replies Ruskin did not make any published rejoinder.[1] He had another controversy and another pamphlet already on hand—*Pre-Raphaelitism*; and he did not resume the public discussion of sectarian topics till a much later date. But in private correspondence he replied to friendly critics, and it is some of these rejoinders that form the subject of Appendix I. to Part III. of this volume.

---

[1] Reviews of *Sheepfolds* appeared, among other places, in the *Prospective Review*, August 1851, vol. 7, pp. 335–343; *Blackwood's Magazine*, September 1851, vol. 70, pp. 326–348 (a review of *Modern Painters*, vols. i. and ii., *Seven Lamps, Stones of Venice*, vol. i., and *Sheepfolds*); *Quarterly Review*, September 1851, vol. 89, pp. 307–332 (an article entitled "Puritanism in the Highlands," Ruskin's pamphlet being noticed on p. 323); *Edinburgh Advertiser*, April 22, 1851; *Free Church Magazine*, (Edinburgh), July 1851, vol. 8, pp. 196–202; and *Tait's Edinburgh Magazine*, May 1851, pp. 286–292: this article, reviewing also the *Stones of Venice*, vol. i., says (p. 292) "we hear that many agriculturists, especially in the Teviots and among the South Downs, have ordered it."

The private controversy which was indirectly the most fruitful in Ruskin's life was that with Frederick Denison Maurice, with Dr. Furnivall as intermediary. This largely turned, as will be seen, on Ruskin's suggestions about Church Discipline (§§ 23, 24); to these he called particular attention in the Preface of 1875, as according with doctrines he was then preaching in *Fors Clavigera*.

With these letters the correspondence between Ruskin and Maurice came to an end for the time, but three years later their intercourse was resumed in a different connexion. Ruskin, as he afterwards said, regarded Maurice as "by nature puzzle-headed;"[1] but though he disliked the opinions, he loved the man, and was in hearty sympathy with the practical efforts of Maurice's Christian Socialism. In 1854 Maurice founded the Working Men's College, then in Red Lion Square (afterwards removed to Great Ormond Street, and now [1904] about to migrate to Camden Town). For the inaugural meeting of the College (October 31, 1854) a reprint of a chapter in *The Stones of Venice* was prepared, as containing an expression of the hopes and ideals of the founders of the College (Vol. X. p. lx.). Ruskin's help did not stop there. He undertook to superintend the art-teaching. An account of his work there is given in the Introduction to Volume V., which in the chronological sequence follows the present volume. Ruskin's work at the College began in the autumn of 1854, and had grown out of the *Notes on the Construction of Sheepfolds*.

It has been said that at the conclusion of the *Notes on the Construction of Sheepfolds*, Ruskin had left over one difficulty which still required solution before his eirenicon could be fulfilled. This was the Baptismal Question. An Essay on this question has been found among Ruskin's papers; it is accordingly printed here, in Appendix II. to Part III. (p. 573), in order to complete his contribution to an attempted Re-Union of the Churches.

The Essay had already been written when he published *Sheepfolds*, and it had obviously been suggested to him by the Gorham controversy, of which a brief résumé may here be given to explain Ruskin's paper. The Rev. G. C. Gorham, a beneficed clergyman in the Diocese of Exeter, was presented by the Lord Chancellor to another living in the same diocese. Before proceeding to institute him, Bishop Phillpotts (the combative "Henry of Exeter") put certain questions with regard to the Sacrament of Baptism, for Gorham was suspected of Calvinistic views on baptismal regeneration. His reply did not

---

[1] *Præterita*, i. ch. i. §§ 13, 14.

satisfy the Bishop, who then refused to institute (1847). Gorham appealed to the Court of Arches, which supported the Bishop. The case was taken to the Judicial Committee of the Privy Council, which, by a majority (with the two Archbishops as assessors), reversed the decision of the Court below, and Gorham was soon afterwards instituted (1850). The case convulsed the religious world. "Were we together," wrote Gladstone to Manning (December 30, 1849), "I should wish to converse with you from sunrise to sunset on the Gorham case. It is a stupendous issue."[1] Onlookers who are not actively enlisted in any one of the hostile parties within the Church Militant may find it difficult to rise to these stupendous heights. But the issues involved were certainly important. On the one hand, if Gorham had not won the day, the expulsion from the Establishment of Calvinists and Evangelicals might have followed. "I am old enough," said Hawkins, the Provost of Oriel, "to remember three baptismal controversies, and this is the first in which one party has tried to eject the other from the Church." On the other side, the High Church Party were indignant at the submission of a question of Church doctrine to a Civil Court. The controversy continued to rage for many months after the Judicial Committee had delivered judgment, and was the immediate reason of Manning's secession to the Church of Rome. Ruskin from his own detached point of view had caught the contagion, and wrote this "Essay on Baptism" as his contribution to the discussion. He did not publish his Essay; he perhaps felt that he had quite enough works at the time in the press or on the stocks. But that he took considerable pains with it, is shown by various notes and fragmentary drafts which have been found among his papers. The Essay itself is undated, but a water-mark on the paper of one piece of rough copy fixes the date as not earlier than 1850. He preserved the fair copy at Brantwood, and in going through his papers at some later date, wrote on the wrapper in which the MS. was rolled up, "Kept to see that I wrote worse once than now." It is probable from other notes of the kind that Ruskin here referred to the handwriting (which in this Essay is somewhat cramped), rather than to the style. But the directly imperative mood in which his points are put is also somewhat lacking in his usual grace; the tone and argument of the Essay, however,—its close reliance upon the text of Scripture, its insistence upon works as evidence of faith—are thoroughly characteristic of his thought at this period, and it completes his contribution to the Church Controversies which then rent

---

[1] Morley's *Life of Gladstone,* i. 378.

the religious and ecclesiastical world, and which in one form or another have been renewed in every generation.

The doctrinal views which he combats or supports are sufficiently set forth in the Essay itself, but it may be well, in order to explain some references in it, to remind the reader of the views which, in the Gorham case, one Party had denounced as heretical. It would not have been a theological controversy if it were possible to formulate Gorham's own views precisely, but the doctrine which the Privy Council extracted from his answers given to the Bishop was this:—

"That Baptism is a sacrament generally necessary to salvation, but that the grace of regeneration does not so necessarily accompany the act of Baptism that regeneration invariably takes place in Baptism; that the grace may be granted before, in, or after Baptism; that Baptism is an effectual sign of grace, by which God works invisibly in us, but only in such as worthily receive it—in them alone it has a wholesome effect; and that without reference to the qualification of the recipient it is not in itself an effectual sign of grace. That infants baptized, and dying before actual sin, are certainly saved; but that in no case is regeneration in Baptism unconditional." [1]

This *Essay on Baptism*, as also the *Notes on Sheepfolds*, illustrates very clearly Ruskin's intimate acquaintance with the Bible. His diaries and MSS. are full of notes on the book—such as are described in Vol. X. p. xxxviii., and such as were utilised in his writings, as, for instance, in the discussion of the Book of Job in this volume (*Lectures on Architecture and Painting*, below, p. 105). Sometimes he studied the Bible book by book, jotting down all the passages which struck him; at other times he collected passages bearing on particular subjects, or illustrating the uses of particular words. But it is ever the hardest workers who are the least satisfied with their work, and in a passage in Ruskin's diary for 1853 there is a note of self-reproach on the ground that his Bible studies were too desultory:—

"*Sunday, 13 Nov., 1853.*— . . . I read thoughtfully part of 1st Genesis, beginning a new course of Bible reading, with greater attention to the marginal readings and interpretations of names than I have attempted yet; this being chiefly in consequence of the wonderful lights thrown upon parts of the Revelations in some conversations I have had lately with a comparatively unlearned man, Mr. Beveridge,[2] from pure Bible reading; and in consequence also of the shame I

[1] The Gorham case figures largely in Memoirs dealing with the time; for fuller particulars see, for instance, the *Life of Bishop Wilberforce*, ii. pp. 34–45; Purcell's *Life of Manning*, i. 517–521; and Morley's *Life of Gladstone*, i. pp. 375–388.

[2] See Vol. XI. p. 133 *n*.

felt yesterday in noticing, as far as I recollect for the first time, that 'Solomon' meant peaceable. How beautifully is this connected with 'The wisdom that cometh from above is first pure, then peaceable.' [1] I have hitherto endeavoured too much to learn the Bible by heart (more, I fear, from vanity than any other feeling) instead of diving into it as I read. I always begin things too eagerly and carelessly, but have prayed I may go on with this."

Notes on the Book of Genesis follow. Ruskin's studies and writings were manifold, as this volume sufficiently shows; but behind them all there was one constant background — an almost daily study of the Bible.

IV

In the last Part of this volume is printed a piece, hitherto unpublished, which is short but pregnant. This is the first, and a portion of the second, of three Letters which Ruskin wrote in 1852, intending to send them to the *Times*, on Political Affairs. The first letter is on Principles of Taxation; the second (of which only an incomplete draft has been found), on Principles of Representation; the third was to have been on Principles of Education. Of this the MS. has not been found; much of it seems to have been utilised by Ruskin in the Notes on Education printed by him as Appendix 7 to the third volume of *The Stones of Venice*. The passages here printed, and the letters from Ruskin to his father in which he further explained his ideas and the importance he attached to them, are of considerable interest in connexion with the development of his political views.

We have traced already some of the occasions and circumstances in which Ruskin had been led to devote thought to social, economic, and political matters. More and more he was becoming convinced that there was something rotten in the state of political society. He was a Republican as against institutions or laws which oppressed the poor; and a Conservative as against theories and reforms which were based on doctrines of liberty and equality. Something must also be allowed for his natural affection for the side of the minority. This is a view he put forward himself in a letter to his father:—

"*Sunday, 16th November* [1851].—In *Galignani* yesterday we had some very wonderful additional accounts of Kossuth, and the address to him by the democrats, signed by a whole man's worth of tailors and a whole bevy of 'Proscrits,' with his polite answer thereto,

[1] James iii. 17.

and his 're-consideration' of his resolution to accept no invitations except from municipal bodies. I do not suppose that at any previous period of history there has been more open Communism coolly announced in the face of all men. The French Revolution was a frenzy begun in a necessary reform of vicious government, but the principles which that frenzy reached at its wildest, becomes now the subject of the after-dinner declamation of our respectable London citizens. There is assuredly a root for all this—desperate abuses going on in governments, and real ground for movement among the lower classes, which of course they are little likely to guide by any very just or rational principle. . . . However, I must mind and not get too sympathising with the Radicals. Effie says with some justice that I am a great conservative in France, because there everybody is radical, and a great radical in Austria, because there everybody is conservative. I suppose that one reason why I am so fond of fish (as creatures, I mean, not as eating) is that they always swim with their heads against the stream. I find it for me the healthiest position."

In this spirit of revolt Ruskin, from his distant eyrie at Venice, surveyed the state of politics in England. Catholic Emancipation had been carried, but Ireland had not been pacified. Chartism had been snuffed out, but the movement for Reform continued. The Corn Laws had been abolished, but the Conservative Party under Disraeli were still hankering after a return to protection.[1] Early in 1851 Lord John Russell's Government had been defeated, but, on Lord Stanley's failure to form an administration, had returned to office. But internal feuds between Lord John and Lord Palmerston had led to the resignation of the latter, and then to the tit for tat which caused the defeat of the former. In February 1852, Lord Stanley (Lord Derby) had by this time become Prime Minister, with Disraeli as Chancellor of the Exchequer and leader in the House of Commons.

It was at this moment that Ruskin wrote his letters. In the first of these, after a passing sneer at Disraeli as a mere novelist, he discussed the policy of Free Trade, and the principles of taxation—stoutly defending the former, and with regard to the latter advocating direct and graduated taxation. The second letter is incomplete, but is partially supplemented by an explanatory letter to his father (see below, p. lxxxiii.). Ruskin seems to have advocated a system of universal suffrage combined with what in later discussions were called "fancy franchises." Every man was

[1] One of the events which Ruskin must have had specially in mind was Disraeli's motion on February 19, 1850, ascribing the agricultural distress to the establishment of free trade, and asking for a Committee of Inquiry.

to have his vote, but votes were to be weighed as well as counted; weight being attached more especially to property and education. This latter test brought him to the subject of a third Letter, in which he discussed the Principles of Education. This letter, as already stated, was ultimately embodied in the last volume of *The Stones of Venice;* to complete his perusal of Ruskin's first scheme of political reform, the reader should, therefore, after reading the Letters now under discussion, refer to that volume (Vol. XI. p. 258). He will there find that Ruskin pleads, in the subject-matter of education, that it should include Natural History, Religion, and the elements of Politics; and, with regard to its scope, that it should be National.

This scheme was set forth by Ruskin two years after Carlyle had published his *Latter-Day Pamphlets,* to which work it doubtless owed something of inspiration; it is, however, worth noticing that the disciple's treatment of the theme, if similar in spirit, was more precise and definite than his stormy teacher's. Ruskin's political writings, now and afterwards, may have been practicable or impracticable—there will be a word to say on that subject presently, and in a later volume; but at any rate they were directed to practical ends; they may have looked towards the sky, but they trod the earth.

Ruskin's father was a Tory of the old school, and an admirer of Disraeli, whose process of educating his Party had as yet hardly begun. The very Radical pill, which, with some Tory gilding, Ruskin proposed to apply to the body politic, was naturally unacceptable at the domestic headquarters; the Letters, to which the son attached great importance, and which he particularly desired to publish in the then year of grace, 1852, were put on the paternal Index, and now see the light of publicity for the first time. The correspondence between father and son is interesting, and, in telling its own story, supplies such further commentary as is necessary on Part IV. of this volume:—

"*March* 6.—These news from England are really too ridiculous, and I can stand it no longer. I am going for three days to give the usual time I set aside for your letter to writing one to the *Times*—on Corn Laws, Election, and Education. George shall copy it. If you like to send it, you can; if not, you can consider it all as written to you, but you must have short letters for a day or two."

"*March* 14.—I don't know whether you have found my *Times* letters worth sending, or whether the *Times* will put them in, but I rather hope so—not in the hope of their doing any good at present, but because I want to be able to refer to them in future. I was a mere boy when the present design for the Houses of Parliament was chosen—but I said in an instant it was vile. I did not say so in print,[1] because I felt that no one would care for a boy's opinion, but I heartily wish now that I had written to the *Times,* and could now refer to my then stated opinion. In like manner I hope the *Times* will put these letters in, for twenty years hence, if I live, I should like to be able to refer to them and say 'I told you so, and now you are beginning to find it out.' And that would give some power—then, however little it may be possible to do at present.

"I have kept these letters as plain and simple as I could. I was tempted to go into the question of cheap wages as connected with that of cheap bread; but found it would lead me too far. In the same way, I should have liked to have gone into some further statements of the mode in which the increasing percentages of income tax were to be fitted to each other; so that a man who had £900 a year, might not be forced to pay £81, and reduced to £819, while a man who had £899 a year paid only £71, 18s. 4¾d. and would have left therefore £827, 1s. 7¼d.; but all this would have taken too much room: I only want to get at the principle."

"*March* 23.—These three letters I want to be able to refer to twenty years hence—people may call them as futile as they like now. I know also how much is said on the subject. When every mouth out of (I know not how many millions there are in) England is talking on the same subject, it is likely the truth will be occasionally said and occasionally admitted. Everything true has been said millions of times, but as long as it is mixed up with falsehood, it will be the better of extrication. Whatever I read of public press shows me the *confusion* of men's heads on simple matters. These three letters do not profess to say anything new, any more than an Eton grammar does. But they profess to give grammatical and common rules in a simple and clear form, and one likely to be useful, as far as they may be attended to, more than a library full of treatises on political economy. If people say they are common truth, let them act upon them; if people suppose them all wrong, there is the more need of them."

Ruskin's father was travelling in the country when the letters reached Denmark Hill; his mother seems to have acknowledged their receipt, and to have deprecated the attack on Disraeli as likely to offend her husband. Ruskin's next letter on the subject is addressed to her:—

"*March* 26.— . . . I am glad you think so well of what is doing in England. But you will see by my last letter[2] that I am not considering England only. There is assuredly over all Europe nothing but

---

[1] Sir Charles Barry's designs were adopted in 1836; Ruskin's earliest criticism of them in print is in vol. ii. of *Modern Painters* (1846), Vol. IV. p. 307 *n.*

[2] The third of the letters intended for the *Times.*

f

mischief; and what is England, when compared with the vast tracts of populous and in some sort civilized territory, which are now falling to decay. But I am very glad the new Government is getting on pretty well. In case you should not yet have sent my letters to *Times*, and should be intending to send them, I wish, as my father likes D'Israeli, that he should put his pen through the sentence about him. The passage will read connectedly without it, better perhaps than with it."

Meanwhile Ruskin's father was reading the letters and lamenting at his son's lapse, as it seemed, from his hereditary Toryism into red Radicalism, or worse. Ruskin replied, defending himself, but acquiescing, though reluctantly, in the suppression, or, at any rate, in the holding back of the letters:—

"*March* 29.—I had yesterday your nice long letter from Leeds, but was sorry to hear from my mother that you were annoying yourself because you did not agree with me, and I am sorry that in the midst of your labour in travelling I have caused you the additional work of these long letters. Keep mine until I get home, and then we will talk about them, but do not vex yourself because you think I am turning republican. I am, I believe, just what I was ten years ago, in all respects but one, that I have not the Jacobite respect for the Stuarts which I had then; when I was at College I used to stand up for James II. I have certainly changed no opinion since I wrote the passage in the *Seven Lamps* about loyalty.[1] I meant the word to signify what it really *does* in the long run signify—*loy*-alty, respect for loy or law; for the King as long as he observes and represents law; and a love, not merely of established laws at a particular time, but of the principles of law and obedience in general. As for the universal suffrage in my letter, if you look over it carefully you will see that I am just as far from universal suffrage as you are—and that by my measure, one man of parts and rank would outweigh in voting a whole shoal of the mob, so that the mob would be no more worth canvassing, and the whole system of bribery would go to the ground at least in its £5 note form. Cabal would take its place, but might be in various ways prevented; into which I do not enter, for my three letters are merely statements of general *theses*, not endeavours to support them. I have purposely not made any specification as to number of votes to be given by property or education, because in order to do that it would be necessary for me to study the average distribution of property and education in order to give it a proper preponderance over the mob. But I hold it a gratuitous and useless

[1] See Vol. VIII. p. 250.

insult to make any man incapable of *giving* an opinion: only let the proper weight be attached to his opinion. In the same way I entered into no discussion of the way in which the land might keep up or increase its value. I said only that *if any* harm was done, that would be *the* harm. As for D'Israeli, you will see by my day before yesterday's letter that I have no animosity against him. I know nothing about Wood.[1] D'Israeli's works give me the idea of his being a coxcomb, but clever; only the last person fit to make a Chancellor of the Exchequer. Perhaps Wood was worse; I think it is very likely there may go as much brains to write a bad novel as to make a very good politician, in the modern sense of the term. . . ."

"*March 30.*—I had yesterday your nice letter from Darlington, and am very glad indeed to hear that you respect the present Ministry. I should be exceedingly sorry if any letters of mine were to do any harm to people whom you respected, and who were doing as well as they could, and I shall be excessively so if anything said in the letters you are just now receiving induces you to publish what may *at present* do harm, though I believe it would in the long run do good. I have thought for three years back over all the points to which you allude respecting election. I should be very glad if it were possible to keep the common people from thinking about governments, but, since the invention of printing, it is not—of all impossibilities that is now the most so; the only question is how to make them of exactly the proper weight in the State, and no more. *At present* the electing body of England is the lower and easily bribable middle class. I want to add to this the mob whom it would be too troublesome to bribe at 2s. 6d. each, and the upper classes, in a mass of weight proportioned to their rank, sense, and wealth. You and I have both our vote, and so has, I suppose, our radical coachman. *I* don't think it worth my while to give in my one vote. *He* does, and the coachmen carry it. According to my system, he would have, being now 70, fifty votes, and I four or five hundred. I should take the trouble to vote, and swamp him and a good many more radicals. As for the difficulty of counting, I believe it is to an accountant as easy to add in hundreds as in tens; for verification, every man should have his name and number of votes given on a seal which should be verified on certain days, called Verification Days, every five years. At an election he should walk into the registering room, show his seal, write its number opposite his candidate's name, his own name being taken at the same time in order of its letter, and walk out again. Not much confusion in this. And there should be no *talking* at elections.

[1] Sir Charles Wood, first Viscount Halifax, Chancellor of the Exchequer in Lord John Russell's Administration, 1846–1852.

"I made the limit of age 70, for I believe many men in very active life have hardly *time* to *think* till they are past 50. I have myself never yet seen any decline in powers of mind, but always increase, in men under 70, unless such a decline as might as well have taken place at 16, from idleness or dissipation. Turner was exactly at his zenith at 70, and not till then. I believe, the mind is never meant to fail under the Seven Weeks[1] appointed for man's proper life, and that all its best and most useful powers will remain if it be properly treated, as long as the body holds together."

"(*April 2.*)— . . . I am very glad indeed the education letter gave you pleasure, and I quite concur in all you say of hitting slightly in order to do the work, not too hard at first. One gets this practical lesson every time one drives a nail into a deal board. At first the great thing is to hit lightly—in the right direction—and to take care of one's own fingers. The least to one side or the other, or the least too hard and the nail will never go in. But once well entered, one may hit harder every minute—get one's finger out of the way—and at last clench the matter with all the swing of one's arm. I consider the public may be very fitly represented by a deal board, and all men who make anything of them may be considered as clever carpenters. It is likely there will be more typical lessons in carpentering than in any other trade, as it was appointed to be St. Joseph's. So keep the letters till we can look them over."

A letter from Ruskin's father (dated Lancaster, 30th March 1852) states his general view on the question, in terms which other and less partial critics have often adopted, and which must have caused no little chagrin and disappointment to a son whose filial affections were now beginning to be separated from complete intellectual sympathy :—

"I shall see to letters for *Times* on my return, as you so wish it. My feelings of attacks on your books and on your newspaper writing differ from yours in this way. I think all attacks on your books are only as the waves beating on Eddystone Lighthouse, whereas your politics are Slum Buildings liable to be knocked down; and no man to whom authority is a useful engine should expose himself to frequent defeat by slender forces.

"Your sneer at the age making a clever novelist Chancellor of Exchequer would already have pained yourself. D'Israeli may end weakly, but at present he commands the House, and is a match for Lord John or any man in it, and his adroitness and information are astonishing."

Here, for the time, the matter rested. Ruskin did not press his

---

[1] A reference, presumably, to the much disputed passage in Daniel ix. 24, 25.

father any further; on the contrary, a month later, he found an occasion for a graceful reconciliation :—

"*Sunday, 26th April* [1852].— . . . *À propos* of cutting out, I found the other day by accident a bit of MS. of the letter which you would not let me send about the Pre-Raphaelites—the *second* to the *Times*, which I re-wrote at your request—cancelling the original draft of it. I am amazed to find how *ill* it now reads to myself, and how right you were in refusing to let it go, so that I am quite ready to trust in your disapproval of the others to the *Times*. Indeed I am very thankful already, since I saw Lord Derby's appeal to the country, that the attack on the Ministry did not appear. It is rather painful to me, however, to find how unequal I am at times, and how little I can judge of what I write, as I write it. I have not any more notice, in any of your letters, of the last on education, which you seem at first to have been much pleased with. I liked that, myself; and some time or other I must re-cast it, in some way, for I want to *have at* our present system—I don't know anything which seems to me so much to require mending."

The Letters, then, were consigned to the shelf, but the views expressed in them remained and developed in Ruskin's mind. Twelve years later they were embodied in his treatise entitled *Unto this Last*. For once his father's judgment was in part at least at fault. So far as Ruskin stood for aristocracy against democracy in the machinery of government, his political edifice has, indeed, been submerged. But the principles of fiscal policy, of taxation, and of national education for which he argued in 1852 have stood, and have been gradually more and more adopted in this country, for fifty years—whatever fate the future may have in store for them. Whether they were indeed firm as Eddystone Lighthouse, the future will show; but the past has already vindicated them from the character of "Slum Buildings."

In closing the Introduction to this volume of Miscellanies, written during the years 1847 to 1854, I may again remind the reader that they were by-works only; pieces thrown off in intervals of other work; excursions into fresh fields; reinforcements of conclusions elsewhere stated. During the same period, Ruskin wrote two of his great books— *The Seven Lamps of Architecture* and *The Stones of Venice*. The collection of these other scattered pieces into a single volume is well calculated to give a forcible impression of his many intellectual activities, and a vivid picture of his strenuous life.

With regard to the *manuscripts* of the various pieces collected in this volume, that of the *Lectures on Architecture and Painting* has been already described above (p. xxxvi.). In the case of the *Reviews of Lord Lindsay* and *Eastlake*, of the article on *Prout*, and of the Letters to the *Times* on *The Pre-Raphaelite Artists*, no manuscripts or notes have been found among Ruskin's papers. They are printed here as they originally appeared. The manuscript of the pamphlet on *Pre-Raphaelitism* has been mentioned above (p. lvii.). A *manuscript* draft of the first part (down to the end of § 6) of the first letter to the *Times* on the National Gallery is in the second MS. volume containing *The Poetry of Architecture* (see Vol. I. p. 2); a draft of portions of the second letter is on the back of some of the sheets of the MS. of *The Stones of Venice*, volumes ii. and iii. It shows once more the care and trouble which Ruskin took even with his occasional work. The letters are here reprinted as they appeared in the *Times*. Bibliographical particulars are given below, p. 396. The manuscript of the pamphlet on *The Opening of the Crystal Palace* has also been mentioned above (p. lxiv.). The *Letters on Painted Glass* and *Notes on the Louvre* are printed from the original letters and diaries respectively; the former were kindly placed at the disposal of the editors by the late Mr. Oldfield. No manuscript of the pamphlet on *The Construction of Sheepfolds* has been found among Ruskin's papers; that of the hitherto unpublished *Essay on Baptism* has been already described (p. lxxvi.); an earlier draft of a small portion of it was among Ruskin's miscellaneous manuscripts. The Letters, in connexion with "Sheepfolds," to Maurice and Furnivall, and the Letters on Politics intended for the *Times*, are printed from the originals.

With regard to the *text*, the reader is referred for particulars to the Bibliographical Note which follows the title of each piece in this volume.

The *illustrations* consist of all those which appeared in *Lectures on Architecture and Painting* (the only piece in the volume published with illustrations by the author), together with several others now introduced.

The *frontispiece* is the portrait of Ruskin by Millais, which has been fully described above (pp. xxiii.–xxv.); Plate I., Ruskin's own drawing of the rocks at the same place, has also been mentioned already (p. xxvi.). The drawing is in the Ruskin Drawing School at Oxford (Reference Series, No. 89). It was exhibited at the Fine Art Society's Rooms in 1878, and is described under the title of " Gneiss, with its weeds, above the stream of Glen-Finlas," in Ruskin *Notes* on that exhibition (No. 45 R. (*a*); it is also referred to in *Præterita* (iii. ch. i. § 10).

Next come the original illustrations in *Lectures on Architecture and Painting*. Of these, seven (including the frontispiece by Millais to that volume) are here printed as separate Plates (II., III., IV., VII., VIII., IX., X.); the others are included in the text. Five additional illustrations to the Lectures have been introduced. Plate V. is from a drawing by Ruskin of the main street of Münster in Germany, which well illustrates what he says in § 18 (p. 36) of the picturesque effect of gables and cornices in street architecture. The drawing, which is in pen and wash ($17\frac{1}{2}$ × 12), is at Brantwood.

Plate VI. is from a drawing by Ruskin of the church of Courmayeur, and illustrates his passage (§ 20, p. 41) about "the grey mountain churches" on the southern slopes of the Alps. The drawing, which is in water-colour ($14\frac{1}{2}$ × 8), is in the possession of Sir John Simon, K.C.B. It was made in 1849.

Plate XI. is from a drawing of an Italian window which may have been intended to illustrate these Lectures, and was perhaps exhibited at them. It is at Brantwood, and is an example of a kind of window described in the Lectures (p. 76 *n*.).

Plate XII. is reproduced from a very large drawing at Brantwood, which also seems to have been exhibited at the Lectures. It is a typical example of various characteristics in the landscape of the Italian painters and more especially of Leonardo da Vinci (see below, p. 112).

Plate XIII. is reproduced from two large drawings, now at Brantwood, which Ruskin similarly made to illustrate the Lectures; it compares the treatment of trees by Turner and Claude respectively (see below, p. 127 *n*.).

The next two Plates illustrate passages in the *Review of Lord Lindsay*. No. XIV. is from a drawing by Ruskin of the south door of the Duomo at Verona. The drawing was reproduced in *Verona and other Lectures* (1894), Plate iv. No. XV. is from a later drawing of Lucca; it is in water-colour (19 × 13), and is at Brantwood.

In addition to the above-mentioned Plates and woodcuts, which either were prepared by Ruskin or are from drawings by him, five other Plates are included which give reproductions of works generally or specifically alluded to in the volume. Under the first head come Plates XVI. and XVII., which are photogravures of drawings by J. F. Lewis (see below, p. 363) which were in Ruskin's collection, and are now in the possession of Mr. and Mrs. Arthur Severn at Herne Hill.

The other Plates, Nos. XVIII., XIX., XX., and XXI., are photogravures from drawings by Turner in the Farnley Collection. They are referred to below (pp. 374, 377, 386), and are not so well known from reproductions as many of the artist's works.

The last Plate, No. XXII., shows the window in the church of St. Giles, Camberwell, which was partly designed by Ruskin, as explained above (p. lxiv.) in the account of the Letters on Painted Glass.

For the Lectures on Colour and Illumination Ruskin prepared numerous illustrations, including several enlargements of initial letters in manuscripts. From six of these, illustrations have been prepared on a reduced scale. Figures 25, 27, and 30 are printed from woodcuts by Mr. W. H. Hooper.

Finally, four facsimiles of Ruskin's manuscript are given. The first (p. xxiv.) is of a letter to Dr. Furnivall from Glenfinlas in 1853, and includes a rough sketch of Ruskin's cottage there; the second is a page of the MS. of the Edinburgh Lectures (p. 128); the third, of a page of the MS. of *Pre-Raphaelitism* (p. 392); and the fourth, of a page from *The Opening of the Crystal Palace* (p. 429).

E. T. C.

[*In the chronological order, this volume is followed in succession by Volumes V. and VI.; the Introduction to Volume V. should, therefore, next be read.*]

PART I

"LECTURES ON ARCHITECTURE
AND PAINTING"

(1854)

LECTURES

ON

ARCHITECTURE AND PAINTING,

DELIVERED AT EDINBURGH

IN

NOVEMBER, 1853.

BY JOHN RUSKIN,

AUTHOR OF "THE STONES OF VENICE," "SEVEN LAMPS OF ARCHITECTURE," "MODERN PAINTERS," ETC.

WITH ILLUSTRATIONS DRAWN BY THE AUTHOR.

LONDON:

SMITH, ELDER, AND CO., 65. CORNHILL.

1854.

[*Bibliographical Note.*—There have been three different editions of this work :—

First Edition (1854).—The title-page is as printed on page 3 of this edition. Crown 8vo, pp. viii. +239. On the reverse of the title-page is the imprint "London : A. and G. A. Spottiswoode, New Street Square," and, in the centre, "[The Author of this Work reserves to himself the right of Translation]." Preface, pp. iii.-vi. (here pp. 7-9) ; Contents, p. vii. (here p. 11) ; List of Illustrations, p. viii. The headline is throughout "Lectures on Architecture | and Painting." At the end is a catalogue (16 pages) of works published by Smith, Elder & Co. On pp. 7, 8, "Works of Mr. Ruskin," the Third Volume of *Modern Painters* is announced as "in preparation." All the illustrations (except the frontispiece, which is numbered Plate XI.) are placed together at the end of the text. As the illustrations are differently arranged in this volume, the original list of "Illustrations" is subjoined :—

Plate	I.	Figs. 1, 3, and 5.	Illustrative diagrams.
,,	II.	,, 2.	Window in Oakham Castle.
,,	III.	,, 4 and 6.	Spray of ash-tree, and improvement of the same on Greek principles.
,,	IV.	,, 7.	Window in Dumblane Cathedral.
,,	V.	,, 8.	Mediæval turret.
,,	VI.	,, 9 and 10.	Lombardic towers.
,,	VII.	,, 11 and 12.	Spires at Coutances and Rouen.
,,	VIII.	,, 13 and 14.	Illustrative diagrams.
,,	IX.	,, 15.	Sculpture at Lyons.
,,	X.	,, 16.	Niche at Amiens.
,,	XI.	,, 17 and 18.	Tiger's head, and improvement of the same[1] on Greek principles.
,,	XII.	,, 19.	Garret window in Hôtel de Bourgtheroude.
,,	XIII.	,, 20 and 21.	Trees, as drawn in the 13th century.
,,	XIV.	,, 22.	Rocks, as drawn by the school of Leonardo da Vinci.
,,	XV.	,, 23.	Boughs of trees, after Titian.

The frontispiece and also Plate III., which similarly consists of two contrasted figures, are furnished with folding flaps attached at the foot. These flaps (often missing in second-hand copies) were provided in order that the lower figure upon each Plate might remain hidden until the points of the upper one had been taken in ; this was evidently done by Ruskin with his original diagrams when delivering his lecture.

Issued in April 1854, in dark brown cloth boards ; price 8s. 6d. (The date of issue is given as April 18 in Wise and Smart's *Bibliography*, i. 47 ; but see below, p. 155 n.)

Second Edition (1855).—The words "Second Edition" are added to the title-page and the back of the cover, and the date is altered, otherwise the general appearance is the same as in the first edition. There were some alterations in the text (see below), and a difference in the setting caused the pages to be 240, instead of 239. Issued on October 4, 1855, at the same price.

---

[1] The other head is, however, supposed to represent a lion : see below, p. 65.

Third Edition (1891).—The title-page is :—

Lectures | on | Architecture and Painting, | delivered at Edinburgh | in November 1853 | By | John Ruskin, LL.D., | Honorary Student of Christ Church, and Honorary Fellow | of Corpus Christi College, Oxford. | With Illustrations. | New Edition. | George Allen, | Sunnyside, Orpington, | and | 8, Bell Yard, Temple Bar, London. | 1891.

Crown 8vo, pp. viii. +256. The imprint—" Printed by Ballantyne, Hanson & Co., Edinburgh & London"—is at the foot of the last page. The text is a reprint of the second edition, and occupied pp. 1–230. The numbering of the paragraphs was introduced. An index was added (pp. 233–256), which is not here reprinted, as the entries are included in the General Index to the edition. The index contains a few editorial notes ; the substance of these is incorporated in this volume. The original Plates were again used, the frontispiece being retouched by Mr. G. Allen ; the folding flaps were discarded "as they usually tore the Plate or were lost in binding" (note by the editor, Mr. W. G. Collingwood), and the Plates of woodcuts, instead of being at the end of the book, were inserted opposite to the references to them in the text. Issued on June 15, 1891, in the usual cloth boards, price 7s. 6d. 3000 copies were printed, and 300 on large hand-made paper at 15s.

Re-issued in 1899 and 1902.

An unauthorised *American Edition* of the book was immediately issued by Messrs. Wiley & Son, New York (being reviewed in *Putman's Monthly*, August 1854). There have been many other American issues, from 50 cents upwards.

Variæ Lectiones.—The following are the variations shown by a collation of the editions ; the list does not, however, mention variations in references to the illustrations caused by the different arrangement of these in 1891, and again in the present edition. It should be noted, further, that in numbering the paragraphs in 1891 the editor broke up several of the longer paragraphs as printed in eds. 1 and 2 ; the arrangement of 1891 is followed in this edition. Also, the titles and dates of the lectures were added at the head of the chapters in 1891.

Preface, in the quotation of Lord Lindsay, line 11, the ed. of 1891, misreads "time" for "kind" ; § 5, line 9, eds. 1 and 2 have the old spelling "goff" for "golf" ; § 14, line 27 and again further on, eds. 1 and 2 read "Dumblane" (and so also in the List of Illustrations) ; § 21, line 8 (see p. 41) ; sixteen lines from the end, ed. 1 reads "occasions" for "occasion" ; § 22, line 42, "towns" in the MS. hitherto misprinted "towers" ; § 37, line 50, "rose" in the MS. printed "roses" in all previous eds. ; § 52, for "Bourgthéroulde" all previous eds. read "Bourgtheroude" (and so also in the List of Illustrations) ; § 66, line 19 (see p. 90) ; § 85, line 2, eds. 1 and 2 read "in the Addenda to this lecture" ; the reference, however, is to the Addenda to Lectures i. and ii. ; § 90, line 36, eds. 1 and 2 read "de" for "du" ; and ed. 1 "Geant" for "Géant" ; § 105 n. (see p. 132) ; § 128, line 5, all previous eds. read "Jullien" for "Julien" ; and in § 130 n. "Steele" for "Steell" ; § 134 (see p. 159).]

PREFACE

THE following Lectures are printed, as far as possible, just as they were delivered. Here and there a sentence which seemed obscure has been mended, and the passages which had not been previously written, have been, of course imperfectly, supplied from memory. But I am well assured that nothing of any substantial importance which was said in the lecture-room, is either omitted, or altered in its signification; with the exception only of a few sentences struck out from the notice of the works of Turner,[1] in consequence of the impossibility of engraving the drawings by which they were illustrated, except at a cost which would have too much raised the price of the volume. Some elucidatory remarks have, however, been added at the close of the second and fourth Lectures, which I hope may be of more use than the passages which I was obliged to omit.

The drawings by which the Lectures on Architecture were illustrated have been carefully reduced, and well transferred to wood by Mr. Thurston Thompson.[2] Those which were given in the course of the notices of schools of painting could not be so transferred, having been drawn in colour; and I have therefore merely had a few lines, absolutely necessary to make the text intelligible, copied from engravings.[3]

I forgot, in preparing the second Lecture for the press, to quote a passage from Lord Lindsay's *Christian Art*,

---

[1] [See below, p. 126.]

[2] [Charles Thurston Thompson (1816–1868), son of John Thompson (the wood-engraver), engraver and photographer, in which latter capacity he was employed by the Science and Art Department; he also took part in the arrangements for the Exhibition of 1851.]

[3] [For the illustrations added in this edition, see above, Introduction, pp. lxxxvi.–lxxxvii.]

illustrative of what is said in that lecture (§ 52), respecting the energy of the mediæval republics. This passage, describing the circumstances under which the Campanile of the Duomo of Florence was built, is interesting also as noticing the universality of talent which was required of architects; and which, as I have asserted in the Addenda (§ 60), always ought to be required of them. I do not, however, now regret the omission, as I cannot easily imagine a better preface to an essay on civil architecture than this simple statement.

"In 1332, Giotto was chosen to erect it (the Campanile), on the ground, avowedly, of the *universality* of his talents, with the appointment of Capo Maestro, or chief Architect (chief Master I should rather write), of the Cathedral and its dependencies, a yearly salary of one hundred gold florins, and the privilege of citizenship, under the special understanding that he was not to quit Florence. His designs being approved of, the republic passed a decree in the spring of 1334, that the Campanile should be built so as to exceed in magnificence, height, and excellence of workmanship whatever in that kind had been achieved by the Greeks and Romans in the time of their utmost power and greatness. The first stone was laid, accordingly, with great pomp, on the 18th of July following, and the work prosecuted with vigour, and with such costliness and utter disregard of expense, that a citizen of Verona, looking on, exclaimed that the republic was taxing her strength too far, that the united resources of two great monarchs would be insufficient to complete it; a criticism which the Signoria resented by confining him for two months in prison, and afterwards conducting him through the public treasury, to teach him that the Florentines could build their whole city of marble, and not one poor steeple only, were they so inclined."

I see that *The Builder*, vol. xi. page 690, has been endeavouring to inspire the citizens of Leeds with some pride of this kind respecting their town-hall. The pride would be well, but I sincerely trust that the tower in question may not be built on the design there proposed.[1] I am sorry to have to write a special criticism, but it must be remembered that the best works, by the best men living, are in this age abused without mercy by nameless critics; and it would be unjust to the public, if those who have given their names as guarantee for their sincerity never had the courage to enter a protest against the execution of designs which appear to them unworthy.

DENMARK HILL, 16th April 1854.

[1] [In the *Builder* of November 12, 1853, an illustrated article was published showing the designs for the Town Hall by Cuthbert Brodrick. The building was erected from his designs and opened by Queen Victoria in 1858. It is surrounded by an open portico with Corinthian columns, and from the centre rises a peculiar tower, covered by a dome.]

CONTENTS

LECTURES ON ARCHITECTURE
AND PAINTING

LECTURE I

ARCHITECTURE[1]

Delivered November 1, 1853

1. I THINK myself peculiarly happy in being permitted to address the citizens of Edinburgh on the subject of architecture, for it is one which, they cannot but feel, interests them nearly. Of all the cities in the British Islands, Edinburgh is the one which presents most advantages for the display of a noble building; and which, on the other hand, sustains most injury in the erection of a commonplace or unworthy one.[2] You are all proud of your city; surely you must feel it a duty in some sort to justify your pride; that is to say, to give yourselves a *right* to be proud of it. That you were born under the shadow of its two fantastic mountains,—that you live where from your room windows you can trace the shores of its glittering Firth, are no rightful subjects of pride. You did not raise the mountains, nor shape the shores; and the historical houses of

---

[1] [The following was Ruskin's Synopsis of the Lecture in the preliminary announcement:—

" General Construction of Domestic Buildings.

General Aspect of Edinburgh—Dependent on its Houses more than its Public Buildings. Interest of its Citizens in Domestic Architecture. Faults of Modern Houses. General Laws of Construction, with respect to Exterior Appearance—Roofs—Windows—Doors and Porches. The Duty of Building with regard to Permanence."]

[2] [Compare Ruskin's early essay on the site for the Scott Monument, Vol. I. p. 258; and see two letters of his addressed to the Edinburgh *Witness* in 1857 (*Arrows of the Chace*, 1880, vol. i. pp. 214–222.]

your Canongate, and the broad battlements of your castle, reflect honour upon you only through your ancestors.[1] Before you boast of your city, before even you venture to call it *yours*, ought you not scrupulously to weigh the exact share you have had in adding to it or adorning it, to calculate seriously the influence upon its aspect which the work of your own hands has exercised? I do not say that, even when you regard your city in this scrupulous and testing spirit, you have not considerable ground for exultation. As far as I am acquainted with modern architecture, I am aware of no streets which, in simplicity and manliness of style, or general breadth and brightness of effect, equal those of the New Town of Edinburgh.[2] But yet I am well persuaded that as you traverse those streets, your feelings of pleasure and pride in them are much complicated with those which are excited entirely by the surrounding scenery. As you walk up or down George Street, for instance, do you not look eagerly for every opening to the north and south, which lets in the lustre of the Firth of Forth, or the rugged outline of the Castle Rock? Take away the sea-waves, and the dark basalt, and I fear you would find little to interest you in George Street by itself. Now I remember a city, more nobly placed even than your Edinburgh, which, instead of the valley that you have now filled by lines of railroad, has a broad and rushing river of blue water sweeping through the heart of it; which, for the dark and solitary rock that bears your castle, has an amphitheatre of cliffs crested with cypresses and olive; which, for the two masses of Arthur's Seat and the ranges of the Pentlands, has a chain of blue mountains higher than the haughtiest peaks of your Highlands; and which, for your far-away Ben Ledi and Ben More, has the great

[1] [Among the "historical houses" of the Canongate are Moray House, built by the Countess of Home in 1628; Canongate Tolbooth, "built in 1591, not exactly 'pro patria et posteris,' but for debtors"; Panmure House, in which Adam Smith lived for some time; and Queensberry House.]

[2] [Compare again the early essay, and the other passages there noted, Vol. I. p. 258.]

central chain of the St. Gothard Alps: and yet, as you go out of the gates, and walk in the suburban streets of that city—I mean Verona—the eye never seeks to rest on that external scenery, however gorgeous; it does not look for the gaps between the houses, as you do here; it may for a few moments follow the broken line of the great Alpine battlements; but it is only where they form a background for other battlements, built by the hand of man. There is no necessity felt to dwell on the blue river or the burning hills. The heart and eye have enough to do in the streets of the city itself; they are contented there; nay, they sometimes turn from the natural scenery, as if too savage and solitary, to dwell with a deeper interest on the palace walls that cast their shade upon the streets, and the crowd of towers that rise out of that shadow into the depth of the sky.[1]

2. *That* is a city to be proud of, indeed; and it is this kind of architectural dignity which you should aim at, in what you add to Edinburgh or rebuild in it. For remember, you must either help your scenery or destroy it; whatever you do has an effect of one kind or the other; it is never indifferent. But, above all, remember that it is chiefly by private, not by public, effort that your city must be

---

[1] [Ruskin here begins to fulfil the intentions he had formed, when at Verona in 1851 and 1852, to celebrate in fitting language the city which he loved so intensely. On revisiting it in 1851 he writes to his father:—

"(*August* 30.)—Verona looks lovelier than ever, or nobler is a better word. Every time I come it makes a most profound impression on me, and I long more and more to have Hunt or Millais, or some such patiently imitative man, to paint me the whole city brick by brick. . . . One of the strangest things to me is its continual *newness*; it is only eighteen months since I was here, yet I feel as if my mind had advanced, and as if every scene had now another story to tell me, so that I should like to go over the whole town again, and again examine every ornament. I should never, never have done."

"(*September* 1.)—. . . Certainly Verona is the finest thing in Italy for general sentiment. Venice is grander and richer, but not so pure in feeling or so lovely in grouping. May it long be spared! I tremble at every fissure in the walls, and fancy them wider and wider every year."

So, again, on returning in the following spring he finds Verona "more and more lovely every time" (June 2), and says (June 4), "if I can put any of my impressions of Verona into good language, they will be worth reading." He made many such attempts; see, e.g., *Verona and its Rivers, A Joy for Ever,* § 76, and *Fors Clavigera,* Letter 84; for other references, see General Index.]

adorned.[1] It does not matter how many beautiful public buildings you possess, if they are not supported by, and in harmony with, the private houses of the town. Neither the mind nor the eye will accept a new college, or a new hospital, or a new institution, for a city. It is the Canongate, and the Princes Street, and the High Street that are Edinburgh. It is in your own private houses that the real majesty of Edinburgh must consist; and, what is more, it must be by your own personal interest that the style of the architecture which rises around you must be principally guided. Do not think that you can have good architecture merely by paying for it. It is not by subscribing liberally for a large building once in forty years that you can call up architects and inspiration. It is only by active and sympathetic attention to the domestic and every-day work which is done for each of you, that you can educate either yourselves to the feeling, or your builders to the doing, of what is truly great.

3. Well, but, you will answer, you cannot feel interested in architecture: you do not care about it, and *cannot* care about it. I know you cannot. About such architecture as is built nowadays, no mortal ever did or could care.[2] You do not feel interested in *hearing* the same thing over and over again;—why do you suppose you can feel interested in *seeing* the same thing over and over again, were that thing even the best and most beautiful in the world? Now, you all know the kind of window which you usually build in Edinburgh: here is an example of the head of one (fig. 1), a massy lintel of a single stone, laid across from side to side, with bold square-cut jambs—in fact, the simplest form it is possible to build. It is by no means a bad form; on the contrary, it is very manly and vigorous, and has a certain dignity in its utter refusal of ornament. But I cannot say it is entertaining. How many windows precisely of this form

do you suppose there are in the New Town of Edinburgh?
I have not counted them all through the town, but I
counted them this morning along this very Queen Street,
in which your Hall is;[1] and on the one side of that street,
there are of these windows, absolutely similar to this example, and altogether devoid of any relief by decoration, six
hundred and seventy-eight.* And your decorations are just
as monotonous as your simplicities. How many Corinthian

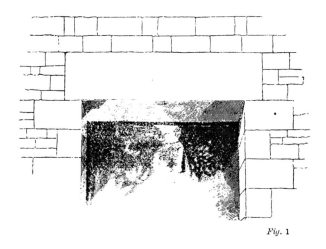

Fig. 1

and Doric columns do you think there are in your banks,
and post-offices, institutions, and I know not what else, one
exactly like another?—and yet you expect to be interested!
Nay, but, you will answer me again, we see sunrises and
sunsets, and violets and roses, over and over again, and we
do not tire of *them*.[2] What! did you ever see one sunrise
like another? does not God vary His clouds for you every
morning and every night? though, indeed, there is enough

* Including York Place, and Picardy Place, but not counting any window
which has mouldings.

[1] [Queen Street Hall, where the lectures of the Philosophical Institution were
delivered.]
[2] [Compare here *Stones of Venice,* vol. ii. ch. vi. § 29 (Vol. X. p. 207); and for
references to passages dealing with variety in nature, see General Index.]
XII. B

in the disappearing and appearing of the great orb above the rolling of the world, to interest all of us, one would think, for as many times as we shall see it; and yet the aspect of it is changed for us daily. You see violets and roses often, and are not tired of them. True! but you did not often see two roses alike, or, if you did, you took care not to put them beside each other in the same nosegay, for fear your nosegay should be uninteresting; and yet you think you can put 150,000 square windows side by side in the same streets, and still be interested by them. Why, if I were to say the same thing over and over again, for the single hour you are going to let me talk to you, would you listen to me? and yet you let your architects *do* the same thing over and over again for three centuries, and expect to be interested by their architecture; with a farther disadvantage on the side of the builder, as compared with the speaker, that my wasted words would cost you but little, but his wasted stones have cost you no small part of your incomes.

4. "Well, but," you still think within yourselves, "it is not *right* that architecture should be interesting. It is a very grand thing, this architecture, but essentially unentertaining. It is its duty to be dull, it is monotonous by law: it cannot be correct and yet amusing."

Believe me, it is not so. All things that are worth doing in art, are interesting and attractive when they are done. There is no law of right which consecrates dulness. The proof of a thing's being right is, that it has power over the heart; that it excites us, wins us, or helps us. I do not say that it has influence over all, but it has over a large class, one kind of art being fit for one class, and another for another; and there is no goodness in art which is independent of the power of pleasing. Yet, do not mistake me; I do not mean that there is no such thing as neglect of the best art, or delight in the worst, just as many men neglect nature, and feed upon what is artificial and base; but I mean, that all good art has the *capacity*

II.

Fig. 2

Window in Oakham Castle.

of pleasing, if people will attend to it; that there is no law against its pleasing; but, on the contrary, something wrong either in the spectator or the art, when it ceases to please. Now, therefore, if you feel that your present school of architecture is unattractive to you, I say there is something wrong, either in the architecture or in you; and I trust you will not think I mean to flatter you when I tell you, that the wrong is *not* in you, but in the architecture. Look at this for a moment (fig. 2);[1] it is a window actually existing—a window of an English domestic building *—a window built six hundred years ago. You will not tell me you have no pleasure in looking at this; or that you could not, by any possibility, become interested in the art which produced it; or that, if every window in your streets were of some such form, with perpetual change in their ornaments, you would pass up and down the street with as much indifference as now, when your windows are of *this* form (fig. 1). Can you for an instant suppose that the architect was a greater or wiser man who built this, than he who built that? or that in the arrangement of these dull and monotonous stones there is more wit and sense than you can penetrate? Believe me, the wrong is not in you; you would all like the best things best, if you only saw them. What is wrong in you is your temper, not your taste; your patient and trustful temper, which lives in houses whose architecture it takes for granted, and subscribes to public edifices from which it derives no enjoyment.

5. "Well, but what are we to do?" you will say to me; "we cannot make architects of ourselves." Pardon me, you can—and you ought. Architecture is an art for

---

* Oakham Castle. I have enlarged this illustration from Mr. Hudson Turner's admirable work on the domestic architecture of England.[2]

---

[1] [Here printed as Plate II.]

[2] [*Some Account of Domestic Architecture in England from the Conquest to the end of the 13th Century*, by T. Hudson Turner, 1851. The window, from the Hall of Oakham Castle, faces p. 30. For another reference to the book, see below, p. 140 *n.*]

all men to learn, because all are concerned with it; and it is so simple, that there is no excuse for not being acquainted with its primary rules, any more than for ignorance of grammar or of spelling, which are both of them far more difficult sciences. Far less trouble than is necessary to learn how to play chess, or whist, or golf, tolerably, —far less than a schoolboy takes to win the meanest prize of the passing year, would acquaint you with all the main principles of the construction of a Gothic cathedral, and I believe you would hardly find the study less amusing. But be that as it may, there are one or two broad principles which need only be stated to be understood and accepted; and those I mean to lay before you, with your permission, before you leave this room.[1]

6. You must all, of course, have observed that the principal distinctions between existing styles of architecture depend on their methods of roofing any space, as a window or door for instance, or a space between pillars;[2] that is to say, that the character of Greek architecture, and of all that is derived from it, depends on its roofing a space with a single stone laid from side to side; the character of Roman architecture, and of all derived from it, depends on its roofing spaces with round arches; and the character of Gothic architecture depends on its roofing spaces with pointed arches, or gables. I need not, of course, in any way follow out for you the mode in which the Greek system of architecture is derived from the horizontal lintel; but I ought perhaps to explain, that by Roman architecture I do not mean that spurious condition of temple form which was nothing more than a luscious imitation of the Greek; but I mean that architecture in which the Roman spirit truly manifested itself, the magnificent vaultings of the aqueduct and the bath, and the colossal heaping of the rough stones in the

---

[1] [On the facility of acquaintance with the leading principles of architecture, and of acquiring judgment on its merits, see *Stones of Venice*, vol. i. (Vol. IX. p. 54); on architecture as a subject of general concern, see *ibid.*, pp. 9, 46.]

[2] [See for a fuller treatment of this subject, *Stones of Venice*, vol. i. (Vol. IX. pp. 76 *seq.*).]

arches of the amphitheatre; an architecture full of expression of gigantic power and strength of will, and from which are directly derived all our most impressive early buildings, called, as you know, by various antiquaries, Saxon, Norman, or Romanesque. Now the first point I wish to insist upon is, that the Greek system, considered merely as a piece of construction, is weak and barbarous compared with the two others.[1] For instance, in the case of a large window or door, such as fig. 1, if you have at your disposal a single large and long stone you may indeed roof it in the Greek manner, as you have done here, with comparative security; but it is always expensive to obtain and to raise to their place stones of this large size, and in many places nearly impossible to obtain them at all: and if you have not such stones, and still insist upon roofing the space in the Greek way, that is to say, upon having a square window, you must do it by the miserably feeble adjustment of bricks, fig. 3.* You are well aware, of course, that this latter is the usual way in which such windows are now built in England; you are fortunate enough here in the north to be able to obtain single stones, and this circumstance alone gives a considerable degree of grandeur to your buildings. But in all cases, and however built, you cannot but see in a moment that this cross bar is weak and imperfect. It may be strong enough for all immediate intents and purposes, but it is not so strong as it might be: however well the house is built, it will still not stand so long as if it had been better constructed; and there is hardly a day passes but you may see some rent or flaw in bad buildings of this kind. You may see one whenever you choose, in one of your most costly, and most ugly buildings, the

Fig. 3

* On this subject, see *The Builder*, vol. xi. p. 709.[2]

---

[1] [Compare *Stones of Venice*, vol. ii. ch. vii. § 47 (Vol. X. p. 312).]

[2] [November 19, 1853; an article referring to the fall of a house in course of erection, and illustrating the weakness of the method of construction shown in Fig. 3 here.]

great church with the dome, at the end of George Street.[1]
I think I never saw a building with a principal entrance so
utterly ghastly and oppressive; and it is as weak as it is
ghastly. The huge horizontal lintel above the door is already
split right through. But you are not aware of a thousandth
part of the evil: the pieces of building that you see are all
carefully done; it is in the parts that are to be concealed
by paint and plaster that the bad building of the day is
thoroughly committed. The main mischief lies in the
strange devices that are used to support the long horizontal
cross beams of our larger apartments and shops, and the
framework of unseen walls; girders and ties of cast iron,
and props and wedges, and laths nailed and bolted together,
on marvellously scientific principles; so scientific, that every
now and then, when some tender reparation is undertaken
by the unconscious householder, the whole house crashes
into a heap of ruin, so total, that the jury which sits on
the bodies of the inhabitants cannot tell what has been the
matter with it, and returns a dim verdict of accidental
death.[2]

[1] [St. George's Established Church at the Charlotte Square end of George Street,
completed in 1814 from the design of Robert Reid at a cost of £33,000. The
entrance consists of a flight of steps leading up to a portico 35 feet high. The dome
is 48 feet across and is surmounted by a cross, the height to the top of which is
160 feet.]

[2] [In the MS.—and possibly in the lecture as delivered—this passage was more
elaborated, and was illustrated by sketches:—

"The other day I was watching the erection of some houses for shops
in a suburb of London—shops that were to make an impression on the
neighbourhood, and to have large plate-glass in their windows, and magnificent
Greek cornices above them. Now, how do you suppose those shops and the
houses above them were built? . . . There were first small square pillars
of brick built up to the height of the shop of as bad bricks as could be got
for money ; and on the top of these pillars was laid a single flat paving-stone
. . . [reference to sketch], and then from pillars was laid a cross beam, but
economy was so strictly studied in this matter that the shortest beams were
chosen which could possibly answer the purpose ; so short that, being laid
from pillar to pillar, the hold here which they had upon the flat stone was
literally not more than two inches—hardly perceptible to the eye at a little
distance . . . [reference to another sketch]. Now, observe, above these
beams was to come the grand Greek cornice—a little bit of the sublime five
orders—in stucco; accordingly, here the bricks were not to be seen, and
both the bricks and brickwork were as bad as they could be *possibly*. . . .
Then, above this row of bad brickwork were laid some more flat stones,
about two inches thick, to be covered with plaster, and form a sort of

7. Did you read the account of the proceedings at the Crystal Palace at Sydenham the other day?[1] Some dozen of men crushed up among the splinters of the scaffolding in an instant, nobody knew why. All the engineers declare the scaffolding to have been erected on the best principles,— that the fall of it is as much a mystery as if it had fallen from heaven, and were all meteoric stones. The jury go to Sydenham and look at the heap of shattered bolts and girders, and come back as wise as they went. Accidental death! Yes, verily; the lives of all those dozen of men had been hanging for months at the mercy of a flaw in an inch or two of cast iron. Very accidental indeed! Not the less pitiable. I grant it not to be an easy thing to raise scaffolding to the height of the Crystal Palace without incurring some danger, but that is no reason why your houses should all be nothing but scaffolding. The common system of support of walls over shops is now nothing but permanent scaffolding; part of iron, part of wood, part of brick: in its skeleton state awful to behold; the weight of three or four stories of wall resting sometimes on two or three pillars of the size of gas pipes, sometimes on a single cross beam of wood, laid across from party wall to party wall in the Greek manner. I have a vivid recollection at this moment of a vast heap

balcony; and above all this was built the entire height of a three-storied house, the whole weight of the walls resting on this single beam which had not two inches of hold at each end ; and the timbers of the first floor being let into it also, so that literally the whole house with its inhabitants depended on this two inches of timber-hold, like a man clinging by his fingers' ends to a precipice. But now mark the consequences. It is indeed probable that the two-inch hold will be found enough for its work, so long as no casualty happens to the house; but let fifty years pass by; let a new drain be opened or a well dug near one of the brick pillars; let the slightest settlement of one of those pillars take place, the timber slips from its hold, and in an instant the house is a mass of ruins. . . . Or suppose no such calamities happen, but the house prolongs its tottering existence in a plastered peace—for a century or so. By that time, at the latest, the wretched work of it begins to give way, the floors slope and bulge, long rambling cracks show themselves through all the external stucco, and reparation after reparation is made, and botch after botch, until the house has cost more than would have built two of its size, and at last the surveyor of the district condemns it as unsafe, and it is pulled down for materials. That will be the history of nearly every house we build in these days of civilization."]

[1] [See the *Times*, August 16, 17, 18, 1853; portion of the main transept gave way, killing and wounding nearly forty men.]

of splinters in the Borough Road, close to St. George's, Southwark, in the road between my own house and London. I had passed it the day before, a goodly shop front, and sufficient house above, with a few repairs undertaken in the shop before opening a new business. The master and mistress had found it dusty that afternoon, and went out to tea. When they came back in the evening, they found their whole house in the form of a heap of bricks blocking the roadway, with a party of men digging out their cook. But I do not insist on casualties like these, disgraceful to us as they are, for it is, of course, perfectly possible to build a perfectly secure house or a secure window in the Greek manner; but the simple fact is, that in order to obtain in the cross lintel the same amount of strength which you can obtain in a pointed arch, you must go to an immensely greater cost in stone or in labour. Stonehenge is strong enough, but it takes some trouble to build in the manner of Stonehenge: and Stonehenge itself is not so strong as an arch of the Colosseum. You could not raise a circle of four Stonehenges, one over the other, with safety; and as it is, more of the cross-stones are fallen upon the plain of Sarum than arches rent away, except by the hand of man, from the mighty circle of Rome. But I waste words;— your own common sense must show you in a moment that this is a weak form; and there is not at this instant a single street in London where some house could not be pointed out with a flaw running through its brickwork, and repairs rendered necessary in consequence, merely owing to the adoption of this bad form; and that our builders know so well, that in myriads of instances you find them actually throwing concealed arches above the horizontal lintels to take the weight off them; and the gabled decoration, at the top of some Palladian windows, is merely the ornamental form resulting from a bold device of the old Roman builders to effect the same purpose.

8. But there is a farther reason for our adopting the pointed arch than its being the strongest form; it is also

the most beautiful form in which a window or door-head can be built. Not the most beautiful because it is the strongest; but most beautiful, because its form is one of those which, as we know by its frequent occurrence in the work of Nature around us, has been appointed by the Deity to be an everlasting source of pleasure to the human mind.

Gather a branch from any of the trees or flowers to which the earth owes its principal beauty. You will find that every one of its leaves is terminated, more or less, in the form of the pointed arch; and to that form owes its grace and character. I will take, for instance, a spray of the tree which so gracefully adorns your Scottish glens and crags—there is no lovelier in the world—the common ash.[1] Here is a sketch of the clusters of leaves which form the extremity of one of its young shoots (fig. 4); and, by the way, it will furnish us with an interesting illustration of another error in modern architectural systems. You know how fond modern architects, like foolish modern politicians, are of their equalities,[2] and similarities; how necessary they think it that each part of a building should be like every other part. Now Nature abhors equality, and similitude, just as much as foolish men love them. You will find that the ends of the shoots of the ash are composed of four * green stalks bearing leaves, springing in the form of a cross, if seen from above, as in fig. 5, and at first you will suppose the four arms of the

Fig. 5

* Sometimes of six; that is to say, they spring in pairs; only the two uppermost pairs, sometimes the three uppermost, spring so close together as to appear one cluster.

[1] [For a more detailed study of the ash leaf, see *Modern Painters*, vol. v. pt. vi. ch. iv. § 5.]

[2] [For a note collecting some of Ruskin's many references to political equality, see Vol. XI. p. 260. The references to the principle, in nature and in art, of diversity in symmetry, are yet more numerous: see General Index, *s.* "Symmetry."]

cross are equal. But look more closely, and you will find that two opposite arms or stalks have only five leaves each, and the other two have seven; or else, two have seven, and the other two nine; but always one pair of stalks has two leaves more than the other pair. Sometimes the tree gets a little puzzled, and forgets which is to be the longest stalk, and begins with a stem for seven leaves where it should have nine, and then recollects itself at the last minute, and puts on another leaf in a great hurry, and so produces a stalk with eight leaves; but all this care it takes merely to keep itself out of equalities; and all its grace and power of pleasing are owing to its doing so, together with the lovely curves in which its stalks, thus arranged, spring from the main bough. Fig. 5 is a plan of their arrangement merely, but fig. 4 is the way in which you are most likely to see them: and observe, they spring from the stalk *precisely as a Gothic vaulted roof springs*, each stalk representing a rib of the roof, and the leaves its crossing stones; and the beauty of each of those leaves is altogether owing to its terminating in the Gothic form, the pointed arch. Now do you think you would have liked your ash trees as well, if Nature had taught them Greek, and shown them how to grow according to the received Attic architectural rules of right? I will try you. Here is a cluster of ash leaves, which I have grown expressly for you on Greek principles (fig. 6, Plate III.). How do you like it?

9. Observe, I have played you no trick in this comparison. It is perfectly fair in all respects. I have merely substituted for the beautiful spring of the Gothic vaulting in the ash bough, a cross lintel; and then, in order to raise the leaves to the same height, I introduce vertical columns; and I make the leaves square-headed instead of pointed, and their lateral ribs at right angles with the central rib, instead of sloping from it. I have, indeed, only given you two boughs instead of four; because the perspective of the crossing ones could not have been given without confusing

III.

Fig. 4

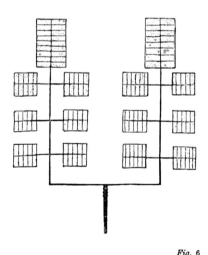

Fig. 6

Spray of Ash-tree, and Improvement of the
same on Greek Principles.

the figure; but I imagine you have quite enough of them as it is.

"Nay, but," some of you instantly answer, "if we had been as long accustomed to square-leaved ash trees as we have been to sharp-leaved ash trees, we should like them just as well." Do not think it. Are you not much more accustomed to grey whinstone and brown sandstone than you are to rubies or emeralds? and yet will you tell me you think them as beautiful? Are you not more accustomed to the ordinary voices of men than to the perfect accents of sweet singing? yet do you not instantly declare the song to be loveliest? Examine well the channels of your admiration, and you will find that they are, in verity, as unchangeable as the channels of your heart's blood; that just as by the pressure of a bandage, or by unwholesome and perpetual action of some part of the body, that blood may be wasted or arrested, and in its stagnancy cease to nourish the frame, or in its disturbed flow affect it with incurable disease, so also admiration itself may, by the bandages of fashion, bound close over the eyes and the arteries of the soul, be arrested in its natural pulse and healthy flow; but that wherever the artificial pressure is removed, it will return into that bed which has been traced for it by the finger of God.[1]

10. Consider this subject well, and you will find that custom has indeed no real influence upon our feelings of the beautiful, except in dulling and checking them;[2] that is to say, it will and does, as we advance in years, deaden in some degree our enjoyment of all beauty, but it in no wise influences our determination of what is beautiful, and what is not. You see the broad blue sky every day over your heads; but you do not for that reason determine blue to be less or more beautiful than you did at first; you are unaccustomed to see stones as blue as the sapphire,

---

[1] [Exodus xxxi. 18; Deuteronomy ix. 10, etc.]

[2] [On the subject of this § 10, compare *Modern Painters*, vol. ii. sec. i. ch. iv. (Vol. IV. pp. 67–75), and the additional passages from the MS. in the same volume, pp. 365–366.]

but you do not for that reason think the sapphire less beautiful than other stones. The blue colour is everlastingly appointed by the Deity to be a source of delight; and whether seen perpetually over your head, or crystallised once in a thousand years into a single and incomparable stone, your acknowledgment of its beauty is equally natural, simple, and instantaneous. Pardon me for engaging you in a metaphysical discussion; for it is necessary to the establishment of some of the greatest of all architectural principles that I should fully convince you of this great truth, and that I should quite do away with the various objections to it, which I suppose must arise in your minds. Of these there is one more which I must briefly meet. You know how much confusion has been introduced into the subject of criticism, by reference to the power of Association over the human heart; you know how often it has been said that custom must have something to do with our ideas of beauty, because it endears so many objects to the affections. But, once for all, observe that the powers of association and of beauty are two entirely distinct powers, — as distinct, for instance, as the forces of gravitation and electricity. These forces may act together, or may neutralise one another, but are not for that reason to be supposed the same force; and the charm of association will sometimes enhance, and sometimes entirely overpower, that of beauty; but you must not confound the two together. You love many things because you are accustomed to them, and are pained by many things because they are strange to you; but that does not make the accustomed sight more beautiful, or the strange one less so. The well-known object may be dearer to you, or you may have discovered charms in it which others cannot; but the charm was there before you discovered it, only needing time and love to perceive it. You love your friends and relations more than all the world beside, and may perceive beauties in their faces which others cannot perceive; but you feel that you would be ridiculous in allowing yourselves to think them the most beautiful persons in the world: you acknowledge that the real beauty of the human countenance depends on fixed laws of form and expression, and not on the affection .you bear to it, or the degree in which you are familiarised with it: and so does the beauty of all other existences.

11. Now, therefore, I think that, without the risk of any farther serious objection occurring to you, I may state what I believe to be the truth,—that beauty has been appointed by the Deity to be one of the elements by which the human soul is continually sustained; it is therefore to be found more or less in all natural objects, but in order that we may not satiate ourselves with it, and weary of it, it is rarely granted to us in its utmost degrees. When we see it in those utmost degrees, we are attracted to it strongly, and remember it long, as in the case of singularly beautiful scenery, or a beautiful countenance. On the other hand, absolute ugliness is admitted as rarely as perfect beauty; but degrees of it more or less distinct are associated with whatever has the nature of death and sin, just as beauty is associated with what has the nature of virtue and of life.[1]

12. This being so, you see that when the relative beauty of any particular forms has to be examined, we may reason, from the forms of Nature around us, in this manner:—what Nature does generally, is sure to be more or less beautiful; what she does rarely, will either be *very* beautiful,[2] or absolutely ugly. And we may again easily determine, if we are not willing in such a case to trust our feelings, which of these is indeed the case, by this simple rule, that if the rare occurrence is the result of the complete fulfilment of a natural law, it will be beautiful; if of the violation of a natural law, it will be ugly. For instance, a sapphire is the result of the complete and perfect fulfilment of the laws of aggregation in the earth of alumina, and it is therefore

[1] [Here, again, compare *Modern Painters*, vol. ii. chs. xii.–xiv., "Of Vital Beauty."]
[2] [On this subject, compare Vol. III. p. 156, Vol. IX. p. 61 *n*.]

beautiful; more beautiful than clay, or any other of the conditions of that earth. But a square leaf on any tree would be ugly, being a violation of the laws of growth in trees,* and we ought to feel it so.

13. Now then, I proceed to argue in this manner from what we see in the woods and fields around us; that as they are evidently meant for our delight, and as we always feel them to be beautiful, we may assume that the forms into which their leaves are cast, are indeed types of beauty, not of extreme or perfect, but average beauty. And finding that they invariably terminate more or less in pointed arches, and are not square-headed, I assert the pointed arch to be one of the forms most fitted for perpetual contemplation by the human mind; that it is one of those which never weary, however often repeated; and that therefore, being both the strongest in structure, and a beautiful form (while the square head is both weak in structure, and an ugly form), we are unwise ever to build in any other.

14. Here, however, I must anticipate another objection. It may be asked why we are to build only the tops of the windows pointed,—why not follow the leaves, and point them at the bottom also?

For this simple reason, that, while in architecture you are continually called upon to do what may be *unnecessary* for the sake of beauty, you are never called upon to do what is *inconvenient* for the sake of beauty. You want the level window sill to lean upon, or to allow the window to open on a balcony: the eye and the common sense of the beholder require this necessity to be met before any laws of beauty are thought of. And besides this, there is in the sill no necessity for the pointed arch as a bearing form; on the contrary, it would give an idea of weak support for the sides of the window, and therefore is at once rejected. Only I

* I am at present aware only of one tree, the tulip tree, which has an exceptional form, and which, I doubt not, every one will admit, loses much beauty in consequence. All other leaves, as far as I know, have the round or pointed arch in the form of the extremities of their foils.

IV.

Fig. 7

Window in Dunblane Cathedral.

beg of you particularly to observe that the level sill, although useful, and therefore admitted, does not therefore become beautiful; the eye does not like it so well as the top of the window, nor does the sculptor like to attract the eye to it; his richest mouldings, traceries, and sculptures are all reserved for the top of the window; they are sparingly granted to its horizontal base. And farther, observe, that when neither the convenience of the sill, nor the support of the structure, are any more of moment, as in small windows and traceries, you instantly *have* the point given to the bottom of the window. Do you recollect the west window of your own Dunblane Abbey?[1] If you look in any common guide-book, you will find it pointed out as peculiarly beautiful,—it is acknowledged to be beautiful by the most careless observer. And why beautiful? Look at it (fig. 7, Plate IV.). Simply because in its great contours it has the form of a forest leaf, and because in its decoration it has used nothing but forest leaves. The sharp and expressive moulding which surrounds it is a very interesting example of one used to an enormous extent by the builders of the early English Gothic, usually in the form seen in fig. 2, Plate II., composed of clusters of four sharp leaves each, originally produced by sculpturing the sides of a four-sided pyramid, and afterwards brought more or less into a true image of leaves, but deriving all its beauty from the botanical form. In the present instance only two leaves are set in each cluster; and the architect has been determined that the naturalism should be perfect. For he was no common man who designed that cathedral of Dunblane. I know not anything so perfect in its simplicity, and so beautiful, as far as it reaches, in all the Gothic with which I am

---

[1] [See *Lectures on Landscape*, § 37, where Ruskin again refers to this window as "one of the prettiest pieces of thirteenth-century carving in the kingdom," and goes on to discuss its imperfect rendering in Turner's *Liber Studiorum* Plate, No. 497 in the National Gallery. Ruskin visited Dunblane shortly before delivering these lectures: see above, Introduction, p. xx. The Cathedral was founded by David I., *circa* 1140, but almost entirely rebuilt, in the pointed style, a century later. It has been repaired in recent years, and is thus used as the parish church of Dunblane.]

acquainted. And just in proportion to his power of mind, that man was content to work under Nature's teaching; and instead of putting a merely formal dogtooth, as everybody else did at the time, he went down to the woody bank of the sweet river beneath the rocks on which he was building, and he took up a few of the fallen leaves that lay by it, and he set them in his arch, side by side, for ever. And, look—that he might show you he had done this,—he has made them all of different sizes, just as they lay; and that you might not by any chance miss noticing the variety, he has put a great broad one at the top, and then a little one turned the wrong way, next to it, so that you must be blind indeed if you do not understand his meaning. And the healthy change and playfulness of this just does in the stone-work what it does on the tree boughs, and is a per-petual refreshment and invigoration; so that, however long you gaze at this simple ornament—and none can be simpler, a village mason could carve it all round the window in a few hours—you are never weary of it, it seems always new.

15. It is true that oval windows of this form are com-paratively rare in Gothic work, but, as you well know, circular or wheel windows are used constantly, and in most traceries the apertures are curved and pointed as much at the bottom as the top. So that I believe you will now allow me to proceed upon the assumption, that the pointed arch is indeed the best form into which the head either of door or window can be thrown, considered as a means of sustaining weight above it. How these pointed arches ought to be grouped and decorated, I shall endeavour to show you in my next lecture. Meantime I must beg of you to con-sider farther some of the general points connected with the structure of the roof.

16. I am sure that all of you must readily acknowledge the charm which is imparted to any landscape by the presence of cottages; and you must over and over again have paused at the wicket gate of some cottage garden, delighted by the simple beauty of the honeysuckle porch

and latticed window.[1] Has it ever occurred to you to ask the question, what effect the cottage would have upon your feelings if it had *no roof?* no visible roof, I mean; — if instead of the thatched slope, in which the little upper windows are buried deep, as in a nest of straw—or the rough shelter of its mountain shales—or warm colouring of russet tiles—there were nothing but a flat leaden top to it, making it look like a large packing-case with windows in it? I don't think the rarity of such a sight would make you feel it to be beautiful; on the contrary, if you think over the matter, you will find that you actually do owe, and ought to owe, a great part of your pleasure in all cottage scenery, and in all the inexhaustible imagery of literature which is founded upon it, to the conspicuousness of the cottage roof—to the subordination of the cottage itself to its covering, which leaves, in nine cases out of ten, really more roof than anything else. It is, indeed, not so much the whitewashed walls—nor the flowery garden—nor the rude fragments of stones set for steps at the door—nor any other picturesqueness of the building which interest you, so much as the grey bank of its heavy eaves, deep-cushioned with green moss and golden stonecrop. And there is a profound, yet evident, reason for this feeling. The very soul of the cottage—the essence and meaning of it—are in its roof; it is that, mainly, wherein consists its shelter; that, wherein it differs most completely from a cleft in rocks or bower in woods. It is in its thick impenetrable coverlid of close thatch that its whole heart and hospitality are concentrated. Consider the difference, in sound, of the expressions "beneath my roof" and "within my walls,"—consider whether you would be best sheltered, in a shed, with a stout roof sustained on corner posts, or in an enclosure of four walls without a roof at all,—and you will quickly see how important a part of the cottage the roof must always be to the mind as well as to the

---

[1] [Compare Ruskin's early essay, *The Poetry of Architecture*, § 12, Vol. I. p. 12.]

eye, and how, from seeing it, the greatest part of our pleasure must continually arise.

17. Now, do you suppose that which is so all-important in a cottage, can be of small importance in your own dwelling-house? Do you think that by any splendour of architecture—any height of stories—you can atone to the mind for the loss of the aspect of the roof? It is vain to say you take the roof for granted. You may as well say you take a man's kindness for granted, though he neither looks nor speaks kindly. You may know him to be kind in reality, but you will not like him so well as if he spoke and looked kindly also. And whatever external splendour you may give your houses, you will always feel there is something wanting, unless you see their roofs plainly. And this especially in the north. In southern architecture the roof is of far less importance; but here the soul of domestic building is in the largeness and conspicuousness of the protection against the ponderous snow and driving sleet. You may make the façade of the square pile, if the roof be not seen, as handsome as you please,—you may cover it with decoration,—but there will always be a heartlessness about it, which you will not know how to conquer; above all, a perpetual difficulty in finishing the wall at top, which will require all kinds of strange inventions in parapets and pinnacles for its decoration, and yet will never look right.

Now, I need not tell you that, as it is desirable, for the sake of the effect upon the mind, that the roof should be visible, so the best and most natural form of roof in the north is that which will render it *most* visible, namely, the steep gable: the best and most natural, I say, because this form not only throws off snow and rain most completely, and dries fastest, but obtains the greatest interior space within walls of a given height, removes the heat of the sun most effectually from the upper rooms, and affords most space for ventilation.[1]

---

[1] [See further on this subject *Stones of Venice*, vol. i. ch. xiii., "The Roof," (Vol. IX. pp. 184–188).]

18. You have then, observe, two great principles, as far
as northern architecture is concerned; first, that the pointed
arch is to be the means by which the weight of the wall
or roof is to be sustained; secondly, that the steep gable
is the form most proper for the roof itself. And now
observe this most interesting fact, that all the loveliest
Gothic architecture in the world is based on the group
of lines composed of the pointed arch and the gable. If
you look at the beautiful apse of Amiens Cathedral—a
work justly celebrated over all Europe—you will find it
formed merely of a series of windows surmounted by pure
gables of open work.[1] If you look at the transept porches
of Rouen, or at the great and celebrated porch of the
Cathedral of Rheims, or that of Strasbourg, Bayeux,
Amiens, or Peterborough, still you will see that these lovely
compositions are nothing more than richly decorated forms
of gable over pointed arch.[2] But more than this, you
must be all well aware how fond our best architectural
artists are of the street effects of foreign cities; and even
those now present who have not personally visited any of
the continental towns must remember, I should think, some
of the many interesting drawings by Mr. Prout, Mr. Nash,[3]
and other excellent draughtsmen, which have for many
years adorned our exhibitions. Now, the principal charm
of all those continental street effects is dependent on the
houses having high-pitched gable roofs. In the Netherlands, and Northern France, where the material for building
is brick or stone, the fronts of the stone gables are raised
above the roofs, and you have magnificent and grotesque
ranges of steps or curves decorated with various ornaments,
succeeding one another in endless perspective along the

[1] [See *Bible of Amiens*, ch. iv., where Ruskin says that the apse of Amiens is
"not only the best, but the very *first* thing done *perfectly* in its manner, by Northern
Christendom . . . the first virgin perfect work . . . of Gothic Architecture."]
[2] [For the porches of Rouen, see *Seven Lamps*, Vol. VIII. pp. 123, 136; for
Bayeux, Vol. VIII. p. 132; for Rheims, Vol. VIII. p. 136, and *Stones of Venice*,
Vol. IX. p. 238; for Peterborough, Vol. I. p. 447, Vol. IX. p. 215.]
[3] [See note on Vol. III. p. 220.]

streets of Antwerp, Ghent, or Brussels. In Picardy and Normandy, again, and many towns of Germany, where the material for building is principally wood, the roof is made to project over the gables, fringed with a beautifully carved cornice, and casting a broad shadow down the house front. This is principally seen at Abbeville, Rouen, Lisieux,[1] and others of the older towns of France. But, in all cases, the effect of the whole street depends on the prominence of the gables ; not only of the fronts towards the streets, but of the sides also, set with small garret or dormer windows, each of the most fantastic and beautiful form, and crowned with a little spire or pinnacle. Wherever there is a little winding stair, or projecting bow window, or any other irregularity of form, the steep ridges shoot into turrets and small spires, as in fig. 8,* each in its turn crowned by a fantastic ornament, covered with curiously shaped slates or shingles, or crested with long fringes of rich ironwork, so that, seen from above and from a distance, the intricate grouping of the roofs of a French city is no less interesting than its actual streets ; and in the streets themselves, the masses of broad shadow which the roofs form against the sky, are a most important background to the bright and sculptured surfaces of the walls.

19. Finally, I need not remind you of the effect upon the northern mind which has always been produced by the heaven-pointing spire, nor of the theory which has been founded upon it of the general meaning of Gothic architecture as expressive of religious aspiration. In a few minutes, you may ascertain the exact value of that theory, and the degree in which it is true.[2]

The first tower of which we hear as built upon the earth,

* This figure is copied from Prout.

---

[1] [See, for instance, Prout's drawing of Lisieux, No. 12 in the *Notes on Prout and Hunt,* reproduced in a later volume of this edition.   Plate V. here shows the effect of an old German town.]

[2] [For another criticism of this theory, see *Stones of Venice,* vol. i. (Vol. IX. p. 185).]

V

J. Ruskin

Münster
1859

Allen & Co. Sc

was certainly built in a species of aspiration; but I do not suppose that any one here will think it was a religious one. "Go to now. Let us build a tower whose top may reach unto heaven."[1] From that day to this, whenever men have become skilful architects at all, there has been a tendency in them to build high; not in any religious feeling, but in mere exuberance of spirit and power —as they dance or sing—with a certain mingling of vanity—like the feeling in which a child builds a tower of cards; and, in nobler instances, with also a strong sense of, and delight in the majesty, height, and strength of the building itself, such as we have in that of a lofty tree or a peaked mountain. Add to this instinct the frequent necessity of points of elevation for watch-towers, or of points of offence, as in towers built on the ramparts of cities, and, finally, the need of elevations for the transmission of sound, as in the Turkish minaret and Christian belfry, and you have, I think, a sufficient explanation of the tower-building of the world in

Fig. 8

general. Look through your Bibles only, and collect the various expressions with reference to tower-building there, and you will have a very complete idea of the spirit in which it is for the most part undertaken. You begin with

---

[1] [Genesis xi. 4.]

that of Babel; then you remember Gideon beating down
the tower of Penuel, in order more completely to humble
the pride of the men of the city; you remember the defence of the tower of Shechem against Abimelech, and
the death of Abimelech by the casting of a stone from it
by a woman's hand; you recollect the husbandman building
a tower in his vineyard, and the beautiful expressions in
Solomon's song,—"The tower of Lebanon, which looketh
towards Damascus;" "I am a wall, and my breasts like
towers;"—you recollect the Psalmist's expressions of love
and delight, "Go ye round about Jerusalem; tell the
towers thereof: mark ye well her bulwarks; consider her
palaces, that ye may tell it to the generation following."[1]
You see in all these cases how completely the tower is a
subject of human pride, or delight, or defence, not in any
wise associated with religious sentiment; the towers of
Jerusalem being named in the same sentence, not with her
temple, but with her bulwarks and palaces.   And thus, when
the tower is in reality connected with a place of worship,
it was generally done to add to its magnificence, but not
to add to its religious expression.   And over the whole of
the world, you have various species of elevated buildings,
the Egyptian pyramid, the Indian and Chinese pagoda, the
Turkish minaret, and the Christian belfry,—all of them
raised either to make a show from a distance, or to cry
from, or swing bells in, or hang them round, or for some
other very human reason.   Thus, when the good people
of Beauvais were building their cathedral, that of Amiens,
then just completed, had excited the admiration of all
France; and the people of Beauvais, in their jealousy and
determination to beat the people of Amiens, set to work to
build a tower to their own cathedral as high as they possibly
could.   They built it so high that it tumbled down, and they
were never able to finish their cathedral at all—it stands a

[1] [The Bible references here are Judges viii. 17, ix. 48–53; Matthew xxi. 33;
Mark xii. 1; Song of Solomon vii. 4, viii. 10; Psalms xlviii. 12, 13. With the last
passage compare *Eagle's Nest,* § 240 *ad fin.*]

wreck to this day.[1] But you will not, I should think, imagine this to have been done in heavenward aspiration. Mind, however, I don't blame the people of Beauvais, except for their bad building. I think their desire to beat the citizens of Amiens a most amiable weakness, and only wish I could see the citizens of Edinburgh and Glasgow inflamed with the same emulation, building Gothic towers * instead of manufactory chimneys. Only do not confound a feeling which, though healthy and right, may be nearly analogous to that in which you play a cricket-match, with any feeling allied to your hope of heaven.

20. Such being the state of the case with respect to tower-building in general, let me follow for a few minutes the changes which occur in the towers of northern and southern architects.

Many of us are familiar with the ordinary form of the Italian bell-tower or campanile. From the eighth century to the thirteenth there was little change in that form : † four-square, rising high and without tapering into the air, story above story, they stood like giants in the quiet fields beside the piles of the basilica or the Lombardic church, in this form (fig. 9), tiled at the top in a flat gable, with open arches below, and fewer and fewer arches on each inferior story, down to the bottom. It is worth while noting the difference in form between these and the towers built for

* I did not, at the time of the delivery of these lectures, know how many Gothic towers the worthy Glaswegians *have* lately built : that of St. Peter's, in particular, being a most meritorious effort.[2]

† There is a good abstract of the forms of the Italian campanile, by Mr. Papworth, in the *Journal of the Archæological Institute*, March 1850.

[1] [The cathedral of Beauvais was commenced in 1225, and the design of its founders and architects, excited to emulation by the splendour of Amiens, which had been begun in 1220, was to surpass in vastness and magnificence all other Gothic edifices. The choir is the loftiest in the world, the elevation of the roof above the pavement being 153 feet, 13 feet higher than that of Amiens. The roof and central tower fell in 1284. A later Gothic tower, 455 feet high, also tumbled down (in 1573). A distant view of Beauvais ("Light in the West") is Plate 66 in *Modern Painters*, vol. v.]

[2] [The church referred to is St. Peter's Free Church, situated at the corner of Mains Street and Waterloo Street; it was designed by the late Mr. Charles Wilson, of Glasgow.]

military service.   The latter were built as in fig. 10, projecting vigorously at the top over a series of brackets or
machicolations, with very small windows, and no decoration
below.   Such towers as these were attached to every important palace in the cities of Italy, and stood in great
circles—troops of towers—around their external walls: their

Fig. 9   *Fig.* 10

ruins still frown along the crests of every promontory of the
Apennines, and are seen from far away in the great Lombardic plain, from distances of half-a-day's journey, dark
against the amber sky of the horizon.   These are of course
now built no more, the changed methods of modern warfare
having cast them into entire disuse; but the belfry or
campanile has had a very different influence on European
architecture.   Its form in the plains of Italy and South
France being that just shown you [fig. 9], the moment we

VI

J. Ruskin.

Allen & Co. Sc

The Church Tower, Courmayeur.

(From the drawing in the possession of Sir John Simon, K.C.B.)

enter the valleys of the Alps, where there is snow to be sustained, we find its form of roof altered by the substitution of a steep gable for a flat one.*　There are probably few in the room who have not been in some parts of South Switzerland, and who do not remember the beautiful effect of the grey mountain churches, many of them hardly changed since the tenth and eleventh centuries, whose pointed towers stand up through the green level of the vines, or crown the jutting rocks that border the valley.[1]

21. From this form to the true spire the change is slight, and consists in little more than various decoration ; generally in putting small pinnacles at the angles, and piercing the central pyramid with traceried windows ; sometimes, as at Fribourg and Burgos[2] throwing it into tracery altogether : but to do this is invariably the sign of a vicious style, as it takes away from the spire its character of a true roof, and turns it merely[3] into an ornamental excrescence.　At Antwerp and Brussels, the celebrated towers (one, observe, ecclesiastical, being the tower of the cathedral, and the other secular),[4] are formed by successions of diminishing towers, set one above the other, and each supported by buttresses thrown to the angles of the one beneath.　At the English cathedrals of Lichfield and Salisbury, the spire is seen in great purity, only decorated by sculpture ; but I am aware of no example so striking in its entire simplicity as that of the towers of the cathedral of Coutances in Normandy.[5]

---

* The form establishes itself afterwards in the plains, in sympathy with other Gothic conditions, as in the campanile of St. Mark's at Venice.

---

[1] [See the drawing of the church of Courmayeur reproduced opposite, Plate VI.]

[2] [Burgos was known to Ruskin only by pictures and engravings ; with Fribourg (Switzerland) he was well familiar : see "The Tower of Fribourg," Plate 24 in *Modern Painters* (vol. iv.) ; the allusion here, however, is to the tower of the Church of St. Nicolas.]

[3] [The MS. reads "merely," which is no doubt the word intended ; hitherto it has been printed "nearly."]

[4] [The Brussels tower is that of the Town Hall, 1401–1448.]

[5] [The Cathedral of Coutances was consecrated in 1056, but no part of the original edifice remains "except perhaps the core of the great piers which carry the central tower," the present structure dating from early in the thirteenth century.　The date of the consecration of Salisbury Cathedral is 1258, but the tower is later ; that of

There is a dispute between French and English antiquaries as to the date of the building, the English being unwilling to admit its complete priority to all their own Gothic. I have no doubt of this priority myself; and I hope that the time will soon come when men will cease to confound vanity with patriotism,[1] and will think the honour of their nation more advanced by their own sincerity and courtesy, than by claims, however learnedly contested, to the invention of pinnacles and arches. I believe the French nation was, in the twelfth and thirteenth centuries, the greatest in the world;[2] and that the French not only invented Gothic architecture, but carried it to a perfection which no other nation has approached, then or since: but, however this may be, there can be no doubt that the towers of Coutances, if not the earliest, are among the very earliest, examples of the fully developed spire. I have drawn one of them carefully for you (fig. 11), and you will see immediately that they are literally domestic roofs, with garret windows, executed on a large scale, and in stone. Their only ornament is a kind of scaly mail, which is nothing more than the copying in stone of the common wooden shingles of the house-roof; and their security is provided for by strong gabled dormer windows, of massy masonry, which, though supported on detached shafts, have weight enough completely to balance the lateral thrusts of the spires. Nothing can surpass the boldness or the simplicity of the plan; and yet, in spite of this simplicity, the clear detaching of the shafts from the slope of the spire, and their great height, strengthened by rude cross-bars of stone, carried back to the wall behind, occasion so

Lichfield (the west front and spires), is given by Willis as about 1275. On the vexed questions, referred to in the text, of the priority between English and French Gothic, the reader may consult the works of M. de Caumont, J. H. Parker's *Introduction to the Study of Gothic Architecture*, Part ii., and C. H. Moore's *Development and Character of Gothic Architecture*, pp. 166–167, 310–313.]

[1] [Compare *Val d'Arno*, § 247, where Ruskin speaks of "the mingling of mean rapacity with meaner vanity which Christian nations now call patriotism;" and see also *A Joy for Ever*, § 81. For Ruskin's views upon patriotism, in a nobler sense of the word, see his article, entitled "Home and its Economies," reprinted in a later volume of this edition.]

[2] [So Ruskin says again in *Modern Painters*, vol. iv. ch. xx. § 23.]

great a complexity and play of cast shadows, that I remember no architectural composition of which the aspect is so completely varied at different hours of the day.* But the main thing I wish you to observe is, the complete *domesticity* of the work ; the evident treatment of the church spire merely as a magnified house-roof ; and the proof herein of the great truth of which I have been endeavouring to persuade you, that all good architecture rises out of good and simple domestic work ; and that, therefore, before you attempt to build great churches and palaces, you must build good house doors and garret windows.

Fig. 11

22. Nor is the spire the only ecclesiastical form deducible from domestic architecture.[1] The spires of France and Germany are associated with other towers, even simpler and more straightforward in confession of their nature, in which, though the walls of the tower are covered with sculpture, there is an ordinary ridged gable roof on the top. The finest example I know of this kind of tower, is that on the north-west angle of Rouen Cathedral (fig. 12) ; but they occur in multitudes in the older towns of Germany ; and the backgrounds of Albert Dürer are full of them, and owe

---

* The sketch was made about ten o'clock on a September morning.[2]

[1] [On the connexion between domestic and ecclesiastical architecture, see *Stones of Venice*, vol. ii. ch. iv. § 53, ch. vi. § 84 (Vol. X. pp. 119, 248).]

[2] [Ruskin was at Coutances in 1848. Writing thence to his father (Sept. 12) he says : " The cathedral here is full of interest, but a little too much like Salisbury ; " and again (Sept. 13) :—

"This is a beautiful place, like all the rest of Normandy that we have seen,—hills and vales and rocks breaking out here and there, and soft

to them a great part of their interest: all these great and magnificent masses of architecture being repeated on a smaller scale by the little turret roofs and pinnacles of every house in the town; and the whole system of them being expressive, not by any means of religious feeling,* but merely of joyfulness and exhilaration of spirit in the inhabitants of such cities, leading them to throw their roofs high into the sky, and therefore giving to the style of architecture with which these grotesque roofs are associated, a certain charm like that of cheerfulness in a human face; besides a power of interesting the beholder which is testified, not only by the artist in his constant search after such forms as the elements of his landscape, but by every phrase of our language and literature bearing on such topics. Have not these words, Pinnacle, Turret, Belfry, Spire, Tower, a pleasant sound in all your ears?

Fig. 12

I do not speak of your scenery, I do not ask you how much you feel that it owes to the grey

* Among the various modes in which the architects, against whose practice my writings are directed, have endeavoured to oppose them, no charge has been made more frequently than that of their self contradiction; the fact being, that there are few people in the world who are capable of seeing the two sides of any subject, or of conceiving how the statements of its opposite aspects can possibly be reconcilable.[1] For instance, in a recent review, though for the most part both fair and intelligent, it is remarked, on this very subject

    fields with avenues of trees between them, and lanes so loaded with blackberries that the hedge on each side looks like a piece of Florentine mosaic of bright black and red. But I am put out by the weather; it has grown so cold that I can only make rapid notes with greatcoat and gloves on. . . . I have pretty well examined this cathedral inside and out, there is not much detail about it, but it is marvellously interesting, a pure and complete example of the very earliest French Gothic."
See also the extract from Ruskin's diary at Coutances, given in Vol. VIII. p. xxxi.]
   [1] [For some other remarks on this charge of the reviewers of his architectural works, see Introduction to *Stones of Venice*, vol. i. (Vol. IX. p. xlii.). On the general subject of his alleged self-contradiction, see above, Introduction, p. li.]

battlements that frown through the woods of Craigmillar,[1] to the pointed turrets that flank the front of Holyrood, or to the massy keeps of your Crichtoun and Borthwick and other border towns. But look merely through your poetry and romances; take away out of your border ballads the word *tower* wherever it occurs, and the ideas connected with it, and what will become of the ballads? See how Sir Walter Scott cannot even get through a description of Highland scenery without help from the idea:—

> "Each purple peak, each flinty *spire*,
> Was bathed in floods of living fire."[2]

Take away from Scott's romances the word and idea *turret*,

of the domestic origin of the northern Gothic, that " Mr. Ruskin is evidently possessed by a fixed idea, that the Venetian architects were devout men, and that their devotion was expressed in their buildings; while he will not allow our own cathedrals to have been built by any but worldly men, who had no thoughts of heaven, but only vague ideas of keeping out of hell, by erecting costly places of worship."[3] If this writer had compared the two passages with the care which such a subject necessarily demands, he would have found that I was not opposing Venetian to English piety; but that in the one case I was speaking of the spirit manifested in the entire architecture of the nation, and in the other of occasional efforts of superstition as distinguished from that spirit; and, farther, that in the one case, I was speaking of decorative features, which are ordinarily the results of feelings, in the other of structural features, which are ordinarily the results of necessity or convenience. Thus it is rational and just that we should attribute the decoration of the arches of St. Mark's with scriptural mosaics to a religious sentiment; but it would be a strange absurdity to regard as an effort of piety the invention of the form of the arch itself, of which one of the earliest and most perfect instances is in the Cloaca Maxima. And thus in the case of spires and towers, it is just to ascribe to the devotion of their designers that dignity which was bestowed upon forms derived from the simplest domestic buildings; but it is ridiculous to attribute any great refinement of religious feeling, or height of religious aspiration, to those who furnished the funds for the erection of the loveliest tower in North France, by paying for permission to eat butter in Lent.[4]

---

[1] [The ruins of Craigmillar Castle, where Mary Queen of Scots lived on her return from France in 1561, lie embossed by trees three miles south-east of Edinburgh, and consist of a square tower in the centre, another in front, and two circular turrets behind—the whole surrounded by a high wall with towers at the corner.]

[2] [*Lady of the Lake*, canto i. 11. For the next passage, see *Rob Roy*, ch. xviii.]

[3] [The passage of Ruskin's on which the criticism is founded is *Stones of Venice*, vol. i. ch. xiii. § 6 (Vol. IX. p. 185).]

[4] [The Tour de Beurre, Rouen; see Vol. VIII. p. 50 n., and for drawings of it by Ruskin, Vol. II. pp. 400, 430.]

and see how much you would lose. Suppose, for instance, when young Osbaldistone is leaving Osbaldistone Hall, instead of saying "The old clock struck two from a *turret* adjoining my bedchamber," he had said, "The old clock struck two from the landing at the top of the stair," what would become of the passage? And can you really suppose that what has so much power over you in words has no power over you in reality? Do you think there is any group of words which would thus interest you, when the things expressed by them are uninteresting?

23. For instance, you know that, for an immense time back, all your public buildings have been built with a row of pillars supporting a triangular thing called a pediment. You see this form every day in your banks and clubhouses, and churches and chapels; you are told that it is the perfection of architectural beauty; and yet suppose Sir Walter Scott, instead of writing, "Each purple peak, each flinty spire," had written, "Each purple peak, each flinty 'pediment,'"*—would you have thought the poem improved? And if not, why would it be spoiled? Simply because the idea is no longer of any value to you; the thing spoken of is a nonentity. These pediments, and stylobates, and architraves never excited a single pleasurable feeling in you —never will, to the end of time. They are evermore dead, lifeless, and useless, in art as in poetry, and though you

---

* It has been objected to this comparison that the form of the pediment does not properly represent that of the rocks of the Trossachs. The objection is utterly futile, for there is not a single spire or pinnacle from one end of the Trossachs to the other. All their rocks are heavily rounded, and the introduction of the word "spire" is a piece of inaccuracy in description, ventured *merely for the sake of the Gothic image.* Farther: it has been said that if I had substituted the word "gable," it would have spoiled the line just as much as the word "pediment," though "gable" is a Gothic word. Of course it would; but why? Because "gable" is a term of vulgar domestic architecture, and therefore destructive of the tone of the heroic description; whereas "pediment" and "spire" are precisely correlative terms, being each the crowning feature in ecclesiastical edifices, and the comparison of their effects in the verse is therefore absolutely accurate, logical, and just.

built as many of them as there are slates on your house-roofs, you will never care for them. They will only remain to later ages as monuments of the patience and pliability with which the people of the nineteenth century sacrificed their feelings to fashions, and their intellects to forms. But on the other hand, that strange and thrilling interest with which such words strike you as are in any wise connected with Gothic architecture—as for instance, Vault, Arch, Spire, Pinnacle, Battlement, Barbican,[1] Porch, and myriads of such others, words everlastingly poetical and powerful whenever they occur,—is a most true and certain index that the things themselves are delightful to you, and will ever continue to be so. Believe me, you do indeed love these things, so far as you care about art at all, so far as you are not ashamed to confess what you feel about them.

24. In your public capacities, as bank directors, and charity overseers, and administrators of this and that other undertaking or institution, you cannot express your feelings at all. You form committees to decide upon the style of the new building, and as you have never been in the habit of trusting to your own taste in such matters, you inquire who is the most celebrated, that is to say, the most em-ployed, architect of the day. And you send for the great Mr. Blank, and the Great Blank sends you a plan of a great long marble box with half-a-dozen pillars at one end of it, and the same at the other;[2] and you look at the Great Blank's great plan in a grave manner, and you daresay it will be very handsome; and you ask the Great Blank what sort of a blank cheque must be filled up before the great plan can be realised; and you subscribe in a generous "burst

[1] [In the city of London "is a street called the Barbican, because sometime there stood on the north side thereof a burgh-kenin, or watch-tower of the city, called in some language a Barbican, as a bikening is called a Beacon" (Stow's *Survey*, p. 113). So the word is used in the *Faërie Queene*, ii. 9, 25 :—

"Within the Barbican a Porter sate,
Day and night duely keeping watch and ward."]

[2] [This seems to refer to the Royal Institution in Edinburgh, an oblong building in the Doric style : see below, pp. 64–65 *n*.]

of confidence" whatever is wanted; and when it is all done, and the great white marble box is set up in your streets, you contemplate it, not knowing what to make of it exactly, but hoping it is all right; and then there is a dinner given to the Great Blank, and the morning papers say that the new and handsome building, erected by the great Mr. Blank, is one of Mr. Blank's happiest efforts, and reflects the greatest credit upon the intelligent inhabitants of the city of so-and-so; and the building keeps the rain out as well as another, and you remain in a placid state of impoverished satisfaction therewith; but as for having any real pleasure out of it, you never hoped for such a thing. If you really make up a party of pleasure, and get rid of the forms and fashion of public propriety for an hour or two, where do you go for it? Where do you go to eat strawberries and cream? To Roslin Chapel, I believe; not to the portico of the last-built institution. What do you see your children doing, obeying their own natural and true instincts? What are your daughters drawing upon their cardboard screens as soon as they can use a pencil? Not Parthenon fronts, I think, but the ruins of Melrose Abbey, or Linlithgow Palace, or Lochleven Castle, their own pure Scotch hearts leading them straight to the right things, in spite of all that they are told to the contrary. You perhaps call this romantic, and youthful, and foolish. I am pressed for time now, and I cannot ask you to consider the meaning of the word "Romance." I will do that, if you please, in next lecture,[1] for it is a word of greater weight and authority than we commonly believe. In the meantime, I will endeavour, lastly, to show you, not the romantic, but the plain and practical conclusions which should follow from the facts I have laid before you.

25. I have endeavoured briefly to point out to you the propriety and naturalness of the two great Gothic forms, the pointed arch and gable roof. I wish now to tell you in what way they ought to be introduced into modern domestic architecture.

[1] [See below, §§ 29–32, pp. 53–56.]

You will all admit that there is neither romance nor comfort in waiting at your own or at any one else's door on a windy and rainy day, till the servant comes from the end of the house to open it. You all know the critical nature of that opening—the drift of wind into the passage, the impossibility of putting down the umbrella at the proper moment without getting a cupful of water dropped down the back of your neck from the top of the doorway; and you know how little these inconveniences are abated by the common Greek portico at the top of the steps. You know how the east winds blow through those unlucky couples of pillars, which are all that your architects find consistent with due observance of the Doric order. Then, away with these absurdities; and the next house you build, insist upon having the pure old Gothic porch, walled in on both sides, with its pointed arch entrance and gable roof above. Under that, you can put down your umbrella at your leisure, and, if you will, stop a moment to talk with your friend as you give him the parting shake of the hand. And if now and then a wayfarer found a moment's rest on a stone seat on each side of it, I believe you would find the insides of your houses not one whit the less comfortable; and, if you answer me, that were such refuges built in the open streets, they would become mere nests of filthy vagrants, I reply that I do not despair of such a change in the administration of the poor laws of this country, as shall no longer leave any of our fellow-creatures in a state in which they would pollute the steps of our houses by resting upon them for a night. But if not, the command to all of us is strict and straight, " When thou seest the naked, that thou cover him, and that thou bring the poor that are cast out to *thy house*." *
Not to the workhouse, observe, but to *thy* house: and I say it would be better a thousandfold, that our doors should be

---

* Isa. lviii. 7.[1]

[1] [Compare *Sesame and Lilies*, § 37 *n.*, where Ruskin quotes this passage again to like effect.]

D

beset by the poor day by day, than that it should be written of any one of us, " They reap every one his corn in the field, and they gather the vintage of the wicked. They cause the naked to lodge without shelter, that they have no covering in the cold. They are wet with the showers of the mountains, and embrace the rock, for want of a shelter." *

26. This, then, is the first use to which your pointed arches and gable roofs are to be put. The second is of more personal pleasurableness. You surely must all of you feel and admit the delightfulness of a bow window; I can hardly fancy a room can be perfect without one. Now you have nothing to do but to resolve that every one of your principal rooms shall have a bow window, either large or small. Sustain the projection of it on a bracket, crown it above with a little peaked roof, and give a massy piece of stone sculpture to the pointed arch in each of its casements, and you will have as inexhaustible a source of quaint richness in your street architecture, as of additional comfort and delight in the interiors of your rooms.

27. Thirdly, as respects windows which do not project. You will find that the proposal to build them with pointed arches is met by an objection on the part of your architects, that you cannot fit them with comfortable sashes. I beg leave to tell you that such an objection is utterly futile and ridiculous. I have lived for months in Gothic palaces, with pointed windows of the most complicated forms, fitted with modern sashes; and with the most perfect comfort.[1] But granting that the objection were a true one—and I suppose it is true to just this extent, that it may cost some few shillings more per window in the first instance to set the fittings to a pointed arch than to a square one—there is not the smallest necessity for the *aperture* of the window being of the pointed shape. Make the uppermost or bearing arch

* Job xxiv. 6–8.

---

[1] [*i.e.* at Venice, 1849–1850, 1851–1852 ; for the comfort of his apartments there, see Vol. X. p. xxix.]

pointed only, and make the top of the window square, filling
the interval with a stone shield, and you may have a perfect
school of architecture, not only consistent with, but eminently conducive to, every comfort of your daily life. The
window in Oakham Castle (fig. 2) is an example of such a
form as actually employed in the thirteenth century; and I
shall have to notice another in the course of next lecture.[1]

28. Meanwhile, I have but one word to say, in conclusion. Whatever has been advanced in the course of this
evening, has rested on the assumption that all architecture
was to be of brick and stone; and may meet with some hesitation in its acceptance, on account of the probable use of
iron, glass, and such other materials in our future edifices.
I cannot now enter into any statement of the possible uses
of iron or glass, but I will give you one reason, which I
think will weigh strongly with most here, why it is not
likely that they will ever become important elements in
architectural effect.[2] I know that I am speaking to a company of philosophers,[3] but you are not philosophers of the
kind who suppose that the Bible is a superannuated book;
neither are you of those who think the Bible is dishonoured
by being referred to for judgment in small matters. The
very divinity of the Book seems to me, on the contrary, to
justify us in referring *every* thing to it, with respect to which
any conclusion can be gathered from its pages.[4] Assuming
then that the Bible is neither superannuated now, nor ever
likely to be so, it will follow that the illustrations which
the Bible employs are likely to be *clear and intelligible illustrations* to the end of time. I do not mean that everything
spoken of in the Bible histories must continue to endure for

---

[1] [See below, p. 74.]

[2] [See on this subject, *Seven Lamps*, Vol. VIII. p. 66; and *Stones of Venice*, Vol. IX. pp. 455–456.]

[3] [The lectures were delivered under the auspices of the Philosophical Institution: see above, Introduction, p. xxvi.]

[4] [In *Modern Painters*, vol. iv. ch. xx. § 44, Ruskin refers to the "great offence" which he gave in these Edinburgh lectures "by supposing, or implying, that scriptural expressions could have any force as bearing upon modern practical questions."]

all time, but that the things which the Bible uses for illustration of eternal truths are likely to remain eternally intelligible illustrations.   Now, I find that iron architecture is indeed spoken of in the Bible.   You know how it is said to Jeremiah, " Behold, I have made thee this day a defenced city, and an iron pillar, and brazen walls, against the whole land."[1]   But I do not find that iron building is ever alluded to as likely to become *familiar* to the minds of men ; but, on the contrary, that an architecture of carved stone is continually employed as a source of the most important illustrations.   A simple instance must occur to all of you at once. The force of the image of the Corner Stone, as used throughout Scripture, would completely be lost, if the Christian and civilised world were ever extensively to employ any other material than earth and rock in their domestic buildings : I firmly believe that they never will ; but that as the laws of beauty are more perfectly established, we shall be content still to build as our forefathers built, and still to receive the same great lessons which such building is calculated to convey ; of which one is indeed never to be forgotten. Among the questions respecting towers which were laid before you to-night, one has been omitted : " What man is there of you intending to build a tower, that sitteth not down first and counteth the cost, whether he have sufficient to finish it ? "[2]   I have pressed upon you, this evening, the building of domestic towers.   You may think it right to dismiss the subject at once from your thoughts ; but let us not do so, without considering, each of us, how far *that* tower has been built, and how truly its cost has been counted.

[1] [Jeremiah i. 18.]
[2] [Luke xiv. 28.]

LECTURE II

ARCHITECTURE[1]

Delivered November 4, 1853

29. BEFORE proceeding to the principal subject of this evening, I wish to anticipate one or two objections which may arise in your minds to what I must lay before you. It may perhaps have been felt by you last evening, that some things I proposed to you were either romantic or Utopian. Let us think for a few moments what romance and Utopianism mean.

First, romance. In consequence of the many absurd fictions which long formed the elements of romance writing, the word romance is sometimes taken as synonymous with falsehood. Thus the French talk of *Des Romans*, and thus the English use the word Romancing.

But in this sense we had much better use the word falsehood at once. It is far plainer and clearer. And if in this sense I put anything romantic before you, pray pay no attention to it, or to me.

30. In the second place. Because young people are particularly apt to indulge in reverie, and imaginative pleasures, and to neglect their plain and practical duties, the word romantic has come to signify weak, foolish, speculative, unpractical, unprincipled. In all these cases it would be much

---

[1] [The following was Ruskin's Synopsis of the Lecture in the preliminary announcement :—

" General Decoration of Domestic Buildings.

The proper Place and Character of Decoration—Motives for Introducing It. Necessity for the Encouragement of Simple Sculpture. Examples of Economical Decoration. Means of Ornamentation at the Disposal of the Scottish Architect. Inlaying. Examples of Mediæval Domestic Work. Future Prospects of Architecture."]

better to say weak, foolish, unpractical, unprincipled. The words are clearer. If in this sense, also, I put anything romantic before you, pray pay no attention to me.

31. But in the third and last place. The real and proper use of the word romantic is simply to characterise an improbable or unaccustomed degree of beauty, sublimity, or virtue. For instance, in matters of history, is not the Retreat of the Ten Thousand romantic? Is not the death of Leonidas? of the Horatii?[1]   On the other hand, you find nothing romantic, though much that is monstrous, in the excesses of Tiberius or Commodus. So again, the battle of Agincourt is romantic, and of Bannockburn, simply because there was an extraordinary display of human virtue in both these battles. But there is no romance in the battles of the last Italian campaign,[2] in which mere feebleness and distrust were on one side, mere physical force on the other. And even in fiction, the opponents of virtue, in order to be romantic, must have sublimity mingled with their vice. It is not the knave, not the ruffian, that are romantic, but the giant and the dragon; and these, not because they are false, but because they are majestic. So again as to beauty. You feel that armour is romantic, because it is a beautiful dress, and you are not used to it. You do not feel there is anything romantic in the paint and shells of a Sandwich Islander, for these are not beautiful.

32. So, then, observe, this feeling which you are accustomed to despise—this secret and poetical enthusiasm in all your hearts, which, as practical men, you try to restrain— is indeed one of the holiest parts of your being. It is the instinctive delight in, and admiration for, sublimity, beauty, and virtue, unusually manifested. And so far from being a dangerous guide, it is the truest part of your being. It is even truer than your consciences. A man's conscience may be utterly perverted and led astray; but so long as

---

[1] [Compare *Stones of Venice*, vol. i. App. 14 (Vol. IX. p. 446).]
[2] [The unsuccessful Italian war of independence against the Austrians, 1848–1849.]

the feelings of romance endure within us, they are unerring,
—they are as true to what is right and lovely as the needle
to the north; and all that you have to do is to add to the
enthusiastic sentiment, the majestic judgment — to mingle
prudence and foresight with imagination and admiration,
and you have the perfect human soul. But the great evil
of these days is that we try to destroy the romantic feeling,
instead of bridling and directing it. Mark what Young
says of the men of the world:—

> " They, who think nought so strong of the romance,
> So rank knight-errant, as a real friend." [1]

And they are right. True friendship is romantic, to the
men of the world—true affection is romantic—true religion
is romantic; and if you were to ask me who of all powerful
and popular writers in the cause of error had wrought most
harm to their race, I should hesitate in reply whether to
name Voltaire, or Byron, or the last most ingenious and
most venomous of the degraded philosophers of Germany,[2]
or rather Cervantes, for he cast scorn upon the holiest
principles of humanity—he, of all men, most helped forward
the terrible change in the soldiers of Europe, from the spirit
of Bayard to the spirit of Bonaparte,* helped to change

---

* I mean no scandal against the *present* Emperor of the French, whose
truth has, I believe, been as conspicuous in the late political negotiations,
as his decision and prudence have been throughout the whole course of
his government.[3]

---

[1] [*Night Thoughts*, viii. 283. Young was a poet much read by Ruskin; see the
passage quoted in his home letters from Venice, Vol. X. p. 405 *n.*; he quotes the
Night Thoughts again in Vol. XI. p. 176.]

[2] [Schopenhauer had just been introduced to the British public (by John Oxenford
in the *Westminster Review*, April 1853), as the leader of a reaction against transcendental and theological philosophy.]

[3] [The reference is to the negotiations in 1853 which set in train the forces
that resulted in the Crimean War. Then, as now, it was the opinion of some ob-
servers that "behind the decorous curtain of the European concert Napoleon III.
was busily weaving scheme after scheme of his own to fix his unsteady diadem
upon his brow." Ruskin, who was to be a warm supporter of the Crimean War
and the French Alliance, had at this time a strong admiration for Napoleon—"a
great Emperor," he calls him (*Modern Painters*, vol. iii. ch. xviii. *ad finem*), and see
p. 421, below. For a later and different view of the Emperor, see *Fors Clavigera*,
Letters 10 and 31.]

loyalty into license, protection into plunder, truth into treachery, chivalry into selfishness; and, since his time, the purest impulses and the noblest purposes have perhaps been oftener stayed by the devil, under the name of Quixotism, than under any other base name or false allegation.[1]

33. Quixotism, or Utopianism; that is another of the devil's pet words. I believe the quiet admission which we are all of us so ready to make, that, because things have long been wrong, it is impossible they should ever be right, is one of the most fatal sources of misery and crime from which this world suffers. Whenever you hear a man dissuading you from attempting to do well, on the ground that perfection is "Utopian," beware of that man. Cast the word out of your dictionary altogether.[2] There is no need for it. Things are either possible or impossible—you can easily determine which, in any given state of human science. If the thing is impossible, you need not trouble yourselves about it; if possible, try for it. It is very Utopian to hope for the entire doing away with drunkenness and misery out of the Canongate; but the Utopianism is not our business—the *work* is. It is Utopian to hope to give every child in this kingdom the knowledge of God from its youth; but the Utopianism is not our business— the *work* is.

34. I have delayed you by the consideration of these two words, only in the fear that they might be inaccurately applied to the plans I am going to lay before you; for, though they were Utopian, and though they were romantic, they might be none the worse for that. But they are neither. Utopian they are not; for they are merely a proposal to do again what has been done for hundreds of years by people whose wealth and power were as nothing compared to ours;—and romantic they are not, in the sense of

---

[1] [Compare, for similar references to *Don Quixote*, *Modern Painters*, vol. iii. ch. xvii. § 29, and *Præterita*, i. § 68.]

[2] [Compare p. 432, below; *Fors Clavigera*, Letters 7 and 8; and *Arrows of the Chace*, 1880, vol. ii. pp. 110, 155.]

self-sacrificing or eminently virtuous, for they are merely the proposal to each of you that he should live in a handsomer house than he does at present, by substituting a cheap mode of ornamentation for a costly one. You perhaps fancied that architectural beauty was a very costly thing. Far from it. It is architectural ugliness that is costly.[1] In the modern system of architecture, decoration is immoderately expensive, because it is both wrongly placed and wrongly finished. I say first, wrongly placed. Modern architects decorate the tops of their buildings. Mediæval ones decorated the bottom.* That makes all the difference between seeing the ornament and not seeing it. If you bought some pictures to decorate such a room as this, where would you put them? On a level with the eye, I suppose, or nearly so? Not on a level with the chandelier? If you were determined to put them up there, round the cornice, it would be better for you not to buy them at all. You would merely throw your money away. And the fact is, that your money *is* being thrown away continually, by wholesale; and while you are dissuaded, on the ground of expense, from building beautiful windows and beautiful doors, you are continually made to pay for ornaments at the tops of your houses, which, for all the use they are of, might as well be in the moon. For instance, there is not, on the whole, a more studied piece of domestic architecture in Edinburgh than the street in which so many of your excellent physicians live—Rutland Street. I do not know if you have observed its architecture; but if you will look at it to-morrow, you will see that a heavy and close balustrade is put all along the eaves of the houses. Your physicians are not, I suppose, in the habit of taking academic and meditative walks on the roofs of their houses; and, if not, this balustrade is altogether useless,—nor merely useless,

* For farther confirmation of this statement see the Addenda at the end of this Lecture [p. 91].

---

[1] [Compare *Stones of Venice*, vol. iii. ch. i. § 44 (Vol. XI. pp. 39–40).]

for you will find it runs directly in front of all the garret windows, thus interfering with their light, and blocking out their view of the street. All that the parapet is meant to do, is to give some finish to the façades, and the inhabitants have thus been made to pay a large sum for a piece of mere decoration. Whether it *does* finish the façades satisfactorily, or whether the physicians resident in the street, or their patients, are in anywise edified by the succession of pear-shaped knobs of stone on their house-tops, I leave them to tell you; only do not fancy that the design, whatever its success, is an economical one.

35. But this is a very slight waste of money, compared to the constant habit of putting careful sculpture at the tops of houses. A temple of luxury has just been built in London for the Army and Navy Club.[1] It cost £40,000, exclusive of purchase of ground. It has upon it an enormous quantity of sculpture, representing the gentlemen of the navy as little boys riding upon dolphins, and the gentlemen of the army—I couldn't see as what—nor can anybody; for all this sculpture is put up at the top of the house, where the gutter should be, under the cornice. I know that this was a Greek way of doing things. I can't help it; that does not make it a wise one. Greeks might be willing to pay for what they couldn't see, but Scotchmen and Englishmen shouldn't.

36. Not that the Greeks threw their work away as we do. As far as I know Greek buildings, their ornamentation, though often bad, is always bold enough and large enough to be visible in its place. It is not putting ornament *high* that is wrong; but it is cutting it too fine to be seen, wherever it is. This is the great modern mistake: you are actually at twice the cost which would produce an

---

[1] [This club-house, built on the site of what was once Nell Gwynne's house, was erected in the years 1846–1851, from the designs of a young Oxford architect, named Parnell. The total cost, inclusive of site and furniture, was £116,000. It is, say its admirers, "a happy combination of Sansovino's Palazzo Cornaro and St. Mark's Library at Venice" (see A. I. Dasent's *History of St. James's Square*, 1895, p. 187 *n*.). For another reference to it, see Vol. IX. p. 348 *n*.]

impressive ornament, to produce a contemptible one; you increase the price of your buildings by one-half, in order to mince their decoration into invisibility. Walk through your streets, and try to make out the ornaments on the upper parts of your fine buildings—(there are none at the bottoms of them). Don't do it long, or you will all come home with inflamed eyes, but you will soon discover that you can see nothing but confusion in ornaments that have cost you ten or twelve shillings a foot.

37. Now, the Gothic builders placed their decoration on a precisely contrary principle, and on the only rational principle. All their best and most delicate work they put on the foundation of the building, close to the spectator, and on the upper parts of the walls they put ornaments large, bold, and capable of being plainly seen at the necessary distance. A single example will enable you to understand this method of adaptation perfectly. The lower part of the façade of the cathedral of Lyons, built either late in the thirteenth or early in the fourteenth century, is decorated with a series of niches, filled by statues of considerable size, which are supported upon pedestals within about eight feet of the ground.[1] In general, pedestals of this kind are supported on some projecting portion of the basement; but at Lyons, owing to other arrangements of the architecture into which I have no time to enter, they are merely projecting tablets, or flat-bottomed brackets of stone, projecting from the wall. Each bracket is about a foot and a half square, and is shaped thus (fig. 13), showing to the spectator, as he walks beneath, the flat bottom of each bracket, quite in the shade, but within a couple of feet of the eye, and lighted by the reflected light from the pavement. The whole of the surface of the wall round the great entrance is covered with bas-relief, as a matter of course; but

[1] [Ruskin was at Lyons, and made the sketches afterwards enlarged for this lecture, in the spring of 1850. See *Stones of Venice*, vol. i. (Vol. IX. p. 433), where he characterises this panelled decoration of Lyons as "the most exquisite piece of Northern Gothic I ever beheld."]

the architect appears to have been jealous of the smallest space which was well within the range of sight; and the *bottom* of every bracket is decorated also—nor that slightly, but decorated with no fewer than *six figures each, besides a flower border*, in a space, as I said, *not quite a foot and a half square.* The shape of the field to be decorated being a kind of quatrefoil, as shown in fig. 13, four small figures are placed, one in each foil, and two larger ones in the centre. I had only time, in passing through the town, to make a drawing of one of the angles of these pedestals; that sketch I have enlarged, in order that you may have some idea of the character of the sculpture. Here is the enlargement of it (fig. 15, Plate VII.). Now observe, this is *one* of the angles of the bottom of a pedestal, not two feet broad, on the outside of a Gothic building; it contains only one of the four little figures which form those angles; and it shows you the head only of one of the larger figures in the centre. Yet just observe how much design, how much wonderful composition, there is in this mere fragment of a building of the great times; a fragment, literally no larger than a schoolboy could strike off in wantonness with a stick: and yet I cannot tell you how much care has been spent—not so much on the execution, for it does not take much trouble to execute well on so small a scale—but on the design, of this minute fragment. You see it is composed of a branch of wild rose, which switches round at the angle, embracing the minute figure of the bishop, and terminates in a spray reaching nearly to the head of the large figure. You will observe how beautifully that figure is thus *pointed to* by the spray of rose, and how all the leaves around it in the same manner are subservient to the grace of its action. Look, if I hide one line, or one rosebud, how the whole is injured, and how much there is to study in the detail of it. Look at this little diamond crown, with a lock of the hair escaping from beneath it; and at the beautiful way in which the tiny leaf at *a*, is set in the angle to prevent its harshness; and having examined this well, consider what a treasure of

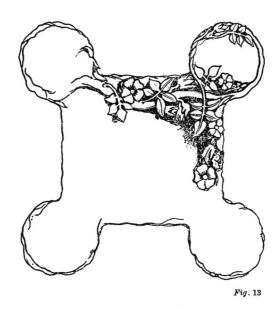

Fig. 13

Fig. 14

thought there is in a cathedral front, a hundred feet wide, every inch of which is wrought with sculpture like this! And every front of our thirteenth century cathedrals is in-wrought with sculpture of this quality![1]   And yet you quietly allow yourselves to be told that the men who thus wrought were barbarians, and that your architects are wiser and better in covering your walls with sculpture of this kind (fig. 14).

38. Walk round your Edinburgh buildings, and look at the height of your eye, what you will get from them. Nothing but square-cut stone—square-cut stone—a wilder-ness of square-cut stone for ever and for ever; so that your houses look like prisons, and truly are so; for the worst feature of Greek architecture is, indeed, not its costliness, but its tyranny.   These square stones are not prisons of the body, but graves of the soul; for the very men who could do sculpture like this of Lyons for you are here! still here, in your despised workmen: the race has not de-generated, it is you who have bound them down, and buried them beneath your Greek stones.   There would be a resurrection of them, as of renewed souls, if you would only lift the weight of these weary walls from off their hearts.*

39. But I am leaving the point immediately in question,

* This subject is farther pursued in the Addenda at the end of this Lecture [p. 85].

---

[1] [In the MS. Ruskin added here :—

"And here, in passing, let me briefly assure you of a fact—beg of you, as you have time and opportunity—to pay your utmost attention to this branch of art, the sculpture of the thirteenth and fourteenth centuries. I cannot tell you how great, how wonderful it is—and that almost every-where.   You are all interested in modern sculpture; you were all delighted with the sculpture in the Great Exhibition : and yet I assure you there is more good and interesting sculpture in a single wing of a good thirteenth-century cathedral, than in ten great exhibitions.   Let me again and again entreat you to pay more attention to this much neglected subject.   You will never make greater progress in art than by close study of thirteenth-century work, and if you do not learn to know its value soon, you will mourn over it when it is too late, for day by day the rage of the Revolutionist and the ignorance of the Restorer are dashing into dust unregretted and unrecognised treasures, for which it will be known in a little while that the contents of the noblest galleries in Europe might cheaply have been exchanged."]

VII.

Fig. 15

Sculpture at Lyons Cathedral.

VIII.

Fig. 16

Niche at Amiens.

which, you will remember, was the proper adaptation of ornament to its distance from the eye. I have given you one example of Gothic ornament, meant to be seen close; now let me give you one of Gothic ornament intended to be seen far off. Here (fig. 16, Plate VIII.) is a sketch of a niche at Amiens Cathedral, some fifty or sixty feet high on the façade, and seven or eight feet wide. Now observe, in the ornament close to the eye, you had *six figures* and a whole wreath of roses in the space of *a foot and a half* square; but in the ornament sixty feet from the eye, you have now only ten or twelve large *leaves* in a space of *eight feet square!* and note also that now there is no attempt whatsoever at the refinement of line and finish of edge which there was in the other example. The sculptor knew that, at the height of this niche, people would not attend to the delicate lines, and that the broad shadows would catch the eye instead. He has therefore left, as you see, rude square edges to his niche, and carved his leaves as massively and broadly as possible : and yet, observe how dexterously he has given you a sense of delicacy and minuteness in the work, by mingling these small leaves among the large ones. I made this sketch from a photograph, and the spot in which these leaves occurred was obscure; I have, therefore, used those of the Oxalis acetosella, of which the quaint form is always interesting.[1]

40. And you see by this example also what I meant just now by saying, that our own ornament was not only wrongly placed, but wrongly FINISHED. The very qualities which *fit* this leaf-decoration for due effect upon the eye, are those which would *conduce to economy* in its execution. A more expensive ornament would be less effective; and it is the very price we pay for finishing our decorations which spoils our architecture. And the curious thing is, that while you all appreciate, and that far too highly, what is called "the bold style" in painting, you cannot appreciate

[1] [For this flower, and Ruskin's love of it, see *Modern Painters*, vol. i. (Vol. III. p. 175 and *n.*).]

it in sculpture. You like a hurried, broad, dashing manner of execution in a water-colour drawing, though that may be seen as near as you choose, and yet you refuse to admit the nobleness of a bold, simple, and dashing stroke of the chisel in work which is to be seen forty fathoms off. Be assured that "handling" is as great a thing in marble as in paint, and that the power of producing a masterly effect with few touches is as essential in an architect as in a draughtsman; though indeed that power is never perfectly attained except by those who possess the power of giving the highest finish when there is occasion.

41. But there is yet another and a weightier charge to be brought against our modern Pseudo-Greek ornamentation. It is, first, wrongly placed; secondly, wrongly finished; and, thirdly, utterly *without meaning*. Observe in these two Gothic ornaments, and in every other ornament that ever was carved in the great Gothic times, there is a definite aim at the representation of some natural object. In fig. 15 you have an exquisite group of rose-stems, with the flowers and buds; in fig. 16, various wild weeds, especially the Geranium pratense; in every case you have an approximation to a natural form, and an unceasing variety of suggestion. But how much of Nature have you in your Greek buildings? I will show you, taking for an example the best you have lately built; and, in doing so, I trust that nothing that I say will be thought to have any personal purpose, and that the architect of the building in question will forgive me; for it is just because it is a good example of the style that I think it more fair to use it for an example. If the building were a bad one of the kind, it would not be a fair instance; and I hope, therefore, that in speaking of the institution on the Mound, just in progress, I shall be understood as meaning rather a compliment to its architect than otherwise.[1] It is not his fault that we force him to build in the Greek manner.

[1] ["The Mound," a raised causeway, connecting the Old and New Towns of Edinburgh, was formed of the earth dug out for the foundations of the latter. The institution referred to is the Royal Institution (containing the National Museum

42. Now, according to the orthodox practice in modern architecture, the most delicate and minute pieces of sculpture on that building are at the very top of it, just under its gutter. You cannot see them in a dark day, and perhaps may never, to this hour, have noticed them at all. But there they are: sixty-six finished heads of lions, all exactly the same; and, therefore, I suppose, executed on some noble Greek type, too noble to allow any modest Modern to think of improving upon it. But whether executed on a Greek type or no, it is to be presumed that, as there are sixty-six of them alike, and on so important a building as that which is to contain your school of design, and which is the principal example of the Athenian style in modern Athens, there must be something especially admirable in them, and deserving your most attentive contemplation. In order, therefore, that you might have a fair opportunity of estimating their beauty, I was desirous of getting a sketch of a real lion's head to compare with them, and my friend Mr. Millais[1] kindly offered to draw both the one and the other for me. You have not, however, at present, a lion in your zoological collection; and it being, as you are probably aware, the first principle of Pre-Raphaelitism, as well as essential to my object in the present instance, that no drawing should be made except from Nature itself, I was obliged to be content with a tiger's head, which, however, will answer my purpose just as well, in enabling you to compare a piece of true, faithful, and natural work with modern architectural sculpture. Here, in the first place, is Mr. Millais' drawing from the *living* beast (fig. 17, Plate IX.). I have not the least fear but that you will at once acknowledge its truth and feel its power. Prepare yourselves next for the Grecian

---

of the Society of Antiquaries of Scotland), of which the north side was finished in 1836; the lions' heads are on that building. To the south stands the National Gallery, which was "in progress" of building 1850–1854. Fergusson greatly extols the Grecian Doric of the Royal Institution, and pronounces it "one of the most faultless of modern buildings" (*History of Modern Architecture*, ed. 1891, ii. p. 85). The architect was W. H. Playfair (1789–1857), who designed many other of the classical buildings which have given to Edinburgh the sobriquet of the "Modern Athens."]

[1] [See above, Introduction, p. xxviii.]

sublimity of the *ideal* beast, from the cornice of your schools of design. Behold it (fig. 18).[1]

43. Now we call ourselves civilised and refined in matters of art, but I assure you it is seldom that, in the very basest and coarsest grotesques of the inferior Gothic workmen, anything so contemptible as this head can be ever found. *They* only sink into such a failure accidentally, and in a single instance; and we, in our civilisation, repeat this noble piece of work threescore and six times over, as not being able to invent anything else so good! Do not think Mr. Millais has caricatured it. It is drawn with the strictest fidelity; photograph one of the heads to-morrow, and you will find the photograph tell you the same tale. Neither imagine that this is an unusual example of modern work. Your banks and public offices are covered with ideal lions' heads in every direction, and you will find them all just as bad as this. And, farther, note that the admission of such barbarous types of sculpture is not *merely* ridiculous; it is seriously harmful to your powers of perceiving truth or beauty of any kind or at any time. Imagine the effect on the minds of your children of having such representations of a lion's head as this thrust upon them perpetually; and consider what a different effect might be produced upon them if, instead of this barren and insipid absurdity, every boss on your buildings were, according to the workman's best ability, a faithful rendering of the form of some existing animal, so that all their walls were so many pages of natural history. And, finally, consider the difference, with respect to the mind of the workman himself, between being kept all his life carving, by sixties, and forties, and thirties, repetitions of one false and futile model,—and being sent, for every piece of work he had to execute, to make a stern and faithful study from some living creature of God.[2]

---

[1] [For the flap with which this Plate is provided, see above, p. 6. Ruskin was a great admirer of Millais' animal-drawing : see *Fors Clavigera* (1877), Letter 79.]

[2] [Compare *Stones of Venice*, vol. ii. ch. vi. ("The Nature of Gothic"), §§ 11–24 (Vol. X. pp. 191–203).]

IX

Fig 17.

Fig 18

J E Millais

Thomson lith?

44. And this last consideration enables me to press this subject on you on far higher grounds than I have done yet.

I have hitherto appealed only to your national pride, or to your common sense; but surely I should treat a Scottish audience with indignity if I appealed not finally to something higher than either of them,—to their religious principles.

You know how often it is difficult to be wisely charitable, to do good without multiplying the sources of evil. You know that to give alms is nothing unless you give thought also: and that therefore it is written, not "blessed is he that *feedeth* the poor," but, "blessed is he that *considereth* the poor."[1] And you know that a little thought and a little kindness are often worth more than a great deal of money.

45. Now this charity of thought is not merely to be exercised towards the poor; it is to be exercised towards all men. There is assuredly no action of our social life, however unimportant, which, by kindly thought, may not be made to have a beneficial influence upon others; and it is impossible to spend the smallest sum of money, for any not absolutely necessary purpose, without a grave responsibility attaching to the manner of spending it. The object we ourselves covet may, indeed, be desirable and harmless, so far as we are concerned, but the providing us with it may, perhaps, be a very prejudicial occupation to some one else. And then it becomes instantly a moral question, whether we are to indulge ourselves or not. Whatever we wish to buy, we ought first to consider not only if the thing be fit for us, but if the manufacture of it be a wholesome and happy one; and if, on the whole, the sum we are going to spend will do as much good spent in this way as it would if spent in any other way. It may be said that we have not time to consider all this before we make a purchase. But no time could be spent in a more important duty; and God never imposes a duty without giving the time to do it. Let us, however, only acknowledge the principle;—once

---

[1] [Psalms xli. 1.]

make up your mind to allow the consideration of the *effect* of your purchases to regulate the *kind* of your purchase, and you will soon easily find grounds enough to decide upon. The plea of ignorance will never take away our responsibilities. It is written, "If thou sayest, Behold, we knew it not; doth not He that pondereth the heart consider it? and He that keepeth thy soul, doth not He know it?"[1]

46. I could press this on you at length, but I hasten to apply the principle to the subject of art.[2]   I will do so broadly at first, and then come to architecture. Enormous sums are spent annually by this country in what is called patronage of art, but in what is for the most part merely buying what strikes our fancies. True and judicious patronage there is indeed; many a work of art is bought by those who do not care for its possession, to assist the struggling artist, or relieve the unsuccessful one. But for the most part, I fear we are too much in the habit of buying simply what we like best, wholly irrespective of any good to be done, either to the artist or to the schools of the country. Now let us remember, that every farthing we spend on objects of art has influence over men's minds and spirits, far more than over their bodies. By the purchase of every print which hangs on your walls, of every cup out of which you drink, and every table off which you eat your bread, you are educating a mass of men in one way or another. You are either employing them healthily or unwholesomely; you are making them lead happy or unhappy lives; you are leading them to look at Nature, and to love her—to think, to feel, to enjoy,—or you are blinding them to Nature, and keeping them bound, like beasts of burden, in mechanical and monotonous employments.[3]   We shall all be asked one day, why we did not think more of this.

---

[1] [Proverbs xxiv. 12.]

[2] [Compare again the passage in *Stones of Venice*, vol. ii. ch. vi. §§ 11–21 (Vol. X. pp. 191 *seq.*), where Ruskin similarly pleads for the life of the workman to be considered in the "patronage of art."]

[3] [For other references to merely mechanical employments—" τέχναι βαναυσικαὶ —see *Lectures on Art*, § 123.]

47. " Well, but," you will say, " how can we decide what we ought to buy, but by our likings ? You would not have us buy what we don't like ? " No, but I would have you thoroughly sure that there *is* an absolute right and wrong in all art, and try to find out the right, and like that; and, secondly, sometimes to sacrifice a careless preference or fancy, to what you know is for the good of your fellow-creatures. For instance, when you spend a guinea upon an engraving, what have you done? You have paid a man for a certain number of hours to sit at a dirty table, in a dirty room, inhaling the fumes of nitric acid, stooping over a steel plate, on which, by the help of a magnifying glass, he is, one by one, laboriously cutting out certain notches and scratches, of which the effect is to be the copy of another man's work. You cannot suppose you have done a very charitable thing in this ! On the other hand, whenever you buy a small water-colour drawing, you have employed a man happily and healthily, working in a clean room (if he likes), or more probably still, out in the pure country and fresh air, thinking about something, and learning something every moment; not straining his eyesight, nor breaking his back, but working in ease and happiness. Therefore if you *can* like a modest water-colour better than an elaborate engraving, do. There may indeed be engravings which are worth the suffering it costs to produce them; but at all events, engravings of public dinners and laying of foundation-stones, and such things, might be dispensed with. The engraving ought to be a first-rate picture of a first-rate subject to be worth buying.

48. Farther, I know that many conscientious persons are desirous of encouraging art, but feel at the same time that their judgment is not certain enough to secure their choice of the best kind of art. To such persons I would now especially address myself, fully admitting the greatness of their difficulty. It is not an easy thing to acquire a knowledge of painting; and it is by no means a desirable thing to encourage bad painting. One bad painter makes

another, and one bad painting will often spoil a great many healthy judgments. I could name popular painters now living, who have retarded the taste of their generation by twenty years. Unless, therefore, we are certain not merely that we like a painting, but that we are *right* in liking it, we should never buy it. For there is one way of spending money which is perfectly safe, and in which we may be absolutely sure of doing good. I mean, by paying for simple sculpture of natural objects, chiefly flowers and animals. You are aware that the possibilities of error in sculpture are much less than in painting; it is altogether an easier and simpler art, invariably attaining perfection long before painting, in the progress of a national mind. It may indeed be corrupted by false taste, or thrown into erroneous forms; but for the most part, the feebleness of a sculptor is shown in imperfection and rudeness, rather than in definite error. He does not reach the fineness of the forms of Nature; but he approaches them truly up to a certain point, or, if not so, at all events an honest effort will continually improve him : so that if we set a simple natural form before him, and tell him to copy it, we are sure we have given him a wholesome and useful piece of education; but if we told him to paint it, he might, with all the honesty in the world, paint it wrongly, and falsely to the end of his days.[1]

49. So much for the workman. But the workman is not the only person concerned. Observe farther, that when you buy a print, the enjoyment of it is confined to yourself and to your friends. But if you carve a piece of stone, and put it on the outside of your house, it will give pleasure to every person who passes along the street—to an innumerable multitude, instead of a few.

Nay, but, you say, we ourselves shall not be benefited by the sculpture on the outsides of our houses. Yes, you

---

[1] [In the MS. draft, and perhaps in the lecture as delivered, Ruskin here reverted to the lions on the Royal Institution :—
" Instead of sixty-six heads cut out of stone—suppose you had two lions cut out of white marble, with their glaring eyes inlaid in cairngorm, and every line studied from nature."]

will, and in an extraordinary degree; for, observe farther, that architecture differs from painting peculiarly in being an art of *accumulation*. The prints bought by your friends, and hung up in their houses, have no collateral effect with yours: they must be separately examined, and if ever they were hung side by side, they would rather injure than assist each other's effect. But the sculpture on your friend's house unites in effect with that on your own. The two houses form one grand mass—far grander than either separately; much more if a third be added—and a fourth; much more if the whole street—if the whole city—join in the solemn harmony of sculpture. Your separate possessions of pictures and prints are to you as if you sang pieces of music with your single voices in your own houses. But your architecture would be as if you all sang together in one mighty choir. In the separate picture, it is rare that there exists any very high source of sublime emotion; but the great concerted music of the streets of the city, when turret rises over turret, and casement frowns beyond casement, and tower succeeds to tower along the farthest ridges of the inhabited hills,—this is a sublimity of which you can at present form no conception; and capable, I believe, of exciting almost the deepest emotion that art can ever strike from the bosoms of men.

And justly the deepest: for it is a law of God and of Nature, that your pleasures—as your virtues—shall be enhanced by mutual aid. As, by joining hand in hand, you can sustain each other best, so, hand in hand, you can delight each other best. And there is indeed a charm and sacredness in street architecture which must be wanting even to that of the temple: it is a little thing for men to unite in the forms of a religious service, but it is much for them to unite, like true brethren, in the arts and offices of their daily lives.

50. And now, I can conceive only of one objection as likely still to arise in your minds, which I must briefly meet. Your pictures, and other smaller works of art, you

can carry with you, wherever you live; your house must be left behind. Indeed, I believe that the wandering habits which have now become almost necessary to our existence, lie more at the root of our bad architecture than any other character of modern times. We always look upon our houses as mere temporary lodgings. We are always hoping to get larger and finer ones, or are forced, in some way or other, to live where we do not choose, and in continual expectation of changing our place of abode. In the present state of society, this is in a great measure unavoidable; but let us remember it is an *evil;* and that so far as it *is* avoidable, it becomes our duty to check the impulse. It is not for me to lead you at present into any consideration of a matter so closely touching your private interests and feelings; but it surely is a subject for serious thought, whether it might not be better for many of us, if, on attaining a certain position in life, we determined, with God's permission, to choose a home in which to live and die,—a home not to be increased by adding stone to stone and field to field, but which, being enough for all our wishes at that period, we should resolve to be satisfied with for ever. Consider this; and also, whether we ought not to be more in the habit of seeking honour from our descendants than our ancestors; thinking it better to be nobly remembered than nobly born; and striving so to live, that our sons, and our sons' sons, for ages to come, might still lead their children reverently to the doors out of which we had been carried to the grave, saying, "Look: This was his house: This was his chamber."[1]

51. I believe that you can bring forward no other serious objection to the principles for which I am pleading. They are so simple, and, it seems to me, so incontrovertible, that I trust you will not leave this room, without determining, as you have opportunity, to do something to advance this long-neglected art of domestic architecture. The reasons I

[1] [With the sentiment of § 50 here, compare *Seven Lamps,* ch. vi. § 3 (Vol. VIII. p. 226).]

have laid before you would have weight, even were I to ask you to go to some considerable expenditure beyond what you at present are accustomed to devote to such purposes; but nothing more would be needed than the diversion of expenditures, at present scattered and unconsidered, into a single and effective channel. Nay, the mere interest of the money which we are accustomed to keep dormant by us in the form of plate and jewellery, would alone be enough to sustain a school of magnificent architecture. And although, in highly wrought plate, and in finely designed jewellery, noble art may occasionally exist, yet in general both jewels and services of silver are matters of ostentation, much more than sources of intellectual pleasure. There are also many evils connected with them—they are a care to their possessors, a temptation to the dishonest, and a trouble and bitterness to the poor. So that I cannot but think that part of the wealth which now lies buried in these doubtful luxuries, might most wisely and kindly be thrown into a form which would give perpetual pleasure, not to its possessor only, but to thousands besides, and neither tempt the unprincipled, nor inflame the envious, nor mortify the poor; while, supposing that your own dignity was dear to you, this, you may rely upon it, would be more impressed upon others by the nobleness of your house-walls than by the glistening of your sideboards.

52.[1] And even supposing that some additional expenditure *were* required for this purpose, are we indeed so much

---

[1] [In the MS. §§ 52 and 53 are different, the illustration referred to in this place being of the window at Oakham (already referred to, p. 19, Plate II.) instead of the one here given. It is probable that the former was the one shown at the lecture, the window from the Hôtel Bourgthéroulde being shown later (see below, p. 77 *n.*). The MS. passage is :—

"You know, on Tuesday [see § 27 above, p. 50], I said that there was no hindrance to your using the pointed arch in common windows, because the sash-fittings would be inconvenient, since you might fill the pointed arch with a shield of stone and yet not lose its effect. Here is an example of existing thirteenth-century work—a window in Oakham Castle—an example which I have taken from Mr. Hudson Turner's admirable work on the domestic architecture of the Middle Ages (a work, by-the-bye, which you would find, I believe, as entertaining as it is useful); and in this window you see the real aperture is a simple oblong, which may be fitted with any

poorer than our ancestors, that we cannot now, in all the
power of Britain, afford to do what was done by every
small republic, by every independent city, in the Middle
Ages, throughout France, Italy, and Germany?[1]   I am not
aware of a vestige of domestic architecture, belonging to
the great mediæval periods, which, according to its material
and character, is not richly decorated.   But look here
(fig. 19, Plate X.), look to what an extent decoration *has*
been carried in the domestic edifices of a city, I suppose
not much superior in importance, commercially speaking, to
Manchester, Liverpool, or Birmingham—namely, Rouen, in
Normandy.   This is a *garret* window, still existing there,—

sash-framework you please, the decoration being completely external to it,
in the shafts, and the bearing arches which sustain the weight of wall.

"Now I am quite sure that at whatever distance you are sitting, you
feel the decoration of this window to be picturesque and effective.   It is
produced by a moulding which is just as universal a characteristic of the
early Gothic style in England, as the so-called egg and arrow moulding is
of the Greek style.   You know the egg and arrow—here is an example of
it, for the accuracy of which I can answer, as it is drawn from one of the
purest Greek cornices in the British Museum.   Now this moulding does
indeed possess, if it be carefully examined, elements of beauty which are
altogether wanting in the Gothic one; but at the distance at which you
are sitting, or examined, even when near, with a careless eye, it is not
half so effective; besides this, the beauty it possesses is of a peculiarly subtle
and abstract kind, while the beauty of the Gothic moulding is perfectly
simple.   You see it represents a succession of groups of four *pointed leaves*.
You must be well aware that all your modern buildings, whenever decorated
at all, are covered with this egg and arrow pattern (executed, indeed, for
the most part in stucco, for it is one of the basenesses of the modern Greek
style that it lends itself easily to every kind of imposture—you can execute
as many Greek mouldings in plaster as you choose—but not Gothic traceries):
but I will not compare the two styles on these terms.   I will suppose, and
in Edinburgh, where your architecture is singularly honest, it is by far
the most probable supposition, that both the buildings to be compared are
in stone.   Well, then, this egg and arrow moulding, for which you are
continually paying, and which you never enjoy—I suppose miles of it are
at this moment being cut at your expense—costs on the average ten shillings
a foot; and this Gothic one, which I know you do enjoy, costs three.   The
framework of the window being precisely the same in both cases, it will cost
to decorate it, in a Gothic and rational way, just one third of what it would
in a Greek and irrational way.

"The entire decoration of such a window as this would therefore cost
about seven or eight pounds; but it is not necessary to go so far, or nearly
so far, as this example, which is a remarkably rich one.   The one thing
generally desirable is to substitute the pointed arch, simply and boldly cut,
for the present square-headed window, and then, according to your means
and inclination, to decorate farther."

For a description of the egg and dart moulding, see *Seven Lamps*, Vol. VIII. p. 144.]
    [1] [See above, Preface, p. 8.]

X.

Fig. 19

Garret Window in Hôtel de
Bourgthéroulde, Rouen.

a garret window built by William de Bourgthéroulde in the early part of the sixteenth century.[1] I show it you, first, as a proof of what may be made of the features of domestic buildings we are apt to disdain; and secondly, as another example of a beautiful use of the pointed arch, filled by the solid shield of stone, and enclosing a square casement. It is indeed a peculiarly rich and beautiful instance, but it is a type of which many examples still exist in France, and of which many once existed in your own Scotland, of ruder work indeed, but admirable always in the effect upon the outline of the building.*

53. I do not, however, hope that you will often be able to go as far as this in decoration; in fact I would rather recommend a simpler style to you, founded on earlier examples; but, if possible, aided by colour, introduced in various kinds of naturally coloured stones. I have observed that your Scottish lapidaries have admirable taste and skill in the disposition of the pebbles of your brooches and other ornaments of dress; and I have not the least doubt that the genius of your country would, if directed to this particular style of architecture, produce works as beautiful as they would be thoroughly national. The Gothic of Florence, which owes at least the half of its beauty to the art of inlaying, would furnish you with exquisite examples; its sculpture is indeed the most perfect which was ever produced by the Gothic schools; but, besides this rich sculpture,

---

* One of the most beautiful instances I know of this kind of window is in the ancient house of the Maxwells, on the estate of Sir John Maxwell of Polloc.[2] I had not seen it when I gave this lecture, or I should have preferred it, as an example, to that of Rouen, with reference to modern possibilities of imitation.

---

[1] [The Hôtel de Bourgthéroulde was constructed in 1506 by William le Roux, Seigneur of Bourgthéroulde.]

[2] [Now the house of Sir John Stirling-Maxwell, great-nephew of the Sir John Maxwell (d. 1865) whom Ruskin had visited. Ruskin here refers not to the mansion-house of Pollok which was built in 1760 by Adam from designs made about twenty years earlier, but either to a sixteenth-century dower-house, known as Haggs Castle, or to Crookston Castle, the tower of which is even older. Both these buildings are on the Pollok estate, and the reference is probably to Haggs, which has some attic windows of the kind mentioned in the text. At the date when Ruskin wrote, the proprietor was endeavouring to revive the ancient spelling Poloc, or Polloc.]

all its flat surfaces are inlaid with coloured stones, much being done with a green serpentine, which forms the greater part of the coast of Genoa. You have, I believe, large beds of this rock in Scotland, and other stones besides, peculiarly Scottish, calculated to form as noble a school of colour as ever existed.*

54. And, now, I have but two things more to say to you in conclusion.

Most of the lecturers whom you allow to address you,

* A series of four examples of designs for windows was exhibited at this point of the lecture, but I have not engraved them, as they were hastily made for the purposes of momentary illustration, and are not such as I choose to publish or perpetuate.[1]

[1] [The omission from the printed lecture of these four examples caused Ruskin to re-write and re-arrange the text. Among his drawings at Brantwood is the one reproduced in Plate XI. opposite, which aptly illustrates the second type of window here described. The four examples were (1) a pointed window with a plain shield; (2) a Giottesque window with coloured stones; (3) a French Gothic window; and (4) the Bourgthéroulde window, or rather (it would seem) a simpler form adapted from that model. The MS. resumes from the passage cited above, § 52 n., p. 74 :—

"I have arranged here four successive examples of the form of the pointed window, filled up by the flat shield of stone, which renders it easily fitted with the modern sash. I don't consider it the best or most beautiful form, but it is the glory of Gothic architecture that it can do *anything*. It does not imperatively demand even the pointed arch above—if you have not room for it. Whatever you really and seriously want, Gothic will do for you; . . . [as in § 55 below] . . . new way of treating it.

"Taking, then, this form of the filling shield, and only adding to it a plain cusp, you would have such a window as this, which would be just as cheap as any that you now build, and though not much in itself, would yet join in the picturesque effect of any richer work in its neighbourhood. The shield is here perfectly plain at the lower edge, because when you have a direct example before you belonging to the fine Gothic times, of the very thing you want, it is unwise to leave it, and the filling shield is not, in any windows I can recollect of this kind, decorated along the lower edge until the upper part of the window has been completely charged with ornament.

"This next arch will strike many of you as strange, but I have given it on purpose, as an example of a Gothic with which we are generally little acquainted—the Giottesque Gothic of Tuscany; and I think it especially deserving of your consideration, because I have observed that your Scottish lapidaries have admirable taste and skill in the disposition of the pebbles of your brooches and other ornaments of dress, and I have not the least doubt that the genius of your country would, if directed to this particular style of architecture, produce works as beautiful as they would be original and national in design. The Giottesque Gothic owes at least the half of its beauty to the art of inlaying; its sculpture is indeed the most perfect which was ever produced by the Gothic schools; but besides this rich sculpture, all its flat surfaces are inlaid with coloured stones, in the manner of this example, but infinitely more richly, as I have limited myself here to such decoration as would be ordinarily achievable. In Tuscany a great deal is

XI

J.Ruskin

M⁙Lagan & Cumming.

Giottesque Window.

lay before you views of the sciences they profess, which are either generally received, or incontrovertible. I come before you at a disadvantage; for I cannot conscientiously tell you anything about architecture but what is at variance with all commonly received views upon the subject. I come before you, professedly to speak of things forgotten or things disputed; and I lay before you, not accepted principles, but questions at issue. Of those questions you are to be the judges, and to you I appeal. You must not, when you leave this room, if you feel doubtful of the truth of what I have said, refer yourselves to some architect of established reputation, and ask him whether I am right or not. You might as well, had you lived in the sixteenth century, have asked a Roman Catholic archbishop his opinion of the first reformer. I deny his jurisdiction; I refuse his decision. I call upon you to be Bereans in architecture, as you are in religion,[1] and to search into these things for yourselves. Remember that, however candid a man may be, it is too much to expect of him, when his career in life has been successful, to turn suddenly on the highway, and to declare that all he has learned has been false, and all he has done, worthless; yet nothing less than such a declaration as this must be made by nearly every existing architect, before he admitted the truth of one word

done with a green serpentine which forms the greater part of the coast of Genoa, and of which the effect is indicated in the drawing; but I have no doubt you have good stones enough in Scotland to form as noble a school of colour as ever existed.

"In the third example the whole effect is produced by sculpture; rich moulding of the early French Gothic being used on the arch and cusps, and the shield filled with an ordinary thirteenth-century current ornament. I do not say such a window as this could be executed cheaply—yet it would not be extravagant; all the sculpture here, though rich in effect, is rude in execution—the whole window would not cost so much as a very common piece of plate, and a few such windows as this would produce a marvellous effect on your streets."

The fourth example is not described in the MS., the lecturer contenting himself with a note: "Lastly, Hôtel de Bourgthéroulde and Roof Oriels." The passage in the MS. about inlaying and its possibilities in Scotland was, it will be seen, used in the printed text.]

[1] [The Bereans, as mentioned in the Acts (xvii. 11), "received the Word with all readiness of mind, and searched the Scriptures daily." The name was adopted by the followers of the Rev. John Barclay, of Kincardineshire (1773).]

that I have said to you this evening. You must be prepared, therefore, to hear my opinions attacked with all the
virulence of established interest, and all the pertinacity of
confirmed prejudice; you will hear them made the subjects
of every species of satire and invective; but one kind of
opposition to them you will never hear; you will never hear
them met by quiet, steady, rational argument; for that is
the one way in which they *cannot* be met. You will constantly hear me accused—you yourselves may be the first
to accuse me—of presumption in speaking thus confidently
against the established authority of ages. Presumption!
Yes, if I had spoken on my own authority; but I have
appealed to two incontrovertible and irrefragable witnesses
—to the nature that is around you—to the reason that is
within you. And if you are willing in this matter to take
the voice of authority *against* that of nature and of reason,
take it in other things also. Take it in religion, as you do
in architecture. It is not by a Scottish audience—not by
the descendants of the Reformer and the Covenanter—that
I expected to be met with a refusal to believe that the
world might possibly have been wrong for *three* hundred
years, in their ways of carving stones and setting up of
pillars, when they know that they were wrong for *twelve*
hundred years, in their marking how the roads divided, that
led to Hell and Heaven.

55. You must expect at first that there will be difficulties and inconsistencies in carrying out the new style;
but they will soon be conquered if you attempt not too
much at once. Do not be afraid of incongruities—do not
think of unities of effect. Introduce your Gothic line by
line and stone by stone; never mind mixing it with your
present architecture; your existing houses will be none the
worse for having little bits of better work fitted to them;
build a porch, or point a window, if you can do nothing
else; and remember that it is the glory of Gothic architecture that it can do *anything*.[1] Whatever you really and

---

[1] [Compare *Stones of Venice*, Vol. XI. p. 228.]

seriously want, Gothic will do for you; but it must be an
earnest want. It is its pride to accommodate itself to your
needs; and the one general law under which it acts is
simply this,—find out what will make you comfortable, build
that in the strongest and boldest way, and then set your
fancy free in the decoration of it. Don't do anything to
imitate this cathedral or that, however beautiful. Do what is
convenient; and if the form be a new one, so much the
better; then set your mason's wits to work, to find out
some new way of treating it. Only be steadily determined
that, even if you cannot get the best Gothic, at least you
will have no Greek; and in a few years' time—·in less time
than you could learn a new science or a new language
thoroughly—the whole art of your native country will be
reanimated.

56. And, now, lastly. When this shall be accomplished,
do not think it will make little difference to you, and that
you will be little the happier, or little the better for it.
You have at present no conception, and can have none,
how much you would enjoy a truly beautiful architecture;
but I can give you a proof of it which none of you will
be able to deny. You will all assuredly admit this principle,—that whatever temporal things are spoken of in the
Bible as emblems of the highest spiritual blessings, must
be *good things* in themselves. You would allow that bread,
for instance, would not have been used as an emblem of
the word of life, unless it had been good, and necessary for
man; nor water used as the emblem of sanctification, unless it also had been good and necessary for man. You
will allow that oil, and honey, and balm are good, when
David says, "Let the righteous reprove me; it shall be an
excellent oil;" or, "How sweet are thy words unto my
taste; yea, sweeter than honey to my mouth;" or, when
Jeremiah cries out in his weeping, "Is there no balm in
Gilead? is there no physician there?" You would admit
at once that the man who said there was no taste in the
literal honey, and no healing in the literal balm, must be

of distorted judgment, since God had used them as emblems of spiritual sweetness and healing. And how, then, will you evade the conclusion, that there must be joy, and comfort, and instruction in the literal beauty of architecture, when God, descending in His utmost love to the distressed Jerusalem, and addressing to her His most precious and solemn promises, speaks to her in such words as these: "Oh, thou afflicted, tossed with tempest, and not comforted,"—What shall be done to her?—What brightest emblem of blessing will God set before her? "Behold, I will *lay thy stones with fair colours*, and thy foundations with sapphires; and I will make thy *windows of agates*, and thy gates of carbuncles, and all thy borders of pleasant stones." Nor is this merely an emblem of spiritual blessing; for that blessing is added in the concluding words, "And all thy children shall be taught of the Lord, and great shall be the peace of thy children."[1]

[1] [The Bible references in § 56 are Psalms cxli. 5, cxix. 103; Jeremiah viii. 22; Isaiah liv. 11, 12, 13.]

ADDENDA TO LECTURES I. AND II

57. THE delivery of the foregoing lectures excited, as it may be imagined, considerable indignation among the architects who happened to hear them, and elicited various attempts at reply.[1] As it seemed to have been expected by the writers of these replies, that in two lectures, each of them lasting not much more than an hour, I should have been able completely to discuss the philosophy and history of the architecture of the world, besides meeting every objection, and reconciling every apparent contradiction, which might suggest itself to the minds of hearers with whom, probably, from first to last, I had not a single exactly correspondent idea relating to the matters under discussion, it seems unnecessary to notice any of them in particular. But as this volume may perhaps fall into the hands of readers who have not time to refer to the works in which my views have been expressed more at large, and as I shall now not be able to write or to say anything·more about architecture for some time to come, it may be useful to state here, and explain in the shortest possible compass, the main gist of the propositions which I desire to maintain respecting that art; and also to note and answer, once for all, such arguments as are ordinarily used by the architects of the modern school to controvert these propositions. They may be reduced under six heads.

1. That Gothic or Romanesque construction is nobler than Greek construction.

---

[1] [One such reply, written in defence of the Greek style, appeared, on the conclusion of the lectures, in the *Edinburgh Advertiser* for November 22, 1853, under the heading " A Few Words on Mr. Ruskin's Art-Opinions."]

2. That ornamentation is the principal part of architecture.

3. That ornamentation should be visible.

4. That ornamentation should be natural.

5. That ornamentation should be thoughtful.

6. And that therefore Gothic ornamentation is nobler than Greek ornamentation, and Gothic architecture the only architecture which should now be built.

58. Proposition 1st.—*Gothic or Romanesque construction is nobler than Greek construction.** That is to say, building an arch, vault, or dome, is a nobler and more ingenious work than laying a flat stone or beam over the space to be covered. It is, for instance, a nobler and more ingenious thing to build an arched bridge over a stream, than to lay two pine-trunks across from bank to bank; and, in like manner, it is a nobler and more ingenious thing to build an arch over a window, door, or room, than to lay a single flat stone over the same space.

No architects have ever attempted seriously to controvert this proposition. Sometimes, however, they say that "of two ways of doing a thing, the best and most perfect is not always to be adopted, for there may be particular reasons for employing an inferior one." This I am perfectly ready to grant, only let them show their reasons in each particular case. Sometimes also they say, that there is a

---

* The constructive value of Gothic architecture is, however, far greater than that of Romanesque, as the pointed arch is not only susceptible of an infinite variety of forms and applications to the weight to be sustained, but it possesses, in the outline given to its masonry at its perfect periods, the means of self-sustainment to a far greater degree than the round arch. I pointed out, for, I believe, the first time, the meaning and constructive value of the Gothic cusp, in [ch. xi.] of the first volume of the *Stones of Venice*. That statement was first denied, and then taken advantage of, by modern architects; and considering how often it has been alleged that I have no *practical* knowledge of architecture, it cannot but be matter of some triumph to me, to find *The Builder* of the 21st January 1854, describing as a new invention, the successful application to a church in Carlow of the principle which I laid down in the year 1851.[1]

---

[1] [The passage referred to in the *Stones of Venice* is in this edition, Vol. IX. p. 167: see note thereon. The church in Carlow is the Bruen Testimonial Church (architect, J. Derick).]

charm in the simple construction which is lost in the scientific one. This I am also perfectly ready to grant. There is a charm in Stonehenge which there is not in Amiens Cathedral, and a charm in an Alpine pine bridge which there is not in the Ponte della Trinità at Florence,[1] and, in general, a charm in savageness which there is not in science. But do not let it be said, therefore, that savageness *is* science.

59. Proposition 2nd.—*Ornamentation is the principal part of architecture.* That is to say, the highest nobility of a building does not consist in its being well built, but in its being nobly sculptured or painted.

This is always, and at the first hearing of it, very naturally, considered one of my most heretical propositions.[2] It is also one of the most important I have to maintain; and it must be permitted me to explain it at some length. The first thing to be required of a building—not, observe, the *highest* thing, but the first thing—is that it shall answer its purposes completely, permanently, and at the smallest expense. If it is a house, it should be just of the size convenient for its owner, containing exactly the kind and number of rooms that he wants, with exactly the number of windows he wants, put in the places that he wants. If it is a church, it should be just large enough for its ´congregation, and of such shape and disposition as shall make them comfortable in it and let them hear well in it. If it be a public office, it should be so disposed as is most convenient for the clerks in their daily avocations; and so on; all this being utterly irrespective of external appearance or æsthetic considerations of any kind, and all being done solidly, securely, and at the smallest necessary cost.

The *sacrifice* of any of these first requirements to external appearance is a futility and absurdity. Rooms must not be darkened to make the ranges of windows symmetrical. Useless wings must not be added on one side, to balance

---

[1] [For a reference to this bridge, see *Stones of Venice*, vol. i. (Vol. IX. p. 161).]
[2] [The proposition is implied both in the *Seven Lamps*, ch. i., and in the *Stones of Venice*, vol. i. ch. ii.]

useful wings on the other, but the house built with one
wing, if the owner has no need of two; and so on.

60. But observe, in doing all this, there is no High, or
as it is commonly called, Fine Art, required at all. There
may be much science, together with the lower form of art,
or "handicraft," but there is as yet no *Fine Art*. House-
building, on these terms, is no higher thing than ship-
building. It indeed will generally be found that the edifice
designed with this masculine reference to utility, will have a
charm about it, otherwise unattainable, just as a ship, constructed with simple reference to its service against powers
of wind and wave, turns out one of the loveliest things that
human hands produce.[1]   Still, we do not, and properly do
not, hold ship-building to be a fine art, nor preserve in
our memories the names of immortal ship-builders; neither,
so long as the mere utility and constructive merit of the
building are regarded, is architecture to be held a fine art,
or are the names of architects to be remembered immortally.
For any one may at any time be taught to build the ship,
or (thus far) the house, and there is nothing deserving of
immortality in doing what any one may be taught to do.

But when the house, or church, or other building is
thus far designed, and the forms of its dead walls and dead
roofs are up to this point determined, comes the divine part
of the work—namely, to turn these dead walls into living
ones. Only Deity, that is to say, those who are taught by
Deity, can do that.

And that is to be done by painting and sculpture, that
is to say, by ornamentation. Ornamentation is therefore
the principal part of architecture, considered as a subject
of fine art.

61. Now observe. It will at once follow from this principle, that *a great architect must be a great sculptor or
painter.*[2]

---

[1] [See Ruskin's preface to *The Harbours of England.*]
[2] [See above, Preface, p. 8.   Compare Vol. I. p. 5 *n.*, where in his earliest
essay on architecture Ruskin ventured on another statement of this kind.   Ruskin

This is a universal law.   No person who is not a great sculptor or painter *can* be an architect.   If he is not a sculptor or painter, he can only be a *builder*.

The three greatest architects hitherto known in the world were Phidias, Giotto, and Michael Angelo; with all of whom, architecture was only their play, sculpture and painting their work.   All great works of architecture in existence are either the work of single sculptors or painters, or of societies of sculptors and painters, acting collectively for a series of years.   A Gothic cathedral is properly to be defined as a piece of the most magnificent associative sculpture, arranged on the noblest principles of building, for the service and delight of multitudes; and the proper definition of architecture, as distinguished from sculpture, is merely "the art of designing sculpture for a particular place, and placing it there on the best principles of building."

Hence it clearly follows, that in modern days we have no *architects*.   The term "architecture" is not so much as understood by us.   I am very sorry to be compelled to the discourtesy of stating this fact, but a fact it is, and a fact which it is necessary to state strongly.

Hence also it will follow, that the first thing necessary to the possession of a school of architecture is the formation of a school of able sculptors, and that till we have that, nothing we do can be called architecture at all.

62. This, then, being my second proposition, the so-called "architects" of the day, as the reader will imagine, are not willing to admit it, or to admit any statement which at all involves it; and every statement, tending in this direction, which I have hitherto made, has of course been met by eager opposition; opposition which perhaps would have been still more energetic, but that architects have not, I think,

here instances Michael Angelo; it is interesting to find (from the recently discovered Dialogues on Painting, in which a Portuguese painter recorded many of the master's words) that Michael Angelo himself laid down the principle that the ideal painter includes the architect and the sculptor (see the Appendix to Sir Charles Holroyd's *Michael Angelo Buonarroti*, 1903).]

till lately, been quite aware of the lengths to which I was prepared to carry the principle.[1]

The arguments, or assertions, which they generally employ against this second proposition and its consequences, are the following:

First.   That the true nobility of architecture consists, not in decoration (or sculpture), but in the "disposition of masses," and that architecture is, in fact, the "art of proportion."[2]

63. It is difficult to overstate the enormity of the ignorance which this popular statement implies.   For the fact is, that *all* art, and all nature, depend on the "disposition of masses."   Painting, sculpture, music, and poetry depend all equally on the "proportion," whether of colours, stones, notes, or words.   Proportion is a principle, not of architecture, but of existence.   It is by the laws of proportion that stars shine, that mountains stand, and rivers flow.   Man can hardly perform any act of his life, can hardly utter two words of innocent speech, or move his hand in accordance with those words, without involving some reference, whether taught or instinctive, to the laws of proportion.   And in the fine arts, it is impossible to move a single step, or to execute the smallest and simplest piece of work, without involving all those laws of proportion in their full complexity.   To arrange (by invention) the folds of a piece of drapery, or dispose the locks of hair on the head of a statue, requires as much sense and knowledge of the laws of proportion, as to dispose the masses of a cathedral.   The one are indeed smaller than the other, but the relations between 1, 2, 4, and 8, are precisely the same as the relations between 6, 12, 24, and 48.   So that the assertion that "architecture

---

[1] [Thus in the pamphlet "by an Architect" already referred to (Vol. IX. p. xliii.), Ruskin was denounced as "obnoxious to the members of the architectural profession, one and all."   He had said so many things, "altogether the reverse of complimentary to the present race of architects, that the entire body cannot but regard him as a common enemy, and a 'malevolent' of the worst description."]

[2] [This traditional definition of architecture had been accepted by the critic in the *Edinburgh Advertiser*, above referred to (p. xxxvi. *n.*), who defended the Greek style against Ruskin's strictures on the ground of its accordance with "geometrical proportion."]

is *par excellence* the art of proportion," could never be made except by persons who know nothing of art in general; and, in fact, never *is* made except by those architects, who, not being artists, fancy that the one poor æsthetic principle of which they *are* cognizant is the whole of art. They find that the "disposition of masses" is the only thing of importance in the art with which they are acquainted, and fancy therefore that it is peculiar to that art; whereas the fact is, that all great art *begins* exactly where theirs *ends*, with the "disposition of masses." The assertion that Greek architecture, as opposed to Gothic architecture, is the "architecture of proportion," is another of the results of the same broad ignorance. First, it is a calumny of the old Greek style itself, which, like every other good architecture that ever existed, depends more on its grand figure sculpture, than on its proportions of parts; so that to copy the form of the Parthenon without its friezes and frontal statuary, is like copying the figure of a human being without its eyes and mouth;[1] and, in the second place, so far as modern pseudo-Greek work *does* depend on its proportions more than Gothic work, it does so, not because it is better proportioned, but because it has nothing *but* proportion to depend upon. Gesture is in like manner of more importance to a pantomime actor than to a tragedian, not because his gesture is more refined, but because he has no tongue. And the proportions of our common Greek work are important to it undoubtedly, but not because they are or ever can be more subtle than Gothic proportion, but because that work has no sculpture, nor colour, nor imagination, nor sacredness, nor any other quality whatsoever in it, but ratios of measures. And it is difficult to express with sufficient force the absurdity of the supposition that there is more room for refinements of proportion in the relations of seven or eight equal pillars, with the triangular end of a roof above them, than between the shafts, and buttresses,

---

[1] [Compare *Stones of Venice,* vol. i. (Vol. IX. p. 284).]

and porches, and pinnacles, and vaultings, and towers, and all other doubly and trebly multiplied magnificences of membership which form the framework of a Gothic temple.

64. Second reply.—It is often said, with some appearance of plausibility, that I dwell in all my writings on little things and contemptible details; and not on essential and large things. Now, in the first place, as soon as our architects become capable of doing and managing little and contemptible things, it will be time to talk about larger ones; at present I do not see that they can design so much as a niche or a bracket, and therefore they need not as yet think about anything larger. For although, as both just now, and always, I have said, there is as much science of arrangement needed in the designing of a small group of parts as of a large one, yet assuredly designing the larger one is *not the easier* work of the two. For the eye and mind can embrace the smaller object more completely, and if the powers of conception are feeble, they get embarrassed by the inferior members which fall *within* the divisions of the larger design.* So that, of course, the best way is to begin with the smaller features; for most assuredly, those who cannot design small things cannot design large ones; and yet, on the other hand, whoever can design small things *perfectly*, can design whatever he chooses. The man who, without copying, and by his own true and original power, can arrange a cluster of rose-leaves nobly, can design anything. He may fail from want of taste or feeling, but not from want of power.

And the real reason why architects are so eager in protesting against my close examination of details, is simply

---

* Thus, in speaking of Pugin's designs, I said, "Expect no cathedrals of him; but no one, at present, can design a better finial, though he will never design even a finial perfectly."[1]   But even this I said less with reference to powers of arrangement, than to materials of fancy; for many men have store enough to last them through a boss or a bracket, but not to last them through a church front.

---

[1] [*Stones of Venice*, vol. i. Appendix 12 (Vol. IX. p. 439).]

that they know they dare not meet me on that ground. Being, as I have said, in reality *not* architects, but builders, they can indeed raise a large building, with copied ornaments, which, being huge and white, they hope the public may pronounce "handsome." But they cannot design a cluster of oak-leaves — no, nor a single human figure — no, nor so much as a beast, or a bird, or a bird's nest![1] Let them first learn to invent as much as will fill a quatrefoil, or point a pinnacle, and then it will be time enough to reason with them on the principles of the sublime.

65. But farther. The things that I have dwelt upon in examining buildings, though often their least parts, are always in reality their principal parts. That is the principal part of a building in which its mind is contained, and that, as I have just shown, is its sculpture and painting. I do with a building as I do with a man, watch the eye and the lips: when they are bright and eloquent, the form of the body is of little consequence.

Whatever other objections have been made to this second proposition, arise, as far as I remember, merely from a confusion of the idea of essentialness or primariness with the idea of nobleness. The essential thing in a building,—its *first* virtue,—is that it be strongly built, and fit for its uses. The noblest thing in a building, and its *highest* virtue, is that it be nobly sculptured or painted.*

66. One or two important corollaries yet remain to be stated. It has just been said that to sacrifice the convenience of a building to its external appearance is a futility

---

* Of course I use the term painting as including every mode of applying colour.

---

[1] [Ruskin was here writing from particular observation, as the following passage in the MS. shows :—

"The other day I was talking to a very intelligent architect's assistant, a young man who, I hope, may do much in his time. But, he inquiring whether I thought he had architectural ability, I asked him to draw me a bit of a leaf moulding out of his head. He said he had 'never done such a thing.' Never designed a bit of moulding? 'No, I never designed anything.' And this at one-and-twenty."]

and absurdity, and that convenience and stability are to be attained at the smallest cost. But when that convenience *has* been attained, the adding the noble characters of life by painting and sculpture, is a work in which all possible cost may be wisely admitted. There is great difficulty in fully explaining the various bearings of this proposition, so as to do away with the chances of its being erroneously understood and applied. For although, in the first designing of the building, nothing is to be admitted but what is wanted, and no useless wings are to be added to balance useful ones, yet in its ultimate designing, when its sculpture and colour become precious, it may be that actual room is wanted to display them, or richer symmetry wanted to deserve them; and in such cases even a useless wall may be built to bear the sculpture, as at San Michele of Lucca, or a useless portico[1] added to complete the cadences, as at St. Mark's of Venice, or useless height admitted in order to increase the impressiveness, as in nearly every noble building in the world. But the right to do this is dependent upon the actual *purpose* of the building becoming no longer one of utility merely; as the purpose of a cathedral is not so much to shelter the congregation as to awe them. In such cases even some sacrifice of convenience may occasionally be admitted, as in the case of certain forms of pillared churches. But for the most part, the great law is, convenience first, and then the noblest decoration possible; and this is peculiarly the case in domestic buildings, and such public ones as are constantly to be used for practical purposes.

67. Proposition 3rd.—*Ornamentation should be visible.*[2]

---

[1] [The sense of this passage has been obscured by the misprint in all previous eds. of "portion" for "portico." The reference is to the two porticoes at the north and south end of the west facade of St. Mark's, "which are of *no use whatever* except to consummate the proportions" (*Stones of Venice,* vol. ii. (Vol. X. p. 152). For San Michele at Lucca, see Plate 1 in Vol. III., and Plate 21 in Vol. IX.]

[2] [This proposition is stated and enforced in *Seven Lamps,* Vol. VIII. pp. 4–8, and *Stones of Venice,* Vol. IX. pp. 292 *seq.*]

The reader may imagine this to be an indisputable position; but, practically, it is one of the last which modern architects are likely to admit; for it involves much more than appears at first sight. To render ornamentation, with all its qualities, clearly and entirely visible in its appointed place on the building, requires a knowledge of effect and a power of design which few even of the best artists possess, and which modern architects, so far from possessing, do not so much as comprehend the existence of. But, without dwelling on this highest manner of rendering ornament " visible," I desire only at present to convince the reader thoroughly of the main fact asserted in the text,[1] that while modern builders decorate the *tops* of buildings, mediæval builders decorated the *bottom*. So singular is the ignorance yet prevailing of the first principles of Gothic architecture, that I saw this assertion marked with notes of interrogation in several of the reports of these Lectures; although, at Edinburgh, it was only necessary for those who doubted it to have walked to Holyrood Chapel,[2] in order to convince themselves of the truth of it, so far as their own city was concerned; and although, most assuredly, the cathedrals of Europe have now been drawn often enough to establish the very simple fact that their best sculpture is in their porches, not in their steeples. However, as this great Gothic principle seems yet unacknowledged, let me state it here, once for all, namely, that the whole building is decorated, in all pure and fine examples, with the most exactly studied respect to the powers of the eye; the richest and most delicate sculpture being put on the walls of the porches, or on the façade of the building, just high enough above the ground to secure it from accidental (not from wanton *) injury. The decoration, as it rises,

* Nothing is more notable in good Gothic than the confidence of its builders in the respect of the people for their work. A great school of

---

[1] [See above, § 34, p. 57.]
[2] [The existing chapel, on the north side of the Palace, consists of the nave of the Abbey Church. The doorway of the west front contains finely sculptured decoration.]

becomes *always* bolder, and in the buildings of the greatest times, *generally* simpler.   Thus at San Zeno and the duomo of Verona, the only delicate decorations are on the porches and lower walls of the façades, the rest of the buildings being left comparatively plain ; in the Ducal Palace of Venice the only very careful work is in the lowest capitals ;[1] and so also the richness of the work diminishes upwards in the transepts of Rouen, and façades of Bayeux, Rheims, Amiens, Abbeville,* Lyons, and Nôtre Dame of Paris.   But in the middle and later Gothic the tendency is to produce an equal richness *of effect* over the whole building, or even to increase the richness towards the top ; but this is done so skilfully that no fine work is wasted ; and when the spectator ascends to the higher points of the building, which he thought were of the most consummate delicacy, he finds them Herculean in strength and rough-hewn in style, the really delicate work being all put at the base.   The general treatment of Romanesque work is to increase the *number* of arches at the top, which at once enriches and lightens the mass, and to put the finest *sculpture* of the arches at the bottom.   In towers of all kinds and periods the *effective* enrichment is towards the top, and most rightly, since their dignity is in their height ; but they are never made the recipients of fine sculpture, with, as far as I know, the single exception of Giotto's campanile, which indeed has fine sculpture, *but it is at the bottom.*

The façade of Wells Cathedral seems to be an exception to the general rule,[2] in having its principal decoration at

architecture cannot exist when this respect cannot be calculated upon, as it would be vain to put fine sculpture within the reach of a population whose only pleasure would be in defacing it.

* The church at Abbeville is late flamboyant, but well deserves, for the exquisite beauty of its porches, to be named even with the great works of the thirteenth century.

---

[1] [For a comparison of the capitals in the lower arcade with those in the upper, and remarks on the adjustment of the latter to their distance from the eye, see *Stones of Venice*, vol. i. (Vol. IX. p. 292).]

[2] [For another reference to Wells, see *Seven Lamps*, Vol. VIII. p. 12.]

the top ; but it is on a scale of perfect power and effective-
ness ; while in the base modern Gothic of Milan Cathedral
the statues are cut delicately everywhere, and the builders
think it a merit that the visitor must climb to the roof
before he can see them ; and our modern Greek and Italian
architecture reaches the utmost pitch of absurdity by placing its fine work *at the top only.* So that the general condition of the thing may be stated boldly, as in the text ;
the principal ornaments of Gothic buildings being in their
porches, and of modern buildings, in their parapets.

68. Proposition 4th. — *Ornamentation should be natural,*
—that is to say, should in some degree express or adopt
the beauty of natural objects. This law, together with its
ultimate reason, is expressed in the statement given in the
Stones of Venice:[1] "All noble ornament is the expression
of man's delight in God's work."

Observe, it does not hence follow that it should be an
exact imitation of, or endeavour in anywise to supersede,
God's work. It may consist only in a partial adoption of,
and compliance with, the usual forms of natural things,
without at all going to the point of imitation ; and it is
possible that the point of imitation may be closely reached
by ornaments, which nevertheless are entirely unfit for their
place, and are the signs only of a degraded ambition and
an ignorant dexterity. Bad decorators err as easily on the
side of imitating nature, as of forgetting her ; and the
question of the exact degree in which imitation should be
attempted under given circumstances, is one of the most
subtle and difficult in the whole range of criticism. I have
elsewhere examined it at some length, and have yet much
to say about it ;[2] but here I can only state briefly that
the modes in which ornamentation *ought* to fall short of

---

[1] [The reference in the original text was to "vol. i. p. 213"; in this edition,
Vol. IX. p. 264.]

[2] [See *Seven Lamps*, Vol. VIII. pp. 169–174, and *Stones of Venice*, Vol. X. pp. 257–
258. Those passages refer to the limits of imitation and abstraction in sculpture.
To the general subject Ruskin returned in the third volume of *Modern Painters.*]

pure representation or imitation are in the main three, namely:—

A. Conventionalism by cause of colour.

B. Conventionalism by cause of inferiority.

C. Conventionalism by cause of means.

69. A. Conventionalism by cause of colour.—Abstract colour is not an imitation of nature, but *is* nature itself; that is to say, the pleasure taken in blue or red, as such, considered as hues merely, is the same, so long as the brilliancy of the hue is equal, whether it be produced by the chemistry of man, or the chemistry of flowers, or the chemistry of skies. We deal with colour as with sound—so far ruling the power of the light, as we rule the power of the air, producing beauty not necessarily imitative, but sufficient in itself, so that, wherever colour is introduced, ornamentation may cease to represent natural objects, and may consist in mere spots, or bands, or flamings, or any other condition of arrangement favourable to the colour.[1]

70. B. Conventionalism by cause of inferiority.—In general, ornamentation is set upon certain services, subjected to certain systems, and confined within certain limits; so that its forms require to be lowered or limited in accordance with the required relations. It cannot be allowed to assume the free outlines, or to rise to the perfection of imitation. Whole banks of flowers, for instance, cannot be carved on cathedral fronts, but only narrow mouldings, having some of the characters of banks of flowers. Also, some ornaments require to be subdued in value, that they may not interfere with the effect of others; and all these necessary *inferiorities* are attained by means of departing from natural forms—it being an established law of human admiration that what is most representative of nature shall, *cœteris paribus*, be most attractive.

All the various kinds of ornamentation, consisting of

---

[1] [On the subject of abstraction in colour, see *Modern Painters*, vol. ii. (Vol. IV. p. 301).]

spots, points, twisted bands, abstract curves, and other such, owe their peculiar character to this conventionalism "by cause of inferiority."

71. C. Conventionalism by cause of means.—In every branch of art, only so much imitation of nature is to be admitted as is consistent with the ease of the workman and the capacities of the material. Whatever shortcomings are appointed (for they are more than permitted, they are in such cases appointed, and meritorious) on account of the untractableness of the material, come under the head of "conventionalism by cause of means."

These conventionalities, then, being duly understood and accepted, in modification of the general law, that law will be, that the glory of all ornamentation consists in the adoption or imitation of the beauties of natural objects, and that no work can be of high value which is not full of this beauty. To this fourth proposition, modern architects have not ventured to make any serious resistance. On the contrary, they seem to be, little by little, gliding into an obscure perception of the fact, that architecture, in most periods of the world, had sculpture upon it, and that the said sculpture generally did represent something intelligible. For instance, we find Mr. Huggins, of Liverpool,[1] lately lecturing upon architecture "in its relations to nature and the intellect," * and gravely informing his hearers, that "in the Middle Ages angels were human figures;" that "some of the richest ornaments of Solomon's temple were imitated from the palm and pomegranate," and that "the Greeks followed the example of the Egyptians in selecting their ornaments from the *plants* of their own country." It is to be presumed that the lecturer has never been in the Elgin or Egyptian room of the British Museum, or it might have occurred to him that the Egyptians and Greeks sometimes also selected their ornaments from the *men* of their own country. But

* See *The Builder*, for January 12, 1854.

---

[1] [Samuel Huggins (1811–1885), President of the Liverpool Architectural Society.]

we must not expect too much illumination at once; and as we are told that, in conclusion, Mr. Huggins glanced at "the error of architects in neglecting the fountain of wisdom thus open to them in nature," we may expect in due time large results from the discovery of a source of wisdom so unimagined.

72. Proposition 5th.—*Ornamentation should be thoughtful.* That is to say, whenever you put a chisel or a pencil into a man's hand for the purpose of enabling him to produce beauty, you are to expect of him that he will think about what he is doing, and feel something about it, and that the expression of this thought or feeling will be the most noble quality in what he produces with his chisel or brush, inasmuch as the power of thinking and feeling is the most noble thing in the man. It will hence follow that as men do not commonly think the same thoughts twice, you are not to require of them that they shall do the same thing twice. You are to expect another and a different thought of them, as soon as one thought has been well expressed.

73. Hence, therefore, it follows also that all noble ornamentation is perpetually varied ornamentation,[1] and that the moment you find ornamentation unchanging, you may know that it is of a degraded kind or degraded school. To this law, the only exceptions arise out of the uses of monotony, as a contrast to change. Many subordinate architectural mouldings are severely alike in their various parts (though never unless they are thoroughly subordinate, for monotony is always deathful according to the degree of it), in order to set off change in others; and a certain monotony or similarity must be introduced among the most changeful ornaments in order to enhance and exhibit their own changes.

The truth of this proposition is self-evident; for no art can be noble which is incapable of expressing thought, and no art is capable of expressing thought which does not

---

[1] [This proposition is implied in *Stones of Venice*, vol. i. (Vol. IX. p. 310), vol. ii. (Vol. X. p. 261).]

change. To require of an artist that he should always reproduce the same picture, would be not one whit more base than to require of a carver that he should always reproduce the same sculpture.

The principle is perfectly clear and altogether incontrovertible. Apply it to modern Greek architecture, and that architecture must cease to exist; for it depends absolutely on copyism.

74. The sixth proposition above stated [§ 57], that *Gothic ornamentation is nobler than Greek ornamentation*, etc., is therefore sufficiently proved by the acceptance of this one principle, no less important than unassailable. Of all that I have to bring forward respecting architecture, this is the one I have most at heart; for on the acceptance of this depends the determination whether the workman shall be a living, progressive, and happy human being, or whether he shall be a mere machine, with its valves smoothed by heart's blood instead of oil,—the most pitiable form of slave.[1]

And it is with especial reference to the denial of this principle in modern and Renaissance architecture, that I speak of that architecture with a bitterness which appears to many readers extreme, while in reality, so far from exaggerating, I have not grasp enough of thought to embrace, the evils which have resulted among all the orders of European society from the introduction of the Renaissance schools of building, in turning away the eyes of the beholder from natural beauty, and reducing the workman to the level of a machine. In the Gothic times, writing, painting, carving, casting,—it mattered not what,—were all works done by thoughtful and happy men; and the illumination of the volume, and the carving and casting of wall and gate, employed, not thousands, but millions, of true and noble *artists* over all Christian lands. Men in the same position are now left utterly without intellectual power or pursuit, and, being unhappy in their work, they rebel against it: hence one of

---

[1] [See again the chapter on "The Nature of Gothic," Vol. X. pp. 194–195.]

the worst forms of Unchristian Socialism.[1] So again, there being now no nature or variety in architecture, the multitude are not interested in it ; therefore, for the present, they have lost their taste for art altogether, so that you can no longer trust sculpture within their reach. Consider the innumerable forms of evil involved in the temper and taste of the existing populace of London or Paris, as compared with the temper of the populace of Florence, when the quarter of Santa Maria Novella received its title of "Joyful Quarter," from the rejoicings of the multitude at getting a new picture into their church,[2] better than the old ones ;—all this difference being exclusively chargeable on the Renaissance architecture. And then, farther, if we remember, not only the revolutionary ravage of sacred architecture, but the immeasurably greater destruction effected by the Renaissance builders and their satellites, wherever they came, destruction so wide-spread that there is not a town in France or Italy but it has to deplore the deliberate overthrow of more than half its noblest monuments, in order to put up Greek porticoes or palaces in their stead; adding also all the blame of the ignorance of the meaner kind of men, operating in thousands of miserable abuses upon the frescoes, books, and pictures, as the architects' hammers did on the carved work, of the Middle Ages ; * and, finally, if we examine the influence which the luxury, and, still more, the heathenism, joined with the essential dulness of these schools, have had

* Nothing appears to me much more wonderful, than the remorseless way in which the educated ignorance, even of the present day, will sweep away an ancient monument, if its preservation be not absolutely consistent with immediate convenience or economy. Putting aside all antiquarian considerations, and all artistical ones, I wish that people would only consider the steps and the weight of the following very simple argument. You allow it is wrong to waste time, that is, your own time ; but then it must be still more wrong to waste other people's ; for you have some right to your own time, but none to theirs. Well, then, if it is thus wrong to waste the time of the living, it

---

[1] [A reference to the then recently adopted phrase "Christian Socialism" ; the first number of *The Christian Socialist*, the organ of the movement, edited by Frederick Denison Maurice, had appeared in November 1850.]
[2] [See for this incident Vol. III. p. 644 n.]

on the upper class of society, it will ultimately be found that no expressions are energetic enough to describe, nor broad enough to embrace, the enormous moral evils which have risen from them.

75. I omitted, in preparing the preceding lecture for the press, a passage referring to this subject, because it appeared to me, in its place, hardly explained by preceding statements. But I give it here unaltered, as being, in sober earnest, but too weak to characterise the tendencies of the " accursed " architecture of which it speaks.

" Accursed, I call it, with deliberate purpose. It needed but the gathering up of a Babylonish garment to trouble Israel;[1]—these marble garments of the ancient idols of the Gentiles, how many have *they* troubled! Gathered out of their ruins by the second Babylon,—gathered by the Papal Church in the extremity of her sin;—raised up by her, not when she was sending forth her champions to preach in the highway, and pine in the desert, and perish in the fire, but in the very scarlet fruitage and fulness of her guilt, when her priests vested themselves not with purple only, but with blood, and bade the cups of their feasting foam not with wine only, but with hemlock;—raised by the hands of the Leos and the Borgias, raised first into that mighty temple where the seven hills slope to the Tiber, that marks by its massy dome the central spot where Rome has reversed the words of Christ, and, as He vivified the stone to the apostleship, she petrifies the apostleship into the stumbling stone; —exalted there first as if to mark what work it had to do, it went forth to paralyse or to pollute, and wherever it came, the lustre faded from the streets of our cities, the grey towers and glorious arches of our abbeys fell by the

must be still more wrong to waste the time of the dead; for the living can redeem their time, the dead cannot. But you waste the best of the time of the dead when you destroy the works they have left you; for to those works they gave the best of their time, intending them for immortality.

---

[1] [Joshua vii. 21.]

river sides, the love of nature was uprooted from the hearts of men, base luxuries and cruel formalisms were festered and frozen into them from their youth; and at last, where, from his fair Gothic chapel beside the Seine, the king St. Louis had gone forth, followed by his thousands in the cause of Christ, another king was dragged forth from the gates of his Renaissance palace,* to die, by the hands of the thousands of his people gathered in another crusade; or what shall that be called—whose sign was not the cross, but the guillotine?"

76. I have not space here to pursue the subject farther, nor shall I be able to write anything more respecting architecture for some time to come. But in the meanwhile, I would most earnestly desire to leave with the reader this one subject of thought—"*The Life of the Workman.*" For it is singular, and far more than singular, that among all the writers who have attempted to examine the principles stated in the *Stones of Venice,* not one † has as yet

---

* The character of Renaissance architecture, and the spirit which dictated its adoption, may be remembered as having been centred and symbolised in the palace of Versailles; whose site was chosen by Louis the Fourteenth, in order that from thence he might *not* see St. Denis, the burial-place of his family. The cost of the palace in twenty-seven years is stated in *The Builder,* for March 18th, 1854, to have been £3,246,000 money of that period, equal to about seven millions now (£900,000 having been expended in the year 1686 alone). The building is thus notably illustrative of the two feelings which were stated in the *Stones of Venice,* to be peculiarly characteristic of the Renaissance spirit, the Pride of State and Fear of Death. Compare the horror of Louis the Fourteenth at the sight of the tower of St. Denis, with the feeling which prompted the Scaligeri at Verona to set their tombs within fifteen feet of their palace walls.[1]

† An article in *Fraser's Magazine,* which has appeared since these sheets were sent to press, forms a solitary exception.[2]

---

[1] [See *Seven Lamps,* ch. vi. (Vol. VIII. p. 247).]

[2] [The reference is to the second of two reviews of *The Stones of Venice,* in *Fraser's Magazine* for April 1854, vol. 49, p. 464. It may be noted that, before this point had been driven home in the second volume of *The Stones of Venice,* one reviewer had noticed the hints of it in the *Seven Lamps,* and had referred to them as a signal instance of Ruskin's "strangeness": see Vol. VIII. p. xxxix. Though the fact was unknown to Ruskin at the time, the chapter in the second volume had made a profound impression on at least one reader, which was to produce much influence in good time: see Vol. X. p. lix.]

made a single comment on what was precisely and accurately the most important chapter in the whole book; namely, the description of the nature of Gothic architecture, as involving the liberty of the workman (vol. ii. ch. vi.). I had hoped that whatever might be the prejudices of modern architects, there would have been found some among them quick-sighted enough to see the bearings of this principle, and generous enough to support it. There has hitherto stood forward not *one*.

But my purpose must at last be accomplished for all this. The labourer among the gravestones of our modern architecture must yet be raised up, and become a living soul. Before he can be thus raised, the whole system of Greek architecture, as practised in the present day, must be annihilated; but it *will* be annihilated, and that speedily. For truth and judgment are its declared opposites, and against these nothing ever finally prevailed, or shall prevail.

LECTURE III

TURNER AND HIS WORKS [1]

Delivered November 15, 1853

77. My object this evening is not so much to give you any account of the works or the genius of the great painter whom we have so lately lost (which it would require rather a year than an hour to do), as to give you some idea of the position which his works hold with respect to the landscape of other periods, and of the general condition and prospects of the landscape art of the present day. I will not lose time in prefatory remarks, as I have little enough at any rate, but will enter abruptly on my subject.

78. You are all of you well aware that landscape seems hardly to have exercised any strong influence, as such, on any pagan nation or pagan artist. I have no time to enter into any details on this, of course, most intricate and difficult subject; [2] but I will only ask you to observe, that wherever natural scenery is alluded to by the ancients, it is either agriculturally, with the kind of feeling that a good Scotch farmer has; sensually, in the enjoyment of sun or shade, cool winds or sweet scents; fearfully, in a mere vulgar dread of rocks and desolate places, as compared with the comfort of cities; or, finally, superstitiously, in the personification or deification of natural powers, generally with much

---

[1] [The following was Ruskin's Synopsis of the Lecture in the preliminary announcement :—

" Turner and his Works.

Progress of Landscape Art from the 13th to the 19th Century :—Its rise through three phases—Giottesque, Leonardesque, and Titianesque—and subsequent Fall. Its peculiar Position in the Modern Mind. Early training of Turner :—Disadvantages to which he was exposed. Mistaken Ideas respecting his Works :— Their true Character and probable future Effect. Character of the Painter."]

[2] [Ruskin returned to the discussion of it in *Modern Painters*, vol. iii. ch. xiii.]

degradation of their impressiveness, as in the paltry fables of Ulysses receiving the winds in bags from Æolus, and of the Cyclops hammering lightning sharp at the ends, on an anvil.* Of course, you will here and there find feeble evidences of a higher sensibility, chiefly, I think, in Plato, Æschylus, Aristophanes, and Virgil.[1] Homer, though in the epithets he applies to landscape always thoroughly graphic, uses the same epithet[2] for rocks, seas, and trees, from one end of his poem to the other, evidently without the smallest interest in anything of the kind; and in the mass of heathen writers, the absence of sensation on these subjects is singularly painful. For instance, in that, to my mind, most disgusting of all so-called poems, the Journey to Brundusium,[3] you remember that Horace takes exactly as much interest in the scenery he is passing through as Sancho Panza would have done.

* Of course I do not mean by calling these fables "paltry," to dispute their neatness, ingenuity, or moral depth; but only their want of apprehension of the extent and awfulness of the phenomena introduced. So also, in denying Homer's interest in nature, I do not mean to deny his accuracy of observation, or his power of seizing on the main points of landscape, but I deny the power of landscape over his heart, unless when closely associated with, and altogether subordinate to, some human interest.[4]

---

[1] [In Plato, however, Ruskin afterwards noted, the affection for the country is confined to its softer aspects (*Modern Painters*, vol. iii. ch. xiii. § 27). For the more modern feeling towards landscape shown in Æschylus and Aristophanes generally, see the same place; for Aristophanes more particularly, see also *Modern Painters*, vol. i. (Vol. III. p. 26 *n.*), vol. iii. ch. xv. § 21, ch. xvi. § 3, vol. v. pt. vii. ch. iv. § 10. To Virgil—"landscape lover, lord of language"—the references in Ruskin's earlier books are few, and do not indicate that same detailed study that he gave to many other classical authors (for other passing allusions to his landscape, see *Modern Painters*, vol. iv. ch. xvi. § 27, vol. v. pt. ix. ch. x. § 22); at a later time Ruskin gave much study to Virgil, and especially to the *Georgics*, which were to be one of the standard books in "St. George's Schools": see *Fors Clavigera*, Letters 5, 8, 18, 61, 84; and for a reference to Virgilian similes—"many thoughts in one," see *Love's Meinie*, § 44.]

[2] [See *Modern Painters*, vol. iii. ch. xiii. § 2, for a fuller discussion of Homeric epithets; the summary statement *here* is not to be taken too literally, for (as Ruskin *there* points out) Homer has several epithets for the sea; so also for rocks, and also for trees.]

[3] [A paraphrase by Ruskin of a few lines of the "*Iter ad Brundusium*" will be found in Vol. II. p. 79; where his appreciation of Horace is also noted.]

[4] [The references are to the *Odyssey*, x. 19, 20; and, for the Cyclops, to Virgil, *G.* iv. 170; *Aen.* viii. 424. Ruskin has some remarks on the ingenuity and deep meaning of the myth of Æolus in *Queen of the Air*, § 19.]

79. You will find, on the other hand, that the language
of the Bible is specifically distinguished from all other early
literature, by its delight in natural imagery;[1] and that the
dealings of God with His people are calculated peculiarly
to awaken this sensibility within them. Out of the monotonous valley of Egypt they are instantly taken into the
midst of the mightiest mountain scenery in the peninsula
of Arabia; and that scenery is associated in their minds
with the immediate manifestation and presence of the
Divine Power; so that mountains for ever afterwards become invested with a peculiar sacredness in their minds:
while their descendants being placed in what was then
one of the loveliest districts upon the earth, full of glorious vegetation, bounded on one side by the sea, on the
north by "that goodly mountain" Lebanon,[2] on the south
and east by deserts, whose barrenness enhanced by their
contrast the sense of the perfection of beauty in their own
land, they became, by these means, and by the touch of
God's own hand upon their hearts, sensible to the appeal
of natural scenery in a way in which no other people
were at the time. And their literature is full of expressions, not only testifying a vivid sense of the power of
nature over man, but showing that *sympathy with natural
things themselves*, as if they had human souls, which is
the especial characteristic of true love of the works of
God. I intended to have insisted on this sympathy at
greater length, but I found, only two or three days ago,
much of what I had to say to you anticipated in a little
book, unpretending, but full of interest, *The Lamp and
the Lantern*, by Dr. James Hamilton;[3] and I will therefore only ask you to consider such expressions as that tender

[1] [Ruskin discussed this aspect of the Bible further in *Modern Painters*, vol. iv.
ch. xx. §§ 46–49.]

[2] [Deuteronomy iii. 25.]

[3] [*The Lamp and the Lantern; or, Light for the Tent and the Traveller*, by James
Hamilton, D.D., 1853; a small volume of lectures on the Bible. The landscape of
the Bible is discussed at pp. 36–43. The author (1814–1867) was for many years
minister of the National Scottish Church, Regent Square, London, and his *Book of
Psalms and Hymns* has been widely adopted in Presbyterian churches.]

and glorious verse in Isaiah, speaking of the cedars on the mountains as rejoicing over the fall of the king of Assyria: "Yea, the fir trees rejoice at thee, and the cedars of Lebanon, saying, Since *thou* art gone down to the grave, no feller is come up against us."[1]   See what sympathy there is here, as if with the very hearts of the trees themselves.   So also in the words of Christ, in His personification of the lilies: "They toil not, neither do they spin."   Consider such expressions as, "The sea saw that, and fled.   Jordan was driven back.   The mountains skipped like rams; and the little hills like lambs."   Try to find anything in profane writing like this; and note farther that the whole book of Job appears to have been chiefly written and placed in the inspired volume in order to show the value of natural history, and its power on the human heart.[2]   I cannot pass by it without pointing out the evidences of the beauty of the country that Job inhabited.*   Observe, first, it was an arable country. "The oxen were ploughing and the asses feeding beside

* This passage, respecting the book of Job, was omitted in the delivery of the Lecture, for want of time.

---

[1] [Isaiah xiv. 8. Ruskin refers to the passage again in *Modern Painters*, vol. iii. ch. xii. § 14. The subsequent Bible references are Matthew vi. 28; Psalms cxiv. 3; Job i. 14, vi. 15–17, ix. 30, viii. 16, 17, v. 23, xiv. 18, v. 9, xxviii. 9.]

[2] [Ruskin had been studying the Book of Job carefully: see Vol. X. p. xxxviii. In a letter to his father from Venice (Nov. 2, 1851), he wrote:—

"By-the-bye, I have been making up my mind that the land of Uz, in which Job lived, must have been close under Lebanon or Caucasus, or in some place at the feet of snowy mountains. All his imagery is that of a mountaineer, but especially the way he dwells on the passing away of the 'snow waters,' (ch. vi. 15–18, ch. xxiv. 19, ch. xii. 15), and all the imagery of ch. xxviii. 4–6, 7, 10, 11, and ch. xiv. 18–19, is exactly that which would occur to a man living in such a place as the valley of St. Martin's. You know how I was disappointed in the autumn when I went to look for my favourite spring at Maglans, that comes out of the limestone strong enough to turn a mill, and there was nothing but the dry stones: it was 'snow waters.' So even the 'great wind from the wilderness,' destroying the house where his sons were feasting [ch. i. 19], was evidently a mountain blast; for in the margin you see it is *not* 'from the wilderness' but 'from aside,' just the expression which Aristophanes uses of wind coming down the hills. I think if you will put Job in among the mountains, the whole book will read much more grandly."

The reference to Aristophanes is to *The Clouds*, 325; the passage is cited and discussed in *Modern Painters*, vol. i. (Vol. III. p. 26 *n*.). There are frequent references to the landscape of the Book of Job in vols. iii., iv., and v. of *Modern Painters*: see General Index.]

them." It was a pastoral country: his substance, besides camels and asses, was 7000 sheep. It was a mountain country, fed by streams descending from the high snows. " My brethren have dealt deceitfully as a brook, and as the stream of brooks they pass away; which are blackish by reason of the ice, and wherein the snow is hid: What time they wax warm they vanish: when it is hot they are consumed out of their place." Again: " If I wash myself with snow water, and make my hands never so clean." Again: " Drought and heat consume the snow waters." It was a rocky country, with forests and verdure rooted in the rocks. " His branch shooteth forth in his garden; his roots are wrapped about the heap, and seeth the place of stones." Again: " Thou shalt be in league with the stones of the field." It was a place visited, like the valleys of Switzerland, by convulsions and falls of mountains. " Surely the mountain falling cometh to nought, and the rock is removed out of his place. The waters wear the stones; thou washest away the things which grow out of the dust of the earth." " He removeth the mountains and they know not: he overturneth them in his anger." " He putteth forth his hand upon the rock: he overturneth the mountains by the roots: he cutteth out rivers among the rocks." I have not time to go farther into this; but you see Job's country was one like your own, full of pleasant brooks and rivers, rushing among the rocks, and of all other sweet and noble elements of landscape. The magnificent allusions to natural scenery throughout the book are therefore calculated to touch the heart to the end of time.

80. Then at the central point of Jewish prosperity, you have the first great naturalist the world ever saw, Solomon; not permitted, indeed, to anticipate, in writing, the discoveries of modern times, but so gifted as to show us that heavenly wisdom is manifested as much in the knowledge of the hyssop that springeth out of the wall[1] as in political and philosophical speculation.

[1] [1 Kings iv. 33.]

The books of the Old Testament, as distinguished from all other early writings, are thus prepared for an everlasting influence over humanity; and, finally, Christ himself, setting the concluding example to the conduct and thoughts of men, spends nearly His whole life in the fields, the mountains, or the small country villages of Judea; and in the very closing scenes of His life, will not so much as sleep within the walls of Jerusalem, but rests at the little village of Bethphage,[1] walking in the morning, and returning in the evening, through the peaceful avenues of the Mount of Olives, to and from His work of teaching in the temple.

81. It would thus naturally follow, both from the general tone and teaching of the Scriptures, and from the example of our Lord himself, that wherever Christianity was preached and accepted, there would be an immediate interest awakened in the works of God, as seen in the natural world: and, accordingly, this is the second universal and distinctive character of Christian art, as distinguished from all pagan work; the first being a peculiar spirituality in its conception of the human form, preferring holiness of expression and strength of character, to beauty of features or of body;[2] and the second, as I say, its intense fondness for natural objects—animals, leaves, and flowers,—inducing an immediate transformation of the cold and lifeless pagan ornamentation into vivid imagery of nature. Of course this manifestation of feeling was at first checked by the circumstances under which the Christian religion was disseminated. The art of the first three centuries is entirely subordinate,—restrained partly by persecution, partly by a high spirituality, which cared much more about preaching than painting; and then when, under Constantine, Christianity became the religion of the Roman empire, myriads of persons gave the aid of their wealth and of their art to the new religion, who were Christians in nothing but the name, and who decorated a

---

[1] [Matthew xxi. 1.]
[2] [Compare "The Relation of Michael Angelo and Tintoret" in *Aratra Pentelici*, §§ 220, 229.]

Christian temple just as they would have decorated a pagan one, merely because the new religion had become Imperial. Then, just as the new art was beginning to assume a distinctive form, down came the northern barbarians upon it; and all their superstitions had to be leavened with it, and all their hard hands and hearts softened by it, before their art could appear in anything like a characteristic form. The warfare in which Europe was perpetually plunged retarded this development for ages; but it steadily and gradually prevailed, working from the eighth to the eleventh century like a seed in the ground, showing little signs of life, but still, if carefully examined, changing essentially every day and every hour: at last, in the twelfth century the blade appears above the black earth; in the thirteenth, the plant is in full leaf.

82. I begin, then, with the thirteenth century, and must now make to you a general assertion, which, if you will note down and examine at your leisure, you will find true and useful, though I have not time at present to give you full demonstration of it.

I say, then, that the art of the thirteenth century is the foundation of all art[1]—nor merely the foundation, but the root of it; that is to say, succeeding art is not merely built upon it, but was all comprehended in it, and is developed out of it. Passing this great century, we find three successive branches developed from it, in each of the three following centuries. The fourteenth century is pre-eminently the age of *Thought*, the fifteenth the age of *Drawing*, and the sixteenth the age of *Painting*.

83. Observe, first, the fourteenth century is pre-eminently the age of thought. It begins with the first words of the poem of Dante;[2] and all the great pictorial poems — the mighty series of works in which everything is done to

---

[1] [Compare *Stones of Venice*, vol. ii. and the note thereon, Vol. X. p. 306.]

[2] [Ruskin refers again to this year—1300, the beginning of the century, the date at which the *Divina Commedia* was commenced, and the middle of the poet's threescore years and ten (had such been his), " nel mezzo del cammin,"—in *Stones of Venice*, vol. ii. (Vol. X. p. 400).]

relate, but nothing to imitate—belong to this century. I should only confuse you by giving you the names of marvellous artists, most of them little familiar to British ears, who adorned this century in Italy; but you will easily remember it as the age of Dante and Giotto[1]—the age of *Thought*.

The men of the succeeding century (the fifteenth) felt that they could not rival their predecessors in invention, but might excel them in execution. Original thoughts belonging to this century are comparatively rare; even Raphael and Michael Angelo themselves borrowed all their principal ideas and plans of pictures from their predecessors; but they executed them with a precision up to that time unseen. You must understand by the word "drawing," the perfect rendering of forms, whether in sculpture or painting; and then remember the fifteenth century as the age of Leonardo, Michael Angelo, Lorenzo Ghiberti, and Raphael[2] —pre-eminently the age of *Drawing*.

The sixteenth century produced the four greatest *Painters*, that is to say, managers of colour, whom the world has seen; namely, Tintoret, Paul Veronese, Titian, and Correggio.[3] I need not say more to justify my calling it the age of *Painting*.

84. This, then, being the state of things respecting art in general, let us next trace the career of landscape through these centuries.

It was only towards the close of the thirteenth century that figure painting began to assume so perfect a condition as to require some elaborate suggestion of landscape background. Up to that time, if any natural object had to be represented, it was done in an entirely conventional way, as you see it upon Greek vases, or in a Chinese porcelain

---

[1] [Dante, 1265–1321; Giotto, 1276–1336.]

[2] [Leonardo, 1452–1519; Michael Angelo, 1475–1564; Raphael, 1483–1520. Ghiberti was earlier, 1378–1455.]

[3] [Tintoret, 1519–1594; Veronese, 1528–1588; Titian, 1477–1576; Correggio, 1494–1534. For a note on Ruskin's other lists of the greatest painters, see Vol. IV. p. xxxv. For Ruskin's diagram showing the dates of the principal Italian artists, arranged in centuries, see *Ariadne Florentina*, Lecture ii.]

pattern; an independent tree or flower being set upon the white ground, or ground of any colour, wherever there was a vacant space for it, without the smallest attempt to imitate the real colours and relations of the earth and sky about it. But at the close of the thirteenth century, Giotto, and in the course of the fourteenth, Orcagna, sought, for the first time, to give some resemblance to nature in their backgrounds, and introduced behind their figures pieces of true landscape, formal enough still, but complete in intention, having foregrounds and distances, sky and water, forests and mountains, carefully delineated, not exactly in their true colour, but yet in colour approximating to the truth. The system which they introduced (for though in many points enriched above the work of earlier ages, the Orcagna and Giotto landscape was a very complete piece of recipe) was observed for a long period by their pupils, and may be thus briefly described:—The sky is always pure blue, paler at the horizon, and with a few streaky white clouds in it, the ground is green even to the extreme distance, with brown rocks projecting from it; water is blue streaked with white. The trees are nearly always composed of clusters of their proper leaves relieved on a black or dark ground, thus (fig. 20).* And observe carefully, with respect to the complete drawing of the leaves on this tree, and the smallness of their number, the real distinction between noble conventionalism and false conventionalism. You will often hear modern architects defending their monstrous ornamentation on the ground that it is "conventional," and that architectural ornament ought to be conventionalised. Remember, when you hear this, that noble conventionalism is not an agreement between the artist and spectator that the one shall misrepresent nature sixty times over, and the other believe the

* Having no memoranda of my own, taken from Giotto's landscape, I had this tree copied from an engraving; but I imagine the rude termination of the stems to be a misrepresentation. Fig. 21 is accurately copied from a MS., certainly executed between 1250 and 1270, and is more truly characteristic of the early manner.[1]

---

[1] [The Psalter of St. Louis; see below, p. 479.]

misrepresentation sixty times over, but it is an agreement
that certain means and limitations being prescribed, only
that *kind of truth* is to be expected which is consistent with
those means.   For instance, if Sir Joshua Reynolds had been
talking to a friend about the character of a face, and there
had been nothing in the room but a deal table and an ink-
bottle—and no pens—Sir Joshua would have dipped his
finger in the ink, and painted a portrait on the table with

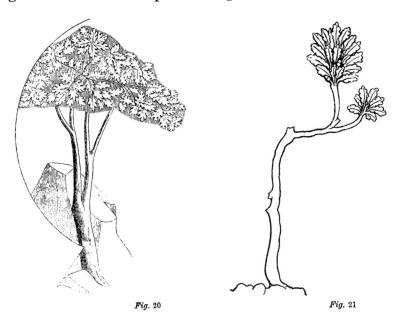

Fig. 20   Fig. 21

his finger, and a noble portrait too ; certainly not delicate
in outline, nor representing any of the qualities of the face
dependent on rich outline, but getting as much of the face
as in that manner was attainable.   That is noble conventionalism, and Egyptian work on granite, or illuminator's
work in glass, is all conventional in the same sense, but not
conventionally false.   The two noblest and *truest* carved
lions I have ever seen, are the two granite ones in the
Egyptian room of the British Museum,[1] and yet in them,

---

[1] [For another reference to these lions, see *Modern Painters*, vol. ii. (Vol. IV.
p. 303).]

the lions' manes and beards are represented by rings of solid rock, as smooth as a mirror!

85. There are indeed one or two other conditions of noble conventionalism, noticed more fully in the Addenda [§§ 68–71]; but you will find that they always consist in *stopping short* of nature, not in falsifying nature; and thus in Giotto's foliage, he *stops short* of the quantity of leaves on the real tree, but he gives you the form of the leaves represented with perfect truth. His foreground also is nearly always occupied by flowers and herbage, carefully and individually painted from nature; while, although thus simple in plan, the arrangements of line in these landscapes of course show the influence of the master-mind, and sometimes, where the story requires it, we find the usual formulæ overleaped, and Giotto at Avignon painting the breakers of the sea on a steep shore with great care,[1] while Orcagna, in his Triumph of Death,[2] has painted a thicket of brambles mixed with teazles, in a manner worthy of the best days of landscape art.

86. Now from the landscape of these two men to the landscape of Raphael, Leonardo, and Perugino, the advance consists principally in two great steps: The first, that distant objects were more or less invested with a blue colour,—the second, that trees were no longer painted with a black ground, but with a rich dark brown, or deep green. From Giotto's old age, to the youth of Raphael, the advance in, and knowledge of, landscape, consisted of no more than these two simple steps; but the *execution* of landscape became infinitely more perfect and elaborate. All the flowers and leaves in the foreground were worked out with the same perfection as the features of the figures; in the middle distance the brown trees were most delicately defined against the sky; the blue mountains in the extreme distance were exquisitely thrown into aërial gradations, and the sky and

---

[1] [See Vol. IX. p. 273 *n.*, where it is pointed out that these frescoes are by Simone Martini, and not (as was once thought) by Giotto.]

[2] [For other references to this fresco at Pisa, see below, p. 146.]

J. Ruskin.

Allen & Co. Sc.

Mediæval Landscape

clouds were perfect in transparency and softness. But still there is no real advance in knowledge of natural objects. The leaves and flowers are, indeed, admirably painted, and thrown into various intricate groupings, such as Giotto could not have attempted, but the rocks and water are still as conventional and imperfect as ever, except only in colour: the forms of rock in Leonardo's celebrated "Vierge aux Rochers"[1] are literally no better than those on a china plate. Fig. 22 shows a portion of them in mere outline, with one cluster of the leaves above, and the distant "ideal" mountains. On the whole, the most satisfactory work of the period is that which most resembles missal painting, that is to say, which is fullest of beautiful flowers and animals scattered among the landscape, in the old independent way, like the birds upon a screen. The landscape of Benozzo Gozzoli is exquisitely rich in incident of this kind.[2]

87. The first man who entirely broke through the conventionality of his time, and painted pure landscape, was Masaccio,[3] but he died too young to effect the revolution of which his genius was capable. It was left for other men to accomplish, namely, for Correggio and Titian. These two painters were the first who relieved the foregrounds of their landscape from the grotesque, quaint, and crowded formalism of the early painters; and gave a close approximation to the forms of nature in all things; retaining, however, thus much of the old system, that the distances were for the most part painted in deep ultramarine blue, the foregrounds in rich green and brown; there were no effects of sunshine and shadow, but a generally quiet glow over the whole scene; and the clouds, though now rolling in irregular masses, and

---

[1] [In the Louvre (see below, p. 460); another version was acquired for the National Gallery (No. 1093) in 1880. Recent researches make it appear probable that Leonardo's landscape was studied from fantastic rocks actually seen and noted by him in his explorations among the mountains: see passages cited in E. T. Cook's *Popular Handbook to the National Gallery*, 6th ed., i. 521.]

[2] [See the descriptions from Ruskin's notebook of 1845, given in Vol. IV. p. 321 n.]

[3] [Masaccio, 1401–1428. See *Modern Painters*, vol. i. pt. ii. sec. i. ch. vii. § 11; the summary sketch of Italian landscape given here should be compared with the longer notices there (Vol. III. pp. 174–184).]

sometimes richly involved among the hills, were never varied in conception, or studied from nature. There were no changes of weather in them, no rain clouds or fair-weather clouds, nothing but various shapes of the cumulus or cirrus,

Fig. 22

introduced for the sake of light on the deep blue sky. Tintoret and Bonifazio introduced more natural effects into this monotonous landscape: in their works we meet with showers of rain, with rainbows, sunsets, bright reflections in water, and so on; but still very subordinate, and carelessly

worked out, so as not to justify us in considering their
landscape as forming a class by itself.

88. Fig. 23, which is a branch of a tree from the background of Titian's " St. Jerome," at Milan,[1] compared with
fig. 20, will give you a distinct idea of the kind of change
which took place from the time of Giotto to that of Titian,

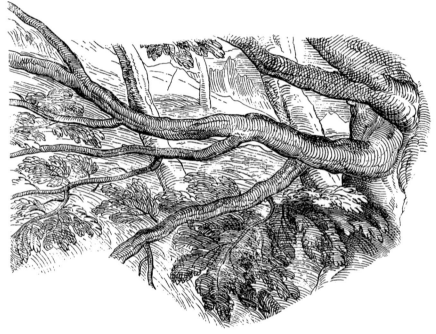

Fig. 23

and you will find that this whole range of landscape may be
conveniently classed in three divisions, namely, *Giottesque,*
Leonardesque, and *Titianesque;* the Giottesque embracing
nearly all the work of the fourteenth, the Leonardesque that
of the fifteenth, and the Titianesque that of the sixteenth
century. Now you see there remained a fourth step to be
taken,—the doing away with conventionalism altogether, so

[1] [For other references to this picture, see Vol. III. p. 181 and *n.*]

as to create the perfect art of landscape painting. The course of the mind of Europe was to do this; but at the very moment when it ought to have been done, the art of all civilised nations was paralysed at once by the operation of the poisonous elements of infidelity and classical learning together, as I have endeavoured to show elsewhere.[1] In this paralysis, like a soldier shot as he is just gaining an eminence, the art of the seventeenth century struggled forward, and sank upon the spot it had been endeavouring to attain. The step which should have freed landscape from conventionalism was actually taken by Claude and Salvator Rosa, but taken in a state of palsy,—taken so as to lose far more than was gained. For up to this time, no painter ever had thought of drawing anything, pebble or blade of grass, or tree or mountain, but as well and distinctly as he could; and if he could not draw it completely, he drew it at least in a way which should thoroughly show his knowledge and feeling of it. For instance, you saw in the oak tree of the Giottesque period, that the main points of the tree, the true shape of leaf and acorn, were all there, perfectly and carefully articulated, and so they continued to be down to the time of Tintoret; both he and Titian working out the separate leaves of their foliage with the most exquisite botanical care. But now observe: as Christianity had brought this love of nature into Paganism, the return of Paganism in the shape of classical learning at once destroyed this love of nature; and at the moment when Claude and Salvator made the final effort to paint the *effects* of nature faithfully, the *objects* of nature had ceased to be regarded with affection; so that, while people were amused and interested by the new effects of sunsets over green seas, and of tempests bursting on rocky mountains, which were introduced by the rising school, they entirely ceased to require on the one side, or bestow on the other, that care and thought by which alone the beauty

---

[1] [See *Stones of Venice*; Vol. X. pp. 207–208, Vol. XI. pp. 225–226.]

of nature can be understood. The older painting had resembled a careful and deeply studied diagram, illustrative of the most important facts; it was not to be understood or relished without application of serious thought; on the contrary, it developed and addressed the highest powers of mind belonging to the human race; while the Claude and Salvator painting was like a scene in a theatre, viciously and falsely painted throughout, and presenting a deceptive appearance of truth to nature; understood, as far as it went, in a moment, but conveying no accurate knowledge of anything, and, in all its operations on the mind, unhealthy, hopeless, and profitless.

89. It was, however, received with avidity; for this main reason, that the architecture, domestic life, and manners of the period were gradually getting more and more artificial; as I showed you last evening [p. 62], all natural beauty had ceased to be permitted in architectural decoration, while the habits of society led them more and more to live, if possible, in cities; and the dress, language, and manners of men in general were approximating to that horrible and lifeless condition in which you find them just before the outbreak of the French Revolution.

Now, observe: exactly as hoops, and starch, and false hair, and all that in mind and heart these things typify and betray, as these, I say, gained upon men, there was a necessary reaction in favour of the *natural*. Men had never lived so utterly in defiance of the laws of nature before; but they could not do this without feeling a strange charm in that which they defied; and, accordingly, we find this reactionary sentiment expressing itself in a base school of what was called *pastoral* poetry; that is to say, poetry written in praise of the country, by men who lived in coffeehouses and on the Mall. The essence of pastoral poetry is the sense of strange delightfulness in grass, which is occasionally felt by a man who has seldom set his foot on it; it is essentially the poetry of the cockney, and for the most part corresponds in its aim and rank, as compared

with other literature, to the porcelain shepherds and shepherdesses on a chimney-piece as compared with great works
of sculpture.

90. Of course all good poetry, descriptive of rural life,
is essentially pastoral, or has the effect of the pastoral on
the minds of men living in cities; but the class of poetry
which I mean, and which you probably understand by the
term pastoral, is that in which a farmer's girl is spoken of
as a "nymph," and a farmer's boy as a "swain," and in
which, throughout, a ridiculous and unnatural refinement
is supposed to exist in rural life, merely because the poet
himself has neither had the courage to endure its hardships,
nor the wit to conceive its realities. If you examine the
literature of the 17th and 18th centuries you will find that
nearly all its expressions, having reference to the country,
show something of this kind; either a foolish sentimentality,
or a morbid fear, both of course coupled with the most
curious ignorance. You will find all its descriptive expressions at once vague and monotonous. Brooks are always
"purling"; birds always "warbling"; mountains always
"lift their horrid peaks above the clouds"; vales always
"are lost in the shadow of gloomy woods"; a few more
distinct ideas about haymaking and curds and cream, acquired in the neighbourhood of Richmond Bridge, serving to
give an occasional appearance of freshness to the catalogue
of the sublime and beautiful which descended from poet
to poet; while a few true pieces of pastoral, like the *Vicar
of Wakefield*, and Walton's *Angler*, relieved the general
waste of dulness. Even in these better productions, nothing is more remarkable than the general conception of
the country merely as a series of green fields, and the combined ignorance and dread of more sublime scenery; of
which the mysteries and dangers were enhanced by the difficulties of travelling at the period. Thus in Walton's *Angler*,
you have a meeting of two friends, one a Derbyshire man,
the other a lowland traveller, who is as much alarmed, and
uses nearly as many expressions of astonishment, at having

to go down a steep hill and ford a brook,[1] as a traveller uses now at crossing the glacier of the Col du Géant. I am not sure whether the difficulties which, until late years, have lain in the way of peaceful and convenient travelling, ought not to have great weight assigned to them among the other causes of the temper of the period; but be that as it may, if you will examine the whole range of its literature—keeping this point in view—I am well persuaded that you will be struck most forcibly by the strange deadness to the higher sources of landscape sublimity which is mingled with the morbid pastoralism. The love of fresh air and green grass forced itself upon the animal natures of men; but that of the sublimer features of scenery had no place in minds whose chief powers had been repressed by the formalisms of the age. And although in the second-rate writers continually, and in the first-rate ones occasionally, you find an affectation of interest in mountains, clouds, and forests, yet whenever they write from their heart, you will find an utter absence of feeling respecting anything beyond gardens and grass. Examine, for instance, the novels of Smollett, Fielding, and Sterne, the comedies of Molière, and the writings of Johnson and Addison, and I do not think you will find a single expression of true delight in sublime nature in any one of them. Perhaps Sterne's *Sentimental Journey*, in its total absence of sentiment on any subject but humanity, and its entire want of notice of anything at Geneva, which might not as well have been seen at Coxwold, is the most striking instance I could give you; and if you compare with this negation of feeling on one side, the interludes of Molière, in which shepherds and shepherdesses are introduced in court dress, you will have a very accurate conception of the general spirit of the age.[2]

---

[1] [See Part ii. ch. ii. For Ruskin's reading of the *Angler*, see Vol. I. p. 412.]
[2] [The MS. continues:—
    ". . . spirit of the age, as far as regards the poetical view of high nature. As respects science, little advance had been made since the time of Pliny, except in astronomy, which had no influence on landscape. Geology was

91. It was in such a state of society that the landscape of Claude, Gaspar Poussin, and Salvator Rosa attained its reputation.   It is the complete expression on canvas of the spirit of the time.   Claude embodies the foolish pastoralism, Salvator the ignorant terror, and Gaspar the dull and affected erudition.

It was, however, altogether impossible that this state of things could long continue.   The age which had buried itself in formalism grew weary at last of the restraint; and the approach of a new æra was marked by the appearance, and the enthusiastic reception, of writers who took true delight in those wild scenes of nature which had so long been despised.

92. I think the first two writers in whom the symptoms of a change are strongly manifested are Mrs. Radcliffe[1] and Rousseau;[2] in both of whom the love of natural scenery, though mingled in the one case with what was merely dramatic, and in the other with much that was pitifully morbid or vicious, was still itself genuine and intense, differing altogether in character from any sentiments previously traceable in literature.   And then rapidly followed a group of writers, who expressed, in various ways, the more powerful or more pure feeling which had now become one of the strongest instincts of the age.   Of these, the principal is

unknown, chemistry in its infancy, botany a mere catalogue of healing herbs, anatomy a catalogue of the muscles of the human frame, uncompared with those of animals.   Archæology was occupied wholly with the remains and the histories of Greece and Rome, and the glorious cathedrals and abbeys of Scotland, England, and France were abandoned to desecration and neglect, or used as quarries of building materials."
With § 90 should be compared *Modern Painters*, vol. iii., chs. xvi., xvii.   In his latest lecture on landscape, 1884 (reported in E. T. Cook's *Studies in Ruskin*, pp. 283–294, and included in a later volume of this edition), Ruskin illustrates his point from Evelyn's *Journal*, which is quoted also in *Præterita*, ii. §§ 2–3, 76.]

[1] [Ann Ward Radcliffe (1764–1823) published *A Sicilian Romance*, 1790; *The Romance of the Forest*, 1791; *The Mysteries of Udolpho*, 1794; and *The Italian*, 1797. It appears that she never saw the Italian scenery which she depicts, but she was devoted to English scenery, making a driving tour with her husband every other year; she was one of the first to celebrate the beauties of the English Lakes.   For other references to her place in the literary history of the romantic movement, see *Modern Painters*, vol. iii. ch. xvii. § 7.]

[2] [For Ruskin's view of Rousseau, see passages collected in Vol. IX. p. xxiii.]

your own Walter Scott.[1] Many writers, indeed, describe nature more minutely and more profoundly; but none show in higher intensity the peculiar passion for what is majestic or lovely in *wild* nature, to which I am now referring. The whole of the poem of the *Lady of the Lake* is written with almost a boyish enthusiasm for rocks, and lakes, and cataracts; the early novels show the same instinct in equal strength wherever he approaches Highland scenery; and the feeling is mingled, observe, with a most touching and affectionate appreciation of the Gothic architecture,[2] in which alone he found the elements of natural beauty seized by art; so that, to this day, his descriptions of Melrose and Holy Island Cathedral, in the *Lay of the Last Minstrel* and *Marmion*, as well as of the ideal abbeys in the *Monastery* and *Antiquary*, together with those of Caerlaverock and Lochleven Castles in *Guy Mannering* and *The Abbot*, remain the staple possessions and text-books of all travellers, not so much for their beauty or accuracy, as for their *exactly expressing that degree of feeling with which most men in this century can sympathise.*

Together with Scott appeared the group of poets—Byron, Wordsworth, Keats, Shelley, and, finally, Tennyson—differing widely in moral principles and spiritual temper, but all agreeing more or less in this love for natural scenery.

93. Now, you will ask me—and you will ask me most reasonably—how this love of nature in modern days can be connected with Christianity, seeing it is as strong in the infidel Shelley as in the sacred Wordsworth. Yes, and it is found in far worse men than Shelley.[3] Shelley was an honest unbeliever, and a man of warm affections; but this new love of nature is found in the most reckless and unprincipled of the French novelists—in Eugène Sue, in Dumas, in George Sand[4]—and that intensely. How is this? Simply

---

[1] [The landscape of Scott is discussed at greater length in *Modern Painters*, vol. iii. ch. xvi.]

[2] [See, however, *Seven Lamps of Architecture*, Preface to ed. 2, Vol. VIII. p. 9.]

[3] [For Ruskin's view of Shelley, see passages collected in Vol. I. p. 253 n.]

[4] [For other references to Eugène Sue, see *Modern Painters*, vol. iii. ch. xvii. §§ 7, 27; vol. iv. ch. xix. § 16; *Academy Notes*, 1857, No. 8; and a letter to Dr.

because the feeling is reactionary; and, in this phase of it, common to the diseased mind as well as to the healthy one. A man dying in the fever of intemperance will cry out for water, and that with a bitterer thirst than a man whose healthy frame naturally delights in the mountain spring more than in the wine cup. The water is not dishonoured by that thirst of the diseased, nor is nature dishonoured by the love of the unworthy. That love is, perhaps, the only saving element in their minds; and it still remains an indisputable truth that the love of nature is a characteristic of the Christian heart, just as the hunger for healthy food is characteristic of the healthy frame.

In order to meet this new feeling for nature, there necessarily arose a new school of landscape painting.[1] That school, like the literature to which it corresponded, had many weak and vicious elements mixed with its noble ones; it had its Mrs. Radcliffes and Rousseaus, as well as its Wordsworths; but, on the whole, the feeling with which Robson drew mountains, and Prout architecture, with which Fielding draws moors, and Stanfield sea—is altogether pure,

Furnivall of May 22, 1855 (given in the privately-printed *Letters from John Ruskin to F. J. Furnivall*, 1897, and reprinted in a later volume of this edition). In the same letter is a reference to Dumas, who is also mentioned in *Modern Painters*, vol. iii. ch. xvii. § 7, and vol. iv. ch. xix. § 16. For George Sand, see *ibid.*, vol. iii. ch. xvii. §§ 7, 27; the letter to Furnivall above cited; and *Fors Clavigera*, Letter 83.]

[1] [At this point Ruskin seems to have read some illustrative passages, for the MS. here inserts :—

"In order that you may have a perfectly clear idea of the distinction on which I have to insist, I will first read to you two passages, from two poets, both great poets, one of the pastoral time, the other of the present time—I mean Pope and Tennyson. I do not mean to disparage Pope : a greater man in many respects never lived, but he lived at the unnatural period; and while his descriptions of men are admirable, his descriptions of scenery are contemptible.

"Now, just the distinction which there is between this worthless description of Pope and the noble one of Tennyson, exists between the Claudesque landscape and the modern landscape. Observe, it is not the distinction between *all* Pope and *all* Tennyson, but between descriptive Pope and descriptive Tennyson. The description of Pope is utterly worthless, so is all landscape of the Claude and Poussin school. The description of Tennyson is always more or less noble, so is all landscape of the modern school."

The MS. does not indicate what passages Ruskin selected; the piece of Pope may have been the lines from his *Pastorals* quoted in *Modern Painters*, vol. iii. ch. xii. § 15. For Ruskin's appreciation of Tennyson's descriptive powers, see *Two Paths*, Appendix I.]

true, and precious, as compared with that which suggested the landscape of the seventeenth century.

94. Now observe, how simple the whole subject becomes. You have, first, your great ancient landscape divided into its three periods—Giottesque, Leonardesque, Titianesque. Then you have a great gap, full of nonentities and abortions; a gulf of foolishness, into the bottom of which you may throw Claude and Salvator, neither of them deserving to give a name to anything. Call it "pastoral" landscape, "guarda e passa,"[1] and then you have, lastly, the pure, wholesome, simple, modern landscape. You want a name for that: I will give you one in a moment; for the whole character and power of that landscape is originally based on the work of one man.

95. Joseph Mallord William Turner was born in Maiden Lane, London, about eighty years ago. The register of his birth was burned, and his age at his death could only be arrived at by conjecture.[2] He was the son of a barber; and his father intended him, very properly, for his own profession. The bent of the boy was, however, soon manifested, as is always the case in children of extraordinary genius, too strongly to be resisted; and a sketch of a coat of arms on a silver salver, made while his father was shaving a customer, obtained for him, in reluctant compliance with the admiring customer's advice,[3] the permission to follow art as a profession.

He had, of course, the usual difficulties of young artists to encounter, and they were then far greater than they are now. But Turner differed from most men in this,—that he was always willing to take anything to do that came in his way. He did not shut himself up in a garret to produce

---

[1] [Dante, *Inferno*, iii. 51. Ruskin quotes the words again in *Cestus of Aglaia*, § 80, and *Præterita*, i. § 254.]

[2] [Subsequent research, however, brought the register and other confirmatory facts to light: see Thornbury's *Life*, pp. 2, 3. Turner was born on April 23 (St. George's Day), 1775, and died on December 19, 1851. The date of his birth was wrongly implied upon the coffin as 1772 ("aged 79"; really aged 76).]

[3] [Mr. Tomkinson, a silversmith: see Thornbury, p. 7.]

unsaleable works of "high art," and starve, or lose his senses.[1] He hired himself out every evening to wash in skies in Indian ink, on other people's drawings, as many as he could, at half-a-crown a-night, getting his supper into the bargain. "What could I have done better?" he said afterwards: "it was first-rate practice." Then he took to illustrating guide-books and almanacks, and anything that wanted cheap frontispieces. The Oxford Almanack, published on a single sheet, with a copper-plate at the top of it, consisting of a "View"—you perhaps, some of you, know the kind of print characteristic of the last century, under which the word "View" is always printed in large letters, with a dedication, obsequious to the very dust, to the Grand Signior of the neighbourhood — well, this Almanack had always such a view of some Oxford College at the top of it, dedicated, I think, always to the head of the College; and it owed this, its principal decoration, to Turner for many years. I have myself two careful drawings of some old seals, made by him for a local book on the antiquities of Whalley Abbey.[2] And there was hardly a gentleman's seat of any importance in England, towards the close of the last century, of which you will not find some rude engraving in the local publications of the time, inscribed with the simple name " W. Turner."[3]

96. There was another great difference between Turner and other men. In doing these drawings for the commonest publications of the day, and for a remuneration altogether contemptible, he never did his work badly because he thought it beneath him, or because he was ill-paid. There does not exist such a thing as a slovenly drawing by Turner. With what people were willing to give him for his work he was content; but he considered that work in its relation to himself, not in its relation to the purchaser. He took

[1] [A reference to Haydon, for whom, see below, pp. 129, 307.]
[2] [T. D. Whitaker's *Parish of Whalley*, 1801. The book contains seven plates by Turner. Ruskin gave the drawings of the seals to Cambridge.]
[3] [Of drawings of "gentlemen's seats" done very early in Turner's career, there are examples in the National Gallery collection; see especially one of Nuneham (No. 852).]

a poor price, that he might *live;* but he made noble drawings, that he might *learn.* Of course some are slighter than
others, and they vary in their materials; those executed
with pencil and Indian ink being never finished to the
degree of those which are executed in colour. But he is
never careless. According to the time and means at his
disposal, he always did his best. He never let a drawing
leave his hands without having made a step in advance,
and having done better in it than he had ever done before;
and there is no important drawing of the period which is
not executed with a *total* disregard of time and price, and
which was not, even then, worth four or five times what
Turner received for it.

Even without genius, a man who thus felt and thus
laboured was sure to do great things; though it is seldom
that, without great genius, men either thus feel or thus
labour. Turner was as far beyond all other men in intellect
as in industry; and his advance in power and grasp of
thought was as steady as the increasing light of sunrise.

97. His reputation was soon so far established that he
was able to devote himself to more consistent study. He
never appears literally to have *copied* any picture; but whenever any master interested him, or was of so established a
reputation that he thought it necessary to study him, he
painted pictures of his own subjects in the style of that
master, until he felt himself able to rival his excellencies,
whatever they were. There are thus multitudes of pictures
by Turner which are direct imitations of other masters;
especially of Claude, Wilson, Loutherbourg, Gaspar Poussin,
Vandevelde, Cuyp, and Rembrandt. It has been argued by
Mr. Leslie[1] that, because Turner thus in his early years
imitated many of the old masters, therefore he must to the
end of his life have considered them greater than himself.
The *non sequitur* is obvious. I trust there are few men
so unhappy as never to have learned anything from their

---

[1] [Probably in some anonymous article, or lecture delivered at the time, by C. R.
Leslie, R.A., then Professor of Painting at the Academy. The remark does not occur
in his subsequently published notices of Turner.]

inferiors; and I fear there are few men so wise as never to have imitated anything but what was deserving of imitation. The young Turner, indeed, would have been more than mortal if, in a period utterly devoid of all healthy examples of landscape art, he had been able at once to see his way to the attainment of his ultimate ends; or if, seeing it, he had felt himself at once strong enough to defy the authority of every painter and connoisseur whose style had formed the taste of the public, or whose dicta directed their patronage.

98. But the period when he both felt and resolved to assert his own superiority was indicated with perfect clearness, by his publishing a series of engravings, which were nothing else than direct challenges to Claude—then the landscape painter supposed to be the greatest in the world —upon his own ground and his own terms. You are probably all aware that the studies made by Claude for his pictures, and kept by him under the name of the *Liber Veritatis*, were for the most part made with pen and ink, washed over with a brown tint; and that these drawings have been carefully fac-similed and published in the form of mezzotint engravings, long supposed to be models of taste in landscape composition. In order to provoke comparison between Claude and himself, Turner published a series of engravings, called the *Liber Studiorum*, executed in exactly the same manner as these drawings of Claude,— an etching representing what was done with the pen, while mezzotint stood for colour. You see the notable publicity of this challenge. Had he confined himself to *pictures* in his trial of skill with Claude, it would only have been in the gallery or the palace that the comparison could have been instituted; but now it is in the power of all who are interested in the matter to make it at their ease.*

.   .   .   .

* When this Lecture was delivered, an enlarged copy of a portion of one of these studies by Claude was set beside a similarly magnified portion of one by Turner. It was impossible, without much increasing the cost of the

XIII

Trees as drawn by Claude and by Turner

99. Now, what Turner did in contest with Claude, he did with every other then-known master of landscape, each in his turn. He challenged, and vanquished, each in his own peculiar field, Vandevelde on the sea, Salvator among rocks, and Cuyp on Lowland rivers; and, having done this, set himself to paint the natural scenery of skies, mountains, and lakes, which, until his time, had never been so much as attempted.

He thus, in the extent of his sphere, far surpassed even Titian and Leonardo, the great men of the earlier schools. In their foreground work neither Titian nor Leonardo *could* be excelled; but Titian and Leonardo were thoroughly conventional in all *but* their foregrounds. Turner was equally great in all the elements of landscape, and it is on him, and on his daring additions to the received schemes of landscape art, that all modern landscape has been founded. You will never meet any truly great living landscape painter who will not at once frankly confess his obligations to Turner, not, observe, as having copied him, but as having been led by Turner to look in nature for what he would otherwise either not have discerned, or discerning, not have dared to represent.

100. Turner, therefore, was the first man who presented us with the *type* of perfect landscape art: and the richness

publication, to prepare two mezzotint engravings with the care requisite for this purpose; and the portion of the Lecture relating to these examples is therefore omitted. It is, however, in the power of every reader to procure one or more plates of each series; and to judge for himself whether the conclusion of Turner's superiority, which is assumed in the next sentence of the text, be a just one or not.[1]

[1] [The two drawings prepared by Ruskin are here reproduced by photogravure (Plate XIII.). The MS. of the omitted portion of the lecture is, however, imperfect; he began writing a few notes, and then decided, it would seem, to extemporise his remarks, suggested by a comparison of the two drawings. They are enlargements of some of the foliage from Claude's *Liber Veritatis* (No. 140, vol. ii., " Angel Comforting Hagar "), and Turner's *Liber Studiorum* (No. 83 : " Stork and Aqueduct ") respectively. He exhibited the two plates at the same time, "in order that you may be sure I have copied them fairly." " You ask me," he said, "is this a fair specimen of Claude? Yes, perfectly. Claude is indeed often more graceful;" but, he seems to have continued, he is never more truthful. Then followed a comparison of the two drawings in that respect—a comparison, we may suppose, such as is worked out in *Modern Painters*, vol. iii. ch. ix., where fig. 7 in Plate 2 is taken from the same piece of Claude.]

of that art, with which you are at present surrounded, and which enables you to open your walls as it were into so many windows,[1] through which you can see whatever has charmed you in the fairest scenery of your country, you will do well to remember as *Turneresque.*

So then you have these five periods to recollect—you will have no difficulty, I trust, in doing so,—the periods of Giotto, Leonardo, Titian, pastoralism, and Turner.

101. But Turner's work is yet only begun. His greatness is, as yet, altogether denied by many; and to the full, felt by very few. But every day that he lies in his grave will bring some new acknowledgment of his power; and through those eyes, now filled with dust, generations yet unborn will learn to behold the light of nature.

You have some ground to-night to accuse me of dogmatism. I can bring no proof before you of what I so boldly assert. But I would not have accepted your invitation to address you, unless I had felt that I had a right to be, in this matter, dogmatic. I did not come here to tell you of my beliefs or my conjectures; I came to tell you the truth which I have given fifteen years of my life[2] to ascertain, that this man, this Turner, of whom you have known so little while he was living among you, will one day take his place beside Shakspeare[3] and Verulam, in the annals of the light of England.

Yes: beside Shakspeare and Verulam, a third star in that central constellation, round which, in the astronomy of intellect, all other stars make their circuit. By Shakspeare, humanity was unsealed to you; by Verulam the *principles* of nature; and by Turner, her *aspect.*[4] All these were sent to unlock one of the gates of light, and to

---

[1] [For pictures as windows, see *Modern Painters,* vol. iii. ch. x.]

[2] [Or even longer, the first essay in defence of Turner (Vol. III. p. 635) dating back to 1836.]

[3] [So in a letter of 1843 Ruskin spoke of "seeing the name of Turner placed on the same impregnable height with that of Shakspeare": see Vol. III. p. 653.]

[4] [See *Modern Painters,* vol. iii. ch. xvii. § 43, where Ruskin explains the comparison with Bacon on the ground that Turner was a master in the science of aspect, as Bacon in that of essence.]

Turner — of whom you have ~~heard~~ known so little while he
was living among you, will one day take his place
beside Shakespeare & Verulam, in the annals of the
~~the~~ light of England.

Yes. beside Shakespeare & Verulam. a third
star in that central constellation, round which, in
the astronomy of intellect — all other stars make their
circuit. ~~Shakespeare is the [illegible]~~ By Shakespeare
humanity was unsealed to you — by Verulam ~~the~~
~~the~~ ~~science~~ the principles of nature — & by Turner ~~[illegible]~~ her
aspect. All these were sent to unlock ~~of~~ ~~the~~ a

FACSIMILE OF A PAGE OF THE MS. OF "LECTURES ON ARCHITECTURE AND PAINTING" (Lecture III., § 101)

pp. 128–129

unlock it for the first time. But of all the three, though not the greatest, Turner was the most unprecedented in his work. Bacon did what Aristotle had attempted; Shakspeare did perfectly what Æschylus did partially; but none before Turner had lifted the veil from the face of nature; the majesty of the hills and forests had received no interpretation, and the clouds passed unrecorded from the face of the heaven which they adorned, and of the earth to which they ministered.

102. And now let me tell you something of his personal character. You have heard him spoken of as ill-natured, and jealous of his brother artists. I will tell you how jealous he was. I knew him for ten years, and during that time had much familiar intercourse with him. I *never once* heard him say an unkind thing of a brother artist, and *I never once heard him find a fault* with another man's work.[1] I could say this of *no other* artist whom I have ever known.

But I will add a piece of evidence on this matter of peculiar force. Probably many here have read a book which has been lately published, to my mind one of extreme interest and value, the life of the unhappy artist, Benjamin Haydon.[2] Whatever may have been his faults, I believe no person can read his journal without coming to the conclusion that his heart was honest, and that he does not *wilfully* misrepresent any fact, or any person. Even supposing otherwise, the expression I am going to quote to you would have all the more force, because, as you know, Haydon passed his whole life in war with the Royal Academy, of which Turner was one of the most influential members. Yet in the midst of one of his most violent

---

[1] [Ruskin repeats this testimony in *Modern Painters*, vol. v. pt. ix. ch. xii. § 4 *n.* ; It is confirmed by the reminiscences of many of his contemporaries which have since seen the light. W. P. Frith, R.A., mentions instances of Turner's appreciation of the work of young artists, and adds, "The severest criticism Turner was ever heard to make was upon a landscape of a brother Academician, whose works sometimes showed signs of weakness. Turner joined a group who were discussing a certain picture's shortcomings, and after hearing much unpleasant remark from which he dissented, he was forced to confess that a very bad passage, to which the malcontents drew his attention, ' *was a poor bit*' " (*Autobiography*, 1887, i. 127).]

[2] [For other references to Haydon (1786–1846), see *Modern Painters*, vol. v. pt. viii. ch. iii. § 3 ; *Academy Notes*, 1858, No. 101 ; *Queen of the Air*, § 159.]

expressions of exultation at one of his victories over the Academy, he draws back suddenly with these words:— "But Turner behaved well, and did me justice."[1]

103. I will give you however besides, two plain facts illustrative of Turner's "jealousy."

You have, perhaps not many of you, heard of a painter of the name of Bird:[2] I do not myself know his works, but Turner saw some merit in them: and when Bird first sent a picture to the Academy, for exhibition, Turner was on the hanging committee. Bird's picture had great merit; but no place for it could be found. Turner pleaded hard for it. No, the thing was impossible. Turner sat down and looked at Bird's picture a long time; then insisted that a place must be found for it. He was still met by the assertion of impracticability. He said no more, but took down one of his own pictures, sent it out of the Academy, and hung Bird's in its place.

Match that, if you can, among the annals of hanging committees. But he could do nobler things than this.

104. When Turner's picture of Cologne was exhibited in the year 1826,[3] it was hung between two portraits, by

---

[1] [Haydon had attended the Academy schools, and his first picture, "Joseph and Mary," was well hung in 1806. His quarrel began in 1809, when he was offended by the position of "Dentatus." He attacked the Academy in the newspapers, started rival schools, and published a book on the pernicious effect of Academies on Art. The book referred to by Ruskin is Haydon's *Autobiography*, edited and completed by Tom Taylor, in three volumes, 1853. Ruskin seems to have relied on his memory, which was here at fault. It is not to Turner, but to Lawrence, that Haydon refers: "Lawrence did me justice like a man of spirit and honour" (vol. i. p. 179). In another passage, however, Haydon, in referring to one of his attacks on the Academy (when he had likened various Academicians to "vinegar cruets," "vipers," "magpies," etc.), adds: "Wilkie and Mulready were spared, and so was Turner" (vol. i. p. 357). In describing his efforts at a later date to be reconciled, and his visits to various Academicians with that object, Haydon does not mention Turner, but again praises Lawrence (vol. ii. pp. 138–149). It is possible, however, that Ruskin may have heard the saying given in the text from some friend of Haydon (*e.g.*, Prout, see below, p. 307), and have confused it in his recollection with the passage in the *Autobiography*. Turner, if generous in recognition of Haydon's talent, could never forget his disloyalty to his "alma mater." When Maclise called on him to tell him of Haydon's suicide (1846), his only words were "He stabbed his mother," repeated several times.]

[2] [Edward Bird (1762–1819), teacher of drawing at Bristol, and an exhibitor of *genre* pictures of homely subjects, was elected A.R.A. in 1812, and R.A. in 1815. A picture by him in the National Gallery collection (No. 323) is now in the Newport Gallery. The story was used by Thornbury in his *Life of Turner*, ed. 1877, p. 272.]

[3] [The full title of the picture was "Cologne: The Arrival of a Packet Boat.

Sir Thomas Lawrence, of Lady Wallscourt and Lady Robert Manners.

The sky of Turner's picture was exceedingly bright, and it had a most injurious effect on the colour of the two portraits. Lawrence naturally felt mortified, and complained openly of the position of his pictures. You are aware that artists were at that time permitted to retouch their pictures on the walls of the Academy. On the morning of the opening of the exhibition, at the private view, a friend of Turner's who had seen the Cologne in all its splendour, led a group of expectant critics up to the picture. He started back from it in consternation. The golden sky had changed to a dun colour. He ran up to Turner, who was in another part of the room. " Turner, *what* have you been doing to your picture ? " " Oh," muttered Turner, in a low voice, " poor Lawrence was so unhappy. It's only lamp-black. It'll all wash off after the exhibition ! " He had actually passed a wash of lamp-black in water - colour over the whole sky, and utterly spoiled his picture for the time, and so left it through the exhibition, lest it should hurt Lawrence's.

You may easily find instances of self - sacrifice where men have strong motives, and where large benefits are to be conferred by the effort, or general admiration obtained by it ; but of pure, unselfish, and perfect generosity, showing itself in a matter of minor interest, and when few could be aware of the sacrifice made, you will not easily find such another example as this.

Evening." It is now in the collection of Mr. John Naylor, of Leighton Hall, Shropshire. For another reference to it, see *Notes on the Turner Gallery at Marlborough House* (1856), under No. 516 (eds. 1–4). Ruskin heard this anecdote from Turner's close friend, George Jones, R.A., and recorded it in his diary (May 22, 1843) :—

> "Jones told me that Turner on one occasion washed his own picture all over with ivory black, utterly spoiling it, that it might not hurt two of Sir T. Lawrence's, and suffered it to remain so through the whole exhibition ; and that having in play painted a picture of the same size and subject as Jones's, and it having got a better place, did all in his power to get the pictures changed. It made me very happy to hear this."

He refers to the anecdote again in *Fors Clavigera* (Letter 26). Thornbury repeats it in his *Life of Turner* (p. 274, ed. 1877), where (p. 347) another anecdote about the picture will be found. Reminiscences of Turner on varnishing days are given in *Dilecta*, § 4.]

105. Thus much for his jealousy of his brother-artists. You have also heard much of his niggardliness in money transactions.   A great part of what you have heard is perfectly true, allowing for the exaggeration which always takes place in the accounts of an eccentric character.   But there are other parts of Turner's conduct of which you have never heard; and which, if truly reported, would set his niggardliness in a very different light.   Every person from whom Turner exacted a due shilling, proclaimed the exaction far and wide; but the persons to whom Turner gave hundreds of pounds were prevented, by their "delicacy," from reporting the kindness of their benefactor.   I may, however, perhaps, be permitted to acquaint you with one circumstance of this nature, creditable alike to both parties concerned.

At the death of a poor drawing master, Mr. Wells,* whom Turner had long known, he was deeply affected, and lent money to the widow until a large sum had accumulated.   She was both honest and grateful, and after a long period was happy enough to be able to return to her benefactor the whole sum she had received from him.   She waited on him with it; but Turner kept his hands in his pockets.   "Keep it," he said, "and send your children to school, and to church."   He said this in bitterness; he had himself been sent to neither.[1]

106. "Well, but," you will answer to me, "we have heard Turner all our lives stigmatised as brutal, and uncharitable, and selfish, and miserly.   How are we to understand these opposing statements?"

Easily.   I have told you truly what Turner was.   You have often heard what to most people he appeared to be.

* Not the Mr. Wells who taught drawing at Addiscombe.   It appears that Turner knew two persons of the same name, and in the same profession.   I am not permitted to name my authority for the anecdote; various egotistic "delicacies," even in this case, preventing useful truth from being clearly assured to the public.[2]

---

[1] [This anecdote also is repeated in Thornbury's *Life*, p. 289; where (ch. xxiii.) other cases in point are recorded.]

[2] [This note was inserted in ed. 2, in answer to a letter in the *Athenæum* of June 10, 1854, denying the anecdote, which had been supposed by the writer of the letter to refer to William Frederick Wells, of the Old Water-Colour Society.]

Imagine what it was for a man to live seventy years in this hard world, with the kindest heart, and the noblest intellect of his time, and never to meet with a single word or ray of sympathy, until he felt himself sinking into the grave. From the time he knew his true greatness all the world was turned against him: he held his own; but it could not be without roughness of bearing, and hardening of the temper, if not of the heart. No one understood him, no one trusted him, and every one cried out against him. Imagine, any of you, the effect upon your own minds, if every voice that you heard from the human beings around you were raised, year after year, through all your lives, only in condemnation of your efforts, and denial of your success. This may be borne, and borne easily, by men who have fixed religious principles, or supporting domestic ties. But Turner had no one to teach him in his youth,[1] and no one to love him in his old age. Respect and affection, if they came at all, came unbelieved, or came too late. Naturally irritable, though kind—naturally suspicious, though generous—the gold gradually became dim, and the most fine gold changed, or, if not changed, overcast and clouded. The deep heart was still beating, but it was beneath a dark and melancholy mail, between whose joints, however, sometimes the slightest arrows found entrance, and power of giving pain. He received no consolation in his last years, nor in his death. Cut off in great part from all society—first, by labour, and at last by sickness—hunted to his grave by the malignities of small critics, and the jealousies of hopeless rivalry, he died in the house of a stranger—one companion of his life, and one only, staying with him to the last. The window of his death-chamber was turned towards the west, and the *sun* shone upon his face in its setting, and rested there, as he expired.[2]

---

[1] [Compare *Modern Painters,* vol. iii. ch. xvii. § 3 *n.*]

[2] [When Turner died, Ruskin was at Venice. But his father sought out Turner's old housekeeper, Mrs. Danby, and from her doubtless learnt the particulars of his last hours, which passed into all the biographies of the painter. The house in which he died still stands at the western end of Cheyne Walk, Chelsea (No. 119). A sketch of the bedroom, showing the window to which he had himself wheeled within an hour of his death, is given opposite p. 359 of Thornbury's *Life* (ed. 1877).]

LECTURE IV

PRE-RAPHAELITISM[1]

Delivered November 18, 1853

107. THE subject on which I would desire to engage your attention this evening, is the nature and probable result of a certain schism which took place a few years ago among our British artists.

This schism, or rather the heresy which led to it, as you are probably aware, was introduced by a small number of very young men; and consists mainly in the assertion that the principles on which art has been taught for these three hundred years back are essentially wrong, and that the principles which ought to guide us are those which prevailed before the time of Raphael; in adopting which, therefore, as their guides, these young men, as a sort of bond of unity among themselves, took the unfortunate and somewhat ludicrous name of " Pre-Raphaelite Brethren."[2]

108. You must also be aware that this heresy has been opposed with all the influence and all the bitterness of art and criticism;[3] but that in spite of these the heresy has gained ground, and the pictures painted on these new principles have obtained a most extensive popularity. These circumstances are sufficiently singular, but their importance

---

[1] [Ruskin's Synopsis of the Lecture in the preliminary announcement was as follows :—

" Pre-Raphaelitism.

Character of Art before and after Raphael. Causes of Decline after Raphael's Time. State of Modern Historical Painting. Nature of the Reaction which is taking Place. Merits and Faults of the Works of HUNT and MILLAIS. Probable Effect of the Movement. Objects now Principally to be kept in View by the Modern Artist and his Patrons."]

[2] [For other references in this sense, see below, p. 321.]

[3] [For specimens, see above, p. xlv., and below, p. 319.]

is greater even than their singularity; and your time will certainly not be wasted in devoting an hour to an inquiry into the true nature of this movement.

I shall first, therefore, endeavour to state to you what the real difference is between the principles of art before and after Raphael's time, and then to ascertain, with you, how far these young men truly have understood the difference, and what may be hoped or feared from the effort they are making.

109. First, then, What is the real difference between the principles on which art has been pursued before and since Raphael? You must be aware, that the principal ground on which the Pre-Raphaelites have been attacked, is the charge that they wish to bring us back to a time of darkness and ignorance, when the principles of drawing, and of art in general, were comparatively unknown; and this attack, therefore, is entirely founded on the assumption that, although for some unaccountable reason we cannot at present produce artists altogether equal to Raphael, yet that we are on the whole in a state of greater illumination than, at all events, any artists who preceded Raphael; so that we consider ourselves entitled to look down upon them, and to say that, all things considered, they did some wonderful things for their time; but that, as for comparing the art of Giotto to that of Wilkie or Edwin Landseer, it would be perfectly ridiculous,—the one being a mere infant in his profession, and the others accomplished workmen.

Now, that this progress has in some things taken place is perfectly true; but it is true also that this progress is by no means the main thing to be noticed respecting ancient and modern art; that there are other circumstances, connected with the change from one to the other, immeasurably more important, and which, until very lately, have been altogether lost sight of.

110. The fact is, that modern art is not so much distinguished from old art by greater skill, as by a radical change in temper. The art of this day is not merely a more

knowing art than that of the thirteenth century,—it is altogether another art.   Between the two there is a great gulf, a distinction for ever ineffaceable.   The change from one to the other was not that of the child into the man, as we usually consider it; it was that of the chrysalis into the butterfly.   There was an entire change in the habits, food, method of existence, and heart of the whole creature. That we know more than thirteenth-century people is perfectly true; but that is not the essential difference between us and them.   We are different kind of creatures from them,—as different as moths are different from caterpillars; and different in a certain broad and vast sense, which I shall try this evening to explain and prove to you;— different not merely in this or that result of minor circumstances,—not as you are different from people who never saw a locomotive engine, or a Highlander of this century from a Highlander of 1745;—different in a far broader and mightier sense than that; in a sense so great and clear, that we are enabled to separate all the Christian nations and tongues of the early time from those of the latter time, and speak of them in one group as the kingdoms of the Middle Ages.   There is an infinite significance in that term, which I want you to dwell upon and work out; it is a term which we use in a dim consciousness of the truth, but without fully penetrating into that of which we are conscious.   I want to deepen and make clear to you this consciousness that the world has had essentially a Trinity of ages—the Classical Age, the Middle Age, the Modern Age; each of these embracing races and individuals of apparently enormous separation in kind, but united in the spirit of their age,—the Classical Age having its Egyptians and Ninevites, Greeks and Romans,—the Middle Age having its Goths and Franks, Lombards and Italians,—the Modern Age having its French and English, Spaniards and Germans; but all these distinctions being in each case subordinate to the mightier and broader distinction, between *Classicalism, Mediævalism,* and *Modernism.*

111. Now our object to-night is indeed only to inquire into a matter of art; but we cannot do so properly until we consider this art in its relation to the inner spirit of the age in which it exists; and by doing so we shall not only arrive at the most just conclusions respecting our present subject, but we shall obtain the means of arriving at just conclusions respecting many other things.

Now the division of time which the Pre-Raphaelites have adopted, in choosing Raphael as the man whose works mark the separation between Mediævalism and Modernism, is perfectly accurate. It has been accepted as such by all their opponents.

You have, then, the three periods: Classicalism, extending to the fall of the Roman empire; Mediævalism, extending from that fall to the close of the fifteenth century; and Modernism thenceforward to our days.

112. And in examining into the spirit of these three epochs, observe, I don't mean to compare their bad men,— I don't mean to take Tiberius as a type of Classicalism, nor Ezzelin[1] as a type of Mediævalism, nor Robespierre as a type of Modernism. Bad men are like each other in all epochs; and in the Roman, the Paduan, or the Parisian, sensuality and cruelty admit of little distinction in the manners of their manifestation. But among men comparatively virtuous, it is important to study the phases of character; and it is into these only that it is necessary for us to inquire. Consider therefore, first, the essential difference in character between three of the most devoted military heroes whom the three great epochs of the world have produced,—all three devoted to the service of their country, —all of them dying therein. I mean, Leonidas in the

---

[1] [Eccelino, or Ezzelino da Romano (1194–1259), fourth of that name, a famous Ghibelline chief, lord of Padua, Vicenza, and Verona, and a faithful servant of the Emperor Frederick II. His "merciless cruelty and callousness to human suffering brand him as an enemy to mankind," and Dante makes him one of those who expiate the sin of cruelty in the lake of blood in the seventh circle of hell (*Inferno*, xii.). Ruskin refers to him again in *Modern Painters*, vol. v. pt. ix. ch. vii. § 7; *Verona and its Rivers*, § 9; *Eagle's Nest*, § 35; *Val d'Arno*, § 96; and *Fors Clavigera*, Letters 84 and 93.]

Classical period,[1] St. Louis in the Mediæval period, and Lord Nelson in the Modern period.

Leonidas had the most rigid sense of duty, and died with the most perfect faith in the gods of his country, fulfilling the accepted prophecy of his death.   St. Louis had the most rigid sense of duty, and the most perfect faith in Christ.   Nelson had the most rigid sense of duty, and——

You must supply my pause with your charity.

Now you do not suppose that the main difference between Leonidas and Nelson lay in the modern inventions at the command of the one, as compared with the imperfect military instruments possessed by the other.   They were not essentially different in that the one fought with lances and the other with guns.   But they were essentially different in the whole tone of their religious belief.

113. By this instance you may be partially prepared for the bold statement I am going to make to you, as to the change which constitutes Modernism.   I said just now that it was like that of the worm to the butterfly.   But the changes which God causes in His lower creatures are almost always from worse to better, while the changes which God allows man to make in himself are very often quite the other way ; like Adam's new arrangement of his nature. And in saying that this last change was like that of a chrysalis, I meant only in the completeness of it, not in the tendency of it.   Instead of from the worm to the butterfly, it is very possible it may have been from the butterfly to the worm.

Have patience with me for a moment after I tell you what I believe it to have been, and give me a little time to justify my words.

---

[1] [For another reference to Leonidas, see above, § 31, and see also *Stones of Venice*, vol. i. (Vol. IX. p. 446); *Modern Painters*, vol. iii. ch. xiii. § 5 ; vol. v. pt. viii. ch. iii. § 4 ; *A Joy for Ever*, § 109 ; *Ethics of the Dust*, § 117 ; other minor references to passages where Ruskin similarly takes Leonidas as the type of classical heroism will be found in the General Index.   For St. Louis, see *Fors Clavigera*, Letter 3, and other references in General Index.   References to Nelson will be found in *Fors Clavigera*, Letters 25 and 66, and *Dilecta*, § 23.]

114. I say that Classicalism began, wherever civilisation began, with Pagan Faith. Mediævalism began, and continued, wherever civilisation began and continued to *confess* Christ. And, lastly, Modernism began and continues, wherever civilisation began and continues to *deny* Christ.

You are startled, but give me a moment to explain. What, you would say to me, do you mean to tell us that *we* deny Christ? we who are essentially modern in every one of our principles and feelings, and yet all of us professing believers in Christ, and we trust most of us true ones? I answer, So far as we are believers indeed, we are one with the faithful of all times,—one with the classical believer of Athens and Ephesus, and one with the mediæval believer of the banks of the Rhone and the valleys of the Monte Viso.[1] But so far as, in various strange ways, some in great and some in small things, we deny this belief, in so far we are essentially infected with this spirit, which I call Modernism.

115. For observe, the change of which I speak has nothing whatever to do with the Reformation, or with any of its effects. It is a far broader thing than the Reformation. It is a change which has taken place, not only in reformed England, and reformed Scotland; but in unreformed France, in unreformed Italy, in unreformed Austria. I class honest Protestants and honest Roman Catholics for the present together, under the general term Christians: if you object to their being so classed together, I pray your pardon, but allow me to do so at present, for the sake of perspicuity, if for nothing else; and so classing them, I say that a change took place, about the time of Raphael, in the spirit of Roman Catholics and Protestants both; and that change consisted in the *denial* of their religious belief, at least in the external and trivial affairs of life, and often in far more serious things.

---

[1] [Ruskin frequently refers in similar terms to the Protestant communities which had their centre at Geneva, and to those of the Vaudois valleys which may be described as lying beneath Monte Viso; see, for instance, for Geneva, *Time and Tide*, § 45, and *Præterita*, ii. § 84; and for the Vaudois valleys, *Præterita*, iii. § 23.]

116. For instance, hear this direction to an upholsterer of the early thirteenth century. Under the commands of the Sheriff of Wiltshire, he is thus ordered to make some alterations in a room for Henry the Third. He is to "wainscot the King's lower chamber, and to paint that wainscot of a green colour, and to put a border to it, and to cause the heads of kings and queens to be painted on the borders; and to paint on the walls of the King's upper chamber the story of St. Margaret, Virgin, and the four Evangelists, and to paint the wainscot of the same chamber of a green colour, spotted with gold." *

Again, the Sheriff of Wiltshire is ordered to "put two small glass windows in the chamber of Edward the King's son ; and put a glass window in the chamber of our Queen at Clarendon; and in the same window cause to be painted a Mary with her Child, and at the feet of the said Mary, a queen with clasped hands."

Again, the Sheriff of Southampton is ordered to "paint the tablet beside the King's bed, with the figures of the guards of the bed of Solomon, and to glaze with white glass the windows in the King's great Hall at Northampton, and cause the history of Lazarus and Dives to be painted in the same."

117. And so on; I need not multiply instances. You see that in all these cases, the furniture of the King's house is made to confess his Christianity.[1] It may be imperfect and impure Christianity, but such as it might be, it was all that men had then to live and die by; and you see there was not a pane of glass in their windows, nor a pallet by their bedside that did not confess and proclaim it. Now, when you go home to your own rooms, supposing them to

---

* Liberate Rolls, preserved in the Tower of London, and quoted by Mr. Turner in his History of the Domestic Architecture of England.[2]

---

[1] [Compare *Stones of Venice*, vol. ii. ch. iv. § 53.]
[2] [For the full title of this work, see above, note on p. 19 ; the quotation here is from p. 211 of the book.]

be richly decorated at all, examine what that decoration consists of. You will find Cupids, Graces, Floras, Dianas, Jupiters, Junos. But you will not find, except in the form of an engraving, bought principally for its artistic beauty, either Christ, or the Virgin, or Lazarus and Dives. And if a thousand years hence, any curious investigator were to dig up the ruins of Edinburgh, and not know your history, he would think you had all been born heathens. Now that, so far as it goes, is denying Christ; it is pure Modernism.

" No," you will answer me, " you misunderstand and calumniate us. We do not, indeed, choose to have Dives and Lazarus on our windows; but that is not because we are moderns, but because we are Protestants, and do not like religious imagery." Pardon me: that is not the reason. Go into any fashionable lady's boudoir in Paris, and see if you will find Dives and Lazarus there. You will find, indeed, either that she has her private chapel, or that she has a crucifix in her dressing-room ; but for the general decoration of the house, it is all composed of Apollos and Muses, just as it is here.[1]

118. Again. What do you suppose was the substance of good education, the education of a knight, in the Middle Ages ? What was taught to a boy as soon as he was able to learn anything ? First, to keep under his body, and bring it into subjection and perfect strength; then to take Christ for his captain,[2] to live as always in His presence, and finally, to do his *devoir*—mark the word—to all men. Now consider, first, the difference in their influence over the

---

[1] [Compare *Stones of Venice*, vol. ii. (Vol. X. p. 325).]

[2] [The MS. inserts : " Do you recollect the words of Shakespeare of the Duke of Norfolk, then at Venice ? " the reference being to the Bishop of Carlisle's reply to Bolingbroke's declaration that Norfolk shall be repealed : " That honourable day shall ne'er be seen," for " banished Norfolk "

> "there at Venice gave
> His body to that pleasant country's earth,
> And his pure soul unto his captain Christ,
> Under whose colours he had fought so long."

(*Richard II.*, iv. 1.) *Cf.* Vol. IX. p. 420 *n.*, Vol. X. p. xxvii.]

armies of France, between the ancient word "devoir," and modern word " gloire." And, again, ask yourselves what you expect your own children to be taught at your great schools and universities. Is it Christian history, or the histories of Pan and Silenus? Your present education, to all intents and purposes, denies Christ, and that is intensely and peculiarly Modernism.

119. Or, again, what do you suppose was the proclaimed and understood principle of all Christian *governments* in the Middle Ages? I do not say it was a principle acted up to, or that the cunning and violence of wicked men had not too often their full sway then, as now; but on what principles were that cunning and violence, so far as was possible, restrained? By the *confessed* fear of God, and *confessed* authority of His law. You will find that all treaties, laws, transactions whatsoever, in the Middle Ages, are based on a confession of Christianity as the leading rule of life; that a text of Scripture is held, in all public assemblies, strong enough to be set against an appearance of expediency; and although, in the end, the expediency might triumph, yet it was never without a distinct allowance of Christian principle, as an efficient element in the consultation. Whatever error might be committed, at least Christ was openly confessed. Now what is the custom of your British Parliament in these days? You know that nothing would excite greater manifestations of contempt and disgust than the slightest attempt to introduce the authority of Scripture in a political consultation. That is denying Christ. It is intensely and peculiarly Modernism.

120. It would be easy to go on showing you this same thing in many more instances; but my business to-night is to show you its full effect in one thing only, namely, in art, and I must come straightway to that, as I have little enough time. This, then, is the great and broad fact which distinguishes modern art from old art; that all ancient art was *religious*, and all modern art is *profane*. Once more, your patience for an instant. I say, all ancient art was

religious; that is to say, religion was its first object; private luxury or pleasure its second. I say all modern art is profane; that is, private luxury or pleasure is its first object; religion its second. Now you all know, that anything which makes religion its second object, makes religion *no* object. God will put ˌup with a great many things in the human heart, but there is one thing He will *not* put up with in it—a second place. He who offers God a second place, offers Him no place. And there is another mighty truth which you all know, that he who makes religion his first object, makes it his whole object; he has no other work in the world than God's work. Therefore I do not say that ancient art was *more* religious than modern art. There is no question of degree in this matter. Ancient art was religious art; modern art is profane art; and between the two the distinction is as firm as between light and darkness.

121. Now, do not let what I say be encumbered in your minds with the objection, that you think art ought not to be brought into the service of religion. That is not the question at present—do not agitate it. The simple fact is, that old art *was* brought into that service, and received therein a peculiar form; that modern art *is not* brought into that service, and has received in consequence another form; that this is the great distinction between mediæval and modern art; and from that are clearly deducible all other essential differences between them. That is the point I wish to show you, and of that there can be no dispute. Whether or not Christianity be the purer for lacking the service of art, is disputable—and I do not mean now to begin the dispute; but that art is the *impurer* for not being in the service of Christianity, is indisputable, and that is the main point I have now to do with.[1]

---

[1] [The MS. here inserts :—

"Now just to show what I mean by arts not now being in the service of religion, take an instance in a little thing. When you go home, look in your libraries and drawing-rooms which books have for the most part the most magnificent bindings and printing. You will find them generally

122. Perhaps there are some of you here who would not allow that the religion of the thirteenth century was Christianity. Be it so; still is the statement true, which is all that is necessary for me now to prove, that art was great because it was devoted to such religion as then existed. Grant that Roman Catholicism was not Christianity —grant it, if you will, to be the same thing as old heathenism—and still I say to you, whatever it was, men lived and died by it, the ruling thought of all their thoughts; and just as classical art was greatest in building to its gods, so mediæval art was great in building to its gods, and modern art is not great, because it builds to *no* God. You have, for instance, in your Edinburgh Library, a Bible of the thirteenth century, the Latin Bible, commonly known as the Vulgate. It contains the Old and New Testaments, complete, besides the books of Maccabees, the Wisdom of Solomon, the books of Judith, Baruch, and Tobit. The whole is written in the most beautiful black-letter hand, and each book begins with an illuminated letter, containing three or four figures, illustrative of the book which it begins. Now, whether this were done in the service of true Christianity or not, the simple fact is, that here is a man's lifetime taken up in writing and ornamenting a Bible, as the sole end of his art; and that doing this, either in a book or on a wall, was the common artist's life at the time; that the constant Bible reading and Bible thinking which this work involved, made a man serious and thoughtful, and a good workman, because he was always expressing those feelings which, whether right or wrong, were the groundwork of his whole being. Now, about the year

annuals, books of ballads, story books, and so on. Then look for the books which have most plain bindings and printings. You find them your Psalm books.

"In the Middle Ages it was the exact reverse. Whatever luxuries a man denied himself, one thing about his house at least was splendid—his Psalter. Do not leave the question in hand, to tell me that you think Psalm books ought to have plain bindings, and plain printings. That is not the question. I do not inquire what effect this modern principle has upon Psalm singing. I only say it has a prejudicial effect upon book-binding."]

1500, this entire system was changed. Instead of the life of Christ, men had, for the most part, to paint the lives of Bacchus and Venus; and if you walk through any public gallery of pictures by the "great masters," as they are called, you will indeed find here and there what is called a Holy Family, painted for the sake of drawing pretty children, or a pretty woman; but for the most part you will find nothing but Floras, Pomonas, Satyrs, Graces, Bacchanals, and Banditti. Now, you will not declare—you cannot believe—that Angelico painting the life of Christ, Benozzo painting the life of Abraham, Ghirlandajo painting the life of the Virgin, Giotto painting the life of St. Francis,[1] were worse employed, or likely to produce a less healthy art, than Titian painting the loves of Venus and Adonis, than Correggio painting the naked Antiope, than Salvator painting the slaughters of the Thirty Years' War?[2] If you will not let me call the one kind of labour Christian, and the other unchristian, at least you will let me call the one moral, and the other immoral, and that is all I ask you to admit.

123. Now observe, hitherto I have been telling you what you may feel inclined to doubt or dispute; and I must leave you to consider the subject at your leisure. But henceforward I tell you plain facts, which admit neither of doubt nor dispute by any one who will take the pains to acquaint himself with their subject-matter.

When the entire purpose of art was moral teaching, it naturally took truth for its first object, and beauty, and the pleasure resulting from beauty, only for its second. But when it lost all purpose of moral teaching, it as naturally took beauty for its first object, and truth for its second.

---

[1] [For Angelico's series of frescoes illustrating the Life of Christ, see Vol. IV. p. 100; for Benozzo Gozzoli's Life of Abraham, *ibid.*, pp. xxxi., 316; Ghirlandajo's Life of the Virgin is the series of frescoes in S. Maria Novella (see *Mornings in Florence*, ch. ii.); for Giotto's Life of St. Francis (at Assisi), see numerous references in *Fors Clavigera*, *e.g.*, Letters 41, 45, and 48.]

[2] [One of Titian's many pictures of Venus and Adonis is in the National Gallery, No. 34; to Correggio's "Antiope" (in the Louvre) Ruskin refers below, p. 472, and in *Modern Painters*, vol. iii. ch. v. § 4; vol. v. pt. vi. ch. v. § 5, ch. x. § 5, pt. vii. ch. iv. § 6 *n.*; for Salvator's battle-pieces, see *Modern Painters*, vol. ii. (Vol. IV. p. 201 and *n.*).]

That is to say, in all they did, the old artists endeavoured, in one way or another, to express the real facts
of the subject or event, this being their chief business:
and the question they first asked themselves was always,
how would this thing, or that, actually have occurred?
what would this person, or that, have done under the
circumstances? and then, having formed their conception,
they work it out with only a secondary regard to grace
or beauty, while a modern painter invariably thinks of the
grace and beauty of his work first, and unites afterwards
as much truth as he can with its conventional graces. I
will give you a single strong instance to make my meaning plainer. In Orcagna's great fresco of the Triumph of
Death, one of the incidents is that three kings,* when
out hunting, are met by a spirit, which, desiring them to
follow it, leads them to a churchyard, and points out to
them, in open coffins, three bodies of kings such as themselves, in the last stages of corruption. Now a modern
artist, representing this, would have endeavoured dimly and
faintly to suggest the appearance of the dead bodies, and

---

* This incident is not of Orcagna's invention, it is variously represented
in much earlier art.   There is a curious and graphic drawing of it, *circa*
1300, in the MS. Arundel 83, Brit. Mus.,[1] in which the three dead persons
are walking, and are met by three queens, who severally utter the sentences,

> "Ich am aferd."
> "Lo, whet ich se?"
> "Me thinketh hit beth develes thre."

To which the dead bodies answer—

> "Ich wes wel fair."
> "Such scheltou be."
> "For Godes love, be wer by me."

It is curious, that though the dresses of the living persons, and the "I
was well fair" of the first dead speaker, seem to mark them distinctly to
be women, some longer legends below are headed "primus *rex* mortuus," etc.

---

[1] [In his notes on the British Museum's collection of illuminated MSS., Ruskin
says of this: "Glorious one, full of odd divinity and quaint lines, especially near
the end," and mentions it as among the three or four which "would be my choice
out of the whole library."   For other references to Orcagna's "Triumph of Death,"
see below (in the Review of Lord Lindsay), p. 224; and *Modern Painters*, vol. iii. ch. iv.
§ 20, ch. viii. § 6.]

would have made, or attempted to make, the countenances of the three kings variously and solemnly expressive of thought. This would be in his, or our, view, a poetical and tasteful treatment of the subject. But Orcagna disdains both poetry and taste; he wants the *facts* only; he wishes to give the spectator the same lesson that the kings had; and therefore, instead of concealing the dead bodies, he paints them with the most fearful detail. And then, he does not consider what the three kings might most gracefully do. He considers only what they actually in all probability *would have done.* He makes them looking at the coffins with a startled stare, and one holding his nose. This is an extreme instance; but you are not to suppose it is because Orcagna had naturally a coarse or prosaic mind. Where he felt that thoughtfulness and beauty could properly be introduced, as in his circles of saints and prophets, no painter of the Middle Ages is so grand. I can give you no better proof of this, than the one fact that Michael Angelo borrowed from him openly—borrowed from him in the principal work which he ever executed, the Last Judgment, and borrowed from him the principal figure in that work.[1] But it is just because Orcagna was so firmly and unscrupulously true, that he had the power of being so great when he chose. His arrow went straight to the mark. It was not that he did not love beauty, but he loved truth first.

124. So it was with all the men of that time. No painters ever had more power of conceiving graceful form, or more profound devotion to the beautiful; but all these gifts and affections are kept sternly subordinate to their moral purpose; and, so far as their powers and knowledge went, they either painted from nature things as they were, or from imagination things as they must have been.

---

[1] [Ruskin describes Orcagna's "Last Judgment," comparing it with Michael Angelo's, in a passage from his diary of 1845, given in Vol. IV. p. 275 *n.*, with which passage should be compared the later discussion of the same matter in *Val d'Arno,* § 256.]

I do not mean that they reached any imitative resemblance to nature. They had neither skill to do it, nor care to do it. Their art was conventional and imperfect, but they considered it only as a language wherein to convey the knowledge of certain facts; it was perfect enough fo. that; and though always reaching on to greater attainments, they never suffered their imperfections to disturb and check them in their immediate purposes. And this mode of treating all subjects was persisted in by the greatest men until the close of the fifteenth century.

125. Now so justly have the Pre - Raphaelites chosen their time and name, that the great change which clouds the career of mediæval art was effected, not only in Raphael's time, but by Raphael's own practice, and by his practice in *the very centre of his available life*.

You remember, doubtless, what high ground we have for placing the beginning of human intellectual strength at about the age of twelve years.* Assume, therefore, this period for the beginning of Raphael's strength. He died at thirty-seven. And in his twenty-fifth year, one half-year only past the precise centre of his available life, he was sent for to Rome, to decorate the Vatican for Pope Julius II., and having until that time worked exclusively in the ancient and stern mediæval manner, he, in the first chamber which he decorated in that palace, wrote upon its walls the *Mene, Tekel, Upharsin* of the Arts of Christianity.

And he wrote it thus: On one wall of that chamber he placed a picture of the World or Kingdom of *Theology*, presided over by *Christ*. And on the side wall of that same chamber he placed the World or Kingdom of *Poetry*, presided over by *Apollo*. And from that spot, and from that hour, the intellect and the art of Italy date their degradation.[1]

* Luke ii. 42, 49.

---

[1] [Compare § 14 of the lecture "Mending the Sieve" in a later volume. The reference is of course to the Stanza del Segnatura, completed by Raphael (d. 1520) in 1511, after three years' labour. On one wall is depicted Theology and the

126. Observe, however, the significance of this fact is not in the mere use of the figure of the heathen god to indicate the domain of poetry. Such a symbolical use had been made of the figures of heathen deities in the best times of Christian art. But it is in the fact, that being called to Rome especially to adorn the palace of the so-called head of the Church, and called as the chief representative of the Christian artists of his time, Raphael had neither religion nor originality enough to trace the spirit of poetry and the spirit of philosophy to the inspiration of the true God, as well as that of theology; but that, on the contrary, *he elevated the creations of fancy on the one wall, to the same rank as the objects of faith upon the other;* that in deliberate, balanced opposition to the Rock of the Mount Zion, he reared the rock of Parnassus, and the rock of the Acropolis; that, among the masters of poetry we find him enthroning Petrarch and Pindar, but not Isaiah nor David, and for lords over the domain of philosophy we find the masters of the school of Athens, but neither of those greater masters [1] by the last of whom that school was rebuked, — those who received their wisdom from heaven

so-called "Dispute on the Sacrament" (more correctly, "The Triumph of Faith"); on another, Mount Parnassus, with Apollo and the Muses; and on a third, representing Philosophy, "The School of Athens." Ruskin refers again to these works, and in the same sense, in *Stones of Venice*, vol. iii. ch. ii. ("Roman Renaissance") § 102 (Vol. XI. p. 130.) In later years, however, he presented the matter in a different light; "Raphael," he says, "painting the Parnassus and the Theology on equal walls of the same chamber of the Vatican, so wrote, under the Throne of the Apostolic power, the harmony of the angelic teaching from the rocks of Sinai and Delphi" (*Preface* to *The Economist of Xenophon*, "Bibliotheca Pastorum," Vol. I., 1876, p. xxiii.). In a note to the passage just quoted, Ruskin corrects his former teaching on this matter. "I imagined at that time," he says, "it had been the honour given to classical tradition which had destroyed the schools of Italy. But it was, on the contrary, the disbelief of it. She fell, not by reverence for the Gods of the Heathen, but by infidelity alike to them, and to her own."]

[1] [Namely, Solomon: "In Gibeon the Lord appeared to Solomon in a dream by night, and God said, Ask what shall I give thee. And Solomon said, . . . Give therefore thy servant an understanding heart. . . . And God said unto him, . . . Behold I have given thee a wise and an understanding heart; so that there was none like thee before thee, neither after thee shall any arise like unto thee" (1 Kings iii. 5), and St. Paul, upon whom as he journeyed near Damascus, "suddenly there shined round about him a light from heaven"; and who standing "in the midst of Mars' Hill said, Ye men of Athens, I perceive that in all things ye are too superstitious" (Acts ix. 3, xvii. 15–23.]

itself, in the vision of Gibeon,* and the lightning of Damascus.

127. The doom of the arts of Europe went forth from that chamber, and it was brought about in great part by the very excellencies of the man who had thus marked the commencement of decline. The perfection of execution and the beauty of feature which were attained in his works, and in those of his great contemporaries, rendered finish of execution and beauty of form the chief objects of all artists ; and thenceforward execution was looked for rather than thought, and beauty rather than veracity.

And as I told you, these are the two secondary causes of the decline of art ; the first being the loss of moral purpose. Pray note them clearly. In mediæval art, thought is the first thing, execution the second ; in modern art execution is the first thing, and thought the second. And again, in mediæval art, truth is first, beauty second ; in modern art, beauty is first, truth second. The mediæval principles led *up* to Raphael, and the modern principles lead *down* from him.

128. Now, first, let me give you a familiar illustration of the difference with respect to execution. Suppose you have to teach two children drawing, one thoroughly clever and active-minded, the other dull and slow ; and you put before them Julien's chalk studies[1] of heads—*études à deux crayons*—and desire them to be copied. The dull child will slowly do your bidding, blacken his paper and rub it white again, and patiently and painfully, in the course of three or four years, attain to the performance of a chalk head, not much worse than his original, but still of less value than the paper it is drawn upon. But the clever child will

---

* 1 Kings iii. 5.

---

[1] [The reference is to the following drawing-books by Julien : *Études d'après l'Antique. Collection des Modèles gradués, depuis les Premier Éléments jusq'aux Figures Académiques pour l'Enseignement du Dessin dans les Lycées* (Paris, n.d.); *Studies of Heads from Paintings of Eminent Artists, or Drawn from Nature* (London, n.d.).]

not, or will only by force, consent to this discipline. He finds other means of expressing himself with his pencil somehow or another; and presently you find his paper covered with sketches of his grandfather and grandmother, and uncles, and cousins,—sketches of the room, and the house, and the cat, and the dog, and the country outside, and everything in the world he can set his eyes on; and he gets on, and even his child's work has a value in it—a truth which makes it worth keeping; no one knows how precious, perhaps, that portrait of his grandfather may be, if any one has but the sense to keep it till the time when the old man can be seen no more up the lawn, nor by the wood. That child is working in the Middle-Age spirit— the other in the modern spirit.

129. But there is something still more striking in the evils which have resulted from the modern regardlessness of truth. Consider, for instance, its effect on what is called historical painting. What do you at present *mean* by historical painting? Now-a-days it means the endeavouring, by the power of imagination, to portray some historical event of past days. But in the Middle Ages, it meant representing the acts of *their own* days; and that is the only historical painting worth a straw.[1] Of all the wastes of time and sense which Modernism has invented—and they are many—none are so ridiculous as this endeavour to represent past history. What do you suppose our descendants will care for our imaginations of the events of former days? Suppose the Greeks, instead of representing their own warriors as they fought at Marathon,[2] had left us nothing but their imaginations of Egyptian battles; and suppose the Italians, in like manner, instead of portraits of Can Grande and Dante, or of Leo the Tenth and Raphael, had left us nothing but imaginary portraits of Pericles and

---

[1] [Compare *Modern Painters*, vol. iii. ch. iii. § 21; ch. vii. § 21.]
[2] [The reference here is generally to Greek reliefs, but more particularly perhaps to the Stelè of Aristion by Aristocles, known as "The Soldier of Marathon." Casts of the original Gravestone of Aristion (in the National Museum at Athens) are in most collections.]

Miltiades? What fools we should have thought them! how bitterly we should have been provoked with their folly! And that is precisely what our descendants will feel towards us, so far as our grand historical and classical schools are concerned. What do we care, they will say, what those nineteenth-century people fancied about Greek and Roman history! If they had left us a few plain and rational sculptures and pictures of their own battles, and their own men, in their everyday dress, we should have thanked them. "Well, but," you will say, "we *have* left them portraits of our great men, and paintings of our great battles." Yes, you have indeed, and that is the only historical painting that you either have, or can have; but you don't *call* that historical painting. You don't thank the men who do it; you look down upon them and dissuade them from it, and tell them they don't belong to the grand schools. And yet they are the only true historical painters, and the only men who will produce any effect on their own generation, or on any other. Wilkie was a historical painter, Chantrey a historical sculptor, because they painted, or carved, the veritable things and men they saw, not men and things as they believed they might have been, or should have been. But no one tells such men they are historical painters, and they are discontented with what they do; and poor Wilkie must needs travel to see the grand school, and imitate the grand school, and ruin himself.[1] And you have had multitudes of other painters ruined, from the beginning, by that grand school. There was Etty, naturally as good a painter as ever lived, but no one told him what to paint, and he studied the antique, and the grand schools, and painted

---

[1] [The two stages in Wilkie's art here described correspond with two in his life. Up to 1822 he had been known as a *genre* painter. In that year, however, he exhibited an "historical" picture, "The Preaching of John Knox" (No. 894 in the Tate Gallery). In 1825 he set out for three years' travel on the Continent (partly for the sake of his health), and it was the admiration he then conceived for the old masters that caused him henceforth to appear exclusively as an historical and portrait painter. For Ruskin's early appreciation of Chantrey, somewhat modified after 1845, see *Præterita*, ii. §§ 26, 113, and compare Vol. III. pp. 653, 654; Vol. IX. p. 289.]

dances of nymphs in red and yellow shawls to the end of his days.[1] Much good may they do you! He is gone to the grave, a lost mind. There was Flaxman, another naturally great man, with as true an eye for nature as Raphael, —he stumbles over the blocks of the antique statues— wanders in the dark valley of their ruins to the end of his days. He has left you a few outlines of muscular men straddling and frowning behind round shields. Much good may they do you! Another lost mind. And of those who are lost namelessly, who have not strength enough even to make themselves known, the poor pale students who lie buried for ever in the abysses of the great schools, no account can be rendered; they are numberless.

130. And the wonderful thing is, that of all these men whom you now have come to call the great masters, there was *not one* who confessedly did not paint his own present world, plainly and truly. Homer sang of what he saw; Phidias carved what he saw; Raphael painted the men of his own time in their own caps and mantles; and every man who has arisen to eminence in modern times has done so altogether by his working in their way, and doing the things he saw. How did Reynolds rise? Not by painting Greek women, but by painting the glorious little living Ladies this, and Ladies that, of his own time. How did Hogarth rise? Not by painting Athenian follies, but London follies. Who are the men who have made an impression upon you yourselves—upon your own age? I suppose the most popular painter of the day is Landseer. Do you suppose he studied dogs and eagles out of the Elgin Marbles? And yet in the very face of these plain, incontrovertible, all-visible facts, we go on from year to year with the base system of Academy teaching, in spite of which every one of these men has risen: I say *in spite* of the entire method and aim of our art-teaching. It destroys the greater number of its pupils altogether; it hinders and paralyses the greatest.

---

[1] [For Ruskin's view of Etty, see passages collected in Vol. III. p. 266 n.; and for Flaxman, *Seven Lamps*, Vol. VIII. p. 44, and *Elements of Drawing*, § 257 n.]

There is not a living painter whose eminence is not in spite of everything he has been taught from his youth upwards, and who, whatever his eminence may be, has not suffered much injury in the course of his victory.   For observe : this love of what is called ideality or beauty in preference to truth, operates not only in making us choose the past rather than the present for our subjects, but it makes us falsify the present when we do take it for our subject.   I said just now that portrait-painters were historical painters ; —so they are ; but not good ones, because not faithful ones.   The beginning and end of modern portraiture is adulation.   The painters cannot live but by flattery ; we should desert them if they spoke honestly.   And therefore we can have no good portraiture ; for in the striving after that which is *not* in their model, they lose the inner and deeper nobleness which *is* in their model.   I saw not long ago, for the first time, the portrait of a man whom I knew well—a young man, but a religious man—and one who had suffered much from sickness.   The whole dignity of his features and person depended upon the expression of serene, yet solemn, purpose sustaining a feeble frame ; and the painter, by way of flattering him, strengthened him, and made him athletic in body, gay in countenance, idle in gesture ; and the whole power and being of the man himself were lost.   And this is still more the case with our public portraits.   You have a portrait, for instance, of the Duke of Wellington at the end of the North Bridge—one of the thousand equestrian statues of Modernism—studied from the show-riders of the amphitheatre, with their horses on their hind-legs in the saw-dust.*   Do you suppose that was the way the Duke sat when your destinies depended on him ? when the foam hung from the lips of his tired horse, and its wet limbs

---

* I intended this last sentence of course to apply to the thousand statues, not definitely to the one in immediate question, which, though tainted with the modern affectation, and the nearest example of it to which I could refer an Edinburgh audience, is the work of a most promising sculptor ; and was indeed so far executed on the principles asserted in the text,

were dashed with the bloody slime of the battle-field, and he himself sat anxious in his quietness, grieved in his fearlessness, as he watched, scythe-stroke by scythe-stroke, the gathering in of the harvest of death? You would have done something had you thus left his image in the enduring iron, but nothing now.

131. But the time has at last come for all this to be put an end to; and nothing can well be more extraordinary than the way in which the men have risen who are to do it. Pupils in the same schools, receiving precisely the same instruction which for so long a time has paralysed

that the Duke gave Mr. Steell[1] a sitting on horseback, in order that his mode of riding might be accurately represented. This, however, does not render the following remarks in the text nugatory, as it may easily be imagined that the action of the Duke, exhibiting his riding in his own grounds, would be different from his action, or inaction, when watching the course of a battle.

I must also make a most definite exception in favour of Marochetti, who seems to me a thoroughly great sculptor; and whose statue of Cœur de Lion, though, according to the principle just stated, not to be considered a *historical* work, is an *ideal* work of the highest beauty and value. Its erection in front of Westminster Hall will tend more to educate the public eye and mind with respect to art, than anything we have done in London for centuries.

⋅   ⋅   ⋅   ⋅   ⋅   ⋅   ⋅   ⋅   ⋅

April 21st, 1854.—I stop the press in order to insert the following paragraph from to-day's *Times :*—" THE STATUE OF CŒUR DE LION.—*Yesterday morning a number of workmen were engaged in pulling down the cast which was placed in New Palace Yard of the colossal equestrian statue of Richard Cœur de Lion. Sir C. Barry was, we believe, opposed to the cast remaining there any longer, and to the putting up of the statue itself on the same site, because it did not harmonise with the building. During the day the horse and figure were removed, and before night the pedestal was demolished and taken away."*[2]

---

[1] [Sir John Steell (1804–1891), knighted on the inauguration of the Scottish memorial to Prince Albert, 1876; appointed sculptor to Queen Victoria for Scotland, 1838. His bronze statue of Wellington was erected in 1852.]

[2] [The statue now stands in Old Palace Yard, between Westminster Hall and the Peers' Entrance. It was first shown at the Great Exhibition of 1851. Baron Carlo Marochetti (1805–1867) had been employed both by Carlo Alberto and by Louis Philippe. He was afterwards patronised by Queen Victoria and Prince Albert, and executed many works in this country, including the Inkerman monument in St. Paul's. He was elected R.A. in 1866.]

every one of our painters,—these boys agree in disliking to copy the antique statues set before them. They copy them as they are bid, and they copy them better than any one else; they carry off prize after prize, and yet they hate their work. At last they are admitted to study from the life; they find the life very different from the antique, and say so. Their teachers tell them the antique is the best, and they mustn't copy the life. They agree among themselves that they like the life, and that copy it they will. They do copy it faithfully, and their masters forthwith declare them to be lost men. Their fellow-students hiss them whenever they enter the room.[1] They can't help it; they join hands and tacitly resist both the hissing and the instruction. Accidentally, a few prints of the works of Giotto, a few casts from those of Ghiberti, fall into their hands, and they see in these something they never saw before—something intensely and everlastingly true.[2] They examine farther into the matter; they discover for themselves the greater part of what I have laid before you to-night; they form themselves into a body, and enter upon that crusade which has hitherto been victorious. And which will be absolutely and triumphantly victorious. The great mistake which has hitherto prevented the public mind from fully going with them must soon be corrected. That mistake was the supposition that, instead of wishing to recur to the *principles* of the early ages, these men wished to bring back the *ignorance* of the early ages. This notion, grounded first on some hardness in their earlier works, which resulted—as it must always result—from the downright and earnest effort to paint nature as in a looking-glass, was fostered partly by the jealousy of their beaten competitors, and partly by the pure, perverse, and hopeless ignorance of the whole body of art-critics, so called, connected with the press. No notion was ever more baseless

---

[1] [This refers to an actual incident, as related by Holman Hunt; see above, Introduction, p. xlv.]

[2] [Compare the Introduction, above, p. xliv.]

or more ridiculous. It was asserted that the Pre-Raphaelites did not draw well, in the face of the fact, that the principal member of their body, from the time he entered the schools of the Academy, had literally encumbered himself with the medals given as prizes for drawing.[1] It was asserted that they did not draw in perspective, by men who themselves knew no more of perspective than they did of astrology; it was asserted that they sinned against the appearances of nature, by men who had never drawn so much as a leaf or a blossom from nature in their lives. And, lastly, when all these calumnies or absurdities would tell no more, and it began to be forced upon men's unwilling belief that the style of the Pre-Raphaelites *was* true and was according to nature, the last forgery invented respecting them is, that they copy photographs. You observe how completely this last piece of malice defeats all the rest. It admits they are true to nature, though only that it may deprive them of all merit in being so. But it may itself be at once refuted by the bold challenge to their opponents to produce a Pre-Raphaelite picture, or anything like one, by themselves copying a photograph.

132. Let me at once clear your minds from all these doubts, and at once contradict all these calumnies.

Pre-Raphaelitism has but one principle, that of absolute, uncompromising truth in all that it does, obtained by working everything, down to the most minute detail, from nature, and from nature only.* Every Pre-Raphaelite landscape background is painted to the last touch, in the

---

* Or, where imagination is necessarily trusted to, by always endeavouring to conceive a fact as it really was likely to have happened, rather than as it most prettily *might* have happened. The various members of the school are not all equally severe in carrying out its principles, some of them trusting their memory or fancy very far; only all agreeing in the effort to make their memories so accurate as to seem like portraiture, and their fancy so probable as to seem like memory.

---

[1] [Millais had been admitted to the Academy schools in 1839, at the age of ten—the youngest student ever admitted there. At thirteen he won a medal for drawing from the antique; at seventeen, the gold medal for painting.]

open air, from the thing itself. Every Pre-Raphaelite figure, however studied in expression, is a true portrait of some living person. Every minute accessory is painted in the same manner. And one of the chief reasons for the violent opposition with which the school has been attacked by other artists, is the enormous cost of care and labour which such a system demands from those who adopt it, in contradistinction to the present slovenly and imperfect style.

133. This is the main Pre-Raphaelite principle. But the battle which its supporters have to fight is a hard one; and for that battle they have been fitted by a very peculiar character.

You perceive that the principal resistance they have to make is to that spurious beauty, whose attractiveness had tempted men to forget, or to despise, the more noble quality of sincerity: and in order at once to put them beyond the power of temptation from this beauty, they are, as a body, characterised by a total absence of sensibility to the ordinary and popular forms of artistic gracefulness; while, to all that still lower kind of prettiness, which regulates the disposition of our scenes upon the stage, and which appears in our lower art, as in our annuals, our commonplace portraits, and statuary, the Pre-Raphaelites are not only dead, but they regard it with a contempt and aversion approaching to disgust. This character is absolutely necessary to them in the present time; but it, of course, occasionally renders their work comparatively unpleasing. As the school becomes less aggressive, and more authoritative—which it will do—they will enlist into their ranks men who will work, mainly, upon their principles, and yet embrace more of those characters which are generally attractive, and this great ground of offence will be removed.

134. Again: you observe that as landscape painters, their principles must, in great part, confine them to mere foreground work; and singularly enough, that they may not

be tempted away from this work, they have been born with comparatively little enjoyment of those evanescent effects and distant sublimities which nothing but the memory can arrest, and nothing but a daring conventionalism portray. But for this work they are not now needed. Turner, the first and greatest of the Pre-Raphaelites, has done it already; he, though his capacity embraced everything, and though he would sometimes, in his foregrounds, paint the spots upon a dead trout, and the dyes upon a butterfly's wing, yet for the most part delighted to begin at that very point where the other branches of Pre-Raphaelitism become powerless.[1]

135. Lastly. The habit of constantly carrying everything up to the utmost point of completion deadens the Pre-Raphaelites in general to the merits of men who, with an equal love of truth up to a certain point, yet express themselves habitually with speed and power, rather than with finish, and give abstracts of truth rather than total truth. Probably to the end of time artists will more or less be divided into these classes, and it will be impossible to make men like Millais understand the merits of men like Tintoret;[2] but this is the more to be regretted because the Pre-Raphaelites have enormous powers of imagination, as well as of realisation, and do not yet themselves know of how much they would be capable, if they sometimes worked on a larger scale, and with a less laborious finish.

136. With all their faults, their pictures are, since Turner's death, the best — incomparably the best — on the

---

[1] [The words claiming Turner as the first and greatest Raphaelite were inserted in ed. 2. Ed. 1 reads:—
"But for this work they are not needed. Turner had done it before them; he, though his capacity . . . yet for the most part delighting to begin at that very point where Pre-Raphaelitism becomes powerless."]

[2] [Millais' views on some of the old masters were expressed in an article entitled "Thoughts on our Art of To-day," which is published in M. H. Spielmann's *Millais and his Works*, 1898 (being there reprinted from the *Magazine of Art* for 1888). He considered that "Time and Varnish are two of the greatest of old masters." He does not mention Tintoret, and seems to rank Rembrandt as first of the portrait-painters among the old masters. The paper is of interest in connexion with the passage in the text as containing Millais' views on the subject of "breadth" and "finish."]

walls of the Royal Academy; and such works as Mr. Hunt's "Claudio and Isabella" have never been rivalled, in some respects never approached, at any other period of art.

This I believe to be a most candid statement of all their faults and all their deficiencies; not such, you perceive, as are likely to arrest their progress. The "magna est veritas"[1] was never more sure of accomplishment than by these men. Their adversaries have no chance with them. They will gradually unite their influence with whatever is true or powerful in the reactionary art of other countries; and on their works such a school will be founded as shall justify the third age of the world's civilisation, and render it as great in creation as it has been in discovery.

137. And now let me remind you but of one thing more. As you examine into the career of historical painting, you will be more and more struck with the fact I have this evening stated to you,[2]—that none was ever truly great but that which represented the living forms and daily deeds of the people among whom it arose—that all precious historical work records, not the past, but the present. Remember, therefore, that it is not so much in *buying* pictures, as in *being* pictures, that you can encourage a noble school. The best patronage of art is not that which seeks for the pleasures of sentiment in a vague ideality, not for beauty of form in a marble image; but that which educates your children into living heroes, and binds down the flights and the fondnesses of the heart into practical duty and faithful devotion.

[1] [Ruskin concluded his Addenda to Lectures I. and II. (§ 76) with this same thought from the Vulgate (1 Esdras iv. 14), there adding "and shall prevail"—"et prævalebit" being the substitution in ordinary citation for the "et prævalet" of the original.]

[2] [See above, § 129, p. 151.]

ADDENDA TO THE FOURTH LECTURE

138. I COULD not enter, in a popular lecture, upon one intricate and difficult question, closely connected with the subject of Pre-Raphaelitism—namely, the relation of invention to observation; and composition to imitation. It is still less a question to be discussed in the compass of a note; and I must defer all careful examination of it to a future opportunity. Nevertheless, it is impossible to leave altogether unanswered the first objection which is now most commonly made to the Pre-Raphaelite work, namely, that the principle of it seems adverse to all exertion of imaginative power. Indeed, such an objection sounds strangely on the lips of a public who have been in the habit of purchasing, for hundreds of pounds, small squares of Dutch canvas, containing only servile imitations of the coarsest nature. It is strange that an imitation of a cow's head by Paul Potter, or of an old woman's by Ostade, or of a scene of tavern debauchery by Teniers, should be purchased and proclaimed for high art, while the rendering of the most noble expressions of human feeling in Hunt's " Isabella," or of the loveliest English landscape, haunted by sorrow, in Millais' " Ophelia,"[1] should be declared " puerile." But, strange though the utterance of it be, there is some weight in the objection. It is true that so long as the Pre-Raphaelites only paint from nature, however carefully selected and grouped, their pictures can never have the characters of the highest class of compositions.[2] But, on the other hand, the shallow and conventional arrangements

---

[1] [For Holman Hunt's "Claudio and Isabella," exhibited 1853, see *Modern Painters*, vol. iii. ch. iv. § 5 ; for " Ophelia " see note in Vol. XI. p. 217.]

[2] [Compare *Modern Painters*, vol. iii. ch. x. § 21, where this remark is referred to and further discussed.]

commonly called "compositions" by the artists of the present day, are infinitely farther from great art than the most patient work of the Pre-Raphaelites. That work is, even in its humblest form, a secure foundation, capable of infinite superstructure; a reality of true value, as far as it reaches, while the common artistical effects and groupings are a vain effort at superstructure without foundation—utter negation and fallacy from beginning to end.

139. But more than this, the very faithfulness of the Pre-Raphaelites arises from the redundance of their imaginative power. Not only can all the members of the school compose a thousand times better than the men who pretend to look down upon them, but I question whether even the greatest men of old times possessed more exhaustless invention than either Millais or Rossetti; and it is partly the very ease with which they invent which leads them to despise invention. Men who have no imagination, but have learned merely to produce a spurious resemblance of its results by the recipes of composition, are apt to value themselves mightily on their concoctive science; but the man whose mind a thousand living imaginations haunt, every hour, is apt to care too little for them; and to long for the perfect truth which he finds is not to be come at so easily. And though I may perhaps hesitatingly admit that it is possible to love this truth of reality too intensely, yet I have no hesitation in declaring that there is *no hope* for those who despise it, and that the painter, whoever he be, who despises the pictures already produced by the Pre-Raphaelites, has himself no capacity of becoming a great painter of any kind. Paul Veronese and Tintoret themselves, without desiring to imitate the Pre-Raphaelite work, would have looked upon it with deep respect, as John Bellini looked on that of Albert Dürer;[1] none but the ignorant could be unconscious of its truth, and none but the insincere regardless of it.

140. How far it is possible for men educated on the

---

[1] [Compare Vol. IX. p. 436.]

severest Pre-Raphaelite principles to advance from their present style into that of the great schools of composition, I do not care to inquire, for at this period such an advance is certainly not desirable. Of great compositions we have enough, and more than enough, and it would be well for the world if it were willing to take some care of those it has. Of pure and manly truth, of stern statement of the things done and seen around us daily, we have hitherto had nothing. And in art, as in all other things, besides the literature of which it speaks, that sentence of Carlyle is inevitably and irreversibly true :—" Day after day, looking at the high destinies which yet await literature, which literature will ere long address herself with more decisiveness than ever to fulfil, it grows clearer to us that the proper task of literature lies in the domain of BELIEF, within which, poetic fiction, as it is charitably named, will have to take a quite new figure, if allowed a settlement there. Whereby were it not reasonable to prophesy that this exceeding great multitude of novel writers and such like, must, in a new generation, gradually do one of two things, either retire into nurseries, and work for children, minors, and semifatuous persons of both sexes, or else, what were far better, sweep their novel fabric into the dust cart, and betake them, with such faculty as they have, *to understand and record what is true,* of which surely there is and for ever will be a whole infinitude unknown to us, of infinite importance to us ? Poetry will more and more come to be understood as nothing but higher knowledge, and the only genuine Romance for grown persons, Reality." [1]

141. As I was copying this sentence, a pamphlet was put into my hand, written by a clergyman, denouncing Woe, woe, woe! to " exceedingly young men of stubborn instincts, calling themselves Pre-Raphaelites." *

---

* *Art, its Constitution and Capacities, etc.* By the Rev. Edward Young, M.A. The phrase " exceedingly young men of stubborn instincts," being twice

[1] [*Diderot,* reprinted in *Miscellanies,* vol. v. p. 2 of the 1872 edition.]

I thank God that the Pre-Raphaelites *are* young, and that strength is still with them, and life, with all the war of it, still in front of them. Yet Everett Millais is this year of the exact age at which Raphael painted the " Disputa," his greatest work ; Rossetti and Hunt are both of them older still—nor is there one member of the body so young as Giotto, when he was chosen from among the painters of Italy to decorate the Vatican.[1] But Italy, in her great period, knew her great men, and did not "despise their youth."[2] It is reserved for England to insult the strength of her noblest children—to wither their warm enthusiasm early into the bitterness of patient battle, and leave to those whom she should have cherished and aided, no hope but in resolution, no refuge but in disdain.

142. Indeed it is woeful, when the young usurp the place, or despise the wisdom, of the aged ; and among the many dark signs of these times, the disobedience and insolence of youth are among the darkest. But with whom is the fault ? Youth never yet lost its modesty where age had not lost its honour ; nor did childhood ever refuse its reverence, except where age had forgotten correction. The cry, " Go up, thou bald head," will never be heard in the land which remembers the precept, " See that ye despise not one of these little ones;"[3] and although indeed youth *may* become despicable, when its eager hope is changed into presumption, and its progressive power into arrested pride, there is something more despicable still, in the old age which has learned neither judgment nor gentleness, which is weak without charity, and cold without discretion.

quoted (carefully excluding the context) from my pamphlet on Pre-Raphaelitism.[4]

---

[1] [Millais in 1854 was 25 ; Rossetti, 26 ; and Hunt, 27.   Giotto was 22 when summoned to Rome—that is, if Vasari's date for the painter's birth (1276) be correct.]

[2] [1 Timothy iv. 12.]

[3] [2 Kings ii. 23 ; Matthew xviii. 10.]

[4] [See below, p. 355.   Mr. Young cites the phrase at pp. 11, 13 of his pamphlet (Bristol, 1854) ; at p. 18 he says of the Pre-Raphaelite movement that " over and above its moral delinquencies, of arrogance, bigotry, and destructiveness," it " panders to the downward tendency of the age," etc.]

PART II

REVIEWS, LETTERS, AND
PAMPHLETS ON ART

(1844–1854)

I

A REVIEW OF LORD LINDSAY'S "SKETCHES OF THE HISTORY OF CHRISTIAN ART"

(*Quarterly Review, June* 1847)

[*Bibliographical Note.*—This review first appeared in *The Quarterly Review* for June 1847 (Vol. 81, pp. 1–57, where it was entitled "Lord Lindsay *on the History of Christian Art.*")

The article was reprinted in *On the Old Road: a Collection of Miscellaneous Essays, Pamphlets, etc., etc., published 1834–1885,* By John Ruskin—(1) in 1885, when it occupied pp. 19–132 (§§ 16–97) of volume i.; (2) in 1899 (second edition), when it occupied pp. 21–135 (§§ 16–97) of volume i.

The numbering of the paragraphs was introduced in the reprint of 1885. As it was there consecutive throughout the volume, the paragraphs are here necessarily re-numbered, and the divisions are in some cases altered. There are no variations in the text, other than a few minor differences of punctuation.]

"THE HISTORY OF CHRISTIAN ART"

1. *Progression by Antagonism: a Theory, involving Considerations touching the Present Position, Duties, and Destiny of Great Britain.* By Lord Lindsay. London, 1846.
2. *Sketches of the History of Christian Art.* By Lord Lindsay. 3 vols. 8vo. London, 1847.

1. THERE is, perhaps, no phenomenon connected with the history of the first half of the nineteenth century, which will become a subject of more curious investigation in after ages, than the coincident development of the Critical faculty, and extinction of the Arts of Design. Our mechanical energies, vast though they be, are not singular nor characteristic; such, and so great, have before been manifested— and it may perhaps be recorded of us with wonder rather than respect, that we pierced mountains and excavated valleys, only to emulate the activity of the gnat and the swiftness of the swallow. Our discoveries in science, however accelerated or comprehensive, are but the necessary development of the more wonderful reachings into vacancy of past centuries; and they who struck the piles of the bridge of Chaos will arrest the eyes of Futurity rather than we builders of its towers and gates—theirs the authority of Light, ours but the ordering of courses to the Sun and Moon.

2. But the Negative character of the age is distinctive. There has not before appeared a race like that of civilized Europe at this day, thoughtfully unproductive of all art— ambitious—industrious—investigative—reflective, and incapable. Disdained by the savage, or scattered by the soldier, dishonoured by the voluptuary, or forbidden by the fanatic, the arts have not, till now, been extinguished by analysis and paralyzed by protection. Our lecturers, learned in

history, exhibit the descents of excellence from school to school, and clear from doubt the pedigrees of powers which they cannot re-establish, and of virtues no more to be revived; the scholar is early acquainted with every department of the Impossible, and expresses in proper terms his sense of the deficiencies of Titian and the errors of Michael Angelo: the metaphysician weaves from field to field his analogies of gossamer, which shake and glitter fairly in the sun, but must be torn asunder by the first plough that passes: geometry measures out, by line and rule, the light which is to illustrate heroism, and the shadow which should veil distress; and anatomy counts muscles, and systematizes motion, in the wrestling of Genius with its angel. Nor is ingenuity wanting—nor patience; apprehension was never more ready, nor execution more exact—yet nothing is of us, or in us, accomplished;—the treasures of our wealth and will are spent in vain—our cares are as clouds without water[1] —our creations fruitless and perishable; the succeeding Age will trample "sopra lor vanita che par persona,"[2] and point wonderingly back to the strange colourless tessera in the mosaic of human mind.

3. No previous example can be shown, in the career of nations not altogether nomad or barbarous, of so total an absence of invention,—of any material representation of the mind's inward yearning and desire, seen, as soon as shaped, to be, though imperfect, in its essence good, and worthy to be rested in with contentment, and consisting self-approval —the Sabbath of contemplation which confesses and confirms the majesty of a style. All but ourselves have had this in measure; the Imagination has stirred herself in proportion to the requirements, capacity, and energy of each race: reckless or pensive, soaring or frivolous, still she has

---

[1] [Jude 12.]
[2] [Dante: *Inferno*, vi. 33–36 :—

    " We, o'er the shades thrown prostrate by the brunt
      Of the heavy tempest passing, set our feet
      Upon their emptiness, that substance seem'd." (Cary.)

Ruskin quotes the words again in *Modern Painters*, vol. iii. ch. v. § 13.]

had life and influence; sometimes aiming at Heaven with brick for stone and slime for mortar—anon bound down to painting of porcelain, and carving of ivory, but always with an inward consciousness of power which might indeed be palsied or imprisoned, but not in operation vain. Altars have been rent, many—ashes poured out,—hands withered —but we alone have worshipped, and received no answer— the pieces left in order upon the wood, and our names writ in the water that runs round about the trench.[1]

4. It is easier to conceive than to enumerate the many circumstances which are herein against us, necessarily, and exclusive of all that wisdom might avoid, or resolution vanquish. First, the weight of mere numbers, among whom ease of communication rather renders opposition of judgment fatal, than agreement probable; looking from England to Attica, or from Germany to Tuscany, we may remember to what good purpose it was said that the magnetism of iron was found not in bars, but in needles. Together with this adversity of number comes the likelihood of many among the more available intellects being held back and belated in the crowd, or else prematurely out-wearied; for it now needs both curious fortune and vigorous effort to give to any, even the greatest, such early positions of eminence and audience as may feed their force with advantage; so that men spend their strength in opening circles, and crying for place, and only come to speech of us with broken voices and shortened time.[2] Then follows the diminution

---

[1] [See 1 Kings xviii. 38.]

[2] [The view here expressed that small states and city communities are more favourable than large states to the production of genius was expounded by Ruskin, with some limitations, in a letter to his father a few years before the date of this review :—

"BAVENO, *Sunday, 24th Aug.* [1845].—. . . Sismondi most truly says that in Florence, where every citizen of common respectability, down to the lowest tradesman, had the chance, the probable chance, of becoming one of the twelve Anziani, of supreme authority, the struggle to obtain this position, to make themselves fit for it, and the faculties developed in the possession of it, gave to the whole nation such force of character for a time as no other exhibited. But I conceive it to be a morbid excitement, and one essentially involving the necessity of following reaction and degradation. Such a government cannot subsist, it can have no settled principles; it is an admirable school for the people, but a miserable instrument in its

of importance in peculiar places and public edifices, as they
engage national affection or vanity; no single city can now
take such queenly lead as that the pride of the whole body
of the people shall be involved in adorning her; the buildings
of London or Munich are not charged with the fulness of
the national heart as were the domes of Pisa and Florence:
—their credit or shame is metropolitan, not acropolitan;
central at the best, not dominant; and this is one of the
chief modes in which the cessation of superstition, so far
as it has taken place, has been of evil consequence to art,
that the observance of local sanctities being abolished, meanness and mistake are anywhere allowed of, and the thoughts
and wealth which were devoted and expended to good purpose in one place, are now distracted and scattered to utter
unavailableness.

5. In proportion to the increasing spirituality of religion,
the conception of worthiness in material offering ceases, and
with it the sense of beauty in the evidence of votive labour;[1]
machine-work[2] is substituted for hand-work, as if the value
of ornament consisted in the mere multiplication of agreeable forms, instead of in the evidence of human care and

own proper function. Besides, even in the former end it must fail, more
or less, according to the scale of the nation ; in a city divided into twenty
companies it works well, but it is absurd altogether in a kingdom divided
into twenty provinces. Independent cities have some reason in being republican, but it must be at the expense of continual jealousies, wars, and
seditions. Peace can only be secured by fixed positions of all ranks, and
settled government of the whole. I want to study the English people
under Elizabeth, for the development of intellect was then great under
an absolute monarchy, and the King-love of Shakespeare is very glorious;
but with that exception there is nothing that the world has ever shown
that can stand—intellectually—beside the power of mind thrown out by
the fighting, falling, insane republicanism of Florence—in Giotto, Orcagna
and Dante, its first-fruits, with all the clusters of the mighty ones, their
satellites, without reckoning the impulse given to the national mind going
on in Ghiberti and Brunelleschi and Masaccio and Ghirlandajo, and
gathering all into one great flash to expire under the Medicis in Michael
Angelo—nothing can be set beside this, I say, except the parallel republicanism of fighting and falling Athens, giving us Æschylus and Phidias
and Aristophanes and Thucydides."]
The reference is to Sismondi's *Histoire des Républiques Italiennes du Moyen Age;*
the Anziani were the twelve elders, who replaced the former consuls.]
    [1] [These were conceptions which Ruskin sought to rekindle in the *Seven Lamps,*
ch. i. ("The Lamp of Sacrifice").]
    [2] [For Ruskin's numerous references to this subject, see General Index, *s.*
"Machinery."]

thought and love about the separate stones; and—machine-work once tolerated—the eye itself soon loses its sense of this very evidence, and no more perceives the difference between the blind accuracy of the engine, and the bright, strange play of the living stroke—a difference as great as between the form of a stone pillar and a springing fountain. And on this blindness follow all errors and abuses—hollowness and slightness of frame-work, speciousness of surface ornament, concealed structure, imitated materials, and types of form borrowed from things noble for things base; and all these abuses must be resisted with the more caution, and less success, because in many ways they are signs or consequences of improvement, and are associated both with purer forms of religious feeling and with more general diffusion of refinements and comforts; and especially because we are critically aware of all our deficiencies, too cognizant of all that is greatest to pass willingly and humbly through the stages that rise to it, and oppressed in every honest effort by the bitter sense of inferiority. In every previous development the power has been in advance of the consciousness, the resources more abundant than the knowledge—the energy irresistible, the discipline imperfect. The light that led was narrow and dim—streakings of dawn—but it fell with kindly gentleness on eyes newly awakened out of sleep. But we are now aroused suddenly in the light of an intolerable day — our limbs fail under the sun-stroke — we are walled in by the great buildings of elder times, and their fierce reverberation falls upon us without pause, in our feverish and oppressive consciousness of captivity; we are laid bedridden at the Beautiful Gate, and all our hope must rest in acceptance of the "such as I have," of the passers by.[1]

6. The frequent and firm, yet modest expression of this hope, gives peculiar value to Lord Lindsay's book on Christian Art; for it is seldom that a grasp of antiquity so comprehensive, and a regard for it so affectionate, have

---

[1] [Acts iii. 6.]

consisted with aught but gloomy foreboding with respect to our own times. As a contribution to the History of Art, his work is unquestionably the most valuable which has yet appeared in England. His research has been unwearied; he has availed himself of the best results of German investigation—his own acuteness of discernment in cases of approximating or derivative style is considerable—and he has set before the English reader an outline of the relations of the primitive schools of Sacred art which we think so thoroughly verified in all its more important ramifications, that, with whatever richness of detail the labour of succeeding writers may illustrate them, the leading lines of Lord Lindsay's chart will always henceforth be followed. The feeling which pervades the whole book is chastened, serious, and full of reverence for the strength ordained out of the lips of infant Art — accepting on its own terms its simplest teaching, sympathizing with all kindness in its unreasoning faith; the writer evidently looking back with most joy and thankfulness to hours passed in gazing upon the faded and faint touches of feeble hands, and listening through the stillness of uninvaded cloisters for fall of voices now almost spent; yet he is never contracted into the bigot, nor inflamed into the enthusiast; he never loses his memory of the outside world, never quits nor compromises his severe and reflective Protestantism, never gives ground of offence by despite or forgetfulness of any order of merit or period of effort. And the tone of his address to our present schools is therefore neither scornful nor peremptory; his hope, consisting with full apprehension of all that we have lost, is based on a strict and stern estimate of our power, position, and resource, compelling the assent even of the least sanguine to his expectancy of the revelation of a new world of Spiritual Beauty, of which whosoever

"will dedicate his talents, as the bondsman of love, to his Redeemer's glory and the good of mankind, may become the priest and interpreter, by adopting in the first instance, and re-issuing with that outward investiture which the assiduous study of all that is beautiful, either in Grecian sculpture, or the later but less spiritual schools of painting, has enabled him to supply, such of its bright ideas as he finds imprisoned in the early and imperfect efforts of art—and secondly, by exploring further on his own account in the untrodden realms of feeling that lie before him, and calling into palpable existence visions as bright, as pure, and as immortal as those that have already, in the golden days of Raphael and Perugino, obeyed their creative mandate, Live!" (Vol. iii. p. 422).[1]

7. But while we thus defer to the discrimination, respect the feeling, and join in the hope of the author, we earnestly deprecate the frequent assertion, as we entirely deny the accuracy or propriety, of the metaphysical analogies, in accordance with which his work has unhappily been arranged.[2] Though these had been as carefully, as they are crudely, considered, it had still been no light error of judgment to thrust them with dogmatism so abrupt into the forefront of a work whose purpose is assuredly as much to win to the truth as to demonstrate it. The writer has apparently forgotten that of the men to whom he must primarily look for the working out of his anticipations, the most part are of limited knowledge and inveterate habit, men dexterous in practice, idle in thought; many of them compelled by ill-ordered patronage into directions of exertion at variance with their own best impulses, and regarding their art only as a means of life; all of them conscious of practical difficulties which the critic is too apt to underestimate, and probably remembering disappointments of early effort rude enough to chill the most earnest heart. The shallow amateurship of the circle of their patrons early disgusts them with theories; they shrink back to the hard teaching of their own industry, and would rather read the book which facilitated their methods than the one that rationalized their aims. Noble exceptions there are, and more than might be deemed; but the labour spent in contest with executive difficulties renders even these better men unapt receivers of a system which looks with little

[1] [Except where otherwise stated, the quotations from Lord Lindsay are always from the *Sketches of the History of Christian Art*.]
[2] [For another reference to Lord Lindsay's metaphysical system, see *Stones of Venice*, vol. i. (Vol. IX. p. 67).]

respect on such achievement, and shrewd discerners of the parts of such system which have been feebly rooted, or fancifully reared. Their attention should have been attracted both by clearness and kindness of promise; their impatience prevented by close reasoning and severe proof of every statement which might seem transcendental. Altogether void of such consideration or care, Lord Lindsay never even so much as states the meaning or purpose of his appeal, but, clasping his hands desperately over his head, disappears on the instant in an abyss of curious and unsupported assertions of the philosophy of human nature: reappearing only, like a breathless diver, in the third page, to deprecate the surprise of the reader whom he has never addressed, at a conviction which he has never stated; and again vanishing ere we can well look him in the face, among the frankincensed clouds of Christian mythology: filling the greater part of his first volume with a *résumé* of its symbols and traditions, yet never vouchsafing the slightest hint of the objects for which they are assembled, or the amount of credence with which he would have them regarded; and so proceeds to the historical portion of the book, leaving the whole theory which is its key to be painfully gathered from scattered passages, and in great part from the mere form of enumeration adopted in the preliminary chart of the schools; and giving as yet account only of that period to which the mere artist looks with least interest—while the work, even when completed, will be nothing more than a single pinnacle of the historical edifice whose ground-plan is laid in the preceding essay, "Progression by Antagonism": —a plan, by the author's confession, "too extensive for his own, or any single hand to execute,"[1] yet without the understanding of whose main relations it is impossible to receive the intended teaching of the completed portion.

8. It is generally easier to plan what is beyond the reach of others than to execute what is within our own;

---

[1] ["Advertisement" to *Progression by Antagonism*, p. v. n.]

and it had been well if the range of this introductory essay had been something less extensive, and its reasoning more careful. Its search after truth is honest and impetuous, and its results would have appeared as interesting as they are indeed valuable, had they but been arranged with ordinary perspicuity, and represented in simple terms. But the writer's evil genius pursues him; the demand for exertion of thought is remorseless, and continuous throughout, and the statements of theoretical principle as short, scattered, and obscure, as they are bold. We question whether many readers may not be utterly appalled by the aspect of an "Analysis of Human Nature"—the first task proposed to them by our intellectual Eurystheus—to be accomplished in the space of six semi-pages,[1] followed in the seventh by the "Development of the Individual Man," and applied in the eighth to a "General Classification of Individuals": and we infinitely marvel that our author should have thought it unnecessary to support or explain a division of the mental attributes on which the treatment of his entire subject afterwards depends, and whose terms are repeated in every following page to the very dazzling of eye and deadening of ear (a division, we regret to say, as illogical as it is purposeless), otherwise than by a laconic reference to the assumptions of Phrenology.

"The Individual Man, or Man considered by himself as an unit in creation, is compounded of three distinct primary elements.
1. Sense, or the animal frame, with its passions or affections.
2. Mind or Intellect;—of which the distinguishing faculties—rarely, if ever, equally balanced, and by their respective predominance determinative of his whole character, conduct, and views of life—are,
　　i. Imagination, the discerner of Beauty,—
　　ii. Reason, the discerner of Truth,—
the former animating and informing the world of Sense or Matter, the latter finding her proper home in the world of abstract or immaterial existences — the former receiving the impress of things Objectively, or *ab externo*, the latter impressing its own ideas on them Subjectively, or *ab interno* — the

[1] [Semi-pages, apparently because there are footnotes which occupy half the text in these pages (1–8) of *Progression by Antagonism.*]

XII.　　　　　　　　　　　　　　　　　　　　M

former a feminine or passive, the latter a masculine or active principle ; and

iii. Spirit—the Moral or Immortal principle, ruling through the Will, and breathed into Man by the Breath of God."—*Progression by Antagonism*, pp. 2, 3.

9. On what authority does the writer assume that the moral is alone the *Immortal* principle—or the only part of the human nature bestowed by the breath of God? Are imagination, then, and reason perishable? Is the Body itself? Are not all alike immortal ; and when distinction is to be made among them, is not the first great division between their active and passive immortality, between the supported body and supporting spirit ; that spirit itself afterwards rather conveniently to be considered as either exercising intellectual function, or receiving moral influence, and, both in power and passiveness, deriving its energy and sensibility alike from the sustaining breath of God—than actually divided into intellectual and moral parts? For if the distinction between us and the brute be the test of the nature of the living soul by that breath conferred, it is assuredly to be found as much in the imagination as in the moral principle. There is but one of the moral sentiments enumerated by Lord Lindsay, the sign of which is absent in the animal creation :—the enumeration is a bald one, but let it serve the turn—" Self-esteem and love of Approbation," eminent in horse and dog ; " Firmness," not wanting either to ant or elephant ; " Veneration," distinct as far as the superiority of man can by brutal intellect be comprehended ; " Hope," developed as far as its objects can be made visible ; and " Benevolence," or Love, the highest of all, the most assured of all—together with all the modifications of opposite feeling, rage, jealousy, habitual malice, even love of mischief and comprehension of jest :—the one only moral sentiment wanting being that of responsibility to an Invisible being, or conscientiousness. But where, among brutes, shall we find the slightest trace of the Imaginative faculty, or of that discernment of beauty which our

author most inaccurately confounds with it, or of the discipline of memory, grasping this or that circumstance at will, or of the still nobler foresight of, and respect towards, things future, except only instinctive and compelled.

10. The fact is, that it is not in intellect added to the bodily sense, nor in moral sentiment superadded to the intellect, that the essential difference between brute and man consists : but in the elevation of all three to that point at which each becomes capable of communion with the Deity, and worthy therefore of eternal life ;—the body more universal as an instrument—more exquisite in its sense—this last character carried out in the eye and ear to the perception of Beauty, in form, sound, and colour—and herein distinctively raised above the brutal sense; intellect, as we have said, peculiarly separating and vast; the moral sentiments like in essence, but boundlessly expanded, as attached to an infinite object, and labouring in an infinite field: each part mortal in its shortcoming, immortal in the accomplishment of its perfection and purpose ; the opposition which we at first broadly expressed as between body and spirit, being more strictly between the natural and spiritual condition of the entire creature—body natural, sown in death, body spiritual, raised in incorruption : Intellect natural, leading to scepticism; intellect spiritual, expanding into faith : Passion natural, suffered from things spiritual ; passion spiritual, centred on things unseen : and the strife or antagonism which is throughout the subject of Lord Lindsay's proof, is not, as he has stated it, between the moral, intellectual, and sensual elements, but between the upward and downward tendencies of all three — between the spirit of Man which goeth upward, and the spirit of the Beast which goeth downward.[1]

11. We should not have been thus strict in our examination of these preliminary statements, if the question had been one of terms merely, or if the inaccuracy of thought

[1] [The Bible references here and in preceding lines are—1 Corinthians xv. 42 ; Hebrews xi. 1 ; Ecclesiastes iii. 21.]

had been confined to the Essay on Antagonism. If upon receiving a writer's terms of argument in the sense—however unusual or mistaken—which he chooses they should bear, we may without further error follow his course of thought, it is as unkind as unprofitable to lose the use of his result in quarrel with its algebraic expression; and if the reader will understand by Lord Lindsay's general term " Spirit " the susceptibility of right moral emotion, and the entire subjection of the Will to Reason; and receive his term " Sense " as not including the perception of Beauty either in sight or sound, but expressive of animal sensation only, he may follow without embarrassment to its close, his magnificently comprehensive statement of the forms of probation which the heart and faculties of man have undergone from the beginning of time. But it is far otherwise when the theory is to be applied, in all its pseudo-organization, to the separate departments of a particular art, and analogies the most subtle and speculative traced between the mental character and artistical choice or attainment of different races of men. Such analogies are always treacherous, for the amount of expression of individual mind which Art can convey is dependent on so many collateral circumstances, that it even militates against the truth of any particular system of interpretation that it should seem at first generally applicable, or its results consistent. The passages in which such interpretation has been attempted in the work before us, are too graceful to be regretted, nor is their brilliant suggestiveness otherwise than pleasing and profitable too, so long as it is received on its own grounds merely, and affects not with its uncertainty the very matter of its foundation. But all oscillation is communicable, and Lord Lindsay is much to be blamed for leaving it entirely to the reader to distinguish between the determination of his research and the activity of his fancy — between the authority of his interpretation and the aptness of his metaphor. He who would assert the true meaning of a symbolical art, in an age of strict inquiry and tardy imagination, ought rather to surrender something of the fulness which his own faith perceives, than expose the fabric of his vision, too finely woven, to the hard handling of the materialist; and we sincerely regret that discredit is likely to accrue to portions of our author's well-grounded statement of real significances, once of all men understood, because these are rashly blended with his own accidental perceptions of disputable analogy. He perpetually associates the present imaginative influence of Art with its ancient hieroglyphical teaching, and mingles fancies fit only for the framework of a sonnet, with the deciphered evidence which is to establish a serious point of history; and this the more frequently and grossly, in the endeavour to force every branch of his subject into illustration of the false division of the mental attributes which we have pointed out.

12. His theory is first clearly stated in the following passage :—

" Man is, in the strictest sense of the word, a progressive being, and with many periods of inaction and retrogression, has still held, upon the whole, a steady course towards the great end of his existence, the re-union and re-harmonizing of the three elements of his being, dislocated by the Fall, in the service of his God. Each of these three elements, Sense, Intellect, and Spirit, has had its distinct development at three distant intervals, and in the personality of the three great branches of the human family. The race of Ham, giants in prowess if not in stature, cleared the earth of primeval forests and monsters, built cities, established vast empires, invented the mechanical arts, and gave the fullest expansion to the animal energies. After them, the Greeks, the elder line of Japhet, developed the intellectual faculties, Imagination and Reason, more especially the former, always the earlier to bud and blossom; poetry and fiction, history, philosophy, and science, alike look back to Greece as their birthplace; on the one hand they put a soul into Sense, peopling the world with their gay mythology— on the other they bequeathed to us, in Plato and Aristotle, the mighty patriarchs of human wisdom, the Darius and the Alexander of the two grand armies of thinking men whose antagonism has ever since divided the battle-field of the human intellect :—While, lastly, the race of Shem, the Jews, and the nations of Christendom, their *locum tenentes* as the Spiritual Israel, have, by God's blessing, been elevated in Spirit to as near and intimate communion with Deity as is possible in this stage of being. Now the peculiar interest and dignity of Art consists in her exact correspondence in her three departments with these three periods of development, and in the illustration she thus affords—more closely and markedly even than literature—to the all-important truth that men stand or fall according as they look up to the

Ideal or not. For example, the Architecture of Egypt, her pyramids and temples, cumbrous and inelegant, but imposing from their vastness and their gloom, express the ideal of Sense or Matter—elevated and purified indeed, and nearly approaching the Intellectual, but Material still; we think of them as of natural scenery, in association with caves or mountains, or vast periods of time; their voice is as the voice of the sea, or as that of "many peoples," shouting in unison:—But the Sculpture of Greece is the voice of Intellect and Thought, communing with itself in solitude, feeding on beauty and yearning after truth:—While the Painting of Christendom—(and we must remember that the glories of Christianity, in the full extent of the term, are yet to come)—is that of an immortal Spirit, conversing with its God. And as if to mark more forcibly the fact of continuous progress towards perfection, it is observable that although each of the three arts peculiarly reflects and characterises one of the three epochs, each art of later growth has been preceded in its rise, progress, and decline, by an antecedent correspondent development of its elder sister or sisters—Sculpture, in Greece, by that of Architecture—Painting, in Europe, by that of Architecture and Sculpture. If Sculpture and Painting stand by the side of Architecture in Egypt, if Painting by that of Architecture and Sculpture in Greece, it is as younger sisters, girlish and unformed. In Europe alone are the three found linked together, in equal stature and perfection." —Vol. i. pp. xii.–xiv.

13. The reader must, we think, at once perceive the bold fallacy of this forced analogy—the comparison of the architecture of one nation with the sculpture of another, and the painting of a third, and the assumption as a proof of difference in moral character, of changes necessarily wrought, always in the same order, by the advance of mere mechanical experience. Architecture must precede sculpture, not because sense precedes intellect, but because men must build houses before they adorn chambers, and raise shrines before they inaugurate idols; and sculpture must precede painting, because men must learn forms in the solid before they can project them on a flat surface, and must learn to conceive designs in light and shade before they can conceive them in colour, and must learn to treat subjects under positive colour and in narrow groups, before they can treat them under atmospheric effect and in receding masses, and all these are mere necessities of practice, and have no more connexion with any divisions of the human mind than the equally paramount necessities that men must gather stones before they build walls, or grind corn before they

bake bread. And that each following nation should take up either the same art at an advanced stage, or an art altogether more difficult, is nothing but the necessary consequence of its subsequent elevation and civilization. Whatever nation had succeeded Egypt in power and knowledge, after having had communication with her, must necessarily have taken up art at the point where Egypt left it—in its turn delivering the gathered globe of heavenly snow to the youthful energy of the nation next at hand, with an exhausted "à vous le dé!"[1] In order to arrive at any useful or true estimate of the respective rank of each people in the scale of mind, the architecture of each must be compared with the architecture of the other—sculpture with sculpture —line with line; and to have done this broadly and with a surface glance, would have set our author's theory on firmer foundation, to outward aspect, than it now rests upon. Had he compared the accumulation of the pyramid with the proportion of the peristyle, and then with the aspiration of the spire; had he set the colossal horror of the Sphinx beside the Phidian Minerva, and this beside the Pietà of M. Angelo;[2] had he led us from beneath the iridescent capitals of Denderah, by the contested line of Apelles,[3] to the hues and the heaven of Perugino or Bellini, we might have been tempted to assoilzie[4] from all staying of question or stroke of partizan the invulnerable aspect of his ghostly theory; but, if, with even partial regard to some of the circumstances which physically limited the attainments of each race, we follow their individual career, we shall find the points of superiority less salient and the connexion between heart and hand more embarrassed.

---

[1] [A phrase from the passing of the dice: " It's you to play." Ruskin probably took it from Molière (*Misanthrope*, v. 4).]

[2] [In *Modern Painters*, vol. ii., Ruskin notices with admiration both the Pietà at Genoa (Vol. IV. pp. 138, 285 *n.*) and that at Florence (*ibid.*, p. 281).]

[3] [A reference to the story of the contest between Apelles and Protagenes—the rival painters alternately showing their skill by the drawing of a line of excessive fineness (Pliny, xxxv. 36, § 11). The Temple of Hathor at Dendera (the Tentyra of the Greeks) is among the best preserved specimens of Egyptian architecture.]

[4] ["To assoilzie," Scottish form of "assoil"; and in Scots law still the proper term for acquittal, or judgment for the defendant.]

14. Yet let us not be misunderstood:—the great gulf between Christian and Pagan art we cannot bridge—nor do we wish to weaken one single sentence wherein its breadth or depth is asserted by our author.[1] The separation is not gradual, but instant and final—the difference not of degree, but of condition ; it is the difference between the dead vapours rising from a stagnant pool, and the same vapours touched by a torch. But we would brace the weakness which Lord Lindsay has admitted, in his own assertion of this great inflaming instant, by confusing its fire with the mere phosphorescence of the marsh, and explaining, as a successive development of the several human faculties, what was indeed the bearing of them all at once over a threshold strewed with the fragments of their idols, into the temple of the One God.

We shall therefore, as fully as our space admits, examine the application of our author's theory to Architecture, Sculpture, and Painting, successively, setting before the reader some of the more interesting passages which respect each art, while we at the same time mark with what degree of caution their conclusions are, in our judgment, to be received.

15. Accepting Lord Lindsay's first reference to Egypt, let us glance at a few of the physical accidents which influenced its types of architecture. The first of these is evidently the capability of carriage of large blocks of stone over perfectly level land. It was possible to roll to their destination along that uninterrupted plain, blocks which could neither by the Greek have been shipped in seaworthy vessels, nor carried over mountain-passes, nor raised except by extraordinary effort to the height of the rock-built fortress or seaward promontory. A small undulation of surface, or embarrassment of road, makes large difference in the portability of masses, and of consequence, in the breadth of the possible intercolumniation, the solidity

---

[1] [Compare *Modern Painters*, vol. ii. *ad fin.* (Vol. IV. p. 331) : "It is vain to attempt to pursue the comparison," etc.]

of the column, and the whole scale of the building. Again, in a hill-country, architecture can be important only by position, in a level country only by bulk. Under the overwhelming mass of mountain-form it is vain to attempt the expression of majesty by size of edifice—the humblest architecture may become important by availing itself of the power of nature, but the mightiest must be crushed in emulating it : the watch-towers of Amalfi are more majestic than the Superga of Piedmont; [1] St. Peter's would look like a toy if built beneath the Alpine cliffs, which yet vouchsafe some communication of their own solemnity to the smallest châlet that glitters among their glades of pine.[2] On the other hand, a small building is in a level country lost, and the impressiveness of bulk proportionably increased; hence the instinct of nations has always led them to the loftiest efforts where the masses of their labour might be seen looming at incalculable distance above the open line of the horizon—hence rose her four-square mountains above the flat of Memphis, while the Greek pierced the recesses of Phigaleia with ranges of columns, or crowned the sea-cliffs of Sunium with a single pediment, bright, but not colossal.[3]

16. The derivation of the Greek types of form from the forest-hut is too direct to escape observation; but sufficient attention has not been paid to the similar petrifaction, by other nations, of the rude forms and materials adopted in the haste of early settlement, or consecrated by the purity of rural life. The whole system of Swiss and German Gothic has thus been most characteristically affected by the structure of the intersecting timbers at the

---

[1] [Ruskin had sketched at Amalfi in 1841 ; for a rough sketch of the Superga at Turin, see *Modern Painters*, vol. v. Fig. 91.]

[2] [Compare on this point *The Poetry of Architecture*, Vol. I. pp. 37, 164, and *Seven Lamps*, Vol. VIII. p. 103.]

[3] [For the situation of the Temple of Apollo Epicurius at Bassæ, in the territory of Phigaleia, see Leake's *Travels in the Morea*, 1830, ii. 9, and Mahaffy's *Rambles in Greece*, p. 318; the sculptures were removed to the British Museum in 1812. The position of the Temple of Athena at Sunium (Cape Colonna) has been sung by Byron—" Place me on Sunium's marble steep," etc. (*Don Juan*, canto iii. st. 86).]

angles of the châlet.[1] This was in some cases directly and without variation imitated in stone, as in the piers of the old bridge at Aarberg;[2] and the practice obtained— partially in the German after-Gothic—universally, or nearly so, in Switzerland—of causing mouldings which met at an angle to appear to interpenetrate each other, both being truncated immediately beyond the point of intersection. The painfulness of this ill-judged adaptation was conquered by association — the eye became familiarized to uncouth forms of tracery—and a stiffness and meagreness, as of cast-iron, resulted in the mouldings of much of the ecclesiastical, and all the domestic Gothic of central Europe; the mouldings of casements intersecting so as to form a small hollow square at the angles, and the practice being further carried out into all modes of decoration—pinnacles interpenetrating crockets, as in a peculiarly bold design of archway at Besançon. The influence at Venice has been less immediate and more fortunate; it is with peculiar grace that the majestic form of the Ducal Palace reminds us of the years of fear and endurance when the exiles of the Prima Venetia settled like homeless birds on the sea-sand, and that its quadrangular range of marble wall and painted chamber, raised upon multiplied columns of confused arcade,* presents but the exalted image of the first pile-supported hut that rose above the rippling of the lagoons.[3]

17. In the chapter on the "Influence of Habit and Religion," of Mr. Hope's Historical Essay,† the reader will find further instances of the same feeling, and, bearing immediately on our present purpose, a clear account of the

---

* The reader must remember that this arcade was originally quite open, the inner wall having been built after the fire, in 1574.

† *An Historical Essay on Architecture*, by the late Thomas Hope (Murray, 1835), chap. iv., pp. 23–31.[4]

---

[1] [This subject is discussed in *Seven Lamps*, Vol. VIII. p. 97, and compare *Notes on Prout and Hunt*.]

[2] [Aarberg on the Aar, between Soleure and Morat.]

[3] [Compare *Stones of Venice*, vol. ii. ch. i. ("The Throne").]

[4] [For other references to this book, see Vol. VIII. p. 63 *n.*, Vol. X. p. 22 *n.*]

derivation of the Egyptian temple from the excavated cavern; but the point to which in all these cases we would direct especial attention, is, that the first perception of the great laws of architectural *proportion* is dependent for its acuteness less on the æsthetic instinct of each nation than on the mechanical conditions of stability and natural limitations of size in the primary type, whether hut, châlet, or tent.

As by the constant reminiscence of the natural proportions of his first forest-dwelling, the Greek would be restrained from all inordinate exaggeration of size—the Egyptian was from the first left without hint of any system of proportion, whether constructive, or of visible parts. The cavern—its level roof supported by amorphous piers—might be extended indefinitely into the interior of the hills, and its outer façade continued almost without term along their flanks—the solid mass of cliff above forming one gigantic entablature, poised upon props instead of columns. Hence the predisposition to attempt in the built temple the expression of infinite extent, and to heap the ponderous architrave above the proportionless pier.

18. The less direct influences of external nature in the two countries were still more opposed. The sense of beauty, which among the Greek peninsulas was fostered by beating of sea and rush of river, by waving of forest and passing of cloud, by undulation of hill and poise of precipice, lay dormant beneath the shadowless sky and on the objectless plain of the Egyptians; no singing winds nor shaking leaves nor gliding shadows gave life to the line of their barren mountains—no Goddess of Beauty rose from the pacing of their silent and foamless Nile. One continual perception of stability, or changeless revolution, weighed upon their hearts—their life depended on no casual alternation of cold and heat—of drought and shower; their giftGods were the risen River and the eternal Sun, and the types of these were for ever consecrated in the lotus decoration of the temple and the wedge of the enduring Pyramid.

Add to these influences, purely physical, those dependent on the superstitions and political constitution; of the overflowing multitude of "populous No"; on their condition of prolonged peace—their simple habits of life—their respect for the dead—their separation by incommunicable privilege and inherited occupation—and it will be evident to the reader that Lord Lindsay's broad assertion of the expression of "the Ideal of Sense or Matter"[1] by their universal style, must be received with severe modification, and is indeed thus far only true, that the mass of Life supported upon that fruitful plain could, when swayed by a despotic ruler in any given direction, accomplish by mere weight and number what to other nations had been impossible, and bestow a pre-eminence, owed to mere bulk and evidence of labour, upon public works which among the Greek republics could be rendered admirable only by the intelligence of their design.

19. Let us, for the present omitting consideration of the debasement of the Greek types which took place when their cycle of achievement had been fulfilled, pass to the germination of Christian architecture, out of one of the least important elements of those fallen forms—one which, less than the least of all seeds, has risen into the fair branching stature under whose shadow we still dwell.

The principal characteristics of the new architecture, as exhibited in the Lombard cathedral, are well sketched by Lord Lindsay :—

"The three most prominent features, the eastern aspect of the sanctuary, the cruciform plan, and the soaring octagonal cupola, are borrowed from Byzantium—the latter in an improved form—the cross with a difference—the nave, or arm opposite the sanctuary, being lengthened so as to resemble the supposed shape of the actual instrument of suffering, and form what is now distinctively called the Latin Cross. The crypt and absis, or tribune, are retained from the Romish basilica, but the absis is generally pierced with windows, and the crypt is much loftier and more spacious, assuming almost the appearance of a subterranean church. The columns of the nave,

[1] [Above, § 12, p. 182.]

no longer isolated, are clustered so as to form compound piers, massive and heavy—their capitals either a rude imitation of the Corinthian, or, especially in the earlier structures, sculptured with grotesque imagery. Triforia, or galleries for women, frequently line the nave and transepts. The roof is of stone, and vaulted. The narthex, or portico, for excluded penitents, common alike to the Greek and Roman churches, and in them continued along the whole façade of entrance, is dispensed with altogether in the oldest Lombard ones, and when afterwards resumed, in the eleventh century, was restricted to what we should now call Porches, over each door, consisting generally of little more than a canopy open at the sides, and supported by slender pillars, resting on sculptured monsters. Three doors admit from the western front; these are generally covered with sculpture, which frequently extends in belts across the façade, and even along the sides of the building. Above the central door is usually seen, in the later Lombard churches, a S. Catherine's-wheel window. The roof slants at the sides, and ends in front sometimes in a single pediment, sometimes in three gables answering to three doors; while, in Lombardy at least, hundreds of slender pillars, of every form and device—those immediately adjacent to each other frequently interlaced in the true lover's knot, and all supporting round or trefoliate arches—run along, in continuous galleries, under the eaves, as if for the purpose of supporting the roof—run up the pediment in front, are continued along the side-walls and round the eastern absis, and finally engirdle the cupola. Sometimes the western front is absolutely covered with these galleries, rising tier above tier. Though introduced merely for ornament, and therefore on a vicious principle, these fairy-like colonnades win very much on one's affections. I may add to these general features the occasional and rare one, seen to peculiar advantage in the cathedral of Cremona, of numerous slender towers, rising, like minarets, in every direction, in front and behind, and giving the east end, specially, a marked resemblance to the mosques of the Mahometans.

"The Baptistery and the Campanile, or bell-tower, are in theory invariable adjuncts to the Lombard cathedral, although detached from it. The Lombards seem to have built them with peculiar zest, and to have had a keen eye for the picturesque in grouping them with the churches they belong to.

"I need scarcely add that the round arch is exclusively employed in pure Lombard architecture.

"To translate this new style into its symbolical language is a pleasurable task. The three doors and three gable ends signify the Trinity, the Catherine-wheel window (if I mistake not) the Unity, as concentrated in Christ, the Light of the Church, from whose Greek monogram its shape was probably adopted. The monsters that support the pillars of the porch stand there as talismans to frighten away evil spirits. The crypt (as in older buildings) signifies the moral death of man, the cross the atonement, the cupola heaven; and these three, taken in conjunction with the lengthened nave, express, reconcile, and give their due and balanced prominence to the leading ideas of the Militant and Triumphant Church, respectively embodied in the architecture of Rome and Byzantium. Add to this, the symbolism of the Baptistery, and the Christian pilgrimage, from the Font to the Door of Heaven, is complete."—Vol. ii. pp. 8–11.

20. We have by-and-bye an equally comprehensive sketch of the essential characters of the Gothic cathedral; but this we need not quote, as it probably contains little that would be new to the reader. It is succeeded by the following interpretation of the spirit of the two styles :—

"Comparing, apart from enthusiasm, the two styles of Lombard and Pointed Architecture, they will strike you, I think, as the expression, respectively, of that alternate repose and activity which characterise the Christian life, exhibited in perfect harmony in Christ alone, who, on earth, spent His night in prayer to God, His day in doing good to man—in heaven, as we know by His own testimony, "worketh hitherto," conjointly with the Father—for ever, at the same time, reposing on the infinity of His wisdom and of His power. Each, then, of these styles has its peculiar significance, each is perfect in its way. The Lombard Architecture, with its horizontal lines, its circular arches and expanding cupola, soothes and calms one ; the Gothic, with its pointed arches, aspiring vaults and intricate tracery, rouses and excites—and why? Because the one symbolises an infinity of Rest, the other of Action, in the adoration and service of God. And this consideration will enable us to advance a step farther:—The aim of the one style is definite, of the other indefinite ; we look up to the dome of heaven and calmly acquiesce in the abstract idea of infinity ; but we only realise the impossibility of conceiving it by the flight of imagination from star to star, from firmament to firmament. Even so Lombard Architecture attained perfection, expressed its idea, accomplished its purpose—but Gothic never; the Ideal is unapproachable."—Vol. ii. p. 23.

21. This idea occurs not only in this passage:—it is carried out through the following chapters;—at page 38, the pointed arch associated with the cupola is spoken of as a "fop interrupting the meditations of a philosopher"; at page 65, the "earlier contemplative style of the Lombards" is spoken of; at page 114, Giottesque art is "the expression of that Activity of the imagination which produced Gothic Architecture"; and, throughout, the analogy is prettily expressed, and ably supported; yet it is one of those against which we must warn the reader: it is altogether superficial, and extends not to the minds of those whose works it accidentally, and we think disputably, characterises. The transition from Romanesque (we prefer using the generic term)[1] to Gothic is natural and straightforward, in many

[1] [So in the *Stones of Venice*, vol. i. (Vol. IX. p. 34) Ruskin divides the styles into Classical, Romanesque, and Gothic.]

points traceable to mechanical and local necessities (of which one, the dangerous weight of snow on flat roofs, has been candidly acknowledged by our author), and directed by the tendency, common to humanity in all ages, to push every newly-discovered means of delight to its most fantastic extreme, to exhibit every newly-felt power in its most admirable achievement, and to load with extrinsic decoration forms whose essential varieties have been exhausted. The arch, carelessly struck out by the Etruscan, forced by mechanical expediencies on the unwilling, uninventive Roman, remained unfelt by either. The noble form of the apparent Vault of Heaven—the line which every star follows in its journeying, extricated by the Christian architect from the fosse, the aqueduct, and the sudarium—grew into long succession of proportioned colonnade, and swelled into the white domes that glitter above the plain of Pisa, and fretted channels of Venice, like foam globes [1] at rest.

22. But the spirit that was in these Aphrodites of the earth was not then, nor in them, to be restrained. Colonnade rose over colonnade; the pediment of the western front was lifted into a detached and scenic wall; story above story sprang the multiplied arches of the Campanile, and the eastern pyramidal fire-type, lifted from its foundation, was placed upon the summit. With the superimposed arcades of the principal front arose the necessity, instantly felt by their subtle architects, of a new proportion in the column; the lower wall enclosure, necessarily for the purposes of Christian worship continuous, and needing no peristyle, rendered the lower columns a mere facial decoration, whose proportions were evidently no more to be regulated by the laws hitherto observed in detached colonnades. The column expanded into the shaft, or into the huge pilaster rising unbanded from tier to tier; shaft and pilaster were associated in ordered groups, and the ideas of singleness and limited elevation once attached to them, swept away for ever; the

[1] [A favourite expression with Ruskin : see Vol. I. pp. 37, 508 ; Vol. II. p. 62.]

stilted and variously centred arch existed already: the pure ogive followed—where first exhibited we stay not to inquire;[1]—finally, and chief of all, the great mechanical discovery of the resistance of lateral pressure by the weight of the superimposed flanking pinnacle. Daring concentrations of pressure upon narrow piers were the immediate consequence, and the recognition of the buttress as a feature in itself agreeable and susceptible of decoration. The glorious art of painting on glass[2] added its temptations; the darkness of northern climes both rendering the typical character of Light more deeply felt than in Italy, and necessitating its admission in larger masses; the Italian, even at the period of his most exquisite art in glass, retaining the small Lombard window, whose expediency will hardly be doubted by any one who has experienced the transition from the scorching reverberation of the white-hot marble front, to the cool depth of shade within, and whose beauty will not be soon forgotten by those who have seen the narrow lights of the Pisan duomo announce by their redder burning, not like transparent casements, but like characters of fire searing the western wall, the decline of day upon Capraja.[3]

23. Here, then, arose one great distinction between Northern and Transalpine Gothic, based, be it still observed, on mere necessities of climate. While the architect of Santa Maria Novella admitted to the frescoes of Ghirlandajo scarcely more of purple lancet light than had been shed by the morning sun through the veined alabasters of San Miniato; and looked to the rich blue of the quinquepartite vault above, as to the mosaic of the older concha, for conspicuous aid in the colour decoration of the whole; the northern builder burst through the walls of his apse, poured over the eastern altar one unbroken blaze, and lifting his shafts like pines, and his walls like precipices, ministered to their miraculous

---

[1] [The evolution of the ogee is traced in *Stones of Venice*, vol. i. ch. x. § 17 (Vol. IX. p. 162), ch. xi. § 20 (*ibid.*, p. 173).]

[2] [See above, Introduction, p. lxv.]

[3] [See note on Vol. IV. p. 288, where Ruskin makes another figure of the island of Capraja.]

XIV

J.Ruskin

Grotesques
South door of the Duomo, Verona.

stability by an infinite phalanx of sloped buttress and glittering pinnacle. The spire was the natural consummation.
Internally, the sublimity of space in the cupola had been
superseded by another kind of infinity in the prolongation of
the nave; externally, the spherical surface had been proved,
by the futility of Arabian efforts, incapable of decoration;
its majesty depended on its simplicity, and its simplicity and
leading forms were alike discordant with the rich rigidity of
the body of the building. The campanile became, therefore,
principal and central; its pyramidal termination was surrounded at the base by a group of pinnacles, and the spire
itself, banded, or pierced into aërial tracery, crowned with
its last enthusiastic effort the flamelike ascent of the perfect pile.

24. The process of change was thus consistent throughout, though at intervals accelerated by the sudden discovery
of resource, or invention of design; nor, had the steps been
less traceable, do we think the suggestiveness of Repose, in
the earlier style, or of Imaginative Activity in the latter,
definite or trustworthy. We much question whether the
Duomo of Verona, with its advanced guard of haughty
gryphons[1]—the mailed peers of Charlemagne frowning from
its vaulted gate,—that vault itself ribbed with variegated
marbles, and peopled by a crowd of monsters—the Evangelical types not the least stern or strange; its stringcourses
replaced by flat cut friezes, combats between gryphons and
chain-clad paladins, stooping behind their triangular shields
and fetching sweeping blows with two-handled swords; or
that of Lucca[2]—its fantastic columns clasped by writhing
snakes and winged dragons, their marble scales spotted with
inlaid serpentine, every available space alive with troops
of dwarfish riders, with spur on heel and hawk in hood,

---

[1] [See the Plate XIV.; and compare *Stones of Venice*, vol. i. (Vol. IX. p. 439),
where these figures are called "the noblest pieces of mediæval sculpture in North
Italy." The Paladins, Roland and Oliver, who guard the entrance, were sculptured
with reference to the traditional building of the first cathedral at Verona by Charlemagne.]
[2] [See the Plate XV., opposite the next page.]

sounding huge trumpets of chase, like those of the Swiss Urushorn, and cheering herds of gaping dogs upon harts and hares, boars and wolves, every stone signed with its grisly beast—be one whit more soothing to the contemplative, or less exciting to the imaginative faculties, than the successive arch, and visionary shaft, and dreamy vault, and crisped foliage, and colourless stone, of our own fair abbeys, chequered with sunshine through the depth of ancient branches, or seen far off, like clouds in the valley, risen out of the pause of its river.[1]

25. And with respect to the more fitful and fantastic expression of the " Italian Gothic," our author is again to be blamed for his loose assumption, from the least reflecting of preceding writers,[2] of this general term, as if the pointed buildings of Italy could in any wise be arranged in one class, or criticised in general terms. It is true that so far as the church interiors are concerned, the system is nearly universal, and always bad ; its characteristic features being arches of enormous span, and banded foliage capitals divided into three fillets, rude in design, unsuggestive of any structural connection with the column, and looking consequently as if they might be slipped up or down, and had been only fastened in their places for the temporary purposes of a festa. But the exteriors of Italian pointed buildings display variations of principle and transitions of type quite as bold as either the advance from the Romanesque to the earliest of their forms, or the recoil from their latest to the cinquecento.

26. The first and grandest style resulted merely from the application of the pointed arch to the frequent Romanesque window, the large semicircular arch divided by three small ones. Pointing both the superior and inferior arches, and adding to the grace of the larger one by striking another

---

[1] [Compare the description of the English Abbeys in *Seven Lamps*, Vol. VIII. p. 99.]
[2] [The phrase "Italian Gothic" is used by Lord Lindsay (vol. ii. p. 39), who justifies his unfavourable opinion of it by reference to Gally Knight.]

XV

J. Ruskin

Allen & Co. Sc.

The Cathedral of Lucca.

arch above it with a more removed centre, and placing the voussoirs at an acute angle to the curve, we have the truly noble form of domestic Gothic, which—more or less enriched by mouldings and adorned by penetration, more or less open of the space between the including and inferior arches—was immediately adopted in almost all the proudest palaces of North Italy—in the Brolettos of Como, Bergamo, Modena, and Siena—in the palace of the Scaligers at Verona —of the Gambacorti at Pisa—of Paolo Guinigi at Lucca[1] —besides inferior buildings innumerable:—nor is there any form of civil Gothic except the Venetian, which can be for a moment compared with it in simplicity or power. The latest is that most vicious and barbarous style of which the richest types are the lateral porches and upper pinnacles of the Cathedral of Como, and the whole of the Certosa of Pavia:[2]—characterised by the imitative sculpture of large buildings on a small scale by way of pinnacles and niches; the substitution of candelabra for columns; and the covering of the surfaces with sculpture, often of classical subject, in high relief and daring perspective, and finished with delicacy which rather would demand preservation in a cabinet, and exhibition under a lens, than admit of exposure to the weather and removal from the eye, and which, therefore, architecturally considered, is worse than valueless, telling merely as unseemly roughness and rustication. But between these two extremes are varieties nearly countless—some of them both strange and bold, owing to the brilliant colour and firm texture of the accessible materials, and the desire of the builders to crowd the greatest expression of value into the smallest space.

27. Thus it is in the promontories of serpentine which meet with their polished and gloomy green the sweep of the

---

[1] [The arches of the Broletto of Como are drawn in Plate 5 of *Stones of Venice*, vol. i.]

[2] [Compare on the Certosa, *Seven Lamps*, ch. i. (Vol. VIII. p. 50 and *n.*), and on the Cathedral of Como, *Stones of Venice*, vol. i. ch. xx. (Vol. IX. p. 263 and *n.*).]

Gulf of Genoa,[1] that we find the first cause of the peculiar spirit of the Tuscan and Ligurian Gothic—carried out in the Florentine duomo to the highest pitch of coloured finish— adorned in the upper story of the Campanile by a trans- formation, peculiarly rich and exquisite, of the narrowly- pierced heading of window already described, into a veil of tracery [2]—and aided throughout by an accomplished precision of design in its mouldings which we believe to be unique. In St. Petronio of Bologna,[3] another and a barbarous type occurs; the hollow niche of Northern Gothic wrought out with diamond-shaped penetrations enclosed in squares; at Bergamo another, remarkable for the same square penetra- tions of its rich and daring foliation;—while at Monza and Carrara the square is adopted as the leading form of decora- tion on the west fronts, and a grotesque expression results —barbarous still;[4]—which, however, in the latter duomo is associated with the arcade of slender niches—the translation of the Romanesque arcade into pointed work, which forms the second perfect order of Italian Gothic, entirely ecclesi- astical, and well developed in the churches of Santa Caterina and Santa Maria della Spina at Pisa.[5]   The Veronese Gothic, distinguished by the extreme purity and severity of its ruling lines, owing to the distance of the centres of circles from which its cusps are struck, forms another, and yet a more noble school—and passes through the richer decoration of Padua and Vicenza to the full magnificence of the Venetian —distinguished by the introduction of the ogee curve with- out pruriency or effeminacy, and by the breadth and decision

---

[1] [Compare *Lectures on Architecture and Painting,* § 53, above, p. 76 and *n.*]

[2] [See *Seven Lamps,* frontispiece and Plate ix., and ch. iii. § 18, ch. iv. § 43 (Vol. VIII. pp. 126, 187).]

[3] [This church was founded in 1390, the architect being Antonio Vincenzi, ambassador of the Bolognese to the Venetian Republic in 1396. Some of its architectural features are drawn and described in Willis' *Architecture of the Middle Ages,* p. 193 and Plate vi.]

[4] [This feature of the Cathedral of Monza is more fully discussed in *Stones of Venice,* vol. i. ch. viii. (Vol. IX. p. 123 and *n.*).]

[5] [For a drawing of the latter church, see Vol. IV., Plate 4.   For Ruskin's special affection for the Veronese Gothic, see *Seven Lamps* (Vol. VIII. p. 13).]

of mouldings as severely determined in all examples of the style as those of any one of the Greek orders.

28. All these groups are separated by distinctions clear and bold—and many of them by that broadest of all distinctions which lies between disorganization and consistency —accumulation and adaptation, experiment and design ;—yet to all one or two principles are common, which again divide the whole series from that of the Transalpine Gothic—and whose importance Lord Lindsay too lightly passes over in the general description, couched in somewhat ungraceful terms, "the vertical principle snubbed, as it were, by the horizontal."[1] We have already alluded to the great school of colour which arose in the immediate neighbourhood of the Genoa serpentine. The accessibility of marble throughout North Italy similarly modified the aim of all design, by the admission of undecorated surfaces. A blank space of freestone wall is always uninteresting, and sometimes offensive ; there is no suggestion of preciousness in its dull colour, and the stains and rents of time upon it are dark, coarse, and gloomy. But a marble surface receives in its age hues of continually increasing glow and grandeur ; its stains are never foul nor dim ; its undecomposing surface preserves a soft, fruit-like polish for ever, slowly flushed by the maturing suns of centuries. Hence, while in the Northern Gothic the effort of the architect was always so to diffuse his ornament as to prevent the eye from permanently resting on the blank material, the Italian fearlessly left fallow large fields of uncarved surface, and concentrated the labour of the chisel on detached portions, in which the eye, being rather directed to them by their isolation than attracted by their salience, required perfect finish and pure design rather than force of shade or breadth of parts ; and further, the intensity of Italian sunshine articulated by perfect gradations, and defined by sharp shadows at the edge, such inner anatomy and minuteness of outline as would have been utterly vain and valueless under the gloom of a northern

[1] [*Sketches of the History of Christian Art*, vol. ii. p. 38.]

sky; while again the fineness of material both admitted of, and allured to, the precision of execution which the climate was calculated to exhibit.

29. All these influences working together, and with them that of classical example and tradition, induced a delicacy of expression, a slightness of salience, a carefulness of touch, and refinement of invention, in all, even the rudest, Italian decorations, utterly unrecognised in those of Northern Gothic: which, however picturesquely adapted to their place and purpose, depend for most of their effect upon bold undercutting, accomplish little beyond graceful embarrassment of the eye, and cannot for an instant be separately regarded as works of accomplished art.   Even the later and more imitative examples profess little more than picturesque vigour or ingenious intricacy.   The oak leaves and acorns of the Beauvais mouldings are superbly wreathed,[1] but rigidly repeated in a constant pattern; the stems are without character, and the acorns huge, straight, blunt, and unsightly. Round the southern door of the Florentine duomo runs a border of fig-leaves, each leaf modulated as if dew had just dried from off it—yet each alike, so as to secure the ordered symmetry of classical enrichment.   But the Gothic fulness of thought is not therefore left without expression; at the edge of each leaf is an animal, first a cicala, then a lizard, then a bird, moth, serpent, snail—all different, and each wrought to the very life—panting—plumy—writhing— glittering — full of breath and power.   This harmony of classical restraint with exhaustless fancy, and of architectural propriety with imitative finish, is found throughout all the fine periods of the Italian Gothic, opposed to the wildness without invention, and exuberance without completion, of the North.

30. One other distinction we must notice, in the treatment of the Niche and its accessories.   In Northern

---

[1] [For these sculptures at Beauvais, see *Stones of Venice*, vol. i. ch. xx. (Vol. IX. p. 278); on the contrast here drawn between Northern and Italian Gothic generally, see Vol. IX. p. 208 and *n.*]

Gothic the niche frequently consists only of a bracket and canopy—the latter attached to the wall, independent of columnar support, pierced into openwork profusely rich, and often prolonged upwards into a crocketed pinnacle of indefinite height. But in the niche of pure Italian Gothic the classic principle of columnar support is never lost sight of. Even when its canopy is actually supported by the wall behind, it is apparently supported by two columns in front, perfectly formed with bases and capitals:—(the support of the Northern niche—if it have any—commonly takes the place of a buttress):—when it appears as a detached pinnacle, it is supported on four columns, the canopy trefoliated with very obtuse cusps, richly charged with foliage in the foliating space, but undecorated at the cusp points, and terminating above in a smooth pyramid, void of all ornament, and never very acute. This form, modified only by various grouping, is that of the noble sepulchral monuments of Verona, Lucca, Pisa, and Bologna; on a small scale it is at Venice associated with the cupola, in St. Mark's, as well as in Santa Fosca, and other minor churches. At Pisa, in the Spina chapel it occurs in its most exquisite form, the columns there being chased with chequer patterns of great elegance. The windows of the Florence cathedral are all placed under a flat canopy of the same form, the columns being elongated, twisted, and enriched with mosaic patterns. The reader must at once perceive how vast is the importance of the difference in system with respect to this member; the whole of the rich, cavernous chiaroscuro of Northern Gothic being dependent on the accumulation of its niches.[1]

31. In passing to the examination of our Author's theory as tested by the progress of Sculpture, we are still struck by his utter want of attention to physical advantages or difficulties. He seems to have forgotten from the first, that

---

[1] [With § 30 here compare *Stones of Venice*, vol. i. ch. xxviii. § 17, and on the subject of niches generally, *ibid.*, ch. xxiv. §§ 7–9 (Vol. IX. pp. 397, 330–331), and *Two Paths*, § 38.]

the mountains of Syene are not the rocks of Paros.[1]   Neither
the social habits nor intellectual powers of the Greek had
so much share in inducing his advance in Sculpture beyond
the Egyptian, as the difference between marble and syenite,
porphyry or alabaster.   Marble not only gave the power, it
actually introduced the *thought* of representation or realization of form, as opposed to the mere suggestive abstraction:
its translucency, tenderness of surface, and equality of tint
tempting by utmost reward to the finish which of all sub-
stances it alone admits:—even ivory receiving not so delicately, as alabaster endures not so firmly, the lightest, latest
touches of the completing chisel.   The finer feeling of the
hand cannot be put upon a hard rock like syenite—the blow
must be firm and fearless — the traceless, tremulous difference between common and immortal sculpture cannot be set
upon it—it cannot receive the enchanted strokes which, like
Aaron's incense,[2] separate the Living and the Dead.   Were
it otherwise, were finish possible, the variegated and lustrous
surface would not exhibit it to the eye.   The imagination
itself is blunted by the resistance of the material, and by
the necessity of absolute predetermination of all it would
achieve.   Retraction of all thought into determined and
simple forms, such as might be fearlessly wrought, necessarily remained the characteristic of the school.   The size
of the edifice induced by other causes above stated, further
limited the efforts of the sculptor.   No colossal figure can
be minutely finished; nor can it easily be conceived except
under an imperfect form.   It is a representation of Impossibility, and every effort at completion adds to the monstrous
sense of Impossibility.   Space would altogether fail us were
we even to name one-half of the circumstances which influence the treatment of light and shade to be seen at vast
distances upon surfaces of variegated or dusky colour; or of

---

[1] [Syene (Assouan, in Upper Egypt); the cliffs of dark granite there were
quarried by the ancient Egyptians, and gave the name to the species of horneblendic
granite known as syenite.   For the influence of the marble quarries at Paros and
other Grecian sites upon the genius of Greek art, see *Aratra Pentelici*, § 159, and
compare *Stones of Venice*, vol. iii. (Vol. XI. p. 38).]

[2] [See Numbers, ch. xvi.]

the necessities by which, in masses of huge proportion, the mere laws of gravity, and the difficulty of clearing the substance out of vast hollows neither to be reached nor entered, bind the realization of absolute form. Yet all these Lord Lindsay ought rigidly to have examined, before venturing to determine anything respecting the mental relations of the Greek and Egyptian. But the fact of his overlooking these inevitablenesses of material is intimately connected with the worst flaw of his theory—his idea of a Perfection resultant from a balance of elements; a perfection which all experience has shown to be neither desirable nor possible.

32. His account of Niccola Pisano, the founder of the first great school of Middle Age sculpture, is thus introduced:—

"Niccola's peculiar praise is this,—that, in practice at least, if not in theory, he first established the principle that the study of nature, corrected by the ideal of the antique, and animated by the spirit of Christianity, personal and social, can alone lead to excellence in art:—each of the three elements of human nature—Matter, Mind, and Spirit—being thus brought into union and co-operation in the service of God, in due relative harmony and subordination. I cannot over-estimate the importance of this principle; it was on this that, consciously or unconsciously, Niccola himself worked—it has been by following it that Donatello and Ghiberti, Leonardo, Raphael, and Michael Angelo have risen to glory. The Sienese school and the Florentine, minds contemplative and dramatic, are alike beholden to it for whatever success has attended their efforts. Like a treble-stranded rope, it drags after it the triumphal car of Christian Art. But if either of the strands be broken, if either of the three elements be pursued disjointedly from the other two, the result is, in each respective case, grossness, pedantry, or weakness:—the exclusive imitation of Nature produces a Caravaggio, a Rubens, a Rembrandt—that of the Antique, a Pellegrino di Tibaldo and a David; and though there be a native chastity and taste in religion, which restrains those who worship it too abstractedly from Intellect and Sense, from running into such extremes, it cannot at least supply that mechanical apparatus which will enable them to soar:—such devotees must be content to gaze up into heaven, like angels cropt of their wings."—Vol. ii. pp. 102–103.

33. This is mere Bolognese eclecticism[1] in other terms,

[1] [Agostino Carracci's sonnet in which he defined the objects of the school—thence called Eclectic—required "him who wishes to be a good painter to acquire the design of Rome, Venetian shade and action, and the dignified colouring of Lombardy; the terrible manner of Michael Angelo, the natural truth of Titian," etc. etc.]

and those terms incorrect.   We are amazed to find a writer usually thoughtful, if not accurate, thus indolently adopting the worn-out falsities of our weakest writers on Taste.   Does he—can he for an instant suppose that the ruffian Caravaggio,[1] distinguished only by his preference of candlelight and black shadows for the illustration and reinforcement of villany, painted nature—mere nature—exclusive nature, more painfully or heartily than John Bellini or Raphael?   Does he not see that whatever men imitate must be nature of some kind, material nature or spiritual, lovely or foul, brutal or human, but nature still?   Does he himself see in mere, external, copiable nature, no more than Caravaggio saw, or in the Antique no more than has been comprehended by David?[2]   The fact is, that all artists are primarily divided into the two great groups of Imitators and Suggestors—their falling into one or other being dependent partly on disposition, and partly on the matter they have to subdue— (thus Perugino imitates line by line with pencilled gold, the hair which Nino Pisano can only suggest by a gilded marble mass, both having the will of representation alike).[3]   And each of these classes is again divided into the faithful and unfaithful imitators and suggestors; and that is a broad question of blind eye and hard heart, or seeing eye and serious heart, always coexistent; and then the faithful imitators and suggestors — artists proper, are appointed, each with his peculiar gift and affection, over the several orders and classes of things natural, to be by them illumined and set forth.

34.   And that is God's doing and distributing; and none is rashly to be thought inferior to another, as if by his own fault; nor any of them stimulated to emulation, and changing places with others, although their allotted tasks be of different dignities, and their granted instruments of different

---

[1] [Compare *Stones of Venice*, vol. ii. ch. vi. § 54.]
[2] [For Jacques Louis David (1748–1825) see Vol. I. p. 278.]
[3] [For Perugino's finish, " even to the gilding of single hairs," see *Modern Painters*, vol. ii. (Vol. IV. p. 138), and the "Notes on the Louvre," § 1, below, p. 449; and for Nino Pisano's gilding of the hair in his statues, *ibid.*, p. 300 and *n.*]

keenness; for in none of them can there be a perfection or balance of all human attributes;—the great colourist becomes gradually insensible to the refinements of form which he at first intentionally omitted; the master of line is inevitably dead to many of the delights of colour; the study of the true or ideal human form is inconsistent with the love of its most spiritual expressions. To one it is intrusted to record the historical realities of his age; in him the perception of character is subtle, and that of abstract beauty in measure diminished; to another, removed to the desert, or enclosed in the cloister, is given, not the noting of things transient, but the revealing of things eternal. Ghirlandajo and Titian painted men, but could not angels; Duccio[1] and Angelico painted Saints, but could not senators. One is ordered to copy material form lovingly and slowly—his the fine finger and patient will: to another are sent visions and dreams upon the bed—his the hand fearful and swift, and impulse of passion irregular and wild. We may have occasion further to insist upon this great principle of the incommunicableness and singleness of all the highest powers;[2] but we assert it here especially, in opposition to the idea, already so fatal to art, that either the aim of the antique may take place together with the purposes, or its traditions become elevatory of the power, of Christian art; or that the glories of Giotto and the Sienese are in any wise traceable through Niccola Pisano to the venerable relics of the Campo Santo.

35. Lord Lindsay's statement, as far as it regards Niccola himself, is true.[3]

" His improvement in Sculpture is attributable, in the first instance, to the study of an ancient sarcophagus, brought from Greece by the ships of Pisa in the eleventh century, and which, after having stood beside the

---

[1] [To Duccio (about 1260–1340), who filled in the school of Siena the place of Cimabue and Giotto, Ruskin does not refer elsewhere than here and in § 44, below.]

[2] [See below, § 52, p. 223.]

[3] [For Ruskin's own account of Niccola Pisano and his work, see Val d'Arno (1874), passim. In § 264 of that book he quotes and "ratifies, as far as my knowledge

door of the Duomo for many centuries as the tomb of the Countess Beatrice, mother of the celebrated Matilda, has been recently removed to the Campo Santo. The front is sculptured in bas-relief, in two compartments, the one representing Hippolytus rejecting the suit of Phædra, the other his departure for the chase :—such at least is the most plausible interpretation. The sculpture, if not super-excellent, is substantially good, and the benefit derived from it by Niccola is perceptible on the slightest examination of his works. Other remains of antiquity are preserved at Pisa, which he may have also studied, but this was the classic well from which he drew those waters which became wine when poured into the hallowing chalice of Christianity. I need scarcely add that the mere presence of such models would have availed little, had not nature endowed him with the quick eye and the intuitive apprehension of genius, together with a purity of taste which taught him how to select, how to modify and how to reinspire the germs of excellence thus presented to him."—Vol. ii. pp. 104, 105.

36. But whatever characters peculiarly classical were impressed upon Niccola by this study, died out gradually among his scholars ; and in Orcagna the Byzantine manner finally triumphed, leading the way to the purely Christian sculpture of the school of Fiesole, in its turn swept away by the returning wave of classicalism. The sculpture of Orcagna, Giotto, and Mino da Fiesole, would have been what it was, if Niccola had been buried in his sarcophagus ;[1] and this is sufficiently proved by Giotto's remaining entirely uninfluenced by the educated excellence of Andrea Pisano,[2] while he gradually bent the Pisan down to his own uncompromising simplicity. If, as Lord Lindsay asserts, " Giotto had learned from the works of Niccola the grand principle of Christian art," the sculptures of the Campanile of Florence would not now have stood forth in contrasted awfulness of simplicity, beside those of the south door of the Baptistery.

permits, the words of my first master in Italian art, Lord Lindsay" (the words, being a passage (pp. 101–102) preceding the one here quoted); while in §§ 19–21 Ruskin describes the sarcophagus here mentioned by Lord Lindsay.]

[1] [For the dates and succession of the artists mentioned here, see the table and remarks in *Ariadne Florentina*, §§ 48–54; and compare *Modern Painters*, vol. iv. ch. xx. §§ 20, 21, where the succession of Italian sculpture is again traced ; for the sculpture of Giotto, see *Mornings in Florence*, §§ 129–130, and *Ariadne Florentina*, § 58; for Mino da Fiesole, *Modern Painters*, vol. ii. (Vol. IV. pp. 101 *n.*, 280), and see also below, § 39.]

[2] [Andrea da Pontadera (about 1270–1348) was the chief pupil of Giovanni (son of Niccola) Pisano ; Andrea's chief pupil was Orcagna. For a notice of Andrea's bas-reliefs on the Campanile, see *Mornings in Florence*, §§ 133–135, 137, 144.]

" Andrea's merit was indeed very great ; his works, compared with those of Giovanni and Niccola Pisano, exhibit a progress in design, grace, composition and mechanical execution, at first sight unaccountable—a chasm yawns between them, deep and broad, over which the younger artist seems to have leapt at a bound,—the stream that sank into the earth at Pisa emerges a river at Florence. The solution of the mystery lies in the peculiar plasticity of Andrea's genius, and the ascendancy acquired over it by Giotto, although a younger man, from the first moment they came into contact. Giotto had learnt from the works of Niccola the grand principle of Christian art, imperfectly apprehended by Giovanni and his other pupils, and by following up which he had in the natural course of things improved upon his prototype. He now repaid to Sculpture, in the person of Andrea, the sum of improvement in which he stood her debtor in that of Niccola : —so far, that is to say, as the treasury of Andrea's mind was capable of taking it in, for it would be an error to suppose that Andrea profited by Giotto in the same independent manner or degree that Giotto profited by Niccola. Andrea's was not a mind of strong individuality ; he became completely Giottesque in thought and style, and as Giotto and he continued intimate friends through life, the impression never wore off :—most fortunate, indeed, that it was so, for the welfare of Sculpture in general, and for that of the buildings in decorating which the friends worked in concert.

" Happily, Andrea's most important work, the bronze door of the Baptistery, still exists, and with every prospect of preservation. It is adorned with bas-reliefs from the history of S. John, with allegorical figures of virtues and heads of prophets, all most beautiful,—the historical compositions distinguished by simplicity and purity of feeling and design, the allegorical virtues perhaps still more expressive, and full of poetry in their symbols and attitudes ; the whole series is executed with a delicacy of workmanship till then unknown in bronze, a precision yet softness of touch resembling that of a skilful performer on the pianoforte. Andrea was occupied upon it for nine years, from 1330 to 1339, and when finished, fixed in its place, and exposed to view, the public enthusiasm exceeded all bounds ; the Signoria, with unexampled condescension, visited it in state, accompanied by the ambassadors of Naples and Sicily, and bestowed on the fortunate artist the honour and privilege of citizenship, seldom accorded to foreigners unless of lofty rank or exalted merit. The door remained in its original position—facing the Cathedral—till superseded in that post of honour by the ' Gate of Paradise,' cast by Ghiberti. It was then transferred to the Southern entrance of the Baptistery, facing the Misericordia." —Vol. ii. pp. 125–128.

37. A few pages farther on, the question of *Giotto's* claim to the authorship of the designs for this door is discussed at length, and, to the annihilation of the honour here attributed to *Andrea*, determined affirmatively, partly on the testimony of Vasari,[1] partly on internal evidence—

---

[1] [According to Vasari, Andrea was appointed "to execute one of the doors for which Giotto had given a most beautiful design" (Bohn's ed., 1855, vol. i. p. 148.]

these designs being asserted by our author to be "thoroughly Giottesque." But, not to dwell on Lord Lindsay's inconsistency, in the ultimate decision his discrimination seems to us utterly at fault. Giotto has, we conceive, suffered quite enough in the abduction of the work in the Campo Santo, which was worthy of him, without being made answerable for these designs of Andrea. That he gave a rough draft of many of them, is conceivable; but if even he did this, Andrea has added cadenzas of drapery, and other scholarly commonplace, as a bad singer puts ornament into an air. It was not of such teaching that came the "Jabal"[1] of Giotto.[1] Sitting at his tent door, he withdraws its rude drapery with one hand: three sheep only are feeding before him, the watchdog sitting beside him; but he looks forth like a Destiny, beholding the ruined cities of the earth become places, like the valley of Achor, for herds to lie down in.[2]

38. We have not space to follow our author through his very interesting investigation of the comparatively unknown schools of Teutonic sculpture. With one beautiful anecdote, breathing the whole spirit of the time—the mingling of deep piety with the modest, manly pride of art—our readers must be indulged :—

"The Florentine Ghiberti gives a most interesting account of a sculptor of Cologne in the employment of Charles of Anjou, King of Naples, whose skill he parallels with that of the statuaries of ancient Greece; his heads, he says, and his design of the naked, were 'maravigliosamente bene,' his style full of grace, his sole defect the somewhat curtailed stature of his figures. He was no less excellent in minuter works as a goldsmith, and in that capacity had worked for his patron a 'tavola d'oro,' a tablet or screen (apparently) of gold, with his utmost care and skill; it was a work of exceeding beauty—but in some political exigency his patron wanted money, and it was broken up before his eyes. Seeing his labour vain and the pride of his heart rebuked, he threw himself on the ground, and uplifting his eyes and hands to heaven, prayed in contrition, 'Lord God Almighty, Governor and disposer of heaven and earth! Thou hast opened mine eyes that I follow from henceforth none other than Thee—Have mercy

---

[1] [One of the sculptures of Giotto's Tower at Florence : see *Mornings in Florence,* §§ 125, 132, where it is described in detail.]
[2] [Isaiah lxv. 10.]

upon me!'—He forthwith gave all he had to the poor for the love of God, and went up into a mountain where there was a great hermitage, and dwelt there the rest of his days in penitence and sanctity, surviving down to the days of Pope Martin, who reigned from 1281 to 1284. 'Certain youths,' adds Ghiberti, 'who sought to be skilled in statuary, told me how he was versed both in painting and sculpture, and how he had painted in the Romitorio [hermitage] where he lived; he was an excellent draughtsman and very courteous. When the youths who wished to improve visited him, he received them with much humility, giving them learned instructions, showing them various proportions, and drawing for them many examples, for he was most accomplished in his art. And thus,' he concludes, 'with great humility, he ended his days in that hermitage.'"—Vol. iii. pp. 257–259.

39. We could have wished that Lord Lindsay had further insisted on what will be found to be a characteristic of all the truly Christian or spiritual, as opposed to classical, schools of sculpture—the scenic or painter-like management of effect. The marble is not cut into the actual form of the thing imaged, but oftener into a perspective suggestion of it—the bas-reliefs sometimes almost entirely under cut, and sharp-edged, so as to come clear off a dark ground of shadow; even heads the size of life being in this way rather shadowed out than carved out, as the Madonna of Benedetto da Majano in Santa Maria Novella,[1] one of the cheeks being advanced half an inch out of its proper place—and often the most

---

[1] [This work by Benedetto (1442–1498) is a group in white marble over the tomb of Filippo Strozzi; Ruskin describes it in his Florence diary of 1845 :—
   "*Maria Novella.*—. . . The first place I used to walk to on entering was the tomb of Filippo Strozzi. It furnishes another instance of a sweet defiance of rule in sculpture, for the countenance of the Madonna (it is a Virgin and Child in a medallion) is so carelessly executed that the two sides are unlike each other; but it is full of sweetness, and almost *too* like flesh, more like a painting than stone. This would be felt more but for the simple hood-like cap, which gives the whole group a Michael Angelesque grandeur of line. The upward look and action of the Christ is superb; the common Madonnas of Raffaelle are all of the earth, earthy, compared to it; but it is not easily felt nor seen neither, for the priests let the people hang garlands of muslin roses and pewter offerings around its neck and the Madonna's arms till the group looks like a chimney sweeper's belle on the first of May. I was much surprised to hear this noble work ascribed to Benedetto da Majano, whose undoubted work in the pulpit of Sta. Croce is far inferior to it, and though cleverly . . . [word missing] comes in my mind rather under the general head of cinquecento work than with any distinctive power. Its under portions are peculiarly rich in quantity and wanting in invention, but its cypress landscapes (representing the birth-place of St. Francis) are pretty and characteristic. The rose border round even this Madonna of Sta. Maria is somewhat poor and commonplace."]

audacious violations of proportion admitted, as in the limbs of Michael Angelo's sitting Madonna in the Uffizii;[1] all artifices, also, of deep and sharp cutting being allowed, to gain the shadowy and spectral expressions about the brow and lip which the mere actualities of form could not have conveyed;—the sculptor never following a material model, but feeling after the most momentary and subtle aspects of the countenance—striking these out sometimes suddenly, by rude chiselling, and stopping the instant they are attained—never risking the loss of thought by the finishing of flesh surface. The heads of the Medici sacristy[2] we believe to have been thus left unfinished, as having already the utmost expression which the marble could receive, and incapable of anything but loss from further touches.   So with Mino da Fiesole and Jacopo della Quercia,[3] the workmanship is often hard, sketchy, and angular, having its full effect only at a little distance; but at that distance the statue becomes ineffably alive, even to startling, bearing an aspect of change and uncertainty, as if it were about to vanish, and withal having a light, and sweetness, and incense of passion upon it that silences the looker-on, half in delight, half in expectation. This daring stroke—this transfiguring tenderness—may be shown to characterize all truly Christian sculpture, as compared with the antique, or the pseudo-classical of subsequent periods.   We agree with Lord Lindsay in thinking the Psyche of Naples[4] the nearest approach to the Christian ideal of all ancient efforts; but even in this the approximation is more accidental than real—a fair type of feature, further exalted by the mode in which the imagination supplies the lost upper folds of the hair.   The fountain of life and emotion remains sealed; nor was the opening of that

---

[1] [The reference is to the circular " Madonna and Child, with the child St. John," formerly in the Uffizi, and now in the Bargello.   A photograph of it is reproduced at p. 120 of Sir Charles Holroyd's *Michael Angelo Buonarroti.*]

[2] [Compare *Modern Painters*, vol. ii. (Vol. IV. p. 118).]

[3] [For Mino da Fiesole, see again *Modern Painters*, vol. ii. (Vol. IV. p. 280 and *n.*; for Jacopo della Quercia, *ibid.* (Vol. IV. p. 122).]

[4] [The well-known fragment, found at the amphitheatre of Capua, in the Hall of the Capolavori in the Museum at Naples.]

fountain due to any study of the far less pure examples accessible by the Pisan sculptors. The sound of its waters had been heard long before in the aisles of the Lombard; nor was it by Ghiberti, still less by Donatello, that the bed of that Jordan was dug deepest, but by Michael Angelo, the last heir of the Byzantine traditions descending through Orcagna, opening thenceforward through thickets darker and more dark, and with waves ever more soundless and slow, into the Dead Sea wherein its waters have been stayed.

40. It is time for us to pass to the subject which occupies the larger portion of the work—the History

"of Painting, as developed contemporaneously with her sister, Sculpture, and (like her) under the shadow of the Gothic Architecture, by Giotto and his successors throughout Italy, by Mino, Duccio, and their scholars at Siena, by Orcagna and Fra Angelico da Fiesole at Florence, and by the obscure but interesting primitive school of Bologna, during the fourteenth and the early years of the fifteenth century. The period is one, comparatively speaking, of repose and tranquillity,—the storm sleeps and the winds are still, the currents set in one direction, and we may sail from isle to isle over a sunny sea, dallying with the time, secure of a cloudless sky and of the greetings of innocence and love wheresoever the breeze may waft us. There is in truth a holy purity, an innocent naïveté, a child-like grace and simplicity, a freshness, a fearlessness, an utter freedom from affectation, a yearning after all things truthful, lovely and of good report, in the productions of this early time, which invest them with a charm peculiar in its kind, and which few even of the most perfect works of the maturer era can boast of,—and hence the risk and danger of becoming too passionately attached to them, of losing the power of discrimination, of admiring and imitating their defects as well as their beauties, of running into affectation in seeking after simplicity and into exaggeration in our efforts to be in earnest,—in a word, of forgetting that in art, as in human nature, it is the balance, harmony, and co-equal development of Sense, Intellect, and Spirit, which constitute perfection."—Vol. ii. pp. 161–163.

41. To the thousand islands, or how many soever they may be, we shall allow ourselves to be wafted with all willingness, but not in Lord Lindsay's three-masted vessel, with its balancing topmasts of Sense, Intellect, and Spirit. We are utterly tired of the triplicity; and we are mistaken if its application here be not as inconsistent as it is arbitrary. Turning back to the introduction, which we have quoted, the reader will find that while Architecture is there taken

for the exponent of Sense, Painting is chosen as the peculiar expression of Spirit. "The painting of Christendom is that of an immortal spirit conversing with its God." But in a note to the first chapter of the second volume, he will be surprised to find painting become a "twin of intellect," and architecture suddenly advanced from a type of sense to a type of spirit :—

"Sculpture and Painting, twins of Intellect, rejoice and breathe freest in the pure ether of Architecture, or Spirit, like Castor or Pollux under the breezy heaven of their father Jupiter."—Vol. ii. p. 14.

42. Prepared by this passage to consider painting either as spiritual or intellectual, his patience may pardonably give way on finding in the sixth letter—(what he might, however, have conjectured from the heading of the third period in the chart of the schools)—that the peculiar prerogative of painting—colour, is to be considered as a *sensual* element, and the exponent of sense, in accordance with a new analogy, here for the first time proposed, between spirit, intellect, and sense, and expression, form, and colour. Lord Lindsay is peculiarly unfortunate in his adoptions from previous writers. He has taken this division of art from Fuseli and Reynolds, without perceiving that in those writers it is one of convenience merely, and, even so considered, is as injudicious as illogical. In what does expression consist but in form and colour? It is one of the ends which these accomplish, and may be itself an attribute of both. Colour may be expressive or inexpressive, like music; form expressive or inexpressive, like words; but expression by itself cannot exist; so that to divide painting into colour, form, and expression, is precisely as rational as to divide music into notes, words, and expression. Colour may be pensive, severe, exciting, appalling, gay, glowing, or sensual; in all these modes it is expressive : form may be tender or abrupt, mean or majestic, attractive or overwhelming, discomfortable or delightsome; in all these modes, and many more, it is expressive; and if Lord Lindsay's analogy be in anywise applicable to either form or colour, we should have colour sensual

(Correggio), colour intellectual (Tintoret), colour spiritual (Angelico)—form sensual (French sculpture), form intellectual (Phidias), form spiritual (Michael Angelo). Above all, our author should have been careful how he attached the epithet "sensual" to the element of colour—not only on account of the glaring inconsistency with his own previous assertion of the spirituality of painting—(since it is certainly not merely by being flat instead of solid, representative instead of actual, that painting is—if it be—more spiritual than sculpture); but also, because this idea of sensuality in colour has had much share in rendering abortive the efforts of the modern German religious painters, inducing their abandonment of its consecrating, kindling, purifying power.[1]

43. Lord Lindsay says, in a passage which we shall presently quote, that the most sensual as well as the most religious painters have always loved the brightest colours. Not so; no painters ever were more sensual than the modern French, who are alike insensible to, and incapable of colour —depending altogether on morbid gradation, waxy smoothness of surface, and lusciousness of line, the real elements of sensuality wherever it eminently exists. So far from good colour being sensual, it saves, glorifies, and guards from all evil: it is with Titian, as with all great masters of flesh-painting, the redeeming and protecting element; and with the religious painters, it is a baptism with fire, an under-song of holy Litanies. Is it in sensuality that the fair flush opens upon the cheek of Francia's chanting angel,* until we think it comes, and fades, and returns, as his voice and his harping are louder or lower—or that the silver light rises upon wave after wave of his lifted hair; or that the burning of the blood is seen on the unclouded brows of the three angels of the Campo Santo, and of folded fire within their wings;[2] or that the hollow blue of the highest

* At the feet of his Madonna, in the Gallery of Bologna.

---

[1] [On this subject see *Modern Painters*, vol. ii. (Vol. IV. p. 197); and *Stones of Venice*, vol. ii. (Vol. X. p. 456).]
[2] [The reference is to the fresco of Benozzo Gozzoli at Pisa, "Abraham parting from the Angels" : see Plate opposite p. 316, in Vol. IV.]

heaven mantles the Madonna with its depth, and falls around her like raiment, as she sits beneath the throne of the Sistine Judgment?[1]   Is it in sensuality that the visible world about us is girded with an eternal iris?[2]—is there pollution in the rose and the gentian more than in the rocks that are trusted to their robing?—is the sea-blue a stain upon its water, or the scarlet spring of day upon the mountains less holy than their snow? As well call the sun itself, or the firmament, sensual, as the colour which flows from the one, and fills the other.

44. We deprecate this rash assumption, however, with more regard to the forthcoming portion of the history, in which we fear it may seriously diminish the value of the author's account of the school of Venice, than to the part at present executed.[3]   This is written in a spirit rather sympathetic than critical, and rightly illustrates the feeling of early art, even where it mistakes, or leaves unanalyzed, the technical modes of its expression.   It will be better, perhaps, that we confine our attention to the accounts of the three men who may be considered as sufficient representatives not only of the art of their time, but of all subsequent; Giotto, the first of the great line of dramatists, terminating in Raffaelle; Orcagna, the head of that branch of the contemplative school which leans towards sadness or terror, terminating in Michael Angelo; and Angelico, the head of the contemplatives concerned with the heavenly ideal, around whom may be grouped first Duccio, and the Sienese, who preceded him, and afterwards Pinturiccio,[4] Perugino, and Leonardo da Vinci.

---

[1] [For other references to "The Last Judgment" by Michael Angelo, see *Modern Painters*, vol. ii. (Vol. IV. p. 281).]

[2] [Compare *Deucalion*, ch. vii., "The Iris of the Earth."]

[3] ["The three volumes now published," said Lord Lindsay in his "Advertisement" to vol. i., "comprise a portion only of my projected work on Christian Art." They did not touch on the Venetian school. but no further volumes were published. Lord Lindsay's chapters, it should be noted, are called "Letters."]

[4] [For references to Pinturicchio, see below, "Notes on the Louvre," p. 453; and compare *Modern Painters*, vol. ii. (Vol. IV. pp. 138, 254 n., 331), and *Stones of Venice*, vol. iii. (Vol. XI. p. 14).]

45. The fourth letter opens in the field of Vespignano. The circumstances of the finding of Giotto by Cimabue are well known.[1] Vasari's anecdote of the fly painted upon the nose of one of Cimabue's figures might, we think, have been spared, or at least not instanced as proof of study from nature "nobly rewarded."[2] Giotto certainly never either attempted or accomplished any small imitation of this kind; the story has all the look of one of the common inventions of the ignorant for the ignorant; nor, if true, would Cimabue's careless mistake of a black spot in the shape of a fly for one of the living annoyances of which there might probably be some dozen or more upon his panel at any moment, have been a matter of much credit to his young pupil. The first point of any real interest is Lord Lindsay's confirmation of Förster's attribution of the Campo Santo Life of Job, till lately esteemed Giotto's, to Francesco da Volterra.[3] Förster's evidence appears incontrovertible; yet there is curious internal evidence, we think, in favour of the designs being Giotto's, if not the execution. The landscape is especially Giottesque, the trees being all boldly massed first with dark brown, within which the leaves are painted separately in light: this very archaic treatment had been much softened and modified by the Giotteschi before the date assigned to these frescoes by Förster. But, what is more singular, the figure of Eliphaz, or the foremost of the three friends, occurs in a tempera picture of Giotto's in the Academy of Florence, the Ascension, among the apostles on the left; while the face of another of the three friends is again repeated in the "Christ disputing with the Doctors" of the

---

[1] [Ruskin tells them in *Giotto and his Works in Padua*, § 4, and again in *Mornings in Florence*, § 66. Vasari's story is that "Giotto, when he was still a boy, and studying with Cimabue, once painted a fly on the nose of a figure on which Cimabue himself was employed, and this so naturally, that when the master returned to continue his work, he believed it to be real, and lifted his hand more than once to drive it away before he should go on with the painting" (*Lives of the Artists*, i. 121 (Bohn's translation, 1855).]

[2] [*Sketches of the History of Christian Art*, ii. 167.]

[3] [See *Modern Painters*, vol. i. (Vol. III. p. 183), and *Giotto and his Works in Padua*, § 6. Lord Lindsay's reference (ii. 168 n.) is to Ernst Förster's *Beiträge zur neuern Kunstge-Schichte*, Leipzig, 1835, p. 115.]

small tempera series, also in the Academy;[1] the figure of Satan shows much analogy to that of the Envy of the Arena chapel; and many other portions of the design are evidently either sketches of this very subject by Giotto himself, or dexterous compilations from his works by a loving pupil. Lord Lindsay has not done justice to the upper division—the Satan before God:[2] it is one of the very finest thoughts ever realized by the Giotteschi. The serenity of power in the principal figure is very noble; no expression of wrath, or even of scorn, in the look which commands the evil spirit. The position of the latter, and countenance, are less grotesque and more demoniacal than is usual in paintings of the time; the triple wings expanded—the arms crossed over the breast, and holding each other above the elbow, the claws fixing in the flesh; a serpent buries its head in a cleft in the bosom, and the right hoof is lifted, as if to stamp.

46. We should have been glad if Lord Lindsay had given

---

[1] [The Envy of the Arena Chapel forms the frontispiece to *Fors Clavigera*, Letter 6. The two series of panels in the Accademia are now sometimes attributed to Taddeo Gaddi—one set is of scenes from the life of St. Francis, the other, scenes from the life of Christ; they were formerly in Santa Croce. In his diary of 1845 Ruskin thus notes them :—

> "One feels the evil of colour perhaps more in the celebrated series of the life of our Lord and St. Francis, by Giotto, than in any other works in Florence. These are all exceedingly beautiful in line, but the colour, though not badly arranged, yet compels the eye to dwell on ugly and shapeless spaces, instead of the beautiful harmony of the contours, and half the value of the design is lost. The colours themselves are not painfully glaring as in Buffalmaco, but there is little in them to satisfy and nothing to please. The design looks like the work of the Campo Santo hand, but the drawing of the features is blunt and bad. In the 'Christ disputing with the Doctors,' one of the faces is the same given to one of the three friends of Job in the Campo Santo. Another, the one I have commonly called Eliphaz, occurs in his picture of the Ascension, in the small room, among the Apostles on the left. This I consider the finest tempera figure of Giotto I have seen; the movement and passion of its figures is not to be surpassed. More, however, is told by the action than the expression. Beside it is an Annunciation of extreme beauty; the Virgin folds her hand over her bosom under her blue robe, which being carried with it, gives a grand angular form. All the Virgins in the other series, as well as this one, have a deep blue mantle, which in the standing figures sometimes cuts them all down in half, but the chastity, severity, and modest intensity of feeling indicated by all the actions of this figure, wherever it occurs, are not to be rivalled."]

[2] [This fresco is also referred to in *Modern Painters*, vol. ii. (Vol. IV. p. 318 *n*.); the description here closely follows the entry from Ruskin's diary of 1845, there cited.]

us some clearer idea of the internal evidence on which he founds his determination of the order or date of the works of Giotto. When no trustworthy records exist, we conceive this task to be of singular difficulty, owing to the differences of execution universally existing between the large and small works of the painter. The portrait of Dante [1] in the chapel of the Podestà is proved by Dante's exile, in 1302, to have been painted before Giotto was six-and-twenty; yet we remember no head in any of his works which can be compared with it for carefulness of finish and truth of drawing; the crudeness of the material vanquished by dexterous hatching; the colour not only pure, but deep—a rare virtue with Giotto; the eye soft and thoughtful, the brow nobly modelled. In the fresco of the Death of the Baptist, in Santa Croce, [2] which we agree with Lord Lindsay in

---

[1] [See, again, *Modern Painters*, vol. ii. (Vol. IV. p. 188 and *n*.).]

[2] [In the chapel of the Peruzzi family, probably painted about 1307; one of a series of scenes from the story of the Baptist. The fresco here noticed had been lately uncovered from a coating of whitewash when Ruskin was at Florence in 1845. The following is the note in his diary :—

"Herod and two other persons are sitting at table under a canopy, of which note that the form is the same with Giotto, whether it be the roof of a manger, or the palace of Herod the King. It is painted blue underneath; and behind the figures, a curtain is let down, striped of various colours, exceedingly rich. A musician on the left, playing on the violin, is a most beautiful figure, very like Perugino's treatment of similar subjects, and full of the same subdued feeling. The Herod is also very grand, though perhaps not a good ideal of Herod, for he is calm, kingly, and free from appearance of evil passion. The Herodias sits on the extreme right, the face is nearly gone, but seems to have been made most wicked and sensual. Her daughter, kneeling, presents her with the head. In the centre of the picture the daughter is dancing, or at least moving softly while she plays the lyre, while a soldier brings in the head of St. John. The two actions are thus curiously involved; the soldier comes in between the musician and the dancing maiden, who is immediately repeated on the right in giving the head to her mother. This second figure of her is exceedingly ugly, and the likeness to her mother wonderfully kept; but the figure with the lyre is fine, and would have been beautiful but that the shaded side of it is in colour so nearly the same as the background that it is lost in it, and hence the half of the face looks a badly drawn profile.

"Take it all in all, it is peculiarly interesting to come to this work after Giottino [whose frescoes are in a preceding chapel, that of S. Silvestro]. The former, unless much repainted, shows all the usual signs of inferior power, greater finish, greater care, darker outline, darker and more forcible shading, fewer errors and less life. Giotto's after it comes fresh, inventive, genuine; he makes you think of the scene and not of the painter, his shades are light, his outlines easy, his eyes softly drawn, not made out by hard lines, his countenances full of motion and sentiment. The last time

attributing to the same early period, the face of the musician is drawn with great refinement, and considerable power of rounding surfaces—(though in the drapery may be remarked a very singular piece of archaic treatment: it is warm white, with yellow stripes; the dress itself falls in deep folds, but the striped pattern does not follow the foldings—it is drawn across, as if with a straight ruler).

47. But passing from these frescoes, which are nearly the size of life, to those of the Arena chapel at Padua, erected in 1303, decorated in 1306, which are much smaller, we find the execution proportionably less dexterous.[1]   Of this famous chapel Lord Lindsay says—

"nowhere (save in the Duomo of Orvieto) is the legendary history of the Virgin told with such minuteness.

" The heart must indeed be cold to the charms of youthful art that can enter this little sanctuary without a glow of delight.   From the roof, with its sky of ultra-marine, powdered with stars and interspersed with medallions containing the heads of our Saviour, the Virgin and the Apostles, to the mock panelling of the nave, below the windows, the whole is completely covered with frescoes, in excellent preservation, and all more or less painted by Giotto's own hand, except six in the tribune, which however have apparently been executed from his cartoons. . . .

"These frescoes form a most important document in the history of Giotto's mind, exhibiting all his peculiar merits, although in a state as yet of immature development.   They are full of fancy and invention; the composition is almost always admirable, although sometimes too studiously symmetrical; the figures are few and characteristic, each speaking for itself, the impersonation of a distinct idea, and most dramatically grouped and contrasted; the attitudes are appropriate, easy, and natural; the action and gesticulation singularly vivid; the expression is excellent, except when impassioned grief induces caricature:—devoted to the study of Nature as he is, Giotto had not yet learnt that it is suppressed feeling which affects one most.   The head of our Saviour is beautiful throughout—that of the Virgin not so good—she is modest, but not very graceful or celestial;—it was long before he succeeded in his Virgins—they are much too matronly: among the accessory figures, graceful female forms occasionally appear, foreshadowing those of his later works at Florence and Naples, yet they

I went to look at this work, I could hardly leave it—the faces of the musician and of Herod are worthy of any period of art.   The draperies are, however, somewhat clumsier, rounder, and less felt than those of the Campo Santo, and it is curious to see the yellow stripe of the musician's carried straight across it without in the least following the folds.   Yet this very piece of simplicity gives a severity and character to the figure, which no correct design of drapery could have given."]

[1] [For the Arena chapel, see *Giotto and his Works in Padua* (1854-1855).]

are always clumsy about the waist and bust, and most of them are under-jawed, which certainly detracts from the sweetness of the female counte-nance. His delineation of the naked is excellent, as compared with the works of his predecessors, but far unequal to what he attained in his later years,—the drapery, on the contrary, is noble, majestic, and statuesque; the colouring is still pale and weak,—it was long ere he improved in this point; the landscape displays little or no amendment upon the Byzantine; the architecture, that of the fourteenth century, is to the figures that people it in the proportion of dolls' houses to the children that play with them,—an absurdity long unthinkingly acquiesced in, from its occurrence in the classic bas-reliefs from which it had been traditionally derived;—and, finally, the lineal perspective is very fair, and in three of the compositions an excellent effect is produced by the introduction of the same background with varied *dramatis personæ*, reminding one of Retzsch's illustrations of Faust. The animals too are always excellent, full of spirit and character." —Vol. ii. pp. 183–199.

48. This last characteristic is especially to be noticed.[1] It is a touching proof of the influence of early years. Giotto was only ten years old when he was taken from following the sheep. For the rest, as we have above stated, the manipulation of these frescoes is just as far inferior to that of the Podestà chapel as their dimensions are less; and we think it will be found generally that the smaller the work the more rude is Giotto's hand. In this respect he seems to differ from all other masters.

"It is not difficult, gazing on these silent but eloquent walls, to repeople them with the group once, as we know—five hundred years ago—assembled within them,—Giotto intent upon his work, his wife Ciuta admiring his progress, and Dante, with abstracted eye, alternately conversing with his friend and watching the gambols of the children playing on the grass before the door. It is generally affirmed that Dante, during this visit, inspired Giotto with his taste for allegory, and that the Virtues and Vices of the Arena were the first-fruits of their intercourse; it is possible, certainly, but I doubt it,—allegory was the universal language of the time, as we have seen in the history of the Pisan school."—Vol. ii. pp. 199, 200.

It ought to have been further mentioned, that the repre-sentation of the Virtues and Vices under these Giottesque figures continued long afterwards. We find them copied, for instance, on the capitals of the Ducal Palace at Venice, with an amusing variation on the "Stultitia," who has neither

---

[1] [On Giotto's rendering of dogs, see *Mornings in Florence*, § 132.]

Indian dress nor club, as with Giotto, but is to the Venetians sufficiently distinguished by riding a horse.[1]

49. The notice of the frescoes at Assisi consists of little more than an enumeration of the subjects, accompanied by agreeable translations of the traditions respecting St. Francis, embodied by St. Buonaventura. Nor have we space to follow the author through his examination of Giotto's works at Naples and Avignon.[2] The following account of the erection of the Campanile of Florence is too interesting to be omitted : —

". . .[3] Giotto made a model of his proposed structure, on which every stone was marked, and the successive courses painted red and white, according to his design, so as to match with the Cathedral and Baptistery; this model was of course adhered to strictly during the short remnant of his life, and the work was completed in strict conformity to it after his death, with the exception of the spire, which, the taste having changed, was never added. He had intended it to be one hundred *braccia*, or one hundred and fifty feet high."—Vol. ii. pp. 247–249.

The deficiency of the spire Lord Lindsay does not regret :—

"Let the reader stand before the Campanile, and ask himself whether, with Michael Scott at his elbow, or Aladdin's lamp in his hand, he would supply the deficiency? I think not."—p. 38.

We have more faith in Giotto than our author—and we will reply to his question by two others—whether, looking down

---

[1] [On Capital No. 12 : see *Stones of Venice*, vol. ii. (Vol. X. p. 408); on the comparison generally, see *ibid.*, p. 385.]

[2] [By the advice of Boccaccio, King Robert the Wise summoned Giotto from Florence to cover his church of Santa Chiara at Naples with frescoes; they were destroyed by whitewash in the eighteenth century, but some other fragments of his work remain in the city. For the frescoes at Avignon, formerly attributed to Giotto, see Vol. IX. p. 273 *n*.]

[3] [The first part of the quotation has already been printed, in the Preface to *Lectures on Architecture and Painting*, above, p. 8. The date "*In 1332* Giotto was chosen*" was not given here; the word *universality*, there italicised, was not so here. On the other hand, a passage lower down—*a criticism which the Signoria resented by confining him for two months in prison*—was italicised here, but not there; and in citing the passage there, Ruskin omitted the Italian "della loro più florida potenza," after "their utmost power and greatness," which was here given.]

upon Florence from the hill of San Miniato, his eye rested oftener and more affectionately on the Campanile of Giotto, or on the simple tower and spire of Santa Maria Novella? —and whether, in the backgrounds of Perugino, he would willingly substitute for the church spires invariably introduced, flat-topped campaniles like the unfinished tower of Florence?

50. Giotto sculptured with his own hand two of the bas-reliefs of this campanile, and probably might have executed them all.[1] But the purposes of his life had been accomplished; he died at Florence on the 8th of January, 1337. The concluding notice of his character and achievement is highly valuable:—

"Painting indeed stands indebted to Giotto beyond any of her children. His history is a most instructive one. Endowed with the liveliest fancy, and with that facility which so often betrays genius, and achieving in youth a reputation which the age of Methuselah could not have added to, he had yet the discernment to perceive how much still remained to be done, and the resolution to bind himself (as it were) to Nature's chariot wheel, confident that she would ere long emancipate and own him as her son. Calm and unimpassioned, he seems to have commenced his career with a deliberate survey of the difficulties he had to encounter and of his resources for the conflict, and then to have worked upon a system steadily and perseveringly, prophetically sure of victory. His life was indeed one continued triumph,—and no conqueror ever mounted to the Capitol with a step more equal and sedate. We find him, at first, slowly and cautiously endeavouring to infuse new life into the traditional compositions, by substituting the heads, attitudes, and drapery of the actual world for the spectral forms and conventional types of the mosaics and the Byzantine painters,— idealising them when the personages represented were of higher mark and dignity, but in none ever out-stepping truth. Advancing in his career, we find year by year the fruits of continuous unwearied study in a consistent and equable contemporary improvement in all the various minuter though most important departments of his art, in his design, his drapery, his colouring, in the dignity and expression of his men and in the grace of his women —asperities softened down, little graces unexpectedly born and playing about his path, as if to make amends for the deformity of his actual offspring— touches, daily more numerous, of that nature which makes the world akin —and ever and always a keen yet cheerful sympathy with life, a playful humour mingling with his graver lessons, which affects us the more as coming from one who, knowing himself an object personally of disgust and ridicule, could yet satirise with a smile.

---

[1] [See above, p. 206 n.]

"Finally, throughout his works, we are conscious of an earnest, a lofty, a religious aim and purpose, as of one who felt himself a pioneer of civilization in a newly-discovered world, the Adam of a new Eden freshly planted in the earth's wilderness, a mouthpiece of God and a preacher of righteousness to mankind.—And here we must establish a distinction very necessary to be recognised before we can duly appreciate the relative merits of the elder painters in this, the most important point in which we can view their character. Giotto's genius, however universal, was still (as I have repeatedly observed) Dramatic rather than Contemplative,—a tendency in which his scholars and successors almost to a man resembled him. Now, just as in actual life—where, with a few rare exceptions, all men rank under two great categories according as Imagination or Reason predominates in their intellectual character—two individuals may be equally impressed with the truths of Christianity and yet differ essentially in its outward manifestation, the one dwelling in action, the other in contemplation, the one in strife, the other in peace, the one (so to speak) in hate, the other in love, the one struggling with devils, the other communing with angels, yet each serving as a channel of God's mercies to man, each (we may believe) offering Him service equally acceptable in His sight—even so shall we find it in art and with artists; few in whom the Dramatic power predominates will be found to excel in the expression of religious emotions of the more abstract and enthusiastic cast, even although men of indisputably pure and holy character themselves; and *vice versâ*, few of the more Contemplative but will feel bewildered and at fault, if they descend from their starry region of light into the grosser atmosphere that girdles in this world of action. The works of artists are their minds' mirror; they cannot express what they do not feel; each class dwells apart and seeks its ideal in a distinct sphere of emotion,—their object is different, and their success proportioned to the exclusiveness with which they pursue that object. A few indeed there have been in all ages, monarchs of the mind and types of our Saviour, who have lived a two-fold existence of action and contemplation in art, in song, in politics, and in daily life; of these have been Abraham, Moses, David, and Cyrus in the elder world—Alfred, Charlemagne, Dante, and perhaps Shakspeare, in the new,—and in art, Niccola Pisano, Leonard [*sic*] da Vinci and Michael Angelo. But Giotto, however great as the patriarch of his peculiar tribe, was not of these few, and we ought not therefore to misapprehend him, or be disappointed at finding his Madonnas (for instance) less exquisitely spiritual than the Sienese, or those of Fra Angelico and some later painters, who seem to have dipped their pencils in the rainbow that circles the throne of God,—they are pure and modest, but that is all; on the other hand, where his Contemplative rivals lack utterance, he speaks most feelingly to the heart in his own peculiar language of Dramatic composition—he glances over creation with the eye of love, all the charities of life follow in his steps, and his thoughts are as the breath of the morning. A man of the world, living in it and loving it, yet with a heart that it could not spoil or wean from its allegiance to God—'non meno buon Cristiano che eccellente pittore,' as Vasari emphatically describes him—his religion breathes of the free air of heaven rather than the cloister, neither enthusiastic nor superstitious, but practical, manly and healthy—and this, although the picturesque biographer of S. Francis!"—Vol. ii. pp. 260-264.

51. This is all as admirably felt as expressed, and to those acquainted with and accustomed to love the works of the painter, it leaves nothing to be asked for; but we must again remind Lord Lindsay, that he has throughout left the *artistical* orbit of Giotto undefined, and the offence of his manner unremoved, as far as regards the uninitiated spectator. We question whether from all that he has written, the un-travelled reader could form any distinct idea of the painter's peculiar merits or methods, or that the estimate, if formed, might not afterwards expose him to severe disappointment. It ought especially to have been stated, that the Giottesque system of chiaroscuro is one of pure, quiet, pervading day-light. No *cast* shadows ever occur, and this remains a marked characteristic of all the works of the Giotteschi. Of course, all subtleties of reflected light or raised colour are unthought of. Shade is only given as far as it is necessary to the articulation of simple forms, nor even then is it rightly adapted to the colour of the light; the folds of the draperies are well drawn, but the entire rounding of them always missed—the general forms appearing flat, and terminated by equal and severe outlines, while the masses of ungradated colour often seem to divide the figure into fragments. Thus, the Madonna in the small tempera series of the Academy of Florence,[1] is usually divided exactly in half by the dark mass of her blue robe, falling in a vertical line. In con-sequence of this defect, the grace of Giotto's composition can hardly be felt until it is put into outline. The colours themselves are of good quality, never glaring, always glad-dening, the reds inclining to orange more than purple, yellow frequent, the prevalent tone of the colour groups warm; the sky always blue, the whole effect somewhat re-sembling that of the Northern painted glass of the same century—and chastened in the same manner by noble neutral tints or greens; yet all somewhat unconsidered and unsystematic, painful discords not unfrequent. The material

---

[1] [See above, § 45, p. 214.]

and ornaments of dress are never particularized, no imitations of texture or jewellery, yet shot stuffs of two colours frequent. The drawing often powerful, though of course uninformed; the mastery of mental expression by bodily motion, and of bodily motion, past and future, by a single gesture, altogether unrivalled even by Raffaelle;—it is obtained chiefly by throwing the emphasis always on the right line, admitting straight lines of great severity, and never dividing the main drift of the drapery by inferior folds; neither are accidents allowed to interfere—the garments fall heavily and in marked angles—nor are they affected by the wind, except under circumstances of very rapid motion. The ideal of the face is often solemn—seldom beautiful; occasionally ludicrous failures occur: in the smallest designs the face is very often a dead letter, or worse: and in all, Giotto's handling is generally to be distinguished from that of any of his followers by its bluntness. In the school work we find sweeter types of feature, greater finish, stricter care, more delicate outline, fewer errors, but on the whole less life.

52. Finally, and on this we would especially insist, Giotto's genius is not to be considered as struggling with difficulty and repressed by ignorance, but as appointed, for the good of men, to come into the world exactly at the time when its rapidity of invention was not likely to be hampered by demands for imitative dexterity or neatness of finish; and when, owing to the very ignorance which has been unwisely regretted, the simplicity of his thoughts might be uttered with a childlike and innocent sweetness, never to be recovered in times of prouder knowledge.[1] The dramatic power of his works, rightly understood, could receive no addition from artificial arrangement of shade, or scientific exhibition of anatomy, and we have reason to be deeply grateful when afterwards " inland far " with Buonaroti and

---

[1] [Compare with this passage that upon Giotto in *Stones of Venice*, vol. iii. (Vol. XI. p. 205).]

Titian, that we can look back to the Giotteschi—to see those children

"Sport upon the shore
And hear the mighty waters rolling evermore."[1]

We believe Giotto himself felt this—unquestionably he could have carried many of his works much farther in finish, had he so willed it; but he chose rather to multiply motives than to complete details. Thus we recur to our great principle of Separate gift.[2] The man who spends his life in toning colours must leave the treasures of his invention untold—let each have his perfect work; and while we thank Bellini and Leonardo for their deeply wrought dyes, and life-laboured utterance of passionate thought; let us remember also what cause, but for the remorseless destruction of myriads of his works, we should have had to thank Giotto, in that, abandoning all proud effort, he chose rather to make the stones of Italy cry out with one voice of pauseless praise, and to fill with perpetual remembrance of the Saints he loved, and perpetual honour of the God he worshipped, palace chamber and convent cloister, lifted tower and lengthened wall, from the utmost blue of the plain of Padua to the Southern wildernesses of the hermit-haunted Apennine.[3]

53. From the head of the Dramatic branch of Art, we turn to the first of the great Contemplative Triad, associated, as it most singularly happens in name as well as in heart; Orcagna = Arcagnuolo; Fra Giovanni—detto Angelico; and Michael Angelo:—the first two names being bestowed by contemporary admiration.

"Orcagna was born apparently about the middle of the (14th) century, and was christened Andrea, by which name, with the addition of that of

---

[1] [Wordsworth's ode, *Intimations of Immortality from Recollections of Early Childhood*:
" Hence in a season of calm weather
Though inland far we be,
Our souls have sight of that immortal sea
Which brought us hither,
Can in a moment travel thither,
And see the children sport," etc.]

[2] [See above, § 34, p. 203.]

[3] [Compare *Giotto and his Works in Padua*, § 18 : "Thus he went, a serene labourer, throughout the length and breadth of Italy."]

his father, Cione, he always designated himself; that, however, of Orcagna, a corruption of Arcagnuolo, or 'The Archangel,' was given him by his contemporaries, and by this he has become known to posterity.

"The earliest works of Orcagna will be found in that sanctuary of Semi-Byzantine art, the Campo Santo of Pisa. He there painted three of the four 'Novissima,' Death, Judgment, Hell, and Paradise—the two former entirely himself, the third with the assistance of his brother Bernardo, who is said to have coloured it after his designs. The first of the series, a most singular performance, had for centuries been popularly known as the 'Trionfo della Morte.' It is divided by an immense rock into two irregular portions. In that to the right, Death, personified as a female phantom, bat-winged, claw-footed, her robe of linked mail [?] and her long hair streaming on the wind, swings back her scythe in order to cut down a company of the rich ones of the earth, Castruccio Castracani and his gay companions, seated under an orange-grove, and listening to the music of a troubadour and a female minstrel; little genii or Cupids, with reversed torches, float in the air above them; one young gallant caresses his hawk, a lady her lap-dog, —Castruccio alone looks abstractedly away, as if his thoughts were elsewhere. But all are alike heedless and unconscious, though the sand is run out, the scythe falling and their doom sealed. Meanwhile the lame and the halt, the withered and the blind, to whom the heavens are brass and life a burthen, cry on Death with impassioned gestures, to release them from their misery,—but in vain; she sweeps past, and will not hear them. Between these two groups lie a heap of corpses, mown down already in her flight—kings, queens, bishops, cardinals, young men and maidens, secular and ecclesiastical—ensigned by their crowns, coronets, necklaces, mitres and helmets—huddled together in hideous confusion; some are dead, others dying,—angels and devils draw the souls out of their mouths; that of a nun (in whose hand a purse, firmly clenched, betokens her besetting sin) shrinks back aghast at the unlooked-for sight of the demon who receives it—an idea either inherited or adopted from Andrea Tafi. The whole upper half of the fresco, on this side, is filled with angels and devils carrying souls to heaven or to hell; sometimes a struggle takes place, and a soul is rescued from a demon who has unwarrantably appropriated it; the angels are very graceful, and their intercourse with their spiritual charge is full of tenderness and endearment; on the other hand, the wicked are hurried off by the devils and thrown headlong into the mouths of hell, represented as the crater of a volcano, belching out flames nearly in the centre of the composition. These devils exhibit every variety of horror in form and feature." —Vol. iii. pp. 130–134.

54. We wish our author had been more specific in his account of this wonderful fresco.[1] The portrait of Castruccio ought to have been signalized as a severe disappointment to the admirers[2] of the heroic Lucchese: the face is flat,

---

[1] [For other references by Ruskin to the "Trionfo della Morte," see *Lectures on Architecture and Painting*, § 123, above, p. 146; and *Modern Painters*, vol. iii. ch. iv. § 20, ch. viii. § 6.]

[2] [Among whom was Ruskin: see *Verona and its Rivers*, § 22. Castruccio Castracani (1283–1328), a native of Lucca having been exiled from his native city,

lifeless, and sensual, though fine in feature. The group of mendicants occupying the centre are especially interesting, as being among the first existing examples of hard study from the model : all are evidently portraits—and the effect of deformity on the lines of the countenance rendered with appalling truth ; the retractile muscles of the mouth wrinkled and fixed—the jaws projecting—the eyes hungry and glaring— the eyebrows grisly and stiff, the painter having drawn each hair separately : the two stroppiati[1] with stumps instead of arms are especially characteristic, as the observer may at once determine by comparing them with the descendants of the originals, of whom he will at any time find two, or more, waiting to accompany his return across the meadow in front of the Duomo : the old woman also, nearest of the group, with grey dishevelled hair and grey coat, with a brown girdle and gourd flask, is magnificent, and the archetype of all modern conceptions of witch. But the crowning stroke of feeling is dependent on a circumstance seldom observed. As Castruccio and his companions are seated under the shade of an orange grove, so the mendicants are surrounded by a thicket of *teazles*, and a branch of ragged thorn is twisted like a crown about their sickly temples and weedy hair.

55. We do not altogether agree with our author in thinking that the devils exhibit every variety of horror ; we rather fear that the spectator might at first be reminded by them of what is commonly known as the Dragon pattern of Wedgwood ware.[2] There is invention in them however — and energy ; the eyes are always terrible, though simply drawn —a black ball set forward, and two-thirds surrounded by a narrow crescent of white, under a shaggy brow ; the mouths are frequently magnificent ; that of a demon accompanying a thrust of a spear with a growl, on the right of the picture,

served as a soldier in England, France, and Lombardy, till he returned to Italy in 1313, when he was chosen chief of the Ghibellines. For other references to him, see *Val d'Arno*, § 278, and *Fors Clavigera*, Letters 18 and 51.]

[1] [Cripples ; literally " maimed."]

[2] [Compare the extract from Ruskin's diary given at Vol. IV. p. 159 *n*.]

is interesting as an example of the development of the canine teeth noticed by Sir Charles Bell (*Essay on Expression*, p. 138 [1])—its capacity of laceration is unlimited: another, snarling like a tiger at an angel who has pulled a soul out of his claws, is equally well conceived; we know nothing like its ferocity except Rembrandt's sketches of wounded wild beasts.[2] The angels we think generally disappointing; they are for the most part diminutive in size, and the crossing of the extremities of the two wings that cover the feet, gives them a coleopterous, cockchafer look, which is not a little undignified; the colours of their plumes are somewhat coarse and dark—one is covered with silky hair, instead of feathers. The souls they contend for are indeed of sweet expression; but exceedingly earthly in contour, the painter being unable to deal with the nude form. On the whole, he seems to have reserved his highest powers for the fresco which follows next, in order, the scene of Resurrection and Judgment.

"It is, in the main, the traditional Byzantine composition, even more rigidly symmetrical than usual, singularly contrasting in this respect with the rush and movement of the preceding compartment. Our Saviour and the Virgin, seated side by side, each on a rainbow and within a vesica piscis, appear in the sky—Our Saviour uttering the words of malediction with uplifted arm, showing the wound in his side, and nearly in the attitude of Michael Angelo, but in wrath, not in fury—the Virgin timidly drawing back and gazing down in pity and sorrow. I never saw this co-equal juxtaposition in any other representation of the Last Judgment."—Vol. iii. p. 136.

56. The positions of our Saviour and of the Virgin are not strictly co-equal; the glory in which the Madonna is seated is both lower and less;[3] but the equality is more complete in the painting of the same subject in Santa M. Novella.[4] We believe Lord Lindsay is correct in thinking

---

[1] [For this book, see *Modern Painters*, vol. ii. (Vol. IV. p. 381).]
[2] [For another reference to Rembrandt's work in this sort, see *Modern Painters*, vol. v. pt. ix. ch. vi. § 19.]
[3] [With § 56 compare Ruskin's detailed description of this fresco, *ibid*. (Vol. IV. p. 275 *n.*).]
[4] [Orcagna's frescoes are in the Strozzi Chapel.]

Orcagna the only artist who has dared it. We question whether even wrath be intended in the countenance of the principal figure; on the contrary, we think it likely to disappoint at first, and appear lifeless in its exceeding tranquillity; the brow is indeed slightly knit, but the eyes have no local direction. They comprehend all things — are set upon all spirits alike, as in that *word-fresco* of our own, not unworthy to be set side by side with this, the Vision of the Trembling Man in the House of the Interpreter.[1] The action is as majestic as the countenance — the right hand seems raised rather to show its wound (as the left points at the same instant to the wound in the side), than in condemnation, though its gesture has been adopted as one of threatening—first (and very nobly) by Benozzo Gozzoli, in the figure of the Angel departing, looking towards Sodom—and afterwards, with unfortunate exaggeration, by Michael Angelo.[2] Orcagna's Madonna we think a failure, but his strength has been more happily displayed in the Apostolic circle. The head of St. John is peculiarly beautiful. The other Apostles look forward or down as in judgment—some in indignation, some in pity, some serene—but the eyes of St. John are fixed upon the Judge Himself with the stability of love—intercession and sorrow struggling for utterance with awe—and through both is seen a tremor of submissive astonishment, that the lips which had once forbidden his to call down fire from heaven should now themselves burn with irrevocable condemnation.

"One feeling for the most part pervades this side of the composition,— there is far more variety in the other; agony is depicted with fearful intensity and in every degree and character; some clasp their hands, some hide their faces, some look up in despair, but none towards Christ; others seem to have grown idiots with horror:—a few gaze, as if fascinated, into the gulf of fire towards which the whole mass of misery are being urged by the ministers of doom—the flames bite them, the devils fish for and catch them with long grappling-hooks:—in sad contrast to the group on the

[1] [*Pilgrim's Progress*, p. 33 (Golden Treasury edition): a description of the Last Judgment.]
[2] [For Gozzoli's angel, see the Plate opposite p. 316 in Vol. IV.; the fresco is described, and Michael Angelo's adoption of the attitude noted, at p. xxx. of the same volume.]

opposite side, a queen, condemned herself but self-forgetful, vainly struggles to rescue her daughter from a demon who has caught her by the gown and is dragging her backwards into the abyss—her sister, wringing her hands, looks on in agony—it is a fearful scene.

"A vast rib or arch in the walls of pandemonium admits one into the contiguous gulf of Hell, forming the third fresco, or rather a continuation of the second—in which Satan sits in the midst, in gigantic terror, cased in armour and crunching sinners—of whom Judas, especially, is eaten and ejected, re-eaten and re-ejected again and again for ever. The punishments of the wicked are portrayed in circles numberless around him. But in everything save horror this compartment is inferior to the preceding, and it has been much injured and repainted."—Vol. iii. p. 138.

57. We might have been spared all notice of this last compartment. Throughout Italy, owing, it may be supposed, to the interested desire of the clergy to impress upon the populace as forcibly as possible the verity of purgatorial horrors, nearly every representation of the *Inferno* has been repainted, and vulgar butchery substituted for the expressions of punishment which were too chaste for monkish purposes. The infernos of Giotto at Padua,[1] and of Orcagna at Florence, have thus been destroyed; but in neither case have they been replaced by anything so merely disgusting as these restorations by Solazzino in the Campo Santo.[2] Not a line of Orcagna's remains, except in one row of figures halfway up the wall, where his firm black drawing is still distinguishable; throughout the rest of the fresco, hillocks of pink flesh have been substituted for his severe forms—and for his agonized features, puppets' heads with roaring mouths and staring eyes, the whole as coarse and sickening, and quite as weak, as any scrabble on the lowest booths of a London Fair.

58. Lord Lindsay's comparison of these frescoes of Orcagna with the great work in the Sistine, is, as a specimen of his writing, too good not to be quoted:—

"While Michael Angelo's leading idea seems to be the self-concentration and utter absorption of all feeling into the one predominant thought, *Am I, individually, safe?* resolving itself into two emotions only, doubt and

---

[1] [For a reproduction of Giotto's "Inferno," see *Giotto and his Works at Padua*.]
[2] [See again *Modern Painters*, vol. ii. (Vol. IV. p. 201 and *n*.). The repainting by Solazzino was done in 1530.]

despair—all diversities of character, all kindred sympathies annihilated under their pressure—those emotions uttering themselves, not through the face but the form, by bodily contortion, rendering the whole composition, with all its overwhelming merits, a mighty hubbub—Orcagna's on the contrary embraces the whole world of passions that make up the economy of man, and these not confused or crushed into each other, but expanded and enhanced in quality and intensity commensurably with the 'change' attend- ant upon the resurrection—variously expressed indeed, and in reference to the diversities of individual character, which will be nowise compromised by that change, yet from their very intensity suppressed and subdued, stilling the body and informing only the soul's index, the countenance. All there- fore is calm; the saved have acquiesced in all things, they can mourn no more—the damned are to them as if they had never been;—among the lost, grief is too deep, too settled for caricature, and while every feeling of the spectator, every key of the soul's organ, is played upon by turns, tenderness and pity form the under-song throughout and ultimately prevail; the curse is uttered in sorrow rather than wrath, and from the pitying Virgin and the weeping archangel above, to the mother endeavouring to rescue her daughter below, and the young secular led to paradise under the approving smile of S. Michael, all resolves itself into sympathy and love.—Michael Angelo's conception may be more efficacious for teaching by terror—it was his object, I believe, as the heir of Savonarola and the representative of the Protestant spirit within the bosom of Catholicism; but Orcagna's is in better taste, truer to human nature, sublimer in philosophy, and (if I mistake not) more scriptural."—Vol. iii. pp. 139–141.

59. We think it somewhat strange that the object of teaching by terror should be attributed to M. Angelo more than to Orcagna, seeing that the former, with his usual dignity, has refused all representation of infernal punishment —except in the figure dragged down with the hand over the face, the serpent biting the thigh, and in the fiends of the extreme angle; while Orcagna, whose intention may be conjectured even from Solazzino's restoration, exhausted him- self in detailing Dante's distribution of torture, and brings into successive prominence every expedient of pain; the prong, the spit, the rack, the chain, venomous fang and rending beak, harrowing point and dividing edge, biting fiend and calcining fire. The objects of the two great painters were indeed opposed, but not in this respect. Orcagna's, like that of every great painter of his day, was to write upon the wall, as in a book, the greatest possible number of those religious facts or doctrines which the Church desired should be known to the people. This he did in the simplest

and most straightforward way, regardless of artistical reputation, and desiring only to be read and understood. But
Michael Angelo's object was from the beginning that of an
artist.   He addresses not the sympathies of his day, but the
understanding of all time, and he treats the subject in the
mode best adapted to bring every one of his own powers
into full play.[1]   As might have been expected, while the
self-forgetfulness of Orcagna has given, on the one hand,
an awfulness to his work, and verity, which are wanting in
the studied composition of the Sistine, on the other it has
admitted a puerility commensurate with the narrowness of
the religion he had to teach.

60. Greater differences still result from the opposed
powers and idiosyncrasies of the two men.   Orcagna was
unable to draw the nude—on this inability followed a coldness to the value of flowing lines, and to the power of
unity in composition—neither could he indicate motion or
buoyancy in flying or floating figures, nor express violence
of action in the limbs—he cannot even show the difference
between pulling and pushing in the muscles of the arm.   In
M. Angelo these conditions were directly reversed.   Intense
sensibility to the majesty of writhing, flowing, and connected
lines, was in him associated with a power, unequalled except
by Angelico, of suggesting aërial motion—motion deliberate
or disturbed, inherent or impressed, impotent or inspired—
gathering into glory, or gravitating to death.   Orcagna was
therefore compelled to range his figures symmetrically in
ordered lines, while Michael Angelo bound them into chains,
or hurled them into heaps, or scattered them before him as
the wind does leaves.   Orcagna trusted for all his expression
to the countenance, or to rudely explained gesture aided by
grand fall of draperies, though in all these points he was
still immeasurably inferior to his colossal rival.   As for his
" embracing the whole world of passions which make up the
economy of man," he had no such power of delineation—

---

[1] [With this comparison, compare the general statement in *Lectures on Architecture
and Painting*, § 123, pp. 145–147.]

nor, we believe, of conception. The expressions on the inferno side are all of them varieties of grief and fear, differing merely in degree, not in character or operation : there is something dramatic in the raised hand of a man wearing a green bonnet with a white plume—but the only really far-carried effort in the group is the head of a Dominican monk [1] (just above the queen in green), who, in the midst of the close crowd, struggling, shuddering, and howling on every side, is fixed in quiet, total despair, insensible to all things, and seemingly poised in existence and sensation upon that one point in his past life when his steps first took hold on hell ; [2] this head, which is opposed to a face distorted by horror beside it, is, we repeat, the only highly wrought piece of expression in the group.

61. What Michael Angelo could do by expression of countenance alone, let the Pietà of Genoa tell, [3] or the Lorenzo, or the parallel to this very head of Orcagna's, the face of the man borne down in the Last Judgment with the hand clenched over one of the eyes. Neither in that fresco is he wanting in dramatic episode ; the adaptation of the Niobe on the spectator's left hand is far finer than Orcagna's condemned queen and princess ; the groups rising below, side by side, supporting each other, are full of tenderness, and reciprocal devotion ; the contest in the centre for the body which a demon drags down by the hair is another kind of quarrel from that of Orcagna between a feathered angel and bristly fiend for a diminutive soul—reminding us, as it forcibly did at first, of a vociferous difference in opinion between a cat and a cockatoo. But Buonaroti knew that it was useless to concentrate interest in the countenances, in a picture of enormous size, ill lighted ; and he preferred giving full play to the powers of line-grouping, for which he could have found no nobler field. Let us not by unwise

---

[1] [With this, compare the passage from Ruskin's diary of 1845 given in Vol. IV. p. 276.]

[2] [Proverbs v. 5.]

[3] [For this medallion, see *ibid.* (Vol. IV. pp. 138 and *n.*, p. 285 *n.*); and for the Lorenzo, p. 285 *n.*]

comparison mingle with our admiration of these two sublime works any sense of weakness in the naïveté of the
one, or of coldness in the science of the other.   Each painter
has his own sufficient dominion, and he who complains of
the want of knowledge in Orcagna, or of the display of it
in Michael Angelo, has probably brought little to his judgment of either.

62. One passage more we must quote, well worthy of
remark in these days of hollowness and haste, though we
question the truth of the particular fact stated in the second
volume respecting the shrine of Or San Michele.[1]   Cement
is now visible enough in all the joints, but whether from
recent repairs we cannot say :—

"There is indeed another, a technical merit, due to Orcagna, which I
would have mentioned earlier, did it not partake so strongly of a moral
virtue.   Whatever he undertook to do, he did well—by which I mean,
better than anybody else.   His Loggia, in its general structure and its
provisions against injury from wet and decay, is a model of strength no
less than symmetry and elegance ; the junction of the marbles in the
tabernacle of Or San Michele, and the exquisite manual workmanship of
the bas-reliefs, have been the theme of praise for five centuries; his colours
in the Campo Santo have maintained a freshness unrivalled by those of
any of his successors there ;—nay, even had his mosaics been preserved at
Orvieto, I am confident the *commettitura* would be found more compact and
polished than any previous to the sixteenth century.   The secret of all
this was that he made himself thoroughly an adept in the mechanism of
the respective arts, and therefore his works have stood.   Genius is too apt
to think herself independent of form and matter—never was there such
a mistake ; she cannot slight either without hamstringing herself.   But
the rule is of universal application ; without this thorough mastery of their
respective tools, this determination honestly to make the best use of them,
the divine, the soldier, the statesman, the philosopher, the poet—however
genuine their enthusiasm, however lofty their genius—are mere empirics,
pretenders to crowns they will not run for, children not men—sporters with
Imagination, triflers with Reason, with the prospects of humanity, with Time,
and with God."—Vol. iii. pp. 148, 149.

A noble passage this,[2] and most true, provided we distinguish always between mastery of tool together with
thorough strength of workmanship, and mere neatness of
outside polish or fitting of measurement, of which ancient
masters are daringly scornful.

[1] [Referred to also in *Modern Painters*, vol. ii. (Vol. IV. p. 300).]
[2] [The passage is also referred to in *Seven Lamps*, Vol. VIII. p. 197.]

63. None of Orcagna's pupils, except Francisco Traini,[1] attained celebrity—

"nothing in fact is known of them except their names. Had their works, however inferior, been preserved, we might have had less difficulty in establishing the links between himself and his successor in the supremacy of the Semi-Byzantine school at Florence, the Beato Fra Angelico da Fiesole. . . . He was born at Vicchio, near Florence, it is said in 1387, and was baptized by the name of Guido. Of a gentle nature, averse to the turmoil of the world, and pious to enthusiasm, though as free from fanaticism as his youth was innocent of vice, he determined, at the age of twenty, though well provided for in a worldly point of view, to retire to the cloister; he professed himself accordingly a brother of the monastery of S. Domenico at Fiesole in 1407, assuming his monastic name from the Apostle of love, S. John. He acquired from his residence there the distinguishing surname 'da Fiesole;' and a calmer retreat for one weary of earth and desirous of commerce with heaven would in vain be sought for;—the purity of the atmosphere, the freshness of the morning breeze, the starry clearness and delicious fragrance of the nights, the loveliness of the valley at one's feet, lengthening out, like a life of happiness, between the Apennine and the sea—with the intermingling sounds that ascend perpetually from below, softened by distance into music, and by an agreeable compromise at once giving a zest to solitude and cheating it of its loneliness—rendering Fiesole a spot which angels might alight upon by mistake in quest of paradise, a spot where it would be at once sweet to live and sweet to die."—Vol. iii. pp. 151–153.

64. Our readers must recollect that the convent where Fra Giovanni first resided is not that whose belfry tower and cypress grove crown the "top of Fésole."[2] The Dominican convent is situated at the bottom of the slope of olives, distinguished only by its narrow and low spire; a cypress avenue recedes from it towards Florence—a stony path, leading to the ancient Badia of Fiesole, descends in front of the three-arched loggia which protects the entrance to the church. No extended prospect is open to it; though over the low wall, and through the sharp, thickset olive leaves, may be seen one silver gleam of the Arno, and, at evening,

---

[1] ["Among all the disciples of Orcagna, none," says Vasari, "was found superior to Francesco Traini" (Bohn's ed., vol. i. p. 217). A picture by him (mentioned by Vasari), of "St. Thomas Aquinas" in the church of St. Catarina at Pisa is still *in situ*. An altar-piece by Traini is in the Accademia at Florence; it was finished in 1346.]

[2] [*Paradise Lost*, i. 289; see Vol. IV. p. 352 and *n*.]

the peaks of the Carrara mountains, purple against the twilight, dark and calm, while the fire-flies glance beneath, silent and intermittent, like stars upon the rippling of mute, soft sea.

"It is by no means an easy task to adjust the chronology of Fra Angelico's works; he has affixed no dates to them, and consequently, when external evidence is wanting, we are thrown upon internal, which in his case is unusually fallacious. It is satisfactory therefore to possess a fixed date in 1433, the year in which he painted the great tabernacle for the Company of Flax-merchants, now removed to the gallery of the Uffizii. It represents the Virgin and child, with attendant Saints, on a gold ground—very dignified and noble, although the Madonna has not attained the exquisite spirituality of his later efforts. Round this tabernacle as a nucleus, may be classed a number of paintings, all of similar excellence—admirable that is to say, but not of his very best, and in which, if I mistake not, the type of the Virgin bears throughout a strong family resemblance."—Vol. iii. pp. 160, 161.

65. If the painter ever increased in power after this period (he was then forty-three), we have been unable to systematize the improvement. We much doubt whether, in his modes of execution, advance were possible. Men whose merit lies in record of natural facts, increase in knowledge; and men whose merit is in dexterity of hand increase in facility; but we much doubt whether the faculty of design, or force of feeling, increase after the age of twenty-five. By Fra Angelico, who drew always in fear and trembling, dexterous execution had been from the first repudiated; he neither needed nor sought technical knowledge of the form, and the inspiration, to which his power was owing, was not less glowing in youth than in age. The inferiority traceable (we grant) in this Madonna[1] results not from its early date, but

---

[1] [There is a long note on this picture in Ruskin's Florentine diary of 1845, from which some of the description in § 66 here is taken. Some additional passages may be given :—

"Perhaps the most valuable single work of Angelico in Florence, except the Judgment of the Accademia. The following points require notice. The Christ is standing on the knees of the Virgin, one hand raised in the usual attitude of benediction, the other holding a globe. The face looks straight forward with the ineffable expression of divinity. The grandeur of this conception as opposed to Raphael's contemptible domesticity needs no comment. . . . [A] fault [in the Madonna] is the hard drawing of the iris and pupil of the eye, terminated by a strong black line, without any dark

from Fra Angelico's incapability, always visible, of drawing the head of life size. He is, in this respect, the exact reverse of Giotto; he was essentially a miniature painter, and never attained the mastery of muscular play in the features

to support it. This is also not an unfrequent error in him; it occurs painfully in the Incoronazione of the Virgin [also in the Accademia] . . . and it is by its entire freedom from this defect that the Madonna of San Domenico in Fiesole assumes such superiority over all his large works. In his smaller works, from necessity, this line is not so conspicuous, and even when not filled in, it only gives greater transparency to the eye. Thus the small dancing angels of the Incoronazione have lovely dark eyes, while the larger figures have the circular line.

" The Madonna of which we are at present speaking, besides these defects, is too calm and cold in expression, and in her gorgeous draperies approaches more to the character of an idol, and less to that of a saint than I like to see. The dress of the Christ is brown, with golden girdle; that of the Madonna blue and red.

" Of the surrounding angels, the first on the right beating the drum is to be noted for the glorious crimson of the plumes of its wings, graduated down to the extremities darker and richer almost to blackness. It seems enamel over the gold. The face is turned full front, the eyes looking forward; the flame of fire on the head is a triangle with concave sides. It is remarkable how much of the refinement of the face would have been lost had these lines been straight instead of curved. There is a curious white baton in the left hand, with which the drum is touched, apparently to modify the sound. The second is blowing a trumpet upwards; the third, which is almost the finest of all, is beating a tambourine with a quiet, continuous motion, the second rising up from beneath his hand as he floats through heaven: the hair in pale ringlets over the brow, falling lower and lower on the neck to the back of the head. These do not so much as tremble, but the tongue of fire on the forehead waves with his motion. The dress, greenish blue, embroidered with gold; the wings, alternately scarlet and brown, starred with gold. These stars, which are frequently used by the painter, are obtained by a single blow with a gouge through the enamel on the gold, which, being indented, reflects the light, which plays on different parts of the wing according to the position of the spectator. The workmanship of this kind throughout his works, considered as mere jewellery, is of the most exquisite kind, and all other jewellery looks coarse beside it. The fourth angel has a psaltery; the fifth bends forward and down, looking up at the same time while he clashes the cymbals; one sees that the whole stoop is in accordance with a cadence of music, a divine figure.

" The angels on the opposite side are perhaps not quite so perfect, except two—the second who is also beating a tambourine, his head bent aside in listening, and who in expression of rapture surpasses all; and the third who has just removed the trumpet from his lips, and with his right hand listens to the last blast of it passing away in space. I have said 'his' and 'he' in speaking of these angels, but they have no sex; they have the power and majesty of men with female delicacy of feature and softness of expression. Of the beauty of their faces no words can give any idea : they are to my mind, after the 'Annunciation' of Sta. Maria Novella, the most exalted and faultless conceptions which the human mind has ever reached of divine things."]

necessary in a full-sized drawing. His habit, almost constant, of surrounding the iris of the eye by a sharp black line, is, in small figures, perfectly successful, giving a transparency and tenderness not otherwise expressible. But on a larger scale it gives a stony stare to the eyeball, which not all the tenderness of the brow and mouth can conquer or redeem.

66. Further, in this particular instance, the ear has by accident been set too far back—(Fra Angelico, drawing only from feeling, was liable to gross errors of this kind,—often, however, more beautiful than other men's truths)—and the hair removed in consequence too far off the brow; in other respects the face is very noble—still more so that of the Christ. The child *stands* upon the Virgin's knees,* one hand raised in the usual attitude of benediction, the other holding a globe. The face looks straightforward, quiet, Jupiter-like, and very sublime, owing to the smallness of the features in proportion to the head, the eyes being placed at about three-sevenths of the whole height, leaving four-sevenths for the brow, and themselves only in length about one-sixth of the breadth of the face, half closed, giving a peculiar appearance of repose. The hair is short, golden, symmetrically curled, statuesque in its contour; the mouth tender and full of life: the red cross of the glory about the head of an intense ruby enamel, almost fire colour; the dress brown, with golden girdle. In all the treatment Fra Angelico maintains his assertion of the authority of abstract imagination, which, depriving his subject of all material or actual being, contemplates it as retaining qualities eternal only—adorned by incorporeal splendour. The eyes of the beholder are supernaturally unsealed: and to this miraculous vision whatever is of the earth vanishes, and all things are seen endowed with an harmonious glory—the garments falling with strange, visionary grace, glowing with indefinite gold—the walls of

---

* In many pictures of Angelico, the Infant Christ appears self-supported—the Virgin not touching the child.

the chamber dazzling as of a heavenly city—the mortal forms themselves impressed with divine changelessness—no domesticity—no jest—no anxiety—no expectation—no variety of action or of thought. Love, all fulfilling, and various modes of power, are alone expressed; the Virgin never shows the complacency or petty watchfulness of maternity; she sits serene, supporting the child whom she ever looks upon, as a stranger among strangers; "Behold the handmaid of the Lord" for ever written upon her brow.

67. An approach to an exception in treatment is found in the Annunciation of the upper corridor of St. Mark's,[1] most unkindly treated by our author:—

"Probably the earliest of the series—full of faults, but imbued with the sweetest feeling; there is a look of naïve curiosity, mingling with the modest and meek humility of the Virgin, which almost provokes a smile."—iii. 176.

Many a Sabbath evening of bright summer have we passed in that lonely corridor—but not to the finding of faults, nor the provoking of smiles. The angel is perhaps something less majestic than is usual with the painter; but the Virgin is only the more to be worshipped, because here, for once, set before us in the verity of life. No gorgeous robe is upon her; no lifted throne set for her; the golden border gleams faintly on the dark blue dress; the seat is drawn into the shadow of a lowly loggia. The face is of no strange, far-sought loveliness; the features might even be thought hard, and they are worn with watching, and severe, though innocent. She stoops forward with her arms folded on her bosom: no casting down of eye nor shrinking of the frame in fear; she is too earnest, too self-forgetful for either: wonder and inquiry are there, but chastened and free from doubt; meekness, yet mingled with a patient majesty; peace, yet sorrowfully sealed, as if the promise of the Angel were already underwritten by the prophecy of Simeon. They

[1] [This fresco at Florence is also described in *Modern Painters*, vol. ii. (Vol. IV. p. 264). The Bible reference above is Luke i. 38.]

who pass and repass in the twilight of that solemn corridor, need not the adjuration inscribed beneath :—

> " Virginis intactae cum veneris ante figuram
> Praetereundo cave ne sileatur Ave." *

We in general allow the inferiority of Angelico's fresco to his tempera works; yet even that which of all these latter we think the most radiant, the Annunciation on the reliquary of Santa Maria Novella,[1] would, we believe, if repeatedly compared with this of St. Mark's, in the end have the disadvantage. The eminent value of the tempera paintings results partly from their delicacy of line, and partly from the purity of colour and force of decoration of which the material is capable.

68. The passage, to which we have before alluded, respecting Fra Angelico's colour in general, is one of the most curious and fanciful in the work :—

> "His colouring, on the other hand, is far more beautiful, although of questionable brilliancy. This will be found invariably the case in minds constituted like his. Spirit and Sense act on each other with livelier reciprocity the closer their approximation, the less intervention there is of Intellect. Hence the most religious and the most sensual painters have always loved the brightest colours—Spiritual Expression and a clearly defined (however inaccurate) outline forming the distinction of the former class; Animal Expression and a confused and uncertain outline (reflecting that lax morality which confounds the limits of light and darkness, right and wrong) of the latter. On the other hand, the more that Intellect, or the spirit of Form, intervenes in its severe precision, the less pure, the paler grow the colours, the nearer they tend to the hue of marble, of the bas-relief. We thus find the purest and brightest colours only in Fra Angelico's pictures, with a general predominance of blue, which we have observed to prevail more or less in so many of the Semi-Byzantine painters, and which, fanciful as it may appear, I cannot but attribute, independently of mere tradition, to an

* The upper inscription Lord Lindsay has misquoted—it runs thus:—

> " Salve Mater Pietatis
> Et Totius Trinitatis
> Nobile Triclinium." [2]

---

[1] [For this picture (now in the Museum of San Marco), see *Modern Painters*, vol. ii. (Vol. IV. p. 263 and *n.*). It is the one of which Ruskin made the pencil sketch engraved as the frontispiece to *Modern Painters*, vol. v.]

[2] [Lord Lindsay (iii. 177) gives the second line as " Eternae Trinitatis."]

inherent, instinctive sympathy between their mental constitution and the colour in question; as that of red, or of blood, may be observed to prevail among painters in whom Sense or Nature predominates over Spirit—for in this, as in all things else, the moral and the material world respond to each other as closely as shadow and substance. But, in Painting as in Morals, perfection implies the due intervention of Intellect between Spirit and Sense—of Form between Expression and Colouring—as a power at once controlling and controlled—and therefore, although acknowledging its fascination, I cannot unreservedly praise the Colouring of Fra Angelico."— Vol. iii. pp. 193, 194.

69. There is much ingenuity, and some truth, here, but the reader, as in other of Lord Lindsay's speculations, must receive his conclusions with qualification. It is the natural character of strong effects of colour, as of high light, to confuse outlines; and it is a necessity in all fine harmonies of colour that many tints should merge imperceptibly into their following or succeeding ones :—we believe Lord Lindsay himself would hardly wish to mark the hues of the rainbow into divided zones, or to show its edge, as of an iron arch, against the sky, in order that it might no longer reflect (a reflection of which we profess ourselves up to this moment altogether unconscious) "that lax morality which confounds the limits of right and wrong." Again, there is a character of energy in all warm colours, as of repose in cold, which necessarily causes the former to be preferred by painters of savage subject—that is to say, commonly by the coarsest and most degraded;—but when sensuality is free from ferocity, it leans to blue more than to red (as especially in the flesh tints of Guido), and when intellect prevails over this sensuality, its first step is invariably to put more red into every colour, and so "rubor est virtutis color." We hardly think Lord Lindsay would willingly include Luca Giordano among his spiritual painters, though that artist's servant was materially enriched by washing the ultramarine from the brushes with which he painted the Riccardi palace ;[1] nor would he,

---

[1] [Luca Giordano (1632–1705), of the Neapolitan school, painted the Great Gallery of the Riccardi Palace in Florence. "The quantity of ultramarine employed was so great, that the assistant, who washed the painter's brushes, is said to have made a large sum by the operation" (Murray's *Handbook for Central Italy*, ed. 1864, p. 150).]

we believe, degrade Ghirlandajo to fellowship with the herd of the sensual, though in the fresco of the vision of Zacharias[1] there are seventeen different reds in large masses, and not a shade of blue. The fact is, there is no colour of the spectrum, as there is no note of music, whose key and prevalence may not be made pure in expression, and elevating in influence, by a great and good painter, or degraded to unhallowed purpose by a base one.

70. We are sorry that our author "cannot unreservedly praise the colouring of Angelico;" but he is again curbed by his unhappy system of balanced perfectibility, and must quarrel with the gentle monk because he finds not in him the flames of Giorgione, nor the tempering of Titian, nor the melody of Cagliari. This curb of perfection we took between our teeth from the first, and we will give up our hearts to Angelico without drawback or reservation. His colour is, in its sphere and to its purpose, as perfect as human work may be: wrought to radiance beyond that of the ruby and opal, its inartificialness prevents it from arresting the attention it is intended only to direct; were it composed with more science it would become vulgar from the loss of its unconsciousness; if richer, it must have parted with its purity, if deeper, with its joyfulness, if more subdued, with its sincerity. Passages are, indeed, sometimes unsuccessful; but it is to be judged in its rapture, and forgiven in its fall: he who works by law and system may be blamed when he sinks below the line above which he proposes no elevation, but to him whose eyes are on a mark far off, and whose efforts are impulsive, and to the utmost of his strength, we may not unkindly count the slips of his sometime descent into the valley of humiliation.

71. The concluding notice of Angelico is true and interesting, though rendered obscure by useless recurrence to the favourite theory.

"Such are the surviving works of a painter, who has recently been as unduly extolled as he had for three centuries past been unduly depreciated,

---

[1] [In the choir of S. Maria Novella.]

—depreciated, through the amalgamation during those centuries of the principle of which he was the representative with baser, or at least less precious matter—extolled, through the recurrence to that principle, in its pure, unsophisticated essence, in the present—in a word, to the simple Imaginative Christianity of the Middle Ages, as opposed to the complex Reasoning Christianity of recent times. Creeds therefore are at issue, and no exclusive partisan, neither Catholic nor Protestant in the absolute sense of the terms, can fairly appreciate Fra Angelico. Nevertheless, to those who regard society as progressive through the gradual development of the component elements of human nature, and who believe that Providence has accommodated the mind of man, individually, to the perception of half-truths only, in order to create that antagonism from which Truth is generated in the abstract, and by which the progression is effected, his rank and position in art are clear and definite. All that Spirit could achieve by herself, anterior to that struggle with Intellect and Sense which she must in all cases pass through in order to work out her destiny, was accomplished by him. Last and most gifted of a long and imaginative race—the heir of their experience, with collateral advantages which they possessed not—and flourishing at the moment when the transition was actually taking place from the youth to the early manhood of Europe, he gave full, unreserved, and enthusiastic expression to that Love and Hope which had winged the Faith of Christendom in her flight towards heaven for fourteen centuries,—to those yearnings of the Heart and the Imagination which ever precede, in Universal as well as Individual development, the severer and more chastened intelligence of Reason."
—Vol. iii. pp. 188–190.

72. We must again repeat that if our author wishes to be truly serviceable to the schools of England, he must express himself in terms requiring less laborious translation. Clearing the above statement of its mysticism and metaphor, it amounts only to this,—that Fra Angelico was a man of (humanly speaking) *perfect* piety — humility, charity, and faith—that he never employed his art but as a means of expressing his love to God and man, and with the view, single, simple, and straightforward, of glory to the Creator, and good to the Creature. Every quality or subject of art by which these ends were not to be attained, or to be attained secondarily only, he rejected; from all study of art, as such, he withdrew; whatever might merely please the eye, or interest the intellect, he despised, and refused; he used his colours and lines, as David his harp, after a kingly fashion, for purposes of praise and not of science. To this grace and gift of holiness were added, those of a fervent imagination, vivid invention, keen sense of loveliness in lines and

colours, unwearied energy, and to all these gifts the crowning one of quietness of life and mind, while yet his convent-cell was at first within view, and afterwards in the centre, of a city which had lead of all the world in Intellect, and in whose streets he might see daily and hourly the noblest setting of manly features.[1]   It would perhaps be well to wait until we find another man thus actuated, thus endowed, and thus circumstanced, before we speak of "unduly extolling" the works of Fra Angelico.

73. His artistical attainments, as might be conjectured, are nothing more than the development, through practice, of his natural powers in accordance with his sacred instincts. His power of expression by bodily gesture is greater even than Giotto's, wherever he could feel or comprehend the passion to be expressed; but so inherent in him was his holy tranquillity of mind, that he could not by any exertion, even for a moment, conceive either agitation, doubt, or fear—and all the actions proceeding from such passions, or, à fortiori, from any yet more criminal, are absurdly and powerlessly pourtrayed by him; while contrariwise, every gesture, consistent with emotion pure and saintly, is rendered with an intensity of truth to which there is no existing parallel; the expression being carried out into every bend of the hand, every undulation of the arm, shoulder, and neck, every fold of the dress and every wave of the hair.   His drawing of movement is subject to the same influence; vulgar or vicious motion he cannot represent; his running, falling, or struggling figures are drawn with childish incapability; but give him for his scene the pavement of heaven, or pastures of Paradise, and for his subject the "inoffensive pace"[2] of glorified souls, or the spiritual speed of Angels,[3] and Michael Angelo alone

---

[1] [For the state of Florence in her prime, see *Mornings in Florence*, §§ 13, 32, 35.]

[2] [*Paradise Lost*, viii. 163 :—

" Her silent course advance
With inoffensive pace, that spinning sleeps
On her soft axle."]

[3] [Compare the passage at the end of *Modern Painters*, vol. ii. (Vol. IV. p. 332).]

can contend with him in majesty,—in grace and musical continuousness of motion, no one. The inspiration was in some degree caught by his pupil Benozzo, but thenceforward for ever lost. The angels of Perugino appear to be let down by cords and moved by wires; that of Titian, in the sacrifice of Isaac, kicks like an awkward swimmer;[1] Raphael's Moses and Elias of the Transfiguration are cramped at the knees; and the flight of Domenichino's angels is a sprawl paralyzed. The authority of Tintoret over movement is, on the other hand, too unlimited; the descent of his angels is the swoop of a whirlwind or the fall of a thunderbolt; his mortal impulses are oftener impetuous than pathetic, and majestic more than melodious.

74. But it is difficult by words to convey to the reader unacquainted with Angelico's works, any idea of the thoughtful variety of his rendering of movement—Earnest haste of girded faith in the Flight into Egypt, the haste of obedience, not of fear; and unweariedness, but through spiritual support, and not in human strength—Swift obedience of passive earth to the call of its Creator, in the Resurrection of Lazarus— March of meditative gladness in the following of the Apostles down the Mount of Olives—Rush of adoration breaking through the chains and shadows of death, in the Spirits in Prison. Pacing of mighty angels above the Firmament, poised on their upright wings, half opened, broad, bright, quiet, like eastern clouds before the sun is up;—or going forth, with timbrels and with dances, of souls more than conquerors, beside the shore of the last great Red Sea, the sea of glass mingled with fire, hand knit with hand, and voice with voice, the joyful winds of heaven following the measure of their motion, and the flowers of the new earth looking on, like stars pausing in their courses.[2]

[1] [On the roof of the sacristy of S. Maria della Salute at Venice. For "the kicking gracefulness" of Raphael's "Transfiguration" at the Vatican, see *Modern Painters*, vol. iii. ch. iv. § 17 *n.*; for Domenichino's "sprawling infants," *ibid.*, vol. ii. (Vol. IV. pp. 327–328). For Tintoret's "authority over movement," see *Modern Painters*, vol. ii., and *Stones of Venice*, vol. iii. (Venetian Index), *passim.*]

[2] [Of the pictures here mentioned, all are at Florence; the "Flight into Egypt" (No. 235), and the "Resurrection of Lazarus" (No. 252), in the Academy; the

75. And yet all this is but the lowest part and narrowest reach of Angelico's conceptions.   Joy and gentleness, patience and power, he could indicate by gesture—but Devotion could be told by the countenance only.   There seems to have been always a stern limit by which the thoughts of other men were stayed; the religion that was painted even by Perugino, Francia, and Bellini, was finite in its spirit—the religion of earthly beings, checked, not indeed by the corruption, but by the veil and the sorrow of clay.   But with Fra Angelico the glory of the countenance reaches to actual transfiguration; eyes that see no more darkly, incapable of all tears, foreheads flaming, like Belshazzar's marble wall,[1] with the writing of the Father's name upon them, lips tremulous with love, and crimson with the light of the coals of the altar —and all this loveliness, thus enthusiastic and ineffable, yet sealed with the stability which the coming and going of ages as countless as sea-sand cannot dim nor weary, and bathed by an ever flowing river of holy thought, with God for its source, God for its shore, and God for its ocean.

76. We speak in no inconsiderate enthusiasm.   We feel assured that to any person of just feeling who devotes sufficient time to the examination of these works, all terms of description must seem derogatory.   Where such ends as these have been reached, it ill becomes us to speak of minor deficiencies as either to be blamed or regretted: it cannot be determined how far even what we deprecate may be accessory to our delight, nor by what intricate involution what we deplore may be connected with what we love. Every good that nature herself bestows, or accomplishes, is given with a counterpoise, or gained at a sacrifice; nor is it to be expected of Man that he should win the hardest battles and tread the narrowest paths, without the betrayal of a weakness, or the acknowledgment of an error.

"Spirits in Prison" (*cf.* Vol. IV. p. 100) and "the Mount of Olives," in the cells of S. Marco.   The passage at the end of § 74 refers to "The Last Judgment," also in the Academy.]
    [1] [Daniel, ch. v.]

77. With this final warning against our author's hesitating approbation of what is greatest and best, we must close our specific examination of the mode in which his design has been worked out. We have done enough to set the reader upon his guard against whatever appears slight or inconsiderate in his theory or statements, and with the more severity, because this was alone wanting to render the book one of the most valuable gifts which Art has ever received. Of the translations from the lives of the saints we have hardly spoken; they are gracefully rendered, and all of them highly interesting—but we could wish to see these, and the enumerations of fresco subjects* with which the other volumes are in great part occupied, published separately for the convenience of travellers in Italy. They are something out of place in a work like that before us. For the rest, we might have more interested the reader, and gratified ourselves, by setting before him some of the many passages of tender feeling and earnest eloquence with which the volumes are replete—but we felt it necessary rather to anticipate the hesitation with which they were liable to be received, and set limits to the halo of fancy by which their light is obscured—though enlarged.

78. One or two paragraphs, however, of the closing chapter must be given before we part:—

"What a scene of beauty, what a flower-garden of art—how bright and how varied—must Italy have presented at the commencement of the sixteenth century, at the death of Raphael! The sacrileges we lament took place for the most part after that period; hundreds of frescoes, not merely of Giotto and those other elders of Christian Art, but of Gentile da Fabriano, Pietro

* We have been much surprised by the author's frequent reference to Lasinio's engravings[1] of various frescoes, unaccompanied by any warning of their inaccuracy. No work of Lasinio's can be trusted for *anything* except the number and relative position of the figures. All masters are by him translated into one monotony of commonplace:—he dilutes eloquence, educates naïveté, prompts ignorance, stultifies intelligence, and paralyses power;

---

[1] ["Execrable engravings," Ruskin calls them, *Modern Painters*, vol. iii. ch. xviii. § 13; "vile and vulgar," *ibid.*, vol. iv. ch. i. § 1 *n.*]

della Francesca, Perugino and their compeers, were still existing, charming the eye, elevating the mind, and warming the heart. Now alas! few comparatively and fading are the relics of those great and good men. While Dante's voice rings as clear as ever, communing with us as friend with friend, theirs is dying gradually away, fainter and fainter, like the farewell of a spirit. Flaking off the walls, uncared for and neglected save in a few rare instances, scarce one of their frescoes will survive the century, and the labours of the next may not improbably be directed to the recovery and restoration of such as may still slumber beneath the whitewash and the daubs with which the Bronzinos and Zuccheros ' et id genus omne' have unconsciously sealed them up for posterity—their best title to our gratitude.—But why not begin at once? at all events in the instances numberless, where merely whitewash interposes between us and them.

"It is easy to reply—what need of this? They—the artists—have Moses and the prophets, the frescoes of Raphael and Michael Angelo—let them study them. Doubtless,—but we still reply, and with no impiety— they will not repent, they will not forsake their idols and their evil ways— they will not abandon Sense for Spirit, oils for fresco—unless these great ones of the past, these Sleepers of Ephesus, arise from the dead. . . . It is not by studying art in its perfection—by worshipping Raphael and Michael Angelo exclusively of all other excellence—that we can expect to rival them, but by re-ascending to the fountain-head—by planting ourselves as acorns in the ground those oaks are rooted in, and growing up to their level—in a word, by studying Duccio and Giotto that we may paint like Taddeo di Bartolo and Masaccio, Taddeo di Bartolo and Masaccio that we may paint like Perugino and Luca Signorelli, Perugino and Luca Signorelli that we may paint like Raphael and Michael Angelo. And why despair of this, or even of shaming the Vatican? For with genius and God's blessing nothing is impossible.

"I would not be a blind partizan, but, with all their faults, the old masters I plead for knew how to touch the heart. It may be difficult at first to believe this; like children, they are shy with us—like strangers, they bear an uncouth mien and aspect—like ghosts from the other world, they have an awkward habit of shocking our conventionalities with home truths. But with the dead as with the living all depends on the frankness with which we greet them, the sincerity with which we credit their kindly qualities; sympathy is the key to truth—we must love, in order to appreciate."— iii. p. 418.

79. These are beautiful sentences; yet this let the young painter of these days remember always, that whomsoever he may love, or from whomsoever learn, he can now no more

takes the chill off horror, the edge off wit, and the bloom off beauty. In all artistical points he is utterly valueless, neither drawing nor expression being ever preserved by him. Giotto, Benozzo, or Ghirlandajo are all alike to him; and we hardly know whether he injures most when he robs or when he redresses.

go back to those hours of infancy and be born again.* About
the faith, the questioning and the teaching of childhood there
is a joy and grace, which we may often envy, but can no
more assume:—the voice and the gesture must not be imitated when the innocence is lost. Incapability and ignorance
in the act of being struggled against and cast away are often
endowed with a peculiar charm—but both are only contemptible when they are pretended. Whatever we have now
to do, we may be sure, first, that its strength and life must
be drawn from the real nature with us and about us always,
and secondly, that, if worth doing, it will be something altogether different from what has ever been done before. The
visions of the cloister must depart with its superstitious peace
—the quick, apprehensive symbolism of early Faith must
yield to the abstract teaching of disciplined Reason. Whatever else we may deem of the Progress of Nations, one character of that progress is determined and discernible. As in
the encroaching of the land upon the sea, the strength of the
sandy bastions is raised out of the sifted ruin of ancient
inland hills—for every tongue of level land that stretches
into the deep, the fall of Alps has been heard among the
clouds, and as the fields of industry enlarge, the intercourse
with Heaven is shortened. Let it not be doubted that as
this change is inevitable, so it is expedient, though the form
of teaching adopted and of duty prescribed be less mythic
and contemplative, more active and unassisted: for the light
of Transfiguration on the Mountain is substituted the Fire
of Coals upon the Shore, and on the charge to hear the

* We do not perhaps enough estimate the assistance which was once
given both to purpose and perception, by the feeling of wonder which with
us is destroyed partly by the ceaseless calls upon it, partly by our habit of
either discovering or anticipating a reason for everything. Of the simplicity
and ready surprise of heart which supported the spirit of the older painters,
an interesting example is seen in the diary of Albert Dürer, lately published
in a work every way valuable, but especially so in the carefulness and richness
of its illustrations, *Divers Works of Early Masters in Christian Decoration*, edited
by John Weale, London, 2 vols. folio, 1846.

Shepherd, follows that to feed the Sheep.[1]   Doubtful we may be for a time, and apparently deserted; but if, as we wait, we still look forward with steadfast will and humble heart, so that our Hope for the Future may be fed, not dulled or diverted by our Love for the Past, we shall not long be left without a Guide:—the way will be opened, the Precursor appointed—the Hour will come, and the Man.

[1] [Luke ix. ; John xxi. 9 ; x. ; xxi. 16.]

II

A REVIEW OF EASTLAKE'S "HISTORY OF OIL-PAINTING"

(*Quarterly Review, March* 1848)

[*Bibliographical Note.*—This Review first appeared in *The Quarterly Review* for March 1848, No. 164, vol. 82, pp. 390–427. It was headed "Eastlake on the History of Painting."

The article has been reprinted in *On the Old Road*—(1) in the first edition (1885), occupying pp. 135–205 (§§ 98–136) of volume i. ; (2) in the second edition (1889), occupying pp. 136–209 (§§ 98–136) of volume i.

The note above (p. 168) on the numbering of the paragraphs applies also here. There are no variations in the text, other than in minor matters of punctuation, etc.]

EASTLAKE'S HISTORY OF OIL-PAINTING

1. *Materials for a History of Oil-Painting.* By Charles Lock Eastlake, R.A., F.R.S., F.S.A., Secretary to the Royal Commission for promoting the Fine Arts in Connexion with the Rebuilding of the Houses of Parliament, etc., etc. London, 1847.

2. *Theophili, qui et Rugerus, Presbyteri et Monachi, Libri III. de Diversis Artibus; seu Diversarum Artium Schedula. (An Essay upon Various Arts, in Three Books, by Theophilus, called also Rugerus, Priest and Monk, forming an Encyclopædia of Christian Art of the Eleventh Century.* Translated, with Notes, by Robert Hendrie.) London, 1847.

1. THE stranger in Florence who for the first time passes through the iron gate which opens from the Green Cloister of Santa Maria Novella into the Spezieria, can hardly fail of being surprised, and that perhaps painfully, by the suddenness of the transition from the silence and gloom of the monastic enclosure, its pavement rough with epitaphs, and its walls retaining, still legible, though crumbling and mildewed, their imaged records of Scripture History, to the activity of a traffic not less frivolous than flourishing, concerned almost exclusively with the appliances of bodily adornment or luxury. Yet perhaps, on a moment's reflection, the rose-leaves scattered on the floor, and the air filled with odour of myrtle and myrrh, aloes and cassia, may arouse associations of a different and more elevated character; the preparation of these precious perfumes may seem not altogether unfitting the hands of a religious brotherhood—or if this should not be conceded, at all events it

must be matter of rejoicing to observe the evidence of intelligence and energy interrupting the apathy and languor of the cloister; nor will the institution be regarded with other than respect, as well as gratitude, when it is remembered that, as to the convent library we owe the preservation of ancient literature, to the convent laboratory we owe the duration of mediæval art.[1]

2. It is at first with surprise not altogether dissimilar, that we find a painter of refined feeling and deep thoughtfulness,[2] after manifesting in his works the most sincere affection for what is highest in the reach of his art, devoting himself for years (there is proof of this in the work before us) to the study of the mechanical preparation of its appliances, and whatever documentary evidence exists respecting their ancient use. But it is with a revulsion of feeling more entire, that we perceive the value of the results obtained—the accuracy of the varied knowledge by which their sequence has been established—and above all, their immediate bearing upon the practice and promise of the schools of our own day.

Opposite errors, we know not which the least pardonable, but both certainly productive of great harm, have from time to time possessed the masters of modern art. It has been held by some that the great early painters owed the larger measure of their power to secrets of material and method, and that the discovery of a lost vehicle or forgotten process might at any time accomplish the regeneration of a fallen school. By others it has been asserted that all questions respecting materials or manipulation are idle and impertinent; that the methods of the older masters were either of no peculiar value, or are still in our power; that a great painter is independent of all but the simplest mechanical aids, and demonstrates his greatness by scorn of system and carelessness of means.

---

[1] [With this description of the Spezieria, compare the letter cited at Vol. IV. p. 352 n., and St. Mark's Rest, § 86.]

[2] [For Ruskin's criticisms on Eastlake, in connexion with the National Gallery, see Vol. III. pp. 670, 675; for a criticism of the painter's own works, see Academy Notes, 1855, No. 120.]

3. It is evident that so long as incapability could shield itself under the first of these creeds, or presumption vindicate itself by the second; so long as the feeble painter could lay his faults on his palette and his panel; and the self-conceited painter, from the assumed identity of materials proceed to infer equality of power—(for we believe that in most instances those who deny the evil of our present methods will deny also the weakness of our present works)—little good could be expected from the teaching of the abstract principles of the art; and less, if possible, from the example of any mechanical qualities, however admirable, whose means might be supposed irrecoverable on the one hand, or indeterminate on the other, or of any excellence conceived to have been either summoned by an incantation, or struck out by an accident. And of late, among our leading masters, the loss has not been merely of the system of the ancients, but of all system whatsoever; the greater number paint as if the virtue of oil pigment were its opacity, or as if its power depended on its polish; of the rest, no two agree in use or choice of materials; not many are consistent even in their own practice; and the most zealous and earnest, therefore the most discontented, reaching impatiently and desperately after better things, purchase the momentary satisfaction of their feelings by the sacrifice of security of surface and durability of hue. The walls of our galleries are for the most part divided between pictures whose dead coating of consistent paint, laid on with a heavy hand and a cold heart, secures for them the stability of dulness and the safety of mediocrity; and pictures whose reckless and experimental brilliancy, unequal in its result as lawless in its means, is as evanescent as the dust of an insect's wing, and presents in its chief perfections so many subjects of future regret.[1]

4. But if these evils now continue, it can only be through

---

[1] [In later writings Ruskin often emphasised the need of more definite and consistent school-teaching in British art; see, for instance, *The Cestus of Aglaia*, § 4, and *The Art of England*, §§ 193, 194; and compare his evidence before the Royal Academy Commission in 1863 (in *On the Old Road*, 1899, vol. ii. § 174, and reprinted in a later volume of this edition.]

rashness which no example can warn, or through apathy which no hope can stimulate, for Mr. Eastlake has alike withdrawn licence from experimentalism and apology from indolence. He has done away with all legends of forgotten secrets;[1] he has shown that the masters of the great Flemish and early Venetian schools possessed no means, followed no methods, but such as we may still obtain and pursue; but he has shown also, among all these masters, the most admirable care in the preparation of materials and the most simple consistency in their use; he has shown that their excellence was reached, and could only have been reached, by stern and exact science, condescending to the observance, care, and conquest of the most minute physical particulars and hindrances; that the greatest of them never despised an aid nor avoided a difficulty. The loss of imaginative liberty sometimes involved in a too scrupulous attention to methods of execution is trivial compared to the evils resulting from a careless or inefficient practice. The modes in which, with every great painter, realization falls short of conception are necessarily so many and so grievous, that he can ill afford to undergo the additional discouragement caused by uncertain methods and bad materials. Not only so, but even the choice of subjects, the amount of completion attempted, nay, even the modes of conception and measure of truth are in no small degree involved in the great question of materials. On the habitual use of a light or dark ground may depend the painter's preference of a broad and faithful, or partial and scenic chiaroscuro; correspondent with the facility or fatality of alterations, may be the exercise of indolent fancy,

---

[1] [Sir Joshua Reynolds, for instance, "believed as confidently in the *Venetian secret*, as ever alchemist did in the philosopher's stone. We ourselves were acquainted with an old painter, a pupil of West's, who in his latter days had devoted himself to repairing pictures, and who possessed portraits by both Titian and Rubens, which he said had belonged to Sir Joshua, and parts of which, to obtain this wished-for secret, had been scraped or rubbed down to the panel, to lay bare the under-paintings or dead colourings. It was this search for the Venetian secret—this constant course of experiments in his pictures, that has caused so many failures" (R. and S. Redgrave: *A Century of Painters*, 1890, p. 50). For an expression of a view in some respects opposite to that of Reynolds, see Millais' "Thoughts on our Art of To-day" (in M. H. Spielmann's *Millais and his Works*).]

or disciplined invention; and to the complexities of a system requiring time, patience, and succession of process, may be owing the conversion of the ready draughtsman into the resolute painter.   Farther than this, who shall say how unconquerable a barrier to all self-denying effort may exist in the consciousness that the best that is accomplished can last but a few years, and that the painter's travail must perish with his life?

5. It cannot have been without strong sense of this, the true dignity and relation of his subject, that Mr. Eastlake has gone through a toil far more irksome, far less selfish than any he could have undergone in the practice of his art. The value which we attach to the volume depends, however, rather on its preceptive than its antiquarian character.   As objects of historical inquiry merely, we cannot conceive any questions less interesting than those relating to mechanical operations generally, nor any honours less worthy of prolonged dispute than those which are grounded merely on the invention or amelioration of processes and pigments.[1]   The subject can only become historically interesting when the means ascertained to have been employed at any period are considered in their operation upon or procession from the artistical aim of such period, the character of its chosen subjects, and the effects proposed in their treatment upon the national mind.   Mr. Eastlake has as yet refused himself the indulgence of such speculation; his book is no more than its modest title expresses.   For ourselves, however, without venturing in the slightest degree to anticipate the expression of his ulterior views—though we believe that we can trace their extent and direction in a few suggestive sentences, as pregnant as they are unobtrusive—we must yet, in giving a rapid sketch of the facts established, assume the privilege of directing the reader to one or two of their most obvious consequences, and, like honest 'prentices, not suffer the abstracted retirement of our master in the back parlour

[1] [For Ruskin's views on discoveries of this kind and their vanity, see *Two Paths*, § 139; *Eagle's Nest*, §§ 33, 74; *Arrows of the Chace*, 1880, i. pp. 277 *seq.*]

to diminish the just recommendation of his wares to the passers-by.

6. Eminently deficient in works representative of the earliest and purest tendencies of art,[1] our National Gallery nevertheless affords a characteristic and sufficient series of examples of the practice of the various schools of painting, after oil had been finally substituted for the less manageable glutinous vehicles which, under the general name of tempera, were principally employed in the production of easel pictures up to the middle of the fifteenth century.   If the reader were to make the circuit of this collection for the purpose of determining which picture represented with least disputable fidelity the first intention of its painter, and united in its modes of execution the highest reach of achievement with the strongest assurance of durability, we believe that—after hesitating long over hypothetical degrees of blackened shadow and yellowed light, of lost outline and buried detail, of chilled lustre, dimmed transparency, altered colour, and weakened force—he would finally pause before a small picture on panel, representing two quaintly dressed figures in a dimly lighted room—dependent for its interest little on expression, and less on treatment—but eminently remarkable for reality of substance, vacuity of space, and vigour of quiet colour; nor less for an elaborate finish, united with energetic freshness, which seem to show that time has been much concerned in its production, and has had no power over its fate.[2]

7. We do not say that the total force of the material is exhibited in this picture, or even that it in any degree possesses the lusciousness and fulness which are among the chief charms of oil-painting; but that upon the whole it would be selected as uniting imperishable firmness with exquisite

[1] [The date of this review must be remembered—1848. In following years the collection received constant accessions illustrative of the art of "the primitives": see above, Introduction, p. lix.]

[2] [No 186: "Portraits of Jan Arnolfini and his Wife," by Jan Van Eyck. For Ruskin's frequent references to Van Eyck, see General Index. The picture was bought for the Gallery in 1842—the first purchase made under Eastlake's keepership (see below, p. 405).]

delicacy; as approaching more unaffectedly and more closely than any other work to the simple truths of natural colour and space; and as exhibiting, even in its quaint and minute treatment, conquest over many of the difficulties which the boldest practice of art involves.

This picture, bearing the inscription " Johannes Van Eyck (fuit ?) [1] hic, 1434," is probably the portrait, certainly the work, of one of those brothers to whose ingenuity the first invention of the art of oil-painting has been long ascribed.   The volume before us is occupied chiefly in determining the real extent of the improvements they introduced, in examining the processes they employed, and in tracing the modifications of those processes adopted by later Flemings, especially Rubens, Rembrandt, and Vandyck.   Incidental notices of the Italian system occur, so far as, in its earlier stages, it corresponded with that of the north; but the consideration of its separate character is reserved for a following volume, [2] and though we shall expect with interest this concluding portion of the treatise, we believe that, in the present condition of the English school, the choice of the methods of Van Eyck, Bellini, or Rubens, is as much as we could modestly ask or prudently desire.

8. It would have been strange indeed if a technical perfection like that of the picture above described (equally characteristic of all the works of those brothers), had been at once reached by the first inventors of the art.   So far was this from being the case, and so distinct is the evidence of the practice of oil-painting in antecedent periods, that of late years the discoveries of the Van Eycks have not

[1] [The word here queried had previously been read "fecit"; it is, however, clearly "fuit," as Eastlake (p. 185 *n.*) correctly stated.   His translation, "John Van Eyck was this man," from which he supposed that the picture was the painter's portrait, is, however, untenable, in view of facts subsequently unearthed about the picture.   The signature, "John Van Eyck was here," is characteristic of the spirit in which the painter worked; "he only professed to come, look, and record what he saw."   On the frame of another portrait in the National Gallery (No. 222) he wrote, "Als ich kan"—the first words of an old Flemish proverb, "As I can, but not as I will."]

[2] [The volume by Eastlake here reviewed was limited to Flemish painting; a discussion of Italian painting being promised hereafter.   This was included in a second volume published posthumously in 1869, under the editorship of Eastlake's widow.]

unfrequently been treated as entirely fabulous; and Raspe,[1] in particular, rests their claims to gratitude on the contingent introduction of amber-varnish and poppy-oil:—"Such *perhaps*," he says, "might have been the misrepresented discovery of the Van Eycks." That tradition, however, for which the great painters of Italy, and their sufficiently vain historian,[2] had so much respect as never to put forward any claim in opposition to it, is not to be clouded by incautious suspicion. Mr. Eastlake has approached it with more reverence, stripped it of its exaggeration, and shown the foundations for it in the fact that the Van Eycks, though they did not create the art, yet were the first to enable it for its function; that having found it in servile office and with dormant power— laid like the dead Adonis on his lettuce-bed[3]—they gave it vitality and dominion. And fortunate it is for those who look for another such reanimation, that the method of the Van Eycks was not altogether their own discovery. Had it been so, that method might still have remained a subject of conjecture; but after being put in possession of the principles commonly acknowledged before their time, it is comparatively easy to trace the direction of their inquiry and the nature of their improvements.

9. With respect to remote periods of antiquity, we believe that the use of a hydrofuge oil-varnish for the protection of works in tempera, the only fact insisted upon by Mr. Eastlake,[4]

---

[1] [R. E. Raspe : *A Critical Essay on Oil-Painting*, 1781, p. 67.]

[2] [The reference is to Vasari, who in his Life of Antonello of Messina attributes the invention to "Giovanni of Bruges" (Jan Van Eyck), and describes the excitement which it caused among Italian painters. The passage is in part cited below, p. 272. For Ruskin's general opinion of Vasari, see *Modern Painters*, vol. iii. ch. ii. § 4; *On the Old Road* (1899 ed.), ii. p. 311 ("an ass with precious things in his panniers"); *Ariadne Florentina*, § 194 ("a very foolish person").]

[3] [The allusion is either to the ritual at the Festival of Adonis : see Theocritus, *Id.* xv., "Here are built for him shadowy bowers of green, all laden with tender anise"; or to the fennel and lettuce-jars, or forcing-beds, called by the Greeks "Adonis Gardens" (see 1 *Henry VI.*, i. 6; *Paradise Lost*, ix. 440; *Faerie Queene*, iii. 6): these also had their place in the Adonis ritual (see Frazer's *Golden Bough*, 1st ed., i. 284).]

[4] ["The movable pictures of the ancients were, for the most part, on wood, and either in tempera or in encaustic. Works executed in either of these methods were, from an early period, often covered with a durable hydrofuge varnish, which, if not indispensible in all cases as a defence against damp, at least served to protect the painting from dust, and allowed of its being washed with safety" (Eastlake, p. 14).]

is also the only one which the labour of innumerable ingenious writers has established: nor up to the beginning of the twelfth century is there proof of any practice of painting except in tempera, encaustic (wax applied by the aid of heat), and fresco. Subsequent to that period, notices of works executed in solid colour mixed with oil are frequent, but all that can be proved respecting earlier times is a gradually increasing acquaintance with the different kinds of oil and the modes of their adaptation to artistical uses.

Several drying oils are mentioned by the writers of the first three centuries of the Christian era—walnut by Pliny and Galen, walnut, poppy, and castor-oil (afterwards used by the painters of the twelfth century as a varnish) by Dioscorides—yet these notices occur only with reference to medicinal or culinary purposes.[1] But at length a drying oil is mentioned in connection with works of art by Aetius, a medical writer of the fifth century. His words are:—

"Walnut oil is prepared like that of almonds, either by pounding or pressing the nuts, or by throwing them, after they have been bruised, into boiling water. The (medicinal) uses are the same: but it has a use besides these, being employed by gilders or encaustic painters; for it dries, and preserves gildings and encaustic paintings for a long time."

"It is therefore clear," says Mr. Eastlake, "that an oil varnish, composed either of inspissated nut oil, or of nut oil combined with a dissolved resin, was employed on gilt surfaces and pictures, with a view to preserve them, at least as early as the fifth century. It may be added that a writer who could then state, as if from his own experience, that such varnishes had the effect of preserving works 'for a long time,' can hardly be understood to speak of a new invention."—P. 22.

Linseed-oil is also mentioned by Aetius, though still for medicinal uses only; but a varnish, composed of linseed-oil mixed with a variety of resins, is described in a manuscript at Lucca, belonging probably to the eighth century:—

"The age of Charlemagne was an era in the arts; and the addition of linseed-oil to the materials of the varnisher and decorator may on the above evidence be assigned to it. From this time, and during many ages, the linseed-oil varnish, though composed of simpler materials (such as sandarach and mastic resin boiled in the oil), alone appears in the recipes hitherto brought to light."—*Ib.*, p. 24.

[1] [The passages in Pliny (xxiii. c. 36), Galen (*De Simpl. Medic.*), and Dioscorides (supposed to have lived in the reign of Augustus) are given by Eastlake on pp. 15–19.]

10. The modes of bleaching and thickening oil in the sun, as well as the siccative power of metallic oxides, were known to the classical writers, and evidence exists of the careful study of Galen, Dioscorides, and others by the painters of the twelfth and thirteenth centuries: the loss (recorded by Vasari) of Antonio Veneziano [1] to the arts, "per che studio in Dioscoride le cose dell' erbe," is a remarkable instance of its less fortunate results.   Still, the immixture of solid colour with the oil, which had been commonly used as a varnish for tempera paintings and gilt surfaces, was hitherto unsuggested; and no distinct notice seems to occur of the first occasion of this important step, though in the twelfth century, as above stated, the process is described as frequent both in Italy and England.   Mr. Eastlake's instances have been selected, for the most part, from four treatises, two of which, though in an imperfect form, have long been known to the public; the third, translated by Mrs. Merrifield, is in course of publication; [2] the fourth, *Tractatus de Coloribus illuminatorum*, is of less importance.

Respecting the dates of the first two, those of Eraclius and Theophilus, some difference of opinion exists between Mr. Eastlake and their respective editors.   The former MS. was published by Raspe,* who inclines to the opinion of its

* *A Critical Essay on Oil-Painting,* London, 1781.

---

[1] [This painter flourished in the latter half of the fourteenth century.   After describing his works in the Campo Santo at Pisa, Vasari continues : "Our artist had meanwhile been always strongly disposed to the study of natural history, and that of the science of botany in particular, which he had studied in Dioscorides.   He took especial pleasure in investigating the nature and properties of plants, and finally abandoning the practice of painting, he betook himself to the distillation of simples, applying himself earnestly to the acquirement of all particulars respecting them. Thus, from a painter Antonio became a physician" (Bohn's ed., 1855, i. 250).]

[2] [(1) The treatise of Eraclius is entitled *De Coloribus et Artibus Romanorum ;* (2) that of Theophilus is described at the head of this Review (above, p. 251); (3) Mrs. Anna Philadelphia Merrifield's work, published in 2 vols., in 1849, brought together all the original documents on the subject ; it was entitled *Original Treatises dating from the XIIth to XVIIIth Centuries on the Arts of Painting in Oil, Miniature, Mosaic, and on Glass.*   (4) The *Tractatus de Coloribus Illuminatorum* is contained in a British Museum MS. (Sloane, No. 1754) ; it is of the fourteenth century (see Eastlake, p. 44).]

having been written soon after the time of St. Isidore of Seville, probably therefore in the eighth century, but insists only on its being prior to the thirteenth. That of Theophilus, published first by M. Charles de l'Escalopier,[1] and lately from a more perfect MS. by Mr. Hendrie, is ascribed by its English editor (who places Eraclius in the tenth) to the early half of the eleventh century. Mr. Hendrie maintains his opinion with much analytical ingenuity, and we are disposed to think that Mr. Eastlake attaches too much importance to the absence of reference to oil-painting in the Mappæ Clavicula (a MS. of the twelfth century),[2] in placing Theophilus a century and a half later on that ground alone. The question is one of some importance in an antiquarian point of view, but the general reader will perhaps be satisfied with the conclusion that in MSS. which cannot possibly be later than the close of the twelfth century, references to oil-painting are clear and frequent.

Nothing is known of the personality of either Eraclius or Theophilus, but what may be collected from their works; amounting, in the first case, to the facts of the author's "language being barbarous, his credulity exceptionable, and his knowledge superficial,"[3] together with his written description as "vir sapientissimus"; while all that is positively known of Theophilus is that he was a monk, and that Theophilus was not his real name. The character, however, of which the assumed name is truly expressive, deserves from us no unrespectful attention: we shall best possess our readers of it by laying before them one or two passages from the preface. We shall make some use of Mr. Hendrie's translation; it is evidently the work of a tasteful man, and in most cases renders the feeling of the original faithfully; but the Latin, monkish though it be, deserved a more accurate following, and many of Mr. Hendrie's deviations

---

[1] [Paris, 1843. For Mr. Hendrie's translation, see above, p. 251.]

[2] [*Mappæ Clavicula* ("A Key to Drawing"); *a MS. Treatise on the Preparation of Pigments, communicated to the Society of Antiquaries:* 1847.]

[3] [Raspe: *A Critical Essay on Oil-Painting*, 1781, p. 44.]

bear traces of unsound scholarship. An awkward instance occurs in the first paragraph :—

"Theophilus, humilis presbyter, servus servorum Dei, indignus nomine et professione monachi, omnibus mentis desidiam animique vagationem utili manuum occupatione, et delectabili novitatum meditatione declinare et calcare volentibus, retributionem cœlestis præmii!"

"I, Theophilus, an humble priest, servant of the servants of God, unworthy of the name and profession of a monk, to all wishing to overcome and avoid sloth of the mind or wandering of the soul, by useful manual occupation and the delightful contemplation of novelties, send a recompense of heavenly price."—*Theophilus*, p. 1.

Præmium is not "price," nor is the verb understood before *retributionem* "send." Mr. Hendrie seems even less familiar with Scriptural than with monkish language, or in this and several other cases he would have recognised the adoption of apostolic formulæ. The whole paragraph is such a greeting and prayer as stands at the head of the sacred epistles: —"Theophilus, to all who desire to overcome wandering of the soul, etc., etc. (wishes) recompense of heavenly reward." Thus also the dedication of the Byzantine manuscript, lately translated by M. Didron,[1] commences "A tous les peintres, et à tous ceux qui, aimant l'instruction, étudieront ce livre, salut dans le Seigneur." So, presently afterwards, in the sentence, "divina dignatio quæ dat omnibus affluenter et non improperat" (translated, "divine *authority* which affluently and not precipitately gives to all"), though Mr. Hendrie might have perhaps been excused for not perceiving the transitive sense of *dignatio* after *indignus* in the previous text, which indeed, even when felt, is sufficiently difficult to render in English; and might not have been aware that the word *impropero* frequently bears the sense of *opprobro ;* he ought still to have recognized the Scriptural "who giveth to all men liberally and *upbraideth* not."[2] "Qui," in the first

---

[1] [The *Manuel d'Iconographie Chrétienne*, 1845, has notes and an introduction by M. Didron, and a translation, by Paul Durand, from a Byzantine MS. of a "Guide to Painting" by Dionysius, Monk of Fourna d'Agrapha. The passage here quoted by Ruskin is at p. 7 of Didron's book.]

[2] [James i. 5. For Ruskin's revised translation of these passages, see next page.]

page,[1] translated "wherefore," mystifies a whole sentence; "ut mereretur," rendered with a schoolboy's carelessness "as he merited," reverses the meaning of another; "jactantia," in the following page, is less harmfully but not less singularly translated "jealousy." We have been obliged to alter several expressions in the following passages, in order to bring them near enough to the original for our immediate purpose:

"Which knowledge, when he has obtained, let no one magnify himself in his own eyes, as if it had been received from himself, and not from elsewhere; but let him rejoice humbly in the Lord, from whom and by whom are all things, and without whom is nothing; nor let him wrap his gifts in the folds of envy, nor hide them in the closet of an avaricious heart; but all pride of heart being repelled,[2] let him with a cheerful mind give with simplicity to all who ask of him, and let him fear the judgment of the Gospel upon that merchant, who, failing to return to his lord a talent with accumulated interest, deprived of all reward, merited the censure from the mouth of his judge of 'wicked servant.'

"Fearing to incur which sentence, I, a man unworthy and almost without name, offer gratuitously to all desirous with humility to learn, that which the divine condescension, which giveth to all men liberally and upbraideth not, gratuitously conceded to me: and I admonish them that in me they acknowledge the goodness, and admire the generosity of God; and I would persuade them to believe that if they also add their labour, the same gifts are within their reach.

"Wherefore, gentle son, whom God has rendered perfectly happy in this respect, that those things are offered to thee gratis, which many, ploughing the sea waves with the greatest danger to life, consumed by the hardship of hunger and cold, or subjected to the weary servitude of teachers, and altogether worn out by the desire of learning, yet acquire with intolerable labour, covet with greedy looks this 'BOOK OF VARIOUS ARTS,' read it through with a tenacious memory, embrace it with an ardent love.

"Should you carefully peruse this, you will there find out whatever Greece possesses in kinds and mixtures of various colours; whatever Tuscany knows of in mosaic-work, or in variety of enamel; whatever Arabia shows forth in work of fusion, ductility, or chasing; whatever Italy ornaments with gold, in diversity of vases and sculpture of gems or ivory; whatever France loves in

---

[1] [The first page of Theophilus; p. xliv. in Mr. Hendrie's book. The passage here referred to is an exordium describing the Fall of Man. He was created a little lower than the angels, *ut rationis capax divinæ prudentiæ consilii ingeniique mereretur participium* ("so that being capable of reason he might be worthy of partaking in the wisdom, counsel, and mind of God"); then it continues, *qui astu diabolico misere deceptus*, etc. ("who nevertheless miserably deceived by diabolical astuteness" fell from his high estate).]

[2] [In the Latin, *omni jactantia repulsa*; Ruskin here corrects Mr. Hendrie's translation: see a few lines above. So seven lines lower, Ruskin re-translates ("that which the divine condescension," etc.) the words *quæ dat affluenter et non improperat divina dignatio*.]

a costly variety of windows; whatever industrious Germany approves in work of gold, silver, copper, and iron, of woods and of stones.

"When you shall have re-read this often, and have committed it to your tenacious memory, you shall thus recompense me for this care of instruction, that as often as you shall have successfully made use of my work, you pray for me for the pity of Omnipotent God, who knows that I have written these things, which are here arranged, neither through love of human approbation, nor through desire of temporal reward, nor have I stolen anything precious or rare through envious jealousy, nor have I kept back anything reserved for myself alone; but in augmentation of the honour and glory of His name, I have consulted the progress and hastened to aid the necessities of many men."—*Ib.*, pp. xlvii.–li.

11. There is perhaps something in the naïve seriousness with which these matters of empiricism, to us of so small importance, are regarded by the good monk, which may at first tempt the reader to a smile. It is, however, to be kept in mind that some such mode of introduction was customary in all works of this order and period. The Byzantine MS., already alluded to, is prefaced still more singularly: "Que celui qui veut apprendre la science de la peinture commence à s'y préparer d'avance quelque temps en dessinant sans relâche . . . puis qu'il adresse à Jesus Christ la prière et oraison suivante," etc.:—the prayer being followed by a homily respecting envy, much resembling that of Theophilus. And we may rest assured that until we have again begun to teach and to learn in this spirit, art will no more recover its true power or place than springs which flow from no heavenward hills can rise to useful level in the wells of the plain. The tenderness, tranquillity, and resoluteness which we feel in such men's words and thoughts found a correspondent expression even in the movements of the hand; precious qualities resulted from them even in the most mechanical of their works, such as no reward can evoke, no academy teach, nor any other merits replace. What force can be summoned by authority, or fostered by patronage, which could for an instant equal in intensity the labour of this humble love, exerting itself for its own pleasure, looking upon its own works by the light of thankfulness, and finishing all, offering all, with the irrespective profusion of flowers

opened by the wayside, where the dust may cover them, and the foot crush them?

12. Not a few passages conceived in the highest spirit of self-denying piety would, of themselves, have warranted our sincere thanks to Mr. Hendrie for his publication of the manuscript. The practical value of its contents is however very variable; most of the processes described have been either improved or superseded, and many of the recipes are quite as illustrative of the writer's credulity in reception, as generosity in communication. The references to the "land of Havilah" for gold, and to "Mount Calybe" for iron,[1] are characteristic of monkish geographical science; the recipe for the making of Spanish gold is interesting, as affording us a clue to the meaning of the mediæval traditions respecting the basilisk. Pliny[2] says nothing about the hatching of this chimera from cocks' eggs, and ascribes the power of killing at sight to a different animal, the catoblepas, whose head, fortunately, was so heavy that it could not be held up. Probably the word "basiliscus" in Theophilus would have been better translated "cockatrice."

"There is also a gold called Spanish gold, which is composed from red copper, powder of basilisk, and human blood, and acid. The Gentiles, whose skilfulness in this art is commendable, make basilisks in this manner. They have, underground, a house walled with stones everywhere, above and below, with two very small windows, so narrow that scarcely any light can appear through them; in this house they place two old cocks of twelve or fifteen years, and they give them plenty of food. When these have become fat, through the heat of their good condition, they agree together and lay eggs. Which being laid, the cocks are taken out and toads are placed in, which may hatch the eggs, and to which bread is given for food. The eggs being hatched, chickens issue out, like hens' chickens, to which after seven days grow the tails of serpents, and immediately, if there were not a stone pavement to the house, they would enter the earth. Guarding against which,

---

[1] [There are many kinds of gold, among which the best kind is produced in the land of Hevilath, which, according to Genesis, the river Phison surrounds (*Theophilus*, p. 265). "Iron is called Calibs, from the Mount Calybe, in which the most is known of its practice" (p. 377). See Genesis ii. 11, 12 : "The name of the first is Pison : that is it which compasseth the whole land of Havilah, where there is gold ; and the gold of that land is good." The Chalybes (in Pontus) were the traditional workers in iron (Virg. *Æn.* viii. 421, etc.).]

[2] [Pliny's description of the basilisk is in *Nat. Hist.*, book viii. c. 33 ; of the catoblepas, in c. 32 : its head is "always bent down towards the earth. Were it not for this circumstance, it would prove the destruction of the human race ; for all who behold its eyes fall dead upon the spot."]

their masters have round brass vessels of large size, perforated all over, the mouths of which are narrow, in which they place these chickens, and close the mouths with copper coverings and inter them underground, and they are nourished with the fine earth entering through the holes for six months. After this they uncover them and apply a copious fire, until the animals' insides are completely burnt. Which done, when they have become cold, they are taken out and carefully ground, adding to them a third part of the blood of a red man, which blood has been dried and ground. These two compositions are tempered with sharp acid in a clean vessel; they then take very thin sheets of the purest red copper, and anoint this composition over them on both sides, and place them in the fire. And when they have become glowing, they take them out and quench and wash them in the same confection; and they do this for a long time, until this composition eats through the copper, and it takes the colour of gold. This gold is proper for all work."
—*Ib.*, p. 267.

Our readers will find in Mr. Hendrie's interesting note the explanation of the symbolical language of this recipe;[1] though we cannot agree with him in supposing Theophilus to have so understood it. We have no doubt the monk wrote what he had heard in good faith, and with no equivocal meaning; and we are even ourselves much disposed to regret and resist the transformation of toads into nitrates of potash, and of basilisks into sulphates of copper.

13. But whatever may be the value of the recipes of Theophilus, couched in the symbolical language of the alchemist, his evidence is as clear as it is conclusive, as far as regards the general processes adopted in his own time. The treatise of Peter de St. Audemar, contained in a volume transcribed by Jehan le Begue in 1431,[2] bears internal evidence

[1] [*Ibid.*, p. 432. "The process which Theophilus describes in this symbolic language appears no other than that for procuring a pure gold by the means of the mineral acids. Let a solution of gold be made by nitro-muriatic acid and copper be introduced, the latter would be dissolved while the gold would re-appear, but in a state of purity, or, as the alchemist would have expressed it, the *copper would* have been transmuted *into pure gold.* . . . The basilisc, the dragon, the red and green lions were (in the symbolic vocabulary of the alchemists) the sulphate of copper and of iron. . . . The toads of Theophilus which hatch the eggs are probably fragments of the mineral salt, nitrate of potash, which would yield one of the elements of the solvent for gold; the blood of a red man, which has been dried and ground, probably a muriate of ammonia; the cocks, the sulphates of copper and iron; the eggs, gold ore; the hatched chickens, which require a stone pavement, sulphuric acid produced by burning them in a stone vessel, collecting the fumes; these are then all digested together, tempered with a sharp acid. The elements of nitro-muriatic acid are all here, the solvent for gold."]

[2] [The treatise of Peter de St. Audemar (Omer) in the Paris library, transcribed in 1431 by Jehan le Beque, is translated in the first volume of the book by Mrs. Merrifield, above referred to (p. 260 *n.*).]

of being nearly coeval with that of Theophilus.   And in addition to these MSS., Mr. Eastlake has examined the records of Ely and Westminster, which are full of references to decorative operations.   From these sources it is not only demonstrated that oil-painting, at least in the broadest sense (striking colours mixed with oil on surfaces of wood or stone), was perfectly common both in Italy and England in the 12th, 13th, and 14th centuries, but every step of the process is determinable.   Stone surfaces were primed with white lead mixed with linseed oil, applied in successive coats, and carefully smoothed when dry.   Wood was planed smooth (or, for delicate work, covered with leather of horse-skin or parchment), then coated with a mixture of white lead, wax, and pulverized tile, on which the oil and lead priming was laid.   In the successive application of the coats of this priming, the painter is warned by Eraclius of the danger of letting the superimposed coat be more oily than that beneath, the shrivelling of the surface being a necessary consequence.

"The observation respecting the cause, or one of the causes, of a wrinkled and shrivelled surface, is not unimportant.   Oil, or an oil varnish, used in abundance with the colours over a perfectly dry preparation, will produce this appearance: the employment of an oil varnish is even supposed to be detected by it. . . . As regards the effect itself, the best painters have not been careful to avoid it.   Parts of Titian's St. Sebastian (now in the Gallery of the Vatican) are shrivelled; the Giorgione in the Louvre is so; the drapery of the figure of Christ in the Duke of Wellington's Correggio [1] exhibits the same appearance; a Madonna and Child by Reynolds, at Petworth, is in a similar state, as are also parts of some pictures by Greuze. It is the reverse of a cracked surface, and is unquestionably the less evil of the two."—*Eastlake*, pp. 36–38.

14. On the white surface thus prepared, the colours, ground finely with linseed oil, were applied, according to the advice of Theophilus, in not less than three successive coats, and finally protected with amber or sandarach varnish: each coat of colour being carefully dried by the aid of heat

---

[1] [This is the picture of "Christ in the Garden of Gethsemane," of which there is a copy in the National Gallery (No. 76).]

or in the sun before a second was applied, and the entire work before varnishing. The practice of carefully drying each coat was continued in the best periods of art, but the necessity of exposure to the sun intimated by Theophilus appears to have arisen only from his careless preparation of the linseed oil, and ignorance of a proper drying medium. Consequent on this necessity is the restriction in Theophilus, St. Audemar, and in the British Museum MS.,[1] of oil-painting to wooden surfaces, because movable panels could be dried in the sun; while, for walls, the colours are to be mixed with water, wine, gum, or the usual tempera vehicles, egg and fig-tree juice; white lead and verdigris, themselves driers, being the only pigments which could be mixed with oil for walls. But the MS. of Eraclius and the records of our English cathedrals imply no such absolute restriction. They mention the employment of oil for the painting or varnishing of columns and interior walls, and in quantity very remarkable. Among the entries relating to St. Stephen's chapel, occur—"For 19 flagons of painter's oil, at 3s. 4d. the flagon, 43s. 4d."[2] (It might be as well, in the next edition, to correct the copyist's reverse of the position of the X and L, lest it should be thought that the principles of the science of arithmetic have been progressive, as well as those of art.) And presently afterwards, in May of the same year, "to John de Hennay, for *seventy* flagons and a half of painter's oil for the painting of the same chapel, at 20d. the flagon, 117s. 6d." The expression "painter's oil" seems to imply more careful preparation than that directed by Theophilus, probably purification from its mucilage in the sun; but artificial heat was certainly employed to assist the drying, and after reading of flagons supplied by the score, we can hardly be surprised at finding charcoal furnished by the cartload—see an entry relating to the Painted Chamber. In one MS. of Eraclius, however, a distinct

---

[1] [The MS. above referred to (p. 260 n.); Sloane, No. 1754 : author unknown.]
[2] [This entry from the records of Westminster Abbey (Sept. 19, 1352) is cited by Eastlake at p. 56; and the following entry at p. 57.]

description of a drying oil in the modern sense, occurs, white lead and lime being added, and the oil thickened by exposure to the sun, as was the universal practice in Italy.

15. Such was the system of oil-painting known before the time of Van Eyck; but it remains a question in what kind of works and with what degree of refinement this system had been applied. The passages in Eraclius refer only to ornamental work, imitations of marble, etc.; and although, in the records of Ely cathedral, the words "pro ymaginibus super columnas depingendis"[1] may perhaps be understood as referring to paintings of figures, the applications of oil, which are distinctly determinable from these and other English documents, are merely decorative; and "the large supplies of it which appear in the Westminster and Ely records indicate the coarseness of the operations for which it was required."[2] Theophilus, indeed, mentions tints for faces—*mixturas vultuum;*[3] but it is to be remarked that Theophilus painted with a liquid oil, the drying of which in the sun he expressly says "in *ymaginibus* et aliis picturis diuturnum et tædiosum nimis est." The oil generally employed was thickened to the consistence of a varnish. Cennini[4] recommends that it be kept in the sun until reduced one half; and in the Paris copy of Eraclius we are told that "the longer the oil remains in the sun the better it will be." Such a vehicle entirely precluded delicacy of execution.

"Paintings entirely executed with the thickened vehicle, at a time when art was in the very lowest state, and when its votaries were ill qualified to contend with unnecessary difficulties, must have been of the commonest description. Armorial bearings, patterns, and similar works of mechanical decoration, were perhaps as much as could be attempted.

"Notwithstanding the general reference to flesh-painting, 'e così fa dello

---

[1] [This record, dated 1325, is given by Eastlake at p. 54.]
[2] [Eastlake, p. 60.]
[3] [*Ibid.*, p. 56.]
[4] [Cennino Cennini's *Treatise on Painting*, written in 1437, and first published in Italian in 1821; translated into English and edited by Mrs. Merrifield in 1844; translated again, with notes, by C. J. Herringham, 1899. For his use of the term *Vernice liquida*, see Eastlake, p. 225.]

incarnare,' in Cennini's directions, there are no certain examples of pictures of the fourteenth century, in which the flesh is executed in oil colours. This leads us to inquire what were the ordinary applications of oil-painting in Italy at that time. It appears that the method, when adopted at all, was considered to belong to the complemental and merely decorative parts of a picture. It was employed in portions of the work only, on draperies, and over gilding and foils. Cennini describes such operations as follows. 'Gild the surface to be occupied by the drapery; draw on it what ornaments or patterns you please; glaze the unornamented intervals with verdigris ground in oil, shading some folds twice. Then, when this is dry, glaze the same colour over the whole drapery, both ornaments and plain portions.'

"These operations, together with the gilt field round the figures, the stucco decorations, and the carved framework, tabernacle, or *ornamento* itself of the picture, were completed first; the faces and hands, which in Italian pictures of the fourteenth century were always in tempera, were added afterwards, or at all events after the draperies and background were finished. Cennini teaches the practice of all but the carving. In later times the work was divided, and the decorator or gilder was sometimes a more important person than the painter. Thus some works of an inferior Florentine artist were ornamented with stuccoes, carving, and gilding, by the celebrated Donatello, who, in his youth, practised this art in connection with sculpture. Vasari observed the following inscription under a picture:—'Simone Cini, a Florentine, wrought the carved work; Gabriello Saracini executed the gilding; and Spinello di Luca, of Arezzo, painted the picture, in the year 1385.'"—*Ib.*, pp. 71, 72, and 80.

16. We may pause to consider for a moment what effect upon the mental habits of these earlier school might result from this separate and previous completion of minor details. It is to be remembered that the painter's object in the backgrounds of works of this period (universally, or nearly so, of religious subject) was not the deceptive representation of a natural scene, but the adornment and setting forth of the central figures with precious work—the conversion of the picture, as far as might be, into a gem, flushed with colour and alive with light. The processes necessary for this purpose were altogether mechanical; and those of stamping and burnishing the gold, and of enamelling, were necessarily performed before any delicate tempera-work could be executed. Absolute decision of design was therefore necessary throughout; hard linear separations were unavoidable between the oil-colour and the tempera, or between each and the gold or enamel. General harmony of effect, aerial perspective, or

deceptive chiaroscuro, became totally impossible; and the dignity of the picture depended exclusively on the lines of its design, the purity of its ornaments, and the beauty of expression which could be attained in those portions (the faces and hands) which, set off and framed by this splendour of decoration, became the cynosure of eyes. The painter's entire energy was given to these portions; and we can hardly imagine any discipline more calculated to ensure a grand and thoughtful school of art than the necessity of discriminated character and varied expression imposed by this peculiarly separate and prominent treatment of the features. The exquisite drawing of the hand also, at least in outline, remained for this reason even to late periods one of the crowning excellences of the religious schools. It might be worthy the consideration of our present painters whether some disadvantage may not result from the exactly opposite treatment now frequently adopted, the finishing of the head before the addition of its accessories. A flimsy and indolent background is almost a necessary consequence, and probably also a false flesh-colour, irrecoverable by any after-opposition.

17. The reader is in possession of most of the conclusions relating to the practice of oil-painting up to about the year 1406.

"Its inconveniences were such that tempera was not unreasonably preferred to it for works that required careful design, precision, and completeness. Hence the Van Eycks seem to have made it their first object to overcome the stigma that attached to oil-painting, as a process fit only for ordinary purposes and mechanical decorations. With an ambition partly explained by the previous coarse applications of the method, they sought to raise wonder by surpassing the finish of tempera with the very material that had long been considered intractable. Mere finish was, however, the least of the excellences of these reformers. The step was short which sufficed to remove the self-imposed difficulties of the art; but that effort would probably not have been so successful as it was, in overcoming long-established prejudices, had it not been accompanied by some of the best qualities which oil-painting, as a means of imitating nature, can command."—*Ib.*, p. 88.

18. It has been a question to which of the two brothers, Hubert or John, the honour of the invention is to be

attributed. Van Mander[1] gives the date of the birth of Hubert 1366 ; and his interesting epitaph in the cathedral of St. Bavon, at Ghent, determines that of his death :—

"Take warning from me, ye who walk over me. I was as you are, but am now buried dead beneath you. Thus it appears that neither art nor medicine availed me. Art, honour, wisdom, power, affluence, are spared not when death comes. I was called Hubert Van Eyck; I am now food for worms. Formerly known and highly honoured in painting; this all was shortly after turned to nothing. It was in the year of the Lord one thousand four hundred and twenty-six, on the eighteenth day of September, that I rendered up my soul to God, in sufferings. Pray God for me, ye who love art, that I may attain to His sight. Flee sin ; turn to the best [objects] : for you must follow me at last."

John Van Eyck appears by sufficient evidence to have been born between 1390 and 1395; and, as the improved oil-painting was certainly introduced about 1410, the probability is greater that the system had been discovered by the elder brother than by the youth of 15. What the improvement actually was is a far more important question. Vasari's account, in the Life of Antonello da Messina, is the first piece of evidence here examined (p. 205); and it is examined at once with more respect and more advantage than the half-negligent, half-embarrassed wording of the passage might appear either to deserve or to promise. Vasari states that "*Giovanni* of Bruges,"[2] having finished a tempera-picture on panel, and varnished it as usual, placed it in the sun to dry —that the heat opened the joinings—and that the artist, provoked at the destruction of his work—

"began to devise means for preparing a kind of varnish which should dry in the shade, so as to avoid placing his pictures in the sun. Having made experiments with many things, both pure and mixed together, he at last found that linseed-oil and nut-oil, among the many which he had tested, were more drying than all the rest. These, therefore, boiled with *other mixtures of his*, made him the varnish which he, nay, which all the painters of the world, had long desired. Continuing his experiments with many other things, he saw that the immixture of the colours with these kinds of oils gave them a very firm consistence, which, when dry, was proof against wet; and, moreover, that the vehicle lit up the colours so powerfully,

---

[1] [Carel Van Mander, in his Life of the Flemish and German Painters (1604). The passages here cited by Ruskin are given by Eastlake, pp. 184, 185.]
[2] [*i.e.*, John Van Eyck.]

that it gave a gloss of itself without varnish; and that which appeared to him still more admirable was, that it allowed of blending [the colours] infinitely better than tempera. Giovanni, rejoicing in this invention, and being a person of discernment, began many works."

19. The reader must observe that this account is based upon and clumsily accommodated to the idea, prevalent in Vasari's time throughout Italy, that Van Eyck not merely improved, but first introduced, the art of oil-painting, and that no mixture of colour with linseed or nut oil had taken place before his time. We are only informed of the new and important part of the invention, under the pointedly specific and peculiarly Vasarian expression—"altre sue misture." But the real value of the passage is dependent on the one fact of which it puts us in possession, and with respect to which there is every reason to believe it trustworthy, that it was in search of a *Varnish* which would dry in the shade that Van Eyck discovered the new vehicle. The next point to be determined is the nature of the Varnish ordinarily employed, and spoken of by Cennini[1] and many other writers under the familiar title of Vernice liquida. The derivation of the word Vernix bears materially on the question, and will not be devoid of interest for the general reader, who may perhaps be surprised at finding himself carried by Mr. Eastlake's daring philology into regions poetical and planetary:—

"Eustathius, a writer of the twelfth century, in his commentary on Homer, states that the Greeks of his day called amber ($\mathring{\eta}\lambda\epsilon\kappa\tau\rho\sigma\nu$) Veronice ($\beta\epsilon\rho\sigma\nu\acute{\iota}\kappa\eta$). Salmasius, quoting from a Greek medical MS. of the same period, writes it Verenice ($\beta\epsilon\rho\epsilon\nu\acute{\iota}\kappa\eta$). In the Lucca MS. (8th century) the word Veronica more than once occurs among the ingredients of varnishes, and it is remarkable that in the copies of the same recipes in the *Mappæ Clavicula* (12th century) the word is spelt, in the genitive, Verenicis and Vernicis. This is probably the earliest instance of the use of the Latinised word nearly in its modern form; the original nominative Vernice being afterwards changed to Vernix.

"Veronice or Verenice, as a designation for amber, must have been common at an earlier period than the date of the Lucca MS., since it there occurs as a term in ordinary use. It is scarcely necessary to remark that the letter β was sounded v by the mediæval Greeks, as it is by their

---

[1] [See above, p. 269 n.]

present descendants.   Even during the classic ages of Greece β represented ϕ in certain dialects.   The name Berenice or Beronice, borne by
more than one daughter of the Ptolemies, would be more correctly written
Pherenice or Pheronice.   The literal coincidence of this name and its
modifications with the Vernice of the Middle Ages, might almost warrant
the supposition that amber, which by the best ancient authorities was
considered a mineral, may, at an early period, have been distinguished by
the name of a constellation, the constellation of Berenice's (golden) hair."—
Eastlake, p. 230.

20. We are grieved to interrupt our reader's voyage
among the constellations; but the next page crystallizes us
again like ants in amber, or worse, in gum-sandarach.   It
appears, from conclusive and abundant evidence, that the
greater cheapness of sandarach, and its easier solubility in
oil rendered it the usual substitute for amber, and that the
word Vernice, when it occurs alone, is the common synonym
for dry sandarach resin.   This, dissolved by heat in linseed
oil, three parts oil to one of resin, was the Vernice liquida
of the Italians, sold in Cennini's time ready prepared, and
the customary varnish of tempera pictures.   Concrete tur-
pentine ("oyle of fir-tree," "Pece Greca," "Pegola"),[1] previously prepared over a slow fire until it ceased to swell,
was added to assist the liquefaction of the sandarach, first
in Venice, where the material could easily be procured, and
afterwards in Florence.   The varnish so prepared, especially
when it was long boiled to render it more drying, was of
a dark colour, materially affecting the tints over which it
was passed.*

"It is not impossible that the lighter style of colouring introduced by
Giotto may have been intended by him to counteract the effects of this
varnish, the appearance of which in the Greek pictures he could not fail to
observe.   Another peculiarity in the works of the painters of the time referred
to, particularly those of the Florentine and Sienese schools, is the greenish

* "The mediæval painters were so accustomed to this appearance in
varnishes, and considered it so indispensable, that they even supplied the
tint when it did not exist.   Thus Cardanus observes that when white of
eggs was used as a varnish, it was customary to tinge it with red lead."
—*Eastlake*, p. 270.

---

[1] [Terms used in various recipes collected by Eastlake : the recipes are indexed
at the end of his second volume.]

tone of their colouring in the flesh; produced by the mode in which they often prepared their works, viz. by a green under-painting. The appearance was neutralized by the red sandarac varnish, and pictures executed in the manner described must have looked better before it was removed."—*Ib.*, p. 252.

Farther on, this remark is thus followed out :—

" The paleness or freshness of the tempera may have been sometimes calculated for this brown glazing (for such it was in effect), and when this was the case, the picture was, strictly speaking, unfinished without its varnish. It is, therefore, quite conceivable that a painter, averse to mere mechanical operations, would, in his final process, still have an eye to the harmony of his work, and, seeing that the tint of his varnish was more or less adapted to display the hues over which it was spread, would vary that tint, so as to heighten the effect of the picture. The practice of tinging varnishes was not even new, as the example given by Cardanus proves. The next step to this would be to treat the tempera picture still more as a preparation, and to calculate still further on the varnish, by modifying and adapting its colour to a greater extent. A work so completed must have nearly approached the appearance of an oil picture. This was perhaps the moment when the new method opened itself to the mind of Hubert Van Eyck. . . . The next change necessarily consisted in using opaque as well as transparent colours; the former being applied over the light, the latter over the darker, portions of the picture; while the work in tempera was now reduced to a light chiaroscuro preparation. . . . It was now that the hue of the original varnish became an objection; for, as a medium, it required to be itself colourless."—*Ib.*, pp. 271–273.

21. Our author has perhaps somewhat embarrassed this part of the argument, by giving too much importance to the conjectural adaptation of the tints of the tempera picture to the brown varnish, and too little to the bold transition from transparent to opaque colour on the lights. Up to this time, we must remember, the entire drawing of the flesh had been in tempera; the varnish, however richly tinted, however delicately adjusted to the tints beneath, was still broadly applied over the whole surface, the design being seen through the transparent glaze. But the mixture of opaque colour at once implies that portions of the design itself were executed with the varnish for a vehicle, and therefore that the varnish had been entirely changed both in colour and consistence. If, as above stated, the improvement in the varnish had been made only after it had been mixed with opaque colour, it does not appear why the idea

of so mixing it should have presented itself to Van Eyck more than to any other painter of the day, and Vasari's story of the split panel becomes nugatory. But we apprehend, from a previous passage (p. 258), that Mr. Eastlake would not have us so interpret him. We rather suppose that we are expressing his real opinion in stating our own, that Van Eyck, seeking for a varnish which would dry in the shade, first perfected the methods of dissolving amber or copal in oil, then sought for and added a good drier, and thus obtained a varnish which, having been subjected to no long process of boiling, was nearly colourless; that in using this new varnish over tempera works he might cautiously and gradually mix it with the opaque colour, whose purity he now found unaffected by the transparent vehicle; and, finally, as the thickness of the varnish in its less perfect state was an obstacle to precision of execution, increase the proportion of its oil to the amber, or add a diluent, as occasion required.

22. Such, at all events, in the sum, whatever might be the order or occasion of discovery, were Van Eyck's improvements in the vehicle of colour, and to these, applied by singular ingenuity and affection to the imitation of nature, with a fidelity hitherto unattempted, Mr. Eastlake attributes the influence which his works obtained over his contemporaries:—

"If we ask in what the chief novelty of his practice consisted, we shall at once recognise it in an amount of general excellence before unknown. At all times, from Van Eyck's day to the present, whenever nature has been surprisingly well imitated in pictures, the first and last question with the ignorant has been—What materials did the artist use? The superior mechanical secret is always supposed to be in the hands of the greatest genius; and an early example of sudden perfection in art, like the fame of the heroes of antiquity, was likely to monopolize and represent the claims of many."—*Ib.*, p. 266.

This is all true; that Van Eyck saw nature more truly than his predecessors is certain; but it is disputable whether this rendering of nature recommended his works to the imitation of the Italians. On the contrary, Mr. Eastlake himself observes in another place (p. 220), that the character of delicate imitation common to the Flemish pictures militated *against* the acceptance of their method :—

"The specimens of Van Eyck, Hugo van der Goes, Memling, and others, which the Florentines had seen, may have appeared, in the eyes of some severe judges (for example, those who daily studied the frescoes of Masaccio), to indicate a certain connection between oil painting and minuteness, if not always of size, yet of style. The method, by its very finish and the possible completeness of its gradations, must have seemed well calculated to exhibit numerous objects on a small scale. That this was really the impression produced, at a later period, on one who represented the highest style of design, has been lately proved by means of an interesting document, in which the opinions of Michael Angelo on the character of Flemish pictures are recorded by a contemporary artist." *

23. It was not, we apprehend, the resemblance to nature, but the abstract power of colour, which inflamed with admiration and jealousy the artists of Italy; it was not the delicate touch nor the precise verity of Van Eyck, but the " vivacita de' colori" (says Vasari) which at the first glance induced Antonello da Messina to "put aside every other

---

* " Si je dis tant de mal de la peinture flamande, ce n'est pas qu'elle soit entièrement mauvaise, mais elle veut *rendre avec perfection* tant de choses, dont une seule suffirait par son importance, qu'elle n'en fait aucune d'une manière satisfaisante." This opinion of M. Angelo's is preserved by Francisco de Ollanda, quoted by Comte Raczynski, *Les Arts en Portugal*, Paris, 1846.[1]

---

[1] [The remarkable dialogues on painting composed by Francisco d'Ollanda, a Portuguese miniature-painter who met Michael Angelo in Rome in 1538, are fully translated into English as an appendix to Sir Charles Holroyd's *Michael Angelo Buonarroti*, 1903. The passage here referred to from Michael Angelo's speech is as follows : "'The painting of Flanders will generally satisfy any devout person more than the painting of Italy, which will never cause him to drop a single tear, but that of Flanders will cause him to shed many ; this is not owing to the vigour and goodness of the painting, but to the goodness of such devout person ; women will like it, especially very old ones or very young ones. It will please likewise friars and nuns, and also some noble persons who have no ear for true harmony. They paint in Flanders, only to deceive the external eye, things that gladden you and of which you cannot speak ill, and saints and prophets. Their painting is of stuffs, bricks and mortar, the grass of the fields, the shadows of trees and bridges and rivers, which they call landscapes, and little figures here and there ; and all this, although it may appear good to some eyes, is in truth done without reasonableness or art, without symmetry or proportion, without care in selecting or rejecting, and finally, without any substance or verve, and in spite of all this, painting in some other parts is worse than it is in Flanders. Neither do I speak so badly of Flemish painting because it is all bad, but because it tries to do so many things at once (each of which alone would suffice for a great work) so that it does not do anything really well."]

avocation and thought, and at once set out for Flanders,"
assiduously to cultivate the friendship of *Giovanni*, presenting to him many drawings and other things, until *Giovanni*,
finding himself already old, was content that Antonello
should see the method of his colouring in oil, nor then to
quit Flanders until he had "thoroughly learned that *process*."
It was this *process*, separate, mysterious, and admirable,
whose communication the Venetian, Domenico, thought the
most acceptable kindness which could repay his hospitality;
and whose solitary possession Castagno thought cheaply
purchased by the guilt of the betrayer and murderer;[1] it
was in this process, the deduction of watchful intelligence,
not by fortuitous discovery, that the first impulse was given
to European art. Many a plank had yawned in the sun
before Van Eyck's; but he alone saw through the rent, as
through an opening portal, the lofty perspective of triumph
widening its rapid wedge;—many a spot of opaque colour
had clouded the transparent amber of earlier times; but the
little cloud that rose over Van Eyck's horizon was "like
unto a man's hand."[2]

What this process was, and how far it differed from
preceding practice, has hardly, perhaps, been pronounced by
Mr. Eastlake with sufficient distinctness. One or two conclusions which he has not marked are, we think, deducible
from his evidence. In one point, and that not an unimportant one, we believe that many careful students of
colouring will be disposed to differ with him : our own
intermediate opinion we will therefore venture to state,
though with all diffidence.

24. We must not, however, pass entirely without notice
the two chapters on the preparation of oils, and on the oleo-
resinous vehicles, though to the general reader the recipes
contained in them are of little interest; and in the absence

---

[1] [Vasari's story (Bohn's ed., 1855, ii. 102) of the murder of Domenico Veneziano,
by Andrea del Castagno, is now disproved by documentary evidence, showing that
Domenico survived his alleged murderer by five years.]
[2] [1 Kings xviii. 44.]

of all expression of opinion on the part of Mr. Eastlake as to their comparative excellence, even to the artist, their immediate utility appears somewhat doubtful. One circumstance, however, is remarkable in all, the care taken by the great painters, without exception, to avoid the yellowing of their oil. Perfect and stable clearness is the ultimate aim of all the processes described (many of them troublesome and tedious in the extreme): and the effect of the altered oil is of course most dreaded on pale and cold colours. Thus Philippe Nunez[1] tells us how to purify linseed oil " for white and blues;" and Pacheco, " el de linaza no me quele mal: aunque ai quien diga que no a de ver el Azul ni el Blanco este Azeite."* De Mayerne[2] recommends poppy oil " for painting white, blue, and similar colours, so that they shall not yellow;" and in another place, " for air-tints and blue;"—while the inclination to green is noticed as an imperfection in hempseed oil: so Vasari—speaking of linseed-oil in contemporary practice — " benchè il noce e meglio, perchè ingialla meno." The Italians generally mixed an essential oil with their delicate tints, including flesh tints (p. 431). Extraordinary methods were used by the Flemish painters to protect their blues; they were sometimes painted with size, and varnished; sometimes strewed in powder on fresh white-lead (p. 456). Leonardo gives a careful recipe for preventing the change of colour in nut oil, supposing it to be owing to neglect in removing the skin of the nut. His words, given at p. 321, are incorrectly translated: " una certa bucciolina," is not a husk or rind—but " a thin skin," meaning the white membranous covering of the nut itself, of which it is almost impossible to detach all the inner

* *Arte de Pintura.* Sevilla, 1649.

---

[1] [*Arte da Pintura*, 1615, p. 58. The recipe is translated by Eastlake at p. 329; and the following passage from Pacheco (who states that his blues and whites were never painted with the universally extolled nut oil, which he was not in the habit of using, but with that of linseed, "although (he adds) some say that blue and white should never see this oil ") at p. 362.]

[2] [In a MS. in the British Museum, Sloane, 2052; cited by Eastlake, p. 360.]

laminæ. This, "che tiene della natura del mallo," Leonardo supposes to give the expressed oil its property of forming a *skin* at the surface.[1]

25. We think these passages interesting, because they are entirely opposed to the modern ideas of the desirableness of yellow lights and green blues, which have been introduced chiefly by the study of altered pictures. The anxiety of Rubens, expressed in various letters, quoted at p. 516, lest any of his whites should have become yellow, and his request that his pictures might be exposed to the sun to remedy the defect, if it occurred, are conclusive on this subject, as far as regards the feeling of the Flemish painters: we shall presently see that the *coolness* of their light was an essential part of their scheme of colour.

The testing of the various processes given in these two chapters must be a matter of time: many of them have been superseded by recent discoveries. Copal varnish is in modern practice no inefficient substitute for amber, and we believe that most artists will agree with us in thinking that the vehicles now in use are sufficient for all purposes, if used rightly. We shall, therefore, proceed in the first place to give a rapid sketch of the entire process of the Flemish school as it is stated by Mr. Eastlake in the 11th chapter, and then examine the several steps of it one by one, with the view at once of marking what seems disputable, and of deducing from what is certain some considerations respecting the consequences of its adoption in subsequent art.

26. The ground was with all the early masters pure *white*, plaster of Paris, or washed chalk with size; a preparation which has been employed without change from remote antiquity—witness the Egyptian mummy-cases. Such a ground, becoming brittle with age, is evidently unsafe on canvas,

---

[1] [The passage cited from Amoretti's *Memorie Storiche, etc., di Leonardo da Vinci,* is thus translated by Eastlake: "Walnuts are covered with a husk or rind [in the original, Le noci sono fasciate da una certa bucciolina che tiene della natura del mallo]; if you do not remove this when you extract oil from them, the colouring matter of this skin becomes separated from the oil and rises to the surface of the picture, and this is what causes the alteration of pictures."]

unless exceedingly thin; and even on panel is liable to crack and detach itself, unless it be carefully guarded against damp. The precautions of Van Eyck against this danger, as well as against the warping of his panel, are remarkable instances of his regard to points apparently trivial:—

"In large altar-pieces, necessarily composed of many pieces, it may be often remarked that each separate plank has become slightly convex in front: this is particularly observable in the picture of the Transfiguration by Raphael. The heat of candles on altars is supposed to have been the cause of this not uncommon defect; but heat, if considerable, would rather produce the contrary appearance. It would seem that the layer of paint, with its substratum, slightly operates to prevent the wood from contracting or becoming concave on that side; it might therefore be concluded that a similar protection at the back, by equalizing the conditions, would tend to keep the wood flat. The oak panel on which the picture by Van Eyck in the National Gallery is painted is protected at the back by a composition of gesso, size, and tow, over which a coat of black oil-paint was passed. This, whether added when the picture was executed or subsequently, has tended to preserve the wood (which is not at all worm-eaten), and perhaps to prevent its warping."—*Ib.*, pp. 373, 374.

On the white ground, scraped, when it was perfectly dry, till it was "as white as milk and as smooth as ivory" (Cennini), the outline of the picture was drawn, and its light and shade expressed, usually with the pen, with all possible care; and over this outline a coating of size was applied in order to render the gesso ground *non*-absorbent. The establishment of this fact is of the greatest importance, for the whole question of the true function and use of the gesso ground hangs upon it. That use has been supposed by all previous writers on the technical processes of painting to be, by absorbing the oil, to remove in some degree the cause of yellowness in the colours. Had this been so, the ground itself would have lost its brilliancy, and it would have followed that a dark ground, equally absorbent, would have answered the purpose as well. But the evidence adduced by Mr. Eastlake on this subject is conclusive:—

"Pictures are sometimes transferred from panel to cloth. The front being secured by smooth paper or linen, the picture is laid on its face, and the wood is gradually planed and scraped away. At last the ground appears; first, the 'gesso grosso,' then, next the painted surface, the 'gesso sottile.' On scraping this it is found that it is whitest immediately next the colours; for on the inner side it may sometimes have received slight stains from the wood, if the latter was not first sized. When a picture which happens to be much cracked has been oiled or varnished, the fluid will sometimes penetrate through the cracks into the ground, which in such parts had become accessible. In that case the white ground is stained in lines only, corresponding in their direction with the cracks of the picture. This last circumstance also proves that the ground was not sufficiently hard in itself to prevent the absorption of oil. Accordingly, it required to be rendered non-absorbent by a coating of size; and this was passed *over* the outline, before the oil-priming was applied."—*Ib.*, pp. *383*, *384*.

The perfect whiteness of the ground being thus secured, a transparent warm oil-priming, in early practice flesh-coloured, was usually passed over the entire picture. This custom, says Mr. Eastlake, appears to have been " a remnant of the old habit of covering tempera pictures with a warm varnish, and was sometimes omitted."[1] When used it was permitted to dry thoroughly, and over it "the shadows were painted in with a rich transparent brown, mixed with a somewhat thick oleo-resinous vehicle;"[2] the lighter colours were then added with a thinner vehicle, taking care not to disturb the transparency of the shadows by the unnecessary mixture of opaque pigments, and leaving the ground bearing bright *through the thin lights.* (?) As the art advanced, the lights were more and more loaded, and afterwards glazed, the shadows being still left in untouched transparency. This is the method of Rubens. The later Italian colourists appear to have laid opaque local colour without fear even into the shadows, and to have recovered transparency by ultimate glazing.

27. Such are the principal heads of the method of the early Flemish masters, as stated by Mr. Eastlake. We have marked as questionable the influence of the ground in supporting the lights: our reasons for doing so we will give,

[1] [Eastlake, p. 388.]
[2] [Quotation marks have in this edition been here inserted, as the words are quoted textually from Eastlake, p. 389; the words following being a summary of Eastlake's pages 389–390.]

after we have stated what we suppose to be the advantages or disadvantages of the process in its earlier stages, guiding ourselves as far as possible by the passages in which any expression occurs of Mr. Eastlake's opinion.

The reader cannot but see that the *eminent* character of the whole system is its predeterminateness. From first to last its success depended on the decision and clearness of each successive step. The drawing and light and shade were secured without any interference of colour; but when over these the oil-priming was once laid, the design could neither be altered nor, if lost, recovered; a colour laid too opaquely in the shadow destroyed the inner organization of the picture, and remained an irremediable blemish; and it was necessary, in laying colour even on the lights, to follow the guidance of the drawing beneath with a caution and precision which rendered anything like freedom of handling, in the modern sense, totally impossible. Every quality which depends on rapidity, accident, or audacity was interdicted; no affectation of ease was suffered to disturb the humility of patient exertion. Let our readers consider in what temper such a work must be undertaken and carried through—a work in which error was irremediable, change impossible—which demanded the drudgery of a student, while it involved the deliberation of a master—in which the patience of a mechanic was to be united with the foresight of a magician—in which no licence could be indulged either to fitfulness of temper or felicity of invention—in which haste was forbidden, yet languor fatal, and consistency of conception no less incumbent than continuity of toil. Let them reflect what kind of men must have been called up and trained by work such as this, and then compare the tones of mind which are likely to be produced by our present practice,—a practice in which alteration is admitted to any extent in any stage—in which neither foundation is laid nor end foreseen—in which all is dared and nothing resolved, everything perilled, nothing provided for— in which men play the sycophant in the courts of their humours, and hunt wisps in the marshes of their wits—a

practice which invokes accident, evades law, discredits application, despises system, and sets forth with chief exultation,
contingent beauty, and extempore invention.

28. But it is not only the fixed nature of the successive
steps which influenced the character of these early painters.
A peculiar *direction* was given to their efforts by the close
attention to drawing which, as Mr. Eastlake has especially
noticed, was involved in the preparation of the design on
the white ground.   That design was secured with a care
and finish which in many instances might seem altogether
supererogatory.*   The preparation by John Bellini[1] in the
Florentine gallery is completed with exhaustless diligence
into even the portions farthest removed from the light, where
the thick brown of the shadows must necessarily have afterwards concealed the greater part of the work.   It was the
discipline undergone in producing this preparation which fixed
the character of the school.   The most important part of
the picture was executed not with the brush, but with the
point, and the refinements attainable by this instrument
dictated the treatment of their subject.   Hence the transition
to etching and engraving, and the intense love of minute
detail, accompanied by an imaginative communication of
dignity and power to the smallest forms, in Albert Dürer
and others.   But this attention to minutiæ was not the only
result; the disposition of light and shade was also affected
by the method.   Shade was not to be had at small cost; its
masses could not be dashed on in impetuous generalization,
fields for the future recovery of light.   They were measured
out and wrought to their depths only by expenditure of

---

* The preparations of Hemling, at Bruges, we imagine to have been in
water-colour, and perhaps the picture was carried to some degree of completion in this material. Van Mander observes that Van Eyck's dead colourings " were cleaner and sharper than the finished works of other painters." [2]

---

[1] [Eastlake refers at p. 381 to this preparation for a picture by Giovanni Bellini
(in the collection of the Uffizi), "drawn and shaded on a white ground preparatory
to its completion in oil colours."]

[2] [Quoted by Eastlake, p. 395.]

toil and time; and, as future grounds for colour, they were necessarily restricted to the *natural* shadow of every object, white being left for high lights of whatever hue. In consequence, the character of pervading daylight, almost inevitably produced in the preparation, was afterwards assumed as a standard in the painting. Effectism, accidental shadows, all obvious and vulgar artistical treatment, were excluded, or introduced only as the lights became more loaded, and were consequently imposed with more facility on the dark ground. Where shade was required in large mass, it was obtained by introducing an object of locally dark colour. The Italian masters who followed Van Eyck's system were in the constant habit of relieving their principal figures by the darkness of some object, foliage, throne, or drapery, introduced behind the head, the open sky being left visible on each side. A green drapery is thus used with great quaintness by John Bellini in the noble picture of the Brera Gallery; a black screen, with marbled veins, behind the portraits of himself and his brother in the Louvre; a crimson velvet curtain behind the Madonna, in Francia's best picture at Bologna.[1] Where the subject was sacred, and the painter great, this system of pervading light produced pictures of a peculiar

---

[1] [For another reference to the Bellini in the Brera Gallery at Milan, see *Modern Painters*, vol. i. (Vol. III. p. 180). The picture referred to in the Louvre is No. 1156, "Portraits of Two Men," now attributed to Gentile Bellini (see below, pp. 453, 454). Francia's "best picture at Bologna" is the "Madonna and Child, with SS. Roch, Bernardino, Anthony, and Sebastian," in the Church of S. Martino. Ruskin describes it in his 1846 diary :—

"The Virgin sits upon an arch, through which is seen a sweet landscape; she looks calmly down to the saints assembled below, turning partly to her right towards the San Rocco, holding the Christ with her left arm. The contour of the figure is, I think, the grandest of all the seated Madonnas I know; perfectly calm, unaffected, and sublime; the right hand holds the Bible open; falling lightly over it, the middle and third finger, just a hair's-breadth more extended than by the mere fall of the hand, *hardly* point to a red-letter text, too high to be read. For grace and simplicity of gesture and quantity of expression put into turns of hands and arms, the figures below are quite unrivalled; the San Rocco pointing to his limb; St. Francis behind, a glorious grey head and most holy countenance; not monkish, and especially another saint leaning with both hands on his staff. It is impossible without seeing the picture, to conceive how much mind may be thrown into this simple action. St. Sebastian on the right; the body most elaborately and exquisitely painted—I think the most finished piece of flesh painting, for finish without forcing of all the muscular markings, and purity of simple colour that I have ever seen. I think this

and tranquil majesty; where the mind of the painter was irregularly or frivolously imaginative, its temptations to accumulative detail were too great to be resisted—the spectator was by the German masters overwhelmed with the copious inconsistency of a dream, or compelled to traverse the picture from corner to corner like a museum of curiosities.

29. The chalk or pen preparation being completed, and the oil-priming laid, we have seen that the shadows were laid in with a transparent *brown* in considerable body. The question next arises—What influence is this part of the process likely to have had upon the *colouring* of the school? It is to be remembered that the practice was continued to the latest times, and that when the thin light had been long abandoned, and a loaded body of colour had taken its place, the brown transparent shadow was still retained, and is retained often to this day, when asphaltum is used as its base, at the risk of the destruction of the picture. The utter loss of many of Reynolds' noblest works has been caused by the lavish use of this pigment. What the pigment actually was in older times is left by Mr. Eastlake undecided :—

"A rich brown, which, whether an earth or mineral alone, or a substance of the kind enriched by the addition of a transparent yellow or orange, is not an unimportant element of the glowing colouring which is remarkable in examples of the school. Such a colour, by artificial combinations at least, is easily supplied; and it is repeated, that, in general, the materials now in use are quite as good as those which the Flemish masters had at their command." —*Ib.*, p. 488.

At p. 446 it is also asserted that the peculiar glow of the brown of Rubens is hardly to be accounted for by any accidental variety in the Cassel earths, but was obtained by the mixture of a transparent yellow. Evidence, however,

picture Francia's finest here, or anywhere. Two angels, one on each side of the Madonna, in the sky, in adoration, are as unequalled as the rest; their passionateness and intensity of action, bending forward with hands lifted, altogether surpasses everything of the kind, except some of the finest things of Angelico's; and it is so utterly free from all attitudinising, so enthusiastic—yet so quiet and full of repose that it may be opposed alike to the artificialness of Perugino's in the Academy here, and yet more to all Raphael's."]

exists of asphaltum having been used in Flemish pictures, and with safety, even though prepared in the modern manner :—

"It is not ground" (says De Mayerne), "but a drying oil is prepared with litharge, and the pulverized asphaltum mixed with this oil is placed in a glass vessel, suspended by a thread (in a water bath). Thus exposed to the fire it melts like butter; when it begins to boil it is instantly removed. It is an excellent colour for shadows, and may be glazed like lake; it lasts well."— *Ib.*, p. 463.

30. The great advantage of this primary laying in of the darks in brown was the obtaining an unity of shadow throughout the picture, which rendered variety of hue, where it occurred, an instantly accepted evidence of light. It mattered not how vigorous or how deep in tone the masses of local colour might be, the eye could not confound them with true shadow; it everywhere distinguished the transparent browns as indicative of gloom, and became acutely sensible of the presence and preciousness of light wherever local tints rose out of their depths. But however superior this method may be to the arbitrary use of polychrome shadows, utterly unrelated to the lights, which has been admitted in modern works; and however beautiful or brilliant its results might be in the hands of colourists as faithful as Van Eyck, or as inventive as Rubens; the principle on which it is based becomes dangerous whenever, in assuming that the ultimate hue of every shadow is brown, it presupposes a peculiar and conventional light.[1] It is true, that so long as the early practice of finishing the underdrawing with the pen was continued, the grey of that preparation might perhaps diminish the force of the upper colour, which became in that case little more than a glowing varnish—even thus sometimes verging on too monotonous warmth, as the reader may observe in the head of Dandolo,[2] by John Bellini, in the National Gallery. But when, by later and more impetuous hands, the point tracing was dispensed with, and

---

[1] [On the subject of colour in shadow, see *Elements of Drawing*, § 55 ; *Lectures on Art*, §§ 134, 175.]

[2] [A slip of the pen for Loredano : No. 189 in the National Gallery.]

the picture boldly thrown in with the brown pigment, it became matter of great improbability that the force of such a prevalent tint could afterwards be softened or melted into a pure harmony; the painter's feeling for truth was blunted; brilliancy and richness became his object rather than sincerity or solemnity; with the palled sense of colour departed the love of light, and the diffused sunshine of the early schools died away in the narrowed rays of Rembrandt. We think it a deficiency in the work before us that the extreme peril of such a principle, incautiously applied, has not been pointed out, and that the method of Rubens has been so highly extolled for its technical perfection, without the slightest notice of the gross mannerism into which its facile brilliancy too frequently betrayed the mighty master.

31. Yet it remains a question how far, under certain limitations and for certain effects, this system of pure brown shadow may be successfully followed. It is not a little singular that it has already been revived in water-colours by a painter who, in his realization of light and splendour of hue, stands without a rival among living schools—Mr. Hunt; his neutral shadows being, we believe, first thrown in frankly with sepia, the colour introduced upon the lights, and the central lights afterwards further raised by body colour, and glazed.[1] But in this process the sepia shadows are admitted only on objects whose local colours are warm or neutral; wherever the tint of the illumined portion is delicate or peculiar, a relative hue of shade is at once laid on the white paper; and the correspondence with the Flemish school is in the use of brown as the ultimate representative of deep gloom, and in the careful preservation of its transparency, not in the application of brown universally as the shade of all colours. We apprehend that this practice represents, in another medium, the very best mode of applying the Flemish system; and that when the result proposed is an effect of vivid colour under bright cool sunshine, it would be impossible to

---

[1] [See, for further notices of William Hunt's artistic method, *Academy Notes*, 1859 ("Water Colour Societies"), and *Notes on Prout and Hunt*.]

adopt any more perfect means. But a system which in any stage prescribes the use of a certain pigment, implies the adoption of a constant aim, and becomes, in that degree, conventional. Suppose that the effect desired be neither of sunlight nor of bright colour, but of grave colour subdued by atmosphere, and we believe that the use of brown for an ultimate shadow would be highly inexpedient. With Van Eyck and with Rubens the aim was always consistent: clear daylight, diffused in the one case, concentrated in the other, was yet the hope, the necessity of both; and any process which admitted the slightest dimness, coldness, or opacity, would have been considered an error in their system by either. Alike, to Rubens, came subjects of tumult or tranquillity, of gaiety or terror; the nether, earthly, and upper world were to him animated with the same feeling, lighted by the same sun; he dyed in the same lake of fire the warp of the wedding-garment or of the winding-sheet; swept into the same delirium the recklessness of the sensualist, and rapture of the anchorite; saw in tears only their glittering, and in torture only its flush. To such a painter, regarding every subject in the same temper, and all as mere motives for the display of the power of his art, the Flemish system, improved as it became in his hands, was alike sufficient and habitual. But among the greater colourists of Italy the aim was not always so simple nor the method so determinable. We find Tintoret passing like a fire-fly from light to darkness in one oscillation, ranging from the fullest prism of solar colour to the coldest greys of twilight, and from the silver tinging of a morning cloud to the lava fire of a volcano: one moment shutting himself into obscure chambers of imagery, the next plunged into the revolutionless day of heaven, and piercing space, deeper than the mind can follow or the eye fathom; we find him by turns appalling, pensive, splendid, profound, profuse; and throughout sacrificing every minor quality to the power of his prevalent mood. By such an artist it might, perhaps, be presumed that a different system of colour would be adopted in almost every picture, and that if a chiaroscuro

T

ground were independently laid, it would be in a neutral grey, susceptible afterwards of harmony with any tone he might determine upon, and not in the vivid brown which necessitated brilliancy of subsequent effect. We believe, accordingly, that while some of the pieces of this master's richer colour, such as the Adam and Eve in the Gallery of Venice, and we suspect also the miracle of St. Mark,[1] may be executed on the pure Flemish system, the greater number of his large compositions will be found based on a grey shadow; and that this grey shadow was independently laid we have more direct proof in the assertion of Boschini,[2] who received his information from the younger Palma: " Quando haveva stabilita questa importante distribuzione, *abboggiava il quadro tutto di chiaroscuro ;* " and we have, therefore, no doubt that Tintoret's well-known reply to the question, " What were the most beautiful colours ? " " *Il nero, e il bianco,*"[3] is to be received in a perfectly literal sense, beyond and above its evident reference to abstract principle. Its main and most valuable meaning was, of course, that the design and light and shade of a picture were of greater importance than its colour; (and this Tintoret felt so thoroughly that there is not one of his works which would seriously lose in power if it were translated into chiaroscuro); but it implied also that Tintoret's idea of a shadowed preparation was in grey, and not in brown.

32. But there is a farther and more essential ground of difference in system of shadow between the Flemish and Italian colourists. It is a well-known optical fact that the colour of shadow is complemental to that of light: and that therefore, in general terms, warm light has cool shadow, and cool light hot shadow. The noblest masters of the

---

[1] [For the " Adam and Eve," see Vol. III. p. 509 ; for the " Miracle of St. Mark," see a passing allusion in *Stones of Venice,* vol. iii., Venetian Index, *s.* " Accademia."]

[2] [*Le Ricche Minere della Pittura Veneziana,* seconda impressione 1674 (in the account of Tintoret in the Introduction).]

[3] [" Dimandato quali fossero i più belli colori, disse, il nero ed il bianco ; perchè l'uno dava forza alle figure profondando le ombre ; l'altre, il rilievo " (Ridolfi: *Le Meraviglie dell' Arte,* 1648, ii. 59). For other references to the saying, see Vol. X. p. xxxv., Vol. XI. p. 364.]

northern and southern schools respectively adopted these contrary keys; and while the Flemings raised their lights in frosty white and pearly greys out of a glowing shadow, the Italians opposed the deep and burning rays of their golden heaven to masses of solemn grey and majestic blue. Either, therefore, their preparation must have been different, or they were able, when they chose, to conquer the warmth of the ground by superimposed colour. We believe, accordingly, that Correggio will be found—as stated in the notes of Reynolds quoted at p. 495—to have habitually grounded with black, white, and ultramarine, then glazing with golden transparent colours; while Titian used the most vigorous browns, and conquered them with cool colour in mass above. The remarkable sketch of Leonardo in the Uffizii of Florence is commenced in brown—over the brown is laid an olive green, on which the highest lights are struck with white.[1]

Now it is well known to even the merely decorative painter that no colour can be brilliant which is laid over one of a corresponding key, and that the best ground for any given opaque colour will be a comparatively subdued tint of the complemental one; of green under red, of violet under yellow, and of *orange* or *brown* therefore under *blue*. We apprehend accordingly that the real value of the brown ground with Titian was far greater than even with Rubens; it was to support and give preciousness to cool colour above, while it remained itself untouched as the representative of warm reflexes and extreme depth of transparent gloom. We believe this employment of the brown ground to be the only means of uniting majesty of hue with profundity of shade. But its value to the Fleming is connected with the management of the lights, which we have next to consider. As we here venture for the first time to disagree in some measure with Mr. Eastlake, let us be sure that we state his opinion fairly. He says:—

"The light warm tint which Van Mander assumes to have been generally used in the oil-priming was sometimes omitted, as unfinished pictures prove.

[1] [For this sketch—an unfinished "Adoration of the Magi"—see *Modern Painters*, vol. i. (Vol. III. p. 183).]

Under such circumstances, the picture may have been executed at once on the sized outline. In the works of Lucas van Leyden, and sometimes in those of Albert Dürer, the thin yet brilliant lights exhibit a still brighter ground underneath (p. 389). . . . It thus appears that the method proposed by the inventors of oil-painting, of preserving light within the colours, involved a certain order of processes. The principal conditions were : first, that the outline should be completed on the panel before the painting, properly so called, was begun. The object, in thus defining the forms, was to avoid alterations and repaintings, which might ultimately render the ground useless without supplying its place. Another condition was to avoid loading *the opaque* colours. *This limitation was not essential with regard to the transparent colours, as such could hardly exclude the bright ground* (p. 398). . . . The system of colouring adopted by the Van Eycks may have been influenced by the practice of glass-painting. They appear, in their first efforts at least, to have considered the white panel as representing light behind a coloured and transparent medium, and aimed at giving brilliancy to their tints by allowing the white ground to shine through them. If those painters and their followers erred, it was in sometimes too literally carrying out this principle. *Their lights are always transparent* (mere white excepted) and their shadows sometimes want depth. This is in accordance with the effect of glass-staining, in which transparency may cease with darkness, but never with light. The superior method of Rubens consisted in preserving transparency chiefly in his darks, and in contrasting their lucid depth with solid lights (p. 408). . . . Among the technical improvements on the older process may be especially mentioned the preservation of transparency in the darker masses, the lights being loaded as required. The system of exhibiting the bright ground through the shadows still involved an adherence to the original method of defining the composition at first ; and the solid painting of the lights opened the door to that freedom of execution which the works of the early masters wanted." —(p. 490.)

33. We think we cannot have erred in concluding from these scattered passages that Mr. Eastlake supposes the brilliancy of the high lights of the earlier schools to be attributable to the under-power of the white ground. This we admit, so far as that ground gave value to the transparent flesh-coloured or brown preparation above it; but we doubt the transparency of the highest lights, and the power of any white ground to add brilliancy to opaque colours. We have ourselves never seen an instance of a *painted brilliant* light that was not loaded to the exclusion of the ground. Secondary lights indeed are often perfectly transparent, a warm hatching over the under-white; the highest light itself may be so—but then it is the white ground itself subdued by transparent *darker* colour, not supporting a light colour.

In the Van Eyck in the National Gallery all the brilliant lights are loaded; mere white, Mr. Eastlake himself admits, was always so; and we believe that the flesh-colour and carnations are painted with colour as *opaque* as the white head-dress, but fail of brilliancy from not being *loaded enough*; the white ground beneath being utterly unable to add to the power of such tints, while its effect on more subdued tones depended in great measure on its receiving a transparent coat of warm colour first. This *may* have been sometimes omitted, as stated at p. 389; when it was so, we believe that an utter loss of brilliancy must have resulted; but when it was used, the highest lights must have been raised from it by opaque colour as distinctly by Van Eyck as by Rubens. Rubens' Judgment of Paris[1] is quoted at p. 388 as an example of the best use of the bright gesso ground:—and how in that picture, how in all Rubens' best pictures, is it used? Over the ground is thrown a transparent glowing brown tint, varied and deepened in the shadow; boldly over that brown glaze, and into it, are struck and painted the opaque grey middle tints, already concealing the ground totally; and above these are loaded the high lights like gems—note the sparkling strokes on the peacock's plumes. We believe that Van Eyck's high lights were either, in proportion to the scale of picture and breadth of handling, as loaded as these, or, in the degree of their thinness, less brilliant. Was then his system the same as Rubens'? Not so; but it differed more in the management of middle tints than in the lights: the main difference was, we believe, between the careful preparation of the gradations of drawing in the one, and the daring assumption of massy light in the other. There are theorists who would assert that their system was the same—but they forget the primal work, with the point underneath, and all that is implied of transparency above. Van Eyck secured his drawing in dark, then threw a pale transparent middle tint over the whole, and recovered

---

[1] [No. 194 in the National Gallery.]

his *highest* lights; all was *transparent* except these. Rubens threw a dark middle tint over the whole at first, and then gave the *drawing* with opaque grey. All was *opaque* except the shadows. No slight difference this, when we reflect on the contrarieties of practice ultimately connected with the opposing principles; above all on the eminent one that, as all Van Eyck's colour, except the high lights, must have been equivalent to a glaze, while the great body of *colour* in Rubens was solid (ultimately glazed occasionally, but not necessarily), it was possible for Van Eyck to mix his tints to the local hues required, with far less danger of heaviness in effect than would have been incurred in the solid painting of Rubens. This is especially noticed by Mr. Eastlake, with whom we are delighted again to concur:—

"The practice of using compound tints has not been approved by colourists; the method, as introduced by the early masters, was adapted to certain conditions, but, like many of their processes, was afterwards misapplied. Vasari informs us that Lorenzo di Credi, whose exaggerated nicety in technical details almost equalled that of Gerard Dow, was in the habit of mixing about thirty tints before he began to work. The opposite extreme is perhaps no less objectionable. Much may depend on the skilful use of the ground. The purest colour in an opaque state and superficially light only, is less brilliant than the foulest mixture through which light shines. Hence, as long as the white ground was visible within the tints, the habit of matching colours from nature (no matter by what complication of hues, provided the ingredients were not chemically injurious to each other) was likely to combine the truth of negative hues with clearness."—*Ib.*, p. 400.

34. These passages open to us a series of questions far too intricate to be even cursorily treated within our limits. It is to be held in mind that one and the same quality of colour or kind of brilliancy is not always the best; the phases and phenomena of colour are innumerable in reality, and even the modes of imitating them become expedient or otherwise, according to the aim and scale of the picture. It is no question of mere authority whether the mixture of tints to a compound one, or their juxtaposition in a state of purity, be the better practice. There is not the slightest doubt that, the ground being the same, a stippled tint is

more brilliant and rich than a mixed one; nor is there doubt on the other hand that in some subjects such a tint is impossible, and in others vulgar. We have above alluded[1] to the power of Mr. Hunt in water-colour. The fruit-pieces of that artist are dependent for their splendour chiefly on the juxtaposition of pure colour for compound tints, and we may safely affirm that the method is for such purpose as exemplary as its results are admirable. Yet would you desire to see the same means adopted in the execution of the fruit in Rubens' Peace and War?[2] Or again, would the lusciousness of tint obtained by Rubens himself, adopting the same means on a grander scale in his painting of flesh, have been conducive to the ends or grateful to the feelings of the Bellinis or Albert Dürer? Each method is admirable as applied by its master; and Hemling and Van Eyck are as much to be followed in the mingling of colour, as Rubens and Rembrandt in its decomposition. If an award is absolutely to be made of superiority to either system, we apprehend that the palm of mechanical skill must be rendered to the latter, and higher dignity of moral purpose confessed in the former; in proportion to the nobleness of the subject and the thoughtfulness of its treatment, simplicity of colour will be found more desirable. Nor is the far higher perfection of drawing attained by the earlier method to be forgotten. Gradations which are expressed by delicate execution of the *darks*, and then aided by a few strokes of recovered light, must always be more subtle and true than those which are struck violently forth with opaque colour; and it is to be remembered that the handling of the brush, with the early Italian masters, approached in its refinement to drawing with the point—the more definitely, because the work was executed, as we have just seen, with little change or play of local colour. And—whatever discredit the looser and bolder practice of later masters may have thrown on the hatched and pencilled execution of earlier periods—we

[1] [§ 31, p. 288.]
[2] [No. 46 in the National Gallery.]

maintain that this method, necessary in fresco, and followed habitually in the first oil pictures, has produced the noblest renderings of human expression in the whole range of the examples of art: the best works of Raphael, all the glorious portraiture of Ghirlandajo and Masaccio, all the mightiest achievements of religious zeal in Francia, Perugino, Bellini, and such others. Take as an example in fresco Masaccio's hasty sketch of himself now in the Uffizii; and in oil, the two heads of monks by Perugino in the Academy of Florence;[1] and we shall search in vain for any work in portraiture, executed in opaque colours, which could contend with them in depth of expression or in fulness of *recorded* life—not mere imitative vitality, but chronicled action. And we have no hesitation in asserting that where the object of the painter is expression, and the picture is of a size admitting careful execution, the transparent system, developed as it is found in Bellini or Perugino, will attain the most profound and serene colour, while it will never betray into looseness or audacity. But if in the mind of the painter invention prevail over veneration,—if his eye be creative rather than penetrative, and his hand more powerful than patient—let him not be confined to a system where light, once lost, is as irrecoverable as time, and where all success depends on husbandry of resource. Do not measure out to him his sunshine in inches of gesso; let him have the power of striking it even out of darkness and the deep.

35. If human life were endless, or human spirit could fit its compass to its will, it is possible a perfection might be reached which should unite the majesty of invention with the meekness of love. We might conceive that the thought, arrested by the readiest means, and at first represented by the boldest symbols, might afterwards be set forth with solemn and studied expression, and that the power might

---

[1] ["Masaccio's sketch of himself in the Uffizii" (in the Gallery of Artists' Portraits by themselves) is now believed to be by and of Filippino Lippi. The heads by Perugino are of Bigio Milanesi, General of the Order of Vallombrosians, and Baldasare, a monk of the same order.]

know no weariness in clothing which had known no restraint in creating. But dilation and contraction are for molluscs, not for men; we are not ringed into flexibility like worms, nor gifted with opposite sight and mutable colour like chameleons. The mind which moulds and summons cannot at will transmute itself into that which clings and contemplates; nor is it given to us at once to have the potter's power over the lump, the fire's upon the clay, and the gilder's upon the porcelain. Even the temper in which we behold these various displays of mind must be different; and it admits of more than doubt whether, if the bold work of rapid thought were afterwards in all its forms completed with microscopic care, the result would be other than painful. In the shadow at the foot of Tintoret's picture of the Temptation, lies a broken rock-boulder.[1] The dark ground has been first laid in, of colour nearly uniform; and over it a few, not more than fifteen or twenty, strokes of the brush, loaded with a light grey, have quarried the solid block of stone out of the vacancy. Probably ten minutes are the utmost time which those strokes have occupied, though the rock is some four feet square. It may safely be affirmed that no other method, however laborious, could have reached the truth of form which results from the very freedom with which the conception has been expressed; but it is a truth of the simplest kind—the definition of a stone, rather than the painting of one—and the lights are in some degree dead and cold—the natural consequence of striking a mixed opaque pigment over a dark ground. It would now be possible to treat this skeleton of a stone, which could only have been knit together by Tintoret's rough temper, with the care of a Fleming; to leave its fiercely-stricken lights emanating from a golden ground, to gradate with the pen its ponderous shadows, and in its completion, to dwell with endless and intricate precision upon fibres of moss, bells of

---

[1] [See *Stones of Venice*, vol. iii., Venetian Index, *s.* "Rocco, Scuola di San," No. 20 (Vol. XI. p. 418).]

heath, blades of grass, and films of lichen. Love like Van Eyck's would separate the fibres as if they were stems of forest, twine the ribbed grass into fanciful articulation, shadow forth capes and islands in the variegated film, and hang the purple bells in counted chiming. A year might pass away, and the work yet be incomplete; yet would the purpose of the great picture have been better answered when all had been achieved? or if so, is it to be wished that a year of the life of Tintoret (could such a thing be conceived possible) had been so devoted?

36. We have put in as broad and extravagant a view as possible the difference of object in the two systems of loaded and transparent light; but it is to be remembered that both are in a certain degree compatible, and that whatever exclusive arguments may be adduced in favour of the loaded system apply only to the ultimate stages of the work. The question is not whether the white ground be expedient in the commencement—but how far it must of necessity be preserved to the close? There cannot be the slightest doubt that, whatever the object, whatever the power of the painter, the white ground, as intensely bright and perfect as it can be obtained, should be the base of his operations; that it should be preserved as long as possible, shown wherever it is possible, and sacrificed only upon good cause. There are indeed many objects which do not admit of imitation unless the hand have power of superimposing and modelling the light; but there are others which are equally unsusceptible of every rendering except that of transparent colour over the pure ground.

It appears from the evidence now produced that there are at least three distinct systems traceable in the works of good colourists, each having its own merit and its peculiar application. First, the white ground, with careful chiaroscuro preparation, transparent colour in the middle tints, and opaque high lights only (Van Eyck). Secondly, white ground, transparent brown preparation, and solid painting of lights above (Rubens). Thirdly, white ground, brown preparation, and solid painting both of lights and shadows above (Titian); on which last method, indisputably the noblest, we have not insisted, as it has not yet been examined by Mr. Eastlake.   But in all these methods the white ground was indispensable.   It mattered not what transparent colour were put over it: red, frequently, we believe, by Titian, before the brown shadows—yellow sometimes by Rubens:— whatever warm tone might be chosen for the key of the composition, and for the support of its greys, depended for its own value upon the white gesso beneath; nor can any system of colour be ultimately successful which excludes it. Noble arrangement, choice, and relation of colour, will indeed redeem and recommend the falsest system: our own Reynolds, and recently Turner, furnish magnificent examples of the power attainable by colourists of high calibre, after the light ground is lost—(we cannot agree with Mr. Eastlake in thinking the practice of painting first in white and black, with cool reds only, " equivalent to its preservation"): —but in the works of both, diminished splendour and sacrificed durability attest and punish the neglect of the best resources of their art.

37. We have stated, though briefly, the major part of the data which recent research has furnished respecting the early colourists; enough, certainly, to remove all theoretical obstacles to the attainment of a perfection equal to theirs. A few carefully conducted experiments, with the efficient aids of modern chemistry, would probably put us in possession of an amber varnish, if indeed this be necessary, at least not inferior to that which they employed; the rest of their materials are already in our hands, soliciting only such care in their preparation as it ought, we think, to be no irksome duty to bestow.   Yet we are not sanguine of the immediate result.   Mr. Eastlake has done his duty excellently; but it is hardly to be expected that, after being long in possession of means which we could apply to no profit, the knowledge that the greatest men possessed no better, should at once urge to emulation and gift with strength.

We believe that some consciousness of their true position already existed in the minds of many living artists; example had at least been given by two of our Academicians, Mr. Mulready and Mr. Etty, of a splendour based on the Flemish system, and consistent, certainly, in the first case, with a high degree of permanence;[1] while the main direction of artistic and public sympathy to works of a character altogether opposed to theirs, showed fatally how far more perceptible and appreciable to our present instincts is the mechanism of handling than the melody of hue.   Indeed we firmly believe, that of all powers of enjoyment or of judgment, that which is concerned with nobility of colour is least communicable: it is also perhaps the most rare.   The achievements of the draughtsman are met by the curiosity of all mankind; the appeals of the dramatist answered by their sympathy; the creatures of imagination acknowledged by their fear; but the voice of the colourist has but the adder's listening, charm he never so wisely.   Men vie with each other, untaught, in pursuit of smoothness and smallness —of Carlo Dolci and Van Huysum;[2] their domestic hearts may range them in faithful armies round the throne of Raphael; meditation and labour may raise them to the level of the great mountain pedestal of Buonarotti—"vestito gia de' raggi del pianeta, che mena dritto altrui per ogni calle;[3] but neither time nor teaching will bestow the sense, when it is not innate, of that wherein consists the power of Titian and the great Venetians.   There is proof of this in the various degrees of cost and care devoted to the preservation of their works.   The glass, the curtain, and the cabinet guard the preciousness of what is petty, guide curiosity to what is popular, invoke worship to what is mighty;—Raphael has his palace—Michael his dome—respect

---

[1] [For other references to Mulready and his executive methods, see passages cited at Vol. IV. p. 336 n.; for Etty, see similarly Vol. III. p. 266 n.]

[2] [For other references to the same qualities in these painters, see—for Dolci— Modern Painters, vol. i. (Vol. III. p. 91), and for Van Huysum, ibid. (p. 672 and n.).]

[3] [Inferno, i. 17–18: "Already vested with that planet's beam, Who leads all wanderers safe through every way" (Cary).]

protects and crowds traverse the sacristy and the saloon; but the frescoes of Titian fade in the solitudes of Padua, and the gesso falls crumbled from the flapping canvas, as the sea-winds shake the Scuola di San Rocco.[1]

38. But if, on the one hand, mere abstract excellence of colour be thus coldly regarded, it is equally certain that no work ever attains enduring celebrity which is eminently deficient in this great respect. Colour cannot be indifferent; it is either beautiful and auxiliary to the purposes of the picture, or false, froward, and opposite to them. Even in the painting of Nature herself, this law is palpable; chiefly glorious when colour is a predominant element in her working, she is in the next degree most impressive when it is withdrawn altogether: and forms and scenes become sublime in the neutral twilight, which were indifferent in the colours of noon. Much more is this the case in the feebleness of imitation; all colour is bad which is less than beautiful; all is gross and intrusive which is not attractive; it repels where it cannot enthral, and destroys what it cannot assist. It is besides the painter's peculiar craft;[2] he who cannot colour is no painter. It is not painting to grind earths with oil and lay them smoothly on a surface. He only is a painter who can melodize and harmonize *hue*—if he fail in this, he is no member of the brotherhood. Let him etch, or draw, or carve: better the unerring graver than the unfaithful pencil—better the true sling and stone than the brightness of the unproved armour. And let not even those who deal in the deeper magic, and feel in themselves the loftier power, presume upon that power — nor believe in the reality of any success unless that which has been deserved by deliberate, resolute, successive operation. We would neither deny nor disguise the influences of sensibility or of imagination, upon this, as upon every other admirable quality of

---

[1] [Titian's frescoes at Padua are in the Scuola del Santo and the Scuola del Carmine; the former now fatally repainted; copies of them have been published by the Arundel Society. For the neglect of the Scuola di San Rocco, see Vol. IV. p. 40.]
[2] [Compare *Ariadne Florentina*, § 21.]

art;—we know that there is that in the very stroke and fall of the pencil in a master's hand, which creates colour with an unconscious enchantment—we know that there is a brilliancy which springs from the joy of the painter's heart—a gloom which sympathizes with its seriousness—a power correlative with its will; but these are all vain unless they be ruled by a seemly caution—a manly moderation—an indivertible foresight. This we think the one great conclusion to be received from the work we have been examining, that all power is vain—all invention vain—all enthusiasm vain—all devotion even, and fidelity vain, unless these are guided by such severe and exact law as we see take place in the development of every great natural glory; and, even in the full glow of their bright and burning operation, sealed by the cold, majestic, deep-graven impress of the signet on the right hand of Time.

III

SAMUEL PROUT

AN ARTICLE IN THE "ART JOURNAL" (1849)

[*Bibliographical Note.*—This essay on Prout first appeared in *The Art Journal* of March 1849, No. 129, pp. 76–77. It was published anonymously. The article was headed by a portrait of Prout and a facsimile of his signature. The following editorial note was appended :—

["Our engraving on wood is from a sketch in crayon by Sir W. Ross, R.A., one of Mr. Prout's many FRIENDS ; no member of the profession has ever lived to be more thoroughly respected—we may add beloved—by his brother artists ; no man has ever given more unquestionable evidence of a gentle and generous spirit, or more truly deserved the esteem in which he is so universally held. His always delicate health, instead of, as it usually does, souring the temper, has made him more considerate and thoughtful of the troubles and trials of others ; ever ready to assist the young by the counsels of experience, he is a fine example of upright perseverance and indefatigable industry, combined with suavity of manners and those endearing attributes of character which invariably blend with admiration of the artist, affection for the man."—*Ed.*]

The essay was reprinted as a pamphlet in 1870, with the following title-page :—

Samuel Prout. | By | John Ruskin, M.A. | Honorary Student of Christ Church | and | Slade Professor of Fine Art. | Oxford . | Printed for Private Circulation Only. | MDCCCLXX.

Crown 8vo, pp. vi. + 10. The imprint on the centre of the reverse of the title-page is "T. & G. Shrimpton, Oxford." On p. v. is the following preface :—

"It is more than twenty years since these admirable remarks appeared in the *Art Journal*. Their author leaves them in silent neglect. They are therefore here revived in print for the benefit of a few friends who are at once hearty admirers of Prout and reverent listeners to Professor Ruskin on this as on all other subjects."—Oxford, 1870.

Issued in dark blue wrappers, with the title-page reproduced upon the front cover.

The essay was next reprinted (with the paragraphs numbered) in *On the Old Road;* (1) in the first edition (1885), vol. i. pp. 206–220 (§§ 137–148); (2) in the second (1899), vol. i. pp. 210–224 (§§ 137–148). The paragraphs are in this edition re-numbered.

There are no various readings to record, except that the spelling of the artist's name "Cozens" has here been substituted for "Cousins" (in all previous editions.)]

SAMUEL PROUT

1. THE first pages in the histories of artists, worthy the name, are generally alike; records of boyish resistance to every scheme, parental or tutorial, at variance with the ruling desire and bent of the opening mind. It is so rare an accident that the love of drawing should be noticed and fostered in the child, that we are hardly entitled to form any conclusions respecting the probable result of an indulgent foresight; it is enough to admire the strength of will which usually accompanies every noble intellectual gift, and to believe that, in early life, direct resistance is better than inefficient guidance. Samuel Prout—with how many rich and picturesque imaginations is the name now associated!—was born at Plymouth, September 17th, 1783, and intended by his father for his own profession;[1] but although the delicate health of the child might have appeared likely to induce a languid acquiescence in his parent's wish, the love of drawing occupied every leisure hour, and at last trespassed upon every other occupation. Reproofs were affectionately repeated, and every effort made to dissuade the boy from what was considered an "idle amusement," but it was soon discovered that opposition was unavailing, and the attachment too strong to be checked. It might perhaps have been otherwise, but for some rays of encouragement received from the observant kindness of his first schoolmaster. To watch the direction of the little hand when it wandered from its task, to draw the culprit

---

[1] [What this was is not known, "but it is believed to have been unconnected with art" (J. L. Roget's *History of the Old Water-Colour Society*, i. 341).]

to him with a smile instead of a reproof, to set him on the high stool beside his desk, and stimulate him, by the loan of his own pen, to a more patient and elaborate study of the child's usual subject, his favourite cat, was a modification of preceptorial care as easy as it was wise; but it perhaps had more influence on the mind and after-life of the boy than all the rest of his education together.

2. Such happy though rare interludes in school-hours, and occasional attempts at home, usually from the carts and horses which stopped at a public-house opposite, began the studentship of the young artist before he had quitted his pinafore. An unhappy accident which happened about the same time, and which farther enfeebled his health, rendered it still less advisable to interfere with his beloved occupation. We have heard the painter express, with a melancholy smile, the distinct recollection remaining with him to this day, of a burning autumn morning, on which he had sallied forth alone, himself some four autumns old, armed with a hooked stick, to gather nuts. Unrestrainable alike with pencil or crook, he was found by a farmer, towards the close of the day, lying moaning under a hedge, prostrated by a sun-stroke, and was brought home insensible. From that day forward he was subject to attacks of violent pain in the head, recurring at short intervals; and until thirty years after marriage not a week passed without one or two days of absolute confinement to his room or to his bed. " Up to this hour," we may perhaps be permitted to use his own touching words, " I have to endure a great fight of afflictions; can I therefore be sufficiently thankful for the merciful gift of a buoyant spirit ? "

3. That buoyancy of spirit—one of the brightest and most marked elements of his character—never failed to sustain him between the recurrences even of his most acute suffering; and the pursuit of his most beloved Art became every year more determined and independent. The first beginnings in landscape study were made in happy truant excursions, now fondly remembered, with the painter Haydon,

then also a youth.[1] This companionship was probably rather cemented by the energy than the delicacy of Haydon's sympathies. The two boys were directly opposed in their habits of application and modes of study. Prout unremitting in diligencé, patient in observation, devoted in copying what he loved in nature, never working except with his model before him; Haydon restless, ambitious, and fiery; exceedingly imaginative, never captivated with simple truth, nor using his pencil on the spot, but trusting always to his powers of memory. The fates of the two youths were inevitably fixed by their opposite characters. The humble student became the originator of a new School of Art, and one of the most popular painters of his age. The self-trust of the wanderer in the wilderness of his fancy betrayed him into the extravagances, and deserted him in the suffering, with which his name must remain sadly, but not unjustly, associated.

4. There was, however, little in the sketches made by Prout at this period to indicate the presence of dormant power. Common prints, at a period when engraving was in the lowest state of decline, were the only guides which the youth could obtain; and his style, in endeavouring to copy these, became cramped and mannered; but the unremitting sketching from nature saved him. Whole days, from dawn till night, were devoted to the study of the peculiar objects of his early interest, the ivy-mantled bridges, mossy watermills, and rock-built cottages, which characterise the valley scenery of Devon. In spite of every disadvantage, the strong love of truth, and the instinctive perception of the chief points of shade and characters of form on which his favourite effects mainly depended, enabled him not only to obtain an accumulated store of memoranda, afterwards valuable, but to publish several elementary works [2] which

---

[1] [For Benjamin Robert Haydon (1786–1846), see above, p. 130. His father was a printer and publisher in Plymouth.]

[2] [*Rudiments of Landscape, in Progressive Studies, Drawn and Etched in imitation of Chalk* (1813); *Prout's Village Scenery* (1813); *A Series of Easy Lessons in Landscape Drawing* (1820); and several other volumes of the kind (see J. L. Roget's *History of the Old Water-Colour Society*, i. 351–353).]

obtained extensive and deserved circulation, and to which many artists, now high in reputation, have kindly and frankly confessed their early obligations.

5. At that period the art of water-colour drawing was little understood at Plymouth, and practised only by Payne, then an engineer in the citadel.[1] Though mannered in the extreme, his works obtained reputation; for the best drawings of the period were feeble both in colour and execution, with commonplace light and shadow, a dark foreground being a *rule absolute*, as may be seen in several of Turner's first productions. But Turner was destined to annihilate such rules, breaking through and scattering them with an expansive force commensurate with the rigidity of former restraint. It happened "fortunately," as it is said,—naturally and deservedly, as it *should* be said,—that Prout was at this period removed from the narrow sphere of his first efforts to one in which he could share in, and take advantage of, every progressive movement.

6. The most respectable of the Plymouth amateurs was the Rev. Dr. Bidlake,[2] who was ever kind in his encouragement of the young painter, and with whom many delightful excursions were made. At his house, Mr. Britton, the antiquarian, happening to see some of the cottage sketches, and being pleased with them, proposed that Prout should accompany him into Cornwall, in order to aid him in collecting materials for his "Beauties of England and Wales." This was the painter's first recognised artistical employment, as well as the occasion of a friendship ever gratefully and fondly remembered.[3] On Mr. Britton's return to London, after sending to him a portfolio of drawings, which were

[1] [William Payne (1769–1843). In 1790 he moved to London, and became a fashionable teacher, as well as a constant exhibitor with the Society of Artists, Royal Academy, and British Institution. Several of his drawings are in the Victoria and Albert (South Kensington) Museum.]

[2] [The Rev. John Bidlake, D.D. (1755–1814), for many years headmaster of the Plymouth Grammar School.]

[3] [John Britton (1771–1857) contributed an account of this tour with Prout to the *Builder* of May 29, 1852; it is cited in Roget's *History*, i. 344. *The Beauties of England and Wales* was published 1801–1804. Prout, on his removal to London, boarded and lodged with Britton for about two years.]

almost the first to create a sensation with lovers of Art, Mr. Prout received so many offers of encouragement, if he would consent to reside in London, as to induce him to take this important step—the first towards being established as an artist.

7. The immediate effect of this change of position was what might easily have been foretold, upon a mind naturally sensitive, diffident, and enthusiastic. It was a heavy discouragement. The youth felt that he had much to eradicate and more to learn, and hardly knew at first how to avail himself of the advantages presented by the study of the works of Turner, Girtin, Cozens,[1] and others. But he had resolution and ambition as well as modesty; he knew that

> " The noblest honours of the mind
> On rigid terms descend." [2]

He had every inducement to begin the race, in the clearer guidance and nobler ends which the very works that had disheartened him afforded and pointed out; and the first firm and certain step was made. His range of subject was as yet undetermined, and was likely at one time to have been very different from that in which he has since obtained pre-eminence so confessed. Among the picturesque material of his native place, the forms of its shipping had not been neglected, though there was probably less in the order of Plymouth dockyard to catch the eye of the boy, always determined in its preference of purely picturesque arrangements, than might have been afforded by the meanest fishing hamlet. But a strong and lasting impression was made upon him by the wreck of the *Dutton* East Indiaman

---

[1] [For other references to Thomas Girtin (1773–1802), see *Modern Painters*, vol. iii. ch. iv. § 18; *Notes on his Drawings by Turner* (Introduction); *Art of England*, §§ 166, 172, and a letter printed in Cosmo Monkhouse's *Earlier English Water-Colour Painters* (1889), and reprinted in a later volume of this edition. For John Robert Cozens (1752–1799), see *Mornings in Florence*, § 118; *Art of England*, § 166.]

[2] [Thomson : *A Poem to the Memory of the Right Hon. Lord Talbot, Lord Chancellor of Great Britain, Addressed to his Son*, lines 288, 289 :—

> " Yet know, these noblest honours of the mind
> On rigid terms descend : . . ."]

on the rocks under the citadel;[1] the crew were saved by the personal courage and devotion of Sir Edward Pellew, afterwards Lord Exmouth. The wreck held together for many hours under the cliff, rolling to and fro as the surges struck her. Haydon and Prout sat on the crags together and watched her vanish fragment by fragment into the gnashing foam. Both were equally awestruck at the time; both, on the morrow, resolved to paint their first pictures; both failed; but Haydon, always incapable of acknowledging and remaining loyal to the majesty of what he had seen, lost himself in vulgar thunder and lightning. Prout struggled to some resemblance of the actual scene, and the effect upon his mind was never effaced.

8. At the time of his first residence in London, he painted more marines than anything else. But other work was in store for him. About the year 1818, his health, which as we have seen had never been vigorous, showed signs of increasing weakness, and a short trial of continental air was recommended. The route by Havre to Rouen was chosen, and Prout found himself, for the first time, in the grotesque labyrinths of the Norman streets. There are few minds so apathetic as to receive no impulse of new delight from their first acquaintance with continental scenery and architecture; and Rouen was, of all the cities of France, the richest in those objects with which the painter's mind had the profoundest sympathy. It was other then than it is now; revolutionary fury had indeed spent itself upon many of its noblest monuments, but the interference of modern restoration or improvement was unknown. Better the unloosed rage of the fiend than the scrabble of self-complacent idiocy. The façade of the cathedral was as yet unencumbered by the blocks of new stonework, never to be carved, by which it is now defaced; the Church of St. Nicholas existed, (the last fragments of the niches of its gateway were seen by the writer dashed upon the pavement in 1840 to make room

---

[1] [Cast ashore under the citadel of Plymouth, January 26, 1796.]

for the new "Hotel St. Nicholas";[1]) the Gothic turret had not vanished from the angle of the Place de la Pucelle, the Palais de Justice remained in its grey antiquity,[2] and the Norman houses still lifted their fantastic ridges of gable along the busy quay (now fronted by as formal a range of hotels and offices as that of the West Cliff of Brighton). All was at unity with itself, and the city lay under its guarding hills, one labyrinth of delight, its grey and fretted towers, misty in their magnificence of height, letting the sky like blue enamel through the foiled spaces of their crowns of open work; the walls and gates of its countless churches wardered by saintly groups of solemn statuary, clasped about by wandering stems of sculptured leafage, and crowned by fretted niche and fairy pediment—meshed like gossamer with inextricable tracery : many a quaint monument of past times standing to tell its far-off tale in the place from which it has since perished—in the midst of the throng and murmur of those shadowy streets — all grim with jutting props of ebon woodwork, lightened only here and there by a sun-beam glancing down from the scaly backs, and points, and pyramids of the Norman roofs, or carried out of its narrow range by the gay progress of some snowy cap or scarlet camisole. The painter's vocation was fixed from that hour. The first effect upon his mind was irrepressible enthusiasm, with a strong feeling of a new-born attachment to Art, in a new world of exceeding interest. Previous impressions were presently obliterated, and the old embankments of fancy gave way to the force of overwhelming anticipations, form-ing another and a wider channel for its future course.

9. From this time excursions were continually made to the Continent, and every corner of France, Germany, the Netherlands, and Italy ransacked for its fragments of carved stone. The enthusiasm of the painter was greater than his ambition, and the strict limitation of his aim to the ren-dering of architectural character permitted him to adopt a

---

[1] [Ruskin describes this destruction in *Modern Painters*, vol. ii. (Vol. IV. p. 37 *n*.).]
[2] [For the restoration of this building, see *Seven Lamps*, Vol. VIII. p. 243 and *n*.]

simple and consistent method of execution, from which he has rarely departed.   It was adapted in the first instance to the necessities of the mouldering and mystic character of Northern Gothic; and though impressions received afterwards in Italy, more especially at Venice, have retained as strong a hold upon the painter's mind as those of his earlier excursions, his methods of drawing have always been influenced by the predilections first awakened.   How far his love of the picturesque, already alluded to, was reconcilable with an entire appreciation of the highest characters of Italian architecture we do not pause to inquire; but this we may assert, without hesitation, that the picturesque *elements* of that architecture were unknown until he developed them, and that, since Gentile Bellini,[1] no one had regarded the palaces of Venice with so affectionate an understanding of the purpose and expression of their wealth of detail.   In this respect the City of the Sea has been, and remains, peculiarly his own.   There is, probably, no single piazza nor sea-paved street from St. Giorgio in Aliga to the Arsenal, of which Prout has not in order drawn every fragment of pictorial material.   Probably not a pillar in Venice but occurs in some one of his innumerable studies; while the peculiarly beautiful and varied arrangements under which he has treated the angle formed by St. Mark's Church with the Doge's palace, have not only made every successful drawing of those buildings by any other hand look like plagiarism, but have added (and what is this but indeed to paint the lily![2]) another charm to the spot itself.

10. This exquisite dexterity of arrangement has always been one of his leading characteristics as an artist.   Notwithstanding the deserved popularity of his works, his greatness in composition remains altogether unappreciated.   Many modern works exhibit greater pretence at arrangement, and a more palpable system; masses of well-concentrated light

---

[1] [See *Modern Painters*, vol. i. (Vol. III. p. 209), where Gentile's painting of architecture is discussed.]
[2] [*King John*, iv. 2.]

or points of sudden and dextrous colour are expedients in the works of our second-rate artists as attractive as they are commonplace. But the moving and natural crowd, the decomposing composition, the frank and unforced, but marvellously intricate grouping, the breadth of inartificial and unexaggerated shadow, these are merits of an order only the more elevated because unobtrusive. Nor is his system of colour less admirable. It is a quality from which the character of his subjects naturally withdraws much of his attention, and of which sometimes that character precludes any high attainment; but, nevertheless, the truest and happiest association of hues in sun and shade to be found in modern water-colour art,* (excepting only the studies of Hunt and De Wint[1]) will be found in portions of Prout's more important works.

11. Of his *peculiar* powers we need hardly speak; it would be difficult to conceive the circle of their influence widened. There is not a landscape of recent times in which the treatment of the architectural features has not been affected, however unconsciously, by principles which were first developed by Prout. Of those principles the most original were his familiarisation of the sentiment, while he elevated the subject, of the picturesque. That character had been sought, before his time, either in solitude or in rusticity; it was supposed to belong only to the savageness of the desert or the simplicity of the hamlet; it lurked beneath the brows of rocks and the eaves of cottages; to seek it in a city would have been deemed an extravagance, to raise it to the height of a cathedral, an heresy. Prout did both, and both simultaneously; he found and proved in the busy shadows and sculptured gables of the Continental street sources of picturesque delight as rich and as

---

* We do not mean under this term to include the drawings of professed oil-painters, as of Stothard or Turner.

---

[1] [For William Hunt and De Wint, see General Index.]

interesting as those which had been sought amidst the darkness of thickets and the eminence of rocks; and he contrasted with the familiar circumstances of urban life, the majesty and the aërial elevation of the most noble architecture, expressing its details in more splendid accumulation, and with a more patient love than ever had been reached or manifested before his time by any artist who introduced such subjects as members of a general composition. He thus became the interpreter of a great period of the world's history, of that in which age and neglect had cast the interest of ruin over the noblest ecclesiastical structures of Europe, and in which there had been born at their feet a generation other in its feelings and thoughts than that to which they owed their existence, a generation which understood not their meaning, and regarded not their beauty, and which yet had a character of its own, full of vigour, animation, and originality, which rendered the grotesque association of the circumstances of its ordinary and active life with the solemn memorialism of the elder building, one which rather pleased by the strangeness than pained by the violence of its contrast.

12. That generation is passing away, and another dynasty is putting forth its character and its laws. Care and observance, more mischievous in their misdirection than indifference or scorn, have in many places given the mediæval relics the aspect and associations of a kind of cabinet preservation, instead of that air of majestic independence, or patient and stern endurance, with which they frowned down the insult of the regardless crowd. Nominal restoration has done tenfold worse, and has hopelessly destroyed what time, and storm, and anarchy, and impiety had spared. The picturesque material of a lower kind is fast departing—and for ever. There is not, so far as we know, one city scene in central Europe which has not suffered from some jarring point of modernisation. The railroad and the iron wheel have done their work, and the characters of Venice, Florence, and Rouen are yielding day by day to a lifeless extension

of those of Paris and Birmingham. A few lustres more, and the modernisation will be complete: the archæologist may still find work among the wrecks of beauty, and here and there a solitary fragment of the old cities may exist by toleration, or rise strangely before the workmen who dig the new foundations, left like some isolated and tottering rock in the midst of sweeping sea. But the life of the Middle Ages is dying from their embers, and the warm mingling of the past and present will soon be for ever dissolved. The works of Prout, and of those who have followed in his footsteps, will become memorials the most precious of the things that have been ; to their technical value, however great, will be added the far higher interest of faithful and fond records of a strange and unreturning era of history. May he long be spared to us, and enabled to continue the noble series, conscious of a purpose and function worthy of being followed with all the zeal of even his most ardent and affectionate mind. A time will come when that zeal will be understood, and his works will be cherished with a melancholy gratitude when the pillars of Venice shall lie mouldering in the salt shallows of her sea, and the stones of the goodly towers of Rouen have become ballast for the barges of the Seine.

IV

THE PRE-RAPHAELITE ARTISTS

LETTERS TO THE "TIMES" (1851, 1854)

[*Bibliographical Note.*—The four letters here given were reprinted in *Arrows of the Chace*, 1880, vol. i. pp. 85–107. Two later letters (1858), given in the same section of that book, are included, in this edition, in the volume containing *Academy Notes*.

The two letters of 1854 had already been reprinted (by the late Mr. Ernest Willett, with Ruskin's permission) in 1876 in pamphlet form, with the following title-page :—

[Reprinted for Private Circulation Only.] | Letters | to | "The Times" | On the Principal | Pre-Raphaelite | Pictures | in the | Exhibition of 1854 | From | The Author of "Modern Painters." | 1876.

8vo, pp. ii. + 9. There is no imprint, nor are there headlines. Issued sewn, without wrappers.

The former letter (that on "The Light of the World") was also printed in 1876 on one side of a single 4to sheet, on the reverse of which was a letter headed: "The following interesting letter from a clergyman is a most complete interpretation of this beautiful allegory."

The greater part of the same letter has also been reprinted on a double sheet (of the size of note-paper); in this form, it is given to visitors who go to see the picture in Keble College, Oxford. There is no date or imprint; the sheet is headed "'The Light of the World,' by Holman Hunt, R.A. [*sic*]. Bequeathed to Keble College by T. Combe, Esq., The University Press, Oxford."

Both were again reprinted (by permission of Ruskin) in *Notes on the Pictures of Mr. Holman Hunt, Exhibited at the Rooms of the Fine Art Society, 1886,* edited by A. Gordon Crawford (pseudonym of A. G. Wise). The letter on "The Light of the World" (with the omission of the last seven lines) was on pp. 15–19 of that pamphlet; that on "The Awakening Conscience," pp. 2–5.

The letter on "The Light of the World" (with the omission of the last seven lines) was again reprinted in 1904 in connexion with the exhibition of the replica (see below, p. 331, *n.*). The reprint occupies pp. 6–11 of a small pamphlet with the following title-page: "'The Light of the World,' by W. Holman Hunt, now exhibiting at the Fine Art Society's, 148, New Bond Street, London."

There are no various readings to record, except that in the third letter "Præ-Raphaelites" has here been altered to "Pre-Raphaelites."]

THE PRE-RAPHAELITE ARTISTS

1. FROM THE *TIMES*, MAY 13, 1851

To the Editor of the " Times"

SIR,—Your usual liberality will, I trust, give a place in your columns to this expression of my regret that the tone of the critique which appeared in the *Times* of Wednesday last on the works of Mr. Millais and Mr. Hunt, now in the Royal Academy, should have been scornful as well as severe.[1]

I regret it, first, because the mere labour bestowed on those works, and their fidelity to a certain order of truth, (labour and fidelity which are altogether indisputable,) ought at once to have placed them above the level of mere contempt; and, secondly, because I believe these young artists to be at a most critical period of their career—at a turning-point, from which they may either sink into nothingness or rise to very real greatness; and I believe also, that whether they choose the upward or the downward path, may in no small degree depend upon the character of the criticism which their works have to sustain. I do not wish in any way to dispute or invalidate the general truth of your critique on the Royal Academy; nor am I surprised at the

---

[1] [The critique appeared on May 7. That it was sufficiently bitter may be gathered from the following portions of it: "These young artists have unfortunately become notorious by addicting themselves to an antiquated style and an affected simplicity in painting. . . . We can extend no toleration to a mere servile imitation of the cramped style, false perspective, and crude colour of remote antiquity. We want not to see what Fuseli termed drapery 'snapped instead of folded'; faces bloated into apoplexy, or extenuated to skeletons; colour borrowed from the jars in a druggist's shop, and expression forced into caricature. . . . That morbid infatuation which sacrifices truth, beauty, and genuine feeling to mere eccentricity, deserves no quarter at the hands of the public."]

319

estimate which the writer formed of the pictures in question when rapidly compared with works of totally different style and aim: nay, when I first saw the chief picture by Millais in the Exhibition of last year,[1] I had nearly come to the same conclusion myself. But I ask your permission, in justice to artists who have at least given much time and toil to their pictures, to institute some more serious inquiry into their merits and faults than your general notice of the Academy could possibly have admitted.

Let me state, in the first place, that I have no acquaintance with any of these artists, and very imperfect sympathy with them. No one who has met with any of my writings will suspect me of desiring to encourage them in their Romanist and Tractarian tendencies.[2]   I am glad to see that Mr. Millais' lady in blue[3] is heartily tired of her painted window and idolatrous toilet table; and I have no particular respect for Mr. Collins' lady in white, because her sympathies are limited by a dead wall, or divided between some gold fish and a tadpole—(the latter Mr. Collins may, perhaps,

---

[1] [A sacred picture (No. 518) upon the text, "And one shall say unto him, What are these wounds in thine hands? Then he shall answer, Those with which I was wounded in the house of my friends" (Zechariah xiii. 6). Ruskin never accounted this among the happier efforts of the painter : see his Notes on the Millais Exhibition of 1886 (now reprinted in the volume containing *Academy Notes*). The picture had no title, but is now called "Christ in the House of His Parents" or "The Carpenter's Shop" (the latter title being originally given to it by hostile critics in derision). Interesting particulars with regard to the production of the picture by the young artist (he was 22 at the time of its exhibition) are given in *The Life and Letters of Sir John Everett Millais*, by J. G. Millais, 1899, i. 76–78. The picture excited the utmost displeasure among the critics. The *Times* pronounced it "revolting," "loathsome," and "disgusting" (May 9, 1850). The *Athenæum* "recoiled" from it "with loathing and disgust" (June 1, 1850). Dickens, in *Household Words* (June 15, 1850), pronounced the female figure "so horrible in her ugliness that she would stand out from the rest of the company as a monster in the vilest cabaret in France." Millais had two other pictures in the Academy of 1850, namely, "Portrait of a gentleman (Mr. James Wyatt, of Oxford) and his grandchild" (No. 429), and " Ferdinand lured by Ariel"—Shakspeare, *Tempest*, Act i. sc. 2 (No. 504). Of these pictures, "The Carpenter's Shop" was recently in the collection of Mr. F. A. Beer ; the "Portrait" is in that of Mr. James Wyatt ; and "Ferdinand," in that of Mr. H. F. Makins.]

[2] [See the next letter, p. 327.]

[3] [The pre-Raphaelite pictures exhibited in the Academy of 1851, and discussed in this and in the following letter, were Millais' "Mariana" (No. 561)—the "lady in blue" here referred to—"The Return of the Dove to the Ark" (No. 651), and "The Woodman's Daughter" (No. 799); Holman Hunt's "Valentine receiving

permit me to suggest *en passant*, as he is already half a frog, is rather too small for his age). But I happen to have a special acquaintance with the water plant, *Alisma Plantago*,[1] among which the said gold fish are swimming; and as I never saw it so thoroughly or so well drawn, I must take leave to remonstrate with you, when you say sweepingly that these men "sacrifice *truth* as well as feeling to eccentricity." For as a mere botanical study of the water lily and *Alisma*, as well as of the common lily and several other garden flowers, this picture would be invaluable to me, and I heartily wish it were mine.

But, before entering into such particulars, let me correct an impression which your article is likely to induce in most minds, and which is altogether false. These pre-Raphaelites (I cannot compliment them on common sense in choice of a *nom de guerre*[2]) do *not* desire nor pretend in any way to imitate antique painting as such. They know very little of ancient paintings who suppose the works of these young artists to resemble them. As far as I can judge of their aim—for, as I said, I do not know the men themselves —the Pre-Raphaelites intend to surrender no advantage

(rescuing?) Sylvia from Proteus" (No. 594); and C. Collins' "Convent Thoughts" (No. 493), to which were affixed the lines from *Midsummer Night's Dream* (Act i. sc. 1)—

> "Thrice blessed they, that master so their blood
> To undergo such maiden pilgrimage;"

and the verse (Psalm cxliii. 5), "I meditate on all Thy works; I muse on the work of Thy hands." The last-named artist also had a portrait of Mr. William Bennett (No. 718) in the Exhibition,—not, however, alluded to in this letter. Charles Allston Collins (1828–1873), son of William Collins, R.A., and the younger brother of Wilkie Collins, subsequently turned his attention to literature; see also *Academy Notes*, 1855, No. 1334, where Ruskin calls attention to a later picture by the artist. "Mariana" is now in the collection of Mr. Farrer; "The Return of the Dove" is in the Oxford University Galleries (bequeathed by Mr. T. Combe); "The Woodman's Daughter" is in the possession of the present Lady Millais.]

[1] [See *Seven Lamps*, Vol. VIII. p. 168 and *n.*]

[2] [Compare *Modern Painters*, vol. i., note added in the edition of 1851 (Vol. III. p. 621), where allusion is made to the painters of a society which "unfortunately, or rather unwisely, has given itself the name of 'Pre-Raphaelite'; unfortunately, because the principles on which its members are working are neither pre- nor post-Raphaelite, but everlasting. They are endeavouring to paint, with the highest possible degree of completion, what they see in nature, without reference to conventional established rules; but by no means to imitate the style of any past epoch."]

which the knowledge or inventions of the present time can afford to their art. They intend to return to early days in this one point only—that, as far as in them lies, they will draw either what they see, or what they suppose might have been the actual facts of the scene they desire to represent, irrespective of any conventional rules of picture-making; and they have chosen their unfortunate though not inaccurate name because all artists did this before Raphael's time, and after Raphael's time did *not* this, but sought to paint fair pictures, rather than represent stern facts; of which the consequence has been that, from Raphael's time to this day, historical art has been in acknowledged decadence.

Now, Sir, presupposing that the intention of these men was to return to archaic *art* instead of to archaic *honesty*, your critic borrows Fuseli's expression respecting ancient draperies "snapped instead of folded," and asserts that in these pictures there is a "*servile* imitation of *false* perspective." To which I have just this to answer:—

That there is not one single error in perspective in four out of the five pictures in question; and that in Millais' "Mariana"[1] there is but this one—that the top of the green curtain in the distant window has too low a vanishing-point; and that I will undertake, if need be, to point out and prove a dozen worse errors in perspective in any twelve pictures, containing architecture, taken at random from among the works of the popular painters of the day.

Secondly: that, putting aside the small Mulready, and the works of Thorburn and Sir W. Ross,[2] and perhaps some others of those in the miniature room which I have not examined, there is not a single study of drapery in the whole Academy, be it in large works or small, which for perfect truth, power, and finish could be compared for an

---

[1] [For other references to Millais' "Mariana," see below, pp. 323, 327; *Academy Notes*, 1857, s. 283; *The Three Colours of Pre-Raphaelitism*, § 19; and *Notes on the Millais Exhibition* of 1886, reprinted in a later volume of this edition.]

[2] [The "small Mulready" was No. 168, "A Music Lesson" (painted in 1809). There were several small works in the exhibition by Robert Thorburn (1818–1885) and Sir William Charles Ross, R.A. (1794–1860).]

instant with the black sleeve of the Julia, or with the velvet on the breast and the chain mail of the Valentine, of Mr. Hunt's picture;[1] or with the white draperies on the table of Mr. Millais' " Mariana," and of the right-hand figure in the same painter's " Dove returning to the Ark."[2]

And further : that as studies both of drapery and of every minor detail, there has been nothing in art so earnest or so complete as these pictures since the days of Albert Dürer. This I assert generally and fearlessly. On the other hand, I am perfectly ready to admit that Mr. Hunt's " Sylvia" is not a person whom Proteus or any one else would have been likely to fall in love with at first sight; and that one cannot feel very sincere delight that Mr. Millais' " Wives of the Sons of Noah" should have escaped the Deluge; with many other faults besides on which I will not enlarge at present, because I have already occupied too much of your valuable space, and I hope to enter into more special criticism in a future letter.

I have the honour to be, Sir,
Your obedient servant,
THE AUTHOR OF " MODERN PAINTERS."

DENMARK HILL, *May 9.*

---

[1] [For this picture, see further, below, pp. 324–325.]
[2] [For other references to this picture—called also " Wives of the Sons of Noah "— see *Academy Notes*, 1858, *s.* 300 ; 1859, *s.* 15 ; 1875, *s.* 218 ; and *The Three Colours of Pre-Raphaelitism*, § 21.]

2. FROM THE *TIMES*, MAY 30, 1851

To the Editor of the " Times"

SIR,—Your obliging insertion of my former letter encourages me to trouble you with one or two further notes respecting the pre-Raphaelite pictures. I had intended, in continuation of my first letter, to institute as close an inquiry as I could into the character of the morbid tendencies which prevent these works from favourably arresting the attention of the public; but I believe there are so few pictures in the Academy whose reputation would not be grievously diminished by a deliberate inventory of their errors, that I am disinclined to undertake so ungracious a task with respect to this or that particular work. These points, however, may be noted, partly for the consideration of the painters themselves, partly that forgiveness of them may be asked from the public in consideration of high merits in other respects.

The most painful of these defects is unhappily also the most prominent—the commonness of feature in many of the principal figures. In Mr. Hunt's " Valentine defending Sylvia,"[1] this is, indeed, almost the only fault. Further examination of this picture has even raised the estimate I had previously formed of its marvellous truth in detail and splendour in colour; nor is its general conception less deserving of praise: the action of Valentine, his arm thrown round Sylvia, and his hand clasping hers at the same instant as she falls at his feet, is most faithful and beautiful, nor

[1] [For other references to this picture—sometimes called "The Two Gentlemen of Verona"—see *Stones of Venice*, vol. iii. (Vol. XI. p. 217), *Academy Notes*, 1859, No. 329, and *The Art of England*, § 6, where Lecture 1 is devoted to the art of " Rossetti and Holman Hunt." The picture is in the collection formed by the late Sir Thomas Fairbairn. See further, Introduction, above, p. xlvii.]

less so the contending of doubt and distress with awakening hope in the half-shadowed, half-sunlit countenance of Julia. Nay, even the momentary struggle of Proteus with Sylvia just past, is indicated by the trodden grass and broken fungi of the foreground.   But all this thoughtful conception, and absolutely inimitable execution, fail in making immediate appeal to the feelings, owing to the unfortunate type chosen for the face of Sylvia.[1]   Certainly this cannot be she whose lover was

" As rich in having such a jewel,
As twenty seas, if all their sands were pearl." [2]

Nor is it, perhaps, less to be regretted that, while in Shakspeare's play there are nominally " Two Gentlemen," in Mr. Hunt's picture there should only be one, — at least, the kneeling figure on the right has by no means the look of a gentleman.   But this may be on purpose, for any one who remembers the conduct of Proteus throughout the previous scenes will, I think, be disposed to consider that the error lies more in Shakspeare's nomenclature than in Mr. Hunt's ideal.

No defence can, however, be offered for the choice of features in the left-hand figure of Mr. Millais' "Dove returning to the Ark."   I cannot understand how a painter so sensible of the utmost refinement of beauty in other objects should deliberately choose for his model a type far inferior to that of average humanity, and unredeemed by any expression save that of dull self-complacency.   Yet let the spectator who desires to be just turn away from this head, and contemplate rather the tender and beautiful expression of the stooping figure, and the intense harmony of colour in the exquisitely finished draperies ; let him note also the ruffling of the plumage of the wearied dove, one

---

[1] [Mr. Holman Hunt, referring to this passage, says : "The letter [by Ruskin] on my 'Valentine' admitted the weak point in my picture.   A man had at the last robbed me of £15 ; this occasioned me to lose my time, and I sent the picture in imperfect in the Sylvia's head.   I afterwards rectified this" (*Contemporary Review,* May 1886, p. 747).]

[2] [*Two Gentlemen of Verona,* Act ii. sc. 4.   The scene of the picture was taken from Act v. sc. 4.]

of its feathers falling on the arm of the figure which holds it, and another to the ground, where, by-the-bye, the hay is painted not only elaborately, but with the most perfect ease of touch and mastery of effect, especially to be observed because this freedom of execution is a modern excellence, which it has been inaccurately stated that these painters despise, but which, in reality, is one of the remarkable distinctions between their painting and that of Van Eyck or Hemling,[1] which caused me to say in my first letter that "those knew little of ancient painting who supposed the works of these men to resemble it."

Next to this false choice of feature, and in connection with it, is to be noted the defect in the colouring of the flesh. The hands, at least in the pictures in Millais, are almost always ill painted, and the flesh tint in general is wrought out of crude purples and dusky yellows. It appears just possible that much of this evil may arise from the attempt to obtain too much transparency—an attempt which has injured also not a few of the best works of Mulready. I believe it will be generally found that close study of minor details is unfavourable to flesh painting; it was noticed of the drawing by John Lewis, in the old water-colour exhibition of 1850,[2] (a work which, as regards its treatment of detail, may be ranged in the same class with the pre-Raphaelite pictures,) that the faces were the worst painted portions of the whole.

The apparent want of shade is, however, perhaps the fault which most hurts the general eye. The fact is, nevertheless, that the fault is far more in the other pictures of the Academy than in the pre-Raphaelite ones. It is the former that are false, not the latter, except so far as every picture must be false which endeavours to represent living sunlight with dead pigments. I think Mr. Hunt has a

---

[1] [See above, Review of Eastlake, § 34, p. 295.]

[2] ["The Hhareem" (No. 147), noticed, partly to the above effect, by the critic of the *Times*, May 1, 1850. It will be remembered that John Lewis is, with Turner, Millais, Prout, Mulready, and Edwin Landseer, one of the artists particularly mentioned in Ruskin's pamphlet on "Pre-Raphaelitism" (1851): see below, p. 363; and see also *Academy Notes*, 1857, Nos. 39, 302.]

slight tendency to exaggerate reflected lights; and if Mr. Millais has ever been near a piece of good painted glass, he ought to have known that its tone is more dusky and sober than that of his Mariana's window. But for the most part these pictures are rashly condemned because the only light which we are accustomed to see represented is that which falls on the artist's model in his dim painting-room, not that of sunshine in the fields.

I do not think I can go much further in fault-finding. I had, indeed, something to urge respecting what I supposed to be the Romanizing tendencies of the painters; but I have received a letter assuring me that I was wrong in attributing to them anything of the kind; whereupon, all I can say is that, instead of the "pilgrimage" of Mr. Collins' maiden over a plank and round a fish-pond, that old pilgrim-age of Christiana and her children towards the place where they should "look the Fountain of Mercy in the face,"[1] would have been more to the purpose in these times. And so I wish them all heartily good speed, believing in sincerity that if they temper the courage and energy which they have shown in the adoption of their systems with patience and discretion in framing it, and if they do not suffer themselves to be driven by harsh or careless criticism into rejection of the ordinary means of obtaining influence over the minds of others, they may, as they gain experience, lay in our England the foundations of a school of art nobler than the world has seen for three hundred years.[2]

I have the honour to be, Sir,

Your obedient servant,

THE AUTHOR OF "MODERN PAINTERS."

DENMARK HILL, *May* 26.

---

[1] [*The Pilgrim's Progress*, Part ii.]

[2] ["I have great hope that they may become the foundation of a more earnest and able school of art than we have seen for centuries."—*Modern Painters*, vol. i. (Vol. III. p. 621).]

"THE LIGHT OF THE WORLD"

3. FROM THE *TIMES*, May 5, 1854

To the Editor of the " Times"

Sir,—I trust that, with your usual kindness and liberality, you will give me room in your columns for a few words respecting the principal Pre-Raphaelite picture in the Exhibition of the Royal Academy this year. Its painter is travelling in the Holy Land, and can neither suffer nor benefit by criticism. But I am solicitous that justice should be done to his work, not for his sake, but for that of the large number of persons who, during the year, will have an opportunity of seeing it, and on whom, if rightly understood, it may make an impression for which they will ever afterwards be grateful.

I speak of the picture called "The Light of the World," by Mr. Holman Hunt.[1] Standing by it yesterday for upwards of an hour, I watched the effect it produced upon the passers-by. Few stopped to look at it, and those who did almost invariably with some contemptuous expression, founded on what appeared to them the absurdity of representing the Saviour with a lantern in his hand. Now, it ought to be remembered that, whatever may be the faults of a Pre-Raphaelite picture, it must at least have taken

---

[1] ["The Light of the World" is well known from the engraving of it by W. H. Simmons. It was originally purchased by Mr. Thomas Combe, of Oxford, who bequeathed it (subject to the life interest of his widow) to Keble College; she, however, presented it at once to the College, where it now hangs in the side-chapel, having been removed there in 1894 from the library. In Ruskin's diary he notes that the price paid was 400 guineas. For other references to the picture, see *Modern Painters*, vol. iii. ch. iii. §§ 9, 23, ch. iv. § 20, ch. vi. § 8, and Appendix 3, in which passages it is cited as an original and imaginative work of ideal religious art, perfect alike in execution and feeling; vol. iv. ch. iv. § 8 *n.*, where a part of this letter is cited; *Academy Notes*, 1856, *s.* 413; 1875, *s.* 196; *Eagle's Nest*, § 115 ("the most true and useful piece of religious vision which realistic art has yet embodied"); and *The Art of England*, § 6.]

much time; and therefore it may not unwarrantably be presumed that conceptions which are to be laboriously realized are not adopted in the first instance without some reflection. So that the spectator may surely question with himself whether the objections which now strike every one in a moment might not possibly have occurred to the painter himself, either during the time devoted to the design of the picture, or the months of labour required for its execution; and whether, therefore, there may not be some reason for his persistence in such an idea, not discoverable at the first glance.

Mr. Hunt has never explained his work to me. I give what appears to me its palpable interpretation.

The legend beneath it is the beautiful verse,—" Behold, I stand at the door and knock. If any man hear my voice, and open the door, I will come in to him, and will sup with him, and he with me."—Rev. iii. 20. On the left-hand side of the picture is seen this door of the human soul. It is fast barred: its bars and nails are rusty; it is knitted and bound to its stanchions by creeping tendrils of ivy, showing that it has never been opened. A bat hovers about it; its threshold is overgrown with brambles, nettles, and fruitless corn,—the wild grass " whereof the mower filleth not his hand, nor he that bindeth the sheaves his bosom." Christ approaches it in the night-time,—Christ, in his everlasting offices of prophet, priest, and king. He wears the white robe, representing the power of the Spirit upon him; the jewelled robe and breastplate, representing the sacerdotal investiture; the rayed crown of gold, inwoven with the crown of thorns; not dead thorns, but now bearing soft leaves, for the healing of the nations.[1]

Now, when Christ enters any human heart, he bears with him a twofold light: first, the light of conscience, which displays past sin, and afterwards the light of peace, the hope of salvation. The lantern, carried in Christ's left

---

[1] [The Bible references here are Psalms cxxix. 7, and Revelation xxii. 2.]

hand, is this light of conscience. Its fire is red and fierce; it falls only on the closed door, on the weeds which encumber it, and on an apple shaken from one of the trees of the orchard, thus marking that the entire awakening of the conscience is not merely to committed, but to hereditary guilt.

The light is suspended by a chain, wrapt about the wrist of the figure, showing that the light which reveals sin appears to the sinner also to chain the hand of Christ.

The light which proceeds from the head of the figure, on the contrary, is that of the hope of salvation; it springs from the crown of thorns, and, though itself sad, subdued, and full of softness, is yet so powerful that it entirely melts into the glow of it the forms of the leaves and boughs, which it crosses, showing that every earthly object must be hidden by this light, where its sphere extends.

I believe there are very few persons on whom the picture, thus justly understood, will not produce a deep impression. For my own part, I think it one of the very noblest works of sacred art ever produced in this or any other age.

It may, perhaps, be answered, that works of art ought not to stand in need of interpretation of this kind. Indeed, we have been so long accustomed to see pictures painted without any purpose or intention whatsoever, that the unexpected existence of meaning in a work of art may very naturally at first appear to us an unkind demand on the spectator's understanding. But in a few years more I hope the English public may be convinced of the simple truth, that neither a great fact, nor a great man, nor a great poem, nor a great picture, nor any other great thing, can be fathomed to the very bottom in a moment of time; and that no high enjoyment, either in picture-seeing or any other occupation, is consistent with a total lethargy of the powers of the understanding.

As far as regards the technical qualities of Mr. Hunt's painting, I would only ask the spectator to observe this difference between true Pre-Raphaelite work and its imitations.[1] The true work represents all objects exactly as they would appear in nature in the position and at the distances which the arrangement of the picture supposes. The false work represents them with all their details, as if seen through a microscope. Examine closely the ivy on the door in Mr. Hunt's picture, and there will not be found in it a single clear outline. All is the most exquisite mystery of colour; becoming reality at its due distance. In like manner examine the small gems on the robe of the figure. Not one will be made out in form, and yet there is not one of all those minute points of green colour, but it has two or three distinctly varied shades of green in it, giving it mysterious value and lustre.[2]

The spurious imitations of Pre-Raphaelite work represent the most minute leaves and other objects with sharp

---

[1] [Compare *Modern Painters*, vol. iv. ch. iv. § 8 and *n.*, where Ruskin quotes this passage in the course of some further remarks on the distinction between true Pre-Raphaelite work, which, in spite of all its detail, yet "suggests more than you can see," and the false imitations by mere definers and delineators.]

[2] [The picture was begun at Worcester Park Farm, near Kingston (Surrey), on the Ewell, where Hunt, Millais, and Collins spent the summer of 1851. It was there that Millais found the scene for his "Ophelia," and the background for his "Huguenot," and Hunt the backgrounds for his "Hireling Shepherd" and "Light of the World." "I had dwelt over and matured my design," writes Hunt, "enough to be able to paint the orchard background at the proper season in the grounds attached to the house. To paint it life-size, as I should have liked, would then have forbidden any hope of sale. It was one of the misfortunes of my position, which I have ever since regretted, but perhaps I should have had greater difficulty in the first work of the painting, which I did from 9 P.M. till 5 A.M. every night, about the time of the full moon, for two or three months. I sat in an open shed made of hurdles, and painted by the light of a candle, a stronger illumination being too blending. On going to bed I slept till ten, and then devoted myself for an hour or two to rectifying any error of colour, and to drawing out the work for the next night." Afterwards the work went on in his studio at Chelsea. "The window which had before served me for sunlight now monthly allowed me to receive moonlight upon the little group of objects that were placed to help me paint the effect of the lantern-light mixing with that of the silvery night. The ivy I had already painted, and the long grass and weeds were completed; but I had made up an imitation door with adjuncts, and had placed a lay-figure for the drapery, with the lantern to shine upon it duly; in the day I could screen out the sun, and at night I removed the blinds to let in the moon. I would sit at my work from 8 or 9 P.M. till 4 A.M. This went on for some months" (*Contemporary Review*, May 1886, p. 749; June, p. 824). In later years Holman Hunt made an enlarged, life-size, version of his picture; this has been purchased by Mr. Charles Booth, who proposes to send it for exhibition in the Colonies and the United States, and to bequeath it to the National Gallery of British Art ; it was exhibited in London in the spring of 1904.]

outlines, but with no variety of colour, and with none of the concealment, none of the infinity of nature.   With this spurious work the walls of the Academy are half covered; of the true school one very small example may be pointed out, being hung so low that it might otherwise escape attention.   It is not by any means perfect, but still very lovely,—the study of a calm pool in a mountain brook, by Mr. J. Dearle, No. 191, "Evening, on the Marchno, North Wales."[1]

I have the honour to be, Sir,
Your obedient servant,
THE AUTHOR OF "MODERN PAINTERS."

DENMARK HILL, *May* 4.

---

[1] [This picture was bought from the walls of the Academy by a prize-holder in the Art Union of London.   The purchaser resided in either America or Australia, and the picture is now, therefore, presumably in one or other of those countries. Ruskin noticed another picture by the same artist in *Academy Notes*, 1855, No. 686.]

"THE AWAKENING CONSCIENCE"

4. FROM THE *TIMES*, May 25, 1854

To the Editor of the " Times"

SIR,—Your kind insertion of my notes on Mr. Hunt's principal picture encourages me to hope that you may yet allow me room in your columns for a few words respecting his second work in the Royal Academy, the "Awakening Conscience."[1] Not that this picture is obscure, or its story feebly told. I am at a loss to know how its meaning could be rendered more distinctly, but assuredly it is not understood. People gaze at it in a blank wonder, and leave it hopelessly; so that, though it is almost an insult to the painter to explain his thoughts in this instance, I cannot persuade myself to leave it thus misunderstood. The poor girl has been sitting singing with her seducer; some chance

---

[1] [This picture—now usually called "The Awakened Conscience"—is in the collection formed by the late Sir Thomas Fairbairn. For other references to it, see *Modern Painters*, vol. iii. ch. vii. § 18, where it is cited as an instance of painting taking "its proper position beside literature"; and *The Art of England*, § 6. In a first note on the picture, in his diary, Ruskin writes: "Hunt's picture, 'Awakening Conscience.' Lear's setting to music of Tennyson's 'Tears, Idle Tears' on the floor; some tangled worsted; her life Bells ringing all round the frame." The music of Lear's setting of "Tears, Idle Tears" is seen, unrolled from the paper, lying on the floor, whilst the music of Moore's poem is on the music-stand of the piano. A frame for embroidery has the worsted with which she is supposed to while away her time when alone. The pattern of the frame is composed of bells swinging at different angles, as though bursting into joyful chimes. The artist, describing the inception of the picture, says : "I had been led to it by the beautiful verse in Proverbs [xxv. 20], 'As he that taketh away a garment in cold weather, so is he that singeth songs to a heavy heart,' when I was seeking for a *material* interpretation of the idea in 'The Light of the World'" (*Contemporary Review*, June 1886, p. 825). In the Academy Catalogue of 1854 Hunt gave the following passages after his title :—

"As of the green leaves on a thick tree, some fall and some grow; so is the generation of flesh and blood."—*Eccles.* xiv. 18.

"Strengthen ye the feeble hands, and confirm ye the tottering knees; say ye to the faint-hearted: Be ye strong; fear ye not; behold your God."—*Isaiah* (Bishop Lowth's translation).]

words of the song, "Oft in the stilly night," have struck upon the numbed places of her heart; she has started up in agony; he, not seeing her face, goes on singing, striking the keys carelessly with his gloved hand.

I suppose that no one possessing the slightest knowledge of expression could remain untouched by the countenance of the lost girl, rent from its beauty into sudden horror; the lips half open, indistinct in their purple quivering; the teeth set hard; the eyes filled with the fearful light of futurity, and with tears of ancient days. But I can easily understand that to many persons the careful rendering of the inferior details in this picture cannot but be at first offensive, as calling their attention away from the principal subject. It is true that detail of this kind has long been so carelessly rendered, that the perfect finishing of it becomes a matter of curiosity, and therefore an interruption to serious thought. But, without entering into the question of the general propriety of such treatment, I would only observe that, at least in this instance, it is based on a truer principle of the pathetic than any of the common artistical expedients of the schools. Nothing is more notable than the way in which even the most trivial objects force themselves upon the attention of a mind which has been fevered by violent and distressful excitement.[1] They thrust themselves forward with a ghastly and unendurable distinctness, as if they would compel the sufferer to count, or measure, or learn them by heart. Even to the mere spectator a strange interest exalts the accessories of a scene in which he bears witness to human sorrow. There is not a single object in all that room—common, modern, vulgar (in the vulgar sense, as it may be), but it becomes tragical, if rightly read. That furniture so carefully painted, even to the last vein of the rosewood—is there nothing to be learnt from that terrible lustre of it, from its fatal newness; nothing there that has the old thoughts of home upon it, or that is ever to become a part of home? Those

---

[1] [Ruskin returned to this subject in *The Two Paths*, § 128.]

embossed books, vain and useless—they also new—marked
with no happy wearing of beloved leaves; the torn and
dying bird upon the floor; the gilded tapestry, with the
fowls of the air feeding on the ripened corn; the picture
above the fireplace, with its single drooping figure—the
woman taken in adultery; nay, the very hem of the poor
girl's dress, at which the painter has laboured so closely,
thread by thread, has story in it, if we think how soon its
pure whiteness may be soiled with dust and rain, her out-
cast feet failing in the street; and the fair garden flowers,
seen in that reflected sunshine of the mirror,—these also
have their language—

> " Hope not to find delight in us, they say,
> For we are spotless, Jessy—we are pure." [2]

I surely need not go on. Examine the whole range
of the walls of the Academy,—nay, examine those of all
our public and private galleries,—and while pictures will
be met with by the thousand which literally tempt to evil,
by the thousand which are directed to the meanest triviali-
ties of incident or emotion, by the thousand to the delicate
fancies of inactive religion, there will not be found one
powerful as this to meet full in the front the moral evil of
the age in which it is painted; to waken into mercy the
cruel thoughtlessness of youth, and subdue the severities
of judgment into the sanctity of compassion.

I have the honour to be, Sir,

Your obedient servant,

THE AUTHOR OF " MODERN PAINTERS."

DENMARK HILL.

---

[1] [Compare the " Notes on the Louvre," below, p. 473.]

[2] [Shenstone : Elegy xxvi. The subject of the poem is that of the picture described
here. The girl speaks,—

> " If through the garden's flowery tribes I stray,
> Where bloom the jasmines that could once allure,
> Hope not," etc.

Ruskin quotes some of the lines in a different connexion in *Modern Painters*, vol. iii.
ch. xii. § 15 (" Of the Pathetic Fallacy ").]

V

PRE-RAPHAELITISM

(1851)

[*Bibliographical Note.*—The *first edition* (1851) has the following title-page :—

Pre-Raphaelitism. | By the Author | of | " Modern Painters." | London : | Smith, Elder, & Co., 65, Cornhill. | 1851.

Octavo, pp. 68. Imprint on the reverse of title-page and at the foot of last page : "London : Spottiswoodes and Shaw, New-Street Square." On p. iii. the following Dedication :—

To Francis Hawkesworth Fawkes, Esq., of Farnley, These pages, which owe their present form to advantages granted By his kindness, Are affectionately inscribed, By his obliged friend, John Ruskin.

Preface, pp. v.–vi. (here p. 339); text, pp. 7–68. Issued on August 13, 1851, at the price of Two Shillings. Some copies were issued without wrappers, and with untrimmed edges ; others in pale-blue coloured wrappers, with cut edges and the title-page (enclosed within a rule) reproduced upon the front cover.

The *second edition* (1862) had a different title-page, as follows :—

Pre-Raphaelitism. | By | John Ruskin, M.A., | Author of "Modern Painters," "Stones of Venice," "Seven Lamps of Architecture," etc. etc. | A New Edition. | London : | Smith, Elder & Co., 65, Cornhill. | M.DCCC.LXII.

Octavo, pp. 67. Imprint upon the reverse of p. 67 : "London : Printed by Smith, Elder & Co., Little Green Arbour Court, Old Bailey, E.C." The Dedication was withdrawn. Preface, p. 3 ; Text, pp. 5–67. Issued on April 13, 1862, at the same price, in pale-blue wrappers, with the title-page (enclosed within a double rule) repeated on the front. For differences of text, see below.

The pamphlet was *reprinted* verbatim from the second edition in *On the Old Road*, 1885, vol. i. pp. 238–309 (§§ 166–225); and again, in the second edition of that work, 1899, vol. i. pp. 241–313 (§§ 166–225).

The headline in both editions of the pamphlet was "Pre-Raphaelitism" throughout. In the reprints it was "Pre-Raphaelitism" on left-hand pages, and "Its Principles" on right-hand pages.

The publication of the pamphlet produced the following replies :—

Obsoletism in Art. A reply to the Author of "Modern Painters," in his defence of "Pre-Raphaelitism." By E. V. Rippingile. London : Richard Bentley, New Burlington Street, M.DCCC.LII. 8vo, pp. 56.

What is Pre-Raphaelitism? By John Ballantyne, A.R.S.A. William Blackwood and Sons, Edinburgh and London. 1856. 8vo, pp. 44.

Variæ Lectiones.—The variations (other than those already described) between the different editions are very slight, being mainly of punctuation, spelling, etc., which are not worth enumerating. In this edition, in § 7 the mark of interrogation at the end of the quotation from Young (wrongly introduced in ed. 2 and thence repeated in *On the Old Road*) is altered; in § 24 the spelling of "Mallard" in Turner's name (in all previous editions) is corrected to "Mallord"; in § 36 the spelling of "Brignal" is altered to "Brignall"; and a correction is made in § 43 (see p. 378 *n*).]

PREFACE

EIGHT years ago, in the close of the first volume of *Modern Painters*, I ventured to give the following advice to the young artists of England:—

" They should go to nature in all singleness of heart, and walk with her laboriously and trustingly, having no other thought but how best to penetrate her meaning; rejecting nothing, selecting nothing, and scorning nothing." Advice which, whether bad or good, involved infinite labour and humiliation in the following it, and was therefore, for the most part, rejected.[1]

It has, however, at last been carried out, to the very letter, by a group of men who, for their reward, have been assailed with the most scurrilous abuse which I ever recollect seeing issue from the public press. I have, therefore, thought it due to them to contradict the directly false statements which have been made respecting their works; and to point out the kind of merit which, however deficient in some respects, those works possess beyond the possibility of dispute.

DENMARK HILL, *August,* 1851.

---

[1] [*Modern Painters,* vol. i. pt. ii. sec. vi. ch. iii. § 21. See note on that passage (Vol. III. p. 624), for some remarks on misconstructions which have been placed upon it. For some reference by Ruskin to criticisms of this Preface, see above, Introduction, pp. lii.–liii.]

PRE-RAPHAELITISM

1. I⊤ may be proved, with much certainty, that God intends no man to live in this world without working: but it seems to me no less evident that He intends every man to be happy in his work. It is written, "in the sweat of thy brow,"[1] but it was never written, "in the breaking of thine heart," thou shalt eat bread: and I find that, as on the one hand, infinite misery is caused by idle people, who both fail in doing what was appointed for them to do, and set in motion various springs of mischief in matters in which they should have had no concern, so on the other hand, no small misery is caused by over-worked and unhappy people, in the dark views which they necessarily take up themselves, and force upon others, of work itself. Were it not so, I believe the fact of their being unhappy is in itself a violation of divine law, and a sign of some kind of folly or sin in their way of life. Now in order that people may be happy in their work, these three things are needed: They must be fit for it: They must not do too much of it: and they must have a sense of success in it—not a doubtful sense, such as needs some testimony of other people for its confirmation, but a sure sense, or rather knowledge, that so much work has been done well, and fruitfully done, whatever the world may say or think about it. So that in order that a man may be happy, it is necessary that he should not only be capable of his work, but a good judge of his work.

2. The first thing then that he has to do, if unhappily his parents or masters have not done it for him, is to find out what he is fit for. In which inquiry a man may be

---

[1] [Genesis iii. 19 : "In the sweat of thy face shalt thou eat bread."]

safely guided by his likings, if he be not also guided by his pride. People usually reason in some such fashion as this: "I don't seem quite fit for a head-manager in the firm of —— & Co., therefore, in all probability, I am fit to be Chancellor of the Exchequer." Whereas, they ought rather to reason thus: "I don't seem quite fit to be head-manager in the firm of —— & Co., but I dare say I might do something in a small greengrocery business; I used to be a good judge of pease;" that is to say, always trying lower instead of trying higher, until they find bottom: once well set on the ground, a man may build up by degrees, safely, instead of disturbing every one in his neighbourhood by perpetual catastrophes. But this kind of humility is rendered especially difficult in these days, by the contumely thrown on men in humble employments. The very removal of the massy bars which once separated one class of society from another, has rendered it tenfold more shameful in foolish people's, *i.e.*, in most people's [1] eyes, to remain in the lower grades of it, than ever it was before. When a man born of an artisan was looked upon as an entirely different species of animal from a man born of a noble, it made him no more uncomfortable or ashamed to remain that different species of animal, than it makes a horse ashamed to remain a horse, and not to become a giraffe. But now that a man may make money, and rise in the world, and associate himself, unreproached, with people once far above him, not only is the natural discontentedness of humanity developed to an unheard-of extent, whatever a man's position, but it becomes a veritable shame to him to remain in the state he was born in, and everybody thinks it his *duty* to try to be a "gentleman." Persons who have any influence in the management of public institutions for charitable education know how common this feeling has become. Hardly a day passes but they receive letters from mothers who want all their six or eight sons to go to

---

[1] [Compare Carlyle's *Latter-day Pamphlets*, No. vi. : "twenty-seven millions, mostly fools."]

college, and make the grand tour in the long vacation, and who think there is something wrong in the foundations of society because this is not possible. Out of every ten letters of this kind, nine will allege, as the reason of the writers' importunity, their desire to keep their families in such and such a "station of life."[1] There is no real desire for the safety, the discipline, or the moral good of the children, only a panic horror of the inexpressibly pitiable calamity of their living a ledge or two lower on the mole-hill of the world—a calamity to be averted at any cost whatever, of struggle, anxiety, and shortening of life itself. I do not believe that any greater good could be achieved for the country, than the change in public feeling on this head, which might be brought about by a few benevolent men, undeniably in the class of "gentlemen," who would, on principle, enter into some of our commonest trades, and make them honourable; showing that it was possible for a man to retain his dignity, and remain, in the best sense, a gentleman, though part of his time was every day occu-pied in manual labour, or even in serving customers over a counter. I do not in the least see why courtesy, and gravity, and sympathy with the feelings of others, and courage, and truth, and piety, and what else goes to make up a gentleman's character, should not be found behind a counter as well as elsewhere, if they were demanded, or even hoped for, there.

3. Let us suppose, then, that the man's way of life and manner of work have been discreetly chosen; then the next thing to be required is, that he do not overwork himself therein. I am not going to say anything here about the various errors in our systems of society and commerce, which appear (I am not sure if they ever do more than appear) to force us to overwork ourselves merely that we may live; nor about the still more fruitful cause of unhealthy toil — the incapability, in many men, of being

---

[1] [Compare *Sesame and Lilies*, § 2. Ruskin was no doubt thinking of the letters he received as a Governor of Christ's Hospital: see *Time and Tide*, §§ 119, 120.]

content with the little that is indeed necessary to their happiness. I have only a word or two to say about one special cause of overwork—the ambitious desire of doing great or clever things, and the hope of accomplishing them by immense efforts: hope as vain as it is pernicious; not only making men overwork themselves, but rendering all the work they do unwholesome to them. I say it is a vain hope, and let the reader be assured of this (it is a truth all-important to the best interests of humanity): *No great intellectual thing was ever done by great effort;* a great thing can only be done by a great man, and he does it *without* effort.[1] Nothing is, at present, less understood by us than this—nothing is more necessary to be understood. Let me try to say it as clearly and explain it as fully as I may.

4. I have said no great *intellectual* thing: for I do not mean the assertion to extend to things moral. On the contrary, it seems to me that just because we are intended, as long as we live, to be in a state of intense moral effort, we are *not* intended to be in intense physical or intellectual effort. Our full energies are to be given to the soul's work—to the great fight with the Dragon—the taking the kingdom of heaven by force.[2] But the body's work and head's work are to be done quietly, and comparatively without effort. Neither limbs nor brain are ever to be strained to their utmost; that is not the way in which the greatest quantity of work is to be got out of them: they are never to be worked furiously, but with tranquillity and constancy. We are to follow the plough from sunrise to sunset, but not to pull in race-boats at the twilight: we shall get no fruit of that kind of work, only disease of the heart.

5. How many pangs would be spared to thousands, if this great truth and law were but once sincerely, humbly understood—that if a great thing can be done at all, it can

---

[1] [Compare on this subject p. 387 below; *Modern Painters,* vol. iii. ch. xvi. § 17; *Two Paths,* App. iv. ; and *Eagle's Nest,* § 85.]

[2] [Matthew xi. 12.]

be done easily; that, when it is needed to be done, there is perhaps only one man in the world who can do it; but *he* can do it without any trouble—without more trouble, that is, than it costs small people to do small things; nay, perhaps, with less. And yet what truth lies more openly on the surface of all human phenomena? Is not the evidence of Ease on the very front of all the greatest works in existence? Do they not say plainly to us, not, "there has been a great *effort* here," but, "there has been a great *power* here"? It is not the weariness of mortality, but the strength of divinity, which we have to recognize in all mighty things; and that is just what we now *never* recognize, but think that we are to do great things, by help of iron bars and perspiration:—alas! we shall do nothing that way but lose some pounds of our own weight.

6. Yet let me not be misunderstood, nor this great truth be supposed anywise resolvable into the favourite dogma of young men, that they need not work if they have genius. The fact is that a man of genius is always far more ready to work than other people, and gets so much more good from the work that he does, and is often so little conscious of the inherent divinity in himself, that he is very apt to ascribe all his capacity to his work, and to tell those who ask how he came to be what he is: "If I *am* anything, which I much doubt, I made myself so merely by labour." This was Newton's way of talking, and I suppose it would be the general tone of men whose genius had been devoted to the physical sciences. Genius in the Arts must commonly be more self-conscious, but in whatever field, it will always be distinguished by its perpetual, steady, well-directed, happy, and faithful labour in accumulating and disciplining its powers, as well as by its gigantic, incommunicable facility in exercising them.[1] Therefore, literally,

[1] [To this effect are the sayings of Reynolds cited by Ruskin in *Lectures on Art*, §§ 48, 145; and compare *Two Paths*, § 98 ("when I hear a young man spoken of as giving promise of high genius . . . I ask 'Does he work?'"). So also Carlyle: "Genius means transcendent capacity of taking trouble" (*Friedrich*, book iv. ch. iii.); and Buffon: "Genius is nothing but a great capacity for patience." Compare also *Lectures on Architecture and Painting*, above, § 96, p. 125.]

it is no man's business whether he has genius or not: work he must, whatever he is, but quietly and steadily; and the natural and unforced results of such work will be always the things that God meant him to do, and will be his best. No agonies nor heart-rendings will enable him to do any better. If he be a great man, they will be great things; if a small man, small things; but always, if thus peacefully done, good and right; always, if restlessly and ambitiously done, false, hollow, and despicable.

7. Then the third thing needed was, I said, that a man should be a good judge of his work; and this chiefly that he may not be dependent upon popular opinion for the manner of doing it, but also that he may have the just encouragement of the sense of progress, and an honest consciousness of victory; how else can he become

> "That awful independent on to-morrow,
> Whose yesterdays look backwards with a smile." [1]

I am persuaded that the real nourishment and help of such a feeling as this is nearly unknown to half the workmen of the present day. For whatever appearance of self-complacency there may be in their outward bearing, it is visible enough, by their feverish jealousy of each other, how little confidence they have in the sterling value of their several doings. Conceit may puff a man up, but never prop him up; and there is too visible distress and hopelessness in men's aspects to admit of the supposition that they have any stable support of faith in themselves.

8. I have stated these principles generally, because there is no branch of labour to which they do not apply: but there is one in which our ignorance or forgetfulness of them has caused an incalculable amount of suffering; and I would endeavour now to reconsider them with special reference to it—the branch of the Arts.

---

[1] ["That blest son of foresight! Lord of fate!
That awful independent on To-morrow!
Whose work is done; who triumphs in the past;
Whose yesterdays look backwards with a smile."
—Young's *Night Thoughts*, ii. 354.]

In general, the men who are employed in the Arts have freely chosen their profession, and suppose themselves to have special faculty for it; yet, as a body, they are not happy men. For which this seems to me the reason—that they are expected, and themselves expect, to make their bread *by being clever*—not by steady or quiet work; and are therefore, for the most part, trying to be clever, and so living in an utterly false state of mind and action.[1]

9. This is the case, to the same extent, in no other profession or employment. A lawyer may indeed suspect that, unless he has more wit than those around him, he is not likely to advance in his profession; but he will not be always thinking how he is to display his wit. He will generally understand, early in his career, that wit must be left to take care of itself, and that it is hard knowledge of law and vigorous examination and collation of the facts of every case entrusted to him, which his clients will mainly demand: this it is which he is to be paid for; and this is healthy and measurable labour, payable by the hour. If he happen to have keen natural perception and quick wit, these will come into play in their due time and place, but he will not think of them as his chief power; and if he have them not, he may still hope that industry and conscientiousness may enable him to rise in his profession without them. Again in the case of clergymen: that they are sorely tempted to display their eloquence or wit, none who know their own hearts will deny, but then they *know* this to *be* a temptation: they never would suppose that cleverness was all that was to be expected from them, or would sit down deliberately to write a clever sermon: even the dullest or vainest of them would throw some veil over their vanity, and pretend to some profitableness of purpose in what they did. They would not openly ask of their hearers—Did you think my sermon ingenious, or my language poetical? They would early understand that they were not paid for being ingenious,

---

[1] [Compare *Modern Painters*, vol. v. pt. viii. ch. iv. § 2 ("mere cleverness or special gift never made an artist").]

nor called to be so, but to preach truth; that if they hap-pened to possess wit, eloquence, or originality, these would appear and be of service in due time, but were not to be continually sought after or exhibited; and if it should happen that they had them not, they might still be serviceable pas-tors without them.

10. Not so with the unhappy artist. No one expects any honest or useful work of him; but every one expects him to be ingenious. Originality, dexterity, invention, ima-gination, everything is asked of him except what alone is to be had for asking—honesty and sound work, and the due discharge of his function as a painter. What function? asks the reader in some surprise. He may well ask; for I sup-pose few painters have any idea what their function is, or even that they have any at all.

11. And yet surely it is not so difficult to discover. The faculties, which when a man finds in himself, he resolves to be a painter, are, I suppose, intenseness of observation and facility of imitation. The man is created an observer and an imitator; and his function is to convey knowledge to his fellow-men, of such things as cannot be taught other-wise than ocularly. For a long time this function remained a religious one: it was to impress upon the popular mind the reality of the objects of faith, and the truth of the histories of Scripture, by giving visible form to both.[1] That function has now passed away, and none has as yet taken its place. The painter has no profession, no purpose. He is an idler on the earth, chasing the shadows of his own fancies.

12. But he was never meant to be this. The sudden and universal Naturalism, or inclination to copy ordinary natural objects, which manifested itself among the painters of Europe, at the moment when the invention of printing superseded their legendary labours, was no false instinct. It was misunderstood and misapplied, but it came at the

---

[1] [Compare *Lectures on Architecture and Painting*, §§ 114 *seq.*]

right time, and has maintained itself through all kinds of abuse; presenting, in the recent schools of landscape, perhaps only the first fruits of its power. That instinct was urging every painter in Europe at the same moment to his true duty—*the faithful representation of all objects of historical interest, or of natural beauty existent at the period;* representation such as might at once aid the advance of the sciences, and keep faithful record of every monument of past ages which was likely to be swept away in the approaching eras of revolutionary change.

13. The instinct came, as I said, exactly at the right moment; and let the reader consider what amount and kind of general knowledge might by this time have been possessed by the nations of Europe, had their painters understood and obeyed it. Suppose that, after disciplining themselves so as to be able to draw, with unerring precision, each the particular kind of subject in which he most delighted, they had separated into two great armies of historians and naturalists;—that the first had painted with absolute faithfulness every edifice, every city, every battlefield, every scene of the slightest historical interest, precisely and completely rendering their aspect at the time; and that their companions, according to their several powers, had painted with like fidelity the plants and animals, the natural scenery, and the atmospheric phenomena of every country on the earth—suppose that a faithful and complete record were now in our museums of every building destroyed by war, or time, or innovation, during these last 200 years—suppose that each recess of every mountain chain of Europe had been penetrated, and its rocks drawn with such accuracy that the geologist's diagram was no longer necessary— suppose that every tree of the forest had been drawn in its noblest aspect, every beast of the field in its savage life— that all these gatherings were already in our national galleries, and that the painters of the present day were labouring, happily and earnestly, to multiply them, and put such means of knowledge more and more within reach of the common

people [1]—would not that be a more honourable life for them, than gaining precarious bread by "bright effects"? They think not, perhaps. They think it easy, and therefore contemptible, to be truthful; they have been taught so all their lives. But it is not so, whoever taught it them. It is most difficult, and worthy of the greatest men's greatest effort, to render, as it should be rendered, the simplest of the natural features of the earth; but also be it remembered, no man is confined to the simplest; each may look out work for himself where he chooses, and it will be strange if he cannot find something hard enough for him. The excuse is, however, one of the lips only; for every painter knows, that when he draws back from the attempt to render nature as she is, it is oftener in cowardice than in disdain.

14. I must leave the reader to pursue this subject for himself; I have not space to suggest to him the tenth part of the advantages which would follow, both to the painter from such an understanding of his mission, and to the whole people, in the results of his labour. Consider how the man himself would be elevated; how content he would become, how earnest, how full of all accurate and noble knowledge, how free from envy—knowing creation to be infinite, feeling at once the value of what he did, and yet the nothingness. Consider the advantage to the people: the immeasurably larger interest given to art itself; the easy, pleasurable, and perfect knowledge conveyed by it, in every subject; the far greater number of men who might be healthily and profitably occupied with it as a means of livelihood; the useful direction of myriads of inferior talents now left fading away in misery. Conceive all this, and then look around at our exhibitions, and behold the "cattle pieces," and "sea pieces," and "fruit pieces," and "family pieces"; the eternal brown cows in ditches, and white sails in squalls, and sliced lemons in

---

[1] [Ruskin often reverted to the wide field which painters might occupy as "historians" and "naturalists." On the former sphere, see, especially, *Modern Painters*, vol. iv. ch. ii. § 6; on the latter, *Lectures on Art*, §§ 105–114, and *Love's Meinie*, § 87.]

saucers, and foolish faces in simpers;—and try to feel what we are, and what we might have been.

15. Take a single instance in one branch of archæology. Let those who are interested in the history of Religion consider what a treasure we should now have possessed, if, instead of painting pots, and vegetables, and drunken peasantry, the most accurate painters of the seventeenth and eighteenth centuries had been set to copy, line for line, the religious and domestic sculpture on the German, Flemish, and French cathedrals and castles; and if every building destroyed in the French or in any other subsequent revolution, had thus been drawn in all its parts with the same precision with which Gerard Dow or Mieris paint bas-reliefs of Cupids. Consider, even now, what incalculable treasure is still left in ancient bas-reliefs, full of every kind of legendary interest, of subtle expression, of priceless evidence as to the character, feelings, habits, histories, of past generations, in neglected and shattered churches and domestic buildings, rapidly disappearing over the whole of Europe—treasure which, once lost, the labour of all men living cannot bring back again; and then look at the myriads of men, with skill enough, if they had but the commonest schooling, to record all this faithfully, who are making their bread by drawing dances of naked women from academy models, or idealities of chivalry fitted out with Wardour Street armour, or eternal scenes from *Gil Blas, Don Quixote,* and the *Vicar of Wakefield,* or mountain sceneries with young idiots of Londoners wearing Highland bonnets and brandishing rifles in the foregrounds. Do but think of these things in the breadth of their inexpressible imbecility, and then go and stand before that broken bas-relief in the southern gate of Lincoln Cathedral,[1] and see if there is no fibre of the heart in you that will break too.

---

[1] [Ruskin had been at Lincoln in the spring of 1851, and he thus noted the cathedral in his diary :—

"Early English. Lincoln the finest example; upper arcade of its west front quite sublime; so exquisite in the curves of its lancet arches, in the breadth and richness of its mouldings and its luxuriant capitals—a type

16. But is there to be no place left, it will be indignantly asked, for imagination and invention, for poetical power, or love of ideal beauty? Yes, the highest, the noblest place—that which these only can attain when they are all used in the cause, and with the aid of truth. Wherever imagination and sentiment are, they will either show themselves without forcing, or, if capable of artificial development, the kind of training which such a school of art would give them would be the best they could receive. The infinite absurdity and failure of our present training consists mainly in this, that we do not rank imagination and invention high enough, and suppose that they *can* be taught. Throughout every sentence that I ever have written, the reader will find the same rank attributed to these powers—the rank of a purely divine gift, not to be attained, increased, or in anywise modified by teaching, only in various ways capable of being concealed or quenched.[1] Understand this thoroughly; know once for all, that a poet on canvas is exactly the same species of creature as a poet in song, and nearly every error in our methods of teaching will be done away with. For who among us now thinks of bringing men up to be poets?—of producing poets by any kind of general recipe or method of cultivation? Suppose even that we see in a youth that which we hope may, in its development, become a power of this kind, should we instantly, supposing that we wanted to make a poet of him, and nothing else, forbid him all quiet, steady, rational labour? Should we force him to perpetual spinning of new crudities out of his boyish brain, and set before him, as the only objects of his study, the laws of versification

of the very best English Gothic. Then the little cinquefoil window in the front, the boss of the arch over it, with a small angel on one side and foliage on the other, and the mouldings of the southern door in the choir are the richest and most delicate I ever saw in England, evidently by the same workman and *travaillées* with a care and profusion altogether unequalled."

See also a note to *Seven Lamps* (Vol. VIII. p. 12) where similar opinions are expressed.]

[1] [As, for instance, in *Modern Painters*, vol. ii. Section II., "Of the Imaginative Faculty." And compare *Seven Lamps*, ch. iii. § 23 (Vol. VIII. p. 134).]

which criticism has supposed itself to discover in the works of previous writers? Whatever gifts the boy had, would much be likely to come of them so treated? unless, indeed, they were so great as to break through all such snares of falsehood and vanity, and build their own foundation in spite of us; whereas if, as in cases numbering millions against units, the natural gifts were too weak to do this, could anything come of such training but utter inanity and spuriousness of the whole man? But if we had sense, should we not rather restrain and bridle the first flame of invention in early youth, heaping material on it as one would on the first sparks and tongues of a fire which we desired to feed into greatness? Should we not educate the whole intellect into general strength, and all the affections into warmth and honesty, and look to heaven for the rest? This, I say, we should have sense enough to do, in order to produce a poet in words: but, it being required to produce a poet on canvas, what is our way of setting to work? We begin, in all probability, by telling the youth of fifteen or sixteen, that Nature is full of faults, and that he is to improve her; but that Raphael is perfection, and that the more he copies Raphael the better; that after much copying of Raphael, he is to try what he can do himself in a Raphaelesque, but yet original manner: that is to say, he is to try to do something very clever, all out of his own head, but yet this clever something is to be properly subjected to Raphaelesque rules, is to have a principal light occupying one-seventh of its space, and a principal shadow occupying one-third of the same; that no two people's heads in the picture are to be turned the same way, and that all the personages represented are to possess ideal beauty of the highest order, which ideal beauty consists partly in a Greek outline of nose, partly in proportions expressible in decimal fractions between the lips and chin; but mostly in that degree of improvement which the youth of sixteen is to bestow upon God's work in general. This I say is the kind of teaching which through various

channels, Royal Academy lecturings, press criticisms, public
enthusiasm, and not least by solid weight of gold, we give
to our young men.   And we wonder we have no painters!

17. But we do worse than this.   Within the last few
years some sense of the real tendency of such teaching has
appeared in some of our younger painters.   It only *could*
appear in the younger ones, our older men having become
familiarised with the false system, or else having passed
through it and forgotten it, not well knowing the degree of
harm they had sustained.   This sense appeared, among our
youths,—increased,—matured into resolute action.   Necessarily, to exist at all, it needed the support both of strong
instincts and of considerable self-confidence, otherwise it
must at once have been borne down by the weight of general
authority and received canon law.   Strong instincts are apt
to make men strange and rude; self-confidence, however
well founded, to give much of what they do or say the
appearance of impertinence.   Look at the self-confidence of
Wordsworth, stiffening every other sentence of his prefaces
into defiance; there is no more of it than was needed to
enable him to do his work, yet it is not a little ungraceful
here and there.   Suppose this stubbornness and self-trust in
a youth, labouring in an art of which the executive part is
confessedly to be best learnt from masters, and we shall
hardly wonder that much of his work has a certain awkward-
ness and stiffness in it, or that he should be regarded with
disfavour by many, even the most temperate, of the judges
trained in the system he was breaking through, and with
utter contempt and reprobation by the envious and the dull.
Consider, further, that the particular system to be overthrown
was, in the present case, one of which the main characteristic
was the pursuit of beauty at the expense of manliness and
truth; and it will seem likely *à priori*, that the men intended
successfully to resist the influence of such a system should
be endowed with little natural sense of beauty, and thus
rendered dead to the temptation it presented.   Summing
up these conditions, there is surely little cause for surprise

that pictures painted, in a temper of resistance, by exceedingly young men, of stubborn instincts and positive self-trust, and with little natural perception of beauty, should not be calculated, at the first glance, to win us from works enriched by plagiarism, polished by convention, invested with all the attractiveness of artificial grace, and recommended to our respect by established authority.

18. We should, however, on the other hand, have anticipated, that in proportion to the strength of character required for the effort, and to the absence of distracting sentiments, whether respect for precedent, or affection for ideal beauty, would be the energy exhibited in the pursuit of the special objects which the youths proposed to themselves, and their success in attaining them.

All this has actually been the case, but in a degree which it would have been impossible to anticipate. That two youths, of the respective ages of eighteen and twenty,[1] should have conceived for themselves a totally independent and sincere method of study, and enthusiastically persevered in it against every kind of dissuasion and opposition, is strange enough; that in the third or fourth year of their efforts they should have produced works in many parts not inferior to the best of Albert Dürer, this is perhaps not less strange. But the loudness and universality of the howl which the common critics of the press have raised against them, the

---

[1] [Millais born in 1829; Holman Hunt in 1827. "The third or fourth year of their efforts" would be 1850 or 1851; for their pictures of those years, see the Letters to the *Times*, above, pp. 319–327. Of Millais' precocity Ruskin made some notes in his diary, recording no doubt what the artist told him :—

"Millais. Born at Southampton; has a dim recollection of country house there and gravel walks, and falling down and hurting his hand. Goes over to Dinant for his mother's health, their house there on a fort—overlooking a deep moat; the children forbidden to go near it; and partly frightened by story of old man who lived at the bottom of it. His sister making a swing which swung right over the edge of it—his intense longing to look over mixed with horror. Never quiet but when he got pieces of paper to draw on. Drew soldiers for a boy he used to play with—the officers saw them and would not believe they were done by the child. They made a bet of a dinner about it—he recollects their calling to him and taking him into the great square under the sycamore trees, and making him draw soldiers and guns; and laughing, and being delighted; and then his being called in to the dinner given by those who had lost the wager, and put in the middle of the table, and made a show of, and all their glasses held in a circle round him."]

utter absence of all generous help or encouragement from those who can both measure their toil and appreciate their success, and the shrill, shallow laughter of those who can do neither the one nor the other—these are strangest of all —unimaginable unless they had been experienced.

19. And as if these were not enough, private malice is at work against them, in its own small, slimy way. The very day after I had written my second letter to the *Times* in the defence of the Pre-Raphaelites, I received an anonymous letter respecting one of them, from some person apparently hardly capable of spelling, and about as vile a specimen of petty malignity as ever blotted paper. I think it well that the public should know this, and so get some insight into the sources of the spirit which is at work against these men: how first roused it is difficult to say, for one would hardly have thought that mere eccentricity in young artists could have excited an hostility so determined and so cruel; hostility which hesitated at no assertion, however impudent. That of the "absence of perspective" was one of the most curious pieces of the hue and cry which began with the *Times*, and died away in feeble maundering in the Art Union; I contradicted it in the *Times*—I here contradict it directly for the second time.[1] There was not a single error in perspective in three out of the four pictures in question. But if otherwise, would it have been anything remarkable in them? I doubt if, with the exception of the pictures of David Roberts,[2] there were one architectural drawing in perspective on the walls of the Academy; I never met but with two men in

---

[1] [For the reply to the *Times*, see above, p. 322. The "maundering in the Art Union" refers to an article in the *Art Journal* for July 1851, headed "'The Pre-Raphaelites," and signed "J. B." (possibly John Ballantyne, the author of the pamphlet noted above, p. 338). The *Art Journal* returned Ruskin's epithet "maundering" in its review of the pamphlet (see above, p. lii. *n*.) The reference in Ruskin's note on the next page is to an engraving of the "Pillars of the Piazzetta" (No. 374 in the Tate Gallery) by R. P. Bonington (1801–1828); the *Art Journal's* remark on the want of aerial perspective is at p. 192, in the number for July 1851; "J. B." had referred to Ruskin (p. 185) as "the Under-graduate of Oxford." For a reply to the charge against Millais' "Huguenot," that it was deficient in "aerial perspective," see *Stones of Venice*, vol. iii. pp. 59, 401.]

[2] [For a notice of his architectural drawing, see *Modern Painters*, vol. i. (Vol. III. p. 223).]

my life who knew enough of perspective to draw a Gothic
arch in a retiring plane, so that its lateral dimensions and
curvatures might be calculated to scale from the drawing.
Our architects certainly do not, and it was but the other
day that, talking to one of the most distinguished among
them, the author of several most valuable works, I found
he actually did not know how to draw a circle in perspective. And in this state of general science our writers for
the press take it upon them to tell us, that the forest-trees in
Mr. Hunt's "Sylvia," and the bunches of lilies in Mr. Collins's
"Convent Thoughts,"[1] are out of perspective.*

20. It might not, I think, in such circumstances, have
been ungraceful or unwise in the Academicians themselves
to have defended their young pupils, at least by the contradiction of statements directly false respecting them,† and

* It was not a little curious, that in the very number of the Art Union
which repeated this direct falsehood about the Pre-Raphaelite rejection of
"linear perspective" (by-the-bye, the next time J. B. takes upon him to
speak of any one connected with the Universities, he may as well first
ascertain the difference between a Graduate and an Under-Graduate), the
second plate given should have been of a picture of Bonington's—a profes-
sional landscape painter, observe—for the want of *aerial* perspective in which
the Art Union itself was obliged to apologise, and in which the artist has
committed nearly as many blunders in *linear* perspective as there are lines
in the picture.

† These false statements may be reduced to three principal heads, and
directly contradicted in succession.

The first, the current fallacy of society as well as of the press, was,
that the Pre-Raphaelites imitated the *errors* of early painters.

A falsehood of this kind could not have obtained credence anywhere
but in England, few English people, comparatively, having ever seen a
picture of early Italian Masters. If they had they would have known that
the Pre-Raphaelite pictures are just as superior to the early Italian in
skill of manipulation, power of drawing, and knowledge of effect, as inferior to them in grace of design; and that in a word, there is not a
shadow of resemblance between the two styles. The Pre-Raphaelites imitate no pictures: they paint from nature only. But they have opposed
themselves as a body, to that kind of teaching above described, which
only began after Raphael's time: and they have opposed themselves as
sternly to the entire feeling of the Renaissance schools; a feeling compounded of indolence, infidelity, sensuality, and shallow pride.[2] Therefore

---

[1] [For these pictures, see above, pp. 320, 325, 327.]
[2] [A characterisation which Ruskin afterwards worked out in the third volume of
the *Stones of Venice*.]

the direction of the mind and sight of the public to such real merit as they possess.   If Sir Charles Eastlake, Mulready, Edwin and Charles Landseer, Cope, and Dyce would each of them simply state their own private opinion respecting their paintings, sign it, and publish it, I believe the act would be of more service to English art than anything the Academy has done since it was founded.[1] But as I cannot hope for this, I can only ask the public to give their pictures careful examination, and to look at them at once with the indulgence and the respect which I have endeavoured to show they deserve.

Yet let me not be misunderstood.   I have adduced them only as examples of the kind of study which I would desire to see substituted for that of our modern schools, and of singular success in certain characters, finish of detail, and brilliancy of colour.   What faculties, higher than imitative, may be in these men, I do not yet venture to say; but I do say, that if they exist, such faculties will manifest themselves in due time all the more forcibly because they have received training so severe.[2]

they have called themselves Pre-Raphaelite.   If they adhere to their principles, and paint nature as it is around them, with the help of modern science, with the earnestness of the men of the thirteenth and fourteenth centuries, they will, as I said, found a new and noble school in England. If their sympathies with the early artists lead them into mediævalism or Romanism, they will of course come to nothing.   But I believe there is no danger of this, at least for the strongest among them.   There may be some weak ones, whom the Tractarian heresies may touch ; but if so, they will drop off like decayed branches from a strong stem.   I hope all things from the schools.

The second falsehood was, that the Pre-Raphaelites did not draw well. This was asserted, and could have been asserted only by persons who had never looked at the pictures.

The third falsehood was, that they had no system of light and shade. To which it may be simply replied that their system of light and shade is exactly the same as the Sun's ; which is, I believe, likely to outlast that of the Renaissance, however brilliant.

---

[1] [It would appear, however, that the Royal Academicians were by no means favourably disposed to the new school.   Mulready and Maclise were alone, it is said, in giving "The Carpenter's Shop" favourable consideration, and an Academician, who was art critic in one of the literary journals, denounced it as "pictorial blasphemy" and "revolting" : see *Life and Letters of Millais*, i. 74–75.]

[2] [See *Modern Painters*, vol. v. pt. vi. ch. x. § 8 (written nearly ten years later), where Ruskin refers to this passage, and adds, "such work can only connect itself with

21. For it is always to be remembered that no one mind is like another, either in its powers or perceptions; and while the main principles of training must be the same for all, the result in each will be as various as the kinds of truth which each will apprehend; therefore, also, the modes of effort, even in men whose inner principles and final aims are exactly the same. Suppose, for instance, two men, equally honest, equally industrious, equally impressed with a humble desire to render some part of what they saw in nature faithfully; and, otherwise, trained in convictions such as I have above endeavoured to induce. But one of them is quiet in temperament, has a feeble memory, no invention, and excessively keen sight. The other is impatient in temperament, has a memory which nothing escapes, an invention which never rests, and is comparatively near-sighted.

22. Set them both free in the same field in a mountain valley. One sees everything, small and large, with almost the same clearness; mountains and grasshoppers alike; the leaves on the branches, the veins in the pebbles, the bubbles in the stream; but he can remember nothing, and invent nothing. Patiently he sets himself to his mighty task; abandoning at once all thoughts of seizing transient effects, or giving general impressions of that which his eyes present to him in microscopical dissection, he chooses some small portion out of the infinite scene, and calculates with courage the number of weeks which must elapse before he can do justice to the intensity of his perceptions, or the fulness of matter in his subject.

23. Meantime, the other has been watching the change of the clouds, and the march of the light along the mountain sides; he beholds the entire scene in broad, soft masses of true gradation, and the very feebleness of his sight is in some sort an advantage to him, in making him more

the great schools by becoming inventive instead of copyist." The point is, as Ruskin says lower down (§ 54), that invention depends on study, and thus " Pre-Raphaelitism and Turnerism " are " one and the same."]

sensible of the aerial mystery of distance, and hiding from him the multitudes of circumstances which it would have been impossible for him to represent. But there is not one change in the casting of the jagged shadows along the hollows of the hills, but it is fixed on his mind for ever; not a flake of spray has broken from the sea of cloud about their bases, but he has watched it as it melts away, and could recall it to its lost place in heaven by the slightest effort of his thoughts. Not only, so, but thousands and thousands of such images, of older scenes, remain congregated in his mind, each mingling in new associations with those now visibly passing before him, and these again confused with other images of his own ceaseless, sleepless imagination, flashing by in sudden troops. Fancy how his paper will be covered with stray symbols and blots, and undecipherable shorthand :—as for his sitting down to " draw from Nature," there was not one of the things which he wished to represent, that stayed for so much as five seconds together : but none of them escaped for all that : they are sealed up in that strange storehouse of his ; he may take one of them out perhaps, this day twenty years, and paint it in his dark room, far away. Now, observe, you may tell both of these men, when they are young, that they are to be honest, that they have an important function, and that they are not to care what Raphael did. This you may wholesomely impress on them both. But fancy the exquisite absurdity of expecting either of them to possess any of the qualities of the other.

24. I have supposed the feebleness of sight in the last, and of invention in the first painter, that the contrast between them might be more striking ; but, with very slight modification, both the characters are real. Grant to the first considerable inventive power, with exquisite sense of colour ; and give to the second, in addition to all his other faculties, the eye of an eagle ; and the first is John Everett Millais, the second Joseph Mallord William Turner.

They are among the few men who have defied all false

teaching, and have therefore, in great measure, done justice to the gifts with which they were intrusted. They stand at opposite poles, marking culminating points of art in both directions; between them, or in various relations to them, we may class five or six more living artists who, in like manner, have done justice to their powers. I trust that I may be pardoned for naming them, in order that the reader may know how the strong innate genius in each has been invariably accompanied with the same humility, earnestness, and industry in study.

25. It is hardly necessary to point out the earnestness or humility in the works of William Hunt;[1] but it may be so to suggest the high value they possess as records of English rural life, and *still* life. Who is there who for a moment could contend with him in the unaffected, yet humorous truth with which he has painted our peasant children? Who is there who does not sympathise with him in the simple love with which he dwells on the brightness and bloom of our summer fruit and flowers? And yet there is something to be regretted concerning him: why should he be allowed continually to paint the same bunches of hot-house grapes, and supply to the Water Colour Society a succession of pineapples with the regularity of a Covent Garden fruiterer? He has of late discovered that primrose banks are lovely, but there are other things grow wild besides primroses: what undreamt-of loveliness might he not bring back to us, if he would lose himself for a summer in Highland foregrounds; if he would paint the heather as it grows, and the foxglove and the harebell as they nestle in the clefts of the rocks, and the mosses and bright lichens of the rocks themselves. And then, cross to the Jura, and bring back a piece of Jura pasture in spring;

---

[1] [William Henry Hunt, of the Old Water-Colour Society (1790–1864). Ruskin had already called frequent attention to his qualities—to his "keen eye for truth," in *Modern Painters*, vol. i. (Vol. III. p. 616); to his "pure Naturalism," in *Stones of Venice*, vol. ii. ch. vi. § 60. For later references, see General Index; for his too frequent painting of grapes, see *Academy Notes*, 1856 (Old Water-Colour Society, Nos. 256, 271).]

with the gentians in their earliest blue, and a soldanelle beside the fading snow! And return again, and paint a gray wall of alpine crag, with budding roses crowning it like a wreath of rubies. That is what he was meant to do in this world; not to paint bouquets in china vases.

26. I have in various other places expressed my sincere respect for the works of Samuel Prout:[1] his shortness of sight has necessarily prevented their possessing delicacy of finish or fulness of minor detail; but I think that those of no other living artist furnish an example so striking of innate and special instinct, sent to do a particular work at the exact and only period when it was possible. At the instant when peace had been established all over Europe, but when neither national character nor national architecture had as yet been seriously changed by promiscuous intercourse or modern "improvement"; when, however, nearly every ancient and beautiful building had been long left in a state of comparative neglect, so that its aspect of partial ruinousness, and of separation from recent active life, gave to every edifice a peculiar interest — half sorrowful, half sublime;—at that moment Prout was trained among the rough rocks and simple cottages of Cornwall, until his eye was accustomed to follow with delight the rents and breaks, and irregularities which, to another man, would have been offensive; and then, gifted with infinite readiness in composition, but also with infinite affection for the kind of subjects he had to portray, he was sent to preserve, in an almost innumerable series of drawings, *every one made on the spot*, the aspect borne, at the beginning of the nineteenth century, by cities which, in a few years more, rekindled wars, or unexpected prosperities, were to ravage, or renovate, into nothingness.

27. It seems strange to pass from Prout to John Lewis;[2]

---

[1] [See Vol. III. p. 217; Vol. IX. pp. 300, 303; and in this volume the separate paper on Prout, published in 1849; and see also (among later passages) Vol. X. p. 301; Vol. XI. p. 24 *n*. (where the present passage is referred to).]

[2] [To J. F. Lewis (1804–1876) also Ruskin had already paid his tribute; see *Modern Painters*, vol. i. (Vol. III. p. 120). Plates XVI. and XVII. here are from drawings by Lewis in Ruskin's collection.]

XVI

J.F.Lewis.RA

Allen&Co.Sc

"After the Vintage".

but there is this fellowship between them, that both seem
to have been intended to appreciate the characters of foreign
countries more than of their own, nay, to have been born
in England chiefly that the excitement of strangeness might
enhance to them the interest of the scenes they had to represent. I believe John Lewis to have done more entire
justice to all his powers (and they are magnificent ones),
than any other man amongst us. His mission was evidently
to portray the comparatively animal life of the southern
and eastern families of mankind. For this he was prepared
in a somewhat singular way—by being led to study, and
endowed with altogether peculiar apprehension of, the most
sublime characters of animals themselves. Rubens, Rembrandt, Snyders, Tintoret, and Titian, have all, in various
ways, drawn wild beasts magnificently;[1] but they have in
some sort humanised or demonised them, making them
either ravenous fiends, or educated beasts, that would draw
cars, and had respect for hermits. The sullen isolation of
the brutal nature; the dignity and quietness of the mighty
limbs; the shaggy mountainous power, mingled with grace
as of a flowing stream; the stealthy restraint of strength
and wrath in every soundless motion of the gigantic frame;
all this seems never to have been seen, much less drawn,
until Lewis drew and himself engraved a series of animal
subjects, now many years ago.[2] Since then, he has devoted
himself to the portraiture of those European and Asiatic
races, among whom the refinements of civilization exist
without its laws or its energies, and in whom the fierceness,
indolence, and subtlety of animal nature are associated with
brilliant imagination and strong affections. To this task
he has brought not only intense perception of the kind of
character, but powers of artistical composition like those
of the great Venetians, displaying, at the same time, a

---

[1] [For a discussion of the animal-painting of the old masters, see *Modern Painters*,
vol. v. pt. ix. ch. vi., where (§ 19) Snyders is more particularly criticised. Compare
also the " Review of Lord Lindsay" above, § 55, p. 226.]

[2] [This was a set of six quarto Plates in mezzotint—*Studies of Wild Animals*—
published by W. B. Cooke in 1824–1825.]

refinement of drawing almost miraculous, and appreciable only, as the minutiæ of nature itself are appreciable, by the help of the microscope. The value, therefore, of his works, as records of the aspect of the scenery and inhabitants of the south of Spain and of the East, in the earlier part of the nineteenth century, is quite above all estimate.

28. I hardly know how to speak of Mulready:[1] in delicacy and completion of drawing, and splendour of colour, he takes place beside John Lewis and the Pre-Raphaelites; but he has, throughout his career, displayed no definiteness in choice of subject. He must be named among the painters who have studied with industry, and have made themselves great by doing so; but, having obtained a consummate method of execution, he has thrown it away on subjects either altogether uninteresting, or above his powers, or unfit for pictorial representation. "The Cherry Woman," exhibited in 1850, may be named as an example of the first kind; the "Burchell and Sophia" of the second (the character of Sir William Thornhill being utterly missed); the "Seven Ages" of the third;[2] for this subject cannot be painted. In the written passage, the thoughts are progressive and connected; in the picture they must be co-existent, and yet separate; nor can all the characters of the ages be rendered in painting at all. One may represent the soldier at the cannon's mouth, but one cannot paint the "bubble reputation"[3] which he seeks. Mulready, therefore, while he has always produced exquisite pieces of painting, has failed in doing anything which can be of true or extensive use. He has, indeed, understood how to discipline his genius, but never how to direct it.

29. Edwin Landseer[4] is the last painter but one whom

---

[1] [See above, p. 300, and for a summary of references to this painter, Vol. IV. p. 336 n.]

[2] [This picture, exhibited at the Academy in 1838, is now in the Victoria and Albert (South Kensington) Museum, being part of the Sheepshanks Gift. "Burchell and Sophia," exhibited in 1847, is noticed in the Addenda to Modern Painters, vol. ii. (Vol. IV. p. 336).]

[3] [As You Like It, ii. 7.]

[4] [For a summary of Ruskin's references to Landseer, see Vol. IV. p. 334 n.]

XVII

J.F.Lewis,R.A.

"At Constantinople."

Allen&Co.Sc.

I shall name: I need not point out to any one acquainted with his earlier works, the labour, or watchfulness of nature which they involve, nor need I do more than allude to the peculiar faculties of his mind. It will at once be granted that the highest merits of his pictures are throughout found in those parts of them which are least like what had before been accomplished; and that it was not by the study of Raphael that he attained his eminent success, but by a healthy love of Scotch terriers.

None of these painters, however, it will be answered, afford examples of the rise of the highest imaginative power out of close study of matters of fact. Be it remembered, however, that the imaginative power, in its magnificence, is not to be found every day. Lewis has it in no mean degree, but we cannot hope to find it at its highest more than once in an age. We *have* had it once, and must be content.

30. Towards the close of the last century, among the various drawings executed, according to the quiet manner of the time, in greyish blue, with brown foregrounds, some began to be noticed as exhibiting rather more than ordinary diligence and delicacy, signed W. Turner.* There was nothing, however, in them at all indicative of genius, or even of more than ordinary talent, unless in some of the subjects a large perception of space, and excessive clearness and decision in the arrangement of masses. Gradually and cautiously the blues became mingled with delicate green, and then with gold; the browns in the foreground became first more positive, and then were slightly mingled with other local colours; while the touch, which had at first been heavy and broken, like that of the ordinary drawing masters of the time, grew more and more refined and expressive, until it lost itself in a method of execution often too delicate for the eye to follow, rendering, with a precision before unexampled, both the texture and the form of every object. The style may be considered as perfectly formed

* He did not use his full signature, "J. M. W.," until about the year 1800.

about the year 1800, and it remained unchanged for twenty years.

During that period the painter had attempted, and with more or less success had rendered, every order of landscape subject, but always on the same principle, subduing the colours of nature into a harmony of which the key-notes are greyish green and brown; pure blues, and delicate golden yellows being admitted in small quantity as the lowest and highest limits of shade and light: and bright local colours in extremely small quantity in figures or other minor accessories.

31. Pictures executed on such a system are not, properly speaking, works in *colour* at all; they are studies of light and shade, in which both the shade and the distance are rendered in the general hue which best expresses their attributes of coolness and transparency; and the lights and the foreground are executed in that which best expresses their warmth and solidity. This advantage may just as well be taken as not, in studies of light and shadow to be executed with the hand; but the use of two, three, or four colours, always in the same relations and places, does not in the least constitute the work a study of colour, any more than the brown engravings of the *Liber Studiorum;* nor would the idea of colour be in general more present to the artist's mind when he was at work on one of these drawings, than when he was using pure brown in the mezzotint engraving. But the idea of space, warmth, and freshness being not successfully expressible in a single tint, and perfectly expressible by the admission of three or four, he allows himself this advantage when it is possible, without in the least embarrassing himself with the actual colour of the objects to be represented. A stone in the foreground might in nature have been cold grey, but it will be drawn nevertheless of a rich brown, because it is in the foreground; a hill in the distance might in nature be purple with heath, or golden with furze; but it will be drawn, nevertheless, of a cool grey, because it is in the distance.

32. This at least was the general theory,—carried out with great severity in many, both of the drawings and pictures executed by him during the period : in others more or less modified by the cautious introduction of colour, as the painter felt his liberty increasing; for the system was evidently never considered as final, or as anything more than a means of progress : the conventional, easily manageable colour, was visibly adopted, only that his mind might be at perfect liberty to address itself to the acquirement of the first and most necessary knowledge in all art—that of form. But as form, in landscape, implies vast bulk and space, the use of the tints which enabled him best to express them, was actually auxiliary to the mere drawing; and, therefore, not only permissible, but even necessary, while more brilliant or varied tints were never indulged in, except when they might be introduced without the slightest danger of diverting his mind for an instant from his principal object. And, therefore, it will be generally found in the works of this period, that exactly in proportion to the importance and general toil of the composition, is the severity of the tint; and that the play of colour begins to show itself first in slight and small drawings, where he felt that he could easily secure all that he wanted in form.

33. Thus the " Crossing the Brook," [1] and such other elaborate and large compositions, are actually painted in nothing but grey, brown, and blue, with a point or two of severe local colour in the figures; but in the minor drawings, tender passages of complicated colour occur not unfrequently in easy places ; and even before the year 1800 he begins to introduce it with evident joyfulness and longing in his rude and simple studies, just as a child, if it could be supposed to govern itself by a fully developed intellect, would cautiously, but with infinite pleasure, add now and then a tiny dish of fruit or other dangerous luxury to the simple order of its daily fare. Thus, in the foregrounds of

[1] [No. 497 in the National Gallery, exhibited in 1815. For other references to the picture, see Vol. III. p. 241 n.]

his most severe drawings, we not unfrequently find him in-
dulging in the luxury of a peacock; and it is impossible to
express the joyfulness with which he seems to design its
graceful form, and deepen with soft pencilling the bloom of
its blue, after he has worked through the stern detail of his
almost colourless drawing.   A rainbow is another of his
most frequently permitted indulgences; and we find him
very early allowing the edges of his evening clouds to be
touched with soft rose-colour or gold; while, whenever the
hues of nature in anywise fall into his system, and can be
caught without a dangerous departure from it, he instantly
throws his whole soul into the faithful rendering of them.
Thus the usual brown tones of his foreground become
warmed into sudden vigour, and are varied and enhanced
with indescribable delight, when he finds himself by the
shore of a moorland stream, where they truly express the
stain of its golden rocks, and the darkness of its clear, Cairn-
gorm-like pools, and the usual serenity of his aerial blue is
enriched into the softness and depth of the sapphire, when
it can deepen the distant slumber of some Highland lake, or
temper the gloomy shadows of the evening upon its hills.[1]

34. The system of his colour being thus simplified, he
could address all the strength of his mind to the accumulation of facts of form; his choice of subject, and his methods
of treatment, are therefore as various as his colour is simple;
and it is not a little difficult to give the reader who is unacquainted with his works, an idea either of their infinitude
of aims, on the one hand, or of the kind of feeling which
pervades them all, on the other.   No subject was too low
or too high for him; we find him one day hard at work on
a cock and hen, with their family of chickens in a farm-
yard; and bringing all the refinement of his execution into
play to express the texture of the plumage; next day he is

---

[1] [See *Modern Painters*, vol. iii. ch. xv. § 12 and *n.*, where Ruskin refers to this
passage, in the course of some further remarks on Turner's colouring: "It is in
these subtle purples that even the more elaborate passages of the earlier drawings
are worked; as, for instance, the Highland streams."]

drawing the Dragon of Colchis. One hour he is much interested in a gust of wind blowing away an old woman's cap; the next, he is painting the fifth plague of Egypt.[1] Every landscape painter before him had acquired distinction by confining his efforts to one class of subject. Hobbima painted oaks; Ruysdael, waterfalls and copses; Cuyp, river or meadow scenes in quiet afternoons; Salvator and Poussin, such kind of mountain scenery as people could conceive, who lived in towns in the seventeenth century. But I am well persuaded that if all the works of Turner, up to the year 1820, were divided into classes (as he has himself divided them in the *Liber Studiorum*), no preponderance could be assigned to one class over another. There is architecture, including a large number of formal "gentlemen's seats," I suppose drawings commissioned by the owners; then lowland pastoral scenery of every kind, including nearly all farming operations—ploughing, harrowing, hedging and ditching, felling trees, sheep-washing, and I know not what else; then all kinds of town life—courtyards of inns, starting of mail coaches, interiors of shops, house-buildings, fairs, elections, etc.; then all kinds of inner domestic life—interiors of rooms, studies of costumes, of still life, and heraldry, including multitudes of symbolical vignettes; then marine scenery of every kind, full of local incident; every kind of boat and method of fishing for particular fish, being specifically drawn, round the whole coast of England— pilchard fishing at St. Ives, whiting fishing at Margate, herring at Loch Fyne; and all kinds of shipping, including studies of every separate part of the vessels, and many marine battle pieces, two in particular of Trafalgar, both of high importance—one of the *Victory* after the battle, now

---

[1] [Ruskin is here referring to various drawings prepared for the *Liber Studiorum*. The *Farm Yard* is No. 507 in the National Gallery; the Dragon (*Jason*), No. 461; "the gust of wind blowing away an old woman's cap" is in the "Yarmouth" in the *England and Wales* Series. On a proof in the Print Room of the British Museum is a note by Turner explaining to the engraver that the white spot in the drawing (which he had evidently not understood) is a "cap," introduced to show the force of the wind. The *Fifth Plague* is No. 875. Turner's own division of the subjects in the *Liber* was into "Historical, Pastoral, Elegant-Pastoral, Mountain, Marine, and Architectural."]

in Greenwich Hospital; another of the death of Nelson, in his own gallery;[1] then all kinds of mountain scenery, some idealized into compositions, others of definite localities; together with classical compositions, Romes, and Carthages, and such others, by the myriad, with mythological, historical, or allegorical figures—nymphs, monsters, and spectres; heroes and divinities.*

35. What general feeling, it may be asked incredulously, can possibly pervade all this? This, the greatest of all feelings—an utter forgetfulness of self. Throughout the whole period with which we are at present concerned, Turner appears as a man of sympathy absolutely infinite—a sympathy so all-embracing, that I know nothing but that of Shakspeare comparable with it.[2] A soldier's wife resting by the roadside is not beneath it; Rizpah, the daughter of Aiah, watching the dead bodies of her sons, not above it.[3] Nothing can possibly be so mean as that it will not interest his whole mind, and carry away his whole heart; nothing so great or solemn but that he can raise himself into harmony with it; and it is impossible to prophesy of him at any moment, whether, the next, he will be in laughter or in tears.

36. This is the root of the man's greatness; and it follows as a matter of course that this sympathy must give him a subtle power of expression, even of the characters of mere material things, such as no other painter ever

---

* I shall give a *catalogue raisonnée* of all this in the third volume of *Modern Painters*.[4]

---

[1] [For the picture in Greenwich Hospital, see *Notes on the Turner Gallery*, 1856 (No. 524), and *Harbours of England*, § 24. The "Death of Nelson" is now No. 480 in the National Gallery: see *Notes on the Turner Gallery, ibid.*]

[2] [For the comparison with Shakspeare, see *Lectures on Architecture and Painting*, § 101, above, p. 128.]

[3] [The "soldier's wife" is in "Winchelsea" (*Liber Studiorum*): see § 52, below. For "Rizpah" (*Liber Studiorum*), see *Modern Painters*, vol. v. pt. ix. ch. xi. § 29.]

[4] [At the time of writing this Ruskin still thought to finish *Modern Painters* in one more volume, the third. The book grew, however, and when he wrote the preface to the third volume, the catalogue here promised had not been given; he there repeated (§ 5 n.) his intention of "forming a systematic catalogue of all his works." This he never completed; but in the fifth volume of *Modern Painters* (pt. ix. ch. xi.) he analysed the order of subjects in *Liber Studiorum*.]

possessed. The man who can best feel the difference between rudeness and tenderness in humanity, perceives also more difference between the branches of an oak and a willow than any one else would; and, therefore, necessarily the most striking character of the drawings themselves is the speciality of whatever they represent—the thorough stiffness of what is stiff, and grace of what is graceful, and vastness of what is vast; but through and beyond all this, the condition of the mind of the painter himself is easily enough discoverable by comparison of a large number of the drawings. It is singularly serene and peaceful: in itself quite passionless, though entering with ease into the external passion which it contemplates. By the effort of its will it sympathises with tumult or distress, even in their extremes, but there is no tumult, no sorrow in itself, only a chastened and exquisitely peaceful cheerfulness, deeply meditative; touched, without loss of its own perfect balance, by sadness on the one side, and stooping to playfulness upon the other. I shall never cease to regret the destruction, by fire, now several years ago, of a drawing which always seemed to me to be the perfect image of the painter's mind at this period,—the drawing of Brignall Church near Rokeby,[1] of which a feeble idea may still be gathered from the engraving (in the Yorkshire series). The spectator stands on the "Brignall banks,"[2] looking down into the glen at twilight; the sky is still full of soft rays, though the sun is gone, and the Greta glances brightly in the valley, singing its even-song; two white clouds, following each other, move without wind through the hollows of the ravine, and others lie couched on the far-away moorlands; every leaf of the woods is still in the delicate air; a boy's kite, incapable of rising, has become entangled in their branches, he is climbing to recover it; and just behind

---

[1] [This drawing was shown in 1824 in Cooke's Exhibition, and engraved in Whitaker's *Richmondshire*. It belonged to Griffith, the picture-dealer, who considered it to be the finest Turner had ever made. Griffith admired it so much that he could never be induced to part with it; and it was burnt in a fire in his house, where Ruskin no doubt had often seen and studied it (see Vol. III. p. xxviii.).]

[2] [Scott: *Rokeby*, iii. 16.]

it in the picture, almost indicated by it, the lowly church is seen in its secluded field between the rocks and the stream; and around it the low churchyard wall, and a few white stones which mark the resting-places of those who can climb the rocks no more, nor hear the river sing as it passes.

There are many other existing drawings which indicate the same character of mind, though I think none so touching or so beautiful: yet they are not, as I said above, more numerous than those which expresses his sympathy with sublimer or more active scenes; but they are almost always marked by a tenderness of execution, and have a look of being beloved in every part of them, which shows them to be the truest expression of his own feelings.[1]

37. One other characteristic of his mind at this period remains to be noticed—its reverence for talent in others. Not the reverence which acts upon the practices of men as if they were the laws of nature, but that which is ready to appreciate the power, and receive the assistance, of every mind which has been previously employed in the same direction, so far as its teaching seems to be consistent with the great text-book of nature itself. Turner thus studied almost every preceding landscape painter, chiefly Claude, Poussin, Vandevelde, Loutherbourg, and Wilson.[2] It was probably by the Sir George Beaumonts and other feeble conventionalists of the period, that he was persuaded to devote his attention to the works of these men; and his having done so will be thought, a few scores of years hence, evidence of perhaps the greatest modesty ever shown by a man of original power. Modesty at once admirable and unfortunate, for the study of the works of Vandevelde and Claude was productive of unmixed mischief to him: he spoiled many of his marine pictures, as for instance

[1] [Compare *Modern Painters*, vol. iv. ch. xvi. § 25, where Ruskin refers to § 36 here in the course of some further remarks about the influence of Yorkshire scenery on Turner.]

[2] [For Turner's study of these painters, see further *Modern Painters*, vol. iii. ch. xviii. ("Of the Teachers of Turner"), and compare *Lectures on Architecture and Painting*, above, § 97.]

Lord Ellesmere's,[1] by imitation of the former; and from the latter learned a false ideal, which, confirmed by the notions of Greek art prevalent in London in the beginning of this century, has manifested itself in many vulgarities in his composition pictures, vulgarities which may perhaps be best expressed by the general term "Twickenham Classicism,"[2] as consisting principally in conceptions of ancient or of rural life such as have influenced the erection of most of our suburban villas. From Nicolo Poussin and Loutherbourg he seems to have derived advantage; perhaps also from Wilson; and much in his subsequent travels from far higher men, especially Tintoret and Paul Veronese. I have myself heard him speaking with singular delight of the putting in of the beech leaves in the upper right-hand corner of Titian's Peter Martyr.[3] I cannot in any of his works trace the slightest influence of Salvator; and I am not surprised at it, for though Salvator was a man of far higher powers than either Vandevelde or Claude, he was a wilful and gross caricaturist. Turner would condescend to be helped by feeble men, but could not be corrupted by false men. Besides, he had never himself seen classical life, and Claude was represented to him as competent authority for it. But he *had* seen mountains and torrents, and knew therefore that Salvator could not paint them.

---

[1] ["Dutch boats in a gale; fishermen endeavouring to put their fish on board," exhibited at the Academy in 1801; in the collection at Bridgewater House. See *Modern Painters*, vol. i. (Vol. III. p. 568), where the picture (which was painted to emulate Vandevelde) is nevertheless spoken of as comparatively "free from the Dutch infection," though still "somewhat heavy in its forms." See also *Harbours of England*, § 39.]

[2] [In a letter to his father with some remarks on Pope, Ruskin wrote :—

"VENICE, *September* 14, 1851.— . . . I have brought my little volume of Pope's poems with me; which I shall read carefully. I hardly know which is most remarkable, the magnificent power and precision of mind, or the miserable corruption of the entire element in which it is educated, and the flatterings, falsenesses, affectations, and indecencies which divert the purpose and waste the strength of the writer, while his natural perception of truth and his carefully acquired knowledge of humanity still render his works of inestimable value. I see he was first educated by a Roman Catholic, and then in *Twickenham* classicism. I am glad to find my term is exactly what I wanted it to be. Pope is the purest example, as well as the highest, of the Cockney classic."]

[3] [For Titian's influence on Turner, see again *Modern Painters*, vol. iii. ch. xviii. For the "Peter Martyr," see note in Vol. III. p. 28.]

38. One of the most characteristic drawings of this period fortunately bears a date, 1818, and brings us within two years of another dated drawing, no less characteristic of what I shall henceforward call Turner's Second period. It is in the possession of Mr. Hawkesworth Fawkes of Farnley, one of Turner's earliest and truest friends; and bears the inscription, unusually conspicuous, heaving itself up and down over the eminences of the foreground—"PASSAGE OF MONT CENIS. J. M. W. TURNER, January 15th, 1820."

The scene is on the summit of the pass close to the hospice, or what seems to have been a hospice at that time,—I do not remember any such at present,—a small square-built house, built as if partly for a fortress, with a detached flight of stone steps in front of it, and a kind of drawbridge to the door. This building, about 400 or 500 yards off, is seen in a dim, ashy grey against the light, which by help of a violent blast of mountain wind has broken through the depth of clouds which hangs upon the crags. There is no sky, properly so. called, nothing but this roof of drifting cloud; but neither is there any weight of darkness—the high air is too thin for it,—all savage, howling, and luminous with cold, the massy bases of the granite hills jutting out here and there grimly through the snow wreaths. There is a desolate-looking refuge on the left, with its number 16, marked on it in long ghastly figures, and the wind is drifting the snow off the roof and through its window in a frantic whirl; the near ground is all wan with half-thawed, half-trampled snow; a diligence in front, whose horses, unable to face the wind, have turned right round with fright, its passengers struggling to escape, jammed in the window; a little farther on is another carriage off the road, some figures pushing at its wheels, and its driver at the horses' heads, pulling and lashing with all his strength, his lifted arm stretched out against the light of the distance, though too far off for the whip to be seen.[1]

---

[1] [For another reference to this drawing, see Ruskin's *Notes on his Drawings by Turner*, No. 9 R.]

XVIII

J.M.W.Turner.R.A

Passage of Mont Cenis. 1820.

From the drawing in the possession of F.H Fawkes. Esquire.

Allen &Co. Sc

39. Now I am perfectly certain that any one thoroughly accustomed to the earlier works of the painter, and shown this picture for the first time, would be struck by two altogether new characters in it.

The first, a seeming enjoyment of the excitement of the scene, totally different from the contemplative philosophy with which it would formerly have been regarded. Every incident of motion and of energy is seized upon with indescribable delight, and every line of the composition animated with a force and fury which are now no longer the mere expression of a contemplated external truth, but have origin in some inherent feeling in the painter's mind.

The second, that although the subject is one in itself almost incapable of colour, and although, in order to increase the wildness of the impression, all brilliant local colour has been refused even where it might easily have been introduced, as in the figures; yet in the low minor key which has been chosen, the melodies of colour have been elaborated to the utmost possible pitch, so as to become a leading, instead of a subordinate, element in the composition; the subdued warm hues of the granite promontories, the dull stone colour of the walls of the buildings, clearly opposed, even in shade, to the grey of the snow wreaths heaped against them, and the faint greens and ghastly blues of the glacier ice, being all expressed with delicacies of transition utterly unexampled in any previous drawings.

40. These, accordingly, are the chief characteristics of the works of Turner's second period, as distinguished from the first,—a new energy inherent in the mind of the painter, diminishing the repose and exalting the force and fire of his conceptions, and the presence of Colour, as at least an essential, and often a principal, element of design.

Not that it is impossible, or even unusual, to find drawings of serene subject, and perfectly quiet feeling, among the compositions of this period; but the repose is in them, just as the energy and tumult were in the earlier period, an external quality, which the painter images by an effort of the will: it is no longer a character inherent in himself. The "Ulleswater," in the England series, is one of those which are in most perfect peace; in the "Cowes," the silence is only broken by the dash of the boat's oars, and in the "Alnwick" by a stag drinking; but in at least nine drawings out of ten, either sky, water, or figures are in rapid motion, and the grandest drawings are almost always those which have even violent action in one or other, or in all; *e.g.* High Force of Tees, Coventry, Llanthony, Salisbury, Llanberis, and such others.[1]

41. The colour is, however, a more absolute distinction; and we must return to Mr. Fawkes's collection in order to see how the change in it was effected. That such a change would take place at one time or other was of course to be securely anticipated, the conventional system of the first period being, as above stated, merely a means of study. But the immediate cause was the journey of the year 1820. As might be guessed from the legend on the drawing above described, "Passage of Mont Cenis, January 15th, 1820," that drawing represents what happened on the day in question to the painter himself. He passed the Alps then in the winter of 1820; and either in the previous or subsequent summer, but on the same journey, he made a series of sketches on the Rhine, in body colour, now in Mr. Fawkes's collection.[2] Every one of those sketches is the almost instantaneous record of an *effect* of colour or atmosphere, taken strictly from nature, the drawing and the

---

[1] [For "Ulleswater," compare Vol. III. p. 490; "Cowes," *ibid.*, p. 547; "Alnwick," *ibid.*, p. 235; "High Force" (or, "The Upper Fall of the Tees"), *ibid.*, pp. 486, 491, 553; "Coventry," *ibid.*, p. 405; "Llanthony," *ibid.*, pp. 401–402 (and plate there); "Llanberis," *ibid.*, p. 410, and *Modern Painters*, vol. v. pt. ix. ch. xi. § 8 *n.* (and plate 80); and for "Salisbury," *Modern Painters*, vol. v. pt. vii. ch. iv. § 19.]

[2] [On his return from this tour "Turner landed at Hull and came straight to Farnley; where, even before taking off his greatcoat, he produced the drawings in a slovenly roll, from his breast-pocket; and Mr. Fawkes bought the lot (some fifty-three in number) for £500, doubtless to Turner's delight, for he could not bear that any series of his should be broken. Then saying that Mr. Fawkes should have no expense in mounting them, he stuck them rudely on cardboard with wafers" (Thornbury's *Life of Turner*, p. 232, 1877 ed.). Two of the Rhine drawings from the Farnley Hall collection—"Johannisberg" and "Sooneck and Baccharach"—are here given.]

XIX

J.M.W.Turner. R.A.

Allen & Co. Sc

Johannisberg, 1824.

From the drawing in the possession of F H. Fawkes Esquire.

details of every subject being comparatively subordinate, and the colour nearly as principal as the light and shade had been before,—certainly the leading feature, though the light and shade are always exquisitely harmonized with it. And naturally, as the colour becomes the leading object, those times of day are chosen in which it is most lovely; and whereas before, at least five out of six of Turner's drawings represented ordinary daylight, we now find his attention directed constantly to the evening: and, for the first time, we have those rosy lights upon the hills, those gorgeous falls of sun through flaming heavens, those solemn twilights, with the blue moon rising as the western sky grows dim, which have ever since been the themes of his mightiest thoughts.

42. I have no doubt, that the *immediate* reason of this change was the impression made upon him by the colours of the continental skies. When he first travelled on the Continent (1800), he was comparatively a young student; not yet able to draw form as he wanted, he was forced to give all his thoughts and strength to this primary object. But now he was free to receive other impressions; the time was come for perfecting his art, and the first sunset which he saw on the Rhine taught him that all previous landscape art was vain and valueless, that in comparison with natural colour, the things that had been called paintings were mere ink and charcoal, and that all precedent and all authority must be cast away at once, and trodden under foot. He cast them away: the memories of Vandevelde and Claude were at once weeded out of the great mind they had en-cumbered; they and all the rubbish of the schools together with them; the waves of the Rhine swept them away for ever: and a new dawn rose over the rocks of the Sieben-gebirge.[1]

43. There was another motive at work, which rendered the change still more complete. His fellow artists were already conscious enough of his superior power in drawing,

[1] [These Seven Mountains—famous in legend and history—of which the Drachen-fels is one, rise inland behind Königswinter, 22 miles south-east of Cologne.]

and their best hope was that he might not be able to colour. They had begun to express this hope loudly enough for it to reach his ears. The engraver of one of his most important marine pictures told me, not long ago, that one day about the period in question, Turner came into his room to examine the progress of the Plate, not having seen his own picture for several years.[1] It was one of his dark early pictures, but in the foreground was a little piece of luxury, a pearly fish wrought into hues like those of an opal. He stood before the picture for some moments; then laughed, and pointed joyously to the fish:—"They say that Turner can't colour!" and turned away.

44. Under the force of these various impulses the change was total. *Every subject thenceforward was primarily conceived in colour;* and no engraving ever gave the slightest idea of any drawing of this period.

The artists who had any perception of the truth were in despair; the Beaumontites, classicalists, and "owl species" in general, in as much indignation as their dulness was capable of. They had deliberately closed their eyes to all nature, and had gone on inquiring, "Where do you put your brown 'tree'?"[2] A vast revelation was made to them at once, enough to have dazzled any one; but to *them,* light unendurable as incomprehensible. They did "to the moon complain,"[3] in one vociferous, unanimous, continuous "Tu whoo." Shrieking rose from all dark places at the same instant, just the same kind of shrieking that is now raised against the Pre-Raphaelites. Those glorious old Arabian Nights, how true they are! Mocking and whispering, and abuse loud and low by turns, from all the black

---

[1] [The picture is "Calais Pier," No. 472 in the National Gallery; the engraver, T. Lupton (see below, § 47). Ruskin described the picture in his *Notes on the Turner Gallery*, 1856, and in a footnote referred to this anecdote, adding that for "several months" he should have written "several years"; the correction is accordingly here made. The picture was exhibited in 1803, and Lupton's engraving of it, which was in hand for many years, never satisfied the painter; an interesting statement on the subject by Lupton is given by Thornbury (p. 196, ed. 1877).]

[2] [See preface to the second edition of *Modern Painters*, vol. i. (Vol. III. p. 45 n.).]

[3] [Gray's *Elegy*, iii.]

J.M.W.Turner.R.A.

Allen & Co.Sc.

Sooneck and Bacharach, 1824

From the drawing in the possession of F.H.Fawkes, Esquire.

stones beside the road, when one living soul is toiling up the hill to get the golden water. Mocking and whispering, that he may look back, and become a black stone like themselves.[1]

45. Turner looked not back, but he went on in such a temper as a strong man must be in, when he is forced to walk with his fingers in his ears. He retired into himself; he could look no longer for help, or counsel, or sympathy from any one; and the spirit of defiance in which he was forced to labour led him sometimes into violences, from which the slightest expression of sympathy would have saved him. The new energy that was upon him, and the utter isolation into which he was driven, were both alike dangerous, and many drawings of the time show the evil effects of both; some of them being hasty, wild, or experimental, and others little more than magnificent expressions of defiance of public opinion.[2]

But all have this noble virtue—they are in everything his own: there are no more reminiscences of dead masters, no more trials of skill in the manner of Claude or Poussin; every faculty of his soul is fixed upon nature only, as he saw her, or as he remembered her.

46. I have spoken above[3] of his gigantic memory: it is especially necessary to notice this, in order that we may understand the kind of grasp which a man of real imagination takes of all things that are once brought within his reach—grasp thenceforth not to be relaxed for ever.

On looking over any catalogues of his works, or of particular series of them, we shall notice the recurrence of the same subject two, three, or even many times. In any other artist this would be nothing remarkable. Probably,

---

[1] [Here Ruskin, it seems, indulges in some little mystification; the reference being not to the *Arabian Nights*, but to his own fairy story, *The King of the Golden River* (see Vol. I.).]

[2] [Compare what Ruskin says above of Wordsworth's Prefaces—"every other sentence stiffened into defiance," § 17, p. 354.]

[3] [§ 21, pp. 359, 360. Ruskin returned to the subject in *Modern Painters*, vol. iv. ch. ii.; see especially § 18, where the passages in this pamphlet are referred to.]

most modern landscape painters multiply a favourite subject twenty, thirty, or sixty fold, putting the shadows and the clouds in different places, and " inventing," as they are pleased to call it, a new " effect" every time. But if we examine the successions of Turner's subjects, we shall find them either the records of a succession of impressions actually received by him at some favourite locality, or else repetitions of one impression received in early youth, and again and again realised as his increasing powers enabled him to do better justice to it. In either case we shall find them records of *seen facts; never* compositions in his room to fill up a favourite outline.

47. For instance, every traveller—at least, every traveller of thirty years' standing—must love Calais, the place where he first felt himself in a strange world.[1] Turner evidently loved it excessively. I have never catalogued his studies of Calais, but I remember, at this moment, five:[2] there is first the " Pas de Calais," a very large oil painting, which is what he saw in broad daylight as he crossed over, when he got near the French side. It is a careful study of French fishing-boats running for the shore before the wind, with the picturesque old city in the distance. Then there is the " Calais Harbour" in the *Liber Studiorum:* that is what he saw just as he was going into the harbour—a heavy brig warping out, and very likely to get in his way or run against the pier, and bad weather coming on. Then there is the " Calais Pier," a large painting, engraved some years ago

---

[1] [The classical passage in Ruskin on Calais is *Modern Painters*, vol. iv. ch. i. §§ 2, 3. In one of his early writings he had also expressed the feelings here described : see Vol. II. p. 341.]

[2] [(1) The " Pas de Calais" was exhibited at the Academy in 1827, under the title "'Now for the Painter': Passengers going on board." It is in the collection of Mr. Naylor at Leighton Hall. (For an anecdote about the title, see Thornbury, p. 293.) (2) "Calais Harbour in the *Liber Studiorum*," called also " Entrance to Calais Harbour," published in No. 11 of the *Liber* (Jan. 1, 1816). (3) For "Calais Pier" (exhibited 1803), see above, p. 378 *n.* (4) The "Fort Rouge" is the "Calais Sands, low water : Poissards collecting bait," exhibited at the Academy in 1830, bought by Messrs. Agnew at the Gillott sale in 1872. There is a sketch of the Fort, and the sands at low water, in the National Gallery collection, No. 421 (*c*). (5) The "Scott" Calais is in Vol. 27 of the *Prose Works* (1834). In the National Gallery collection there are several sketches at Calais, described by Ruskin in his *Catalogue of the Sketches and Drawings, etc.*, 1857-1858 (see Vol. XIII.).]

by Mr. Lupton:* that is what he saw when he had landed, and ran back directly to the pier to see what had become of the brig. The weather had got still worse, the fishwomen were being blown about in a distressful manner on the pier head, and some more fishing-boats were running in with all speed. Then there is the "Fort Rouge," Calais: that is what he saw after he had been home to Dessein's,[1] and dined, and went out again in the evening to walk on the sands, the tide being down. He had never seen such a waste of sands before, and it made an impression on him. The shrimp-girls were all scattered over them too, and moved about in white spots on the wild shore; and the storm had lulled a little, and there was a sunset—such a sunset!—and the bars of Fort Rouge seen against it, skeleton-wise. He did not paint that directly; thought over it—painted it a long while afterwards.

48. Then there is the vignette in the illustrations to Scott. That is what he saw as he was going home, meditatively; and the revolving lighthouse came blazing out upon him suddenly, and disturbed him. He did not like that so much; made a vignette of it, however, when he was asked to do a bit of Calais, twenty or thirty years afterwards, having already done all the rest.

Turner never told me all this, but any one may see it if he will compare the pictures. They might, possibly, not be impressions of a single day, but of two days or three; though, in all human probability, they were seen just as I have stated them;† but they *are* records of successive impressions, as plainly written as ever traveller's diary. All of them pure veracities. Therefore immortal.

49. I could multiply these series almost indefinitely from the rest of his works. What is curious, some of them have

---

* The Plate was, however, never published.[2]

† And the more probably because Turner was never fond of staying long at any place, and was least of all likely to make a pause of two or three days at the beginning of his journey.

---

[1] [This very old-established inn at Calais figures in Sterne's *Sentimental Journey.* See also Ruskin's metrical "Tour" of 1835, Vol. II. p. 398, and *Præterita*, ii. ch. x. § 186.]

[2] [See note above, p. 378.]

a kind of private mark running through all the subjects. Thus, I know three drawings of Scarborough, and all of them have a starfish in the foreground: I do not remember any others of his marine subjects which have a starfish.[1]

The other kind of repetition — the recurrence to one early impression — is, however, still more remarkable. In the collection of F. H. Bale, Esq., there is a small drawing of Llanthony Abbey.[2] It is in his boyish manner, its date probably about 1795; evidently a sketch from nature, finished at home. It had been a showery day; the hills were partially concealed by the rain, and gleams of sunshine breaking out at intervals. A man was fishing in the mountain stream. The young Turner sought a place of some shelter under the bushes; made his sketch; took great pains when he got home to imitate the rain, as he best could; added his child's luxury of a rainbow; put in the very bush under which he had taken shelter, and the fisherman, a somewhat ill-jointed and long-legged fisherman, in the courtly short breeches which were the fashion of the time.

50. Some thirty years afterwards, with all his powers in their strongest training, and after the total change in his

---

[1] [In Ruskin's diary at Farnley he notes this observation:—

" 'Scarborough.' I now know three of this subject: Mr. Fawkes's large water-colour, where the principal object on the left is a great pile of common beach posts, with a pool of dark green water in front, beautifully painted, and a *starfish* large, and a dark ship ashore. The wet sand in distance quite unrivalled.

"The second is the one engraved by Lupton. It is founded on the first, only the pile of posts is gone, and all depends on the dark ship, distant cliffs, white figure, and *starfish*.

"The third, rough seas (Lady Barnes'), where a large cliff has taken the place of the posts, and the dark ship is gone, and we have rough sea. But the starfish still."

The Farnley "Scarborough" is engraved in *Ruskin and Turner*, vol. ii. p. 216. Lupton's engraving is in the *Harbours of England*; Ruskin notes the starfish in his description of the Plate (XII.) in that work; the original drawing is No. 169 in the National Gallery. Lady Barnes' "Scarborough" sketch is probably one of those which afterwards passed into Ruskin's collection—perhaps the sketch (with a starfish conspicuous on the sand) which he sold in 1869 (see Vol. XIII.); two others remained in his collection (*Notes on his Drawings by Turner*, Nos. 81 and 82).]

[2] [The drawing of 1795, formerly in the Bale collection, afterwards passed into that of Mr. John Edward Taylor. The "Llanthony" for the *England and Wales* Series (*circa* 1834) is described, and a photogravure of it is given, in *Modern Painters*, vol. i. (Vol. III. p. 402); there is another very early drawing of Llanthony Abbey in the National Gallery (No. 638).]

feelings and principles, which I have endeavoured to describe, he undertook the series of "England and Wales," and in that series introduced the subject of Llanthony Abbey. And behold, he went back to his boy's sketch and boy's thought. He kept the very bushes in their places, but brought the fisherman to the other side of the river, and put him, in somewhat less courtly dress, under their shelter, instead of himself. And then he set all his gained strength and new knowledge at work on the well-remembered shower of rain, that had fallen thirty years before, to do it better. The resultant drawing is one of the very noblest of his second period.

51. Another of the drawings of the England series, Ulleswater, is the repetition of one in Mr. Fawkes's collection,[1] which, by the method of its execution, I should conjecture to have been executed about the year 1808 or 1810: at all events, it is a very quiet drawing of the first period. The lake is quite calm; the western hills in grey shadow, the eastern massed in light; Helvellyn rising like a mist between them, all being mirrored in the calm water. Some thin and slightly evanescent cows are standing in the shallow water in front; a boat floats motionless about a hundred yards from the shore; the foreground is of broken rocks, with some lovely pieces of copse on the right and left.

This was evidently Turner's record of a quiet evening by the shore of Ulleswater, but it was a feeble one. He could not at that time render the sunset colours: he went back to it, therefore, in the England Series, and painted it again with his new power. The same hills are there, the same shadows, the same cows,—they had stood in his mind, on the same spot, for twenty years,—the same boat, the same rocks, only the copse is cut away—it interfered with the masses of his colour. Some figures are introduced bathing; and what was grey, and feeble gold in the first drawing, becomes purple and burning rose-colour in the last.

---

[1] [For the "Ulleswater" in the *England and Wales*, see *Modern Painters*, vol. i. (Vol. III. pp. 490, 541), and vol. iv. ch. xviii. § 12.]

52. But perhaps one of the most curious examples is in the series of subjects from Winchelsea.[1] That in the *Liber Studiorum*, " Winchelsea, Sussex," bears date 1812, and its figures consist of a soldier speaking to a woman, who is resting on the bank beside the road. There is another small subject, with Winchelsea in the distance, of which the engraving bears date 1817. It has *two* women with bundles, and *two* soldiers toiling along the embankment in the plain, and a baggage waggon in the distance. Neither of these seems to have satisfied him, and at last he did another for the England Series, of which the engraving bears date 1830. There is now a regiment on the march; the baggage waggon is there, having got no farther on in the thirteen years, but one of the women is tired, and has fainted on the bank; another is supporting her against her bundle, and giving her drink; a third sympathetic woman is added, and the two soldiers have stopped, and one is drinking from his canteen.

53. Nor is it merely of entire scenes, or of particular incidents that Turner's memory is thus tenacious. The slightest passages of colour or arrangement that have pleased him— the fork of a bough, the casting of a shadow, the fracture of a stone—will be taken up again and again, and strangely worked into new relations with other thoughts. There is a single sketch from nature in one of the portfolios at Farnley, of a common wood-walk on the estate, which has furnished passages to no fewer than three of the most elaborate compositions in the *Liber Studiorum*.[2]

54. I am thus tedious in dwelling on Turner's powers of memory, because I wish it to be thoroughly seen how all

---

[1] [(1) The drawing for the *Liber Studiorum* Plate is No. 487 in the National Gallery. (2) The second drawing, " Winchelsea from the Rye Road " (now in the possession of Mr. Abel Buckley), was etched by W. B. Cooke for the *Southern Coast*, but the plate was never finished. The drawing has since been engraved in *Hastings and its Vicinity*; see for another reference to it, Ruskin's *Notes on his Drawings by Turner*, No. 34. (3) The third drawing (for which see also above, p. 370), made for the *England and Wales* Series, was given to Ruskin by his father in 1840 : see *Præterita*, vol. ii. ch. i., and the *Notes* just mentioned, No. 34.]

[2] [One of the *Liber* compositions referred to is doubtless the "Procris and Cephalus"; probably another is the unpublished "Huntsman in a Wood."]

his greatness, all his infinite luxuriance of invention, depends on his taking possession of everything that he sees,—on his grasping all, and losing hold of nothing,—on his forgetting himself, and forgetting nothing else. I wish it to be understood how every great man paints what he sees or did see, his greatness being indeed little else than his intense sense of fact. And thus Pre-Raphaelitism and Raphaelitism, and Turnerism, are all one and the same, so far as education can influence them. They are different in their choice, different in their faculties, but all the same in this, that Raphael himself, so far as he was great, and all who preceded or followed him who ever were great, became so by painting the truths around them as they appeared to each man's own mind, not as he had been taught to see them, except by the God who made both him and them.

55. There is, however, one more characteristic of Turner's second period, on which I have still to dwell, especially with reference to what has been above advanced respecting the fallacy of overtoil; namely, the magnificent ease with which all is done when it is *successfully* done. For there are one or two drawings of this time which are *not* done easily.[1] Turner had in these set himself to do a fine thing to exhibit his powers; in the common phrase, to excel himself; so sure as he does this, the work is a failure. The worst drawings that have ever come from his hands are some of this second period, on which he has spent much time and laborious thought; drawings filled with incident from one side to the other, with skies stippled into morbid blue, and warm lights set against them in violent contrast; one of Bamborough Castle, a large water-colour, may be named as an example.[2] But the truly noble works are those in which, without effort, he has expressed his thoughts as they came, and forgotten himself; and in these the

---

[1] [See above, p. 344. With the following passage, compare *Modern Painters*, vol. iii. ch. iii. § 3.]

[2] [The same criticism is made on this drawing of Bamborough in *Modern Painters*, vol. i. (Vol. III. p. 248).]

outpouring of invention is not less miraculous than the swiftness and obedience of the mighty hand that expresses it. Any one who examines the drawings may see the evidence of this facility, in the strange freshness and sharpness of every touch of colour; but when the multitude of delicate touches, with which all the aërial tones are worked, is taken into consideration, it would still appear impossible that the drawing could have been completed with *ease*, unless we had direct evidence on the matter: fortunately, it is not wanting. There is a drawing in Mr. Fawkes's collection of a man-of-war taking in stores: it is of the usual size of those of the England Series, about sixteen inches by eleven: it does not appear one of the most highly finished, but it is still farther removed from slightness. The hull of a first-rate occupies nearly one-half of the picture on the right, her bows towards the spectator, seen in sharp perspective from stem to stern, with all her port-holes, guns, anchors, and lower rigging elaborately detailed; there are two other ships of the line in the middle distance, drawn with equal precision; a noble breezy sea dancing against their broad bows, full of delicate drawing in its waves; a store-ship beneath the hull of the larger vessel, and several other boats, and a complicated cloudy sky. It might appear no small exertion of mind to draw the detail of all this shipping down to the smallest ropes, from memory, in the drawing-room of a mansion in the middle of Yorkshire, even if considerable time had been given for the effort. But Mr. Fawkes sat beside the painter from the first stroke to the last. Turner took a piece of blank paper one morning after breakfast, outlined his ships, finished the drawing in three hours, and went out to shoot.[1]

56. Let this single fact be quietly meditated upon by our ordinary painters, and they will see the truth of what

---

[1] [This drawing is here reproduced, Plate XXI. The term "a first-rate," which Ruskin uses above (as in Campbell's poem, "The Launch of a First-Rate"; for another reference to the drawing, see *Harbours of England*, § 41), has gone out of use in these days, belonging as it does to the time when the British Navy was divided into six rates of vessels, according to the number of guns carried.]

XX1

J.M.W.Turner,R.A.

Allen&Co.Sc.

Man-of-War taking in Stores, 1818.

From the drawing in the possession of F.H.Fawkes, Esquire

was above asserted,[1]—that if a great thing can be done at all, it can be done easily; and let them not torment themselves with twisting of compositions this way and that, and repeating, and experimenting, and scene-shifting. If a man can compose at all, he can compose at once, or rather he must compose in spite of himself. And this is the reason of that silence which I have kept in most of my works, on the subject of Composition.[2] Many critics, especially the architects, have found fault with me for not "teaching people how to arrange masses;" for not "attributing sufficient importance to composition." Alas! I attribute far more importance to it than they do;—so much importance, that I should just as soon think of sitting down to teach a man how to write a *Divina Commedia*, or *King Lear*, as how to "compose," in the true sense, a single building or picture. The marvellous stupidity of this age of lecturers is, that they do not see that what they call, "principles of composition," are mere principles of common sense in everything, as well as in pictures and buildings;—A picture is to have a principal light? Yes; and so a dinner is to have a principal dish, and an oration a principal point, and an air of music a principal note, and every man a principal object. A picture is to have harmony of relation among its parts? Yes; and so is a speech well uttered, and an action well ordered, and a company well chosen, and a ragout well mixed. Composition! As if a man were not composing every moment of his life, well or ill, and would not do it instinctively in his picture as well as elsewhere, if he could. Composition of this lower or common kind is of exactly the same importance in a picture that it is in anything else,—no more. It is well that a man should say what he has to say in good order and sequence, but the main thing is to say it truly. And

---

[1] [See p. 344.]

[2] [The subject had, however, been glanced at in *Modern Painters*, volumes i. and ii. (see, *e.g.*, Vol. III. p. 334, Vol. IV. p. 231), and in *Stones of Venice*, vol. ii. (Vol. X. pp. 215–216 *n.*). Ruskin afterwards dealt with it more fully in *The Elements of Drawing*, Letter iii., and *Modern Painters*, vol. v. pt. viii. ch. i.]

yet we go on preaching to our pupils as if to have a principal light was everything, and so cover our academy walls with Shacabac feasts,[1] wherein the courses are indeed well ordered, but the dishes empty.

57. It is not, however, only in invention that men overwork themselves, but in execution also ; and here I have a word to say to the Pre-Raphaelites specially. They are working too hard. There is evidence in failing portions of their pictures, showing that they have wrought so long upon them that their very sight has failed for weariness, and that the hand refused any more to obey the heart. And, besides this, there are certain qualities of drawing which they miss from over-carefulness. For, let them be assured, there is a great truth lurking in that common desire of men to see things done in what they call a " masterly," or " bold," or " broad," manner : a truth oppressed and abused, like almost every other in this world, but an eternal one nevertheless ; and whatever mischief may have followed from men's looking for nothing else but this facility of execution, and supposing that a picture was assuredly all right if only it were done with broad dashes of the brush, still the truth remains the same :— that because it is not intended that men shall torment or weary themselves with any earthly labour, it is appointed that the noblest results should only be attainable by a certain ease and decision of manipulation. I only wish people understood this much of sculpture, as well as of painting, and could see that the finely finished statue is, in ninety-nine cases out of a hundred, a far more vulgar work than that which shows rough signs of the right hand laid to the workman's hammer : but at all events, in painting it is felt by all men, and justly felt. The freedom of

---

[1] ["Barmecide feasts" is the better-known expression, referring to the tale in *The Arabian Nights* of "The Barber's Sixth Brother," of how Shacabac was invited to a feast, when starving, by the wealthy Barmecide, and finding the dishes and goblets empty, had "to cloy the hungry edge of appetite with bare imagination of the feast." He at once entered into the humour of the thing, which so pleased the Barmecide that he then provided Shacabac with a substantial banquet.]

the lines of nature can only be represented by a similar
freedom in the hand that follows them; there are curves
in the flow of the hair, and in the form of the features, and
in the muscular outline of the body, which can in no wise
be caught but by a sympathetic freedom in the stroke of
the pencil. I do not care what example is taken; be it
the most subtle and careful work of Leonardo himself, there
will be found a play and power and ease in the outlines,
which no *slow* effort could ever imitate. And if the Pre-
Raphaelites do not understand how this kind of power, in
its highest perfection, may be united with the most severe
rendering of all other orders of truth, and especially of those
with which they themselves have most sympathy, let them
look at the drawings of John Lewis.

58. These then are the principal lessons which we have
to learn from Turner, in his second or central period of
labour. There is one more, however, to be received; and
that is a warning; for towards the close of it, what with
doing small conventional vignettes for publishers, making
showy drawings from sketches taken by other people of
places he had never seen, and touching up the bad engravings from his works submitted to him almost every day,—
engravings utterly destitute of animation, and which had to
be raised into a specious brilliancy by scratching them over
with white, spotty lights, he gradually got inured to many
conventionalities, and even falsities; and, having trusted for
ten or twelve years almost entirely to his memory and invention, living, I believe, mostly in London, and receiving
a new sensation only from the burning of the Houses of
Parliament,[1] he painted many pictures between 1830 and
1840 altogether unworthy of him. But he was not thus to
close his career.

59. In the summer either of 1840 or 1841, he undertook
another journey into Switzerland. It was then at least forty

[1] [In the year following the fire of 1834, Turner exhibited two large pictures of
this scene. One of them (formerly in the collection of Mr. Victor Marshall of Coniston)
is now in the possession of Mr. Ponsford; the other, in that of Mr. Holbrook Gaskell.]

years since he had first seen the Alps; (the source of the Arveron, in Mr. Fawkes's collection, which could not have been painted till he had seen the thing itself, bears date 1800,)[1] and the direction of his journey in 1840 marks his fond memory of that earliest one; for, if we look over the Swiss studies and drawings executed in his first period, we shall be struck by his fondness for the pass of the St. Gothard; the most elaborate drawing in the Farnley collection is one of the Lake of Lucerne from Fluelen;[2] and, counting the *Liber Studiorum* subjects, there are, to my knowledge, six compositions taken at the same period from the pass of St. Gothard, and, probably, several others are in existence.[3]   The valleys of Sallenches and Chamouni, and Lake of Geneva, are the only other Swiss scenes which seem to have made very profound impressions on him.

He returned in 1841 to Lucerne; walked up Mont Pilate on foot, crossed the St. Gothard, and returned by Lausanne and Geneva.   He made a large number of coloured sketches on this journey, and realised several of them on his return. The drawings thus produced are different from all that had preceded them, and are the first which belong definitely to what I shall henceforward call his Third period.

The perfect repose of his youth had returned to his mind, while the faculties of imagination and execution appeared in renewed strength; all conventionality being done away by the force of the impression which he had received from the Alps, after his long separation from them.   The drawings are marked by a peculiar largeness and simplicity

---

[1] [The reading of the dates on the Farnley drawings is matter of some dispute. It is, however, now generally agreed that 1802 was the date of Turner's first Continental journey.   Ruskin in his last catalogue of the Turner drawings at the National Gallery (Group VIII.) gives the date as 1803 (see Vol. XIII., and compare Vol. III. p. 235 *n*.).]

[2] [Now in the collection of Sir Donald Currie.]

[3] [There are five such compositions, of Turner's early period, in the National Gallery alone—namely Nos. 476 and 477 (the drawings for *Liber Studiorum*), No. 320 ("The Old Road, Pass of St. Gothard"), No. 321 ("The Old Devil's Bridge"), and No. 324 ("On the Pass of the St. Gothard above Amsteg").   The "profound impression" made upon Turner from the first by the valleys of Sallenches, Chamouni, and the Lake of Geneva may similarly be traced in the National Gallery, as also in the catalogue of Ruskin's collection (see Vol. XIII.).]

of thought: most of them by deep serenity, passing into melancholy; all by a richness of colour, such as he had never before conceived. They, and the works done in following years, bear the same relation to those of the rest of his life that the colours of sunset do to those of the day; and will be recognized, in a few years more, as the noblest landscapes ever yet conceived by human intellect.[1]

60. Such has been the career of the greatest painter of this century. Many a century may pass away before there rises such another; but what greatness any among us may be capable of, will, at least, be best attained by following in his path;—by beginning in all quietness and hopefulness to use whatever powers we may possess to represent the things around us as we see and feel them; trusting to the close of life to give the perfect crown to the course of its labours, and knowing assuredly that the determination of the degree in which watchfulness is to be exalted into invention, rests with a higher will than our own. And, if not greatness, at least a certain good, is thus to be achieved; for though I have above spoken of the mission of the more humble artist, as if it were merely to be subservient to that of the antiquarian or the man of science, there is an ulterior aspect, in which it is not subservient, but superior. Every archæologist, every natural philosopher, knows that there is a peculiar rigidity of mind brought on by long devotion to logical and analytical inquiries. Weak men, giving themselves to such studies, are utterly hardened by them, and become incapable of understanding anything nobler, or even of feeling the value of the results to which they lead. But even the best men are in a sort injured by them, and pay a definite price, as in most other matters, for definite advantages. They gain a peculiar strength, but lose in tenderness, elasticity, and impressibility. The man who has gone,

---

[1] [Compare with this estimate of Turner's latest Swiss drawings (1841–1842) what Ruskin says in *Modern Painters*, vol. i. (Vol. III. p. 250); a passage added in the fifth edition, which was published in the same year as this pamphlet (1851). In volumes iv. and v. of *Modern Painters* Ruskin analysed some of the drawings in detail, and see also the Epilogue to the *Notes on his Drawings by Turner* (Vol. XIII.).]

hammer in hand, over the surface of a romantic country, feels no longer, in the mountain ranges he has so laboriously explored, the sublimity or mystery with which they were veiled when he first beheld them, and with which they are adorned in the mind of the passing traveller. In his more informed conception, they arrange themselves like a dissected model: where another man would be awe-struck by the magnificence of the precipice, he sees nothing but the emergence of a fossiliferous rock, familiarised already to his imagination as extending in a shallow stratum, over a perhaps uninteresting district; where the unlearned spectator would be touched with strong emotion by the aspect of the snowy summits which rise in the distance, he sees only the culminating points of a metamorphic formation, with an uncomfortable web of fan-like fissures radiating, in his imagination, through their centres.* That in the grasp he has obtained of the inner relations of all these things to the universe, and to man, that in the views which have been opened to him of natural energies such as no human mind would have ventured to conceive, and of past states of being, each in some new way bearing witness to the unity of purpose and everlastingly consistent providence of the Maker of all things, he has received reward well worthy the sacrifice, I would not for an instant deny; but the sense of the loss is not less painful to him if his mind be rightly constituted; and it would be with infinite gratitude that he would regard the man, who, retaining in his delineation of natural scenery a fidelity to the facts of science

---

* This state of mind appears to have been the only one which Wordsworth had been able to discern in men of science; and in disdain of which, he wrote that short-sighted passage in the *Excursion*, Book III. l. 165–190, which is, I think, the only one in the whole range of his works which his true friends would have desired to see blotted out. What else has been found fault with as feeble or superfluous, is not so in the intense distinctive relief which it gives to his character. But these lines are written in mere ignorance of the matter they treat; in mere want of sympathy with the men they describe: for, observe, though the passage is put into the mouth of the Solitary, it is fully confirmed, and even rendered more scornful, by the speech which follows.

FACSIMILE OF THE CONCLUDING PASSAGE OF THE MS. OF "PRE-RAPHAELITISM"

pp. 392–393

so rigid as to make his work at once acceptable and credible to the most sternly critical intellect, should yet invest its features again with the sweet veil of their daily aspect; should make them dazzling with the splendour of wandering light, and involve them in the unsearchableness of stormy obscurity; should restore to the divided anatomy its visible vitality of operation, clothe the naked crags with soft forests, enrich the mountain ruins with bright pastures, and lead the thoughts from the monotonous recurrence of the phenomena of the physical world, to the sweet interests and sorrows of human life and death.

VI

LETTERS TO THE "TIMES" ON THE NATIONAL GALLERY

(1847, 1852)

[*Bibliographical Note.* — These two letters first appeared in the *Times* of January 7, 1847, and December 29, 1852.

The first letter was reprinted, with comments by "Verax," in pp. 44–58 of *The Abuses of the National Gallery,* etc. etc., by Verax, 1847.

Both letters were reprinted in *Arrows of the Chace,* 1880, vol. i. pp. 53–66, and 67–77. The numbering of the paragraphs is introduced in the present edition.

There is also a reprint of them, bearing the date 1852, of which no mention is made in Shepherd's Bibliography (1881), though it appears in that edited by T. J. Wise in 1889. The title-page is :—

> The National Gallery. | Two Letters | to the Editor of the *Times* | By | The Author of "Modern Painters." | London : | 1852.

Octavo, pp. 16. The imprint at the foot of p. 16 reads : "London : Printed by Stewart and Murray, Old Bailey." Issued stitched and without wrappers.

That this reprint belongs to a much later date than 1852 is proved by a collation of the *Variæ Lectiones.* Thus in line 5 of § 3, "Dust an inch thick accumulated upon the *frames*" is the reading in Ruskin's MS. and in the *Times.* In *Arrows of the Chace* (1880) the word is *panes,* an obvious misprint, for one of Ruskin's grievances was that at this time the pictures were not glazed. Yet *panes* is the word in the reprint which professes to be of the year 1852. So, again, in § 2, line 19, the dash (—) after "old canvass," which does not appear in the *Times,* was introduced in *Arrows of the Chace,* and reappears in the reprint. In § 4, line 9, a superfluous comma after "warned" figures in both reprints. In § 7, line 2, a comma in the original becomes a semicolon in both reprints ; as also in line 13. In line 26, the comma after "brilliancy" is inserted in the present edition. In § 8, line 9, a comma in the original is changed into a semicolon in both reprints (here followed) ; line 22, the comma after "this" disappeared in both reprints ; line 32, a superfluous comma after "large" was inserted in both reprints ; line 41, the word "only" was similarly inserted, and a comma after "attributable." In § 9, line 4, the words "the various purchases made in" were omitted in both reprints, and in line 7 "utility" was misprinted "ability" in both. Some other minor variations in punctuation, in which again the alleged reprint of 1852 follows the alterations made in 1880, need not be enumerated ; but finally, in § 9, line 38, "or" in the *Times* was printed "and" in *Arrows of the Chace,* and this misprint also appears in the reprint of "1852." It thus follows that the reprint "of extreme scarcity" is what is known in the trade as a "fake," being an unauthorised reprint from *Arrows of the Chace* at some date later than 1880.

A collation of the second letter shows a similar result. The reprint of "1852" omits the two footnotes by the author, which appeared as such in the *Times ;* the publisher not perceiving that these notes, unlike others in *Arrows of the Chace,* were the author's and not the editor's. In the first author's note, last line, "Claudes" in the *Times* is printed "Claude's" in both reprints. In § 2, line 9, "curators" is printed with a capital C in both ; line 25, "chill" printed "dirt" in both ; and there are again several minor variations in punctuation, which it is unnecessary to enumerate ; in all cases the alterations introduced in *Arrows of the Chace* (1880) appear in the reprint of "1852."]

THE NATIONAL GALLERY

I

DANGER TO THE NATIONAL GALLERY [1]
(1847)

To the Editor of the " Times "

1. SIR,—As I am sincerely desirous that a stop may be put to the dangerous process of cleaning lately begun in our National Gallery, and as I believe that what is right is most effectively when most kindly advocated, and what is true most convincingly when least passionately asserted, I was grieved to see the violent attack upon Mr. Eastlake in your columns of Friday last; yet not less surprised at the attempted defence which appeared in them yesterday.[2] The outcry which has arisen upon this subject has been just, but it has been too loud; the injury done is neither so great nor so wilful as has been asserted, and I fear that the respect which might have been paid to remonstrance may be refused to clamour.

2. I was inclined at first to join as loudly as any in the hue and cry. Accustomed, as I have been, to look to England as the refuge of the pictorial as of all other distress, and to hope that, having no high art of her own, she would at least protect what she could not produce, and respect

---

[1] [From the *Times*, January 7, 1847. For the circumstances in which this letter was written, see Introduction, above, p. lviii.]

[2] [The " violent attack " alludes to a letter of " Verax " in the *Times* of Thursday (not Friday), December 31, 1846, and the " attempted defence " to another letter signed " A. G." in the *Times* of January 4, two days (not *the* day) before Ruskin wrote the present letter. For " Verax," see again Introduction, p. lviii.]

what she could not restore, I could not but look upon the attack which has been made upon the pictures in question as on the violation of a sanctuary. I had seen in Venice the noblest works of Veronese painted over with flake-white with a brush fit for tarring ships; I had seen in Florence Angelico's highest inspiration rotted and seared into fragments of old wood, burnt into blisters, or blotted into glutinous maps of mildew;[1] I had seen in Paris Raphael restored by David and Vernet; and I returned to England in the one last trust that, though her National Gallery was an European jest, her art a shadow, and her connoisseurship an hypocrisy, though she neither knew how to cherish nor how to choose, and lay exposed to the cheats of every vendor of old canvass, yet that such good pictures as through chance or oversight might find their way beneath that preposterous portico, and into those melancholy and miserable rooms, were at least to be vindicated thenceforward from the mercy of republican, priest, or painter, safe alike from musketry, monkery, and manipulation.

3. But whatever pain I may feel at the dissipation of this dream, I am not disposed altogether to deny the necessity of some illuminatory process with respect to pictures exposed to a London atmosphere and populace. Dust an inch thick, accumulated upon the frames in the course of the day, and darkness closing over the canvass like a curtain, attest too forcibly the influence on floor and air of the "mutable, rank-scented, many."[2] It is of little use to be over-anxious for the preservation of pictures which we cannot see; the only question is, whether in the present instance the process may not have been carried perilously far, and

---

[1] [For the repainting of Veronese's pictures in S. Sebastiano at Venice, see Vol. XI. p. 432. For the maltreatment of Fra Angelico's "Vita di Cristo" at Florence, see Vol. IV. p. 100 and n. Several of Raphael's pictures in the Louvre have at one time or another been subjected to repainting—such as "La Belle Jardinière," and the "St. Margaret." Vernet, the elder (1714–1789), was much employed by Louis XV., and David (1748–1825) by Napoleon. Information with regard to the cleaning and repainting of pictures in the Louvre at a later date was given to the Select Committee of 1853 (Questions 2625–2657).]

[2] [Shakespeare : *Coriolanus,* iii. 1. 66.]

whether in future simpler and safer means may not be adopted to remove the coat of dust and smoke, without affecting either the glazing of the picture, or, what is almost as precious, the mellow tone left by time.

4. As regards the " Peace and War," [1] I have no hesitation in asserting that for the present it is utterly and for ever partially destroyed. I am not disposed lightly to impugn the judgment of Mr. Eastlake, but this was indisputably of all the pictures in the Gallery that which least required, and least could endure, the process of cleaning. It was in the most advantageous condition under which a work of Rubens can be seen; mellowed by time into more perfect harmony than when it left the easel, enriched and warmed without losing any of its freshness or energy. The execution of the master is always so bold and frank as to be completely, perhaps even most agreeably, seen under circumstances of obscurity, which would be injurious to pictures of greater refinement; and, though this was, indeed, one of his most highly finished and careful works, (to my mind, before it suffered this recent injury, far superior to everything at Antwerp, Malines, or Cologne,) [2] this was a more weighty reason for caution than for interference. Some portions of colour have been exhibited which were formerly untraceable; but even these have lost in power what they have gained in definiteness,—the majesty and preciousness of all the tones are departed, the balance of distances lost. Time may perhaps restore something of the glow, but never the subordination; and the more delicate portions of flesh tint, especially the back of the female figure on the left, and of the boy in the centre, are destroyed for ever.

---

[1] [No. 46. The cleaning of this picture was one of the principal counts in Mr. Morris Moore's indictment (see his letter to the *Times*, and Questions 2477–2479 in his evidence before the Select Committee of 1853. Sir Charles Eastlake's reply was that the picture had been already "restored" in 1802 (*ibid.*, Questions 4484–4847). For another reference to it, see above, "Review of Eastlake," § 34, p. 295.]

[2] [For Rubens' principal work at Cologne see Vol. II. p. 352; at Malines, in the Church of St. John, is his famous altar-piece, the "Adoration of the Magi"; and at Antwerp, in the Church of Notre Dame, his yet more celebrated "Descent from the Cross."]

5. The large Cuyp[1] is, I think, nearly uninjured. Many portions of the foreground painting have been revealed, which were before only to be traced painfully, if at all. The distance has indeed lost the appearance of sunny haze, which was its chief charm, but this I have little doubt it originally did not possess, and in process of time may recover.

6. The "Bacchus and Ariadne"[2] of Titian has escaped so scot free that, not knowing it had been cleaned, I passed it without noticing any change. I observed only that the blue of the distance was more intense than I had previously thought it, though, four years ago, I said of that distance that it was "difficult to imagine anything more magnificently impossible, not from its vividness, but because it is *not faint and aerial enough* to account for its purity of colour. There is so total a want of atmosphere in it, that but for the difference of form it would be impossible to distinguish the mountains from the robe of Ariadne."*

Your correspondent is alike unacquainted with the previous condition of this picture, and with the character of Titian distances in general, when he complains of a loss of aerial quality resulting in the present case from cleaning.

7. I unfortunately did not see the new Velasquez[3] until

---

* *Modern Painters*, vol. i. p. 146 [Vol. III. p. 269].

---

[1] ["Landscape, with Cattle and Figures—Evening" (No. 53). Since the bequest of the somewhat higher "large Dort" in 1876 (No. 961), it has ceased to be "the large Cuyp."]

[2] [No. 35. This and the two pictures already mentioned were the typical instances of "spoilt pictures" quoted by "Verax."]

[3] ["Philip IV. of Spain, hunting the Wild Boar" (No. 197), purchased in 1846, and thereupon cleaned. The Committee of 1853 elicited some curious information about this picture. Lord Cowley, its former owner, had sent it to a Mr. Thane, a picture-dealer, to be relined. A too hot iron was used, and a portion of the paint entirely disappeared. Thane was in despair. The picture haunted him at nights. He saw the figure of it in his dreams becoming more and more attenuated until at length it appeared a skeleton. He was near going mad over it, when a good angel came to his rescue in the shape of Lance, the flower and fruit painter, who offered to restore the missing parts out of his head. The parts which Lance claimed to have thus painted in were the groups on the left of the foreground, and some of the middle distance. "I endeavoured," he says, "to fill up the canvas, such as I supposed Velasquez would have done; and I had great facility in doing that, because if there was a man without a horse here, there was a horse without a man there, so I could easily

it had undergone its discipline, but I have seldom met with an example of the master which gave me more delight, or which I believed to be in more genuine or perfect condition. I saw no traces of the retouching which is hinted at by your correspondent "Verax," nor are the touches on that canvass such as to admit of very easy or untraceable interpolation of meaner handling. His complaint of loss of substance in the figures of the foreground is, I have no doubt, altogether groundless. He has seen little southern scenery if he supposes that the brilliancy and apparent nearness of the silver clouds is in the slightest degree overcharged, and shows little appreciation of Velasquez in supposing him to have sacrificed the solemnity and might of such a distance to the inferior interest of the figures in the foreground. Had he studied the picture attentively, he might have observed that the position of the horizon suggests, and the *lateral* extent of the foreground *proves*, such a distance between the spectator and even its nearest figures as may well justify the slightness of their execution.

Even granting that some of the upper glazings of the figures had been removed, the tone of the whole picture is so light, gray, and glittering, and the dependence on the power of its whites so absolute, that I think the process hardly to be regretted which has left these in lustre so precious, and restored to a brilliancy, which a comparison with any modern work of similar aim would render

take his execution as nearly as possible, and my own style of painting enabled me to keep pretty near the mark" (!). But he particularly added that the high lights of the sky (on which Ruskin here lays special stress) were untouched by him. So that there Ruskin was right. The picture, when restored to its owner, gave complete satisfaction, and Lance's share in it was kept a secret. A year or two later he must have felt a proud man. The picture was being exhibited at the British Gallery. In front of it Lance met two *cognoscenti* of his acquaintance. "It looks to me," he said, testing them, "as if it had been a good deal repainted."—"No! you're wrong there," they said; "it is remarkably free from repaints." It should be added that soon after the Parliamentary inquiry referred to above, a tracing of Goya's copy, procured from Madrid, showed in fact that the restored work differed but slightly from the copy, and Lance's work was probably far less important and extensive than he asserted. An idea of the original condition of the picture may be had from a reduced replica, or first sketch, now in the Wallace Collection.]

apparently supernatural, the sparkling motion of its figures and the serene snow of its sky.

8. I believe I have stated to its fullest extent all the harm that has yet been done, yet I earnestly protest against any continuance of the treatment to which these pictures have been subjected. It is useless to allege that nothing but discoloured varnish has been withdrawn, for it is perfectly possible to alter the structure and continuity, and so destroy the aerial relations of colours of which no part has been removed. I have seen the dark blue of a water-colour drawing made opaque and pale merely by mounting it; and even supposing no other injury were done, every time a picture is cleaned it loses, like a restored building, part of its authority; and is thenceforward liable to dispute and suspicion, every one of its beauties open to question, while its faults are screened from accusation. It cannot be any more reasoned from with security; for, though allowance may be made for the effect of time, no one can calculate the arbitrary and accidental changes occasioned by violent cleaning. None of the varnishes should be attacked; whatever the medium used, nothing but soot and dust should be taken away, and that chiefly by delicate and patient friction; and, in order to protract as long as possible the necessity even for this, all the important pictures in the gallery should at once be put under glass,[1] and closed, not merely by hinged doors, like the Correggio, but permanently and securely. I should be glad to see this done in all rich galleries, but it is peculiarly necessary in the case of pictures exposed in London, and to a crowd freely admitted four days in the week; it would do good also by necessitating the enlargement of the rooms, and the bringing down of all the pictures to the level of the eye. Every picture that is worth buying or retaining is worth exhibiting in

---

[1] [On this and other collateral subjects the reader is referred to the next letter; to Ruskin's evidence before the National Gallery Commission in 1857; and to the Appendix to his *Notes on the Turner Gallery at Marlborough House, 1856–1857*. With regard to the other strictures here pronounced, see above, Introduction, p. lix.]

its proper place, and if its scale be large and its handling rough, there is the more instruction to be gained by close study of the various means adopted by the master to secure his distant effect. We can certainly spare both the ground and the funds which would enable us to exhibit pictures for which no price is thought too large, and for all purposes of study and for most of enjoyment pictures are useless when they are even a little above the line. The fatigue complained of by most persons in examining a picture gallery[1] is attributable not to the number of works, but to their confused order of succession, and to the straining of the sight in endeavouring to penetrate the details of those above the eye. Every gallery should be long enough to admit of its whole collection being hung in one line, side by side, and wide enough to allow of the spectators retiring to the distance at which the largest picture was intended to be seen. The works of every master should be brought together and arranged in chronological order; and such drawings or engravings as may exist in the collection, either of, or for, its pictures, or in any way illustrative of them, should be placed in frames opposite each, in the middle of the room.

9. But, Sir, the subjects of regret connected with the present management of our national collection are not to be limited either to its treatment or its arrangement. The principles of selection which have been acted upon in the various purchases made in the course of the last five or six years have been as extraordinary as unjustifiable. Whatever may be the intrinsic power, interest, or artistical utility of the earlier essays of any school of art, it cannot be disputed that characteristic examples of every one of its most important phases should form part of a national collection: granting them of little value individually, their collective teaching is of irrefragable authority, and the exhibition of perfected results alone, while the course of national progress through which these were reached is altogether concealed,

---

[1] [Compare the letter of 1852 below, § 8, p. 413.]

is more likely to discourage than to assist the efforts of
an undeveloped school.   Granting even what the shallow-
est materialism of modern artists would assume, that the
works of Perugino were of no value but as they taught
Raphael, that John Bellini is altogether absorbed and over-
mastered by Titian—that Nino Pisano was utterly superseded
by Bandinelli[1] or Cellini, and Ghirlandajo sunk in the shadow
of Buonaroti—granting Van Eyck to be a mere mechanist,
and Giotto a mere child, and Angelico a superstitious monk,
and whatever you choose to grant that ever blindness deemed
or insolence affirmed, still it is to be maintained and proved,
that if we wish to have a Buonaroti or a Titian of our
own, we shall with more wisdom learn of those of whom
Buonaroti and Titian learned, and at whose knees they
were brought up, and whom to their day of death they
ever revered and worshipped, than of those wretched pupils
and partisans who sank every high function of art into a
form and a faction, betrayed her trusts, darkened her traditions, overthrew her throne, and left us where we now
are, stumbling among its fragments.   Sir, if the canvasses
of Guido, lately introduced into the gallery,[2] had been
works of the best of those pupils, which they are not—if
they had been good works of even that bad master, which
they are not,—if they had been genuine or untouched
works, even though feeble, which they are not—if, though
false and retouched remnants of a feeble and fallen school,
they had been endurably decent or elementarily instructive, some conceivable excuse might perhaps have been by
ingenuity forged, and by impudence uttered, for their introduction into a gallery where we previously possessed two
good Guidos[3] and no Perugino (for the attribution to him

---

[1] [For Bandinelli, see Vol. III. p. 618; for Cellini, Vol. IV. p. 318.]

[2] ["Lot and his Daughters leaving Sodom" (No. 193), purchased for the Gallery
in 1844; and "Susannah and the Elders" (No. 196), purchased in the same year.
For another criticism of these purchases, see Vol. III. p. 670.]

[3] [The "two good Guidos" previously possessed are the "St. Jerome" (No. 11)
and the "Magdalen" (No. 177).   The "wretched panel" is No. 181, "The Virgin
and Infant Christ with St. John": it is by some attributed to Perugino's scholar,
Lo Spagna.   In 1856 a very fine Perugino was purchased for the Gallery—"The

of the wretched panel which now bears his name is a mere insult), no Angelico, no Fra Bartolomeo, no Albertinelli, no Ghirlandajo, no Verrochio, no Lorenzo di Credi—(what shall I more say, for the time would fail me?)—but now, Sir, what vestige of apology remains for the cumbering our walls with pictures that have no single virtue, no colour, no drawing, no character, no history, no thought? Yet 2000 guineas were, I believe, given for one of those encumbrances,[1] and 5000 for the coarse and unnecessary Rubens,[2] added to a room half filled with Rubens before, while a mighty and perfect work of Angelico was sold from Cardinal Fesch's collection for 1500.[3] I do not speak of the spurious Holbein,[4] for though the veriest tyro might well be ashamed of such a purchase, it would have been a judicious addition had it been genuine; so was the John Bellini, so was the Van Eyck; but the mighty Venetian master who alone of all the painters of Italy united purity of religious aim with perfection of artistical

Virgin adoring the Infant Christ, the Archangel Michael, the Archangel Raphael and Tobias" (No. 288)—an acquisition which greatly delighted Ruskin (see, *e.g.*, *Elements of Drawing*, § 199). Other examples were afterwards added. The Gallery boasts also two Angelicos, "The Adoration of the Magi" (No. 582), and "Christ amid the Blessed" (No. 663), purchased in 1857 and 1860;—one Albertinelli, "Virgin and Child" (No. 645), also purchased in 1860;—and two Lorenzo di Credis, both of the "Virgin and Child" (Nos. 593 and 648), purchased in 1857 and 1865. A work which is attributed to Fra Bartolommeo—"Virgin and Child with St. John" (No. 1694)—was purchased in 1900. The Gallery still possesses no D. Ghirlandajo, and no Verrocchio.]

[1] [For Guido's "Lot and his Daughters" the sum of £1680 was paid.]

[2] ["The Judgment of Paris" (No. 194), purchased from Mr. Penrice's collection in 1846. The price was £4200.]

[3] ["The Last Judgment";—its purchaser was the Earl of Dudley, from whom it was subsequently acquired by the Berlin Museum. A photographic reproduction of this work (pronounced the most important of all Angelico's representations of the subject), is given at p. 132 of Mr. Langton Douglas' *Fra Angelico*, and an engraving of it in Mrs. Jameson's *History of Our Lord*, ii. 414. Cardinal Fesch was Archbishop of Lyons, and the uncle of Napoleon Buonaparte. His gallery contained in its time the finest private collection of pictures in Rome.]

[4] [The "libel on Holbein" was bought as an original, from Mr. Rochard, in 1845, for £630. And very much ashamed the Trustees were, when immediately after the purchase the facts were discovered; they subscribed £100 between them, which they offered to the dealer, "to induce him to annul the bargain, but he declined, and there was an end of it" (*Report of the Select Committee*, 1853, Q. 6181). It now figures in the National Gallery as "A Medical Professor," German school, sixteenth century (No. 195).]

power, is poorly represented by a single head;[1] and I ask, in the name of the earnest students of England, that the funds set apart for her Gallery may no longer be played with like pebbles in London auction-rooms. Let agents be sent to all the cities of Italy; let the noble pictures which are perishing there be rescued from the invisibility and ill-treatment which their position too commonly implies, and let us have a national collection which, however imperfect, shall be orderly and continuous, and shall exhibit with something like relative candour and justice the claims to our reverence of those great and ancient builders, whose mighty foundation has been for two centuries concealed by wood, and hay, and stubble, the distorted growing, and thin gleaning of vain men in blasted fields.

I have the honour to be, Sir,

Your obedient servant,

THE AUTHOR OF "MODERN PAINTERS."

Jan. 6.

---

[1] [The Bellini is the "Portrait of Doge Leonardo Loredano" (No. 189), purchased in 1844 : for another remark on the picture, see p. 287 ; and for Ruskin's estimate of Bellini, compare especially *The Relation between Michael Angelo and Tintoret*. Several other examples of Bellini have since been added to the Gallery (Nos. 280, 599, 726, 803, 812, 1233, 1440, 1455). The Van Eyck is the "Portrait of Jean Arnolfini and his Wife" (No. 186), purchased in 1842 ; for a description of it, see above, p. 256.]

II

THE NATIONAL GALLERY [1]

1852

To the Editor of the "Times"

1. SIR,—I trust that the excitement which has been caused by the alleged destruction of some of the most important pictures in the National Gallery will not be without results, whatever may be the facts of the case with respect to the works in question. Under the name of "restoration," the ruin of the noblest architecture and painting is constant throughout Europe. We shall show ourselves wiser than our neighbours [2] if the loss of two Claudes and the injury of a Paul Veronese [3] induce us to pay so much attention to the preservation of ancient art as may prevent it from becoming a disputed question in future whether they are indeed pictures which we possess or their skeletons.

2. As to the facts in the present instance, I can give no opinion. Sir Charles Eastlake and Mr. Uwins [4] know more than I of oil paintings in general, and have far more profound respect for those of Claude in particular. I do not suppose they would have taken from him his golden

---

[1] [From the *Times*, December 29, 1852; the letter was headed as above : see above, Introduction, p. lix.]

[2] [See above, p. 398 *n*.]

[3] [Claude's " Marriage of Isaac and Rebecca " (No. 12), and his " Queen of Sheba " picture (No. 14, Seaport, with figures). The only pictures of Veronese which the Gallery at this time contained, were the " Consecration of St. Nicholas " (No. 26), and the " Rape of Europa " (No. 97). It is the former of these two that is here spoken of as injured. Much evidence was taken by the Select Committee of 1853 on the " restoration " of these pictures in the preceding year.]

[4] [Mr. Thomas Uwins, R.A., had succeeded Sir Charles Eastlake as Keeper of the National Gallery in 1847 ; and resigned, in part owing to hostile criticism, in 1855.]

armour that Turner might bear away a dishonourable victory in the noble passage of arms to which he has challenged his rival from the grave.* Nor can the public
suppose that the curators of the National Gallery have
any interest in destroying the works with which they are
intrusted. If, acting to the best of their judgment, they
have done harm, to whom are we to look for greater
prudence or better success? Are the public prepared to
withdraw their confidence from Sir C. Eastlake and the
members of the Royal Academy, and intrust the national
property to Mr. Morris Moore, or to any of the artists and
amateurs who have inflamed the sheets of the *Times* with
their indignation? Is it not evident that the only security
which the nation can possess for its pictures must be found
in taking such measures as may in future prevent the
necessity of their being touched at all? For this is very
certain, that all question respecting the effects of cleaning
is merely one of the amount of injury. Every picture
which has undergone more friction than is necessary at
intervals for the removal of dust or chill[1] has suffered injury
to some extent. The last touches of the master leave
the surface of the colour with a certain substantial texture,
the bloom of which, if once reached under the varnish,
must inevitably be more or less removed by friction of any
kind,—how much more by friction aided by solvents? I
am well assured that every possessor of pictures who truly
loves them, would keep—if it might be—their surfaces from

---

* The public may not, perhaps, be generally aware that the condition
by which the nation retains the two pictures bequeathed to it by Turner,
and now in the National Gallery, is that "they shall be hung beside
Claudes."[2]

---

[1] [The word "chill" in the *Times* was printed "dirt" in *Arrows of the Chace*. In
the MS. draft the word is "damp." Chill or damp seems to be what Ruskin meant:
see the end of § 6, below.]
[2] ["Dido building Carthage" (No. 498), and "The Sun rising in a Mist" (No. 479).
The actual wording of Turner's will on the matter ran thus: "I direct that the said
pictures, or paintings, shall be hung, kept, and placed, that is to say, always between
the two pictures painted by Claude, the Seaport and the Mill." Accordingly they
now hang side by side with these two pictures (Nos. 5 and 12) in the National Gallery.]

being so much as breathed upon, which may, indeed, be done, and done easily.

3. Every stranger who enters our National Gallery, if he be a thoughtful person, must assuredly put to himself a curious question. Perceiving that certain pictures—namely, three Correggios, two Raphaels, and a John Bellini—are put under glass,[1] and that all the others are left exposed, as oil pictures are in general, he must ask himself,—"Is it an ascertained fact that glass preserves pictures; and are none of the pictures here thought worth a pane of glass but these five?[2] Or is it unascertained whether glass is beneficial or injurious, and have the Raphaels and Correggios been selected for the trial—'*Fiat experimentum in corpore vili?*'" Some years ago it might have been difficult to answer him; now the answer is easy, though it be strange. The experiment has been made. The Raphaels and Correggios have been under glass for many years: they are as fresh and lovely as when they were first enclosed; they need no cleaning, and will need none for half a century to come; and it must be, therefore, that the rest of the pictures are left exposed to the London atmosphere and to the operations which its influence renders necessary, simply because they are not thought worth a pane of plate glass. No. There is yet one other possible answer,—that many of them are hung so high, or in such lights, that they could not be seen if they were glazed. Is it then absolutely necessary that they should be hung so high? We are about to build a new National Gallery;[3] may it not be so arranged as that the pictures we place therein may at once be safe and visible?

---

[1] [See above, Introduction, p. lix.]

[2] [Apparently a misprint, as *six* pictures are mentioned.]

[3] [The existing National Gallery was opened in 1838, but only six of the rooms were at first devoted to the collection, the remaining space being allotted to the Royal Academy of Arts (whose inscription may still be seen over a disused doorway). The enlargement or removal of the Gallery had for some years been mooted, and the Select Committee of 1853 suggested a site at Kensington. This recommendation, however, was not adopted. In 1860, 1876, and 1884 the Gallery was enlarged, and in 1869 the Royal Academy removed to Burlington House.]

4. I know that this has never yet been done in any gallery in Europe, for the European public have never yet reflected that a picture which was worth buying was also worth seeing. Some time or other they will assuredly awake to the perception of this wonderful truth, and it would be some credit to our English common sense if we were the first to act upon it.

5. I say that a picture which is worth buying is also worth seeing; that is, worth so much room of ground and wall as shall enable us to see it to the best advantage. It is not commonly so understood. Nations, like individuals, buy their pictures in mere ostentation, and are content, so that their possessions are acknowledged, that they should be hung in any dark or out-of-the-way corners which their frames will fit. Or, at best, the popular idea of a national gallery is that of a magnificent palace, whose walls must be decorated with coloured panels, every one of which shall cost £1000, and be discernible, through a telescope, for the work of a mighty hand.

6. I have no doubt that in a few years more there will be a change of feeling in this matter, and that men will begin to perceive, what is indeed the truth—that every noble picture is a manuscript book, of which only one copy exists, or ever can exist; that a national gallery is a great library, of which the books must be read upon their shelves; that every manuscript ought, therefore, to be placed where it can be read most easily;[1] and that the style of the architecture and the effect of the saloons are matters of no importance whatsoever, but that our solicitude ought to begin and end in the two imperative requirements—that every picture in the gallery should be perfectly seen and perfectly safe; that none should be thrust up, or down, or aside, to make room for more important ones; that all

---

[1] ["The Art of a nation is, I think, one of the most important points of its history, and a part which, if once destroyed, no history will ever supply the place of; and the first idea of a National Gallery is that it should be a Library of Art, in which the rudest efforts are, in some cases, hardly less important than the noblest."—*National Gallery Commission*, 1857,—Ruskin's evidence. Compare also *St. Mark's Rest*, Preface.]

should be in a good light, all on a level with the eye, and all secure from damp, cold, impurity of atmosphere, and every other avoidable cause of deterioration.

7. These are the things to be accomplished; and if we set ourselves to do these in our new National Gallery, we shall have made a greater step in art-teaching than if we had built a new Parthenon. I know that it will be a strange idea to most of us that Titians and Tintorets ought, indeed, all to have places upon "the line," as well as the annual productions of our Royal Academicians;[1] and I know that the *coup d'œil* of the Gallery must be entirely destroyed by such an arrangement. But great pictures ought not to be subjects of "*coups d'œil*." In the last arrangement of the Louvre, under the Republic, all the noble pictures in the gallery were brought into one room, with a Napoleon-like resolution to produce effect by concentration of force; and, indeed, I would not part willingly with the memory of that saloon, whose obscurest shadows were full of Correggio; in whose out-of-the-way angles one forgot, here and there, a Raphael; and in which the best Tintoret on this side of the Alps was hung sixty feet from the ground![2] But Cleopatra dissolving the pearl was nothing to this; and I trust that in our own Gallery our poverty, if not our will,[3] may consent to a more modest and less lavish manner of displaying such treasures as are intrusted to us, and that the very limitation of our possessions may induce us to make that the object of our care which can hardly be a ground of ostentation. It might, indeed, be a matter of some difficulty to conceive an arrangement of the collections in the Louvre or the Florence Gallery which should

---

[1] [It will be remembered that the exhibitions of the Royal Academy were at this time held in the National Gallery.]

[2] [The galleries of the Louvre were reorganized on their being declared national instead of Crown property, after the Revolution of 1848; and the choicest pictures were then collected together in the "grand salon carré," which, although since re-arranged, still contains a similar selection. The "best Tintoret on this side of the Alps" is the "Susannah and the Elders," now No. 349 in that room : for a description of it, see below, p. 459. Ruskin refers again to the position of the picture in *Cestus of Aglaia*, § 4.]

[3] [*Romeo and Juliet*, v. 1.]

admit of every picture being hung upon the line. But the works in our own, including the Vernon and Turner bequests,[1] present no obstacle in their number to our making the building which shall receive them a perfect model of what a National Gallery ought to be. And the conditions of this perfection are so simple that if we only turn our attention to these main points it will need no great architectural ingenuity to attain all that is required.

8. It is evident, in the first place, that the building ought to consist of a series of chambers or galleries lighted from above, and built with such reference to the pictures they are to contain, as that opposite a large picture room enough should be allowed for the spectator to retire to the utmost distance at which it can ever be desirable that its effect should be seen; but, as economy of space would become a most important object when every picture was to be hung on a level with the eye, smaller apartments might open from the larger ones for the reception of smaller pictures, one condition being, however, made imperative, whatever space was sacrificed to it—namely, that the works of every master should be collected together, either in the same apartment or in contiguous ones. Nothing has so much retarded the advance of art as our miserable habit of mixing the works of every master and of every century. More would be learned by an ordinarily intelligent observer in simply passing from a room in which there were only Titians to another in which there were only Caraccis, than by reading a volume of lectures on colour. Few minds are strong enough first to abstract and then to generalize the characters of paintings hung at random. Few minds are so dull as not at once to perceive the points of difference, were the works of each painter set by themselves. The fatigue of which most persons complain in passing

---

[1] [The *gift* of Mr. Robert Vernon, in 1847, consisted of 157 pictures, all of them, with two exceptions only, of the British school. The Turner bequest included 105 finished oil paintings, in addition to the numerous sketches and drawings. Works of the British school were at this time shown in Marlborough House; it was not till 1876 that the whole collection was housed under a single roof.]

through a picture gallery,[1] as at present arranged, is indeed partly caused by the straining effort to see what is out of sight, but not less by the continual change of temper and of tone of thought, demanded in passing from the work of one master to that of another.

9. The works of each being, therefore, set by themselves,* and the whole collection arranged in chronological and ethnological order, let apartments be designed for each group large enough to admit of the increase of the existing collection to any probable amount. The whole gallery would thus become of great length, but might be adapted to any form of ground-plan by disposing the whole in a labyrinthine chain, returning upon itself.[2] Its chronological arrangement would necessitate its being continuous, rather than divided into many branches or sections. Being lighted from above, it must be all on the same floor, but ought at least to be raised one story above the ground, and might admit any number of keepers' apartments, or of schools, beneath; though it would be better to make it quite independent of these, in order to diminish the risk of fire. Its walls ought on every side to be surrounded by corridors, so that the interior temperature might be kept equal, and no outer surface of wall on which pictures were hung exposed to the weather. Every picture should be glazed, and the horizon which the painter had given to it placed on a level with the eye.

10. Lastly, opposite each picture should be a table, containing, under glass, every engraving that had ever been made from it, and any studies for it, by the master's own hand,

---

* An example of a cognate school might, however, be occasionally introduced for the sake of direct comparison, as in one instance would be necessitated by the condition above mentioned attached to part of the Turner bequest.

---

[1] [See above, p. 403; and compare what Ruskin says in Vol. III. pp. 651–652, of the strain of passing from one painter to another.]

[2] [Ruskin is here working out an idea which occurred to him at Venice, on first hearing of Turner's bequest: see the letter to his father given in the Introduction to Vol. XIII.]

that remained, or were obtainable. The values of the study and of the picture are reciprocally increased—of the former more than doubled—by their being seen together; and, if this system were once adopted, the keepers of the various galleries of Europe would doubtless consent to such exchanges of the sketches in their possession as would render all their collections more interesting.

I trust, Sir, that the importance of this subject will excuse the extent of my trespass upon your columns, and that the simplicity and self-evident desirableness of the arrangement I have described may vindicate my proposal of it from the charge of presumption.

I have the honour to be, Sir,
Your obedient servant,
THE AUTHOR OF "MODERN PAINTERS."

HERNE HILL, DULWICH, *Dec.* 27.

VII

THE OPENING

OF

THE CRYSTAL PALACE

CONSIDERED IN SOME OF ITS RELATIONS TO
THE PROSPECTS OF ART

BY

JOHN RUSKIN

(1854)

[*Bibliographical Note.*—Of this pamphlet there has been only one separate edition, in 1854. The title-page is :—

The Opening | of | The Crystal Palace | considered in some of its Relations | to the prospects of Art. | By | John Ruskin, M.A., | Author of | "The Stones of Venice," "The Seven Lamps of Architecture," "Modern Painters," etc. | London : | Smith, Elder & Co., 65. Cornhill. | 1854.

Octavo, pp. 21. The imprint is on the reverse of the title-page : " London : A. and G. A. Spottiswoode, New Street Square." It is repeated on the reverse of p. 21, where also is an announcement that the Third Volume of *Modern Painters* was "preparing for publication." Issued on July 22, 1854, in stiffened, buff-coloured wrappers, with the title-page (enclosed in a ruled frame) repeated on the front cover. Price one shilling.

The pamphlet was reprinted in *On the Old Road*, 1885, vol. i. pp. 349–370 (§§ 253–273), and again in the second edition of that collection, 1899, vol. i. pp. 355–375 (§§ 253–273).]

The variations in the text are these : § 1, line 5, "Simmenthal" misprinted "Simnenthal" in the first reprint; line 9, "those low larch huts" misprinted "those lowland huts" in both reprints; line 12, "power" in all previous editions, is here altered, as required by the context, to "powers"; in § 8, line 5, "possible" was misprinted "impossible" in both reprints; so also in § 12, line 4, "without" was misprinted "with"; in § 13, line 12, "be indeed" was misprinted "indeed be"; and in § 14, line 6, "prolongations," "prolongation." A few variations in punctuation are not enumerated.

The numbering of the paragraphs was introduced in *On the Old Road,* the numbers being consecutive throughout the volume. In this edition, the paragraphs in the pamphlet are numbered independently (§§ 1–21).]

THE OPENING OF
THE CRYSTAL PALACE

CONSIDERED IN SOME OF ITS RELATIONS TO
THE PROSPECTS OF ART

1. I READ the account in the *Times* newspaper of the opening of the Crystal Palace at Sydenham as I ascended the hill between Vevay and Châtel St. Denis,[1] and the thoughts which it called up haunted me all day long, as my road wound among the grassy slopes of the Simmenthal. There was a strange contrast between the image of that mighty palace, raised so high above the hills on which it is built as to make them seem little less than a basement for its glittering stateliness, and those low larch huts, half hidden beneath their coverts of forest, and scattered like grey stones along the masses of far-away mountain. Here, man contending with the powers of Nature for his existence; there commanding them for his recreation: here, a feeble folk nested among the rocks with the wild goat and the coney,[2] and retaining the same quiet thoughts from generation to generation; there, a great multitude triumphing in the splendour of immeasurable habitation, and haughty with hope of endless progress and irresistible power.

2. It is indeed impossible to limit, in imagination, the beneficent results which may follow from the undertaking

---

[1] [The opening of the Palace by Queen Victoria and the Prince Consort was on June 10, 1854. Ruskin was in Switzerland with his parents at the time. In the middle of June they went from Vevay to Thun, by the Simmenthal; Châtel St. Denis is about ten miles on the road from Vevay.]

[2] [See Proverbs xxx. 26.]

thus happily begun.[1] For the first time in the history of the world, a national museum is formed in which a whole nation is interested; formed on a scale which permits the exhibition of monuments of art in unbroken symmetry, and of the productions of nature in unthwarted growth,—formed under the auspices of science which can hardly err, and of wealth which can hardly be exhausted; and placed in the close neighbourhood of a metropolis overflowing with a population weary of labour, yet thirsting for knowledge, where contemplation may be consistent with rest, and instruction with enjoyment.   It is impossible, I repeat, to estimate the influence of such an institution on the minds of the working-classes.   How many hours once wasted may now be profitably dedicated to pursuits in which interest was first awakened by some accidental display in the Norwood palace; how many constitutions, almost broken, may be restored by the healthy temptation into the country air,—how many intellects, once dormant, may be roused into activity within the crystal walls, and how these noble results may go on multiplying and increasing and bearing fruit seventy times seven-fold, as the nation pursues its career, — are questions as full of hope as incapable of calculation.   But with all these grounds for hope there are others for despondency, giving rise to a group of melancholy thoughts, of which I can neither repress the importunity nor forbear the expression.

3. For three hundred years, the art of architecture has been the subject of the most curious investigation; its principles have been discussed with all earnestness and acuteness; its models in all countries and of all ages have been examined with scrupulous care, and imitated with unsparing expenditure.   And of all this refinement of inquiry,—this lofty search after the ideal,—this subtlety of investigation

---

[1] [Ruskin, as we have seen, was interested in the scheme of the Crystal Palace as a museum, and especially in its casts of mediæval architecture : see *Stones of Venice*, vol. ii. (Vol. X. p. 416).   For other allusions to the Palace, see *Stones of Venice*, vol. i. (Vol. IX. p. 456), and *Aratra Pentelici*, § 53.]

and sumptuousness of practice,—the great result, the admirable and long-expected conclusion is, that in the centre of the nineteenth century, we suppose ourselves to have invented a new style of architecture, when we have magnified a conservatory!

4. In Mr. Laing's speech,[1] at the opening of the Palace, he declares that "*an entirely novel order of architecture*, producing, by means of unrivalled mechanical ingenuity, the most marvellous and beautiful effects, sprang into existence to provide a building." *   In these words, the speaker is not merely giving utterance to his own feelings.   He is expressing the popular view of the facts, nor that a view merely popular, but one which has been encouraged by nearly all the professors of art of our time.

It is to this, then, that our Doric and Palladian pride is at last reduced!   We have vaunted the divinity of the Greek ideal—we have plumed ourselves on the purity of our Italian taste—we have cast our whole souls into the proportions of pillars and the relations of orders—and behold the end!   Our taste, thus exalted and disciplined, is dazzled by the lustre of a few rows of panes of glass; and the first principles of architectural sublimity, so far sought, are found all the while to have consisted merely in sparkling and in space.

Let it not be thought that I would depreciate (were it possible to depreciate) the mechanical ingenuity which has been displayed in the erection of the Crystal Palace, or that I underrate the effect which its vastness may continue to produce on the popular imagination.   But mechanical ingenuity is *not* the essence either of painting or architecture,[2] and largeness of dimension does not necessarily involve nobleness of design.   There is assuredly as much ingenuity

* See the *Times* of Monday, June 12th.

---

[1] [Samuel Laing (1812-1897), at that time chairman of the Crystal Palace Company, and also for many years of the London, Brighton, and South Coast Railway.   The words quoted are from the Address to the Queen.]

[2] [See *Seven Lamps*, ch. i. § 1 (Vol. VIII. pp. 27–28).]

required to build a screw frigate, or a tubular bridge, as a hall of glass;—all these are works characteristic of the age; and all, in their several ways, deserve our highest admiration, but not admiration of the kind that is rendered to poetry or to art. We may cover the German Ocean with frigates, and bridge the Bristol Channel with iron, and roof the county of Middlesex with crystal, and yet not possess one Milton, or Michael Angelo.

5. Well, it may be replied, we need our bridges, and have pleasure in our palaces; but we do not want Miltons, nor Michael Angelos.

Truly, it seems so; for, in the year in which the first Crystal Palace was built, there died among us a man whose name, in after-ages, will stand with those of the great of all time. Dying, he bequeathed to the nation the whole mass of his most cherished works; and for these three years, while we have been building this colossal receptacle for casts and copies of the art of other nations, these works of our own greatest painter have been left to decay in a dark room near Cavendish Square,[1] under the custody of an aged servant.

This is quite natural. But it is also memorable.[2]

6. There is another interesting fact connected with the history of the Crystal Palace as it bears on that of the art of Europe, namely, that in the year 1851, when all that glittering roof was built, in order to exhibit the paltry arts of our fashionable luxury—the carved bedsteads of Vienna, and glued toys of Switzerland, and gay jewellery of France[3]

---

[1] [That is, in Turner's own gallery in his house in Queen Anne Street. The disposition of his pictures under his will, long litigated, was not settled till March 1856.]

[2] [The MS. continues:—

"The Florentines exiled their Dante, and whitewashed the paintings of their Giotto. Five hundred years passed by, and they scrape the whitewash away in crumbs, bring to light the faded portrait of the exile, to exclaim in triumph 'l'abbiamo, il nostro poeta.' Is this indeed the course of nature? Must it be so for ever?"

For the discovery of Giotto's portrait of Dante, see Vol. IV. p. 188 n.]

[3] [In the MS. there is an additional passage—a digression on the Great Exhibition of 1851—which is of interest:—

"I cannot help noticing with some surprise the conclusions said to have been arrived at by the thinking portion of the English public, in the course

—in that very year, I say, the greatest pictures of the Venetian masters were rotting at Venice in the rain, for want of roof to cover them, with holes made by cannon shot through their canvass.[1]

There is another fact, however, more curious than either of these, which will hereafter be connected with the history of the palace now in building; namely, that at the very period when Europe is congratulated on the invention of a new style of architecture, because fourteen acres of ground have been covered with glass, the greatest examples in existence of true and noble Christian architecture are being resolutely destroyed; and destroyed by the effects of the very interest which was beginning to be excited by them.

7. Under the firm and wise government of the third Napoleon,[2] France has entered on a new epoch of prosperity, one of the signs of which is a zealous care for the preservation of her noble public buildings. Under the influence of

of their examination of the contents of the former Exhibition. I say with surprise — not because those conclusions are in any wit false — but because, unless I had been told so, I should not have fancied them *new*. For instance, one of these important conclusions is said to be, that articles of foreign manufacture are in better taste than those of English. Did it verily need a Great Exhibition to assure us of this? Have we been a nation of travellers for the last forty years, and have we absolutely come to no conclusion respecting the manufactures of the Continent. When we land at Calais or Boulogne, and enter the chambers of an hotel, it requires no very acute intelligence to discover that the locks will not fasten, and the knives will not cut, that the curtains hang prettily, and the furniture is fashioned and arranged with an aim at agreeable effect, not found in the respectable but tasteless rooms of our English hostelries. And it might surely from these facts enter into the traveller's mind, nor would his further inquiries fail to confirm the impression, that possibly Sheffield cutlery, and French embroidery might both be good of their kind; but that Bar Iron ought not in general to be purchased at Paris, nor the patterns of silks to be accepted from Yorkshire. Had, indeed, no such conclusion as this been arrived at before the year 1851?"]

[1] [See *Modern Painters*, vol. ii. (Vol. IV. pp. 40, 395).]
[2] [For other expressions of Ruskin's admiration for Napoleon III., see above, *Lectures on Architecture and Painting*, § 32, p. 55 n. He approved even of the *coup d'état* of December 2, 1851, as appears from the following letter to his father :—

"VENICE, *December* 23 [1851].— . . . I quite agree with you in rejoicing at L. Napoleon's piece of despotism, and am only sorry he let Thiers go—the greatest mischief-maker of the set. . . . I am surprised to hear the Austrians here expressing fear of 'war with France in three months.' They seem to think Napoleon cannot keep his place except by war. I begin, however, to pay little attention to anybody's anticipations, and never to expect anything that *is expected*."]

this healthy impulse, repairs of the most extensive kind are at this moment proceeding, on the cathedrals of Rheims, Amiens, Rouen, Chartres, and Paris; (probably also in many other instances unknown to me). These repairs were, in many cases, necessary up to a certain point; and they have been executed by architects as skilful and learned as at present exist,—executed with noble disregard of expense, and sincere desire on the part of their superintendents that they should be completed in a manner honourable to the country.

8. They are, nevertheless, more fatal to the monuments they are intended to preserve, than fire, war, or revolution. For they are undertaken, in the plurality of instances, under an impression, which the efforts of all true antiquaries have as yet been unable to remove, that it is possible to reproduce the mutilated sculpture of past ages in its original beauty.

"Reproduire avec une exactitude mathematique," are the words used, by one of the most intelligent writers on this subject,* of the proposed regeneration of the statue of Ste. Modeste, on the north porch of the Cathedral of Chartres.

Now it is not the question at present, whether thirteenth century sculpture be of value, or not. Its value is assumed by the authorities who have devoted sums so large to its so-called restoration, and may therefore be assumed in my argument. The worst state of the sculptures whose restoration is demanded may be fairly represented by that of the celebrated group of the Fates, among the Elgin Marbles in the British Museum. With what favour would the guardians of those marbles, or any other persons interested in Greek art, receive a proposal from a living sculptor to "reproduce with mathematical exactitude" the group of the Fates, in a perfect form, and to destroy the original? For with exactly such favour, those who are interested in Gothic

---

* M. l'Abbé Bulteau, *Description de la Cathédrale de Chartres* (8vo, Paris, Sagnier et Bray, 1850), p. 98, *note*.

art should receive proposals to reproduce the sculpture of Chartres or Rouen.

9. In like manner, the state of the architecture which it is proposed to restore may, at its worst, be fairly represented to the British public by that of the best preserved portions of Melrose Abbey.[1] With what encouragement would those among us who are sincerely interested in history, or in art, receive a proposal to pull down Melrose Abbey, and "reproduce it mathematically"? There can be no doubt of the answer which, in the instances supposed, it would be proper to return. "By all means, if you can, reproduce mathematically, elsewhere, the group of the Fates, and the Abbey of Melrose. But leave unharmed the original fragment, and the existing ruin."[2] And an answer of the same tenour ought to be given to every proposal to restore a Gothic sculpture or building. Carve or raise a model of it in some other part of the city; but touch not the actual edifice, except only so far as may be necessary to sustain, to protect it. I said above that repairs were in many instances necessary. These necessary operations consist in substituting new stones for decayed ones, where they are absolutely essential to the stability of the fabric; in propping, with wood or metal, the portions likely to give way; in binding or cementing into their places the sculptures which are ready to detach themselves; and in general care to remove luxuriant weeds and obstructions of the channels for the discharge of the rain. But no modern or imitative sculpture ought *ever*, under any circumstances, to be mingled with the ancient work.

10. Unfortunately, repairs thus conscientiously executed are always unsightly, and meet with little approbation from the general public; so that a strong temptation is necessarily felt by the superintendents of public works to execute the required repairs in a manner which, though indeed fatal

---

[1] [Compare above, *Lectures on Architecture and Painting*, § 24, p. 48.]
[2] [Compare Ruskin's letter on the restoration of Ribbesford Church, reprinted in *Arrows of the Chace*, 1880, vol. i. pp. 235–236, and in a later volume of this edition.]

to the monument, may be, in appearance, seemly. But a far more cruel temptation is held out to the architect. He who should propose to a municipal body to build in the form of a new church, to be erected in some other part of their city, models of such portions of their cathedral as were falling into decay, would be looked upon as merely asking for employment, and his offer would be rejected with disdain. But let an architect declare that the existing fabric stands in need of repairs, and offer to restore it to its original beauty, and he is instantly regarded as a lover of his country, and has a chance of obtaining a commission which will furnish him with a large and ready income, and enormous patronage, for twenty or thirty years to come.

11. I have great respect for human nature. But I would rather leave it to others than myself to pronounce how far such a temptation is always likely to be resisted, and how far, when repairs are once permitted to be undertaken, a fabric is likely to be spared from mere interest in its beauty, when its destruction, under the name of restoration, has become permanently remunerative to a large body of workmen.

Let us assume, however, that the architect is always conscientious—always willing, the moment he has done what is strictly necessary for the safety and decorous aspect of the building, to abandon his income, and declare his farther services unnecessary. Let us presume, also, that every one of the two or three hundred workmen who must be employed under him is equally conscientious, and, during the course of years of labour, will never destroy in carelessness what it may be inconvenient to save, or in cunning what it is difficult to imitate. Will all this probity of purpose preserve the hand from error, and the heart from weariness? Will it give dexterity to the awkward—sagacity to the dull—and at once invest two or three hundred imperfectly educated men with the feeling, intention, and information of the freemasons of the thirteenth century? Grant that it can· do all this, and that the new building

is both equal to the old in beauty, and precisely correspondent to it in detail. Is it, therefore, altogether *worth*
the old building? Is the stone carved to-day in their
masons' yards altogether the same in value to the hearts
of the French people as that which the eyes of St. Louis
saw lifted to its place? Would a loving daughter, in mere
desire for gaudy dress, ask a jeweller for a bright facsimile
of the worn cross which her mother bequeathed to her on
her deathbed?—would a thoughtful nation, in mere fondness
for splendour of streets, ask its architects to provide for it
facsimiles of the temples which for centuries had given joy
to its saints, comfort to its mourners, and strength to its
chivalry?

12. But it may be replied, that all this is already admitted by the antiquaries of France and England; and that
it is impossible that works so important should now be
undertaken without due consideration and faithful superintendence.

I answer, that the men who justly feel these truths are
rarely those who have much influence in public affairs. It
is the poor abbé, whose little garden is sheltered by the
mighty buttresses from the north wind, who knows the
worth of the cathedral. It is the bustling mayor and the
prosperous architect who determine its fate.

I answer farther, by the statement of a simple fact. I
have given many years, in many cities, to the study of
Gothic architecture; and of all that I know, or knew, the
entrance to the north transept of Rouen Cathedral was,
on the whole, the most beautiful—beautiful, not only as
an elaborate and faultless work of the finest time of Gothic
art, but yet more beautiful in the partial, though not
dangerous, decay which had touched its pinnacles with
pensive colouring, and softened its severer lines with unexpected change and delicate fracture, like sweet breaks in a
distant music. The upper part of it has been already
restored to the white accuracies of novelty; the lower
pinnacles, which flanked its approach, far more exquisite in

their partial ruin than the loveliest remains of our English abbeys, have been entirely destroyed, and rebuilt in rough blocks, now in process of sculpture. This restoration, so far as it has gone, has been executed by peculiarly skilful workmen; it is an unusually favourable example of restoration, especially in the care which has been taken to preserve intact the exquisite, and hitherto almost uninjured sculptures which fill the quatrefoils of the tracery above the arch. But I happened myself to have made, five years ago, detailed drawings of the buttress decorations on the right and left of this tracery, which are part of the work that has been completely restored, And I found the restorations as inaccurate as they were unnecessary.[1]

13. If this is the case in a most favourable instance, in that of a well-known monument, highly esteemed by every antiquary in France, what, during the progress of the now almost universal repair, is likely to become of architecture which is unwatched and despised?

Despised! and more than despised—even hated! It is a sad truth, that there is something in the solemn aspect of ancient architecture which, in rebuking frivolity and chastening gaiety, has become at this time literally *repulsive* to a large majority of the population of Europe. Examine the direction which is taken by all the influences of fortune and of fancy, wherever they concern themselves with art, and it will be found that the real, earnest effort of the upper classes of European society is to make every place in the world as much like the Champs Elysées of Paris as possible. Wherever the influence of that educated society is felt, the old buildings are relentlessly destroyed; vast hotels, like barracks, and rows of high, square-windowed dwelling-houses, thrust themselves forward to conceal the hated antiquities of the great cities of France and Italy. Gay promenades, with fountains and statues, prolong themselves along the quays once dedicated to commerce; ball-rooms

---

[1] [For some of Ruskin's drawings of details on this porch, see *Seven Lamps of Architecture*, Plate 1 (Fig. 2), 10 (Figs. 1–4).]

and theatres rise upon the dust of desecrated chapels, and thrust into darkness the humility of domestic life.   And when the formal street, in all its pride of perfumery and confectionery, has successfully consumed its way through wrecks of historical monuments, and consummated its symmetry in the ruin of all that once prompted a reflection, or pleaded for regard, the whitened city is praised for its splendour, and the exulting inhabitants for their patriotism— patriotism which consists in insulting their fathers with forgetfulness, and surrounding their children with temptation.

14. I am far from intending my words to involve any disrespectful allusion to the very noble improvements in the city of Paris itself, lately carried out under the encouragement of the Emperor.   Paris, in its own peculiar character of bright magnificence, had nothing to fear, and everything to gain, from the gorgeous prolongations of the Rue Rivoli.[1] But I speak of the general influence of the rich travellers and proprietors of Europe on the cities which they pretend to admire, or endeavour to improve.   I speak of the changes wrought during my own lifetime on the cities of Venice, Florence, Geneva, Lucerne, and chief of all on Rouen,[2] a city altogether inestimable for its retention of mediæval character in the infinitely, varied streets in which one half of the existing and inhabited houses date from the fifteenth or early sixteenth century, and the only town left in France in which the effect of old French domestic architecture can yet be seen in its collective groups.   But when I was there, this last spring,[3] I heard that these noble old Norman houses are all, as speedily as may be, to be stripped of the dark slates which protected their timbers, and deliberately whitewashed over all their sculptures and ornaments, in order to bring the interior of the town into

[1] [See *Stones of Venice*, vol. i. (Vol. IX. p. 257).]
[2] [Compare the summary of such changes up to 1845 given by Ruskin in *Modern Painters*, vol. ii. (Vol. IV. pp. 37–41) ; and for a description of the old Rouen, the Essay on Prout, above, p. 310.]
[3] [Ruskin visited some of the French towns on his way to Switzerland in the spring of 1854 (see Introduction to Vol. V.).]

some conformity with the "handsome fronts" of the hotels and offices on the quay.

Hotels and offices, and "handsome fronts" in general— they can be built in America or Australia—built at any moment, and in any height of splendour. But who shall give us back, when once destroyed, the habitations of the French chivalry and bourgeoisie, in the days of the Field of the Cloth of Gold?

15. It is strange that no one seems to think of this! What do men travel for, in this Europe of ours? Is it only to gamble with French dies [1]—to drink coffee out of French porcelain—to dance to the beat of German drums, and sleep in the soft air of Italy? Are the ball-room, the billiard-room, and the Boulevard, the only attractions that win us into wandering, or tempt us to repose? And when the time is come, as come it will, and that shortly, when the parsimony—or lassitude—which, for the most part, are the only protectors of the remnants of elder time, shall be scattered by the advance of civilization—when all the monuments, preserved only because it was too costly to destroy them, shall have been crushed by the energies of the new world, will the proud nations of the twentieth century, looking round on the plains of Europe, disencumbered of their memorial marbles,—will those nations indeed stand up with no other feeling than one of triumph, freed from the paralysis of precedent and the entanglement of memory, to thank us, the fathers of progress, that no saddening shadows can any more trouble the enjoyments of the future,—no moments of reflection retard its activities; and that the new-born population of a world without a record and without a ruin may, in the fulness of ephemeral felicity, dispose itself to eat, and to drink, and to die?

16. Is this verily the end at which we aim, and will the mission of the age have been then only accomplished, when the last castle has fallen from our rocks, the last cloisters

---

[1] [So written by Ruskin for "dice," the more usual form of the plural in this sense.]

noted. Are then no new countries — on all the earth ... uncrowned by the thorns of cathedral spires — untormented by the consciousness of a Past.

... this little ... Europe ... small ... of our globe. gilded with the blood of old battles, and grey with the temples of old priests ... this narrow floor ... mosques of the future. Is not America wide enough ... in — ... for the elasticities of our humanity? Asia not rich enough — for its ...? Or, in the ... meadowlands and solitary ... hills of ... itself — is there not room enough for the ... and the indulgences of magnificence, without ... foundation ... of all glory upon ruin; and prefacing all progress with obliteration.

We must answer these questions ... speedily — or we answer in vain. The peculiar character of the evil which is ... wrought by this age is its utter inseparableness. Its schools of art — and ... its extending galleries ... museums of ... and ...

44.

faded from our valleys, the last streets, in which the dead have dwelt, been effaced from our cities, and regenerated society is left in luxurious possession of towns composed only of bright saloons, overlooking gay parterres? If this be indeed our end, yet why must it be so laboriously accomplished? Are there no new countries on the earth, as yet uncrowned by Thorns of cathedral spires, untenanted by the consciousness of a past? Must this little Europe— this corner of our globe, gilded with the blood of old battles, and grey with the temples of old pieties — this narrow piece of the world's pavement, worn down by so many pilgrims' feet, be utterly swept and garnished for the masque of the Future? Is America not wide enough for the elasticities of our humanity? Asia not rich enough for its pride? or among the quiet meadow-lands and solitary hills of the old land, is there not yet room enough for the spreadings of power, or the indulgences of magnificence, without founding all glory upon ruin, and prefacing all progress with obliteration?

17. We must answer these questions speedily, or we answer them in vain. The peculiar character of the evil which is being wrought by this age is its utter irreparableness. Its newly formed schools of art, its extending galleries, and well-ordered museums will assuredly bear some fruit in time, and give once more to the popular mind the power to discern what is great, and the disposition to protect what is precious. But it will be too late. We shall wander through our palaces of crystal, gazing sadly on copies of pictures torn by cannon-shot, and on casts of sculpture dashed to pieces long ago. We shall gradually learn to distinguish originality and sincerity from the decrepitudes of imitation and palsies of repetition; but it will be only in hopelessness to recognize the truth, that architecture and painting can be "restored" when the dead can be raised,— and not till then.

18. Something might yet be done, if it were but possible thoroughly to awaken and alarm the men whose studies of

archæology have enabled them to form an accurate judgment of the importance of the crisis. But it is one of the strange characters of the human mind, necessary indeed to its peace, but infinitely destructive of its power, that we never thoroughly feel the evils which are not actually set before our eyes. If, suddenly, in the midst of the enjoyments of the palate and lightnesses of heart of a London dinner-party, the walls of the chamber were parted, and through their gap, the nearest human beings who were famishing, and in misery, were borne into the midst of the company—feasting and fancy-free—if, pale with sickness, horrible in destitution, broken by despair, body by body, they were laid upon the soft carpet, one beside the chair of every guest, would only the crumbs of the dainties be cast to them—would only a passing glance, a passing thought be vouchsafed to them? Yet the actual facts, the real relations of each Dives and Lazarus, are not altered by the intervention of the house wall between the table and the sick-bed—by the few feet of ground (how few!) which are indeed all that separate the merriment from the misery.

19. It is the same in the matters of which I have hitherto been speaking. If every one of us, who knows what food for the human heart there is in the great works of elder time, could indeed see with his own eyes their progressive ruin; if every earnest antiquarian, happy in his well-ordered library, and in the sense of having been useful in preserving an old stone or two out of his parish church, and an old coin or two out of a furrow in the next ploughed field, could indeed behold, each morning as he awaked, the mightiest works of departed nations mouldering to the ground in disregarded heaps; if he could always have in clear phantasm before his eyes the ignorant monk trampling on the manuscript, the village mason striking down the monument, the court painter daubing the despised and priceless masterpiece into freshness of fatuity, he would not always smile so complacently in the thoughts of the little learnings and petty preservations of his own immediate

sphere. And if every man, who has the interest of Art and of History at heart, would at once devote himself earnestly —not to enrich his own collection—not even to enlighten his own neighbours or investigate his own parish-territory —but to far-sighted and *fore*-sighted endeavour in the great field of Europe, there is yet time to do much. An association might be formed,[1] thoroughly organized so as to maintain active watchers and agents in every town of importance, who, in the first place, should furnish the society with a *perfect* account of every monument of interest in its neighbourhood, and then with a yearly or half-yearly report of the state of such monuments, and of the changes proposed to be made upon them; the society then furnishing funds, either to buy, freehold, such buildings or other works of untransferable art as at any time might be offered for sale, or to assist their proprietors, whether private individuals or public bodies, in the maintenance of such guardianship as was really necessary for their safety ; and exerting itself, with all the influence which such an association would rapidly command, to prevent unwise restoration and unnecessary destruction.

20. Such a society would of course be rewarded only by the consciousness of its usefulness. Its funds would have to be supplied, in pure self-denial, by its members, who would be required, so far as they assisted it, to give up the pleasure of purchasing prints or pictures for their own walls, that they might save pictures which in their lifetime they might never behold ;—they would have to forego the enlargement of their own estates, that they might buy, for a European property, ground on which their feet might never tread. But is it absurd to believe that men are capable of doing this ? Is the love of art altogether a selfish principle in the heart ? and are its emotions altogether incompatible with the exertions of self-denial, or enjoyments of generosity ?

---

[1] [See Introduction, above, p. lxiii.]

21. I make this appeal at the risk of incurring only contempt for my Utopianism. But I should for ever reproach
myself if I were prevented from making it by such a risk ;[1]
and I pray those who may be disposed in any wise to
favour it to remember that it must be answered at once
or never. The next five years determine what is to be
saved—what destroyed. The restorations have actually
begun like cancers on every important piece of Gothic
architecture in Christendom ; the question is only how
much can yet be saved. All projects, all pursuits, having
reference to art, are at this moment of less importance than
those which are simply protective. There is time enough for
everything else. Time enough for teaching—time enough
for criticising—time enough for inventing. But time little
enough for saving. Hereafter we can create, but it is now
only that we can preserve. By the exertion of great
national powers, and under the guidance of enlightened
monarchs, we may raise magnificent temples and gorgeous
cities ; we may furnish labour for the idle, and interest for
the ignorant. But the power neither of emperors, nor
queens, nor kingdoms, can ever print again upon the sands
of time the effaced footsteps of departed generations, or
gather together from the dust the stones which had been
stamped with the spirit of our ancestors.

---

[1] [See above, *Lectures on Architecture and Painting*, § 33, p. 56.]

APPENDIX TO PART II

I

LETTERS ON PAINTED GLASS [1]

(1844)

1

MY DEAR OLDFIELD,—As we always travel slowly, in order not to fatigue my mother, and went round by Dieppe, we arrived here only this forenoon. I found no glass at Abbeville—at Eu, the pet church of Louis Philippe has some modern glass, of the worst kind; as bad as Ward's [2] in design, and worse in colour, but in the private chapel there were some good heads after Perugino. No glass at Dieppe. But when I got into the Cathedral here this evening, I was grievously vexed with all that I had done, and rendered almost hopeless by the dazzling beauty of form of the windows of the choir, and, to make the matter worse, I came upon some bits of restoration, which, though apparently adhering in all points to the original design, had utterly lost its effect, so that I find we are entirely in Ward's power, and however good the design we give him may be, he can altogether spoil it in execution. I set myself to consider the difference between the ancient and modern work, which I find chiefly to consist in these points (the design, size, etc., being in all points the same).

First, the modern glass admits much more light, producing a glaring and painful impression on the eye, so that I could not look at it long—the old glass soothed, attracted, and comforted the eye, not dazzling it, but admitting of long contemplation without the least pain. On closer examination, I found that the *whites* of the modern glass were very bright, looking like the ground glass of a lamp, and were all inclined to *pink* in their hue; while the whites of the old glass were dead, and wanting in transparency, looking like the ground of a picture (*i.e.* like real *colour*, instead of mere *ground* glass), and that they were all inclined to *green* in their hue. Note this, please, especially.

Again, I found that all the blues of the old glass had a *grey* or *black* quality of colour, black stains occurring upon them, so as to make them in places almost opaque, very pure indeed in places, but always tending to

---

[1] [For particulars about these letters, see above, Introduction, pp. lxiv.-lxv., where also other references on the subject are collected.]

[2] [Messrs. Ward and Nixon of Frith Street, Soho, having submitted a design which was not approved, for filling the large east window of Camberwell Church with painted glass, were instructed by the Church Committee to execute a new design, to be prepared by Mr. Ruskin and Mr. Oldfield.]

grey; whereas the modern blues were much more transparent—like the blues of a druggist's bottles—and instead of tending to grey, tended to *purple.*

Again, the yellows of the old glass were always *pale,* passing into grey— sometimes stained with black, the yellows of the modern glass *invariably orange* in a very high degree. Again, the *reds* of the old glass were pure crimson in their general tone, and occasionally so dark as to pass into black, while the reds of the modern glass were invariably a tone more inclined to scarlet, and more pale. Now I want you to go to Ward, and insist especially on this want of *transparency* in the old glass, which it appears to me is a very, *very* important point. I find universally that the eye rests on it as on a quiet picture, while with the modern it is tormented by violence of transmitted light.

I imagine, therefore, the modern glass is much thinner, and that there is less lead in it. The old glass seems opaque without grinding—by actual body of colour.

Again, let me beg of you to criticise the colours of the glass which Ward shows you most strictly, and in the yellows, to avoid like poison the orange tint, in the blues, to shun with equal horror the *purple* tint, and choose rather a dead grey or black than a bright purple. In the reds, look for pure *crimson,* and avoid scarlet, though *real* scarlet is used in some places sparingly—only take care that your crimson *be* crimson, not scarlet*tish.* In the whites, take them very dark and green in hue. And in the greens themselves, don't take *grapy* hues, but doubtful, greyish, blackish, sea-water looking tones.

Lastly, I find the iron bars twice as thick in the old glass as in the modern, and running through every bit of the window. If ever Ward gives you a bit of whole glass, four inches over, make him smash it, and stick it together again. I think the putty, or the rust of the iron, gives quality to the edges of the glass. I am quite certain, from what I have seen, that Ward will make a mess of the window, but if you hold tight in these points of colour it will be at least endurable. I thought, when I made the design, that I had filled it too full of little bits, but I find the windows here are divided and divided again, down to even smaller fragments. So don't stand any nonsense about making the figures larger. If you do, you will spoil all. Break it well up, stick it together with iron, and select *dirty* colours, blacks, and greens, and greys, and browns, to fill up gaps with. In my design all the colours are too intense—too gaudy, rather—they want chastening—all but the little bits in the angles.

So much for general principles. On Monday, we stay here till twelve o'clock. All the morning I shall be drawing from these windows. I will send you the results straightway. They are of the thirteenth century, and by the *same man* who did the windows at Chartres. I hope to be at Chartres on Tuesday, and the whole of Wednesday, and then I will send you fillings for the circles, etc., which Ward must not alter. My father says the old whites are *fishy.*

> All send their kind regards.
> Yours ever very truly,
> J. RUSKIN.

Make Ward put iron into the smallest circles, bind the winepress with it, and the door-posts, and the ark—or with strong, painted black lines if he can't put iron. Don't let him tell you that the old windows have been broken and mended; all the windows I have been studying are absolutely perfect and uninjured, not a pane lost. Now pray take care to have *dark* whites, *very* dark.

2

CHARTRES, *22nd May.*

DEAR OLDFIELD,—I have been all day in the cathedral, doing nothing. The vivid impression it had left upon me was far beneath the truth, and the little attention I have lately given to the subject has so far opened my eyes to the value of these windows that I could do nothing for two hours together but walk round and round again, wondering. Ward ought to come here before he is an hour older; for all the cathedrals of Europe could scarcely, together, furnish such a mass of colour as I have been dazzling myself with to-day.[1]

I was delighted to find, in the first place, that two of the best windows here were grounded with the very chequer which you proposed to have for our central light, and that I was wrong in supposing that the gold should be in the centre of the squares. I hope, therefore, that no alteration has been made, and that the central light will be this ground with five circular subjects; we can have nothing better, provided Ward keeps his blue pure and deep in the circles, and opposes it with pale yellows and rich purply *browns* in the figures.

All the windows here have subjects of the richest and fullest kind, the ground of chequer appearing only in small spaces. Had it been in our power—either pecuniarily or in consistence with our plan of subject—to have done so, I should have wished to have copied one of them, bit by bit, in our central light, without alteration; but as they, without exception, represent quaint Romish legends, unsuited either to the comprehension or faith of a Camberwell congregation, I think it needless to send you any of the designs; neither have I found anything to assist me in supplying the vacancies of the upper parts, for all the subjects here are so quaint and grotesque that they do not admit of being separated from the blaze of colour with which they are surrounded, or of being brought to close quarters. They are indeed, to my mind, the perfection of glass-painting; but still, they will scarcely do for the nineteenth century. Take, for instance, the "Temptation on the Pinnacle," which, as you are going to have a "Temptation," I sketched for Mr. Ward's edification [reference to an enclosed sketch, which is not available]. I'm afraid Ward will think he can do better. I am sure he can't; but I think the congregation might object to a devil with so neat a pair of legs, and so I suppose he had better give us his own design. This is one of three—in the last, the devil is going off in a passion, with his arms a-kimbo—a figure of most admirable expression and life.

---

[1] [For the windows of Chartres—especially the west window, "upon which 'gouts' of blood appear to have been dropped"—see below, "Lectures on Colour," § 37, p. 504. Other references to the windows occur in *Two Paths*, § 82; and *Lectures on Landscape* (the west window again), § 74.]

Fig. 2 [again reference to a sketch] may perhaps give you some idea of the intense richness and fulness of these windows. Three such crosses, each containing, as you see, six figure subjects, form the centre of the window, one above another, and three square figure subjects of the same richness fill up each vacant lateral space; giving thirty-six figure subjects in the window. The elegance of the cross design, marked by the blue spaces in the arms, is unrivalled by anything I remember. But in both these drawings you must allow for my having no good red by me. The reds here are intense and glorious beyond description, and I have nothing in my box but a little dead pink madder; where you see the pale rose colour in the drawings, you must suppose intense ruby.

Of all the beautiful windows in this church, which I consider unimpeachable standards of perfection, the following propositions are universally true. The *ground* of all is blue, and in much the same proportion as in my design, in some a little less. The figure subjects are very small, and subdivided, as you see in fig. 2, and in most cases, quite incomprehensible, as you see this one is. I have faithfully copied it, but have not the slightest idea what it means.

There cannot be found six square inches of unbroken blue in any window, though most of them are, I suppose, about 7 feet wide by 25 high. Ward's great spaces of blank blue will be much diminished by his subjects being put into circles, and, I pray you, show him how the blue is cut up by the iron, and graduated in depth, in the "Temptation" I send. Make him do the same. This graduation is a very great point in exhibiting colour. All the blues here vary perpetually from sky blue to nearly black, thus giving additional entertainment to the eye, even in a single colour. Modern windows are much too uniform in tint. The *prevalent* colours of the figure subjects are here a rich madder brown, a pale vivid green, and straw yellow, red occurring chiefly in the grounds and borders. The devil's head in the "Temptation" is of the most radiant scarlet ruby.

ORLEANS, *May 23rd.*—On going again to the cathedral [Chartres] this morning, I was yet more struck with the palpitation of the ground colour. It is, to the modern glass, what the varying complexion of life is to rouge. Would you be so good as to go to Mr. Tennant's in the Strand,[1] close by Somerset House, and ask him for a small piece of *Labrador* felspar of the richest *blue*, taking care to avoid streaks of green or orange, and show it to Ward, and tell him to match it. Tell Tennant to put it down to my account.

The finest windows in colour in the cathedral are three of the twelfth century, in perfect preservation, and their colour is entirely unique. I never saw anything approaching it, not for depth, but for refinement and purity; and it is their blue which the Labrador felspar resembles. In his circular subjects below, Ward must take a dark smalt blue, but if he can reach this Labrador tint in the pale parts of the upper lights, it will be very valuable.

This blue is so luminous that the ruby reds of the window come upon

---

[1] [Mr. Tennant, mineralogist, then of 149 Strand. Compare *Fors Clavigera*, Letters 64, and 70 (Notes and Correspondence).]

it as distinct *shades*, looking as if it had been spotted with rich blood. In this respect it differs from all the windows I ever saw. Points of scarlet are used, nearly that of the scarlet geranium, but more pure. These, in chiaroscuro, are about the pitch of the blue. I fear, however, that any attempt to imitate such colour in modern times would end in coarse glare. The wonder of this window is that all its hues are luminous without being transparent. It deadens the light totally, or rather becomes imbued with light itself, letting none through, and so glowing like a precious stone in darkness.

It would be worth your while to come to Chartres merely for the sake of seeing this single window. I counted this morning the number of painted windows in the cathedral, and measured them as well as I could, by taking a man's height with the pencil and applying it to them. One is apt to *under*estimate size in so enormous a building; but as nearly as I can guess their dimensions, the windows are as follows:—

Thirty-seven lancet windows of purple toned glass in the lower chapels round the choir and nave, each about 7 feet in width by 25 in height. The example, fig. 2, is from one of these. They vary in number of figure subjects: that which had fewest had twenty-eight, and that which had most, forty-two. There are, I think, forty-four or forty-six windows, but seven or nine are without coloured glass, having only dead white with a pattern, and coloured border, leaving thirty-seven of perfect colour.

Fifty-four lancet windows in the upper story of the choir, nave, and transepts, each about 5 feet by 20, containing larger figure subjects of intense glow, grotesque in character, with legends underneath, and shields.

Thirty-four large rose windows in the nave and transepts, each 12 feet in diameter.

Six small roses, perfect gems, in the chapel, 4 feet in diameter.

Three large roses (west end and transepts), each not less than 40 feet in diameter, charged with the most intense hues, purple ground with azure medallions.

Ten lancet windows, five under each transept rose, of about 4 feet by 16 long, with large figure subjects.

Seven lancet windows, 6 feet by 40 at the east end of the choir, with purple glass very rich, but of more modern tone than the rest.

And three of the twelfth century at the west end, the centre one of 10 by 30, containing twenty-seven figure subjects; the two others, 7 by 20, containing fourteen.

I wish you could find time to run over and look at this, before finishing Camberwell.

Well, now you will want to know what all this has to do with *our* window. Not much, certainly, for, as I told you, the subjects in Chartres are too quaint to be used in conspicuous places, chiefly legendary. At the bottom of each window is a representation of the trade of the body by which it was presented. One—the tailors'—gives a capital shop-boy measuring the cloth, and another hanging up a shirt. The legend of St. Hubert is delightfully given in another, hounds in leash, galloping horses, and a stag of the size of a mouse, with a cross as big as a cathedral. Another has the Deluge, in which I expected to get something to suit me, but no.

The water is given thus—with the ark so, on the top of it. The belt
a is red, b is green, c is gold. So you see I am left to my own devices,
and I have but little time; but there

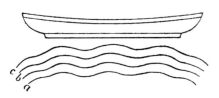

are three or four points which we
must alter.

In· the first place—the Paradise
on the left is horribly insipid. I
intend, if Mr. Storie[1] will allow me,
to substitute the angel coming down
from heaven, with the chain and key,
to bind the dragon for a thousand
years; the dragon will give me red to set against the purgatory, and I
shall put some repentant leopards and converted cockatrices above, which
will give me some more; so keep that open, please.

In the second place, I have been looking for lambs everywhere; but
find none that I like. I don't know how it is, but a lamb with a flag
over its shoulder reminds me much more of Camberwell Fair than the
Day of Judgment.

At Rouen I found in St. Vincent a Christ coming to judgment, which
pleased me, robed in crimson, showing the wound in the side, after a design
of Albert Dürer's. There is some grandeur about it, and I see no objection to putting the seven lamps before it; so that we take away the
emerald rainbow. The sword is on one side in the sky; a bunch of some
flowers, which I have faithfully copied, on the other. I shall add a point or
two of colour, and send it you. If we do not put a powerful piece of
colour in this centre, the church on the left will overbalance us. But if
you can get a rich design from Ward with the Lamb, do not hesitate to
put it in if you like it better than the Albert Dürer. I leave the choice
entirely to Mr. Storie and you; I mean, don't do a *single* thing out of
complaisance to me, as I only wish to lay as much material before you
as I can, to enable you to choose; and this Albert Dürer may, from its
grotesqueness, be offensive to you; if so, don't write to me, but get another
design put in hand. I cannot yet tell what to do with the angel on the
right, but I shall think of something.

I hope also to send you a better " Baptism of the Sea," or to substitute
something for it of clearer form. All this I will do as soon as I can; but
travelling leaves one little time. If Ward goes on with the smaller circles,
triangular spaces, or with his own part, no time need be lost.

Finally, let me repeat again the great and important watchword—
"Smash." All the Chartres windows are one series of breaking and rivet-
ing. I looked at St. Patrice, Rouen, tell Ward, and admire it much for
purity of colour, and originality and expression in design; but the *tout
ensemble* is scattered, and altogether wanting in solemnity and repose. I
will write again soon.

Yours ever very truly,

J. Ruskin.

---

[1] [The Vicar of Camberwell at that date.]

XXII

Allen & Co. Sc.

Window in St. Giles' Church, Camberwell.
(The glass designed by J. Ruskin and E. Oldfield.)

3

ORLEANS, *May 24th.*

I HAVE been a little reconciled to beading, by finding it used in these twelfth siècle windows, and in some others, with excellent effect; but it is always *very* small in proportion to the subject, not greater than is shown at the bottom of fig. 1 (there *was* no beading here, I only put it for illustration), while Ward's are about as big as any people's heads would be. But in *almost* all the windows of Chartres and Rouen the border is like that which occurs on the right and left of fig. 1, a plain band jointed with iron [word missing—? rivets] one or more of which occur according to the pattern. You see the border of the circle in fig. 2 is red, blue, and white, and of the lozenge red and pale yellow, no beading. This is what I want for my subjects. Apropos of white, there are all shades of it in these windows, but invariably green in hue. There is no marked distinction between the whites and greens, they pass perpetually into one another. The palest white, seen by itself, would be a beautiful clear chrysoprase green.

I don't know that I have anything more to say. Ward must design the horsemen with jacinth breastplates, for they puzzle me.

We start for Briare to-day; I hope to send you the designs from Auxerre or Dijon. The cathedral here is so frightful that when I walk in the town I keep my head turned the other way lest I should see it.[1] It is unquestionably the most intensely barbarous building in Europe, covered with work of the most vicious and vile kind. Every fault that can possibly be committed in architecture may be illustrated from it. Nothing in England is so bad, old or new.

There was a fair at Chartres while we were there. On one of the booths, —like Richardson's—there was the following inscription :—

THEATRE

Ici on represente

La Passion de N. S. J. C.

Tragedie en cinq actes.

Suivie de la resurrection, avec un Apotheose.

Aujourd'hui

Paul et Virginie

Point de Vue Maritime.

Terminé par le Naufrage et l'Apotheose.

In another part of the fair a grocer had for a sign a large devil made of plums riding on a pig made of figs. Would not this be a nice devil for Ward, peculiarly illustrative of temptation? I am in hopes, if we do our window nicely, that the congregation will have the other lights filled. In that case we would come over to Chartres, and copy our windows, and give them some nice legends. If Mr. Langar would put in his shopman and a shirt, and Mr. Partington his, with some barley-sugar, we could get on gloriously.

[1] [Compare the *Letters to a College Friend,* Vol. I. p. 430, and *Stones of Venice,* vol. i. (Vol. IX. p. 124).]

4

DIJON, *29th May.*

DEAR OLDFIELD,—You will be surprised at not hearing from me, but indeed I have had little time; the afternoons in this country are so lovely that I cannot miss my walk, and we travel all the mornings. I write, however, hurriedly, to put you in mind of what I forgot to mention in my last letter—Ward's *rosette*, joining his circles in the long light. It was vulgar and disagreeable in the last degree. I hope it is not too late to alter it. I send these patterns, fig. 1 [below], merely to give you some types of the class of ornament employed in the Chartres glass, and of what I think may be called good *manner* in this kind of decoration, as opposed to Ward's flourishes. You will observe the rudeness and bluntness of the pattern: its sharp angular lines, and delicate introduction of bars of one colour on fields of another. As a further standard I send fig. 2 [p. 443],

Fig. 24

faithfully copied in Rouen Cathedral, in which you will see how full the circles are of figures, how rude and undistinguishable these figures are, and how coarse and severe the species of ornament by which the circles are joined.

I send this, also, because it gives an example of the border which I recommended for this light, and which I find frequently repeated, and always with good effect. I don't send the circular and square patterns as good; for indeed I saw *no* isolated figures of this kind in either Chartres or Rouen. The figure subjects are always put close together, and linked by a pattern which interferes with, and is part of, them, as in the example I send; so that I have been obliged to adapt their decorations to these three patterns; the Chartres windows are all filled in this sort of way, each large space having figure subject. I send you the Albert Dürer, and hope the face won't be quite rubbed out on the way; but as it is to be so small it does not much matter. I have put in the seven lamps, because I think them sufficiently warranted by Rev. ii. 1, and iii. 1. The lightning I put in on account of Matt. xxiv. 27, and other such passages. The red things I intended for falling stars, Matt. xxiv. 29, Rev. vi. 13, and so the blackened sun and moon becoming blood; but I don't much like the stars, they look like fireworks. Many such subjects have a background of blue, with circular spots, in the old windows; it always looks rich. I think if you and Ward put your heads together you will be able to put in a good background. As I said before, if you don't like the figure don't think of taking it. The sword and branch are in the original, and so I leave them. Oh, remember that the robe is of the richest possible *carmine* hue, dark blood-red in the folds. I have no red that can come within dreaming distance of it.

A letter sent to 7 Billiter Street,[1] with "to be forwarded" upon it, will reach me by the first post. There are some fine windows at Auxerre, which confirm all my former positions. I forgot to say, however, that the windows at Chartres have blues of more purple cast, sometimes, than those of Rouen, and that these blues are very glorious; nevertheless, the most solemn effect, I still feel convinced, is to be gained by blackish blues.

Yours ever very truly,

J. RUSKIN.

5

GENEVA, *3rd June.*

DEAR OLDFIELD,—I send you at last two rude designs, one for the angel in the circle, the other for the side;[2] both rudely drawn, because to try and get a little purer red, I used this white paper, which takes colour badly: my drawing-paper is all grey. I was obliged to alter my plan in the side piece. I tried the tigers, but it made the angel at the top look like Mr. Wombwell, and the angel at the bottom like Mr. Van Amberg;[3] so I put in a row of gates, which you will please to take for the celestial city, and a bit of unintelligible figure from St. Radegonde to fill up, which looks something between a monk and an angel, and may be typical of general felicity. The chaining of the dragon I suppose people will understand. You perceive he holds with his tail tight round an apple-tree. If Mr. Ward could make him look a little less like a gamecock, it would be desirable.

I thought a long while over the other, but could find nothing which would balance the other two single figures except this subject. It isn't easy to make anybody look dignified with their legs so far asunder, but if you don't like the action, Ward can supply a better figure. I expect him at any rate to improve on this; and the landscape below will,

---

[1] [The city office of Ruskin's father.]
[2] [These designs are not available.]
[3] [The reference is of course to a performer in Wombwell's menagerie.]

I think, give opportunity for some fine solemn greys and quiet tones to take off from the glare of the dress, which must be pure ruby, with shades of deeper red ; the sky nearly black at the top, passing down through intense blue.   The broken scythe and hour-glass mean—"there shall be time no longer."[1]   I think the angel is crooked ; tell Ward to put his spine right. We leave this place for Chamouni to-morrow, and henceforward I believe I shall have my time so fully occupied that I shall be unable to think more of the window.   I leave it with perfect confidence in Mr. Storie's hands and yours.   The Ark and cloud circles I have not had time to think of ; the latter puzzles me.   Try something yourself.   And with all the rest, alter and add as you see fit, and especially with those things last sent, as I have no books by me to study them from.   I think the colour of this millennium side is tolerably good, and will match the purgatory ; only the dragon looks as if he had just come off the handle of some dragon china, and the celestial *city* looks like the wall of the celestial *empire ;* but I daresay Ward will make them more decent.   The resurrection in the third segment below I do not think wants altering, it will look ghastly and spectral beside the others, and so it should.   It will be valuable also to set off the richness of the others.   I should like to hear from you when you have time.   All our kindest regards to all at Champion Hill.

Ever very truly yours,
J. RUSKIN.

I send you also the St. Radegonde bit ; you will find it in Lasteyrie.[2] If Ward has any prints from St. Patrice, he can take the " death" there for the model of the fighting angel, altering the head and bosom ; it is a fine figure.

6

CHAMOUNI, June 31st.

DEAR OLDFIELD,—I wished to send you a long letter, but find it impossible to sit down quietly here.   I have only three days more of it, and every moment of it will be employed ; so I can only send you a short note to tell you how delighted I am with your design for the long light. I think it in every way beautiful and good.   But I much dread Ward's nasty figures in the circles.   He hasn't much room, which is a mercy. I am sorry the chequers must be larger, but I see it cannot be helped ; indeed, I doubt rather if it will be found possible to get the rest of the design and border clear in the space, but I hope Ward will make an effort, and draw delicately.   I am obliged to you also for pointing out the optical effect of the crosses, which is to me both new and inexplicable.

I fully agree with you in every word you say about the last drawings I sent, and I am thoroughly glad that I happened to leave town, as it has put you on your mettle, and made me much more easy as to the

---

[1] [Revelation x. 6.]

[2] [Ferdinand de Lasteyrie : *Histoire de la Peinture sur verre d'après des monuments en France :* 1838-1857.   A window representing the Last Judgment in the Abbey Church of St. Radegonde at Poictiers, is the subject of Plates 19 and 20 in that work.]

result. I don't think that between us we shall do anything very bad, though I might have fallen into sad mistakes alone. By all means select from the Bourges windows for the Paradise subject; mine has no expression in it at all. Only I should still like a little red if you can get it in; not but that I have precisely the same feeling which you have respecting it, as a [word indecipherable] and fiery colour, expressive of anger and power; but that without it I think the Purgatory on the other side will look entirely detached and isolated, inharmonious, drawing all eyes to it, and throwing the whole window off its balance; while the subjects must in both cases be so very small that I hardly calculate on either the Purgatory or Paradise being intelligible as such, and therefore I think it more important that the window should be symmetrical and complete in general effect than that the Paradise should be expressive on close examination. In fact, not one of the Chartres subjects in the upper parts of the windows is intelligible without a ladder ; they are one mass of confusion, and it was from observing this that I ventured to send the new Paradise, thinking that if the play of colour were good, it did not matter whether it were calculated to please the few people who would take telescopes or ladder to it. But I should be exceedingly obliged to you if you would get some more expressive figures from Bourges, retaining only a little red somewhere, which appears to me farther valuable because it will give, by opposition to the Resurrection subject, a pallid and fearful tone to this latter, which will be effective, especially as it is the nearest the eye.

All the other designs I am sure you will arrange a great deal better than I can here, as I have no books to assist me or give tone to the eye. In fact, I do not care how much you alter, now that I have seen your design for the chief light; this latter I return in case you should want it. If you should be inclined to favour me with another letter, my address for a fortnight is Poste Restante, Geneva.

Sτ. Martins, *5th July.*—You see I pay you back, for being so long in sending me any news, in your own coin. I have been very busy, and wanted to think over the subject a little more than I could when I wrote the above, half asleep. However, I still hold to the opinion that we ought to have a little red in Paradise somehow, though how to introduce anything so inappropriate I don't know. The worst of it is that red is the colour of sin—"red like crimson." [1]

Ward is preposterously slow in execution. I wish we had happened to fall into other hands ; but perhaps if we had had a better man to deal with, we might have been more modest and less determined to have our own way, in which case let us hope that the window would have been worse off in the end. It don't matter to us now how long he takes, it is neither our fault nor our affair.

I like all your alterations in the Albert Dürer ; especially the reversing of the sword ; but you need not have altered the clouds unless their form was *per se* disagreeable, as the white throne is given to Christ in Judgment, Rev. xx. 11, and I intended the clouds to assume the form of it. The round

---

[1] [Isaiah i. 18.]

object is in the original a globe and cross; it is unnecessary I think, as from its size it must certainly be indistinguishable. By-the-bye, is it usual to see angels' heads as completely turned (upside down) as every other couple of yours will be in the central light. I should have been disposed myself to reverse them in direction (rather than to treat them as if one were catching turtle) as at figure 2. Will you see if there is authority for the complete reverse? When visibly floating in air it is another thing; but I am afraid it will look a little awkward in a half circle.

My address will be for a fortnight after you receive this, Geneva, but I cannot *receive* my letters till the end of the time, as I shall be engaged in the valleys of the Monte Rosa, so you must not be surprised if I am long in answering. My Father and Mother join with me in kindest regards to yourself and all at Champion Hill. I am very sorry to leave all the trouble on your hands, while I am idling here.

I don't understand what the Bishop has got to do with the pulpit of Herne Hill Church, or what objection he has to the Evangelists. It is very abominable. Our Bishops seem to prefer the profane to the Popish, and would admit into their cathedrals the statue of an actor rather than of an Apostle.

Ever most truly yours,
J. RUSKIN.

I hope to be home in about six weeks, unless I stop in Paris.

7

DIJON, *7th August.*

DEAR OLDFIELD,—When I received your last letter, I had on my hands several which it was absolutely necessary I should dispatch, as they were to old friends to whom I had not sent a single line since my departure, and I was also taking advantage of every moment to finish the tasks I had set myself at Chamouni in the way of climbing, the heaviest of which I had reserved to the last, that I might be in better training for them, and therefore I was obliged to leave your important letter unanswered. In fact my head was so full of ice and chamois that I could not in any way bring it to bear on things artistical. I never spent so delightful a time in Switzerland, for by keeping myself in constant training, I was able at last to walk with the best guides and knock up all the bad ones; and so obtained access to some of the real arcana of the Alps. Last Saturday week I came upon a herd of thirty or more chamois, high on the Aiguille d'Argentière; a thing rare even in the memory of old guides. I am happy to find there *are* so many yet, as there was some fear of the race diminishing. I was away at Monte Rosa when your letter came,[1] which made further delay; but I hope the window has been going on. I quite agree with all your remarks; only one or two things we

---

[1] [For particulars of Ruskin's excursions among the Alps in 1844, see Vol. III. pp. xxv.–xxvii., Vol. IV. pp. xxii., xxiii.]

shall have, I think, to remember in introducing new designs. First, that I believe you will find your blues very much more *prominent* in glass than on paper, and reds *vice versâ;* so at least I was told by an Oxford authority the other day; so that the quantity of blue being in the present window very great, we must be careful not to knock out too much red. I thought that I had fully expressed my concurrence with you in putting the angel and dragon into C. I intended to do so at least; and I am sure your group of saints will answer well for the segment. I thought the Baptism had been knocked out long ago, and that Ward was designing another. I had much rather you would, however. All that you say respecting my borrowings from M. Angelo is perfectly just. I borrowed not from taste but from weakness, because I found I could not design quaint or characteristic figures without an original. I found that mine looked absurd without being expressive. Indeed, in the whole design I had no view to its actual execution, but merely to the giving Ward an illustration of the kind of colour and character we wanted. I fully feel that you have too much on your hands, but how can I help you? I am just going to Paris. I have only a week to spare—put a day for Versailles, one for La Madeleine, Notre Dame, etc., and four for the Louvre. How am I to do anything for windows?

I shall be home on the 24th, *D.V.,* but I am afraid I shall still have enough to do. I think the *Jonah* a very pretty bit of colour, well mingled, and so far useful in varying the dead blue ground of the other designs. In altering it will it not be as well to keep the gourd and whale pretty much as they are for this reason? To be sure, as a baptismal emblem, one doesn't want the gourd. Put it as you think best; only before determining on a new design, it is, I think, well to try a little one in the *place* of the other, on the whole design, as sometimes a bit too much blue or yellow will unbalance the rest. If I should meet with anything in Notre Dame or Amiens useful, I will try to find time to note it.

All our kindest regards to your circle at Champion Hill. Are you going to dissolve this Autumn?[1] and where are you thinking of going to? I wish you would look at Chartres.

Ever most sincerely yours,

J. Ruskin.

---

[1] [A reference to current politics, the Government of Sir Robert Peel being at that time supposed to be in a critical position (see Greville's *Memoirs,* second part, vol. ii. p. 248).]

NOTES ON THE LOUVRE

[These Notes are extracted from Ruskin's Diaries of 1844, 1849, and 1854; the side headings, except where they are enclosed in brackets, are in the MS. The numbers have been altered to those which the frames now bear. The following is an index to all the pictures mentioned. The substitution of the new numbers for the old, and the titles added in this index, will enable readers to identify the pictures, but it should be borne in mind that the galleries have been frequently re-arranged since Ruskin wrote; his remarks, therefore, about the position of pictures do not in most cases apply to the present state of things. Some of the pictures referred to cannot, for a like reason, be identified.]

Pinturicchio :—
   1417 (" Virgin and Child "), p. 453.
Potter, Paul :—
   2527 (" The Mead "), p. 471.
Poussin, N. :—
   710 ("The Philistines struck with Plague "), p. 454.
   722 (" The Ecstasy of St. Paul "), p. 454.
   727 (" Mars and Venus "), p. 453.
   728 ("Mars and Rhea Sylvia"), p. 454.
   729 (" Bacchanal "), p. 456.
   730 (" Bacchanal "), p. 472.
   732 (" The Triumph of Flora "), p. 470.
   734 (" The Shepherds in Arcadia "), p. 454.
   736 (" Spring, or the Earthly Paradise "), p. 469.
   739 (" Winter, or the Great Flood "), p. 469.
   741 (" Diogenes "), p. 469.
Raphael :—
   1496 (" La Belle Jardinière"), pp. 453, 473.
   1498 (" Holy Family of Francis I."), p. 450.
Rembrandt :—
   2541 ("The Philosopher in Meditation "), p. 454.
Rubens :—
   2100 (" The Majority of Louis XIII."), p. 472.
   2115 (" Village Fête "), pp. 470, 473.
   2116 (" Tournament "), p. 456.
   2085–2108 (Medici Series), pp. 472, 473.

Ruysdael :—
   2558 ("Storm "), p. 454.
Teniers :—
   2164 (" Heron Hawking "), p. 454.
Tintoretto :—
   1464 ("Susannah and the Elders "), p. 459.
Titian :—
   1577 ("Virgin and Child adored by Saints "), p. 452.
   1578 (" La Vierge au Lapin "), p. 452.
   1580 (" Holy Family "), p. 450.
   1581 (" The Disciples at Emmaus "), pp. 450, 451, 471.
   1583 ("The Flagellation "), p. 452.
   1584 ("The Entombment"), pp. 452, 453, 469, 473.
   1589 (" Allegory "), p. 458.
   1590 ("Alphonso di Ferrara and Laura di Dianti "), p. 450.
   1593 (" Portrait of a Man "), p. 458.
Vandyck :—
   1962 ("The Virgin with the Donors "), p. 468.
   1971 (" Portrait of Francis of Moncade "), p. 468.
   1973 ("Portrait of a Man and a Child "), p. 468.
   1976 (" Portrait of a Man "), p. 468.
Veronese, Paolo :—
   1187 (" Lot leaving Sodom "), p. 471.
   1188 ("Susanna and the Elders "), pp. 455, 460.
   1192 ("The Wedding Feast at Cana "), pp. 451, 452, 456, 473.
   1193 ("The Dinner at Simon the Pharisee's"), pp. 451, 452, 461, 465, 467, 473.
   1196 (" The Disciples at Emmaus "), pp. 451, 452, 465.

1. NOTES OF 1844 [1]

§ 1. PARIS, *Aug. 14th.*—Note of the Louvre. Perugino [No. 1565: "The Holy Family "]. All the chiaroscuro of the faces is given either with pen or crayon, cross hatched like engraving; but with a prevalence of perpendicular strokes. The colour appears originally almost to have concealed this, but to have let it through with time. The outlines firm and hard with pen, and deepened with the brush in brown. Hair exquisitely delicate. It is generalised into soft masses in the greater part, but its extremities are *bonâ fide* gilt, by individual hairs, so as to look like golden wires,[2]

---

[1] [This visit to the Louvre was made on Ruskin's return from the tour noticed in the preceding appendix : compare Vol. IV., Introduction, p. xxiii.]

[2] [Compare the " Review of Lord Lindsay," § 33, above, p. 202.]

pretty thick. The glory of the St. Catherine, a single line, follows the flow of the hair so as to take the shape of a cup, and that of the Madonna in a less degree. The form of the female heads is too square, their expression finer than Raffaelle. Draperies crimson, green, and black ; rigid, but very fine.

§ 2. The horse part of Guido's Nessus [No. 1454] is dappled, and the dappling of a grey which looks exactly like shadow. It confuses the eye improperly, as if it were an ill-shaped shadow cast by Deianira's dress and foot. The unity of the body is fine—there is a straining at the thighs of the man which sympathises with the lines of the horse's dewlap into which they fall.

§ 3. A singular instance of refinement in Titian [No. 1590 : "Alphonso di Ferrara and Laura di Dianti"], a mirror held to the back of a lady dressing her hair. The mirror is nearly black and invisible, only one square bright light upon it, but on looking close, the light is found to be truly the image of the window given by vertical strokes chiefly, and to be interrupted by a curve below ; that of the woman's head reflected. On looking close, the whole figure is seen in the shade of the mirror ; the half light on the back, the dark dress, the clasp or knot on the shoulder, and a reflected light on the edge of this shoulder all clear and sharp, no slurring. The face and head-dress of Flora are also reflected in front of the *armour* of the man.[1]

§ 4. Leonardo's "Bacchus" [No. 1602], very fine ; remarkable for the exquisite drawing of all the botanical details ; almost a Flemish delicacy superadded to Italian treatment. The columbine is used in it extensively, and a campanula, whose bell is blue and expansive, whose stalk separates at joints, marked by triple groups of leaves. The ivy leaves around the head of Bacchus of fine cold green.

§ 5. Francesco di Bianchi, il Frari [No. 1167 : "Virgin and Child"], very fine ; a grand head of a monk on the left ; a child, as an angel, playing guitar ; of most perfect beauty. Background a pure, warm, marvellous grey blue, but tone of flesh rather earthy and cold. In front of the Madonna, a hole in the pavement like a grave, with flowers growing out of it.[2]

§ 6. Note leaf and flower [reference to drawing] used in foreground of Titian's small "Holy Family" [No. 1580]. The flower is of a dull yellowish brown—may perhaps have been yellow. On the table-cloth in his "Supper at Emmaus" [No. 1581], some flowers are strewed, of which the principal is a blue one with white heart and black stripes (in the heart). In the great stalactite Leonardo ["La Vierge aux Rochers," No. 1599] flags and aloes are used beside the above mentioned flowers. The same flower is, I think, used [reference to drawing]. Its centre is also white, but its colour is of a much fainter grey blue, with a strong tinge of green. Possibly Leonardo's, allowing for change, may be the true colour, and Titian's purified, as he did the columbine.[3] In Raphael's chief Madonna (child leaping out of cradle) [No. 1498—"The Holy Family of Francis I."], the flowers are articulated (with which the Angel is crowning the Madonna) even to harshness, like a hard

---

[1] [Here in the diary follow the notes on Tintoret's "Susannah" and "a rascally Canaletti," given below, pp. 459 *n.*, 468 *n.*]

[2] [Ruskin again noted this picture in 1854, but the page in the diary is torn at the side : see below, p. 471.]

[3] [In his Notes of 1854 Ruskin again notes these flowers, adding, "Leonardo is wrong ; it is the common borage."]

Dutch painting, and their forms are perhaps a little vulgar. The bunch is held loosely in his hands; it is a handful, not a garland. The cross in St. John's hand is hollow, like two pieces of bark nailed together.

§ 7. Titian [No. 1581 : "The Pilgrims of Emmaus "] very noble.[1] Sunset in distance—the head of Christ, raised half against a column, is detached dark from the dark column, and light from the light sky, the dark part being relieved slightly by faint rays behind it. Monk with lilac robe on the right, with the hands clasped in the usual prescribed attitude for receiving the Sacrament. The trace of column is left, showing the original intention. The alteration is bold and sweeping, different from the rest of the sky. Christ, in blessing, lifts the second and first finger and thumb, the other two bent. A page is introduced with plume, waiting; the rigid pattern of the embroidered table-cloth is entirely given, as well as the flower shapes.

§ 8. The same subject by Paul Veronese [No. 1196]. The action of the hand is the same; so also in the little Christ of the Vierge aux Rochers (Leonardo). It is crowded with figures in full Venetian costume, but those of the disciples are simple and rather grand. The Christ is miserable, looking up like Rubini[2] in a last act. Parts of the sky, which by the position they hold would seem to have been blue, are now perfectly black. The tone of the greater part of the picture is not agreeable, but two little girls playing with a dog in the centre of the foreground, forming indeed the principal subject, are perfectly divine—the one on the left above all, her hand just laid on dog's neck, lightly, and her face lifted in a pause of serious thought.

§ 9. *August 17th.*—I was a long while yesterday studying the execution of the two large Paul Veroneses,[3] and noting the difference between their manly, fearless, fresco-like attainment of vast effect, in spite of details, and Landseer's, or any other of our best manipulators' paltry dwelling upon them. I have had a change wrought in me, and a strong one, by this visit to the Louvre, and know not how far it may go; chiefly in my full understanding of Titian, John Bellini, and Perugino, and my being able to abandon everything for them, or rather being *unable* to look at anything else.

I had a long ramble to-day among the churches; a fine Albert Dürer in one :[4] and much pleased with the quaint interior of St. Geneviève. The Sainte Chapelle was blocked up with scaffolding, but it is a glorious thing, the crypt by far the most elegant I ever saw—characterised especially by the two vertical columns which support the circular groining of West end.

§ 10. To go on with the Louvre. Of the two large Paolo Veroneses, that of the Magdalen washing feet [No. 1193] is far the mellowest and noblest in tone, and the most careful in execution. The side figure of the woman with child in her arms on the left, is unrivalled, in my mind; whether for

---

[1] [For another notice of this picture, see *Modern Painters*, vol. iii. ch. ix. § 18 ; and for the Veronese (§ 36), *ibid.*, ch. iv. § 4, and vol. v. ch. vi. § 18.]

[2] [The great operatic tenor of the time (b. 1795, d. 1854.]

[3] [*i.e.*, the "Marriage at Cana" (No. 1192) and the "Dinner at Simon the Pharisee's" (No. 1193), fully noted in 1849 : see below, p. 461.]

[4] [This may refer to St. Gervais, where, in one of the side chapels, is a " Passion," a work of the German school, but not now attributed to Dürer.]

grace, or for daylight, in the upper part at least. Beyond her the wall is completely covered with rows of pewter plates, but grandly treated in the extreme; so also the comfits and almonds lying in flat round dishes along the horse-shoe table. By-the-bye, the centre figure of the upper row in the opposite Cana marriage [No. 1192] seems to be the cook beating beefsteaks tender.

In both these pictures the multiplicity of costume, though grotesque and startling, is not revolting; for the impression of feasting, and of various guests, was necessary or allowable in both subjects. But in the one of Emmaus [No. 1196], in the solemn recognition of their risen Master by the two disciples who were walking together, and were *sad*, the introduced extra figures are altogether unendurable and reprehensible, and mark truly depraved taste, or utter want of thought. The lower parts of the Cana are very much more careless in handling, and more thick in paint, than those of the Pharisee [No. 1193], so much so that I should scarcely have supposed them by the same hand; the Pharisee one is peculiarly thin, the canvas showing almost disagreeably throughout.

§ 11. The finest Titian in the Gallery [No. 1584: "The Entombment"], glowing, simple, broad and grand. It is to be opposed to "The Flagellation" [No. 1583], in which the shades are brown instead of grey, the outlines strong brown lines, the draperies broken up by folds, the light very round and vivid, and foiled by deep shades; the flesh forms the highest lights, and the draperies are subdued.

In "The Entombment" every one of these conditions is reversed. Even the palest flesh is solemn, and dark, in juxtaposition with bright golden white drapery. All the masses broad and flat, the shades grey, the outlines chaste and severe. May be taken as an example of the highest dignity of impression, wrought out by mere grandeur of colour and composition, for the head of Christ is entirely sacrificed, being put in the deepest possible shade, against clear sky, and it is disagreeable in itself. The head of the St. John and St. Joseph are however grand conceptions, and the foliage of the landscape graceful in the extreme. It is curious that in this broadest of all broad pictures there should be one of the most delicate transitions of colour I remember. It begins with St. John's robe —crimson, in shade intensely dark; then same in light. Then St. Joseph's face nearly purely crimson, carried off by the juxtaposition of the robe. Then his neck, paler; then his arm, paler still, which joins robe of Magdalen, which is *warmed* near it by a few reflected lights, but in its palest part, joins and unites with the corpse-cold hand of the Madonna.

The colour throughout amounts to little more than exquisite staining. The bright draperies and the chequers upon them exquisitely delicate, and finished and full of hue, appear the result of the same operation as the dark retiring ground; incorporated with it, and showing no edge in many places. The most palpable piece of painting is the white drapery under the Christ which is visibly superimposed, and has a raised edge.

§ 12. Titian's white in No. 1577 ["The Virgin and Child adored by Saints"], which is another grand one, is as nearly as possible the colour of one of Turner's yellow sunsets. The Infant in this picture, as well as in 1578 ["La Vierge au Lapin"] is remarkable for the fine tapering of the limbs and excessive smallness of the feet.

A snail shell is carefully drawn on the ground in "The Entombment."

§ 13. I found myself finally in the Louvre, fixed opposite this Titian, and turning alternately to it and to the one exactly opposite—John and Gentile Bellini, by John Bellini.[1] I was a long time hesitating between this and Raphael's dark portrait[2] but decided for the John Bellini.

§ 14. No. 1417 is Pinturicchio's exquisite and pure Madonna. I like the execution almost as well as, almost better than, Raphael, especially of the Belle Jardinière [No. 1496], which is to my mind singularly coarse, as compared with the tribune Madonna or with one St. Cecilia.[3] The St. John is in this respect most faulty, and his left hand so offensive in its plastery and diseased look, that it made me give up looking at the picture.

§ 15. AMIENS.—I proceed with Louvre notes. 1566 [Perugino: "St. Paul"] is very noble, but hung too high to be judged of. 1319, Benozzo Gozzoli, is a Thomas Aquinas, with Plato on left, Aristotle on right; the heads of all these refined and somewhat majestic, but wanting in intensity. A crowd below, containing many refined and delicate expressions of small heads.

§ 16. MONTREUIL (August 21).—The Standish Gallery in the Louvre contains much which I could not examine—in drawings.[4]

The Spanish pictures on the way to it seem second, or third-rate, except a few Velasquez's; among which, with a small landscape, in which the trees are completely mixed with the sky by the sweeping lightness of the brush, and yet stand clear enough at a little distance. I like the manner of this landscape better than Salvator's, but there is not much in it. There is a good head by him, for red reflected lights, and grey full lights—an impressive Murillo, a ghastly coloured monk, sitting writing, white, hearse-like plumes in his cap, solemn and masterly; and a good bit of painting of Christ as a boy, giving bread to a begging friar (the head shaped like present French); also a monk in full canonicals, being crowned by an angel. But I could not look, even for a moment, at pictures of this school after the Italians.[5]

§ 17. Of Nicolas Poussin, 727 ["Mars and Venus"] is a singularly fine example for execution, the canvass being the coarsest I ever saw used for a small picture, the interstices being the tenth or eighth of an inch broad, and the paint is so thin on the features of the Venus that the face can scarcely be seen on looking close—nothing but network ; yet on retiring the beauty and refinement of the face is equal to any in his most careful works—

[1] [No. 1156—now called "Portraits of Two Men," and ascribed to Gentile Bellini ; for another notice of the picture see next page.]

[2] [Perhaps the beautiful and well-known "Portrait of a Young Man," No. 1644 (in the Salon Carré), formerly attributed to Raphael, now more commonly to Franciabigio.]

[3] [The "Tribune Madonna" is the "Madonna del Cardellino" in the Tribuna at the Uffizi ; for Ruskin's notice of it, see Vol. IV. p. 85. The St. Cecilia is at Bologna : see Vol. II. p. 167, Vol. IV. p. 212. The St. John is in the "Belle Jardinière."]

[4] [For the Standish Gallery see below, p. 459 n. A few stray notes on the sculptures here follow in the diary.]

[5] [The pictures above noticed cannot now be identified, and probably many of them are no longer exhibited at the Louvre ; the Standish Gallery, as such, has been dispersed, and the Spanish pictures are differently placed.]

its smile most exquisite, and its cast and chiselling lovely to a degree. Pictures so painted would be good copies for tapestry workers. In 710, the plague of Philistines, the coarse gesture is used, noted by Richmond, but it is a picture worth two of ours.[1]

734 ["The Shepherds in Arcadia"] is very fine in tone; only part of the sky (which is now generally green in hue) is altered to a crude blue. Is it possible that this blue, or anything like it, was the original tint; that the other hues were raw in proportion, and that we owe our majesty of tone to time?

§ 18. Calais, *22nd August*.—A heavy and dull day from Montreuil. All bleak and desolate here.

722 ["The Ecstasy of St. Paul"] is a valuable N. Poussin, from its freshness of colour. It is a landscape seen through a stone arch. The distance dark and forcible, the stone tones subdued and faint, and yet distance kept; a sword laid across the near stone is a fine incident.

728 ["Mars and Rhea Sylvia"] I have marked as very grand, but forget it. Two works by N. Poussin, in the Gallery, one of large size figures rather above life, and finely treated.

562 [Le Sueur: "St. Scholastica appearing to St. Benedict"] is a lovely floating Madonna, with attendant angels beautifully buoyant and graceful and tender, but not religious nor sublime.

1135 ["The Holy Family"]: a most beautiful Giorgione. The distance, though green, luminous, and well toned, seems to me crudely and freshly painted, coarse in handling, but the head of St. Catherine is glorious pure warm brown in shade; and the whole picture operates very perilously on the black forced dead light and shade of the large Raphael, hung near it.[2]

1136 ["Concert Champêtre"] is also very valuable; the standing woman a graceful thought, and the red cap a marvellous colour, warming the whole landscape.

In my favourite picture, the Bellini portraits [No. 1156], I have noted at first a cunning expression from the askance look in John himself. It wore off, and, I fancy, was false. Note that the screen which brings out these two heads appears a dead black, veined in imitation of marble, with white, but it is in reality a greenish and subdued black, against which the two caps—pure black—detach themselves vigorously; and also, though less forcibly, the hair of John Bellini. The execution of the flesh is at once the most delicate and forcible in the whole gallery. Raphael looks laborious after it, and Titian careless.

2541 ["The Philosopher in Meditation"]. With spiral stair; a most precious Rembrandt.

2558 ["A Storm on the Dykes of Holland"]. Ruysdael's sea, action good, well sympathized with by reeds on shore, foam fairly broken; not the remotest degree either of lustre or transparency. But far finer than Vandevelde.

2164 ["Heron Hawking"]. A well painted game piece by Teniers, with agreeable landscape.

---

[1] [No. 165 in the National Gallery, a picture by Poussin of the same subject.]

[2] [Owing to the re-arrangements of the Gallery since Ruskin wrote, it is impossible now to say which picture by Raphael he here refers to.]

2313 [Berchem : "View of the Environs of Nice "]. Note for future copying with reference to false sublime.[1]

1986 [Van Eyck : "The Virgin with the Donor "]. The man very intense and fine.

2341. A large and important genuine Cuyp, which may be given as an instance of his disjointed, cold, and imperfect effect in the whole, with successful parts. A bad picture in every sense of the word.

2011 [" Jesus Driving the Dealers out of the Temple "]. Jacques Jordaens —may be given as an instance of Dutch taste. Christ is kicking over a table with one foot, and laying about Him with the cord at the same time, with an indifferent air, as if He were doing it to amuse Himself, or for the sake of exercise.

1284 [Lorenzo di Pavia : " The Family of the Virgin "]. Very grand.

1188 [Paolo Veronese]. Magnificent. I think the best and most expressive Susannah I recollect—not much dignity, but refinement, delicacy, and life.

—— A fine portrait by Tintoret utterly spoiled by an unlucky and obtrusive coat of arms, hung on a column beside it.[2]

§ 19. No. 2416 (Jeunes Filles Picking Flowers). A landscape by Van Huysum,[3] who seems to me the most delicate of the Dutch painters, in which individual leaves of trees and foreground are given or attempted, and the futility of the effort shown by the entire spottiness and pettiness of all the near objects, though the nearest, especially the details of leafage on the right, are delightful from their delicacy and precision being there in their place. The man has fine feeling ; the distance is rich, glowing, and full of Italian dignity, and his knowledge of details is here useful to him, from his being at once compelled and able to avoid them, or analyze and generalize them. The following names I counted in the Louvre, of painters giving details with perfect and microscopic precision and painting for them. Those crossed are the ablest, those marked o are a little inferior to the average :—

Teniers.	Vander Venne.
× Henri Rokes (or Zorg).	Van Breda.
× Guillaume Kalff.	Jan Wynants.
× Abraham Mignon.	Peeter Neefs.
× × Jean Van Huysum.	× David de Heem.
Herman Zachtleven.	Gaspard Netscher.
Gabriel Metsu.	Breughel.
Jean Van Kessel.	Pierre de Hooch.
Pierre Van Slingelandt.	Guillme Van Mieris.
Adrian Vanderwerff.	Van Os.
Henri Van Steenwick, fils.	Paul Bril.
o N. Brekelenkam.	o Jan Miel.

Besides all the commonly instanced ones, Ostade, G. Dow, Wouvermans, etc.[4]

[1] [For later references to Berchem's works as typical of the " hybrid " school of landscape, see *Modern Painters*, vol. v. pt. ix. ch. 1 § 3, ch. viii. §§ 2, 11.]

[2] [This note fits the Venetian portrait of a man (No. 1185), with a column on which is the coat of arms of the del Buono family. The picture is, however, by Calcker (1499–1546), a pupil and successful imitator of Titian.]

[3] [Compare Vol. III. p. 672.]

[4] [The diary here refers to "a cold sketch of Guido's—distance pure pale blue, the rest in same key," and two "interesting Berghems," which cannot now be identified.]

§ 20. ——[1] is a fine Annibale [Caracci] ("The Resurrection") sunrise; orb just half up, a solemn luminous and imaginative passage full of truth. A soldier is sleeping on the top of the tomb; the others undisturbed around it. The seal is on it unbroken, as at *a* [reference to sketch]; Christ has risen *through* the stone, not, as is usually represented, cleaving it.

2116. Tournament by Rubens—its distance a sunset as above [reference to a sketch],[2] most vigorously conceived and every way fine, but remarkable for the impossible position of the sun's rays, and for the heavy lightless brick-red used in the orb itself.

729 ["The Education of Bacchus"]. The finest Poussin in the Gallery; recumbent nymph and exquisite distance, a little coarse in handling, but thoroughly grand.

1302. Taddeo Gaddi: execution not delicate, but occasional heads very fine, though to me it seems indiscriminately so. The Herod in one has a very good head; the Madonna is poor.

1569. ["Jesus Appearing"? Perugino]. Note for its exquisite trees.

1604. [School of Leonardo: "The Virgin with the Scales"]. Violent simpering in all the faces. Virgin with elaborate curls, yet looks like a man. The St. Michael has a female expression. Both would have been fine if the Madonna had been a Christ, and the St. Michael a Madonna. The other three figures wretched.

In 1599 ["La Vierge aux Rochers"] the Jesus is very solemn, and the picture has grown upon me exceedingly.

2. NOTES OF 1849

§ 21. PARIS, *8th September.*—I entered the Louvre this morning[3] under the peculiar advantage of having been utterly separated from humanity, and from all manifestation of human mind, for full 120 days, and I was suddenly therein brought into contact with perhaps the most varied exhibition of the powers of the human mind in Europe—(for there is a local colour and character about the Florentine and Roman galleries utterly wanting in the *mélange* of Dutch, Spanish, French, and Italian work—all first-rate—presented by the Louvre). I felt as if I had been plunged into a sea of wine of thought, and must drink to drowning. But the first distinct impression which fixed itself on me was that of the entire superiority of Painting to Literature as a test, expression, and record of human intellect, and of the enormously greater quantity of Intellect which might be forced into a picture—and read there—compared with that which might be expressed in words. I felt this strongly as I stood before the Paul Veronese.[4] I felt assured that more of Man, more of awful and inconceivable intellect, went to the making of that picture than of a thousand poems. I saw at once the whole life of the man—his religion, his conception of humanity, his reach of conscience, of moral feeling, his kingly

---

[1] [? No. 1223; it is not now in the Louvre.]

[2] [See *Modern Painters*, vol. iii. ch. xviii. § 22, fig. 6, where the sketch was used.]

[3] [This visit to the Louvre was made on Ruskin's way home from a Swiss tour in the summer of 1849; compare Vol. IX., Introduction, p. xxiii.]

[4] [The "Wedding Feast at Cana," No. 1192.]

imaginative power, his physical gifts, his keenness of eye, his sense of colour, his enjoyment of all that was glorious in nature, his chief enjoyment of that which was especially fitted to his sympathies, his patience, his memory, his thoughtfulness—all that he was, that he had, that he could, was there. And as I glanced away to the extravagances, or meannesses, or mightinesses, that shone or shrank beneath my glance along the infinite closing of that sunset-coloured corridor, I felt that painting had never yet been understood as it is—an Interpretation of Humanity.

§ 22. It is vain to talk of a man's being a great or a little Painter. There is no Greatness of Manhood and of mind too vast to be expressed by it. No meanness nor vileness too little or too foul to be arrested by it. And what the man is, such is his picture: not the achievement of an ill or well practised art, but the magnificent or miserable record of divine or decrepit mind. There is first the choice of subject and the thought of it, in which the whole soul of the man may be traced—his love, his moral principle, his modes of life, the kind of men among which he moved, and whose society he preferred, the degree of understanding he had of these men; and all this to a degree and with an exactitude which no words could ever reach. For the best Poet—use what expressions he may, [is] yet in a sort dependent upon his reader's acceptance and rendering of such expressions. He may talk of nobility of brow or of mien: but the painter alone can show us the exact contour of brow and bearing of limb which he himself felt to be noble; the painter only can show us the very hues and lines he loved, the very cast of thought he most honoured. Let all this be read aright, and then add to it the expression of the less profound gifts, and feelings of the man—of his caprices, his fancies, his prejudices, his wildnesses of imagination, his favourite and familiar branches of knowledge—all stealing in in their due place—and more or less harmonized with his subject according to the degree in which that, or his Art, was predominant. Finally, the colossal power of the Art itself—of mere pictorial invention and execution—how many strange qualities of mind are there not involved in this alone, which in the poet must lie dormant. How feeble are his means of expressing *colour*, at the best, and if the music of words be thought equivalent to it, yet how little and miserable is the Art of arranging syllables and rhyme (often at some sacrifice of meaning), compared with that awful self-command, that lordly foresight and advance, by which the great painter gathers together his glory of deep-dyed light.

§ 23. Nor as an expression of Vice or Folly is it less distinct, for in exact proportion to the powers which it can express, are the powers it demands. With less than it can receive, it is incomplete. A man who is not a great man from the heart outwards, has no chance—I say not of being a great painter—but of being a painter at all. Cast into a field of contest of giants, he displays nothing but his own minuteness. And utterly and basely is the nakedness of most men discovered therein. For as in no poem is so much mystery of intellect concentrated as in this work of Veronese, and in many of Titian, Tintoret, M. Angelo, and Raffaelle, so in no book is it possible to display the amount of absolute idiocy which is exhibited in modern French or Italian work. Men may be taught to write grammar, not to draw steadily. For decency's or for learning's sake, they are forced in writing to abstain from *some* words and thoughts, but there is no grossness which pictorial precedent cannot excuse, and in which therefore a gross painter does not indulge himself. There are some ideas of vulgarity or of crime which no words, however laboured, would succeed in suggesting to a gentle heart or a pure mind. But the brutal painter has the eyes at his mercy; and as Kingliness and Holiness, and Manliness and Thoughtfulness were never by words so hymned or so embodied or so enshrined as they have been by Titian, and Angelico, and Veronese, so never were Blasphemy and cruelty and horror and degradation and decrepitude of Intellect—and all that has sunk and will sink Humanity to Hell—so written in words as they are stamped upon the canvasses of Salvator and Jordaens and Caravaggio and modern France.

§ 24. I was singularly struck with one exemplification of all this that I felt in two pictures of Titian, side by side, which showed the entire grasp the man had of the whole range of the joys and the [*Titian: "Por-* efforts of the grace and the gloom of human life. The one, *trait of a Man,"* a portrait of a man in a dark dress, the darkest possible *No.* 1593.] warm green, passing into coal black, the background dark— the light falling, with Rembrandt simplicity and singleness, on the head and hands (note that Rembrandtism in its truth and in its right application to solemn subject is practised by the greatest men): one arm leaned against the plinth of a grey cold column of stone with an Attic base [a rough sketch of this base], the hand falling over the edge of it in perfect rest—the other, right hand, laid on the sword hilt, the back of the hand upmost; the black hilt, ebony black with one or two intense white flashes on it, like those of Turner on the chains in the "Slaver,"[1] rising between the forefinger and the second; the front of the thumb seen below, all at rest—the face dark, the hair short, and as black as night; the eye lightless, calm, but sternly set and fixed, the beard dark brown, and full from the lip—almost the only flowing line admitted in the picture (for the sleeve that rounds to the pendent hand is foreshortened—in a series of short waves as below [rough sketch of piece of sleeve], the white of the column being rudely loaded over its flat intense black in a series of apparently inconsiderate sweeps); the mouth curled and scornful, yet not exaggerated, all quiet and self subdued, yet lurid and wrathful in its single wreathed line of burning red—seen through the shade of the hand like a gleam of angry sunset through a thunder cloud.

§ 25. Beside this picture hangs that of Titian with his mistress:[2] she, all softness and gentleness, her light hair half bound, half bedewed, [*Titian's "Alle-* with pearl, her shoulders heaving under the brown kerchief *gory in honour* which is falling from them—and her full breast rising out of *of Alfonso* the light white loose dress—yet grandly always—not sensually. *d'Avalos," No.* Pure womanhood—tender and voluptuous, but sublime, not 1589.] sensual—her round and glowing arm, clasped at the shoulder by an armlet of ruby and gold, bent over the bright, ideal, substanceless

[1] [For this picture, once in Ruskin's collection, see *Modern Painters*, vol. i. (Vol. III. p. 571, and Plate 12).]

[2] [This picture is now known as "An Allegory in honour of Alfonso d'Avalos, Marquis of Guast" (1502–1546), the generalissimo of Charles V.'s armies. A letter is extant from the Marquis to the painter's friend, Aretino, in which he states his wish to have his portrait painted by Titian, along with that of his wife, and that

ball which seems to mark at once the lustre and the mystery and the hollow-ness of life and of the world—the Cupid with his arrow sheaf, and azure wings—above,—another bright haired and most lovely nymph, clasping her hands as if in worship of the higher loveliness—her hair wreathed with a sharp laurel-like leaf and white starry flowers—but *both* small and lustrous —and full of grace and purity—her eyes wet, and the light flashing upon them, while those of the Queen of Titian are set on soft and brooding darkness—the brows of both the fair creatures nearly alike—that subdued horizontal arch which has so much at once of grace and power: the dress of one crimson and green, of the other, the Magdalen-like Grace, grey and gold—between them, their Lord, the head in shadow, the white light flashing from his dark cuirass. Note, by-the-bye, this armour is actually more con-spicuous than the head of the wearer ; reason, first, that the sentiment is chiefly of colour, to which that of the armour is precious ; secondly, that the steel gives the greatest possible contrast to the feminine tenderness.

§ 26. Two pictures of Susannah. Tintoret and Veronese, the first in Standish gallery ;[1] Susannah in attitude of robing Venus of Guido in our gallery ;[2] face quite calm and somewhat animal —she does not see that she is watched ; a magnificent grey grove, in which the bending and twining symmetry of suc-cessive trunks, wreathed with lovely, sharp-edged, exquisitely *[Tintoret : " Susannah bathing," No. 1464.]* drawn ivy, is more like architecture than ever architecture was like vege-tation (how utterly different in its sculpture-like severity of sentiment from flowing trunks of the same kind with Rubens) leads back in steep perspective to an opening to the sky [sketch of the trunks], whence the two elders, with Tintoret's usual caprice, look in over a kind of altar cloth ; the foreground is occupied by a water full of reeds and flags, and frogs, and two white nondescript fish tails; but close to the spectator, down among the reeds and water, is a dark grey animal like a rabbit, with long ears, and a malignant human face. There is no doubt, no obscurity about it, it is as plain as the Susannah herself—adding another to my catalogue

of his child as a Cupid. It is supposed that in this picture Titian executed the commission in a semi-allegorical form, symbolising the return of the general from a campaign to enjoy the fruits of peace and victory. The date usually assigned to the picture is 1533, but see *The Later Work of Titian*, by Claude Phillips, p. 18.]

[1] [The gallery which at that time contained the pictures and other objects of art be-queathed to King Louis-Philippe by Frank Hall Standish (1799–1840), an English author and connoisseur. The "Susannah" (not itself one of the Standish pictures) now hangs in the "Grande Gallerie." Ruskin had noted this picture also in his diary of 1844 :—

> "Tintoret's 'Susannah' is very noble, and especially remarkable for the grand landscape, large tree trunks enriched with ivy, most delicately drawn and finished, forming an entire, unbroken, square mass of shade over two-thirds of the picture, in spite of the complete details."

It is the picture referred to by Ruskin above (p. 411) as "the best Tintoret this side of the Alps." When the editor of *Arrows of the Chace* (1880) wrote to ask him to which picture these words referred, Ruskin replied (May 19), "Susannah and the Elders. I am still of the same mind. It is one of the sorrows of my life never to have seen that picture close. ... The Susannah," he adds, "is one of the great mystic pictures with a landscape of lovely arbour and trellis, and *such* frogs in the water."]

[2] [This must be a slip of the pen for the Susannah of Guido ; in that picture in the National Gallery (No. 196) the attitude—that of screening the breast with the arm—resembles Tintoret's.]

of the Meaning caprice of the painter. This figure, however, unless it be a white Devil, sent to tempt Susannah, is nearly as inexplicable as the skeleton one of the Crucifixion.[1]

§ 27. Veronese's treatment is utterly different. The water falls from a dolphin-mouthed fountain—Susannah, sitting on a bench which [*Veronese: "Susannah and the Elders," No. 1188.*] is under the statue of a faun, is addressed by the elders, grand senatorial figures, the expression of passion thoroughly marked on their otherwise not ignoble features, Susannah gathering her dress about her bosom—looks up to them neither in fear nor shame—but in the most fiery indignation, the face as expressive as one so much side-shortened can possibly be; the background of the most exquisitely painted laurel leaves, natural size.

§ 28. Outline of upper portion of cave in Leonardo's " Vierge aux Rochers " . . . [references to a sketch]; the light from under the dark [*Leonardo's " Vierge aux Rochers," No. 1599.*] edge strikes on their crude and artificial cleavage. What kind of mind could lead Leonardo to adopt such an ideal? . . . [further reference to sketches]. Under this cavernous line, in the distance, a whole range apparently of blue icebergs, seen against horizon light, and I think water below. Above, the dark rocks, after the hole has been pierced in them, are rounded off into a kind of haystack shape; beams also run from one to the other. The blue, however, is not so blue as Titian's, nor the brown so brown. [Later notes:—] Those blue icebergs appear to be his universal distance. In the St. Anne [No. 1598] they rise out of a kind of sea, or wide river, with a weir upon it—these men who never drew landscape from nature *could* not get on without weirs—and form a cloudy, unfinished distance far away behind the heads, like an old map, some idea of snow in extreme distance. The foreground is a kind of oolite-like rock . . . [reference to sketches], covered with loose, painfully elaborated pebbles; one, or a zoned flint, nearly an agate, carefully veined. Behind the head of Monna Lisa [No. 1601], same thing, equally grotesque, blue and unfinished.[2]

§ 29. Titian's drapery seems an exception to the general rule I had hoped to establish, that artists might at once be known, whether of [*Noble and Ignoble Drapery.*] great or mean mind, by the sense of *gravity* and of *generalization* in its treatment. Yet the thought deserves development. I imagine the *seriousness* of the mind, as distinguished from its simple *power*, is to a certain degree shown by its choice of heavily gravitating folds: provided this choice be natural, not affected. Nothing can be more grand— more quiet—more simple—more material than its falls in Veronese. In the French fresco picture of the Magdalen washing Christ's feet in the Madeleine[3] here, the blue drapery of Christ, by way of being grand, hangs like a blanket between two posts, and all the draperies are square at the top, and hang in dead verticals and gigantic masses, off which the spectator cannot take his eye; the blue drapery specified between the knees of the Christ, is the principal object in the semicircle. Consider this peculiar blanketty

---

[1] [For a description of Tintoret's " Crucifixion " at Venice, see Vol. IV. pp. 270, 271, where, however, the figure here referred to is not noticed.]

[2] [For a further discussion of Leonardo's landscape, see above, pp. 112, 113 ; also Plate 12 and figure 22.]

[3] [In the first chapel on the left side ; by L. C. F. Couder (1790–1873).]

drapery—Corbould[1] has it in the manner rudely shown . . . [reference to a sketch], and some Germans, and partly the clumsy monks of monument at Dijon. It is affected verticality. Then consider the true and highest sublimity of verticality in M. Angelo, mixed with vast bounding curves. Then the pure and graceful verticality of Angelico passing into affectation in Perugino, etc. All of them different from the manly, simple, everyday natural grandeur of Veronese. Then Titian sometimes majestic, but often, too, mean and broken, marking, I think, a lower sanctity of mind than Veronese—as also his more sensual pictures, his mighty intellect atoning for want of seriousness. Then the various degrees of flutter and of common-place—the drapery of Jordaens happened to be next to Veronese's—one fold of it is enough to show the inanity, baseness, and disquietude of the fellow's mind, and to prepare one beforehand for his *Kicking* over the Money tables.[2] Note that exaggerated Verticality in drapery is usually associated with exaggerated Horizontality in sky — and has been run hard by late pursuers of sublime (worth a separate paragraph, this Abuse).

§ 30. In Paul Veronese's smaller of the two grand pictures—the Magdalene washing Christ's feet—note style of architecture a good deal debased : the principal figures are set under a rotunda supported by Corinthian columns, with a rich, modern French-looking cornice : the acanthus leaves have *blunt, round* lobes, and the circles of the round shafts at the top are all out of perspective. Note, by-the-bye, in the new treatment of the Corinthian capital generally, the difference between leaves and [*Veronese: "The Feast in the House of Simon the Pharisee," No. 1193.*]
feathers, between the natural bend of a living leaf—and the crisped curl up of a blighted one : and the exaggerated twist of feather filaments. This subject I must inquire into, and consider the structures of feathers in ostrich, etc., as opposed to that of leaves ; it is connected closely with the entire subject of Morbid decoration, and the Corinthian capitals of the Madeleine here, inside, are entirely spoiled by their ends curling right round and becoming absolute feathers. Consider this in connection with early and severe capitals. It is perhaps worth a chapter, associated with curls of waves, etc. The principal evil is, I think, when the end of the leaf loses its living connection with stem, and curls on its own account.[3]

As regards the general taste of the rest of the architecture, its balus-trades are very beautiful, graceful, and light in lines of balusters, or even lighter : a circular temple in distance, with garlands (festoons) hung from pillar to pillar. Statues in semicircular niches rather loose and French. On the whole, grand, rather by suggested size, and by the accidental associa-tion of its outlines, than by real design.

§ 31. As regards its Painting, it is invariably kept in the lightest and palest neutral tint possible ; the columns being exquisitely rounded, the first ruled outlines often left almost in black, and the high lights touched on them in pure white, as well as on the capitals: the whole tone being a close approximation to Turner's [*Architecture of Veronese.*]

---

[1] [For other references to Corbould, see *Academy Notes*, 1858.]

[2] [Jacob Jordaens (1593–1678) : " Jesus driving the dealers out of the Temple," No. 2011 ; see also above, p. 455.]

[3] [Ruskin worked out this subject in *The Stones of Venice*, vol. iii. : see Vol. XI. pp. 8–11.]

in our Venice;[1] only not quite generally so white; and with this further exception, that while Turner gets his dark side dark upon cloudy white sky, Veronese boldly throws his entire building light and dark, white out from the blue sky behind : and only brings the dark side of the cupola in the distance dark against distant sky, by which he gives solidity to the whole. Turner, keeping the same building tone, gets his nearer building dark; his distant one light against sky, and so gives distance and dreaminess to the whole. The most essential difference is in the cast shadows, Turner being, though not darker, more decided. There is a degree of false assumption in this, as the general white tone of Veronese is far more possible without, than with, cast shadows. Yet I saw to-day (Monday, 10th September) that Veronese was very nearly right, even in sunshine. After a vain attempt to get into Library, we drove to the Arc de l'Etoile, when a little, very little exercise of self-denial on my part was rewarded by my verifying this important effect of Veronese. The Arc de l'Etoile is of a warm limestone (marble ?), not very pure or fine in colour; but whiter than Caen stone. The sky was blue, varied with white clouds. The sun-

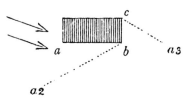

light in the direction of the arrows giving a broad dark side with comparatively little reflected light — no walls near, but the ground, observe, very dry and white. Standing at a and looking at the corner b, the base of it came vigorously dark against the pale blue of horizon, while the top, where the eye was very much dimmed, appeared as though a Daguerreotype would have pronounced it to be as nearly as possible of the pitch of the sky at that angle perhaps 35–40, with, nevertheless, a *nuance* of *light* on the stone; while to the eye undimmed, it was pronounced in clear warm light upon the blue. On this pale dark side the ornaments were, for the most part, traced in darkness; the richer ones and under cornices as dark masses; partly owing to the crowding of their line, partly to discoloration, but for the most part, they might be drawn with a grey pencil in pure lines upon the warm dark; looking from a^3 towards the side b c, that side appeared of a pure transparent ochre, much warmer than a b, and *all of it* vigorously dark against the sunlight sky at bottom and *top*. White clouds, by their opposition, threw the feeblest of the darks into deep shade on the one hand, and the figures, especially coloured ones, threw them all into clear light on the other, almost in the Veronese key. This principality of figure tone is a most characteristic feature with Veronese, and I was delighted to see him thus confirmed, as well as Turner in his Venice. Yet note that this truth referred only—or rather was seen only—in the two dark sides : retiring so as to see the illumined sides, another key came into the picture, a warm strong light nearly up to that of clouds, casting all the rest into dark grey, and touched like fire on the shelly crests of the cornice. Turner endeavours to unite this with the pearly grey : being perfectly true in the

¹ ["The Grand Canal, Venice," sometimes called "Shylock," exhibited at the Academy in 1837, and afterwards bought by Ruskin's father; sold by Ruskin in 1872; now in the collection of Mr. Ralph Brocklebank.]

pitch of his Shadow, his light is necessarily as white as he can get it, and yet not nearly raised enough, nor warm enough in comparison, making his shadows, though of perfectly true pitch, look ghostly. Veronese, on the contrary, assumes the luminous chalk side, accessible without difficulty, for his total key; only altering it by introducing a feeble *direction* of general light—nothing like so much as that which there is from a window into the inside of a room—which on the distant buildings casts no shadow at all. (Q. is there not a worse falsity than Turner's, by-the-bye, in having a dark side without a shadow in the open air?) *Vide* page 320 [reference to another sketch] which in the near figures, the shadow of a black dwarf, within about three feet of the white table-cloth, is *not* traceable on the marble of the floor, all the way from his foot to the table but only to about the length of his foot, and on the table-cloth itself is a most ætherial grey, just like one of Turner's feeblest, only not so sharp, and lighter than the dark side of said table-cloth. His whole purpose, therefore, is to represent character, action, and local colour, with as little of accidental light and shade as possible, except as it is necessary to explain form; while, nevertheless, as a group of lights and shades the picture is magnificent; but all its shadows are local tints —hence his fondness for negroes, who give him a rich brown: one of them places his hand on a white column; it is like a Benvenuto Cellini's mingling of bronze and alabaster; their hair gives him the most vigorous black—together with local blacks occurring in dresses and patterns, as, for instance, on the under table-cloth, where the black remains intense and full in full light, though the red of a lilac dress in front of it remains red (and lighter than that, local black) in full shade.

§ 32. Consider, then, if this be not a further instance of the necessity of Contentment with, and of aiming *at*, a single object, if any great perfection is to be reached. Veronese desires glory *Contentment;* and truth of colour, and he gets it, adding all the majesty *Singleness of* of shadow by local colour; the French painters have vainly *Purpose.* tried to join force of light and shade with colour; note especially the sharp divisions of draperies in blue and white, as sharp as candlelight shadow, in fresco of Ascending Magdalen over altar of La Madeleine.[1] Now, to get this, they have sacrificed a certain portion of colour, whitening their blues and reds on the lights, and using much light colour; the result is a kind of statuesque block in a sickly candlelight, drawing the eye to all its bits and divisions, and entirely picturesque in *treatment* without the shadow of picturesqueness in *conception*. They are, in fact, bad imitations of Greek statues, seen by a feeble sunlight (for the shadows have the sharpness of the highest sunlight without its force or energy), and dressed up in opaque and artificial colour (I never thought of this necessary sympathy between shadow and Form or Fancy in the Picturesque before). Tintoret, on the other hand, as he *Picturesque;* increases the force of his shadow, increases that of colour *Sympathy re-* also; his main difference from Veronese and Titian being less *quired in it.* in the force of cast shadows than in the increased vigour of dark sides. But then, as he increases this vigour, in draperies, etc., with the Frenchman,

---

[1] [By C. J. Ziegler (1804–1856).]

he not only introduces sympathetic picturesqueness of form, but a vast mass of relative shade, out of which his fierce lights in pure colour rise in due relation. The Frenchman leaves *light* in mass, like Paul Veronese, and therefore draws the eye only to his break-up petits shadows: again, Tintoret never sacrifices the truth of a colour, but reaches his light and shade through his colour as far as he can with truth and no further, and in his cast shadows he rather uses one here and there for a ghastly or expressive effect than admits them as a necessity. This comparison, however, I must work out with much thought.[1]

§ 33. Meantime, note further of Veronese, as we saw that the black outlines were much left, so the painting seems extremely *Architecture of* thin; being on the floor, I saw the picture divinely, out of *Veronese;* its frame. At the bottom, the canvass where the frame had *Thinness of* gone over it, appeared covered with a very thin film of gesso, *colour.* and over this a rich, somewhat dark brown was scratched very rudely in small touches, not like the hand of a master, unless done so on purpose. Nevertheless, all the greys of the architecture, and blues of sky, appeared to me ,to be painted over this brown, and to have its dark gleaming through them continually, and giving depth. The greys themselves were the most pearly and lovely possible, and, to my amazement, of pure colour blended as finely as Turner's own—how, on such a scale, heaven knows; but there were pure blues, and gold and rose colour, and the under brown—all most ætherial and amalgamating, and melting into the opalescent grey which made me write in my small note-book, when I first sat down before this architecture, that it had properties which in nature were "almost peculiar to snow." The touching of the high lights is not so confused as Turner's, more like scene-painting—fitter for background—as less studied, quite as *white* but more commonplace in stroke. The strong darks, throughout the pictures, are dreadfully chilled, only a patch here and there showing their original intensity. The vermilions are just as raw and bad as in Cuyp.[2]

§ 34. The Modified and Sublime Picturesqueness, in exact harmony with *Picturesqueness.* the grand colour, is very delicious; consider especially the quaint form of the sandal . . . [reference to a sketch-book]. It is white; and it seems to me a curious circumstance that the female figure to which it belongs, the one which I have always so much admired at the side of the picture, being a kind of chorus figure lifting her foot so as (apparently), propping it on the base of the column, to rest the child upon it which she seems about to take from her shoulder, brings the lines of the cavetto of the sandal into exact correspondence with the base of the column, as in the upper sketch: the base is shown more carefully at . . . [reference to another sketch], with the opponent line given by the foot of the little girl peeping round the pillar, who forms the chorus on the other (right) side. Thus there is a kind of statuesque quietness given to the figure; it is, at least in the foot . . . [reference to sketch]: (the same base is used in the Titian portrait above described), half turned into stone, and endowed with a grand metamorphic repose, contrasting with the full life of all the rest.

---

[1] [Here, it will be seen, Ruskin is making some of the studies which he worked out in *Modern Painters*, vol. iv. ch. iii. ("Of Turnerian Light").]
[2] [See *Modern Painters*, vol. i. (Vol. III. p. 271).]

§ 35. Observe also that nothing is thought by Veronese beneath his notice, or beneath his pains. It is impossible to fix any general rule as to what is grand or not, in his hands: Sir Joshua Reynolds' rule of "it is drapery and nothing more," [1] is set at utter defiance: indeed I am beginning to think it ought to be. The sitting figure on the extreme left, next the column in a brown tambour, has a dress up to his neck, of green and warm buff in vertical stripes, very broad; the buff has a narrow pink *satin* bar in the centre, and this, where the dress is wrinkled at the neck, is touched with excessive care and delight, the points of its lustre flashing like sparks of fire. So in the picture of the "Supper at Emmaus," with the two little girls [No. 1196], the figure of the matron on the left has a drapery of blue satin, with touches of gold (by-the-bye, look at this again: an example of disunity— yet beautiful in *colour*, though it would be wretched in form) which is studied as carefully as a bit of Chalon [2]—but in such a manly and magnificent way. The damask white and gold of the two children marvellous also—the pattern so thoroughly drawn without stiffness, so also in the table-cloth of the Magdalen—every bit of its pierced border painted thoroughly.

Drapery, Texture of.

§ 36. It struck me, on Saturday, that Veronese and such other men were afraid to give colour to their architecture, lest it should become too important and too solid, but felt that they might give it to their draperies, and yet keep them subordinate,* by the various superimpositions of the colours. The negro boy so often

Colour in Architecture.

---

* I think his usual practice is to keep his high lights colder than his middle tints in draperies. In order to arrive at something like a general conclusion, I set down to-day what was clearest of the colour of the figures in the large Magdalen picture [No. 1193], in doing which I first noted the difference between the heavy monkish drapery with narrow square shadows and masses of light and the feminine drapery with broad masses of middle tint, or even full shadow with wrinkled narrow lights on edges . . . [references to sketches]. In the succeeding list 1 is high light, 2 middle tint, 3 deep shadow, *a* prefixed to the draperies markedly massed in light, *b* to those markedly narrowed in light: those without a letter are of intermediate character or unnoted :—

Colour of Veronese.

Drapery.

1. *b.*   Orange dress of Chorus figure on left my favourite, 1 coldest, 2 full warm orange, 3 greyer, but full colour still.
2. —   Petticoat of same figure above feet, an orange green, 1 and 2 warm orange green, 3 full green.
3. —   Yellow, full, of sitting figure—1 full pure yellow, 2–3 greyish yellow, *i.e.* a kind of colour between yellow lake and Roman ochre; 2 more greenish, 3 (all broad and none dark) more brownish or reddish.
4. —   Lilac—1 cold lilac—3 crimson.
5. *a.*   Whitish yellow ground of a turban striped with red (vermilion), a very dull, yet not dirty colour, most difficult either to copy and describe : 1 full, 3 greyed down.
6. —   Another more crimsony lilac, 1 cold passing into purply white, 2 purply grey, 3 crimsony purple.
7. *a.*   Vermilion, note it has been painted over a grey : 1 pure and high, too

---

[1] [See *Stones of Venice*, vol. iii. (Vol. XI. p. 417 *n.*), for this passage.]
[2] [For this painter, see Vol. X. p. 87 *n.*]

mentioned, has assuredly been painted over two plates, and the crease of the table-cloth at the edge of the table, and yet the *final* white of the table-cloth is *most certainly* painted up to it, and stops at it (as also it does, and this is especially remarkable, at the plates of fruit on the other side, the outline of the flat cherries being sharply given by the circum-dragged white): and the head is most marvellously brought out; there has (I am not *quite* sure of any of these assertions respecting method, except in the particular spots described, which may be sometimes ex-ceptional) first been a black ground, part of the figures on the other side of table; on this a yellow wine-glass has been painted, leaving at one side, as it was struck on, the outline of the negro's most marked features in the black ground. Over this left space, the complexion and such drawing as is required, are given by one coat of the peculiar negro brown of Veronese, which is, of course, struck on and modelled as a light, leaving just an edge of the original black ground between it and the glass yellow, which touched with a vivid brown about the lips serves for an outline.

		uniform, and full throughout, 2 brownish heavy and very disagree-able, 3 hardly existent.
8.	*a.*	Grave orange yellow, sleeve of St. Peter, 1 full in mass, 2 browner, 3 grey nearly positive.
9.	*a.*	Full orange of Magdalene—1, 2, together and much confused, broad and full, 2 I *think* warmest, 3 greyish brown.
10.	*a.*	Deep blue lilac, 1 and 2 together in mass, but 1 coldest, 3 the same as 2, deepened.
11.	—	Full crimson, 1 full, 2 variously subdued brownish or purplish, 3 the same deepened almost to black.
12.	*b.*	Golden green, dress of (Martha?) the principal standing female figure, 1 on edges, highest nearly gold, 2 greener, 3 same passing into black.
13.	*b.*	Lining of the above green at the neck, a shot colour very square in its folds, 1 pink, 2 lilac, 3 greenish grey.
14.	—	Bluish russet green—lower petticoat in same figure, 1 full blue green, struck over brown ground, 2 the said brown ground, more or less lightly touched with the green, 3 full brown and clear.
15.	*a.*	White 1 warm not up to yellow, 2, 3, cold grey.
16.	—	Cold grey—1, 2, 3 alike.
17.	*a.*	Lilac of negro boy (pantaloons) before table, 1 white passing into cool lilac very broad, 2 full, 3 same deepened to crimson, 2 and 3 both narrow.
18.	—	Bluish green—Kneeling boy in front of column—1 blue passing into blue green (struck over) 2 full warm green, 3 same deepened to black.
19.	—	Orange, in upper dress of negro boy, 1 full gold, rising in one place to golden white, 2 warm orange brown, 3 grey brown, a little greenish.
20.	—	White, of a dress; seems confused or repainted, but has assuredly been painted over pink, which is seen through a crack. It is disagreeable. The more I looked, the more thoroughly I was puzzled.

Reds 7, 11, *unvaried.* Lilacs, 4, 6, 10, 13, 17 (Blues, mem, all dark and doubt-ful); I think greens 2, 12, 14, 18, orange 1, 9, 19, yellow, 3, 5, 8, white and grey, 15, 16, 20.

[This note is from an entry made in the diary a day or two after the notes in the text.]

The square creases of the table-cloth, where it has been folded, are elaborately and carefully drawn : they have value as dividing the broad white mass by a kind of masonry, and their formality is varied at the side by the crescent shape of the table. The square and oblong dividing of pavement in red (brownish) and white marble, is also very beautiful and careful . . . [reference to a sketch]. The broadest of the small compartments, though all is thrown into sharp level perspective, are evidently intended to be square, and the long broad ones about four squares ; the narrower are, I think, short, or about a third of the width ; at . . . [reference to another notebook] are their relations rudely taken by bringing edge of book against the picture. All the three narrow bands are of course equal in breadth.

§ 37. I am a little wrong above [p. 463], in denying all cast shadow. The statement about that of dwarf is true, but there are several sharper shadows where they can be ventured—one *Chiaroscuro.* especially down the middle distance architecture, cast from the right, quite sharp ; and from the statues in niches on their hollows ; and in the effects at the proper distance, say the full length of the picture, all the shadows, which seem so faint when one is close, come out broad and clear ; and as nearly as possible Turner's pitch on the side of the white post-office [1] —their faintness seems rather the result of the quantity of reflected and diffused light, than of the feebleness of the sun ray. There is, however, a decided conventionalism, as like Turner as can be—except that Turner makes his diffused light dusty and sunny ; Veronese clear and quiet. The shadow of the wall on the right, tier above tier of silver and gold plate, giving lustrous grey, with a negro in profile—a brown mass of vigorous yet retired shade leaning over and brought against the white distant palace ; while in the foreground the first column of the rotunda is brought in luminous rounded white and grey, one mass of light, out of the retiring shade of the silver wall, all most marvellous. The distant white palace, note, Ionic with Corinthian above, and the acanthus leaves of the near capitals, just turn their very tips, and no more—no feathering or bending about them. The more I looked at the architecture the better I liked it—excepting only the garland on distant rotunda.

§ 38. On the whole, my study this time has caused me to attach less importance to mere *quality* of colour. It seems to me that there is nothing *very* inimitable in particular spaces of it, and *Colour of* that much, even in the best pictures, is a little heavy ; the *Venetians.* pillars in the Magdalen have been painted entirely first ; and the noble figures of the women. . . [reference to sketch] and the rest, painted over them—the mouldings cause a projection in the colour plainly enough seen. (The white of the table-cloth is however painted up to and about the other figures : as, for instance, up to the dark brown negro hand of the dwarf on the right ; and this entire painting of one distance of the picture first, and then another, must, I think, have been a fine aid, as well as discipline of the imagination.) In Annibale Caracci's landscapes the dark hills and distances are all boldly painted first, and the trees struck over them in brown, or green :—in places this causes curious transparent effects when the picture ages : but consider what manly freedom of hand and thought and stroke,

___
[1] [*i.e.,* the Casa Grimani in his picture of Venice above referred to.]

and what purity of colour it admits as opposed to our blundering practice
on the one hand, though it may also necessitate heavy colour as opposed
to pure Van Eyckism on the other. This, however, is evidently one of the
little understood *uses* of oil colour, as enabling superimposition.

§ 39. But to return: *repentirs* are not infrequent in Veronese—often
covered with heavy colour. Titian's child in the Holy Family[1]—with the
magnificent red-capped figure, luminous as a star at a little distance, is apparently heavy and opaque, seen near, or at least nothing very difficult to
reach. Bits, however, there are occasionally, which make one hopeless, like the
hand of the Madonna laid on the white rabbit in the small Holy Family:[2] a
perfect lamp of light. I never saw a piece of more exquisite colour sentiment
than this: in its quaintness and purity, and simplicity and light.

§ 40. Vandyck has a portrait of singular power—a man bareheaded, with
arm on side, akimbo, and slashed sleeve—and light distant
[Vandyck's sky; painted most impetuously and magnificently, but the colour
"Portrait of as opaque and heavy as can be—in hands as much so as a bit
a Man," of deal—and owing all its power to its visible hastiness and
No. 1976.] masterly dragging and striking; each hand, I suppose, might take the painter
from a minute to a minute and a half to finish. The colour of the whole is
fine, but it is by choice, opposition, and execution, not quality. I return to
Mulready's maxim:[3] the fine colour seems to me to come naturally from the
manly hand and eye, and to depend much on everything being done simply,
unaffectedly, and at *once*.

§ 41. Vandyck's "Holy Family," the chief one here, like that at Dulwich,[4]
is a total failure; the child looks like George the Fourth. Now
Religious and nothing can be more exquisite than his little Dutch-faced girl
Aristocratic asking her father, a black senator, to come out with her.[5] On
Sentiment. the other side of the gallery, nothing more lordly or gentle
than a head, one of two, of a prince in armour[6] near this Holy Family. How
is it that he could conceive a gentleman and a child, but not a Madonna?
Note that all his dignity becomes vulgarity when he approaches the Sacred
infant.[7]

§ 42. Observe in Canaletto's La Salute,[8] one has to look for the Doge's
Palace. Not a ray of light, not a spark of wave, leads to or
Canaletto. illustrates it. How cold is this, how utterly lifeless—a man
deserves chastisement for making truth so contemptible.[9]

---

[1] [No. 1577.]

[2] ["La Vierge au Lapin," by Titian, No. 1578.]

[3] [See *Seven Lamps*, Vol. VIII. p. 19.]

[4] ["La Vierge aux Donateurs," No. 1962. The picture in the Dulwich Gallery
is No. 90, "The Madonna and Infant Saviour" (a replica of the picture in the
Bridgewater Gallery).]

[5] [No. 1973: "Portrait of a Man and a Child."]

[6] [No. 1971: "Equestrian Portrait of Francis of Moncade." No. 1972 is a bust portrait of the same. But here, again, the arrangement of the pictures has been altered.]

[7] [With these notes on Vandyck compare *Modern Painters*, vol. v. pt. ix. ch. iv.
§ 14; ch. vi. §§ 5, 10.]

[8] ["View of the Church of La Madonna della Salute," No. 1203.]

[9] [So in the 1844 notes:
    "A rascally Canaletti, all the shaded parts of the boats cast a faint insipid
    reflection: the bright beaks and high lights none whatever, nor any of the
    vertical lines."]

§ 43. The cold grey of the flesh of the body in Titian's "Entombment" [No. 1584] is brought in the uppermost hand against the cheek of the bronzed face—an intense brown, then against scarlet—below against white, and under the arm against dark blue; the flesh outlines of the child above noticed are in greyish brown, not pink like Northcote—no exaggeration.

Colour opposition.

§ 44. After looking carefully at three of his important landscapes—the Deluge, the Eden, and the Gideon—and generally at those scattered through the rooms,[1] I was thoroughly puzzled as to his character, intellectual or moral. In the three landscapes he is cold, artificial, lifeless, feeble, ignorant, conventional, yet always of course a painter; the thing is well painted from beginning to end, and there is always the same quaint power of composition about certain passages. But no words are too strong to reprobate the vileness and meanness of the oak branches and general outline (the foliage being characteristically painted—thorough oak). On the left of the "Gideon" they are as meanly, as they are visibly, *composed,* and the cottage or town architecture in the valley beyond that on the hill looking like La Riccia, and rather grand, is a curious example of the selection exactly of those forms which I should have called the ugliest, both in feeling and line, in the world, all tiled roofs over half-built walls, with windows exactly in the middle . . . [reference to a sketch-book]; the windows, one straight ruled square of grey, *flat grey paint,* neither varied on edge nor surface, tiles ruled straight, eaves straight—all formalized to a physically impossible degree, as if that could idealize such buildings. Consider this as the very and literal anti-picturesque spirit, without grandeur or quaintness or anything else to recommend it.

Nicolo Poussin.

The trees and hills and water and sky are all grey, the first greenish, the last bluish, passing down into good, though lifeless and joyless, gold in the left-hand corner of horizon, the best bit on the whole of the picture; the sky is cloudy, the clouds *cirro-cumuli,* neither grand nor mean, not absolutely commonplace, but far less striking or sublime, and very cold in colour; the ground goes down into the water in the usual formal bank, a dull coloured gravel appearing in places, the water not ill painted, reflections rather studied; but *enfin,* a bit of stagnant water, and there an end. The sentiment of the picture, however, has been well intended; for Poussin has taken the most extraordinary pains to paint the pebbles under the water, in the stream of the foreground, and not only so, but, to my delight, a trunk of a tree has fallen across the stream; it goes under the water, whose flow across it is marked by a gleam of white at the edge, and casts its shadow, detached from it, beneath across the *bottom,* none on the surface; the pebbles are all of the usual commonplace ill-grouped ellipse — the water lowers their tone a little, and shows chiefly by white touches at edge. Poussin has evidently made a study for it; but with all, it is quite uninteresting, and has none of the ripple or brightness or murmur of a stream.

Water Painting.

1 ["The Deluge" is No. 739 ("Winter, or the Great Flood"); and "The Eden," No. 736 ("Spring, or the Earthly Paradise"). By "the Gideon" it is clear from the description that Ruskin meant No. 741, the landscape entitled "Diogenes throwing his bowl away." A young man, standing near Diogenes, is drinking out of his hand; hence Ruskin's reference to Gideon (Judges vii.).]

§ 45. A few rooms on, facing this landscape — which throughout may
be described as the very type of a painter-like frigidity, the
Poussin's Flora Niobe of landscapes, the dullest, flattest, joylessest formality
[No. 732.] of propriety in wood and water: the trees and grass afraid
to be green, the sky too grand to be blue, the water too polite to be noisy
or to move, the moss taken off the tiles, and the beads out of the timbers
and the cracks out of the stones, and the whole thing coloured like the
world in a fainting fit, as if the man who did it had never seen a brighter
colour than a Dutch fog, and had painted an Italian landscape by hearsay;
or as if he had never seen, or at any rate never enjoyed, a tint of colour
or an energetic form in his life, and had about as much sensation as a tortoise
and as much hilarity as a Quaker—opposite this picture, I say, is that one
of the Triumph of Flora [1] with a sky as blue as a gentian, and massy white
clouds, as pure as snow; and a burning distance, all orange gold, as if all
summer and autumn were gathered into one sunset over deep, deep blue
hills, carried down by fiery flakes among the figures; the trees filling all
the blue sky with stars of blossom, and the figures one bright, unrestrainable riot of pure delight—a Keats-like revel of body and soul of most
heavenly creatures—limbs and raiment, thoughts and feelings all astir, one
laugh of life and of colour; two blue-winged Cupids dancing as they drag
the car, or dragging it rather by their dancing unconsciously; a nymph with
dusky yellow dress, and bright brown hair with a white rose in it, and fair,
light limbs—a very autumnal sunbeam, made mortal, dancing first of all;
Flora herself, a sweet throned intense personified gladness; another nymph
stooping as she flies along to gather a (celandine?), but all so pure and
yet so wildly glad, that one might think the spring wind had turned a
drift of loose rose leaves into living creatures.

Note especially of the tree above, it has more white blossoms than
leaves, and they are like hawthorn blossom exaggerated—much larger than
real hawthorn—I think, compared with the figures, they would be about the
size of a wine-glass each flower, and the leaves smaller than flowers. It is an
ideal of spring blossom; compare that which I saw at Vevay, apple-blossom
against blue hills. The celandine is almost white, best in shade, and may
have been meant for a daisy; if it ever were, it is very coarse and large,
and square petalled. [*Note.*] I forgot that the figures which come against
the sunset in this picture increase its heat in a glorious way; they have
red dresses, or fragments of dress, their limbs are burning orange red—
half sunshine, half bronzed flesh; and just between the limbs and (under
the arm?) of one or two fragments of the most intense orange dress complete sparks of fire, which bring the colour of the sky down among them.
As an example of increase of warmth of colour by sympathy into one
flash, it would be difficult to match it.

§ 46. Compare with this spirit of pure revelry, true classic—nay, better
than true classic—the revel of Rubens, a crowd of peasants,
Rubens: "The near some place, drinking, dancing like baboons, hauling
Village Fête," each other by the part of the body where a waist should
No. 2115. be, kissing, and—men and women alike—fighting for pots
of beer. I never thought Rubens vulgar till to-day; but as, yesterday, I

---

[1] [For another reference to this picture, see *Modern Painters*, vol. iii. ch. xviii. § 28.]

found a problem about Vandyck,[1] so I have to consider to-day how strange it is that Rubens could paint a picture like that of his mother, in our Gallery,[2] and such a thing as this. For there is no joy of colour, no fine form, no drollery; it is unmitigated brutality: if meant as a satire on drunkenness, well; but I cannot conceive a good man enduring to paint it, bearing the sight of his own imaginations. A pig puts its snout out of a stye in the corner; and two ducks, carefully painted, occupy the nearest gutter. I did not enough note the landscape background.

§ 47. The most impressive picture of the Sphinx and Pyramids[3] I have ever seen—modern French in Standish Gallery—deep blue sky, ground nearly white, pyramids, light side, nearly white and ghostly like Turner, dark side just dark on sky and no more. Very sweeping, far away, and fine—and *real* withal!

§ 48. *Grass-painting.*—Giorgione's picture[4] I had not time to examine— it is in bad light. Pure blue distance and golden sky, then brown cottages against it, full green in foreground, changing Titian's last two steps. The grass on which figures sit has puzzled him—it is exquisitely touched, but not like grass, covered with slender curved lines, like hay left after carrying; Paul Potter's, in large cow piece [No. 2527], execrable, all like this . . . [reference to sketch] touched on in light.

3. NOTES OF 1854[5]

§ 49. No. 1187 [Paolo Veronese: " Lot leaving Sodom "]. I have before noted this picture. The action of one of the daughters pulling her sandal up at the heel to be compared with Turner's old woman at Turin.[6]

Titian, " Supper at Emmaus " [No. 1581]. The table-cloth covered with the blue flower I found at Sion with the conical centre as opposite [reference to a drawing], mixed with heart's-ease.

Domenichino, 1614 [" Hercules and Achelous"]. A hero stopping bull in full career, which he does standing on *tip-toe*, on one leg, the bull utterly out of proportion, utterly meagre, base, and like the worst toy in a child's Noah's Ark, with its leg *forward* under it, as at [reference to a sketch]; could a bull possibly fall in such a position? Two kings standing by shrug their shoulders and lift up their hands, as people are represented at a show of a dwarf or giantess, on the canvass outside.[7]

---

[1] [See above, § 41, p. 468.]

[2] [*i.e.*, in this case, the Dulwich Gallery; the reference being to the " Portrait of an Old Lady " (now No. 29), formerly entitled "The Mother of Rubens," now ascribed to his school.]

[3] [Here, again, the picture cannot now be identified, as there is none in the Louvre corresponding to the description.]

[4] [The " Concert Champêtre," No. 1136 (now well hung) : see above, p. 454.]

[5] [This visit to the Louvre was made on Ruskin's return from his summer tour in 1854 : see above, Introduction, p. xxxvii.]

[6] [The figure in the corner of Turner's drawing of "Turin from the Superga": see Ruskin's *Notes on his Drawings by Turner*, No. 17.]

[7] [Ruskin next notices Francesco di Bianchi's " Madonna and Child " (No. 1167) and Lorenzo di Costa (No. 1261 or 1262); but the page in the diary is greatly torn, and the extracts cannot be given.]

Mantegna, 1376 ["Wisdom victorious over the Vices"]. Very important from its good rendering of distant low hills; flat and true, not all knots and humps, but low and soft.

Perugino (?), 1567 ["The Fight between Love and Chastity"]. Very like him, but a profane subject; showing inroads of classicalism: Nymphs assailed by Cupids.

Cima da Conegliano, 1259 ["Virgin and Child"]. Has hanging rock at side, with house on it, as opposite.[1] It is curious how many pictures depend on rocks with holes through them. Count, to-morrow.

Flemish (?), 2202 [Painter unknown: "The Angelic Salutation"]. Snowy mountains, in clear distance; very pretty; the best of Alps in all Flemish [school]—gem-like and finished, never sublime.

Rubens, 2100, Dolphin swimming after ship,[2] and red fish on top of water close by: compare with Turner.

Observe that at present in the Louvre one whole side of a room is given to Eustache Le Sueur; and Karl Dujardin, and Albert van Everdingen, and Balthazar Denner are on the line, and their only Tintoret, 60 feet high.[3]

Poussin, 730 ["Bacchanal"]. Poussin's best bold landscape; nearly blue hills, one mass of blue against yellow, and brown rocks in front; the sky, first white clouds on greenish blue ground, which, as it goes away to the horizon, takes the character of leaden clouds on a golden distance—the painter seeming not clearly to have made up his mind what he meant it for.

Mountains.—Multitudes of mountains painted blue on one side, and white on the other: Watteaus on this principle.

The grand impression on me in walking through the Louvre often after Switzerland is the utter *coarse*ness of painting—especially as regards mountains. The universal principle of blue mass behind, and green or brown banks or bushes in front. No real sense of height or distance—no care, no detail, no affection. To think of the soft purple dawns melting along the heights of the Valais, and then of such things as these!

§ 50. *Sept.* 28.—I thought, in the Louvre, yesterday, that it would be well to have separate chapters, showing in art how all things successively depend on—Truth, Refinement, Confusion. That is, I found that truth was an absolute measure of the goodness of art, that the greatest men were always those who gave most truth. Secondly, that refinement was also an absolute measure, all the greatest men being, according to their scale, exquisitely tender and refined and subtle. Thirdly, confusion is also an absolute measure, all the greatest men being confused. Correggio's "Antiope" [No. 1118] is much bolder and more vague in execution than I thought—a wonderful example of effect of finish got through sketchy touches in

---

[1] [The sketch on the opposite page of the diary is cut out. Beneath it Ruskin had written, "Put my cottages at Zermatt with this." The sketch was used as Fig. 86 in *Modern Painters*, vol. iv. ch. xvi. § 36.]

[2] [The subject is "The Majority of Louis XIII."; the King is shown standing on the ship of State.]

[3] [Now rearranged.]

the foreground. Paul Veronese's mystery through all his decision; lightness of touch and intense refinement, through all his power.

1416, Cosimo Rosselli.[1] An exquisite branch of white blossom of some kind, something like cherry, its flowers drawn dark in perfect perspective of every curve against the golden sky in foreground. It is a crowning of the Virgin.

2115, Rubens ["The Village Fair"]. Get engraving of some part of Rubens' drunken festival to put beside Angelico: show quality in both.

I did not think Rubens could have been so ignoble as he is in the Frances and Victories, and above all Minervas, with tucked-up petticoats and bare muscular legs, and half-boots, in the Medici series.[2]

Veronese [No. 1192]. In the great Cana picture it appears to me difficult to decide whether irony or insult is intended by the cats playing with the handle of the vase of water. Is it to show the irreverence with which the most solemn gifts of God are treated by man; as in like manner the head of clown with bells, and then the hour-glass just under Christ. The patterns on the dresses of the Veronese, unless they are of gold, or damask, or something lustrous, are, when dark, just as dark in light as in shade, if not a little darker.

1598. In Leonardo's St. Anne (a villainous piece of rubbish now, whatever it may have been) there are some good bits, and those Pre-Raphaelite. The pebbles under the feet of St. Anne are now more laboured than the figures, some of the flints being agatescent, and every vein of the agate drawn in pebbles not an inch wide.[3] In Titian's "Entombment" [No. 1584] the two snail shells on the ground are painted as carefully as any part of the picture.[4] In Veronese's "Dinner in Simon's House" [No. 1193] the interwoven lace of the hem of the table-cloth most laborious; the meshes being carefully varied in size, quite as careful as Hunt's hem in "The Awakening Conscience."[5]

---

[1] [The picture described is, however, No. 1416, by Piero di Cosimo.]

[2] [The series of pictures, representing the history of Mary of Medici, painted by Rubens, 1620–1625, for the old gallery of the Luxembourg; Nos. 2085–2108 in the Louvre. Ruskin notices them in more detail in *The Harbours of England*, § 30 and *n.*; see also *Modern Painters*, vol. iii. ch. viii. § 6.]

[3] [See *Modern Painters*, vol. iii. ch. ix. § 18, where Ruskin notices this detail in his discussion of Finish in art.]

[4] [In a later diary (1856) Ruskin notes:—
  "Besides the snail shells in Titian's 'Entombment' there are two alchemilla leaves in the left-hand bottom corner, beautifully drawn—quite as laboured as the foot of the Christ. The foreground of the 'Belle Jardinière' is worked out in the hardest way with conspicuous columbine, rose and plaintain—all in brownish green with black shadows."]

[5] [For this picture, and for the details here mentioned, see above, p. 335.]

ADDRESSES ON DECORATIVE COLOUR [1]

(1854)

I. THE DISTINCTION BETWEEN ILLUMINATION
AND PAINTING

[Delivered on Saturday, November 11th, 1854]

1. Mr. Ruskin commenced by stating that he was not going to read a paper, or to speak from notes, and it was a mistake in the advertisement [2] to say that he intended to deliver a lecture. It was not a lecture, but a little friendly talk, and his object was to address himself to the students present, and place before them, in a familiar way, things which were useful.

Before entering upon this subject, however, he wished to glance at one or two historical points, with the view of explaining the examples he proposed to set before them. In these days it was a very common practice to laugh at the Middle Ages and hold them up to ridicule. Truly they were ridiculous in many senses, but certainly they were not ridiculous in their way of writing. They did not write in those days so much as we do now, but they wrote much better when they did write. Even so far back as the seventh century, the Saxon writing began to acquire character and dignity and beauty, though the writing of that period differed materially from anything that we did now. The specimen he now submitted

---

[1] [The three following addresses, on "Decorative Colour as applicable to Architectural and other Purposes," were given by Ruskin, in 1854, at the Architectural Museum, as stated above (Introduction, p. lxvi.). They were not written out by him, nor were they printed in any of his works. They were, however, reported at the time in the press; and especially in the *Morning Chronicle* (November 13, 27, and December 11), and the *Builder* (November 25, December 2, 16). A fuller report, collated from these and other sources, was given in Part II., pp. 125–153, of *Ruskiniana* (privately printed in 1892). The present report is based on this last version, but has been somewhat amended (see above, p. lxvi.). The numbering of the paragraphs is now introduced.]

[2] [The lecture had been advertised in the *Athenæum* of October 21, 1854, and elsewhere. It appears that a printed synopsis was also issued—at any rate of the second and third lectures—(see §§ 14, 29), but the editors have not been able to find a copy of it.]

(an initial letter) was written as an ornament to a psalter belonging to a lady who died in the year 656, St. Salaberga.[1] It would be perceived that the colours employed in writing in that day were simply black, yellow and red. The design in the example was a continuous scroll, beginning in a bird's beak, and terminating in a sort of yellow dragon. It never encountered itself at a turn, but it glanced off and met again in some different part of its progress, and never doubled simply upon itself. Such was the general character of the MS. of that century. It was not very easy to imitate. He had himself tried it, but found it difficult; and to do it well considerable practice would be required. He wished, however, to draw attention to the fact that there was a character and a finish about this writing which was not found in common penmanship.

2. From these yellow and black scrolls they went on improving until the great masters of the time of Charlemagne, when the art of illuminated writing received a great impulse. Then more and more colour was introduced in the finish, and greater variety in the outline. It had been frequently said that Charlemagne could not write, but that was very imperfectly true. True, he could not write in what would be called writing now; for what we now understand as writing would not have been called writing in the days of Charlemagne. Here was an example of the writing of that age. This (the specimen exhibited) was written in the eighth century, and it was the beginning of one of the books of the Gospel. It would be observed that more colour was introduced about this time; and they would notice how it was stolen in, as it were, upon the gold. But though it was said Charlemagne could not write, though he could not write as we write now, yet he could write after a fashion. He always carried tablets about with him, upon which he from time to time put down anything he desired to remember. He could not, however, write like the specimen the meeting were now examining; but he employed those who could, and paid great respect to them. Immense respect was paid to the writers of those days. He (the lecturer) would much like that respect paid to the art of writing now. As showing the kind of respect which this art commanded in the Middle Ages, he would read an anecdote respecting an eminent writer who lived in the time of Charlemagne.

"There was in the monastery of Arnisberg a writer named Richard, an Englishman, who had with his own hand copied a great number of books, hoping to receive in heaven a recompense for his labours. When he quitted this life his brother monks buried him in a place of honour. Twenty years afterwards his tomb was opened, and his right hand was found in as perfect a state of preservation as though it were alive, and appeared to have been recently cut off from an animated body, while all the rest of the corpse was dust. This hand is shown as a great miracle to this day in the monastery of Arnisberg."

3. This showed the honour with which a good writer was regarded at that period; and not only was the art honourable and profitable to those who practised it, but its effect was profitable and valuable to others. We had an instance of this in the history of one to whom we were indebted for

---

[1] [This Psalter was one of the MSS. in the Duke of Hamilton's library, which Ruskin had examined in 1853 (see above, p. lxvii.).]

all our English literature—he alluded to King Alfred. Alfred himself was honoured in France for his writing; and the best writing of that period came from France. It was well known that the French princess Judith, who was Alfred's stepmother, took great pains to teach him; but it would seem that he had naturally no more taste for study than other children, for it was recorded of him that he lived to twelve years old before he was taught to read. How he was induced to learn was, according to Mr. Sharon Turner, in this wise: "When Alfred was twelve years old, she (Judith) was sitting one day surrounded by her family with a MS. of Saxon poetry in her hands. . . . With a happy judgment she proposed it as a gift to him who would be the soonest to learn to read it. The whole incident may have been chance play, but it was fruitful of consequences. The elder princes—one then a king, the other in mature youth or manhood—thought the reward inadequate to the task, and were silent. But the mind of Alfred, captivated by the prospect of information, and pleased with the beautiful decoration of the first letter of the writing, inquired if she actually intended to give it to such of her children as would the soonest learn to understand and repeat it. His mother repeating the promise, with a smile of joy at the question, he took the book, found out an instructor, and learned to read it. When his industry had crowned his wishes with success, he recited it to her. To this important though seemingly trivial incident we owe all the intellectual cultivation and all the literary works of Alfred, and all the benefits which by these he imparted to his countrymen."[1] In this case the beautiful initial letter was the attraction—a letter, probably, like that which he (the lecturer) had just exhibited as characteristic of the date of Charlemagne. This was the first inducement to study with our English Alfred, and he was not quite sure whether it would not be better generally that children should remain until they were twelve years of age, and then be tempted to read by such inducements as these, rather than that we should go on impressing upon their minds in infancy the enormous fallacy that "A" ever was, or under any circumstances could become, an apple-pie.

4. The main idea of the age of which he was now speaking, however, was that a book was a noble and a sacred thing, to be respected and revered. It became precious because it was written with so much labour and with so much beauty; and then came the idea of its sanctity. It was noble, inasmuch as it was the means of making human thought—the most transient and evanescent of all things — the most permanent of all things. The mountains of the earth would fall sooner than some of the noblest thoughts perpetuated by books would perish. Well, this being the idea of books, which then obtained in men's minds, they worked, and worked on, to attain greater excellence in their writing, by systematising their colour more and more, until they arrived at a perfect system, which, however, they might have found out long before they did, and which [it] was strange that we ourselves had not discovered. It was strange that those who were familiar with the Bible, wherein they were told that the colours directed to be used for ornamenting the tabernacle were gold (or yellow), and blue, and purple,

---

[1] [The passage is quoted from Sharon Turner's *History of England*, 1839, vol. i. pp. 500–501. For a further reference to it, see below, § 19, p. 493. For a sketch by Ruskin of the Life of Alfred, see *The Pleasures of England*, §§ 103 *seq.*]

and scarlet,[1] as being those calculated to form the basis of the richest, most harmonious, and glorious combination, should not have adopted them in all cases where such results were required. The thirteenth-century people, however, had not, it appeared, derived their knowledge from the Bible; they went on working and experimenting until they found it out. Here (exhibiting it) was a Bible of the year 1220; it was but a common example, but worth exhibiting, on account of the clerkly manner in which the letters were written and the intense delicacy of the writing generally.

5. He now came to the middle of the thirteenth century, when an immense development of the art took place. It was well known that the whole spirit of the Middle Ages was to be found in the writings of Dante: there it must be sought.[2] Dante was the prophet of the Middle Ages. In his *Purgatory* * he introduced a description of certain people suffering the penalty of pride. He represented them as being crushed under great stones, in the position of which we have so many examples in the architectural decorations of that period, as in figures bearing corbels, brackets, etc. That accounted for the painful attitudes and contortions of the figures bearing brackets to be found in and about ancient ecclesiastical edifices. It was curious to see what Dante appeared to think most calculated to create the feeling of pride in the human breast. It was not valour, nobility, or success in battles, but excellence in writing. These were his words:—

> " Listening, I bent my visage down : and one
> (Not he who speaks) twisted beneath the weight
> That urged him, saw me, knew me straight, and call'd,
> Holding his eyes with difficulty fix'd
> Intent upon me, stooping as I went,
> Companion of their way. 'Oh!' I exclaim'd,
> 'Art thou not Oderigi? Art not thou
> Agobbio's glory?—glory of that art
> Which they of Paris call the limner's skill?'
> 'Brother,' said he, 'with tints that gayer smile,
> Bolognian Franco's pencil lines the leaves.
> His all the honour now—my light obscured.' "[3]

* Canto XI., ll. 73 *seqq.*

---

[1] [Exodus xxvi.; referred to again in *Seven Lamps* (Vol. VIII. p. 34).]

[2] [So, above, in *Lectures on Architecture and Painting*, p. 108.]

[3] [The lines about Oderigi, the illuminator, a friend of Giotto and Dante, are quoted again in the second lecture (§ 20, p. 494). "There lived in Rome," says Vasari in his Life of Giotto, "a certain Oderigi of Agobbio, an excellent miniature-painter, with whom Giotto lived on terms of close friendship; and who was therefore invited by the Pope to illuminate many books for the library of the palace. . . . In my book of ancient drawings I have some few remains from the hand of this artist, who was certainly a clever man, although much surpassed by Franco of Bologna, who executed many admirable works in the same manner, for the same pontiff (and which were also destined for the library of the palace), at the same time with Oderigi. From the hand of Franco, also, I have designs, both in painting and illuminating, which may be seen in my book above cited; among others, are an eagle, perfectly well done, and a lion tearing up a tree, which is most beautiful" (Bohn's edition, 1855, i. 104).]

The line which is given by Cary (for this is his translation)—

"Which they of Paris call the limner's skill"—

is not properly translated." [1] The word, which in the original is *"alluminare,"* does not mean the limner's art, but the art of the illuminator—the writer and illuminator of books. The passage gave a peculiar interest to the illuminated works of the date in which Dante wrote. His book contained

---

[1] [In criticism of this remark, "M.A.," writing to the *Builder* (December 2, 1854) from Cambridge, defended Cary's translation by referring to Johnson's dictionary to show that "limner" was after all corrupted from "enlumineur," *i.e.,* "a decorator of books with initial pictures." His letter concluded by remarking upon another of Ruskin's statements in the second lecture (§ 18, below), namely, that "Black letter is not really illegible, it is only that we are not accustomed to it. . . . The fact is, *no* kind of character is really illegible. If you wish to see real illegibility, go to the Houses of Parliament and look at the inscriptions there !" In reply to "M.A." Ruskin wrote the following letter, which appeared in the *Builder* of December 9 :—

"LIMNER" AND ILLUMINATION.

"I do not usually answer objections to my written statements, otherwise I should waste my life in idle controversy ; but as what I say to the workmen at the Architectural Museum is necessarily brief, and in its words, though not in its substance, unconsidered, I will answer, if you will permit me, any questions or cavils which you may think worthy of admission into your columns on the subject of these lectures.

"I do not know if the Cambridge correspondent, whose letter you inserted last week, is more zealous for the honour of Cary, or anxious to detect me in a mistake. If the former, he will find, if he take the trouble to look at the note in the 264th page of the second volume of the *Stones of Venice* [Vol. X. p. 307 *n.*], that Cary's reputation is not likely to suffer at my hands. But the translation, in the instance quoted, is inadmissible. It does not matter in the least whence the word 'limner' is derived. I did not know when I found fault with it that it was a corruption of 'illuminator,' but I knew perfectly that it did not in the existing state of the English language *mean* 'illuminator.' No one talks of 'limning a missal,' or of a 'limned missal.' The word is now universally understood as signifying a painter or draughtsman in the ordinary sense, and cannot be accepted as a *translation* of the phrase of which it is a *corruption*.

"Touching the last clause of the letter, I should have thought that a master of arts of Cambridge might have had wit enough to comprehend that characters may be illegible by being far off, as well as by being ill-shaped ; and that it is not less difficult to read what is too small to be seen, than what is too strange to be understood. The inscriptions on the Houses of Parliament are illegible, not because they are in black letters, but because, like all the rest of the work on that, I suppose, the most effeminate and effectless heap of stones ever raised by man, they are utterly unfit for their position.

"J. RUSKIN."

This letter was reprinted in *Arrows of the Chace*, 1880, ii. 245. It elicited a further letter, together with one from "Vindex," in defence of Sir Charles Barry and the Houses of Parliament (see the *Builder*, Dec. 16, 1854). But Ruskin did not pursue the controversy.]

passages which must have given a material direction to the art of illuminated writing, and especially in the effective introduction of colour.[1]

6. This period—the middle of the thirteenth century—was marked also by the career of St. Louis, and the next example which he (the lecturer) had to produce was from a psalter[2] emblazoned by the fleur de lis and castle, which were on all works done for St. Louis, which was peculiar in having, in addition to the names of the saints, the names of the members of St. Louis's family, with the dates of their deaths, but not that of St. Louis himself. First, there was the name of Count Robert of Artois, St. Louis's brother, who lost his life while charging the Saracens at Mansourah—just as our light cavalry had charged the Russians at Balaklava. There was thus a note of his death which was put down as a sort of martyrdom. Then there were the names of King Philip II., then that of Louis VIII.,[3] the father, and of Blanche of Castile, the mother of St. Louis, but not his own. Now, Queen Blanche died in 1252, and St. Louis himself in 1270, so that it was evident this psalter was written between those two periods, and the different portions of it at some distance of time from each other. The leaf exhibited was one of the common leaves taken from the beginning of the book. The flourish of the initial letter he had enlarged, in order to show more clearly what sort of a thing it was. The prevailing colours were blue, purple, and scarlet, with gold, and black and white were introduced in smaller quantities. Leaves were introduced, and the ornament, it would be perceived, was constantly changing in form and in the curve and life of the leaf. If there were no change there could be no life. A person could not live without change; not a tree or a leaf could live without growth. That might be taken as the great rule of all living art. He might, while upon this point, remark, that one of the great evils of the day was an intense love of symmetry. Nothing in nature was perfectly symmetrical. No two sides of any animal, tree, or other natural object, were exactly alike. Try to brush your hair exactly alike on both sides, and you will find it could not be done. A statue to be graceful must not have the arms and legs in the same action on both sides; they must be in different actions. In nature they always *were* in different actions. In sculpture, in painting, as in everything else, in art as in nature, without dissimilarity there could be no grace. That, too, was one of the laws of capital illumination.

7. The next specimen he would present to their notice was a capital letter at the beginning of a psalm. In this they would observe that animals, as well as natural leaves, were introduced. Up to this period nature had not been followed in writing to the same extent, but had been treated in the manner represented in the previous examples. The little Bible he had in his hand, in which the initial capital, of which the letter he exhibited was an enlargement, occurred, was a good example of the style of writing of the year 1230. Here, they would observe, the prevailing colours were

---

[1] [For Dante's care in defining colours, see *Modern Painters*, vol. iii. ch. xiv. § 49.]

[2] [This was Ruskin's Psalter of St. Louis, for which see above, Introduction, p. lxix.]

[3] [Robert, Count of Artois, brother of Louis IX., slain at the battle of Mansourah in Egypt, 1250 ; Philip II. reigned 1189–1223 ; Louis VIII. reigned 1223–1226.]

the same, blue, purple, and scarlet, with white introduced at intervals, telling like beautiful pearls. It was a great point in the arts—which many did not seem to be aware of—to know how precious white was. Here were two of the introductory leaves of a psalter which he wished to bring to notice, on account of the human faces introduced in the ornament of the letters.[1] One of these illuminations represented Solomon, having been named David's successor, being made to ride upon the king's own mule, and the burial of King David with Solomon watching at the bier. Both

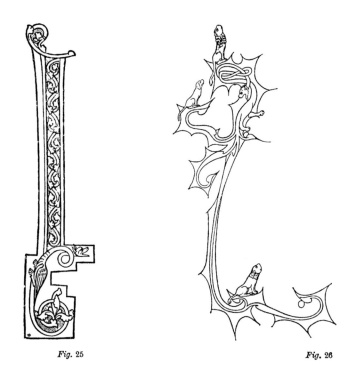

Fig. 25   Fig. 26

of these examples were remarkable for the beauty of the faces. Outline and colour were, however, the principles of these examples; beyond that there was no imitation of nature. The introduction of nature was the culminating point of the art.

8. But from this time they began to enrich their MSS. more and more; the systemisation of colour went on until they reached a point of enormous luxury. With that luxury of ornament and colour came carelessness and the gradual degradation and decline of the art. The manuscript now produced,

[1] [Figures 25, 26, and 27, here introduced, have been engraved on wood from large drawings found at Brantwood. Fig. 25 may serve to illustrate the decorative scroll; fig. 26, the introduction of animals; fig. 27, the addition of human figures.]

one belonging to the sixteenth century, exhibited that carelessness and degradation in a marked degree. The art having reached its culminating point about the middle or towards the close of the thirteenth century, from that period began to decay, the principles of it having been lost sight of in the attempt to attain greater luxuriousness of drawing and effect, those principles which he insisted upon as the fundamental principles of the art being clearness of outline and simplicity of colour, without the introduction of light and shade.[1]

Fig. 27

9. He had said that writers were not reverenced sufficiently in these days,—he said also that neither were painters reverenced as they ought to be. It was a very difficult thing to paint well — much more so than most people imagined ; and to lay on light and shade properly, to realise and to convey upon canvas a thorough impression of the varying effects of sunshine and shadow, in the colour of the air, and in the tints given in every object in nature, was a far more difficult thing than most men were capable of accomplishing. This was the reason why we had so few really good painters, and so many bad paintings. There had been never more than three or four really good painters in the world in any one age, and no wonder, for it required talent of a very rare order to be a painter in the higher sense of the term. The fault of the present age was that we never knew the difference between good and bad painting, and it was a miserable thing to see a

---

[1] [In connection with this lecture, it may be noted that seven years later (June 1861) Ruskin addressed the Society of Antiquaries of London upon the subject of illuminated MSS. This address was in connexion with an Exhibition arranged by the Society. In the *Proceedings of the Society of Antiquaries* (1861, p. 408) it is recorded that—

"John Ruskin, Esq., made some observations on the gradual development, both in colour and form, of the art of illuminating till it reached its culminating point in the 13th century ; and thence traced its gradual decay, from the introduction of principles at variance with what he considered the proper functions of this beautiful art."

In "an interesting and characteristic address" (says the *Times*, June 10, 1861), "he proceeded to trace the gradual development of the art, both in colour and form, down to the period when, in his opinion, the art of illumination abandoned its proper function, and by the application of shading effected the final decay of what had constituted its essential principles and glory in the 13th century."

"He showed" (says the *Guardian* of June 12, 1861) "how the art of illumination

2 H

number of men passing their time in futile painting. It was as difficult, and required a natural capacity as extraordinary, to be a good painter, as it did to be a Duke of Wellington; but though it was necessary to possess a first-rate capacity and talents of the highest order to be a painter, it was not so to enable persons to outline truly from nature, and to lay on simple colour beautifully. This also was a peculiar gift not possessed by every one; but it was a gift which hundreds of persons possessed naturally. Amongst dressmakers there were many who instinctively, as it were, evinced an aptitude at arranging flowers and putting on colour, so as to throw in depth or light as required, for the purpose of producing harmonious combinations, and the instinct to arrange bouquets of flowers, so as to combine in harmony the various hues, was common. A child of twelve often knew how to do that well. But the mischief was that, when young people were found to possess talent of outlining or arranging colour in more than an ordinary degree, they were pressed to learn to draw, though they might not have brains enough to draw well.

10. He would urge upon those of his audience who had the gift of colour not to allow it to be checked or run away with by pursuing that which it was more than doubtful that they would ever succeed in. There might be first-rate art exhibited in the pursuit of colour only. The field was narrow, no doubt; but if a man made up his mind to be an illu-minator—if he possessed the gift of arranging colour, and his opportunities and time did not admit of his making himself a good painter—then let him take up this principle, that every form he drew must be in pure colour, without shadow. He might use what colours he pleased; but let him not resort to shadow in any shape—the object should always be represented in gradated pure colour, with true outline. The first step was to be perfect master of outline. "The first thing to tell you is always to look for out-line; the first thing I shall tell the young artists, whom I mean to lecture after you, is never to look for outline,—that there is no such thing as out-line in nature. And then people will say I am inconsistent." Outline was susceptible of great beauty and infinite variety; but it must be firm and true, not thickened on the side opposite to the light, with a view of showing something like a shadow. It must not be shadowed at all. Nothing could be more absurd than to attempt to throw in shadow by thickening the line; for if the outline was ever lost, it would oftener be on the dark side than on the light side. Besides, the veracity of the line would lie within the compass of a hair. It must be right or wrong. If right, the thickening of the line destroyed the correctness, and the thickness must be removed before the outline could be true, the truth lying somewhere within the thick line. The first thing to practise was perfectly faithful outline, and an important thing to know was how much could be expressed by it. Here

grew out of that of writing, and that when the two became separated they rapidly declined. Illuminations lost their flat, unshaded character, and degenerated into picture-books, and the letters became less perfectly formed. He thought the art of illumination might well be revived at the present day and employed in the ornamenta-tion of those books for which we feel a sort of personal affection."

"The most beautiful specimen" (says the *Guardian*) "exhibited on this occasion was some leaves of a psalter, executed for the use of St. Louis, and shown by Mr. Ruskin. There is a great deal of character in the figures, and nothing can exceed the delicacy of the outlines and colours."]

was an example of the fourteenth century, containing nothing but outline. They would observe that there was a blue bird in the composition, which appeared all but animated because it was, as far as it went, so beautifully drawn. This example, and some of the others, would, however, appear to those who were close to them somewhat coarse, in consequence of their having been considerably enlarged from the original MS. But there might be as much perception of nature in working out these mere outlines as in working out a fully shadowed drawing, like one he now exhibited (a bunch of leaves very far inferior as a work of art to either of the examples of MS. shown), and it was much better that they should possess, for the purposes of decoration generally, the daring conventionality of colour shown in other specimens he submitted to them with pure outline, than that they should be imitators of the spurious examples produced by painters who could not paint, and which violated the eye wherever they were seen. He had said that the peculiar character of the decorative work of the thirteenth century was the introduction of nature, and that was the circumstance that would make it especially agreeable to those who pursued this art now, if it could (as he hoped) be revived amongst us. In practising it, they need not limit themselves to birds and leaves, as in the examples before them, but might avail themselves of every natural object. As soon as they could trace an outline correctly, he wanted them to watch closely every living object around them—groups of children in the streets, leaves, trees, birds, and the animals in the Zoological Gardens; but he would warn them against introducing too much; and when they were painting, let them never introduce the same letter twice, or the same figure or animal twice in the same composition.

11. Now, what were the fields for an occupation of this kind? This was a serious question, and unless the change took place which he was now striving to bring about, he found himself wedged in between two difficulties. He frequently received letters from persons who said to him, "Build us a house, or paint us a room in this way." The reply he was compelled to make was, that he had not the workmen who could do it; and then it was said, naturally enough, that he was a humbug. He went to the workmen, and they said, "We cannot devote our time to that kind of work; there is no demand for it, and we could not earn our money by it." Now, he had asked the students and workmen to come together there that day, that they might aid him in the attempt to revive the art to which he had been directing their attention, by recommending to those by whom they were employed to introduce this kind of decoration wherever opportunity offered. There was a great field for it in ornamenting the interiors of churches. There was the lettering of the Commandments, and the writing over the Communion-table, the windows, or other ornamental work, where illuminated letters might be introduced with great effect. The patterns might be perpetually varied, and animals, birds, leaves, trees, and other natural objects might be made to give life and diversity to them. But he would urge upon them, whenever they were required to paint anything in a church, to do it as well as they could, and to introduce as much of nature as they could in a graceful manner. Then there was the decoration of rooms —though upon that point he confessed he was much at sea and saw considerable difficulty, for he liked good pictures and prints in rooms, and

would, as far as he could, induce people to buy them, and the examples he had exhibited certainly would not look well with those. He would say nothing further upon this point, therefore, except that he should like to receive the advice and suggestions of workmen themselves upon it. In the lettering on the outside of shop-fronts illuminated letters might appropriately be employed, and would form a pleasing change from the dingy appearance which many of the shop-fronts, especially in the Metropolis, presented. He would urge upon them, when they had shop-fronts to decorate, to endeavour to induce the shopkeeper to allow them to introduce such letters. He believed the effect would be good, and our streets greatly warmed by it; but he was not over-sanguine when he looked at that unhappy thing in Leicester Square,[1] which was abominably ugly, in spite of its colour.

12. Another and a most important field for the exercise of this art, was the decoration of books. He did not say that every book should be illuminated,—some books, as the Bible, should, he thought, be as simple in lettering as possible; but books of poetry or art might be very appropriately decorated as suggested. He was anxious to see a taste for decorating books in this manner, because he believed we were falling into a very careless way of regarding our books. It might be that we had so many books now as compared with what persons in similar positions in life formerly possessed. It had been said that it was better to have a few books than many; he could not say that that was his feeling; he considered it a most delightful thing to have a library. At the same time, he should like people to value and love their books more than they did, and feel in the manufacture of a book what the people of the Middle Ages felt. The feeling that prevailed in the Middle Ages with regard to books was, that they were holy things, and those who were employed upon them felt that they were engaged upon a holy work. He would like to bring back something of that feeling; and he would also like to bring back for the workmen the employment of illuminating books, for he thought it must have been a most happy employment. He did not know at what cost now an illuminator might be able to produce a finely illuminated page. That was a subject on which he was anxious to obtain information. He wanted to have the data, and if the workmen would furnish him with that, he would endeavour to bring the subject before the public. What he wanted was the information to enable him to say, when asked, what would be the cost of illuminating some beloved book, which it might be desired to preserve as a valued work in a family. He thought very many persons would gladly avail themselves of the opportunity, if it were offered them, to have books of this character so decorated to be preserved as heirlooms. For his own part, he would infinitely rather have a finely illuminated book than a picture. He would like to have a book of which every page was a picture. The great point was to make this art of book illumination fashionable: if that were done, it would go on as a matter of course. A new school of art would be introduced; the eye for colour would become disciplined; the perception of truth and form in outline would become disciplined; and the art of painting would be more and more appreciated. A Titian

---

[1] [The " Royal Panopticon of Science and Art," built (1852–1853) in the Moorish style as a Polytechnic, afterwards converted into a Music Hall and renamed " The Alhambra "; burnt down in 1882; rebuilt 1883–1884.]

could only be appreciated by those who understood harmony of colour. It was not the extraordinary effects of the light and shade—beautiful though they were—that marked the true Titian, so much as the beautiful harmony of his colours; and by disciplining the eye to those harmonies a feeling would be created in the public mind which was now almost dead.

13. There was another advantage that would result from the rival of this art to the student and illuminator. He could not imagine a happier life than that which would be led by any person of quiet and studious habits with something like the disposition of the old monks who were the illuminators in past times, while following this occupation. If it were cultivated, a totally new impulse would be given to art in every direction, and possibly also to literature; for people would feel that it was better to have a monument in the shape of an illuminated book than in that of an illuminated window; and many a man engaged in writing a book would feel more interest in his work, and take more care in its composition, if he knew that it was to be beautifully illuminated, to be placed in a library as a be-loved thing, to be handed down from father to son, and from generation to generation, than if it were printed in the ordinary way, tossed about and scattered all over the world with all the errors committed in it by printers' devils, and thrown aside as soon as read. As showing the kind of life he would encourage, he would ask permission to read a passage from Longfellow, describing the Friar Pacificus transcribing and illuminating the Gospel of St. John : [1]—

> " It is growing dark! Yet one line more,
> And then my work for to-day is o'er ;
> I come again to the name of the Lord !
> Ere I that awful name record,
> That is spoken so lightly among men,
> Let me pause awhile, and wash my pen ;
> Pure from blemish and blot must it be
> When it writes that word of mystery !
> Thus have I laboured on and on,
> Nearly through the Gospel of St. John.
> Can it be that from the lips
> Of this same gentle Evangelist,
> That Christ himself perhaps has kissed,
> Came the dread Apocalypse ?
> It has a very awful look,
> As it stands there at the end of the book,
> Like the sun in an eclipse.
> Ah me ! when I think of that vision divine,
> Think of writing it, line by line,
> I stand in awe of the terrible curse,
> Like the trump of doom in the closing verse !
> God forgive me ! if ever I
> Take aught from the book of that Prophecy ;
> Lest my part, too, should be taken away
> From the Book of Life on the Judgment Day."

[1] [*The Golden Legend* : iv., "The Scriptorium." Compare *Modern Painters*, vol. iv. ch. xx. § 32, where Ruskin says that Longfellow, in *The Golden Legend*, "has entered more closely into the temper of the Monk, for good and for evil, than ever yet theological writer or historian."]

Then notice the change of feeling—how natural !

> " This is well written, though I say it !
> I should be not afraid to display it
> In open day, on the self-same shelf
> With the writings of St. Thecla herself,
> Or of St. Theodosius, who of old
> Wrote the Gospels in letters of gold !
> That goodly folio standing yonder,
> Without a single blot or blunder,
> Would not bear away the palm from mine,
> If we should compare them line for line.
> There, now, is an initial letter !
> King René himself never made a better !
> Finished down to the leaf and the snail,
> Down to the eyes on the peacock's tail !
> And now, as I turn the volume over,
> And see what lies between cover and cover,
> What treasures of art these pages hold,
> All ablaze with crimson and gold,
> God forgive me ! I seem to feel
> A certain satisfaction steal
> Into my heart and into my brain,
> As if my talent had not lain
> Wrapped in a napkin, and all in vain.
> Yes, I might almost say to the Lord,
> Here is a copy of Thy word,
> Written out with much toil and pain ;
> Take it, O Lord, and let it be
> As something I have done for Thee."

He looks from the window.

> " How sweet the air is ! How fair the scene !
> I wish I had as lovely a green
> To paint my landscapes and my leaves !
> How the swallows twitter under the eaves !
> There, now, there is one in her nest ;
> I can just catch a glimpse of her head and her breast,
> And will sketch her thus, in her quiet nook,
> For the margin of my Gospel Book."

This was the kind of life he wished the students of this art to follow. He proposed to leave the various examples he had exhibited in the Museum, that those who desired to do so, might come in if they pleased, and work from them between then and the next lecture. In the next lecture he proposed to explain the general principles of outline, and to exhibit examples ; and in the third lecture he intended to explain the principles of colour.

II. THE GENERAL PRINCIPLES OF OUTLINE

[Delivered Saturday, November 25th, 1854]

14. The subject of this lecture was the general principle of outline; and the points which it was the purpose of Mr. Ruskin to illustrate, as stated in the syllabus, were—" Wherein dignity of outline consists; probability that many persons are possessed of outline talent who are incapable of drawing in the full sense of the term; and natural objects, how to be studied with a view to skill in illumination."

He commenced by observing that, as it was probable there were many persons present who had not attended the previous lecture, it would be necessary for him to repeat what he had then said—viz., that he had come there to tell working people plain things in a plain way, and that he must be pardoned, therefore, if his so-called lecture—which, however, was not really a lecture, but a talk—was less entertaining than it would perhaps otherwise be. The business of that morning would be to ascertain, as far as possible, the real nature and merits of outline. First, however, it was necessary to agree upon the important point of what that which was generally called outline really was. The first thing they knew about it was, that it was something that did not exist in nature. There was no such thing as outline in nature, and for this simple reason, that every object, whether placed near to or at a distance from the eye, had something which could not be clearly appreciated or described. On looking at a leafy tree, at first sight you would think you saw its form clearly and sharply defined against the sky; but try and count the leaves, and you found that what appeared to be an outline was but a mere mist of dots, expressible by no lines or series of lines you could lay down. Go farther still, and examine a forest of trees, and you would find that if the single tree had no outline, still less had the aggregate of trees, of which the forest was composed, anything like outline. The grey mountain ridge appeared at first sight to form a distinct line against the background of the sky: examine it more closely, and the apparent outline resolves itself into the verdure of countless blades of grass and mosses, which no pen can trace, no line describe. The vast forest had no outline, nor had the leaves which grew on its lordly trees, nor the cattle which were sheltered beneath their shade. There were blades of grass, leaves, hairs, and fibres in infinite number, but nothing that could be accurately expressed by a line; and it was the same with everything in nature that had any organic structure —there was something which the eye recognised, but nothing that it could accurately define or the hand trace; nothing that could be expressed by human skill or human art. When a man, by the exercise of great ingenuity, succeeded in making an ugly thing like the specimen in his hand (showing the frame of a drawing), even that was not an outline—it was like a line traced against a background; but if they attempted to describe any objects in nature by means of a black line, they put down something that there was not.

15. What, then, was an outline? It was not a fact—it was simply the

assertion of a fact: namely, that if an outline were well drawn, within the breadth of the lines, whatever it might be, the termination of the thing took place. The line might be thick, or it might be thin, but the end of the thing represented was within it, and if it were pure and perfect outline, each side of the line would be true to the contour of the thing intended to be represented. Take, for instance, a round ball. If you attempted to draw an outline of it, and that outline were correct, it did not matter how thick or thin the line was: it would be true to the contour of the ball. The real surface and contour would fall between the two sides of the outline were it truly drawn. But if, by way of giving effect, any part of the outline were darkened or thickened more than another, then they would have an utter fallacy—one of its outside lines must necessarily be wrong; and the eye, instantly embarrassed, did not know which it was to follow—it lost itself, and did not know how to go right. They knew how much people had been of late in the habit of publishing outlines which depended for half of what was called the effect, on being thicker on the side away from the light than on the other side. It was very curious how they could have fallen into such a habit, for nothing could be more absurd; but he apprehended the main reason was that, when people were drawing things at all spiritedly, they had a tendency to add pieces of shadow on the side farthest away from the light. Here was an instance (exhibiting a drawing), and here was a true outline (exhibiting another drawing). Outline might, indeed, if judiciously shaded, be made to convey increased expression and effect; but what he wished to impress upon them was that, in drawing outline, they should draw it correctly. If they drew shadows, they should draw freely. But before they began, let them understand what they were going to draw. No great draughtsman who understood his business ever thickened his outline on the side away from the light; for, as a general thing, outline was most visible on the side next the light, and though the real object was to get pure outline in all cases, the thorough master of his craft would, if he thickened at all, be apt to thicken the line turned towards the light. He would show them some instances of this. Take an example of a man whom they would admit to have been a master of his craft—Raffaelle. Here was an etching of the head of St. Katherine done with a pen. The only dark side of the outline, as they would observe, was next to the light. Towards the opposite side the line vanished almost into nothing, whilst under the nose and round the eyes the shadows were marked as in the leaf which he had just exhibited. Here was another specimen, one of Albert Dürer's. He was a man, too, who knew his business. Here was a woodcut by that master (exhibiting it). It was coarse and bold, but it was true. It was not cut as they cut now, and perhaps so much the better. They could see plainly on what side the light came there. The shadows were all perfectly and freely drawn, and they would see that when the object of Albert Dürer was to draw outline, he stuck to outline, and that when he did thicken his line, it was next the light. Such was the practice of Raffaelle and Albert Dürer. But here, perhaps, was a better specimen still (exhibiting another of Albert Dürer's). They could not tell on which side the light was, for it was clear and pure outline only. If they looked at the clouds presented in this example, they would see that they were the most aerial things imaginable, but that where there were dark lines they were all turned towards the light. Then there was another man who knew his business—Turner (an etching of Turner's was here produced). This was done by Turner with the point of an old fork, he believed. The effect was beautiful. All these were first-rate specimens of outline. There was yet another specimen, executed by a noble fellow, a German—who had done some greater things than any other artist of the present day.[1] He was not so good as Albert Dürer, but he was mighty in his way, and ought to be universally known; and the woodcuts of Death the Avenger, and Death the Friend, were worthy of being known to the whole civilised world. He was glad to be able to make them acquainted with this example, for there was in it the effect of a sunset expressed with almost unexampled power, and in the sleeve of the principal figure, which was outlined with the most perfect accuracy, the strongest lines were those which came against the light.

16. Outline, then, was the production of certain effects in a certain way. It was opposed to light and shadow in this respect—that light and shadow altered, but outline, the statement of material form, did not alter. Many persons had the gift of seeing and producing effects in light and shadow, which did not exist in outline; while others had the gift of perceiving and expressing the contour of a thing in outline. They were aware that many people, before the invention of photography, gained their bread by cutting black-paper portraits. He had always been struck by the marvellous gift which had enabled these persons with a pair of scissors to cut out instantaneously and with the greatest accuracy the profile of a human face. Again, they knew how many people were enabled, with marvellous accuracy, to portray features, and even expression,—and this gift was frequent in children,—in outline upon paper. But these persons stopped short, partly from want of opportunity, and more frequently from a failing of character,—that was, they had not the disposition to go into the nicer subtleties of light and shade, not only because they were subtleties, and uncertain in their results, but because there was a peculiar delicacy in light and shade, the expression of which required enormous study and practice. Even to appreciate this delicacy and softness required a peculiar sympathy, almost an effeminacy, of mind; and those who loved it most, and followed it most,—those who attained the greatest eminence in expressing it,—had often been led into sensuality. To some extent sensuality was, though not necessarily so, the result of that peculiar state of mind; as in Correggio, who, though he had painted some of the most sublime of sacred subjects, had, in many of his works, displayed the grossest sensuality—sensuality of which any man ought to be ashamed.[2] He was not in this saying anything against light and shadow; but there was this difference between it and outline, that the love of outline was a pure love of truth, and assuredly it was better for those who possessed the gift of outline and had not the time, or

---

[1] [Alfred Rethel, born at Aix-la-Chapelle, 1816; studied at Düsseldorf and Frankfort; designed and partly executed the designs for the decoration of the " Kaisersaal " at Aix-la-Chapelle; made drawings for a " Dance of Death," to which Reinick wrote verses; died in an asylum at Düsseldorf, 1859. For other references to him, see *Modern Painters*, vol. iii. ch. viii. § 8, where these same woodcuts are described as " inexpressibly noble and pathetic grotesques "; *Elements of Drawing*, Appendix ii., § 257 ("Things to be Studied "); and *Art of England*, § 100.]

[2] [See *Modern Painters*, vol. ii. (Vol. IV. p. 197 and *n*.).]

opportunity, or the mind to pursue light and shadow, to cultivate the gifts they possessed, than to endeavour to produce effects which they would never be capable of expressing. Whether or not there was a peculiar character in these people, he did not know; but assuredly it would be better that they should be able to express themselves accurately in pure outline than to follow after effects which they could not realise. With outline it was possible to unite to a certain extent pure colour or pure shadow. Instinctively this might be done. In the Raffaelle sketch which he had exhibited, there was a certain degree of light and shade added to the outline; but when both shadow and colour were added, then a mighty question was opened. Colour varied with every phase—with every turn in the contour of a subject. And if in addition to colour it were desired to express light and shade in its true and subtle connection with colour, a whole lifetime must be devoted to it. Painting was very much like music. A musician for whom he had great respect, who was present at the previous meeting, and from whom he had learned all he knew of the art, Mr. Hullah,[1] had spoken of the difficulty of teaching people to sing and to play, and especially of the skill which was required in the management of an orchestra. There was great similarity between the two arts, painting and music, in this respect. Drawing an outline correctly corresponded very much with plain clear speaking. Drawing in outline with colour corresponded with clear articulation in singing. If to outline they added light and shade, they arrived at something corresponding to clear articulation, coupled with playing upon an instrument. But if upon true outline they gave light and shadow and true colour in their due proportions, that was like the skilful management of the full orchestra. There were not many who could do that.

17. Persons who, commenting on what he had said on the art of illumination, and not understanding the requirements of a great painter, but supposing that from the mere ornamentation of a page, or the clear drawing of an outline, they could go on to imitate the truths of nature in light and shade and colour, were mistaken as to the views which he had expressed. He had shown that the art of illumination was distinct from that of true painting, and had produced examples from missals, showing the falling off in that art, after it had attained its culminating point in the thirteenth century, and attributing its decline to the attempt to introduce more and more light and shadow. Here was a specimen of this (exhibiting a page fully illuminated, containing fruit, scarlet strawberries, flowers, and other things). Had this been put into his hand by the artist, he would have said to him, "You are not going to be an ornamental painter any more, then? You are going to be a painter of fruit: if you want to paint fruit, that is the way to do it (showing a pear painted in water-colours): unless you can paint fruit as well as that, I will have nothing to do with you, and to do that you must paint for six hours every day for forty years." This was first-rate fruit painting by W. Hunt, of the Old Water-colour Society. It

---

[1] [John Pyke Hullah (1812–1884), musical composer and teacher, began singing classes on the Tonic Sol-fa system in 1841, and wrote manuals on the method. Ruskin refers to "Mr. Hullah's admirable observations on the use of the study of music" in a letter of 1857; reprinted in *Arrows of the Chace*, 1880, i. 39, and included in a later volume of this edition.]

was a glorious thing to be able to paint like that, and yet it was but a single pear; on the human face there were at least a million of shades of colours, and not less in the ripened pear, and there were half-a-dozen scarlet strawberries in every page of the missal; and yet the one was bad painting, while the other was all but perfection. These later missals were full of faults and incongruities, arising from the attempt to produce paintings when the writers should have limited themselves to ornaments. It would have been far better if they had confined themselves to what they could do well, instead of attempting great things to which they were unequal. He had been subjected to criticism because he had expressed an opinion more favourable to the works of the thirteenth century than those of a later period; but an examination of the works of the two periods would show that he was fully borne out by the facts. In his opinion no doubt could exist in the minds of any persons who had seen the architecture of Rheims, Amiens, and Notre Dame of Paris, and had compared them with the contemporary works of Lincoln and Wells Cathedrals, that during the thirteenth century architecture was in a much higher state in France than in England: indeed, the purest Gothic in the world was the French Gothic with the square abacus of that period.[1] What he had spoken of was the fall of art, as respected missal painting; and he had shown, from the causes which he had stated, that the art had from that period continued to decline. It had gone on falling, becoming worse and worse, until the time of Giulio Clovio[2] which was the worst of all. He did not mean to say that a painter should not illuminate a book or paint a wall, but it must be when he was at rest. But because a great painter might have painted a magnificent picture on the wall of a palace, we must not expect to have all our rooms painted by great artists, nor could we expect generally to have good paintings in our books. If we had, the attention would be carried away from the work of the author to the work of the artist, and he had no idea of having books that would not be read. What he wished was, to endeavour, by introducing appropriate decoration, to make books more attractive, and not to fill libraries with works so highly decorated that the owners were afraid to touch them. His object in introducing illuminations into books was not to lead the mind away from the text, but to enforce it.

18. Whilst upon this subject, he would notice some remarks which had appeared in last week's *Builder*. It was said, in an article signed " Illuminator," that he had shown illustrations of letters surrounded and mixed up with so many ornaments and forms as to render them illegible.[3] He was

---

[1] [This sentence is expanded below, p. 493; compare with it *Lectures on Architecture and Painting*, above, p. 62 n.]

[2] [Giorgio Giulio Clovio (called Macedo), born in Croatia in 1498; died in Rome in 1578; the great miniaturist of his age. There are examples of his work in the Library of the British Museum.]

[3] [The writer of this letter (*Builder*, November 18), said : "I was induced by the prospectus, issued from the Architectural Museum, to attend there on the 11th inst., for the purpose of hearing Mr. Ruskin lecture on 'decorative colour, as applicable to architectural and other purposes.' This is a very grand announcement for a very subordinate purpose, when we come to read the small printing, which says that 'these lectures will be exclusively addressed to workmen who are in the habit of executing designs (more especially letterings) on walls and shop-fronts. . . .' I found

afraid that many of the specimens which he had exhibited were, to some extent, illegible ; but that was only because we were not used to them. Probably there were not many persons present who could read Greek or Hebrew, and to them the text of a book in either of these languages would be equally illegible ; but that was only because they were unacquainted with the Greek and Hebrew alphabets. If they were to study Greek and Hebrew, the letters would no longer be strange ; and so, when they became accustomed to illuminated lettering, it would be read with facility. He had never recommended that every letter, or every initial letter, should be illuminated, but that the illumination should be appropriately introduced to illustrate, not to obscure, the text. There were many present who probably could not read black letter. Here was (exhibiting it) a black-letter manuscript of 1290. It was plain enough to those who were accustomed to it, although to many it would be perfectly illegible. Of all persons he was the last who ought to be charged with desiring to introduce illegibility ; for he had published his opinions upon the subject. He had said in his *Seven Lamps*,—" Place them, therefore (inscriptions), where they will be read, and there only ; and let them be plainly written—not turned upside down, nor wrong end first. It is an ill sacrifice to beauty to make that illegible whose only merit is in its sense. Write the Commandments on the church walls, where they may be plainly seen, but do not put a dash and a tail to every letter, and remember that you are an architect, not a writing-master." [1] His opinions in this respect, therefore, ought not to have been mistaken. If they wanted to see writing perfectly illegible, he would recommend them to go and look at the inscriptions in the Houses of Parliament.

19. Passing from that subject, what he desired to impress upon them was to endeavour to express themselves clearly and legibly in outline ; but, above all, truly. The first thing to be done was to understand the difference between a true outline and a false one ; and this led him back to the Parisian MS. to which he had previously referred. He was glad that he had been led back to this subject, for he had been told that it had been said of him in a newspaper—he himself never looked at these things, for if he read everything that was said against him, he should have no time for anything else,—but a friend of his had told him that the *Morning Chronicle* had accused him of knowingly misrepresenting the circumstances of the teaching of Alfred,[2]—that he had said it was the stepmother of

---

at a very early step he declared, 'that he wanted us to teach him how his theories were to be carried out.' " The rest of the letter shows that Ruskin's lecture had fallen on some stony ground. The writer much preferred the plain, honest letters supplied by the trade to " birds or animals, whose heads or tails ran a race all round the letter."]

[1] [See Vol. VIII. p. 147, and the author's note there.]

[2] [The reference is to a characteristic letter from E. A. Freeman, which appeared in the *Morning Chronicle* of November 16. Freeman detected in Ruskin's passing allusions to Charlemagne and Alfred an intention to poach. " I perceive," he wrote, " from your paper that Mr. Ruskin in a lecture at the Architectural Museum has been deserting his ordinary subjects of ' lamps,' ' stones,' and ' sheepfolds,' to communicate information about the two greatest sovereigns of Western Europe. Unfortunately Mr. Ruskin's facts are entirely apocryphal, and his inferences far from trustworthy." Freeman's objections were (1) that according to the better authorities,

the Saxon king, a French princess, instead of his own mother, who was an Englishwoman, who induced him to learn to read by exhibiting to him a beautifully illuminated French missal, and promising it as the reward of his success. Now, he would give this advice to all who heard him, and especially to young persons—let them never suspect a man of wilful misrepresentation until they had *proof* that he had said what he knew to be incorrect. If they did so, they not only insulted the person, but they insulted themselves irreparably. People were often led into misrepresentations and sophistries in the eagerness of argument; but he did not believe, and none but those who were in the habit of misrepresenting could believe, that people would deliberately state a fact one way when they knew it to be another. As it happened, in this case he could have no motive for misrepresentation. He did not care a straw whether it was a French princess or an English princess who was the means of teaching Alfred. That was not his affair, but Sharon Turner's, whose book he had quoted,[1] and whom he considered an authority on the point. But that in the illuminated works of the thirteenth century France stood pre-eminent, any person acquainted with the subject must be aware. Whenever he entered a museum, or examined any collection of old illuminated writing, if he saw any specimens which were first-rate, he always said they were French; if he saw any MSS. second-rate in character, but still showing great intellectual power, though not wrought up with great refinement, he concluded that it was probably English work; if other specimens showed some intellectual power, but at the same time a great clinging to precedent, then he set them down as German; and if they were irretrievably coarse, he concluded they were Dutch. What was true with regard to MSS. was true also with respect to sculpture and architectural decoration. The best specimen we had of the Gothic architecture of that century was Lincoln Cathedral, and the next was that of Wells.[2] The specimens of sculpture from Lincoln Cathedral, so justly brought forward by Mr. Cockerell,[3] were probably the finest examples that could be found in the country. But although they exhibited great boldness of outline and vigour of invention, they were by no means equal to the architectural sculpture of the French cathedrals of the same period: they were not equal to the compositions at Rheims, Amiens, and especially at Notre Dame (Mr. Ruskin here handed round some beautiful calotype views of the sculptured arches and columns of the French and English cathedrals of the thirteenth century, evidencing the superiority of the former in point of refinement). The fact,

---

Charlemagne never succeeded in learning to write, though he was constantly trying. Ruskin was referred to "Eginhart, p. 140, ed. Frankf. 1707. Hallam's *Middle Ages*, ii. 352, 9th ed., and Milman's *Gibbon*, ix. 178. Sismondi, *Hist. des Français*, i. 423, ed. (I am sorry to say) Bruxelles, 1847." (2) Secondly, as appears in the text, Freeman objected that it was Alfred's own mother who taught him to read: "Pauli's Life of Alfred, p. 86 (Eng. ed.), or Mr. Thorpe's Note on Florence, i. 86." This was criticised as a mistake by intention. "Mr. Ruskin's motive is obvious, being of a piece with the anti-national character of his writings in general. . . . Mr. Ruskin is said to know something about modern painters; he evidently knows as little of mediæval kings as of English architecture."]

1 [See above, p. 476.]
2 [See above, p. 92.]
3 [For Cockerell, see Vol. IX. p. 430 *n.*]

too, was proved by Dante [who, meeting in purgatory Oderigi, the famous illuminator, and friend of Giotto and of Dante, addressed him—

> " Art thou not Oderigi?   Art not thou
> Agubbio's glory—glory of that art
> Which they of Paris call the limner's skill ?"][1]

Dante spoke also of England, but not as equally distinguished in art as France.   He represented the people of England as remarkable for qualities of a more simple character [as a troop retired under the rocks in happy converse ; and of the great Plantagenet monarch he said—]

> " Behold the king of simple life and plain,
> Harry of England." [2]

And he characterised them as a people distinguished by force of character,

veracity, and simplicity, but not celebrated for great pre-eminence in the arts.

20. He would now revert to the subject of illuminated letters.   Here was a page of an illuminated missal hymn (exhibiting it), written in the year 1290, for the nuns of the monastery of Beaupré.[3] It was very beautifully executed, and in a free style.   He wished them to look at the little figure at the foot of the page, of an archer shooting at a bird with an arrow.   The outline, notwithstanding its minuteness, was most accurately drawn, and evidently by a man who had thought it worth while to study the art he practised.   He had made an enlargement of the little scarlet figure, and it would be seen from that, that although the writer did not, perhaps, know much of anatomy, he had taken care to study an archer drawing a bow before he drew the outline.   It was quite evident that the artist knew something of the manner of drawing the bow, and desired to represent it accurately.   Let them compare this outline with the base outline which he would now exhibit (producing it), by a man who did not

Fig. 28

care to know anything about drawing a bow before he began to trace his outlines.   The arrow was altogether out of proportion—it was almost as long

---

[1] [Already quoted in the former address, § 5, p. 477, above.]
[2] [See *Purgatory*, vii. 131.   The reference is to Henry III.]
[3] [*Antiphonarium Ecclesiæ S. Marie de Bello Prato.*   Two of the folio volumes of this MS. are now in the library of Mr. Henry Yates Thompson ; the third remaining

as the man. The stags appeared as if waiting to be shot, their horns looking so much like the branches of the trees under which they stood, that it
was scarcely possible to distinguish one from the other. There was not a
line in the whole composition that was not false, and yet this was a correct
copy of one of the most celebrated works of Claude Lorraine, a drawing in the
possession of the Duke of Devonshire.[1]

21. Mr. Ruskin then exhibited a Parisian MS. of the time of St. Louis,
which he said was one of the best specimens in his possession. It was full
of animals, figures, and ornaments. He particularly pointed out a white bird,
too small to be appreciated without the aid of a glass, but of which he exhibited an enlarged copy, calling attention to the humorous expression of
self-satisfaction in the bird's eye, the ease of its position, and other merits.
The whole MS., he observed, was full of figures equally ingenious, and
equally beautiful.

22. In many of the examples of the early illuminated writings was to be
found much of humour, almost
amounting to wit; and the
lesson to be deduced from
them was, that humour, as far
as it was expressible by art,
would be best expressed by a
few free lines quickly and
easily drawn, for nothing was
so disgusting as laboured humour, whether in words or
painting.   He could never
laugh at what had been called
the humour of Hogarth.   Hogarth had humour, but much more than
humour; his pictures were not to be laughed at, they easily made him serious
the whole day after; they were bitter, agonising satire.[2]   The gift of
humour was peculiar to Englishmen. They could often express it in a few
lines; and although he would not have this humour so conspicuous in
books as to interfere with the text, yet it would be delightful if people,
when dealing with books, could have the power of expressing the humour
and wit which arises in their mind, illustrative of the text.

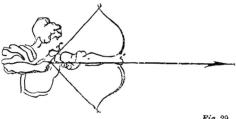

Fig. 29

23. That was one thing to which outline drawing might be applied.
Another was the grotesque. It was not mere humour that was expressed
in a grotesque. A grotesque was often the expression of truths in a small
compass. The grotesque was as available in poetry as in painting. The
poet and the painter, be it remembered, were essentially the same. He

at Brantwood. Mr. Thompson has identified the place of origin at Beaupré near
Brussels. Ruskin refers to the MS. at some length in *The Pleasures of England,*
§ 99, where a *facsimile* of a page from it is given in this edition.]

[1] [The diagrams here mentioned have been found at Brantwood, and reduced
reproductions of them are here given. The Claude is from No. 180 in the *Liber
Veritatis* ("Landscape with Æneas shooting.") It is given with more detail, and
is analysed, in *Modern Painters,* vol. iii. ch. xviii. § 26 and fig. 7.]

[2] [For Ruskin elsewhere on Hogarth, see *Lectures on Architecture and Painting,*
§ 130, above, p. 153; *Seven Lamps* (Vol. VIII. p. 212); *Stones of Venice,* vol. ii.
(Vol. X. p. 223); *Inaugural Address at the Cambridge School of Art,* § 22.]

would give them a definition of the poet and the painter together, which they would remember, though it was a hissing one.   The poet or the painter was a man who concentrated sermons into sights.   If they could not do this, they deserved not the name of poet or painter.   A few strokes from the pen or the pencil should convey to the mind in a moment what it would take an hour to describe.   Supposing he was to attempt to describe the vice of gluttony, it would take him a long time to bring before them the hardness of heart, the degradation of intellect, and all the evils which resulted from it.   But Spenser did this in twenty-seven lines in grotesque. The Red Cross Knight in the course of his chivalry is led unhappily to the House of Pride.   The poet there displays to him the Seven Mortal Sins, one of whom, Gluttony, is thus described : [1]—

> " And by his side rode loathsome Gluttony,
> Deformèd creature, on a filthy swine ;
> His belly was up-blowne with luxury,
> And eke with fatnesse swollen were his eyne,
> And like a crane his neck was long and fyne,
> With which he swallowed up excessive feast.
>
> .   .   .   .
>
> " In greene vine leaves he was right fitly clad ;
> For other clothes he could not wear for heat ;
> And on his head an yvie girland had,
> From under which fast trickled down the sweat ;
> Still as he rode, he somewhat still did eat,
> And in his hande did bear a bouzing can,
> Of which he supt so oft, that in his seat
> His dronken corse he scarse upholden can.
>
> .   .   .   .   .   .
>
> Full of diseases was his carcass blew,
> And a dry dropsie through his flesh did flow."

Here evils, which would take a long sermon to work out, were described in not twenty-seven lines, as he had said, but in sixteen, and were fixed in the memory in such a way as not to be forgotten.   Take another example from the same poet,—his description of Avarice : [2]—

> " And greedy Avarice by him did ride
> Upon a camell loaden all with gold ;
> Two iron coffers hong on either side,
> With precious metall full as they might hold ;
> And in his lap an heap of coine he told ;
>
> .   .   .   .   .   .
>
> And thred-bare cote and cobbled shoes he ware ;
> Ne scarse good morsell all his life did tast ;
> But both from backe and belly still did spare,
> To fill his bags, and richesse to compare."

24. In both these cases, and throughout the greater parts of Spenser and

---

[1] [*Faerie Queene*, book i. canto iv. 21–23.   Ruskin cites some of the lines in *Stones of Venice*, vol. ii. (Vol. X. p. 402).]

[2] [*Ibid.*, book i. canto iv. 27–28.   See, again, *Stones of Venice*, vol. ii. (Vol. X. p. 403), where Ruskin compares Spenser's " Avarice " with that on the Ducal Palace.]

of Dante, it would be observed how strongly the evil to be avoided was impressed upon the mind, by being brought prominently before the *vision*. This could be done to some extent in outline, but not in finished painting. The painter could not represent in detail the long crane's neck of the glutton, nor place the disgusting wretch upon the swine's back. By means, however, of a few roughly and freely drawn outlines, something like a representation could be given of these more conspicuous personages in the motley train of the proud and haughty Lucifera.[1] The grotesque was much used in the Middle Ages, and it was a means of conveying truths to the mind which we had ignorantly passed over.[2]

25. Again, how could spiritual beings be so fitly represented as by outline? To portray spiritual existences with success on the canvas had ever been one of the greatest problems in art; but a solution of the difficulty could be found in the judicious use of outline, nor was it necessary to study anatomy and muscles in order to paint either an angel or a demon. A man of first-rate merit and ability (Stothard),[3] but, unfortunately, trammelled by academic rules, had been selected to illustrate Milton, and, among other subjects, to delineate Satan. Look at the result. (The lecturer here exhibited an engraving from the work referred to.) The only idea which the painter had formed of his hero was that he was an extremely muscular man, with a remarkably handsome calf to his leg, and handsome, tight-fitting shoes, to protect his feet from the "burning marle,"[4] and his steel armour made to bend in and out, in order to show the development of his muscles. Was there ever such an absurdity? Could anybody think for a moment that that was a spirit? But when abstract outline was combined with beautiful colour, the main effects were obtained. The imagination took them up, and suggested to itself something noble which could be conveyed by no other means.

26. Take another illustration. (Ruskin here exhibited two leaves from illuminated MSS. representing the story of St. John the Baptist.) One, he said, was the initial letter of a hymn, and the object was to bring the story prominently before the eye of the reader or the singer to stimulate him in the performance of his duty—to tell all that could be told in the space of a single leaf. It would be seen how the same subject was treated at different periods. The one showed a St. John, seated in a meadow, reading a book, with a lamb by his side—a charming little picture, most elaborately finished; the other a St. John of an earlier date and of rougher execution.[5] The object of each work was to illustrate the principal events in the life of the forerunner of the Messiah; but in the case of the less laboured work of the earlier period, the story was told by an outlined figure walking upon the kingly head of Herod and the head of Herodias. In one hand the saint bore the representation, not of the mere ordinary lamb, but of the

---

[1] [*Faerie Queene*, book i. canto iv.]

[2] [Ruskin further discusses the concentrated symbolism of grotesques, again illustrating the subject from Spenser, in *Modern Painters*, vol. iii. ch. viii. (see especially § 5).]

[3] [For other references to Stothard, see note in Vol. IV. p. 194.]

[4] [*Paradise Lost*, i. 292.]

[5] [The latter of the two illustrations here referred to has been found at Brantwood, and is here given on reduced scale.]

Lamb of God; while with the other, he pointed to the sacred object of his mission. A calm and holy serenity beamed around the features of the martyr, and though walking in triumph upon the heads, he still appeared divinely unconscious of the fallen and prostrate condition of his murderers. There was a peculiar expression, too, in the face of Herodias. She appeared to be too much astonished to be in pain. "I thought I had his head in a charger—it is not so!—he has mine at his feet for ever and ever." Now, which of these illuminations told the story in the best manner—the man in the meadow with the book and the lamb, or the more vigorous and poetic treatment of the subject by the artist of the thirteenth century?

Fig. 30

27. So much for the recommendation of outline. He now came to the more practical question of how to acquire it. In a letter published in the *Builder*,[1] one of his pupils objected that he had referred to them for help in carrying out his idea. The help he had asked was that they should inform him at what price such ornamentation of walls and books and shop-fronts as he had suggested could be executed. If he went to an artist and asked him for how much he could paint a picture two feet by two feet six inches, he should think it strange if he received for answer that it was not a practical question. All he wanted from the workmen was to know at what price the work could be done, and what he wanted to tell the workmen was how to do the work. Than this there was nothing more easy and simple. To those who had the gift and the liking—and those who had the gift would have the liking—he would say, Take a blunt pen, and common ink, and. draw with it everything, every figure, that came in their way, observing, however, these two important points: that no line was ever to be drawn loosely, without a meaning or a use; and that every characteristic shade or local colour, or stains that might be useful when they came to fill up with colour, were to be carefully noted. As in the bird he had exhibited, the pupil of the eye must be observed and marked, and also the black legs. Everything must be noted that could be useful in filling up with pure colour afterwards. If they drew a lion and a leopard, the leopard must especially be marked as a *spotted* creature. In everything they did they must note the local, not the accidental, colour.

28. After observing that the specimens which he had produced would remain at the Museum for the inspection of those who felt an interest in

----

[1] [See above, p. 491 *n.*]

the subject and desired to follow up the study, Mr. Ruskin concluded by stating that the whole of his remarks had been dictated by a desire to impress upon his audience the *practicable* nature of his suggestions. He had frequently heard himself called a visionary and an unpractical man. Nothing could be more erroneous.   His whole life had been devoted to bringing people down from idealisms and fancies to practical truths. He felt certain that if all who had heard him would acquire the habit of drawing everything that came before them, and which they saw with their own eyes, they would soon attain a power which would make them infinitely happy and honoured by all whose esteem they valued, make them capable of doing a vast amount of good, give them a power of communing with nature, and implant in them a reverence for Him who made both nature and their hearts.

III. THE GENERAL PRINCIPLES OF COLOUR.

[Delivered Saturday, December 9th, 1854.]

29. THE special points of the lecture were—"The general principles of colour; dignity of pure colour; whereon its power depends; the colours which are the basis of illumination are blue, purple and scarlet, with gold; peculiar power of crimson; value of green, white and black, and modes of their necessary introduction; refinements of intermediate hues in delicate work; review of subject."

The speaker commenced his remarks by broadly stating that the subject upon which he was about to address his audience was one upon which neither he himself nor anybody else could tell anything which would be of the least value, beyond what every person present could find out for himself by the exercise of that noble faculty which taught Falstaff to run away—he meant "instinct." [1] Under the circumstances in which Falstaff was placed, to run away was undoubtedly the best thing which he could do. By "instinct," however, he did not wish to be understood as implying that by which an animal performed acts like to those of men, but that peculiar faculty by which all creatures did particularly that which it was their function to do, as the bee built its combs. In the construction of those hexagonal combs philosophers had discovered certain rules, which they had expressed in mathematical and logical formulæ. But, although the bee constructed his cells in such a manner as most successfully to economise the consumption of wax, yet he was perfectly ignorant of the laws of numerical series, by which the principles upon which he acted could be explained and illustrated by the philosopher. The bee did not know, and did not want to know, these rules: he built his cells by a higher and a nobler teaching. Take a bluebottle, and try to make it build a cell, and all attempts would end as they began—in buzz. Why, then, because we were higher animals, should we act differently from the bee in endeavouring to attain our ends?   Neither did higher animals ever do any great

[1] [See 1 *Henry IV.*, Act ii. sc. 4: "Instinct is a great matter. I was a coward on instinct."]

thing but by instinct. Did the brave and gallant soldiers in the Crimea act upon any other than instinct as they stood by their death-dealing guns? Did they entertain for a moment the question of the expediency of their running away? Far from it. Running away was not in them: they were animated solely by the instinct of courage. Ask a man of honour why he told the truth, or why he was not in the habit of telling lies. His reply would be, that it was not in him to act other than truthfully. Ask the man of compassion why he picked up the ragged boy from the gutter, who had been run over in the street, and his answer would be that he could not help doing it—it was his instinct to do so. He could, in fact, be no other than a compassionate man.

30. And this was especially the case in the arts. Everything to be well done must be done by instinct. If we went to any noble colourist, to any real man of talent, and asked him why he did such or such a thing, his answer would be, "I don't know: I do it because it appears to me to look well." The other day he was seated by the side of one of the greatest living colourists, Mr. Hunt;[1] and, in reply to a question put to him as to why he put on a certain colour [which appeared to be against all rules], he said "he did not know; *he was just aiming at it.*" He had had frequent opportunities of conversing with Turner, but had never heard him utter a single rule of colour, though he had frequently heard him, like all great men, talk of "trying" to do a thing. This was ever the language of great genius. A man of no talent, a bad colourist, would be ready to give you mathematical reasons for every colour he put on the canvas. Mulready was another great colourist, and he had once asked him whether he had any principles or rules of colour. The reply of the colourist was, "Know what you have to do, and do it;" but he could not tell by what rules he was to know what to do to a certain thing. The same thing prevailed in poetry. The master poets, who wrote the best verses, could not tell their way of doing it. Tennyson was, in his opinion, the leading master of versification at the present day, and he knew of no rules to guide him. An intimate friend of the poet set himself one day to find out all the rules of Tennyson's versification, and collected together, from his verses, an immense number of laws and examples. "Look here," said he, "what wonderful laws you observe." "It's all true," replied the poet, "I do observe them, but I never knew it." Take, again, the case of music. Haydn was one of the greatest of geniuses, as well as an ardent lover of true harmony. An admirable French work, containing the lives of Haydn and other composers, gave a striking instance of the perfect independence of mind and freedom from fetters of rule which characterised this fine composer. Checked in his youth by masters, this rare person had yet "taken science out of his own heart; he had found it there, and remarked the feelings which passed within his own breast, and he acted upon its suggestions and native promptings." When in London, a young lord called upon Haydn, and sought his instruction. In the course of the

---

[1] [William Hunt, of the Old Water-Colour Society; see *Modern Painters*, vol. iii. ch. vii. §§ 12, 13, where these anecdotes of Hunt, Turner, and Haydn are repeated. The remark of Mulready had been enforced in the *Seven Lamps*, Introd., § 1 (Vol. VIII. p. 19). The "admirable French work" is De Stendhal's *Vies de Haydn, de Mozart, et de Metastase;* compare the passages quoted from it in *Modern Painters*, vol. iii. ch. vii. §§ 11, 12.]

interview the young man pointed out to the composer a number of faults and departures from the established rules of harmony which he had marked in one of his overtures.   He inquired the cause of these errors, and why such a note had been used, when a different one would have been the more correct. Haydn replied that he had done so because it had a good effect, and pleased his taste.   The Englishman disapproved of the alterations, when Haydn told him to play the passages as he would wish them to be altered, and see which would produce the best effect.   After a good deal of argument on each side, the great composer, becoming perfectly impatient, said, " My lord, you have the goodness to give me lessons, and I do not deserve the honour of receiving them from you," and bowed him out of the room.

31. He was anxious to get his hearers entirely quit of the notion of supposing that they could do nothing without " rule."   We were told, as a rule, that there were three primary colours—red, blue and yellow—and that these primaries should occur in every composition ; that these three colours always existed in a ray of light in the proportions of eight, five, and three, and that in these proportions they neutralised each other, and produced white light.   Then, said the scientific gentleman, " Because these colours occur in a ray of light, you should always put them into your colour compositions in just such a manner as that each colour may be neutralised by its neighbour." How absurd was all this !   Were there not also acids and alkalies in chemistry which neutralised each other ? and would it not be equally reasonable for a man to say to his cook, " Whenever you squeeze a lemon on my veal, put a pinch of magnesia with it, in order that the alkali may neutralise the acid " ?   There, said the lecturer (producing at the same time an orange), is as fine a yellow as you can have.   If the scientific man were asked what colours should be introduced with it in a composition, he would reply, " Well, eight of red, and five of blue."   But what said Nature ?   She gave neither red nor blue, but, placing the orange in the midst of bright green leaves, enabled you to look on one of the most beautiful objects in exist- ence—an orange grove.   Look, too, at the beautiful little sky-blue flowers of the gentian.[1]   Did Nature give that eight of blue, five of red, and a touch of yellow ?   No such thing.   There were the green grass, the white lilies of the valley, and the grey rock, but not a touch of red or yellow ; yet that flower always looked beautiful.   Some fine specimens of water- colour drawings of Turner and others were exhibited, for the purpose of showing that beautiful effects might be obtained without adherence to these arbitrary rules, and could often only be obtained by defiance of them ; and the lesson which the lecturer deduced from these examples, as well as from a careful study of the finest works of the old masters, was that a close observance of these laws would most assuredly lead the scholar in a wrong direction.

32. But not only were these laws calculated to lead people wrong, but they would make those who followed them immoderately conceited.   He was talking the other day to a man [2] who, of all others, had, perhaps, been the most successful in pursuing these laws of colour, and, in the course of conversation, the lawgiver said, " Well, I find, upon the whole, that there

<hr />

[1] [For Ruskin's love of the gentian, see Vol. II. p. 431 n.]
[2] [No doubt, Sir David Brewster, F.R.S. (1781–1868).]

is no harmony except between red and green." That was very odd, Mr. Ruskin replied, for his impression was, that Titian, and some others who knew something of the matter, had used red and blue. "No," said the philosopher, "it will not do—Titian is all wrong." On asking him whether there was any picture in the Academy which came up to his views of harmony in colour, the philosopher said that he had been carefully through the whole collection, and had only found one picture which was painted on scientific principles. That picture the lecturer had seen ; he would not mention its name, but it was one of the chief daubs in the collection in the Academy. The worst of all this intermeddling of science was, that not only the artist derived no help from it, but it prevented science from doing the work which really came within its own province. Science could not give the artist the colours which it told him to use. We had no crimsons or scarlets which would stand ; but (producing an illuminated MS.) there were pieces of scarlet which had stood upon that page for more than 500 years, and still remained perfectly bright. On the best modes of working in gold and preparing colours, which was the work of the scientific man, no attempt was made to help the colourist.

33. But if not by science, how was skill in colouring to be obtained ? Only by instinct. Man is a being differing from the lower animals, he having two kinds of instinct, one which aimed at higher, and the other at baser ends ; and he had also his noble reason, to enable him to find out which of his acts would elevate the one or depress the other. The most efficient mode by which a knowledge of colour could be obtained by the artist was by casting all rules behind his back, and trusting to his own instincts when in a calm and healthy state. Watch for everything, look carefully for everything in nature which was beautiful. Whenever any combination of colours or a colour particularly beautiful was found, note it carefully. If this kind of work be enjoyed and continued in, depend upon it, the student would soon begin to invent, and having put down two or three colours, others would soon suggest themselves as necessary. Pass not a single thing, however small or despised, for no colour was so contemptible but that it might furnish some hint, and there was no hour of the day in which something might not be learned. Fettered by rules, all these opportunities of gaining knowledge would be lost to the student. He was most anxious, in any remarks which he had made, that he should not be understood as depreciating the value of any of those ably illustrated works of Mr. Owen Jones[1] and others who had studied the subject of the law of colour—a subject, in the abstract, of great interest. All he meant to convey was, that these rules would never teach any one to colour ; and the artist who submitted himself to the law of these three primaries was lost for ever.

34. In connection with colouring there were, however, three necessities which should never be lost sight of by the student. They were the necessity of gradation, of subtlety, and of surprise ; and these it would be found were most sedulously and carefully acknowledged by the most successful of colourists, whether ancient or modern. No colour was really valuable until

---

[1] [Owen Jones (1809–1874), architect and ornamental designer ; author of *Plans of the Alhambra* (1842–1845), *The Polychromatic Ornament of Italy* (1846), and *The Grammar of Ornament* (1856). For a reference to the former work, see *Stones of Venice*, vol. i. (Vol. IX. p. 469 n.).]

it was gradated. The great beauty of colour consisted in a sort of twilight melancholy—a dying away ; no colour was, in fact, of use till it appeared to be dying. Colour might be gradated by passing into other colours, or by becoming paler or darker. Instances of subtle gradation of colour[1] were shown in the flowers of the scarlet cactus, and in some of the beautiful water-colour drawings of Turner. This same law was pre-eminently to be found among the illuminated works of the thirteenth century, where white lines or dots were most judiciously and effectively introduced for the purpose of gradating colours.

35. A second and not less important point always observed by the successful colourist was the excessive delicacy to which he strove to bring all the hues he laid on, whether the working was large or small. When a person had coloured rightly, a grain more or a grain less would injure the whole. This delicacy was carried to such an extent by Paul Veronese, that in one of his largest pictures, now in Paris, a small white hair upon the paw of a cat playing with a vase in the foreground was essential to the completeness of the picture.[2] Another striking instance of this extreme delicacy was to be seen in a plum painted by the greatest of living fruit-painters, Mr. Hunt, where a minute spot of scarlet was plainly seen upon the surface, and produced a most pleasing and agreeable effect to the eye. It was this extreme delicacy of all good colour, and the care which was taken in its application even to architectural decoration, that rendered fruitless and unsuccessful all attempts to restore or to represent the old decorations upon any architectural works of the past centuries. We know nothing of what colours were employed by the Egyptians, or by any of the ancient decorators. We had found a bit of red in one place and a powder of blue or yellow upon some other, and we know nothing more. There were nearly twenty different reds now known to us ; which one did the Egyptians use ? Most certainly not that one which was now employed to represent the revived monuments of that age and country. Till we knew this we could not restore the rudest monument of past ages ! Until we knew absolutely and certainly what colours they used,—till, in fact, we could call the men up from the dead,—we had no right to touch what they had left behind.

36. Another important law to be always kept in mind was the law of surprise. This law in colour was one of the chief sources of pleasure,—just as in music, the change to one note, when another was expected, formed the principal cause of the delight experienced in listening to the finest works of the composers. To the works of the old masters this "law of surprise" was uniformly acted upon, and the painters appear to have set themselves certain laws, and then suddenly to have transgressed them in a most playful and effective manner. An instance of this was shown in an illuminated MS. On one side was a number of heads within ovals, following each other regularly, when suddenly, towards the close of the series, an irregularly minded angel clapped his wing over his head, outside the oval. In another

---

[1] [On this subject compare *Modern Painters*, vol. ii. (Vol. IV. p. 89).]

[2] [The picture referred to is the "Marriage in Cana." Compare what Ruskin says of the delicacy of effect in "The Family of Darius," No. 294 in the National Gallery (*Modern Painters*, vol. v. pt. viii. ch. iv. § 18, and *Lectures on Landscape*, § 68).]

part a disobedient leaf suddenly appeared out of the ordinary and expected line, and all who saw the change could not but feel thankful to the unruly leaf for the excellent effect it had produced.

37. Passing from the laws affecting the management of colour, he proceeded to point out what colours ought to be used. The best lesson in colour to which he could point was a sunset. The clouds were *scarlet, golden, purple, white, grey*, but not *crimson*, except in stormy weather. Crimson was a colour which rarely occurred,—when it did, almost always giving the idea of a bloody hue ; and it was curious to notice how, in the cactus speciosissimus and some other flowers, the purple, passing from scarlet, rarely, if ever, touched crimson. But one, at least, of the most beautiful of flowers in nature was crimson—viz., the rose ; and the blush on the cheek was the most beautiful of colours, but the crimson which they displayed was always associated with the idea of life.[1] There were undoubtedly cases in which crimson could be used with the greatest success, and one of the finest windows which he had ever seen was one at the western end of Chartres Cathedral,[2] of the twelfth century, upon which "gouts" of blood appeared to have been dropped. Nothing could exceed the richness and beauty of this window beneath the gorgeous rays of the sunset. Blues, whites, scarlets, yellows, and greys were all colours of the clouds — of heaven ; fixed green and a particular kind of ashy buff were the colours of the earth. All that was calculated to attract the mind in this peculiar art of illumination was to be found in the colours of heaven. The golden, scarlet, white, russet, purple, and grey colours all kept to the sky; the greens and the buffs to earth. There was, too, a sort of bluish green in the sky; and, as a general rule, greens should be always tinted and tempered with blue. The earthy, ashy, buff colour of earth—the ugliest of all colours—was preeminently the one used in this boasted nineteenth century. Some attempts of a most praiseworthy nature were being made to improve the colour of the ordinary tiles for architectural purposes, and a manufacturer of those tiles had covered the whole front of his house with them, where they would have had a most excellent effect, had he not, with the worst possible taste, made the ground of the whole of them this ugliest of all colours.

38. The purple was a colour to which great importance was attached by the ancients.[3] The old Greek purple was unquestionably not of a scarlet hue, but a deep and sombre colour. In the *Odyssey*, Menelaus, in his interview with the sea-king Proteus, when told of the assassination of Agamemnon, is represented as going away sad. Homer says his mind became *purple*.[4] Many persons would suppose it meant "crimsoned" over with blood. But this was not the meaning intended to be conveyed; for in one part of the *Iliad* he describes the sinking and darkness which came

---

[1] [Compare *Modern Painters*, vol. iv. ch. iii. § 24.]
[2] [See Letters, above, on "Painted Glass," p. 438.]
[3] [Compare *Modern Painters*, vol. iii. ch. xiv. §§ 43, 44, and *Queen of the Air*, §§ 91 *seq.*]
[4] [πολλὰ δέ μοι κραδίη πόρφυρε κιόντι: *Odyssey*, iv. 572. The following references are *Iliad*, v. 83 (πορφύρεος θάνατος); xiv. 16 (ὡσ δ' ὅτε πορφύρῃ πέλαγος); xiii. 703 (βόε οἴνοπε) ; i. 350 (οἴνοπα πόντον); iv. 141 (ὡσ δ' ὅτε τίς τ' ἐλέφαντα γυνὴ φοίνικι μιήνῃ Μῃονὶς ἠὲ Κάειρα). Ruskin quotes this last passage in *Modern Painters*, vol. ii. (Vol. IV. p. 130 *n.*]

over a dying soldier's eyes, as he faints with his wound, and death comes to him as "purple death." The words are weak as given by Pope :—

> " Down sinks the priest, the purple hand of death
> Closed his dim eyes, and fate suppressed his breath."

But there were other passages where this purple was referred to, which proved that it could have had nothing of the scarlet about it—as in a description of the sea. When dark brown clouds pass over the blue Mediterranean, they give a dark, leaden-like purple to the waters as they lie motionless. Homer thus describes the sea when in this state :—

> " As when old Ocean's silent surface sleeps,
> The waves just heaving on the purple deeps,
> While yet the expected tempest hangs on high,
> Weighs down the clouds, and blackens all the sky."

There could be no question but that the purple here referred to was a dark leaden colour. The same epithet of "purple" has been applied by Homer to the face of oxen, and they certainly had not scarlet faces; but they had a peculiar russet passing into blue, which could frequently be seen in their dark foreheads. When Achilles went to the sea to seek his mother Thetis, Homer says that the sea appeared to him of this dark strange bloody purple. The ideal of blood among the Greeks was that of a dark, rich colour. Homer said of Menelaus, when wounded by Pandarus, that his blood distilled down his thigh, as when a Tyrian girl stained the ivory. Reverting to the strange manner in which in nature the purple gradated into scarlet, without touching the crimson, Mr. Ruskin urged upon the student of illumination the propriety of not using the sacred colour, crimson, the symbol of life, without extreme caution.

39. Passing from that colour itself, the lecturer next called attention to the necessity of a careful study of the abstract lines which were to inclose it, instancing the noble and graceful curves which were to be met with in many of the illuminated letters of the thirteenth century. As instances of such, he exhibited an enlarged drawing of a small letter from one of the missals, the curves in which were of the most graceful character, and could only be drawn by the most skilful hand. Having pointed out the grace and beauty of the original, Mr. Ruskin produced, amid the laughter of his audience, the same graceful design vulgarised by the use of combined mathematical curves, and showed, by adding a few strokes, that this vulgarisation was, in fact, the form of an Ionic capital. Mr. Ruskin intimated that he had placed in the adjoining room, under the care of Mr. Allen,[1] to whom he confessed himself deeply indebted for the very valuable assistance he had rendered him, several examples of this class of curves, taken from MSS., which they might glance at now and then ; and expressed his readiness to attend at the Museum upon stated days, to look over any examples which might be brought to him, in order as far as he was able to help the student forward in his work.

40. It was grievous to think how large an amount of power was lying

---

[1] [Not Mr. George Allen, but a Mr. Allen then employed at the Museum.]

dormant at this time of the world, because bound down and darkened by the absurd scientificalities which it was the fashion of the day to promulgate and insist upon as indispensable. A day or two since a person who had attended his previous lectures had sent him some books of sketches, stating that he had been in the habit of illuminating, not for profit, but merely because he found it satisfied his mind. These books were filled with the most marvellous sketches and most felicitous ideas. Among the various sketches he had found one which was a perfectly new thought, even on the subject of " The Lord's Supper," a theme which had exhausted the genius of some of the finest painters of ancient and modern time. "And when they had sung a hymn, they went up to the Mount of Olives." [1] The sketch represents the group of the disciples singing the hymn—a most beautiful and charming subject for the painter. A few days since he had set some boys to work to produce some specimens of illuminated letters; they had been most successful in their work, and the lecturer exhibited the results of their labours in two large initial letters for the " Kyrie Eleison." There was, therefore, none of that insuperable difficulty about the use of ornamental letters which some persons had imagined, and he was most anxious to impress upon those of his audience who might be engaged in the execution of ornamental designs, and lettering on walls and shop-fronts, how easily and with what success they might introduce initial letters of this description. It was surprising to see the dexterity and skill with which many of these writers could strike the curves of the letters they were painting. It was a most marvellous power, one which could only be attained by constant and long practice; but he was anxious to see this sleight of hand turned to greater advantage, and used to more effect. They might depend upon it, that if they once introduced these ornamental letters, they would achieve for themselves a vast amount of success, and carry the public along with them to an extent of which they could at present form no adequate opinion.

41. There were two points about the art of illumination which, in closing, he desired to refer to: they were the uniform attention which was paid to purity of colour, and the vast power of the grotesque which could be advantageously employed by those who were in the habit of using the art. An examination of the works of the old illuminators would show in the most striking manner the great attention which they always paid to purity of colour. Between the good colourist and the layer-on of paint there was the widest possible difference. The Dutch excelled in the art of laying on paint, but their work was far different from that careful system of colouring adapted by the illuminators of the thirteenth century. Observe how carefully, and with what exquisite taste, the small lines and dots of white are introduced in order to produce harmonious effects where the immediate contrast of strong or bright colours would offend the eye. In some of the smaller work of these illuminated missals, the white was introduced in such small quantities as to be only visible by the aid of a microscope. Some specimens illustrative, in a high degree, of the great care and labour bestowed in this respect, were handed to the audience. In the works of the old masters of painting, the holiest subjects were always depicted in the most powerful and purest of colours; as the subjects lowered in character, they gradually lost their dignity of colour, until they came to the lowest

---

[1] [Matthew xxvi. 30.]

character of all in colour—the works of Salvator Rosa, which were nothing more than mere drabs and browns.

42. The second highly important consideration in connection with this art, was that to which he had alluded on a previous occasion [1]—viz., the vast powers of grotesque which it afforded. This power of the grotesque was one which ought not to be overlooked by people of this country, for most undoubtedly the faculty belonged peculiarly to the northern nations. Carlyle, to whom he (the lecturer) owed more than to any other living writer,[2] in his *Hero Worship* thus referred to the exercise of this power. "It is strange," said he, "after our beautiful Apollo statues, and clear smiling mythuses, to come down upon the Norse gods 'brewing ale,' to hold their feast with Ægir, the Sea-Jötun, sending out Thor to get the cauldron for them in the Jötun country; Thor, after many adventures, clapping the pot on his head like a huge hat, and walking off with it,—quite lost in it, the ears of the Pot reaching down to his heels! A kind of vacant hugeness, large, awkward gianthood, characterises that Norse system; enormous force, as yet altogether untutored, stalking helpless with large uncertain strides. Consider only their primary mythus of the creation! The gods, having got their giant Ymer slain, —a giant made by 'warm wind,' and much confused work, out of the conflict of Frost and Fire—determined on constructing a world with him. His blood made the Sea, his flesh was the Land, the Rocks his bones"—good geology that!—"of his eyebrows they formed Asgard, their God's dwelling; his skull was the great blue vault of Immensity, and the brains of it became the Clouds. What a hyper-Brobdignagian business! Untamed thought, great, giant-like, enormous, to be turned in due time into the compact greatness, not giant-like, but god-like, and stronger than gianthood, of the Shakespeares, the Goethes! Spiritually, as well as bodily, these men are our progenitors."[3]

43. The works of Albert Dürer, and the great German artist, to whom allusion had been made in the previous lectures,[4] were also full of this power of the grotesque. The plates of "Death the Avenger," and "Death the Friend," were the most remarkable modern instances of the grotesque in its peculiar *moral* power he knew. In the one Death appears suddenly as a masquer [among the gay throng] in a masked ball at Paris; and, although the subject was similar to that which had been previously treated by Dr. Young, he did not think that the German artist was indebted to Dr. Young for the idea. Dr. Young was remarkable for this power.

> "'Twas in a circle of the gay I stood.
> Death would have enter'd; nature pushed him back."

Now mark the grotesque,—

> "Supported by a doctor of renown,
> His point he gain'd. Then artfully dismissed

---

[1] [See above, § 23, p. 495.]

[2] [This was Ruskin's first public admission of Carlyle as his "master." In the third volume of *Modern Painters*, written a few months later, Ruskin names Carlyle as the author to whom he is most of all indebted, and speaks of "Carlyle's stronger thinking colouring mine continually" (Appendix iii.). For the numerous later references, see General Index.]

[3] [Carlyle's *Hero-Worship*, in the lecture on "The Hero as Divinity."]

[4] [Rethel: see above, p. 489 n.]

The sage ; for Death design'd to be conceal'd.
He gave an old vivacious usurer
His meagre aspect and his naked bones ;
In gratitude for plumping up his prey,
A pamper'd spendthrift ; whose fantastic air,
Well-fashion'd figure, and cockaded brow,
He took in change, and underneath the pride
Of costly linen, tuck'd his filthy shroud.
His crooked bow he straighten'd to a cane ;
And hid his deadly shafts in Myra's eyes." [1]

The other plate, " Death the Friend," showed the grotesque in its gentler power of teaching. The old sexton sits quietly in his chair beneath the belfry, at the window of the church tower; the summer evening is falling— Death has come for him, his lean and ghostly horse is waiting in the clouds; and he stands and tolls at once the vesper and the passing bell, while a little bird on the window-sill sings as the good man dies. The whole is full of that poetry and that feeling which were so characteristic of the thirteenth-century art, of the period when Walter, the Minnesinger, left this charge in his testament, " Let the little birds be fed daily on my grave." [2]

---

[1] [*Night Thoughts*, v. 846–859. For Ruskin's constant reading of Young, see Vol. X. p. 405 *n.*]

[2] [Herr Walter von der Vogelweide (about 1190–1240), Walter of the bird-meadow ; see *Lays of the Minnesingers* (by Edgar Taylor, 1825, p. 213). See Longfellow's poem " Walter von der Vogelweide " :—

" And he gave the monks his treasures,
Gave them all with this behest :
They should feed the birds at noontide
Daily on his place of rest."]

PART III

"NOTES ON THE CONSTRUCTION OF SHEEPFOLDS"

(1851)

NOTES

ON THE

CONSTRUCTION OF SHEEPFOLDS

BY

JOHN RUSKIN, M.A.,

AUTHOR OF "THE SEVEN LAMPS OF ARCHITECTURE," ETC.

LONDON

SMITH, ELDER AND CO., 65, CORNHILL

1851

[Bibliographical Note.—The following is the list of editions, etc. :—

First Edition (1851).—The title-page of this edition is as shown on p. 511 here. Octavo, pp. 50, followed by a leaf containing an advertisement of "Mr. Ruskin's Works on Art," and on the reverse (and also on the reverse of the title-page), the imprint " London : Printed by Stewart and Murray, Old Bailey." A Prefatory Note, styled " Advertisement," is on p. 3 (here p. 517). Issued without wrappers on March 6, 1851. Price One Shilling.

Second Edition (1851).—The title-page is different, thus : —

Notes | on the | Construction of Sheepfolds. | By | John Ruskin, M.A., | Author of | "The Stones of Venice," "The Seven Lamps of Architecture," etc. | Second Edition. | London : | Smith, Elder and Co., 65, Cornhill. | 1851.

Octavo, pp. iv. + 50. Imprint on reverse of title-page as before. Preface to the Second Edition, pp. 1, 2 (here p. 519) ; " Advertisement," p. 3. The leaf of advertisements at the end of the first edition does not reappear. Issued, in the same style and at the same price, in April 1851.

Third Edition (1875).—The existence of the second edition had escaped the author's memory ; the preface to that edition was accordingly not reprinted ; and this was erroneously described "Second Edition" on the title-page :—

Notes | on the | Construction of Sheepfolds. | By | John Ruskin, LL.D., | Honorary Student of Christ Church, Oxford ; Honorary Fellow of | Corpus Christi College, Oxford ; and Slade Professor | of Fine Art, Oxford. | Second Edition. | George Allen, | Sunnyside, Orpington, Kent. | 1875.

Octavo, pp. 52. Imprint (on reverse of title-page and at foot of p. 52) "Watson and Hazell, Printers, London and Aylesbury." The "Preface (called 'Advertisement') to the First Edition" occupies p. iii., with an addition (pp. iii.-iv.) of 1875 (here p. 521). Issued on October 1, 1875, in white paper wrappers, with the title-page (enclosed in a ruled frame) repeated on the front, and an announcement of "Works by Ruskin" on pages 3 and 4. Price One Shilling. (1000 copies printed.)

Fourth Edition (1879).—The alterations here are (1) the date, (2) "Fourth Edition" instead of "Second," (3) a new imprint "Chiswick Press :— Charles Whittingham, Tooks Court, Chancery Lane," and (4) buff wrappers instead of white, and removal of the Advertisements. Otherwise, this edition is identical with the Third. (1000 copies printed.)

The text of the "Notes" was the same in all editions, except for a few printers' alterations noticed below.

The pamphlet was *reprinted* (with all three Prefaces) in *On the Old Road*, 1885, vol. ii. pp. 249–301 (§§ 182–301), and again in the Second Edition of that collection, 1899, vol. iii. pp. 255–309 (§§ 182–301). The numbering of the paragraphs (first introduced in 1885) is altered in this edition.

Variæ Lectiones.—The differences in the text between the various editions of the pamphlet (other than those already described) are very slight, and are mostly matters of punctuation, etc. ; *e.g.*, in § 9, line 14, for "one seven-thousandth part," ed. 1 reads "the $\frac{1}{7000}$th part"; § 13, line 11, ed. 3 mis-reads "the people" for "people"—a misprint followed in both editions of *On the Old Road;* § 25, note, line 7, eds. 1 and 2 read "had," ed. 3 reads "has." The paragraphs are in this edition renumbered.

The publication of the pamphlet in 1851 produced the following *replies:*—

Notes on Shepherds and Sheep. A letter to John Ruskin, Esq., M.A. By William Dyce, M.A., Royal Academician ; Professor of the Theory of the Fine Arts, King's College, London. "Si intellixisti spiritualiter (verba Christi) spiritus et vita tibi sunt ; si in-tellixisti carnaliter, etiam spiritus et vita sunt, sed tibi non sunt" (S. August.—Tract xxvii.). London : Longmans, Brown, Green and Longmans. MDCCCLI. 8vo, pp. 36.

A Reply to "Notes on the Construction of Sheepfolds." By a Graduate of the University of Cambridge. London : C. Goodall and Son, 30 Great Pulteney Street, Golden Square ; and Thomas Bosworth, 215 Regent Street. 1851. 8vo, pp. 16.

A privately-printed volume, referring to the Notes, has the following title-page :—

Two Letters | Concerning | "Notes on the Construction of Sheepfolds." | Addressed to | The Rev. F. D. Maurice, M.A., | in 1851. | By | John Ruskin, LL.D., D.C.L. | Author of "Modern Painters," etc., and Honorary Fellow of Corpus | Christi College, Oxford | With Forewords by | F. J. Furnivall, M.A., Hon. Dr. Phil. | London. | Printed for Private Distribution only. | 1890.

Crown 8vo, pp. 30. On the reverse of the title-page "*Not for Sale*" and the imprint "R. Clay and Sons, Limited, London and Bungay." "Forewords," signed "F. J. Furnivall, 3 St. George's Square, Primrose Hill, N.W. 8 October, 1890," occupy pp. 7–14. These begin with some personal reminis-cences of Ruskin and his wife in 1848–1850 ; the description of Ruskin has been cited at Vol. VIII. p. 34, and the rest is cited in the later volume con-taining Ruskin's other letters to Furnivall. Passages from F. D. Maurice's letters cited in later pages of the "Forewords" are given, and Dr. Furnivall's account of the correspondence is incorporated, in the Appendix to Part III. of this volume, below, pp. 561, 565, 568. Ruskin's Letter I. (pp. 17–22) is here given, pp. 562–565 ; Letter II. (pp. 23–26), pp. 566–568 ; his first letter to Dr. Furnivall (given as Appendix to the book now being de-scribed, pp. 29–30) is given on p. 569 here. Issued in white "vellum" boards, lettered in gilt up the back —" Two Letters—John Ruskin, 1890 " ; 40 copies on Whatman's hand-made paper, and four on vellum.

Another privately-printed volume, again dealing with the Notes, has the following title-page :—

John Ruskin | and | Frederick Denison Maurice | on | " Notes on the Construction of Sheepfolds," | Edited by | Thomas J. Wise. | London : | Privately Printed | 1896.

Small 4to, pp. 52. On p. 5, " This is to certify that of this book thirty copies only have been printed." No imprint. The Editor's Preface occupies pp. 9–12 ; this consists for the most part of extracts from the " Forewords " by Dr. Furnivall, above described. Maurice's letter to Furnivall, criticising " Sheepfolds " (March 25, 1851) is there given at length (pp. 13–22) ; Ruskin's letter of March 30 follows (pp. 22–28); then, Maurice's rejoinder of April 4 (pp. 28–40) ; Ruskin's letter of " Easter Sunday " and " April 25 " (pp. 41–45) ; Maurice's letter closing the correspondence (pp. 45–50); and finally, Ruskin's letter to Furnivall of March 17 (pp. 50–52, here pp. 569–570). On the last page is a further extract from Furnivall's " Forewords." So much of Maurice's letters as is necessary to understand Ruskin's replies is here given (see pp. 561, 565, 568), the extracts being supplementary to those included in the volume last described.

The text of Ruskin's Letters, as printed in the later volume, shows many slight variations from that given in the earlier. Dr. Furnivall printed his book from transcripts, into which numerous variations in minor matters of punctuation, paragraphing, etc., had crept. Also on p. 563 here, five lines from the bottom, the words " whom you think such dreadful sinners " had dropped out. Mr. Wise's book followed the original letters, and his text is reprinted here. A name, however, which Dr. Furnivall had left blank (p. 564 here), and which Mr. Wise printed, is here again left blank ; the case referred to may be identified in the House of Lords' Journals, for May 28, 1850.]

ADVERTISEMENT

(1851)

MANY persons will probably find fault with me for publishing opinions which are not new: but I shall bear this blame contentedly, believing that opinions on this subject could hardly be just if they were not 1800 years old. Others will blame me for making proposals which are altogether new: to whom I would answer, that things in these days seem not so far right but that they may be mended. And others will simply call the opinions false and the proposals foolish—to whose good-will, if they take it in hand to contradict me, I must leave what I have written— having no purpose of being drawn, at present, into religious controversy. If, however, any should admit the truth, but regret the tone of what I have said, I can only pray them to consider how much less harm is done in the world by ungraceful boldness, than by untimely fear.

DENMARK HILL,
February, 1851.

PREFACE TO THE SECOND EDITION

(1851)

SINCE the publication of these Notes, I have received many letters upon the affairs of the Church, from persons of nearly every denomination of Christians; for all these letters I am grateful, and in many of them I have found valuable information, or suggestion: but I have not leisure at present to follow out the subject farther; and no reason has been shown me for modifying or altering any part of the text as it stands. It is republished, therefore, without change or addition.

I must, however, especially thank one of my correspondents for sending me a pamphlet, called "Sectarianism, the Bane of Religion and the Church,"* which I would recommend, in the strongest terms, to the reading of all who regard the cause of Christ; and, for help in reading the Scriptures, I would name also the short and admirable arrangement of parallel passages relating to the offices of the clergy, called "The Testimony of Scripture concerning the Christian Ministry." †

* London: 1846. Nisbet & Co., Berners Street.
† London: 1847. T. K. Campbell, 1, Warwick Square.

PREFACE TO THE THIRD EDITION

(1875)

I HAVE only to add to this first preface, that the boldness of the pamphlet,—ungraceful enough, it must be admitted, —has done no one any harm, that I know of; but on the contrary, some definite good, as far as I can judge; and that I republish the whole now, letter for letter, as originally printed, believing it likely to be still serviceable, and, on the ground it takes for argument (Scriptural authority), incontrovertible as far as it reaches; though it amazes me to find on re-reading it, that, so late as 1851, I had only got the length of perceiving the schism between sects of Protestants to be criminal, and ridiculous, while I still supposed the schism between Protestants and Catholics to be virtuous and sublime.

The most valuable part of the whole is the analysis of governments, pp. 551–552; the passages on Church discipline, pp. 545, 546, being also anticipatory of much that I have to say in *Fors*,[1] where I hope to re-assert the substance of this pamphlet on wider grounds, and with more modesty.

BRANTWOOD,
3rd August, 1875.

---

[1] [See note on p. 538, below, for a reference in *Fors Clavigera*, Letter 49. See also Letter 20 (on the neglect of Discipline by the Church). Those passages, however, were written before this preface; in later numbers of *Fors*, there are many passing references to the Church and to Bishops and their duties (see General Index, under those headings).]

NOTES

1. THE following remarks were intended to form part of the appendix to an essay on Architecture:[1] but it seemed to me, when I had put them into order, that they might be useful to persons who would not care to possess the work to which I proposed to attach them: I publish them, therefore, in a separate form; but I have not time to give them more consistency than they would have had in the subordinate position originally intended for them. I do not profess to teach Divinity; and I pray the reader to understand this, and to pardon the slightness and insufficiency of notes set down with no more intention of connected treatment of their subject than might regulate an accidental conversation. Some of them are simply copied from my private diary;[2] others are detached statements of facts, which seem to me significative or valuable, without comment; all are written in haste, and in the intervals of occupation with an entirely different subject. It may be asked of me, whether I hold it right to speak thus hastily and insufficiently respecting the matter in question? Yes. I hold it right to *speak* hastily; not to *think* hastily. I have not thought hastily of these things; and, besides, the haste of speech is confessed, that the reader may think of me only as talking to him, and saying, as shortly and simply as I can, things which, if he esteem them foolish or

---

[1] [See *The Stones of Venice*, vol. i., Appendix 12, and the author's note (Vol. IX. p. 437).]

[2] [See above, Introduction, p. lxxiii.]

idle, he is welcome to cast aside; but which, in very truth,
I cannot help saying at this time.

2. The passages in the essay which required notes, described the repression of the political power of the Venetian
Clergy by the Venetian Senate; and it became necessary
for me—in supporting an assertion made in the course of
the inquiry, that the idea of separation of Church and State
was both vain and impious—to limit the sense in which it
seemed to me that the word "Church" should be understood, and to note one or two consequences which would
result from the acceptance of such limitation. This I may
as well do in a separate paper, readable by any person interested in the subject; for it is high time that *some* definition of the word should be agreed upon. I do not mean
a definition involving the doctrine of this or that division
of Christians, but limiting, in a manner understood by all
of them, the sense in which the *word* should thenceforward
be used. There is grievous inconvenience in the present
state of things. For instance, in a sermon lately published
at Oxford, by an anti-Tractarian divine, I find this sentence,
—"It is clearly within the province of the State to establish a national *church*, or *external institution of certain forms
of worship.*" Now suppose one were to take this interpretation of the word "Church," given by an Oxford divine,
and substitute it for the simple word in some Bible texts,
as, for instance, "Unto the angel of the external institution
of certain forms of worship of Ephesus, write," etc. Or,
"Salute the brethren which are in Laodicea, and Nymphas,
and the external institution of certain forms of worship
which is in his house,"[1]—what awkward results we should
have, here and there! Now I do not say it is possible
for men to agree with each other in their religious *opinions*,
but it is certainly possible for them to agree with each
other upon their religious *expressions;* and when a word
occurs in the Bible a hundred and fourteen times, it is
surely not asking too much of contending divines to let it

---

[1] [Revelation ii. 1; Colossians iv. 15.]

stand in the sense in which it there occurs; and when they want an expression of something for which it does *not* stand in the Bible, to use some other word. There is no compromise of religious opinion in this; it is simply proper respect for the Queen's English.

3. The word occurs in the New Testament, as I said, a hundred and fourteen times.* In every one of those occurrences, it bears one and the same grand sense: that of a congregation or assembly of men. But it bears this sense under four different modifications, giving four separate meanings to the word. These are—

(I.) The entire Multitude of the Elect; otherwise called the Body of Christ; and sometimes the Bride, the Lamb's Wife; including the Faithful in all ages;—Adam, and the children of Adam yet unborn.

In this sense it is used in Ephesians v. 25, 27, 32; Colossians i. 18; and several other passages.

(II.) The entire multitude of professing believers in Christ, existing on earth at a given moment; including false brethren, wolves in sheep's clothing, goats and tares, as well as sheep and wheat, and other forms of bad fish with good in the net.

In this sense it is used in 1 Cor. x. 32, xv. 9; Galatians i. 13; 1 Tim. iii. 5, etc.

(III.) The multitude of professed believers, living in a certain city, place, or house. This is the most frequent sense in which the word occurs, as in Acts vii. 38, xiii. 1; 1 Cor. i. 2, xvi. 19, etc.

(IV.) Any assembly of men: as in Acts xix. 32, 41.

4. That in a hundred and twelve out of the hundred and fourteen texts, the word bears some one of these four meanings, is indisputable.† But there are two texts in

---

* I may, perhaps, have missed count of one or two occurrences of the word; but not, I think, in any important passages.

† The expression "House of God," in 1 Tim. iii. 15, is shown to be used of the congregation by 1 Cor. iii. 16, 17.

I have not noticed the word κυριακὴ (οἰκία), from which the German "Kirche," the English "Church," and the Scotch "Kirk" are derived, as it is not used with that signification in the New Testament.

which, if the word had alone occurred, its meaning might have been doubtful.   These are Matt. xvi. 18, and xviii. 17.[1]

The absurdity of founding any doctrine upon the inexpressibly minute possibility that, in these two texts, the word might have been used with a different meaning from that which it bore in all the others, coupled with the assumption that the meaning was this or that, is self-evident: it is not so much a religious error as a philological solecism; unparalleled, so far as I know, in any other science but that of divinity.

Nor is it ever, I think, committed with open front by Protestants.   No English divine, asked in a straightforward manner for a Scriptural definition of "the Church," would, I suppose, be bold enough to answer "the Clergy."   Nor is there any harm in the common use of the word, so only that it be distinctly understood to be not the Scriptural one; and therefore to be unfit for substitution in a Scriptural text.   There is no harm in a man's talking of his son's "going into the Church;" meaning that he is going to take orders: but there is much harm in his supposing this a Scriptural use of the word, and therefore, that when Christ said, "Tell it to the Church," He might possibly have meant, "Tell it to the Clergy."

5. It is time to put an end to the chance of such misunderstanding.   Let it but be declared plainly by all men, when they begin to state their opinions on matters ecclesiastical, that they will use the word "Church" in one sense or the other;—that they will accept the sense in which it is used by the Apostles, or that they deny this sense, and propose a new definition of their own.   We shall then know what we are about with them—we may perhaps grant them their new use of the term, and argue with them on that understanding; so only that they will not pretend to make

---

[1] ["Thou art Peter, and upon this rock I will build my church." "And if he shall neglect to hear them, tell it unto the church." For a short commentary on the latter text, see *Stones of Venice*, vol. i. (Vol. IX. p. 437 *n.*), and compare below, § 24.]

use of Scriptural authority, while they refuse to employ Scriptural language. This, however, it is not my purpose to do at present. I desire only to address those who are willing to accept the Apostolic sense of the word Church; and with them, I would endeavour shortly to ascertain what consequences must follow from an acceptance of that Apostolic sense, and what must be our first and most necessary conclusions from the common language of Scripture * respecting these following points :—

(1) The distinctive characters of the Church.

(2) The Authority of the Church.

(3) The Authority of the Clergy over the Church.

(4) The Connection of the Church with the State.

6. These are four separate subjects of question; but we shall not have to put these questions in succession with each of the four Scriptural meanings of the word Church, for evidently its second and third meaning may be considered together, as merely expressing the general or particular conditions of the Visible Church, and the fourth signification is entirely independent of all questions of a religious kind. So that we shall only put the above inquiries successively respecting the Invisible and Visible Church; and as the two last—of authority of Clergy, and connection with State—can evidently only have reference to the Visible Church, we shall have, in all, these six questions to consider :—

(1) The distinctive characters of the Invisible Church.

(2) The distinctive characters of the Visible Church.

(3) The Authority of the Invisible Church.

(4) The Authority of the Visible Church.

(5) The Authority of Clergy over the Visible Church.

(6) The Connection of the Visible Church with the State.

* Any reference, *except* to Scripture, in notes of this kind would, of course, be useless: the argument from, or with, the Fathers, is not to be compressed into fifty pages. I have something to say about Hooker; but I reserve that for another time, not wishing to say it hastily, or to leave it without support.[1]

---

[1] [Ruskin had made many notes on Hooker (see Introduction, p. lxxiii.), but he did not publish anything further on the subject.]

7. (1) What are the distinctive characters of the Invisible Church? That is to say, What is it which makes a person a member of this Church, and how is he to be known for such? Wide question—if we had to take cognizance of all that has been written respecting it, remarkable as it has been always for quantity rather than carefulness, and full of confusion between Visible and Invisible: even the Article of the Church of England being ambiguous in its first clause: "The *Visible* Church is a congregation of Faithful men." As if ever it had been possible, except for God, to see Faith, or to know a Faithful man by sight! And there is little else written on this question, without some such quick confusion of the Visible and Invisible Church;—needless and unaccountable confusion. For evidently, the Church which is composed of Faithful men is the one true, indivisible, and indiscernible Church, built on the foundation of Apostles and Prophets, Jesus Christ Himself being the chief cornerstone.[1] It includes all who have ever fallen asleep in Christ, and all yet unborn, who are to be saved in Him: its Body is as yet imperfect; it will not be perfected till the last saved human spirit is gathered to its God.

A man becomes a member of this Church only by believing in Christ with all his heart; nor is he positively recognizable for a member of it, when he has become so, by any one but God, not even by himself. Nevertheless, there are certain signs by which Christ's sheep may be guessed at. Not by their being in any definite Fold—for many are lost sheep at times; but by their sheep-like behaviour; and a great many are indeed sheep which, on the far mountainside, in their peacefulness, we take for stones. To themselves, the best proof of their being Christ's sheep is to find themselves on Christ's shoulders; and, between them, there are certain sympathies (expressed in the Apostles' Creed by the term "communion of Saints"), by which they may in a sort recognize each other, and so become verily visible to each other for mutual comfort.

---

[1] [Ephesians ii. 20 ; 1 Corinthians xv. 18.]

8. (2) The Limits of the Visible Church, or of the Church in the Second Scriptural Sense, are not so easy to define: they are awkward questions, these, of stake-nets. It has been ingeniously and plausibly endeavoured to make Baptism a sign of admission into the Visible Church: but absurdly enough; for we know that half the baptized people in the world are very visible rogues, believing neither in God nor devil; and it is flat blasphemy to call these Visible Christians; we also know that the Holy Ghost was some-times given before Baptism,* and it would be absurdity to call a man, on whom the Holy Ghost had fallen, an Invisible Christian. The only rational distinction is that which prac-tically, though not professedly, we always assume. If we hear a man profess himself a believer in God and in Christ, and detect him in no glaring and wilful violation of God's law, we speak of him as a Christian; and, on the other hand, if we hear him or see him denying Christ, either in his words or conduct, we tacitly assume him not to be a Christian. A mawkish charity prevents us from outspeaking in this matter, and from earnestly endeavouring to discern who are Christians and who are not; and this I hold † to be one of the chief sins of the Church in the present day; for thus wicked men are put to no shame; and better men are encouraged in their failings, or caused to hesitate in their virtues, by the example of those whom, in false charity,

---

* Acts x. 44.

† Let not the reader be displeased with me for these short and ap-parently insolent statements of opinion. I am not writing insolently, but as shortly and clearly as I can; and when I seriously believe a thing, I say so in a few words, leaving the reader to determine what my belief is worth. But I do not choose to temper down every expression of personal opinion into courteous generalities, and so lose space, and time, and intelligi-bility at once. We are utterly oppressed in these days by our courtesies, and considerations, and compliances, and proprieties. Forgive me them, this once, or rather let us all forgive them to each other, and learn to speak plainly first, and, if it may be, gracefully afterwards; and not only to speak, but to stand by what we have spoken. One of my Oxford friends heard, the other day, that I was employed on these notes, and forthwith wrote to me, in a panic, not to put my name to them, for fear I should 'compromise myself.' I think we are most of us compromised

they choose to call Christians. Now, it being granted that it is impossible to know, determinedly, who are Christians indeed, that is no reason for utter negligence in separating the nominal, apparent, or possible Christian, from the professed Pagan or enemy of God. We spend much time in arguing about efficacy of sacraments and such other mysteries; but we do not act upon the very certain tests which are clear and visible. We know that Christ's people are not thieves—not liars—not busybodies—not dishonest— not avaricious—not wasteful—not cruel. Let us then get ourselves well clear of thieves — liars — wasteful people— avaricious people—cheating people—people who do not pay their debts. Let us assure them that they, at least, do not belong to the Visible Church; and having thus got that Church into decent shape and cohesion, it will be time to think of drawing the stake-nets closer.

I hold it for a law, palpable to common sense, and which nothing but the cowardice and faithlessness of the Church prevents it from putting in practice, that the conviction of any dishonourable conduct or wilful crime, of any fraud, falsehood, cruelty, or violence, should be ground for the excommunication of any man: — for his publicly declared separation from the acknowledged body of the Visible

to some extent already, when England has sent a Roman Catholic minister to the second city in Italy, and remains herself for a week without any government, because her chief men cannot agree upon the position which a Popish cardinal is to have leave to occupy in London.[1]

---

[1] [The pamphlet was passing through the press during the Ministerial crisis which followed the defeat of Lord John Russell's Government in February 1851. The defeat was on a Franchise resolution, but the difficulty in the way of forming a new Government was the Ecclesiastical Titles Bill which Lord John, following up his famous Durham Letter, had introduced; declaring null and void the Papal Bull of 1850 creating Roman Catholic dioceses in England, and appointing Cardinal Wiseman Archbishop of Westminster. The Peelites refused to join Lord John on account of the Bill; Lord Aberdeen declined to form an Administration, recognising that some measure of the kind was required by the state of public feeling; Lord Stanley failed to form one, and in the end Lord John returned to office (March) and passed his Bill (July). "The Roman Catholic Minister" was the Right Hon. R. Lalor Sheil, who, on October 24, 1850, had been appointed Her Majesty's Minister Plenipotentiary to the Grand Duke of Tuscany. In the previous year, as Master of the Mint, he had issued "the Godless florin."]

Church : and that he should not be received again therein without public confession of his crime and declaration of his repentance. If this were vigorously enforced, we should soon have greater purity of life in the world, and fewer discussions about high and low churches. But before we can obtain any idea of the manner in which such law could be enforced, we have to consider the second question respecting the Authority of the Church. Now Authority is twofold : to declare doctrine, and to enforce discipline; and we have to inquire, therefore, in each kind,—

9. (3) What is the authority of the Invisible Church? Evidently, in matters of doctrine, all members of the Invisible Church must have been, and must ever be, at the time of their deaths, right in the points essential to Salvation. But, (A), we cannot tell who *are* members of the Invisible Church.

(B) We cannot collect evidence from death-beds in a clearly stated form.

(C) We can collect evidence, in any form, only from some one or two out of every sealed thousand of the Invisible Church. Elijah thought he was alone in Israel ; and yet there were seven thousand invisible ones around him.[1] Grant that we had Elijah's intelligence ; and we could only calculate on collecting one seven-thousandth part of the evidence or opinions of the part of the Invisible Church living on earth at a given moment: that is to say, the seven-millionth or trillionth of its collective evidence. It is very clear, therefore, we cannot hope to get rid of the contradictory opinions, and keep the consistent ones, by a general equation. But, it has been said, these are no contradictory opinions ; the Church is infallible. There was some talk about the infallibility of the Church if I recollect right, in that letter of Mr. Bennett's to the Bishop of London.[2] If any Church is infallible, it is assuredly the

---

[1] [1 Kings xix. 14, 18.]

[2] [See *Resignation of the Rev. W. J. E. Bennett, M.A.; Correspondence of the Lord Bishop of London with the Rev. Mr. Bennett*, 1850, p. 9. Mr. Bennett (1804–1886), first Incumbent of St. Paul's, Knightsbridge, and one of the founders of St. Barnabas',

Invisible Church, or Body of Christ: and infallible in the main sense it must of course be by its definition. An Elect person must be saved, and therefore cannot eventually be deceived on essential points: so that Christ says of the deception of such, "If it were *possible*,"[1] implying it to be impossible. Therefore, as we said, if one could get rid of the variable opinions of the members of the Invisible Church, the constant opinions would assuredly be authoritative: but, for the three reasons above stated, we cannot get at their constant opinions: and as for the feelings and thoughts which they daily experience or express, the question of Infallibility—which is practical only in this bearing—is soon settled. Observe, St. Paul, and the rest of the Apostles, write nearly all their epistles to the Invisible Church:— those epistles are headed,—Romans, "To the beloved of God, called to be saints;" 1 Corinthians, "To them that are sanctified in Christ Jesus;" 2 Corinthians, "To the saints in all Achaia;" Ephesians, "To the saints which are at Ephesus, and to the faithful in Christ Jesus;" Philippians, "To all the saints which are at Philippi;" Colossians, "To the saints and faithful brethren which are at Colosse;" 1 and 2 Thessalonians, "To the Church of the Thessalonians, which is in God the Father, and the Lord Jesus;" 1 and 2 Timothy, "To his own son in the faith;" Titus, to the same; 1 Peter, "To the Strangers, Elect according to the foreknowledge of God;" 2 Peter, "To them that have obtained like precious faith with us;" 2 John, "To the Elect lady;" Jude, "To them that are sanctified by God the Father, and preserved in Jesus Christ, and called."

10. There are thus fifteen epistles, expressly directed to the members of the Invisible Church. Philemon and Hebrews, and 1 and 3 John, are evidently also so written, though not so expressly inscribed. That of James, and

---

Pimlico, was one of the conspicuous Ritualists of the time. His practices were referred to in Lord John Russell's Durham Letter. He resigned his incumbency at Bishop Tait's request in 1850.]
    [1] [Matthew xxiv. 24.]

that to the Galatians, are as evidently to the Visible Church: the one being general, and the other to persons "removed from Him that called them." Missing out, therefore, these two epistles, but including Christ's words to His disciples, we find in the Scriptural addresses to members of the Invisible Church, fourteen, if not more, direct injunctions "not to be deceived." * So much for the "Infallibility of the Church."

Now, one could put up with Puseyism more patiently, if its fallacies arose merely from peculiar temperaments yielding to peculiar temptations. But its bold refusals to read plain English; its elaborate adjustments of tight bandages over its own eyes, as wholesome preparation for a walk among traps and pitfalls; its daring trustfulness in its own clairvoyance all the time, and declarations that every pit it falls into is a seventh heaven; and that it is pleasant and profitable to break its legs;—with all this it is difficult to have patience. One thinks of the highwayman with his eyes shut in the *Arabian Nights;*[1] and wonders whether any kind of scourging would prevail upon the Anglican highwayman to open "first one and then the other."

11. (4) So much, then, I repeat, for the infallibility of the *In*visible Church, and for its consequent authority. Now, if we want to ascertain what infallibility and authority there is in the Visible Church, we have to alloy the small wisdom and the light weight of Invisible Christians, with the large percentage of the false wisdom and contrary weight of Undetected Anti-Christians. Which alloy makes up the current coin of opinions in the Visible Church, having such value as we may choose—its nature being properly assayed —to attach to it.

There is, therefore, in matters of doctrine, *no such thing*

---

* Matt. xxiv. 4; Mark xiii. 5; Luke xxi. 8; 1 Cor. iii. 18, vi. 9, xv. 33; Eph. iv. 14, v. 6; Col. ii. 8; 2 Thess. ii. 3; Heb. iii. 13; 1 John i. 8, iii. 7; 2 John 7, 8.

---

[1] [Night 31; the Story of the Barber's Second Brother.]

as the Authority of the Church. We might as well talk of the authority of a morning cloud. There may be light *in* it, but the light is not of it; and it diminishes the light that it gets; and lets less of it through than it receives, Christ being its sun. Or, we might as well talk of the authority of a flock of sheep—for the Church is a body to be taught and fed, not to teach and feed: and of all sheep that are fed on the earth, Christ's Sheep are the most simple, (the children of this generation are wiser): always losing themselves; doing little else in this world *but* lose themselves;—never finding themselves; always found by Some One else; getting perpetually into sloughs, and snows, and bramble thickets, like to die there, but for their Shepherd, who is for ever finding them and bearing them back, with torn fleeces and eyes full of fear.

12. This, then, being the No-Authority of the Church in matter of Doctrine, what Authority has it in matters of Discipline?

Much, every way. The sheep have natural and wholesome power (however far scattered they may be from their proper fold) of getting together in orderly knots; following each other on trodden sheepwalks, and holding their heads all one way when they see strange dogs coming; as well as of casting out of their company any whom they see reason to suspect of not being right sheep, and being among them for no good. All which things must be done as the time and place require, and by common consent. A path may be good at one time of day which is bad at another, or after a change of wind; and a position may be very good for sudden defence, which would be very stiff and awkward for feeding in. And common consent must often be of such and such a company on this or that hillside, in this or that particular danger,—not of all the sheep in the world: and the consent may either be literally common, and expressed in assembly, or it may be to appoint officers over the rest, with such and such trusts of the common authority, to be used for the common advantage. Conviction of crimes, and excommunication, for instance, could neither be effected except before, or by means of, officers of some appointed authority.

13. (5) This then brings us to our fifth question. What is the Authority of the Clergy over the Church?

The first clause of the question must evidently be,— Who *are* the Clergy? And it is not easy to answer this without begging the rest of the question.

For instance, I think I can hear certain people answering, that the Clergy are folk of three kinds;—Bishops, who overlook the Church;[1] Priests, who sacrifice for the Church; Deacons, who minister to the Church: thus assuming in their answer, that the Church is to be sacrificed *for*, and that people cannot overlook and minister to her at the same time;—which is going much too fast. I think, however, if we define the Clergy to be the "Spiritual Officers of the Church,"—meaning, by Officers, merely People in office,—we shall have a title safe enough and general enough to begin with, and corresponding too, pretty well, with St. Paul's general expression προϊστάμενοι, in Rom. xii. 8, and 1 Thess. v. 13.

Now, respecting these Spiritual Officers, or office-bearers, we have to inquire, first, What their Office or Authority is, or should be? secondly, Who gave, or should give, them that Authority? That is to say, first, What is, or should be, the *nature* of their office? and secondly, What the *extent*, or force, of their authority in it? for this last depends mainly on its derivation.

14. First, then, What should be the offices, and of what kind should be the authority, of the Clergy?

I have hitherto referred to the Bible for an answer to every question. I do so again; and, behold, the Bible gives me no answer. I defy you to answer me from the Bible. You can only guess, and dimly conjecture, what the offices of the Clergy *were* in the first century. You cannot show

---

[1] [For Bishops as overseers, see below, § 25, p. 547.]

me a single command as to what they shall be. Strange,
this; the Bible gives no answer to so apparently important
a question! God surely would not have left His word
without an answer to anything His children ought to ask.
Surely it must be a ridiculous question—a question we
ought never to have put, or thought of putting. Let us
think of it again a little. To be sure,—It *is* a ridiculous
question, and we should be ashamed of ourselves for having
put it:—What should be the offices of the Clergy? That
is to say, What are the possible spiritual necessities which
at any time may arise in the Church, and by what means
and men are they to be supplied?—evidently an infinite
question. Different kinds of necessities must be met by
different authorities, constituted as the necessities arise.
Robinson Crusoe, in his island, wants no Bishop, and makes
a thunderstorm do for an Evangelist.[1] The University of
Oxford would be ill off without its Bishop; but wants
an Evangelist besides; and that forthwith.[2] The authority
which the Vaudois shepherds need is of Barnabas, the Son
of Consolation;[3] the authority which the city of London
needs is of James, the Son of Thunder. Let us then alter
the form of our question, and put it to the Bible thus:
What are the necessities most likely to arise in the Church?
and may they be best met by different men, or in great
part by the same men acting in different capacities? and
are the names attached to their offices of any consequence?
Ah, the Bible answers now, and that loudly. The Church
is built on the Foundation of the Apostles and Prophets,
Jesus Christ Himself being the corner-stone. Well; we
cannot have two foundations, so we can have no more

---

[1] ["On the 16th of May (according to my wooden calendar) the wind blew exceeding hard, accompanied with abundance of lightning and thunder all day, and
was succeeded by a very stormy night. The seeming anger of the heavens made me
have recourse to my Bible," etc. (p. 154, ed. 1818.).]

[2] [Samuel Wilberforce, Bishop of Oxford, 1845–1869; the Bishop's attitude on the
Hampden Controversy, the presence of Dr. Pusey in his diocese, and other circumstances, had at this time made him "suspect" to the Evangelical Party.]

[3] [For the persecution of the Vaudois Church, see Vol. I. pp. 392–393.]

Apostles nor Prophets:—then, as for the other needs of the Church in its edifying upon this foundation, there are all manner of things to be done daily;—rebukes to be given; comfort to be brought; Scripture to be explained; warning to be enforced; threatenings to be executed; charities to be administered; and the men who do these things are called, and call themselves, with absolute indifference, Deacons, Bishops, Elders, Evangelists, according to what they are doing at the time of speaking. St. Paul almost always calls himself a deacon, St. Peter calls himself an elder, 1 Peter v. 1; and Timothy, generally understood to be addressed as a bishop, is called a deacon in 1 Tim. iv. 6— forbidden to rebuke an elder, in v. 1, and exhorted to do the work of an evangelist, in 2 Tim. iv. 5. But there is one thing which, as officers, or as separate from the rest of the flock, they *never* call themselves,—which it would have been impossible, as so separate, they ever *should* have called themselves; that is—*Priests*.

15. It would have been just as possible for the Clergy of the early Church to call themselves Levites, as to call themselves (ex-officio) Priests. The whole function of Priesthood was, on Christmas morning, at once and for ever gathered into His Person who was born at Bethlehem; and thenceforward, all who are united with Him, and who with Him make sacrifice of themselves; that is to say, all members of the Invisible Church become, at the instant of their conversion, Priests; and are so called in 1 Peter ii. 5, and Rev. i. 6, and xx. 6, where, observe, there is no possibility of limiting the expression to the Clergy; the conditions of Priesthood being simply having been loved by Christ, and washed in His blood. The blasphemous claim on the part of the Clergy of being *more* Priests than the godly laity — that is to say, of having a higher Holiness than the Holiness of being one with Christ,— is altogether a Romanist heresy, dragging after it, or having its origin in, the other heresies respecting the sacrificial power of the Church officer, and his repeating the oblation of Christ,

and so having power to absolve from sin:—with all the other endless and miserable falsehoods of the Papal hierarchy; falsehoods for which, that there might be no shadow of excuse, it has been ordained by the Holy Spirit that no Christian minister shall once call himself a Priest from one end of the New Testament to the other, except together with his flock; and so far from the idea of any peculiar sanctification, belonging to the Clergy, ever entering the Apostles' minds, we actually find St. Paul defending himself against the possible imputation of inferiority: "If any man trust to himself that he is Christ's, let him of himself think this again, that, as he is Christ's, even so are we Christ's" (2 Cor. x. 7). As for the unhappy retention of the term Priest in our English Prayer-book, so long as it was understood to mean nothing but an upper order of Church officer, licensed to tell the congregation from the reading-desk, what (for the rest) they might, one would think, have known without being told,—that "God pardoneth all them that truly repent," — there was little harm in it; but, now that this order of Clergy begins to presume upon a title which, if it mean anything at all, is simply short for Presbyter, and has no more to do with the word Hiereus than with the word Levite, it is time that some order should be taken both with the book and the Clergy.[1] For instance, in that dangerous compound of halting poetry with hollow Divinity, called the *Lyra Apostolica*,[2] we find much versification on the sin of Korah and his company: with suggested parallel between the Christian and Levitical Churches, and threatening that there are "Judgment Fires, For high-voiced Korahs in their day." There are indeed such fires. But when Moses said, "a

---

[1] [Compare *Fors Clavigera*, Letter 49, where Ruskin refers to this passage and denounces the "equivocation" between Priest and Presbyter, and *Letters on the Lord's Prayer and the Church* (vol. i. § 237 of *On the Old Road* (1899), reprinted in a later volume.]

[2] [*Lyra Apostolica*; a volume of Poems (by J. W. Bowden, R. H. Froude, J. Keble, J. H. Newman, R. I. Wilberforce, and I. Williams), subscribed a, β, γ, δ, ε, ζ respectively, 1836. The piece here referred to is No. cli., "Korah, Dathan, and Abiram," by Keble (γ).]

Prophet shall the Lord raise up unto you, like unto me," did he mean the writer who signs γ in the *Lyra Apostolica?* The office of the Lawgiver and Priest is now for ever gathered into One Mediator between God and man; and THEY are guilty of the sin of Korah who blasphemously would associate themselves in His Mediatorship.

16. As for the passages in the "Ordering of Priests" and "Visitation of the Sick" respecting Absolution, they are evidently pure Romanism, and might as well not be there, for any practical effect which they have on the consciences of the Laity; and had much better not be there, as regards their effect on the minds of the Clergy. It is indeed true that Christ promised absolving powers to His Apostles: He also promised to those who believed, that they should take up serpents; and if they drank any deadly thing, it should not hurt them.[1] His words were fulfilled literally; but those who would extend their force to beyond the Apostolic times, must extend both promises, or neither.

Although, however, the Protestant laity do not often admit the absolving power of their clergy, they are but too apt to yield, in some sort, to the impression of their greater sanctification; and from this instantly results the unhappy consequence that the sacred character of the Layman himself is forgotten, and his own Ministerial duty is neglected. Men not in office in the Church suppose themselves, on that ground, in a sort unholy; and that, therefore, they may sin with more excuse, and be idle or impious with less danger, than the Clergy: especially they consider themselves relieved from all ministerial function, and as permitted to devote their whole time and energy to the business of this world. No mistake can possibly be greater. Every member of the Church is equally bound to the service of the Head of the Church; and that service is pre-eminently the saving of souls. There is not a moment of a man's

---

[1] [Mark xvi. 18.]

active life in which he may not be indirectly preaching; and throughout a great part of his life he ought to be *directly* preaching, and teaching both strangers and friends; his children, his servants, and all who in any way are put under him, being given to him as special objects of his ministration. So that the only difference between a Church officer and a lay member is either a wider degree of authority given to the former, as apparently a wiser and better man, or a special appointment to some office more easily discharged by one person than by many: as, for instance, the serving of tables by the deacons; the authority or appointment being, in either case, commonly signified by a marked separation from the rest of the Church, and the privilege or power,* of being maintained by the rest of the Church, without being forced to labour with his hands, or encumber himself with any temporal concerns.

17. Now, putting out of the question the serving of tables, and other such duties, respecting which there is no debate, we shall find the offices of the Clergy, whatever names we may choose to give to those who discharge them, falling mainly into two great heads:—Teaching; including doctrine, warning, and comfort: Discipline; including reproof and direct administration of punishment. Either of which functions would naturally become vested in single persons, to the exclusion of others, as a mere matter of convenience: whether those persons were wiser and better than others or not; and respecting each of which, and the authority required for its fitting discharge, a short inquiry must be separately made.

18. Teaching.—It appears natural and wise that certain men should be set apart from the rest of the Church that they may make Theology the study of their lives: and that they should be thereto instructed specially in the Hebrew and Greek tongues; and have entire leisure granted them for the study of the Scriptures, and for obtaining general

---

* ἐξουσία in 1 Cor. ix. 12. 2 Thess. iii. 9.

knowledge of the grounds of Faith, and best modes of its defence against all heretics: and it seems evidently right, also, that with this Scholastic duty should be joined the Pastoral duty of constant visitation and exhortation to the people; for, clearly, the Bible, and the truths of Divinity in general, can only be understood rightly in their practical application; and clearly, also, a man spending his time constantly in spiritual ministrations, must be better able, on any given occasion, to deal powerfully with the human heart than one unpractised in such matters.   The unity of Knowledge and Love, both devoted altogether to the service of Christ and His Church, marks the true Christian Minister; who, I believe, whenever he has existed, has never failed to receive due and fitting reverence from all men,—of whatever character or opinion; and I believe that if all those who profess to be such were such indeed, there would never be question of their authority more.

19. But, whatever influence they may have over the Church, their authority never supersedes that of either the intellect or the conscience of the simplest of its lay members.   They can assist those members in the search for truth, or comfort their over-worn and doubtful minds; they can even assure them that they are in the way of truth, or that pardon is within their reach: but they can neither manifest the truth, nor grant the pardon.   Truth is to be discovered, and Pardon to be won, for every man by himself.   This is evident from innumerable texts of Scripture, but chiefly from those which exhort every man to seek after Truth, and which connect knowing with doing.   We are to seek after knowledge as silver, and search for her as for hid treasures; therefore, from every man she must be naturally hid, and the discovery of her is to be the reward only of personal search.   The kingdom of God is as treasure hid in a field;[1] and of those who profess to help us to seek for it, we are not to put confidence in those who

---

[1] [Proverbs ii. 4 ; Matthew xiii. 44.]

say,—Here is the treasure, we have found it, and have it, and will give you some of it; but in those who say,—We think that is a good place to dig, and you will dig most easily in such and such a way.

20. Farther, it has been promised that if such earnest search be made, Truth shall be discovered: as much truth, that is, as is necessary for the person seeking. These, therefore, I hold, for two fundamental principles of religion, —that, without seeking, truth cannot be known at all; and that, by seeking, it may be discovered by the simplest. I say, without seeking it cannot be known at all. It can neither be declared from pulpits, nor set down in Articles, nor in anywise "prepared and sold" in packages, ready for use. Truth must be ground for every man by himself out of its husk, with such help as he can get, indeed, but not without stern labour of his own. In what science is knowledge to be had cheap? or truth to be told over a velvet cushion, in half-an-hour's talk every seventh day? Can you learn chemistry so?—zoology?—anatomy? and do you expect to penetrate the secret of all secrets, and to know that whose price is above rubies; and of which the depth saith,—It is not in me,[1]—in so easy fashion? There are doubts in this matter which evil spirits darken with their wings, and that is true of all such doubts which we were told long ago—they can "be ended by action alone."*

21. As surely as we live, this truth of truths can only so be discerned: to those who act on what they know,

---

* (Carlyle, *Past and Present,* chapter xi.) Can anything be more striking than the repeated warnings of St. Paul against strife of words; and his distinct setting forth of Action as the only true means of attaining knowledge of the truth, and the only sign of men's possessing the true faith? Compare 1 Timothy vi. 4, 20, (the latter verse especially, in connection with the previous three,) and 2 Timothy ii. 14, 19, 22, 23, tracing the connection here also; add Titus i. 10, 14, 16, noting "*in works* they deny him," and Titus iii. 8, 9, "affirm constantly that they be careful to maintain good works; but avoid foolish questions;" and finally, 1 Timothy i. 4–7: a passage which seems to have been especially written for these times.

---

[1] [Job xxviii. 14, 18.]

more shall be revealed; and thus, if any man will do His will, he shall know the doctrine whether it be of God.[1] Any man:—not the man who has most means of knowing, who has the subtlest brains, or sits under the most orthodox preacher, or has his library fullest of most orthodox books, —but the man who strives to know, who takes God at His word, and sets himself to dig up the heavenly mystery, roots and all, before sunset, and the night come, when no man can work.[2] Beside such a man, God stands in more and more visible presence as he toils, and teaches him that which no preacher can teach—no earthly authority gainsay. By such a man, the preacher must himself be judged.

22. Doubt you this? There is nothing more certain nor clear throughout the Bible: the Apostles themselves appeal constantly to their flocks, and actually *claim* judgment from them, as deserving it, and having a right to it, rather than discouraging it. But, first notice the way in which the discovery of truth is spoken of in the Old Testament: " Evil men understand not judgment; but they that seek the Lord understand all things," Proverbs xxviii. 5. God overthroweth, not merely the transgressor or the wicked, but even " the words of the transgressor," Proverbs xxii. 12, and " the counsel of the wicked," Job v. 13, xxi. 16; observe again, in Proverbs xxiv. 14, " My son, eat thou honey, because it is good—so shall the knowledge of wisdom be unto thy soul, when thou hast *found it*, there shall be a reward;" and again, " What man is he that feareth the Lord? him shall He teach in the way that He shall choose;" so Job xxxii. 8, and multitudes of places more; and then, with all these places, which express the definite and personal operation of the Spirit of God on every one of His people, compare the place in Isaiah, which speaks of the contrary of this human teaching: a passage which seems as if it had been written for this very day and hour. " Because their fear towards me is taught by the *precept of*

---

[1] [John vii. 17.]
[2] [John ix. 4. Compare *Sesame and Lilies*, Preface (1871), § 7.]

men; therefore, behold, the wisdom of their wise men shall perish, and the understanding of their prudent men shall be hid" (xxix. 13, 14). Then take the New Testament, and observe how St. Paul himself speaks of the Romans, even as hardly needing his epistle, but able to admonish one another: "*Nevertheless, brethren, I have written the more boldly unto you in some sort, as putting you in mind*" (xv. 15). Any one, we should have thought, might have done as much as this, and yet St. Paul increases the modesty of it as he goes on; for he claims the right of doing as much as this, only "because of the grace given to me of God, that I should be the minister of Jesus Christ to the Gentiles." Then compare 2 Cor. v. 11, where he appeals to the consciences of the people for the manifestation of his having done his duty; and observe in verse 21 of that, and 1 of the next chapter, the "pray" and "beseech," not "command"; and again in chapter vi. verse 4, "approving ourselves as the ministers of God." But the most remarkable passage of all is 2 Cor. iii. 1, whence it appears that the churches were actually in the habit of giving letters of recommendation to their ministers; and St. Paul dispenses with such letters, not by virtue of his Apostolic authority, but because the power of his preaching was enough manifested in the Corinthians themselves. And these passages are all the more forcible, because if in any of them St. Paul had claimed absolute authority over the Church as a teacher, it was no more than we should have expected him to claim, nor could his doing so have in anywise justified a successor in the same claim. But now that he has not claimed it,—who, following him, shall dare to claim it? And the consideration of the necessity of joining expressions of the most exemplary humility, which were to be the example of succeeding ministers, with such assertion of Divine authority as should secure acceptance for the epistle itself in the sacred canon, sufficiently accounts for the apparent inconsistencies which occur in 2 Thess. iii. 14, and other such texts.

23. So much, then, for the authority of the Clergy in matters of Doctrine. Next, what is their authority in matters of Discipline? It must evidently be very great, even if it were derived from the people alone, and merely vested in the clerical officers as the executors of their ecclesiastical judgments, and general overseers of all the Church. But granting, as we must presently, the minister to hold office directly from God, his authority of discipline becomes very great indeed; how great, it seems to me most difficult to determine, because I do not understand what St. Paul means by "delivering a man to Satan for the destruction of the flesh."[1] Leaving this question, however, as much too hard for casual examination, it seems indisputable that the authority of the Ministers or court of Ministers should extend to the pronouncing a man Excommunicate for certain crimes against the Church, as well as for all crimes punishable by ordinary law. There ought, I think, to be an ecclesiastical code of laws; and a man ought to have jury trial, according to this code, before an ecclesiastical judge; in which, if he were found guilty, as of lying, or dishonesty, or cruelty, much more of any actually committed violent crime, he should be pronounced Excommunicate; refused the Sacrament; and have his name written in some public place as an excommunicate person, until he had publicly confessed his sin and besought pardon of God for it. The jury should always be of the laity, and no penalty should be enforced in an ecclesiastical court except this of excommunication.

24. This proposal may seem strange to many persons; but assuredly this, if not much more than this, is commanded in Scripture, first in the (much-abused) text, "Tell it unto the Church;"[2] and most clearly in 1 Cor. v. 11–13; 2 Thess. iii. 6 and 14; 1 Tim. v. 8 and 20; and Titus iii. 10; from which passages we also know the two proper degrees of the penalty. For Christ says, Let him who

---

[1] [1 Corinthians v. 5.]
[2] [See above, § 4.]

refuses to hear the Church, "be unto thee as an heathen man and a publican."[1] But Christ ministered to the heathen, and sat at meat with the publican; only always with declared or implied expression of their inferiority; here, therefore, is one degree of excommunication for persons who "offend" their brethren, committing some minor fault against them; and who, having been pronounced in error by the body of the Church, refuse to confess their fault or repair it; who are then to be no longer considered members of the Church; and their recovery to the body of it is to be sought exactly as it would be in the case of an heathen. But covetous persons, railers, extortioners, idolaters, and those guilty of other gross crimes, are to be entirely cut off from the company of the believers; and we are not so much as to eat with them. This last penalty, however, would require to be strictly guarded, that it might not be abused in the infliction of it, as it has been by the Romanists. We are not, indeed, to eat with them, but we may exercise all Christian charity towards them, and give them to eat, if we see them in hunger, as we ought to all our enemies; only we are to consider them distinctly as our *enemies:* that is to say, enemies of our Master, Christ; and servants of Satan.

25. As for the rank or name of the officers in whom the authorities, either of teaching or discipline, are to be vested, they are left undetermined by Scripture. I have heard it said by men who know their Bible far better than I, that careful examination may detect evidence of the existence of three orders of Clergy in the Church. This may be; but one thing is very clear, without any laborious examination, that "bishop" and "elder" sometimes mean the same thing; as, indisputably, in Titus i. 5 and 7, and 1 Peter v. 1 and 2, and that the office of the bishop or overseer was one of considerably less importance than it is with us. This is palpably evident from 1 Timothy iii.,

---

[1] [Matthew xviii. 17. For a discussion of this text, see below, p. 564. Other Bible references in § 24 are 1 Corinthians viii. 13; and v. 11.]

for what divine among us, writing of episcopal proprieties, would think of saying that bishops "must not be given to wine," must be "no strikers," and must not be "novices"? We are not in the habit of making bishops of novices in these days; and it would be much better that, like the early Church, we sometimes ran the risk of doing so; for the fact is we have not bishops enough—by some hundreds. The idea of overseership has been practically lost sight of, its fulfilment having gradually become physically impossible, for want of more bishops. The duty of a bishop is, without doubt, to be accessible to the humblest clergymen of his diocese, and to desire very earnestly that all of them should be in the habit of referring to him in all cases of difficulty; if they do not do this of their own accord, it is evidently his duty to visit them, live with them sometimes, and join in their ministrations to their flocks, so as to know exactly the capacities and habits of life of each; and if any of them complained of this or that difficulty with their congregations, the bishop should be ready to go down to help them, preach for them, write general epistles to their people, and so on: besides this, he should of course be watchful of their errors—ready to hear complaints from their congregations of inefficiency or aught else; besides having general superintendence of all the charitable institutions and schools in his diocese, and good knowledge of whatever was going on in theological matters, both all over the kingdom and on the Continent. This is the work of a right overseer;[1] and I leave the reader to calculate how many additional bishops—and those hard-working men, too —we should need to have it done, even decently. Then our present bishops might all become archbishops with advantage, and have general authority over the rest.*

* I leave, in the main text, the abstract question of the fitness of Episcopacy unapproached, not feeling any call to speak of it at length at present; all that I feel necessary to be said is, that bishops being granted,

[1] [On Bishops as overseers, see *Stones of Venice*, vol. ii. (Vol. X. p. 25); *Sesame and Lilies*, § 22; *Time and Tide*, § 72; and *Fors Clavigera*, Letter 62.]

26. As to the mode in which the officers of the Church should be elected or appointed, I do not feel it my business to say anything at present, nor much respecting the extent of their authority, either over each other or over the congregation, this being a most difficult question, the right solution of which evidently lies between two most dangerous extremes—insubordination and radicalism on one hand, and ecclesiastical tyranny and heresy on the other: of the two, insubordination is far the least to be dreaded—for this reason, that nearly all real Christians are more on the watch against their pride than their indolence, and would sooner obey their clergyman, if possible, than contend with him; while the very pride they suppose conquered often returns masked, and causes them to make a merit of their humility and their abstract obedience, however unreasonable: but they cannot so easily persuade themselves there is a merit in abstract *dis*obedience.

27. Ecclesiastical tyranny has, for the most part, founded itself on the idea of Vicarianism, one of the most pestilent of the Romanist theories, and most plainly denounced in Scripture. Of this I have a word or two to say to the modern " Vicarian." All powers that be are unquestionably ordained of God; so that they that resist the Power, resist the ordinance of God. Therefore, say some in these offices, We, being ordained of God, and having our credentials, and being in the English Bible called ambassadors for God,[1] do, in a sort, represent God.   We are Vicars of

it is clear that we have too few to do their work.   But the argument from the practice of the Primitive Church appears to me to be of enormous weight,—nor have I ever heard any rational plea alleged against Episcopacy, except that, like other things, it is capable of abuse, and has sometimes been abused; and as, altogether clearly and indisputably, there is described in the Bible an episcopal office, distinct from the merely ministerial one; and, apparently, also an episcopal officer attached to each church, and distinguished in the Revelation as an Angel, I hold the resistance of the Scotch Presbyterian Church to Episcopacy to be unscriptural, futile, and schismatic.

[1] [2 Corinthians v. 20: "Now then we are ambassadors for Christ." The preceding Bible reference is Romans xiii. 1, 2.]

Christ, and stand on earth in place of Christ.   I have heard this said by Protestant clergymen.

28. Now the word ambassador has a peculiar ambiguity about it, owing to its use in modern political affairs; and these clergymen assume that the word, as used by St. Paul, means an Ambassador Plenipotentiary; representative of his King, and capable of acting for his King.   What right have they to assume that St. Paul meant this? St. Paul never uses the word ambassador at all.   He says, simply, " We are in embassage from Christ; and Christ beseeches you through us."   Most true.   And let it further be granted, that every word that the clergyman speaks is literally dictated to him by Christ; that he can make no mistake in delivering his message; and that, therefore, it is indeed Christ Himself who speaks to us the word of life through the messenger's lips.   Does, therefore, the messenger represent Christ?   Does the channel which conveys the waters of the Fountain represent the Fountain itself?   Suppose, when we went to draw water at a cistern, that all at once the Leaden Spout should become animated, and open its mouth and say to us, See, I am Vicarious for the Fountain.   Whatever respect you show to the Fountain, show some part of it to me.   Should we not answer the Spout, and say, Spout, you were set there for our service, and may be taken away and thrown aside * if anything goes wrong with you?   But the Fountain will flow for ever.

29. Observe, I do not deny a most solemn authority vested in every Christian messenger from God to men.   I am prepared to grant this to the uttermost; and all that George Herbert says, in the end of " The Church-porch,"[1]

---

* " By just judgment be deposed," Art. 26.

[1] [Stanzas lxviii.–lxxiv., where Herbert says of the preacher—
"God sent him, whatsoe'er he be; O, tarry,
   And love him for his Master; his condition,
   Though it be ill, makes him no ill physician."
Compare a passage in *Letters to a College Friend,* Vol. I. p. 489.]

I would enforce, at another time than this, to the utter-most. But the Authority is simply that of a King's *Messenger*; not of a King's *Representative*. There is a wide difference; all the difference between humble service and blasphemous usurpation.

Well, the congregation might ask, grant him a King's messenger in cases of doctrine,—in cases of discipline, an officer bearing the King's Commission. How far are we to obey him? How far is it lawful to dispute his commands?

For, in granting, above, that the Messenger always gave his message faithfully, I granted too much to my adversaries, in order that their argument might have all the weight it possibly could. The Messengers rarely deliver their message faithfully; and sometimes have declared, as from the King, messages of their own invention. How far are we, knowing them for King's messengers, to believe or obey them?

30. Suppose for instance, in our English army, on the eve of some great battle, one of the colonels were to give this order to his regiment: " My men, tie your belts over your eyes, throw down your muskets, and follow me as steadily as you can, through this marsh, into the middle of the enemy's line," (this being precisely the order issued by our Puseyite Church officers). It might be questioned, in the real battle, whether it would be better that a regiment should show an example of insubordination, or be cut to pieces. But happily in the Church there is no such difficulty; for the King is always with His army: not only with His army, but at the right hand of every soldier of it. Therefore, if any of their colonels give them a strange command, all they have to do is to ask the King; and never yet any Christian asked guidance of his King, in any difficulty whatsoever, without mental reservation or secret resolution, but he had it forthwith. We conclude then, finally, that the authority of the Clergy is, in matters of discipline, large (being executive, first, of the written laws of God, and secondly, of those determined and agreed upon by the body of the Church), in matters of doctrine,

dependent on their recommending themselves to every man's conscience, both as messengers of God, and as themselves men of God, perfect, and instructed to good works.*

31. (6) The last subject which we had to investigate was, it will be remembered, what is usually called the connection of "Church and State." But, by our definition of the term Church, throughout the whole of Christendom, the Church (or society of professing Christians) *is* the State, and our subject is therefore, properly speaking, the connection of lay and clerical officers of the Church; that is to say, the degrees in which the civil and ecclesiastical governments ought to interfere with or influence each other.

It would of course be vain to attempt a formal inquiry into this intricate subject;—I have only a few detached points to notice respecting it.

32. There are three degrees or kinds of civil government. The first and lowest, executive merely; the government in this sense being simply the National Hand, and composed of individuals who administer the laws of the nation, and execute its established purposes.

The second kind of government is deliberative; but in its deliberation, representative only of the thoughts and will of the people or nation, and liable to be deposed the instant it ceases to express those thoughts and that will. This, whatever its form, whether centred in a king or in any number of men, is properly to be called Democratic. The third and highest kind of government is deliberative, not as representative of the people, but as chosen to take separate counsel for them, and having power committed to it, to enforce upon them whatever resolution it may adopt,

* The difference between the authority of doctrine and discipline is beautifully marked in 2 Timothy ii. 25, and Titus ii. 12–15. In the first passage, the servant of God, teaching divine doctrine, must not strive, but must "in *meekness* instruct those that oppose themselves;" in the second passage, teaching us "that denying ungodliness and worldly lusts he is *to live soberly, righteously, and godly* in this *present world*," the minister is to speak, exhort, and rebuke with ALL AUTHORITY—both functions being expressed as united in 2 Timothy iv. 3.

whether consistent with their will or not.   This government is properly to be called Monarchical, whatever its form.

33. I see that politicians and writers of history continually run into hopeless error, because they confuse the Form of a Government with its Nature. A Government may be nominally vested in an individual; and yet if that individual be in such fear of those beneath him, that he does nothing but what he supposes will be agreeable to them, the Government is Democratic; on the other hand, the Government may be vested in a deliberative assembly of a thousand men, all having equal authority, and all chosen from the lowest ranks of the people; and yet if that assembly act independently of the will of the people, and have no fear of them, and enforce its determinations upon them, the Government is Monarchical; that is to say, the Assembly, acting as One, has power over the Many, while in the case of the weak king, the Many have power over the One.

A Monarchical Government, acting for its own interest, instead of the people's, is a tyranny.   I said the Executive Government was the hand of the nation:—the Republican Government is in like manner its tongue.   The Monarchical Government is its head.

All true and right government is Monarchical, and of the head.   What is its best form, is a totally different question; but unless it act *for* the people, and not as representative of the people, it is no government at all; and one of the grossest blockheadisms of the English in the present day, is their idea of sending men to Parliament to "represent *their* opinions."   Whereas their only true business is to find out the wisest men among them, and send them to Parliament to represent their *own* opinions, and act upon them.   Of all puppet-shows in the Satanic Carnival of the earth, the most contemptible puppet-show is a Parliament with a mob pulling the strings.[1]

---

[1] [In connexion with what Ruskin says of Carlyle constantly colouring his thoughts (*Modern Painters,* vol. iii. App. iii.), it may here be recalled that *Latter-Day Pamphlets* (ch. vi., " Parliaments ") had appeared in 1850.]

34. Now, of these three states of Government, it is clear that the merely executive can have no proper influence over ecclesiastical affairs. But of the other two, the first, being the voice of the people, or voice of the Church, must have such influence over the Clergy as is properly vested in the body of the Church. The second, which stands in the same relation to the people as a father does to his family, will have such farther influence over ecclesiastical matters, as a father has over the consciences of his adult children. No absolute authority, therefore, to enforce their attendance at any particular place of worship, or subscription to any particular Creed. But indisputable authority to procure for them such religious instruction as he deems fittest,* and to recommend it to them by every

---

* Observe, this and the following conclusions depend entirely on the supposition that the Government is part of the Body of the Church, and that some pains have been taken to compose it of religious and wise men. If we choose, knowingly and deliberately, to compose our Parliament, in great part, of infidels and Papists, gamblers and debtors, we may well regret its power over the Clerical officer; but that we should, at any time, so compose our Parliament, is a sign that the Clergy themselves have failed in their duty, and the Church in its watchfulness;—thus the evil accumulates in reaction. Whatever I say of the responsibility or authority of Government, is therefore to be understood only as sequent on what I have said previously of the necessity of closely circumscribing the Church, and then composing the Civil Government out of the circumscribed Body. Thus, all Papists would at once be rendered incapable of share in it, being subjected to the second or most severe degree of excommunication [1]—first, as idolaters, by 1 Cor. v. 10; then as covetous and extortioners (selling absolution,) by the same text; and, finally, as heretics and maintainers of falsehoods, by Titus iii. 10, and 1 Tim. iv. 1.

I do not write this hastily, nor without earnest consideration both of the difficulty and the consequences of such Church Discipline. But either the Bible is a superannuated book, and is only to be read as a record of past days; or these things follow from it, clearly and inevitably. That we live in days when the Bible has become impracticable, is (if it be so) the very thing I desire to be considered. I am not setting down these plans or schemes as at present possible. I do not know how far they are possible; but it seems to me that God has plainly commanded them, and that, therefore, their impracticability is a thing to be meditated on.

---

[1] [For Ruskin's views at this time on the admission of Roman Catholics to Parliament, see Vol. VIII. pp. 267–269, Vol. IX. p. 423.]

means in his power; he not only has authority, but is under obligation to do this, as well as to establish such disciplines and forms of worship in his house as he deems most convenient for his family: with which they are indeed at liberty to refuse compliance, if such disciplines appear to them clearly opposed to the law of God; but not without most solemn conviction of their being so, nor without deep sorrow to be compelled to such a course.

35. But it may be said, the Government of a people never does stand to them in the relation of a father to his family. If it do not, it is no Government. However grossly it may fail in its duty, and however little it may be fitted for its place, if it be a Government at all, it has paternal office and relation to the people. I find it written on the one hand,—"Honour thy Father;" on the other, —"Honour the King:" on the one hand,—"Whoso smiteth his Father, shall be put to death;"* on the other,—"They that resist shall receive to themselves damnation."[1] Well, but, it may be farther argued, the Clergy are in a still more solemn sense the Fathers of the People, and the People are their beloved Sons; why should not, therefore, the Clergy have the power to govern the civil officers?

36. For two very clear reasons.

In all human institutions certain evils are granted, as of necessity; and, in organizing such institutions, we must allow for the consequences of such evils, and make arrangements such as may best keep them in check. Now, in both the civil and ecclesiastical governments there will of necessity be a certain number of bad men. The wicked civilian has comparatively little interest in overthrowing ecclesiastical authority; it is often a useful help to him, and presents in itself little which seems covetable. But the wicked ecclesiastical officer has much interest in overthrowing the civilian, and getting the political power into

---

* Exod. xxi. 15.

[1] [The other Bible references are Exodus xxi. 2; 1 Peter ii. 17; Romans xiii. 2.]

his own hands. As far as wicked men are concerned, therefore, it is better that the State should have power over the Clergy, than the Clergy over the State.

Secondly, supposing both the Civil and Ecclesiastical officers to be Christians; there is no fear that the civil officer should underrate the dignity or shorten the serviceableness of the minister; but there is considerable danger that the religious enthusiasm of the minister might diminish the serviceableness of the civilian. (The History of Religious Enthusiasm[1] should be written by some one who had a life to give to its investigation; it is one of the most melancholy pages in human records, and one the most necessary to be studied.) Therefore, as far as good men are concerned, it is better the State should have power over the Clergy than the Clergy over the State.

37. This we might, it seems to me, conclude by unassisted reason. But surely the whole question is, without any need of human reason, decided by the history of Israel. If ever a body of Clergy should have received independent authority, the Levitical Priesthood should; for they were indeed a Priesthood, and more holy than the rest of the nation. But Aaron is always subject to Moses. All solemn revelation is made to Moses, the civil magistrate, and he actually commands Aaron as to the fulfilment of his priestly office, and that in a necessity of life and death: " Go, and make an atonement for the people."[2] Nor is anything more remarkable throughout the whole of the Jewish history than the perfect subjection of the Priestly to the Kingly Authority. Thus Solomon thrusts out Abiathar from being priest, 1 Kings ii. 27; and Jehoahaz administers the funds of the Lord's House, 2 Kings xii. 4, though that money was actually the Atonement Money, the Ransom for Souls (Exod. xxx. 12).

38. We have, however, also the beautiful instance of Samuel uniting in himself the offices of Priest, Prophet, and

---

[1] [For an actual work on this subject, see Vol. X. p. 452.]
[2] [Leviticus ix. 7.]

Judge; nor do I insist on any special manner of subjection of Clergy to civil officers, or *vice versâ;* but only on the necessity of their perfect unity and influence upon each other in every Christian kingdom. Those who endeavour to effect the utter separation of ecclesiastical and civil officers, are striving, on the one hand, to expose the Clergy to the most grievous and most subtle of temptations from their own spiritual enthusiasm and spiritual pride; on the other, to deprive the civil officer of all sense of religious responsibility, and to introduce the fearful, godless, conscienceless, and soulless policy of the Radical and the (so-called) Socialist. Whereas, the ideal of all government is the perfect unity of the two bodies of officers, each supporting and correcting the other; the Clergy having due weight in all the national councils; the civil officers having a solemn reverence for God in all their acts; the Clergy hallowing all worldly policy by their influence; and the magistracy repressing all religious enthusiasm by their practical wisdom. To separate the two is to endeavour to separate the daily life of the nation from God, and to map out the dominion of the soul into two provinces—one of Atheism, the other of Enthusiasm. These, then, were the reasons which caused me to speak[1] of the idea of separation of Church and State as Fatuity; for what Fatuity can be so great as the not having God in our thoughts; and, in any act or office of life, saying in our hearts, "There is no God"?[2]

39. Much more I would fain say of these things, but not now: this only I must emphatically assert, in conclusion:—That the schism between the so-called Evangelical and High Church Parties in Britain, is enough to shake many men's faith in the truth or existence of Religion at all. It seems to me one of the most disgraceful scenes in Ecclesiastical history, that Protestantism should be paralyzed at its very heart by jealousies, based on little else than

[1] [See *Stones of Venice,* vol. i. App. 12 (Vol. IX. p. 437).]
[2] [Psalms xiv. 1, liii. 1.]

mere difference between high and low breeding. For the essential differences in the religious opinions of the two parties are sufficiently marked in two men whom we may take as the highest representatives of each—George Herbert and John Milton; and I do not think there would have been much difficulty in atoning those two, if one could have got them together. But the real difficulty, nowadays, lies in the sin and folly of both parties; in the superciliousness of the one, and the rudeness of the other. Evidently, however, the sin lies most at the High Church door, for the Evangelicals are much more ready to act with Churchmen than they with the Evangelicals; and I believe that this state of things cannot continue much longer; and that if the Church of England does not forthwith unite with herself the entire Evangelical body, both of England and Scotland, and take her stand with them against the Papacy, her hour has struck. She cannot any longer serve two masters;[1] nor make courtesies alternately to Christ and Antichrist. That she *has* done this is visible enough by the state of Europe at this instant. Three centuries since Luther—three hundred years of Protestant knowledge—and the Papacy not yet overthrown! Christ's truth still restrained, in narrow dawn, to the white cliffs of England and white crests of the Alps;—the morning star paused in its course in heaven;—the sun and moon stayed, with Satan for their Joshua.[2]

40. But how to unite the two great sects of paralyzed Protestants? By keeping simply to Scripture. The members of the Scottish Church have not a shadow of excuse for refusing Episcopacy; it has indeed been abused among them, grievously abused; but it is in the Bible; and that is all they have a right to ask.

They have also no shadow of excuse for refusing to employ a written form of prayer. It may not be to their taste—it may not be the way in which they like to pray;

---

[1] [Matthew vi. 24; Luke xvi. 13.]
[2] [Joshua x. 13.]

but it is no question, at present, of likes or dislikes, but of duties; and the acceptance of such a form on their part would go half-way to reconcile them with their brethren. Let them allege such objections as they can reasonably advance against the English form, and let these be carefully and humbly weighed by the pastors of both churches: some of them ought to be at once forestalled. For the English Church, on the other hand, *must* cut the term Priest entirely out of her Prayer-book, and substitute for it that of Minister or Elder; the passages respecting Absolution must be thrown out also, except the doubtful one in the Morning Service, in which there is no harm; and then there would be only the Baptismal question left, which is one of words rather than of things, and might easily be settled in Synod, turning the refractory Clergy out of their offices, to go to Rome if they chose. Then, when the Articles of Faith and form of worship had been agreed upon between the English and Scottish Churches, the written forms and articles should be carefully translated into the European languages, and offered to the acceptance of the Protestant churches on the Continent, with earnest entreaty that they would receive them, and due entertainment of all such objections as they could reasonably allege; and thus the whole body of Protestants, united in one great Fold,[1] would indeed go in and out, and find pasture; and the work appointed for them would be done quickly, and Antichrist overthrown.

41. Impossible: a thousand times impossible!—I hear it exclaimed against me. No — not impossible. Christ does not order impossibilities, and He *has* ordered us to be at peace one with another. Nay, it is answered—He came not to send peace, but a sword. Yes, verily: to send a sword upon earth, but not within His Church; for to His Church He said, " My peace I leave with you."

---

[1] [John x. 9; in § 41 the Bible references are Matthew x. 34; John xiv. 27.]

APPENDIX TO PART III

I

LETTERS ON "THE CONSTRUCTION OF SHEEPFOLDS"

1. LETTERS TO F. D. MAURICE

[WHEN this pamphlet appeared, a copy of it was sent by Dr. F. J. Furnivall to the Rev. F. D. Maurice. Maurice at that time knew Ruskin only by his books. He wrote to Dr. Furnivall (March 25, 1851) saying that he found himself in agreement with Ruskin on some points, but in sharp disagreement on others. Dividing his criticism of the pamphlet under heads, he *agreed* with Ruskin (1) that the sense of the word Church is to be obtained from the Bible, and that its use there is uniform; (2) that the clergy are not separate from the laity as "the Church"; (3) that the Church and State are united, and that civil governors have dominion over the clergy. But he *disagreed* on the following points: (1) alleging that Ruskin had missed the Scriptural Sense of "Church" (*ecclesia*) as "a body called out"; (2) had not perceived what this calling out means. (3) In a third clause, Maurice noted the successive "calls" from Abraham to Christ; (4) "that of this method Mr. Ruskin, professing to follow Scripture exactly, has taken no notice, but has tried to deduce a meaning from isolated texts, so sanctioning a vulgar practice"; (5) that Ruskin's nomenclature (Visible and Invisible Church) was unscriptural. Maurice protested that we were wilfully and shamefully perverting God's purpose "when we speak of an invisible Church, meaning a set of men taken out of the condition of law and humanity, and made possessors of a peculiar privilege appertaining to themselves! Against this accursed doctrine—which I believe is undermining all faith, holiness, love, among us, and is making us all in our different sections and departments a set of exclusive contemptuous Pharisees —may God give me grace to bear witness in life and in death! I am sure the Bible is refuting it in every line. I am sure that it is teaching us that men are brought out of narrowness, selfishness, into that which is free, large, universal. I am sure it is saying that those who yield to God's Spirit, and believe in Him, only come to believe that which is as true of every publican and harlot as it is of themselves." (6) Maurice next, referring to § 24 of the pamphlet, called Ruskin's account of Christ's dealing with publicans and sinners "most frightful and detestable misrepresentation. . . . I say he ought to sit in sackcloth and ashes for uttering such a sentence." (7) He complains that Ruskin makes havoc of the Epistles, "decreeing that St. Paul shall mean only true believers, though he speaks in those very Epistles of fornicators," etc. (8) He objected to Ruskin making "so entirely light of Baptism," which to Maurice "is a witness for the universality of God's goodwill." (9) Next, on Ruskin's scheme of excommunication (§ 23), Maurice was severe: "I never read any scheme better contrived for enthroning, if not canonizing, respectability and decency; and any scheme which *less* levels the hills and exalts the valleys, which less affronts Scribes and Pharisees with the rude and terrible sentence, 'Oh generation of vipers! who hath bidden you to flee from the wrath to come?'" With Maurice's other points we are not concerned, as they do not arise in the subsequent correspondence. Maurice's letter to Furnivall of March 25 was sent on to Ruskin, who replied as follows:—]

I

Sunday evening, 30th March [1851].

MY DEAR MR. MAURICE,—I have been reading with much respect and interest your letter to Furnivall, and comparing it with some of your published writings:—I am much grieved, on one side, that what I have written should so far offend you; and happy that it should, on the other, for I should be most thankful to be proved wrong in much of what I believe:— My faith is a dark one; yours, so far as I can understand it, a glorious and happy one. I said, in the beginning of what I wrote, that I should not allow myself to be drawn into controversy: nor should I, unless in the *hope* of being convinced of error. If I thought your opposition to me futile, or if I did not wish to think with you, I should not have made any comment on your letter. But I covet that wide-world spirit of yours; and if you do not think you have spent too much time on me already, I would fain ask you to devote still an hour or two. For in your present letter you have been too indignant to reason. I like your indignation; but I must have something more out of you than indignation before I can come to be of your mind.

1. You find fault with me for not enough considering the etymological force of ἐκκλησία—truly I did not, nor have I ever done so enough: I have always thought the word was simply used as we should use the word "assembly," and that when the idea of calling was to be implied, it was separately expressed as in 1 Cor. i. 2; and I so far think so still; that is, I believe the word in St. Paul's time to have been one of such common use that it would never have expressed, *per se*, any idea of calling by God: nor do I think it was ever intended to do so. I may be very wrong in this, and will consider of it.

2. But while I do not enough attach the idea of "calling" to this word, do not think I ever lost sight of the calling itself. All that you say in your 3rd Clause, I hold to the full: but it did not appear to me to bear in the least on the matter in question. I do not—throughout the Pamphlet —speak of the methods of Conversion: I had nothing to do with them. All I had to examine was the practical method of associating and governing men pretending to be converted.

3. Answer to your 4th Clause.

This exclamation against "Isolated Texts" I always look upon with suspicion. For I believe the Bible to have been written for simple people, and that simple people *can* only look at isolated texts. I think that every necessary doctrine is to be proved by positive texts, and not by subtle reasonings, of which most poor Christians are quite incapable.

This *vulgar* practice I think, therefore, the right one, just because it *is* vulgar. And I have always found the Tractarians shrink in horror from these same "Isolated Texts."

4. Answer to your 5th Clause.

I give up my nomenclature at once, if it displeases you. I used Visible and Invisible[1] merely as convenient and generally recognised expressions for the Church in heaven and on earth—or rather for my first and second senses of the word. Had I not done so, I should have been obliged to write "Church in the first sense," "Church in the second sense," all through, which would have been inconvenient; but make this substitution, if you like it.

5. What follows, I do not in the least understand. I certainly never deduced invisibility from visibility. I mean, very simply, that I see a man behave decently and hear him talk like a Christian. He is to me visible and hearable an ascertainable creature — so far. His membership with Christ I cannot see: I call it therefore invisible. I never spoke of "men taken out of the condition of humanity." I said that I could not see their hearts, and that the Lord looketh upon the heart: I meant that the Lord knoweth them that are His[2]—and that we don't. What is there "accursed" in this doctrine; or what is the doctrine which you suppose me to have meant, and which you call "accursed"? I have read this indignant passage three times over, and I do not in the smallest degree understand what you are attacking. You say "you are sure that those who yield to God's spirit only come to believe *that* which is *as true of every publican and harlot as it is of themselves.*"

That . . . What?

6. Answer to your sixth Clause.

Let me restate somewhat more clearly what I said, or meant to say, of Christ's Excommunication—and have patience with me.

I said that Christ always implied the inferiority of such; and I meant to say that He proved His infinite Mercy and the all-atoning power of His Death in the very fact of His being willing to associate with—ready to hear, and able to save—the most degraded of mankind. The whole power and beauty of His ministry depends upon the first admission, that those whom He came to save were indeed chief of sinners. I now repeat that Christ invariably implies this inferiority—

"What do ye more than others? Do not *even* the Publicans, whom you think such dreadful sinners, so?"[3] "The publicans and harlots—believed on Him." "Go into the Kingdom before *you*"—in which passages the whole force depends upon their being considered as inferior. These—Christ says—lost and sinful though they were—yet believed. Again of the Heathen, "It is not meet to take the children's bread," etc.[4]

---

[1] [See above, §§ 6, 7.]
[2] [1 Samuel xvi. 7; 2 Timothy ii. 19.]
[3] [Matthew v. 47.]
[4] [Matthew xxi. 31, 32, xv. 26.]

And finally and chiefly, the main text: "Let him be unto thee as an heathen man," etc.

Now, my dear Sir, you have called my representation of this text[1] frightful and detestable: What is yours? It *has* a meaning, I suppose—isolated though it be:—and to give it a plain and practicable meaning is all I ask of you; and that you must do, before you have any right to be indignant with me.

But permit me once more to put my interpretation of it into clear form. I find Christ associate constantly in one breath—the heathen, publican, and harlot. Now, there is a harlot's house within six doors of me. There was a ball there—four nights ago; and many other harlots met there on the occasion. I did not go myself; I would not have allowed my wife to go, if she had asked leave. I call that excommunication; and I prevailed upon a young man of my acquaintance, who had intended to go to the meeting, to join in my excommunication—and stay away also. Was there anything wrong in this?

But further: if I had my way, this person's name should be written up as excommunicate at the church door up the street. Would this be very dreadful?

If, however, this same person were sick, or in sorrow, and happened to hear of me as able to assist her, and asked me to come and talk to her, I should go instantly—and eat with her—or do anything that I could for her, without the least fear of, or care for, compromising my own character, and I would make my wife do the same.

In the same manner I would not ask a pickpocket to dine with me, unless for some special purpose—but if the pickpocket were suffering or repentant, I would associate with him to any extent.

Is there anything detestable in all this?

Again—Lady —— ran away from her husband last year; she is received into all the best English society of Italy together with her paramour. I don't think she is received as a Magdalene, but as an agreeable person. I think this is wrong: and would not receive her, until she parted from her paramour, and declared herself penitent. I don't think this unmerciful or horrible. I do but desire that some sense of the awfulness of presumptuous sin should be manifested by the Church; and behold, you fly in my face like a wild creature, and upset a whole scuttleful of ashes on my head— as if I had said that sinners were of different flesh and blood from the apparently righteous. I do not mean the separation to be expressed as a "stand aside—for I am holier," but as "I serve God—you do not. Do not therefore wear my livery."

7. Answer to your 7th Clause.

I have nothing to do with the contents of the Epistles, except as they bear on the question in hand:—and as to the character of those to whom they were written, I suppose the directions to be warrant for it: and that the writers knew whom they intended to address.

I could give you a longer answer, but have not time.

8. Answer to your 8th Clause.

Precisely because I believe conversion to *be* an act of God, and not of our own, I make light of Baptism. For Baptism I consider an act of man.

---

[1] [See above, § 24.]

But this following page is the one which induced me to answer your letter at all—you speak of the redemption "not of us but of the whole world" in Christ. What *do* you—what *can* you—mean by this? It would be, I do not say the happiest day of my life, but the beginning of another life to me, if you could justify those words. I will not go further—the rest of your letter touches on minor points; but pray answer me this—or if you like better to write to Furnivall—and call me hard names to your better content when not addressing me directly—do so, though I should not think it rude if you called me them to my face, any more than I think an Alpine stream rude when I throw a stone into it, and it splashes me. Only do not speak so as to make Furnivall excommunicate *me*. This "being defamed, we entreat." [1]

Ever respectfully and faithfully yours,

J. RUSKIN.

[Maurice rejoined in a second letter (April 4, 1851) from which the following passage is an extract: "You will see, I think, why I can most heartily sympathise with all your rules of conduct about your neighbours and Lady ——, admiring especially your distinctions respecting sickness and suffering, and yet dissent altogether from your apparent interpretation of our Lord's acts, and from the doctrine of excommunication which you attempted in your pamphlet to deduce from them. I suspected that there *was* this essential hearty humanity lurking under your exclusiveness, and that made me stamp and swear the more fiercely at the wolf's clothing in which you had thought fit to hide the true fleece. I never said, or dreamed, that our Lord loved publicans *qua* extortioners, or harlots *qua* unchaste women; I should have thought that blasphemy. But I said He loved publicans *qua* men, and harlots *qua* women; and that, instead of excommunicating them, He went straight to them, ate and drank with them, claimed them as men and women. I cannot use your language exactly, and say that He waited till they were penitents. He says the contrary Himself: 'I am not come to *call* the righteous, but sinners, to repentance'—the repentance was not necessarily there, nor was it the ground of His sympathy. He owned them as having the nature He took, as being His brothers and sisters; and on that ground, and in that way, He awakened their repentance. They *did* repent when they acknowledged Him as their Lord and Brother. But when the maxim and practice of the Pharisees and respectable Jews generally went to the direct excommunication of them as excluded from God's covenant and mercy, is it not a strange turning of things upside down to call those parts of our Lord's conduct which most offended them (the Pharisees) and outraged all their prejudices, an excommunication? And if I am taught by the Gospels to consider these acts as a direct assertion of communion with men as men, and so, as an exhibition of Himself in His character of the Son of Man and of the Son of God also revealing the mind of His Father, may I not storm a little when you seem to me wholly to pervert and reverse the nature and object of them?" On the text of which Ruskin had made so much (see above, p. 564), Maurice thus replied: "But the great stumbling-block is 'Let him be unto thee as an heathen man and a publican.' And this occurs in the Gospel of Matthew

<hr>

[1] [1 Corinthians iv. 13.]

the publican! Suppose he had taken our Lord to say, 'Deal with the sinful brother as I deal with the class of publicans'—what must he have thought? 'Why, there can be no excommunication at all! For He has called me, a publican, to the highest office in His Kingdom.' Of course he took Him to mean, 'Exclude the guilty brother from your society, as the well-behaved Jews, who are constantly denouncing me for keeping company with publicans, exclude them.'"

Maurice then passed on to "state his faith—his gospel of "Inclusiveness," as Ruskin called it. The essence of Conversion, he says, is "God revealing or unveiling His Son IN him;" and he continues: "The revelation or unveiling of Christ as the real ground of Humanity, as the Son of Man and the Son of God, in whom and for whom all things were created, whether things in Heaven or things on earth, in whom all things consist, and in whom all things are to be gathered up, who is the first-born of every creature, the first-begotten from the dead, the Prince of all the Kings of the earth—this I hold to be the subject of Scripture; this is what I see evolving itself from the first book of it to the last. The Gospel, as I understand it, is the good news to man of this Revelation. . . . It declares that the Spirit of the Father and the Son, the Spirit in whom they are and have ever been one, is given to men that they may be one, that they may be a Society of redeemed creatures, sacrificed, consecrated to God, that Baptism into the name of the Father, the Son, and the Holy Ghost is the divine witness and assurance that this is the true condition and order of the Universe."

To this letter Ruskin replied as follows:—]

II

MATLOCK,
Easter Sunday [1851].

MY DEAR MR. MAURICE,—I cannot enough thank you for your kind letter. I have not answered it hitherto, having been in a stranger's house [1]—my mind much taken up with other matters. I wished to think over your letter carefully, that I might, if possible, save you further labour in answering or refuting me. But, interesting as your reply is, it is not a solution of the question which troubles me: there is much in it which I hope to talk over with you some day, having no time to write about it. The main points in which as an answer to my askings, it seems insufficient to me, I can state quickly. I asked for a practical explanation of Christ's meaning in the "Let him be unto thee," etc. It appears to be connected with the Sermon on the Mount—it seems to me as much a practical and simple order as any therein. I ask you merely how I am to put it into practice.

You evade the question: you say, What must Matthew the Publican have thought, who had been called to one of the highest offices of the Church?

What Matthew's thoughts were is by no means to the point. I want our Lord's *meaning*. Are you prepared to substitute this, which you say Matthew

---

[1] [At Farnley Hall: see above, Introduction, p. liv.]

must have supposed to have been his meaning in the text itself—and read it thus ?

"If thy brother—&c.—go and tell him his fault, &c. If he will not hear thee,—&c.—(take two or three others). And if he will not hear them, tell it unto the Church. But if he will not hear the Church—*call him to one of the highest offices of the Church.*"

If you are not prepared to read the text thus, Matthew's thoughts are not to the purpose; and you have given no interpretation to the text.

Now, that text should *have* an interpretation. At present it lies dormant in the Bible—not a soul quotes it—thinks of it—far less acts upon it. Everybody quotes "Judge not that ye be not judged."[1] It is a pleasant text that for most people, being a pious expression for—"Let *me* alone, and I'll let *you*." But the counter-text might as well not have been written for any use we make of it.

But the main point I would press upon you is, your inclusiveness. You ask me what I make of those texts, "Gave himself a ransom for *all*," etc.

Those texts are, it seems to me, as simple as they are necessary.

If you had bought a shipload of slaves, and offered them their freedom, I suppose you would do it in these terms—"I have paid for you *all;* you are all free to come with me or stay where you are, as you choose."

How Christ could otherwise express Himself than thus, I see not. He has purchased us *all*. But why, for this reason, you should put in the same category those who accept His offer—who hold out their arms to Him to have their fetters struck off, and then wash His feet with tears—and those who shrink out of His way into the hold of the ship, and with blasphemies and defiances declare they will stay by their old owner—I see not either.

DENMARK HILL,
25th April [1851].

I KEPT the letter by me for some days more—hoping to be able to follow out your argument more closely. But it now seems to me useless; for you miss the plain, simple, and straightforward statements of Scripture to reason abstractedly into far distance from such obscure ones as the "to Reveal His Son in me."

You, as a minister, are called upon to read some portions of the Psalms every Sunday, and to wait for the congregation's taking up every alternate verse. I always supposed that the language of the Psalms was therefore intended to be personally adopted by both minister and people;— but you cannot adopt five verses together, I suppose, from one end of the book to the other, without calling yourself a separate person in some way or other, and declaring, if not invoking, God's wrath against persons not in such separate state. The distinction between the righteous and wicked is the end, in express words, of both the Old and New Testaments— it echoes in terrific decision and inevitable plainness through every verse of them both: as plainly as the voice of mercy which calls to the one class

---

[1] [Matthew vii. 1. Following Bible references are—1 Timothy ii. 6; Luke vii. 38. With what Ruskin here says about picking and choosing texts, compare *Ethics of the Dust*, § 59.]

to become as the other—and as surely as I believe the Bible, I must believe in a man's power to know to which class he belongs—and often to know to which class others belong also.

And all this plain and positive Scriptural assertion you calmly ignore—to pursue a speculative ratiocination on the " Reveal His Son in me."

In the same manner you pass over, utterly without explanation, the plain texts on which I based my positions. "With such an one not to eat" is thorough, short, unmistakable English, and so are the other texts I alleged. All I ask is practical instruction how to obey those texts. I do not care to call the obedience excommunication, it is an ugly word; but I want to have the texts understood and practised, and you have not told me how you practise them. The fact is, I always longed to meet with any one who could explain in a merciful way the Scriptural language of condemnation. I did conceive some hope from those very texts you quote that there might be some ray of hope for all mankind—that, as you express it, one might be saved "only as a man." Therefore I wrote in answer to your first letter. But the thought I have been induced by this correspondence to give to this special subject ends in a more fixed conviction that, if indeed all men are to be saved, the Bible is the falsest Book ever written by human hand.

I rose just now from my writing-table, feeling so wonderstruck at the doctrine of your letter that I hardly knew how to speak of it more. I went mechanically to my Bible, and it opened—where think you? At the twenty-sixth Psalm.[1]

But I will write no more. Your most humble and tender feeling cannot make you less useful—and God forbid I should argue against it; and may He also give me strength to make the Choice betwixt His love and His anger, which is, I believe, offered to us all in the Strait of Life.

Thank you again and again for your letter,

Respectfully and faithfully yours,

J. RUSKIN.

[Maurice wound up the correspondence by a short reply, dated April 28, of which the gist was as follows: " I was not denouncing our Lord's doctrine of excommunication, I was denouncing yours. *He* says, 'If your *brother* trespass against you, tell him his fault alone ; then, take with you two or three men ; then, if he neglect them, tell it to the Church ; then, if he refuse the Church, give up all intercourse with him.' Beautiful and divine method! for which you and this age substitute the method of not acknowledging men as brothers at all, of refusing intercourse with them, *without* telling them their fault or going to the Church, on the assumption that they are publicans and sinners, and therefore have no part or lot in the matter."]

---

[1] ["4. I have not dwelt with vain persons : neither will I have fellowship with the deceitful.

"5. I have hated the congregation of the wicked ; and will not sit among the ungodly," etc.]

2. LETTERS TO F. J. FURNIVALL

[DR. FURNIVALL, who was the intermediary between Maurice and Ruskin in the foregoing correspondence, also himself joined in the fray. His letters are not available; but he has explained his point of view. Ruskin had sent him a copy of *Sheepfolds*. "I did not at all like the Discipline and Excommunication part of it," he writes, "as I thought it would lead to ministers and neighbours poking their noses into every man's private affairs, and to a lot of hypocrisy and intolerance." [1] Other points made by Dr. Furnivall sufficiently appear from Ruskin's letters.]

I

[*Postmark: March 17th, 1851.*]

MY DEAR FURNIVALL,—Many thanks for *your* notes on *mine*. To answer them fully would take much more time than I have this morning—almost another pamphlet—but to their main purport I answer briefly.

(1) I allow the Church (ii.), p. 2,[2] to include tares, because with all the scrutiny that human eyes can give it, *it always must*. (Remember St. Bruno's conversion.)[3] But that is no excuse for not turning out people who are plainly *not* of it. All who look like sheep will not be sheep, but at least turn out all who do not wear sheep's clothing.

(2 and 3) The Epistles written to the invisible Church therefore necessarily address with it multitudes not for the time living up to their profession. This might be in ignorance, and all the passages you quote addressed to persons living in crime presume this ignorance, and are the rebuking of the fault previous to excommunication.

Otherwise the *Church is always* used in my sense of it—as including only persons living up to their profession.

(4) You may see that I quote Thess. iii. 15, as the first degree of excommunication, not the second.

(5) I said in all *Christian* States, *i.e.*, in Christen*dom*. If you let the *Dom* be unchristian, it is Unchristendom. Wherever the State calls itself Christian, its government should be pre-eminently Christian, therefore pre-eminently part of the Church, and the State or whole people is either a

---

[1] ["Forewords" to *Two Letters* (see Bibliographical Note, above, p. 514), p. 9. The first of Ruskin's Letters to Furnivall was the Appendix to that book (pp. 29–30). The second and third are reprinted from pp. 7–13 of *Letters from John Ruskin to F. J. Furnivall* (privately printed, 1897), where also the first letter is again given.]

[2] [The reference is to the pamphlet; § 3 in this edition, p. 525.]

[3] [St. Bruno's conversion is dated from the funeral of the renowned doctor, Raymond, under whom Bruno had studied theology at Paris. Raymond was celebrated for apparent holiness of life; but in the midst of the funeral service the dead man sat up, and cried, "By the justice of God I am condemned." Twice more the same thing happened: Raymond's body was cast into an unhallowed grave; and Bruno retired into the wilderness. The story is depicted in the series of pictures, now in the Louvre, painted by La Sueur for the cloisters of the Chartreuse at Paris.]

majority Christian or a majority Pagan. If the majority and government are Pagan, of course the State is not the Church.

The rest of your note refers to the endless question of Authority of Scripture, into which it is vain to enter. I say only this—If the Bible does not speak plain English enough to define the articles of saving faith, burn it, and write another, but don't talk of *Interpreting* it. I will keep your note to talk it over with you.

Ever affectionately yours,
J. RUSKIN.

P.S.—I ended my note in some indignation, because really a man of your intelligence ought to be above repeating the stale, and a thousand times over stale, equivocation between Authority and Belief. Is it possible you don't see the difference between having Authority to *Pro*nounce an unwritten Truth and to *An*nounce your belief of a written one. I lay my hand on the Bible and say I believe I read this here. You say *you don't*. I say— Then it seems to me you either lie or are judicially struck blind, and I will have no company with you. The retort is of course the same. Both parties call, and *should* call, each other Heretics, and God will see which is right at the last day.

II

TRINITY LODGE, *Sunday*.
[*Postmark: March 28th, 1851.*]

MY DEAR FURNIVALL,—I really have not been able to answer so much as a word, either to your letter or card, until now. Nor now will I answer at any length, for, as you rightly say, the differences between us lie deep, and could not be argued out in less than a volume of letters on either side. But I will answer your one question—Dare you say "I serve God" —for the answer to this will *express* the difference between us clearly, and that will be always something gained.

Yes. Whenever I *do* serve Him, I dare to say so; whenever I do *not* serve Him, I *know* that I do not. How often I do not, is not your question. Be it enough to say that there are some *moments* of my life in which I try to serve Him (and to try to do it, is to do it); and that I perfectly know the difference between those moments, and the innumerable other moments in which I serve the Devil and my own Lusts. Farther, I believe with all my heart and soul that His children do, on this Earth, "diligently serve God day and night;"[1] that they are just as certain that they are in His Service, as any Footman is who receives daily wages for daily work done. And that these His children can say, and *must* say, to many men around them, *I serve* God, *you* do *not*.

I believe that all men are God's children, in the sense in which dogs, mice, and rats are His children; but until they are converted, or born again, in no other sense; only, the offer of salvation, by *becoming* His children, is held out to them all. And if you call this doctrine Pharisaical, I cannot help it. But I would ask you this—whether a child snatched by

---

[1] [Acts xxvi. 7 : "Instantly serve God day and night."]

its father out of a burning house, and shrieking out that its brother or sister is still left behind, has any Pharisaical feeling towards such brother or sister? For its feeling towards them is that which I believe every saved Christian has towards those whom God has not converted, with this exception, that God becomes the Father only of those whom He saves, *adopting* them in Christ: He is the Father of others as He is of all beasts. That Pharisaical feeling will mingle itself with this, and that there will always be Accursed Pharisees mixed among Blessed Believers, I believe and admit as surely as you do. That does not in the least affect the firmness of my trust.

That those who are God's Children know themselves for such; that there are, indeed, many men of whom they dare not pronounce whether they be His or no; but that of others, they may at once declare that they are *not* His—I will not argue this with you. You may find full statements of the doctrine and support of it, a thousand times better than I could give you, in the works of Calvin, Luther, Milton, Bunyan, Baxter, Boston, Newton,[1] and such others, to whom I refer you, for I can write no more — unless there is something in Maurice's letter which I may desire to answer. Please send it me here, if you get it by Tuesday; after Tuesday, you had better keep it till you hear from me.

Effie joins me in kindest regards.

Yours most truly,
J. RUSKIN.

Be so kind as to keep this line, for perhaps my only answer to Maurice may be to ask him to read it.

III

[*Postmark: March 28th*, 1851.]

MY DEAR FURNIVALL,—I am very sorry I was impatient in the morning; I am now in less hurry, and can explain myself better.

You are like many other good people whom I know—who, having strong feelings, refuse the passages of Scripture which are plain and clear, in order to help themselves to those which are mystic.[2] There is, and can be, no doubt respecting what St. Paul means by not eating with a man, or having no company with him. This plain command you reject, and try to palliate your rejection by those mystical expressions of parables. I would read Scripture with the other side uppermost, I say, when the word and command is plain—*do* first what you are bid, and afterwards think about the meaning of parables.

But to me the parables themselves are also perfectly plain. You see, the gathering up of the tares would be, in the parable, a *previous* infliction

---

[1] [Thomas Boston (1677–1732), Scottish divine, author of *Marrow of Modern Divinity*; John Newton (1725–1807), divine and friend of Cowper, much influenced by Whitefield and Wesley.]

[2] [Compare the reply to Maurice, above, p. 567.]

of their *final* judgment. The parallel to such gathering, in the world, would be the "in flaming fire taking vengeance on them that know not God."[1]

This *vengeance* we are forbidden to exercise. You know the "*field* is the world."[2] To gather the tares out of it, would be to destroy the wicked out of the world. You are not to do this, but to let both live, and grow together—not confusing the one with the other—never calling wheat tares, nor tares wheat — so far as you can know one from the other. You know, probably, that the word translated 'tares' does in reality mean *bad wheat*, a kind of weed which to this day is employed in the East to spoil land with. You are therefore to let both good and bad wheat *live*—grow in God's great field—trying to make good wheat of the bad. But you are to keep the separation distinct, as far as in you lies, and to know the one from the other.

I hope that whatever Good was proposed to me to be done by any man—Hindoo, Turk, Greek, Romanist, or English Pagan—I should, without hesitation, join him in doing, according to the close of your letter. All I want to be plainly understood is, that he *is* a Greek, Turk, or what else—and, therefore, that I am not to have fellowship with him as a Christian.

Ever yours affectionately,
J. Ruskin.

---

[1] [2 Thessalonians i. 8.]
[2] [Matthew xiii. 38.]

II

ESSAY ON BAPTISM[1]

[1850–1851]

§ 1. IF one of the angels of God were this day to descend from His presence, or to pause from journeying through the places of His dominions—that he might follow the course of our Earth, and watch the obscure planet as it whirled—how strange would its aspect be to him, if the counsels of the Almighty were secret to him, as to us!

He might delight himself for a time in tracing the laws of a Natural system perhaps before unknown to him; worshipping again and again at each renewed delight. But he would quickly turn to observe the race of beings for whom his Creator and theirs once descended on the Earth, and then was slain. And what would be his wonder, as he beheld their multitudes, wandering amidst sands, and mountains, and islands, savage or sensual, erring or imbecile, idolatrous or Godless—hateful and hating one another.

The Earth but twenty-four thousand miles round.

Eighteen hundred and fifty years since God came down upon it.

And half of its inhabitants have never heard of this yet!

If a bank breaks in London, those whom it concerns in India hear of it in six weeks.

God comes down to save men in Syria, and those whom *this* concerns do not get the news in eighteen hundred years. This would be strange to His Angel, though natural to us.

§ 2. But he would see stranger things yet. He would presently look to the place where Christ had suffered, and to the cities where His Apostles taught — and when he saw room for Christ's faith hardly yet made in Jerusalem, and the Syrian still ready to perish * where once Christ's folds were enclosed—when he saw the dust of the desert lie white upon Pergamos and Thyatira—Ephesus and Laodicea—Sardis and Philadelphia—and Smyrna —driving a goodly trade with Christian London in Figs!—would not this be strange to the Angel, though natural to us?

§ 3. But he would see stranger things yet.

He would turn to the group of capes and peninsulas where the name of Christ is named, and where God's providence has granted the knowledge

* Deuteronomy xxvi. 5.

[1] [For the circumstances in which this Essay was written, see above, Introduction, p. lxxv. It has not hitherto been published.]

and power which might have hallowed that name, and taught it to all the world. And there he would see the abomination of the Papacy standing in the holy place, and Christ forgotten as soon as named in a Woman-worship more gross than ever Ephesus gave Diana; and the dull monk fretting away his life in uselessness, and the subtle priest selling souls for money; and the fields trodden down by armies, and the cities sunk in dissipation and distress, and the bold Atheist lifting his head as the only Honest man among them all. And this the state of Christendom, after eighteen centuries of Christianity!

§ 4. But he would see stranger things yet.

He would look to our own Island, knowing that *there* at least the pure word of God was preached. He would see a race of men gifted by God's kindness with intense energy and clear intelligence — with every earthly means of doing good at their disposal. Peace—freedom—knowledge—wealth —and guarded by God's Providence, by a series of all but miraculous interpositions, from every form of danger — and every effort of hostility—and perhaps the Angel would be surprised to find that the idea of religious motives or of Christian charities, as in any wise connected with or influencing political acts, would be scouted as the last fanaticism in the Parliament of this favoured nation; perhaps also he would be surprised to find that for two years back the only mode in which we had exercised influence on foreign nations had been stealthily to stir up strife, and clumsily to encourage rebellion.[1] But if he passed by all this, if he looked disdainfully past Parliaments and policies, as the World's business more than his, and turned to the flock of Christ's faithful people, there, assuredly, strangest of all that he had witnessed, would be to him—angry words of God's ministers one to the other—paralysed efforts of Christian teachers one by the other—contending congregations, obstinate about forms of words and films of opinion, and God's servants giving themselves leisure to dispute about times and methods of conversion, while the whole earth is still lying in wickedness. Imagine the firemen at the great Fire of London stopping from their work at the engines to dispute about the way in which water put out fire. Fancy them getting irritated respecting the Equivalents of Hydrogen and Oxygen in the elements, and finally fighting across the leathern pipes until one half of them were disabled: a stranger sight than this it must be to the Angels of God to see the Christians of Great Britain quarrel about Baptismal Regeneration, while half the world is unbaptized, and the other half blaspheming Christ.

§ 5. Nor less strange to hear them say, meanwhile, that this fire is of God's kindling and this evil on the Earth is His sending. Yes; it *is* His sending—but it is your fault. It must needs be that the offence come— woe to you by whom it comes;[2] and all this misery has come by you Christians. You, polite and gentle ministers, who trip mincingly up pulpit stairs, and read fair sermons out of fair black books on fair velvet cushions; you, hot Presbyterians, who will not let a plain man pray a good prayer

---

[1] [This remark, again, helps to fix the date of the Essay (compare p. lxxvi., above); the reference obviously being to what Palmerston described as his attitude of "judicious bottle-holding" towards the insurrectionary movements in Europe which followed the Revolution of 1848.]

[2] [Luke xvii. 1.]

twice over;[1] you, artistical Christians, who paint windows and carve capitals; you, ignorant Christians, who deface cathedrals which you ought to bless your brethren for having built; you, logical and erudite Christians, who hunt for red letters, and block out God's light with old vellum; you, heady and high-minded Christians, who, so only that you obey Evangelist,[2] never care to enter the house of the Interpreter. All this has been your fault. You have been praying to Christ for a thousand years that He would grant you unity among yourselves, and confirm His Kingdom. You pray every day, and some of you in set forms, for Unity, peace and concord,[3] and for the influences of the Holy Spirit. And you see day by day that God does not grant your prayer, and that you are further from Unity than ever. Do you verily suppose that God refuses the prayers of His people, if they have not done something specially to displease Him? Not casual prayers for worldly things—those God *may* refuse and bless you in refusing. But prayers for Unity and for the shedding of the Holy Ghost He never refused, except in sorrow. Does a Father refuse his son bread, except in sorrow? He might refuse it, if he had ordered the son to go into his field and plough, and the son would not; the Father might wisely and justly say, "You would not work for your bread to-day; and to-day I will not give it you. You shall feel what it is to hunger." So you Christians continue asking God for bread; but you will not plough for it. You quarrel over your ploughs, and your Heavenly Father day after day refuses you your bread, until you think it a matter of course that He should do so. But He is angry with you, and you are mocking Him. Mocking Him, by praying to Him without exerting yourselves. Mocking Him, by asking for what He has said He will not give you, unless you do this—or that, which you refuse to do. Ask your own consciences what your sin and your failure is—it is not for me to tell you, each man should discover that for himself, and may if he will. But have you so much as taken God's *advice* in anything? Have you been wise as serpents—as harmless as doves?[4] Harmless! You are hindering each other. Wise! You are despising each other. Is your wisdom (such as you have) pure and peaceable, gentle, and easy to be entreated?[5] or does it stand astride upon texts, as Apollyon straddled over the road before Christian?[6] Is it utterly without partiality, and without Hypocrisy? Look to it, you Low Church Christians, how much Radicalism, and Socialism, and Liberalism, and Republicanism, and worldly spite and petty jealousy, and small self-admiration, the Devil has managed to mix up with your honest objections to Episcopacy, and wholesome love of field preaching. Look to it, you High Church Christians, how much Schoolmaster's respect for the Queen's English, how much gentlemanly regard for white hands and smooth manners, how much taste for good music well sung, how much impertinent pride in your University learning, ay, and how much downright love of quiet lives and good livings, the Devil uses to help your

---

[1] [Compare *Notes on Sheepfolds*, § 40, p. 557, above.]
[2] [See *The Pilgrim's Progress* for Evangelist and the Interpreter.]
[3] [The Second Collect in the Order for Morning Prayer.]
[4] [Matthew x. 16.]
[5] [James iii. 17.]
[6] [See, again, *The Pilgrim's Progress*: "Then *Apollyon* straddled quite over the breadth of the way," etc. (p. 61, Golden Treasury edition).]

fiery defences of ecclesiastical authority and Apostolic succession. Look to it, for in these the evil must lie. Consider with yourselves whether God ever commands anything impossible. He has commanded you to be at peace with one another, yet you say you cannot be; and He has commanded you to prove all things and hold fast the good,[1] and yet you deliberately allow, and expect, schism to take place concerning points of serious— well-nigh of saving—belief; tacitly thereby accusing God of having made the Scripture so obscure that it cannot be understood, or of withholding the help of His Spirit from those who ask it. Either the Bible must be a lie altogether, or else whatsoever is necessary to Salvation in heaven and to peace on earth may be gathered therefrom, by every man who asks and desires God's help as he reads. Dispute about a serious point of doctrine, and you prove the Bible false, or yourselves hypocrites—conscious or un-conscious—for pretending to believe it when you do not. For if it be true, what is necessary for your Life may be found in it; and, touching what is unnecessary, it has told you not to dispute.

§ 6. Hypocrites, or else culpably, inconceivably careless; careless either to discern the true meaning of what you read, or to receive in patience the sense of your opponent's terms. At least one half of the dint and violence of every religious dispute between people commonly honest depends upon their not understanding, not choosing to understand each other's language. And this evil I may surely take so much upon myself as to endeavour to lessen. I have neither authority nor knowledge for this handling of doctrine. I have neither time nor strength for the attack of prejudice. But I may at least plead with you for the prudence, and prove to you the ease, of receiving each other's words in the sense in which they are used. There is war enough in the world without the additional and heavier calamity of war of the fold of Christ; and there are some questions, even of principles and Faith, which I believe we might well for a time suffer to remain at rest; but if any of our disputes arise out of false acceptation of terms, and might be calmed in an instant if men did but understand each other, how imperative is the duty to make our thoughts clear, and our expressions simple!

§ 7. Now the whole question of Baptismal Regeneration is one which I could be well pleased to see left at rest. The great question for every man—"Whether he be Now serving God or not?"—is one as easily answered as it is rarely asked. If he be, it matters little whether he were converted at his Baptism or after it. If he be not, whatever the Grace bestowed on him in Baptism might have been, he is now in need of more. It is a questionless fact that the greater number of baptized persons are serving the World and the Devil: it is of more importance to teach them what grace it is still in their power to receive, than how much they have hitherto received in vain.

I could wish, then, that this question were left at rest, but if this cannot be, at least let us take care that we do not dispute about the *Term* "regeneration," a term occurring twice only in the Bible, and then in two different senses.[2] The greater number of persons who hotly deny the doctrine

[1] [1 Thessalonians v. 21.]

[2] [Matthew xix. 28 : "Ye which have followed me in the regeneration, when the Son of man shall sit in the throne of his glory, ye shall also sit upon thrones."

of Baptismal Regeneration, understand by Regeneration the Saving Unity with Christ, the final conversion of the sinner to God, the consummate Grace after the bestowal of which they cannot perish.

It is nevertheless as clear as noonday, since it is admitted that the greater number of baptized persons throughout Europe are Godless sinners, that the Church (if you suppose her to assert Regeneration to be the necessary consequence of the Baptismal Rites) does *Not* mean by Regeneration anything of this kind. Quarrel with her, therefore, if you will, for improper use of the English language, and for attaching to the word Regeneration a sense different from yours; but do not quarrel with her *doctrine* until you quietly reflect what she really means: it may be that after reflection, you will have two quarrels with her instead of one—one for unscriptural doctrine, another for inaccurate language—only do not confound your two accusations together. Examine her doctrine first, and if you can accept that, for the sake of peace in Christendom, forgive her language.

§ 8. Now there are three distinct ways in which the Church's words may be understood: since that all baptized persons are saved, she cannot mean—

(1) She may be understood that a certain degree of Grace is given at Baptism, but a degree not amounting to entire conversion.

(2) She may be understood that all persons are regenerated or converted at Baptism, but that regenerate persons are not safe for ever, some or many of them afterwards falling away from Christ.

(3) She may be understood that conversion entire and secure is the result of Baptism, but only of some Baptism; that is to say, of Baptism "rightly received." [1]

That these several views may each be supposed consistent with acceptance of the Church's words, is evident from the tone of the disputes on this subject, which presume sometimes one to be her doctrine—sometimes another.

Whichever view be right, it is certain that the Church's words ought not to bear interpretation into all or any. Examine, therefore, these several creeds. If you can hold none of them, you can be no member of the Church of England (though I do not see why that should be a reason for your contradicting her, or shortening her powers). But if you can conscientiously hold any one of them, express that one clearly both to yourself and others, and be ready to give your support in case of need, distinctly and calmly to that particular view, considering at the same time how far you may esteem those as fellow Churchmen or fellow Christians, who hold in sincerity some other of the above Creeds, and how far it would be right to break with them in order to formally establish your own.

§ 9. And in first approaching the subject take care of two things. Do not confuse the question "What Baptism *is* and conveys?" with the question

---

Titus iii. 5 : "Not by works of righteousness which we have done, but according to his mercy he saved us by the washing of regeneration, and renewing of the Holy Ghost." See below, § 15, p. 581.]

[1] [Article xxvii. : "Baptism is not only a sign of profession, and mark of difference, whereby Christian men are discerned from others that be not christened, but it is also as a sign of Regeneration or new Birth, whereby, as by an instrument, they that receive Baptism rightly are grafted into the Church," etc.]

" Whether children should be baptized or not ? " Above all do not argue that *because* children *are* baptized, *therefore* Baptism can only mean this, or that. You are not told distinctly in the Bible that children ought to be baptized, but you are told very distinctly what Baptism is, and does.   Receive, therefore, from the Bible, as you would from any other book, what you are told distinctly before what you are told obscurely, and what you are told directly before what you are told by implication.   Treat the question of Infant Baptism separately ; determine first what baptism is, and then whether it should be given to children, but do not assume the fitness of a practice which rests for a great part of its justification on the mere opinion and custom of the Church, and, on the strength of it, weaken or dispute the meaning of the words of the Bible.   Take the words of the Bible as they are written, and by them judge the practice of the Church.

§ 10. Again, do not tacitly admit the thought that there may be two kinds of Baptism—one for infants, another for adults.   I have not seen this thought definitely expressed, but I have traced it in many persons' minds. I only ask that you will not admit it *tacitly*.   Write it out, and express it clearly.   You perhaps think that the modern baptism of Infants is a totally different thing from the serious Baptism of St. Paul or Cornelius ; or you think that infant baptism is only semi-baptism, and is completed in Confirmation.   Whichever of these views you entertain, state it distinctly, and consider what will follow from it : in the first case, that the Baptism should be repeated at mature age ; in the second, that the Grace of Baptism may perhaps be withheld by God till the time of Confirmation.   Consider these points separately, but do not confuse either of them with the plain question, What is this grace of perfect baptism, received at its proper time ?

§ 11. With these precautions, let us in order examine the views stated above (page 577).   I am not going to assert any of them.   I shall only endeavour to put such questions to you as may help you in defining them, and in applying Scripture to test them.

(I.) That a certain degree of Grace is given at Baptism, but a degree
          not amounting to entire conversion.

Here we at once find the argument respecting baptism complicated by one respecting the nature of Conversion ; and the fact is that in all disputes of the kind, every approach to an understanding on the one head has always been prevented by misunderstanding on the other.   The two questions cannot be settled at once, and yet they are so closely connected that it is difficult to reason out either of them without a side reference to the influence which its decision is likely to have upon the other.   The High Churchman will not think out the meaning of Conversion, lest its explanation should interfere with his notion of the efficacy of Baptism ; the Evangelical Churchman explains away every text respecting Baptism, which appears likely to diminish the importance he has been accustomed to attach to the idea of Conversion.   Let us get rid of this chameleon fashion of looking at this thing with one eye up and another down.   Let us take up the Evangelical word and idea of Conversion candidly, and see how far either of them may be defined.

§ 12. Many experienced Christians look back to this period, and some even to the moment, when they first became servants of Christ.   Doubtless, whether remembered or not, there has been such a moment for all Christians who have not, like Obadiah, feared the Lord from their youth [1]—a literal and mathematically definable *moment*. For it is certain there was one time when, if they had died, their souls would have perished; and another time when, if they had died, their souls were safe: you may approximate into actual contact the limits of these conditions, for there is no neutral ground. A man is either Christ's friend or enemy; there cannot therefore be so much as an instant in which he is neither the one nor the other. Therefore the change from being the one to being the other must be instantaneous.

Now it is also true that a man must be either alive or dead, and that the change from a state of Life to a state of death is instantaneous. Yet we have no difficulty in understanding what is meant when it is said that a man is "Dying." He may be dying for some hours, for some days, or for some years, but he is certainly to be considered dying from the time he is first struck by mortal disease, or at least all the time such disease is making progress.

May not this be true also of Conversion? Is not a man converting, as we say he is dying? May not his Spiritual frame die to sin just as slowly, and with as long a struggle, as his physical frame sickens, wastes, and expires? Does not his Christian soul give up the world grievously and agonisingly, till it comes to the last gasp of sin, and is dead to it?

Some persons are doubtless converted as a man is killed by Lightning; but are not others converted they know not when, as men die in their sleep; do not some struggle with their conversion, and thrust it off by strength of heart, as men do their deaths; and do not some pass through a lingering conversion of many wearing years?

§ 13. Now I ask the Evangelical Christian, whether, in the natural body, he would say that God's hand was more stretched out against a man at the instant of his death, than in the disease which brought about the death? When Ahaziah fell through the lattice,* or at least when Elijah received God's message for him, was God's wrath less definitely gone forth against him than at the moment of his death? Was God's power less exerted upon Herod, when the worms first began to gnaw him, than at the instant of his giving up the Ghost? †

Now put the parallel question.

Is the Grace of God acting less definitely upon a man when the worm first begins to gnaw his conscience, than at the instant when he dies to the world? When first the fear and the foreboding seize him, which are to bring him to Christ, is God dealing with him less affectionately than at the moment in which he comes to Christ? Consider this analogy carefully, and see whether this Moment of Conversion, upon which you lay so much stress, be anything more than the time of the last, and perhaps the lightest blow which God strikes at a man's heart to cut it from the world. You watch a woodman hewing a tree, and you are thrilled as the tree nods, and appalled as it falls. But in God's eyes the first blow of the axe is

* 2 Kings i. 2, 4.
† Acts xii. 13.

---

[1] [1 Kings xviii. 12.]

perhaps as important as the last, and He saw how little held the tree to its old roots long before *you* saw it nod.

Consider, further, if you think that the wrath of God was the same against Herod when he first fainted on his throne as when he expired, whether God's love is not as great to a man when first He strikes at his heart, or goes forth to seek him on the dark mountains, as when He brings him home to His fold? Consider, also, since you say that a work which God begins He always finishes, and infer thence that a man once converted is safe, whether these first strokes be not the *true* beginning of God's work, and whether God is likely to stop when the tree is only cut half-way through.

§ 14. But I have to press another Analogy. As in Conversion we Die to Sin, so we are Born to Christ. This is the Analogy in accordance with which you Evangelical Christians restrict the term "Regeneration" to the moment of Conversion. Consider, therefore, this analogy carefully.

Are you quite sure, in the first place, that the moment of the natural birth is a more important one in God's eyes than any other of the child's existence? It is with Astrologers, but is it with God? Are you quite sure that the child receives its soul at that moment—neither after nor before? Does the mere fact of its breathing air with its lungs, and of light being admitted to its eyes, make this difference between mortality and immortality? Is there any real sign or evidence of more of a soul being put into it at that moment, than there was before? Might it not have had what you call its soul a month sooner, if you had frightened its mother; and if you now fasten a ring of iron round its skull, will it ever show more evidence of a soul than it did by its motions in the womb? nay, was not the peculiar disposition of its soul influenced by the mother's thoughts, before you admit that its soul existed? But grant it otherwise, grant that though it draw only two breaths and so expires, it is an immortal being, and that if it had lost life ten seconds before it was but a piece of clay, was God's power then less exerted in framing its bones and sinews, and preparing it for an habitation of the soul, than at the moment of birth, or more especially at that moment than afterwards in developing the intelligence and affections of this New Creature? It indeed is a date of some peculiar importance to *us* when the child is first trusted to our care; but in God's eyes perhaps the moment of conception is as important as this, and the direction which He gives to the thoughts of the mother, while the Child is still in her bosom, as important a part of the creation of the Child's soul as the admission of air to its lungs.

§ 15. Now apply this analogy. It is an important moment to Us, in our short-sighted Humanity, when we first see that our friends have become Christians, or feel that we are New Creatures ourselves. But is that moment much more important in God's sight than any of the others in which He was preparing us and them for the change, or in which, after that change, He leads us to further perfection? And if not, and if the Grace of God is effectually exerted upon us perhaps many years before outward evidence of it appear to ourselves or others, is there any sign by which we may so much as *conjecture* when this Grace is first extended to us and called into active operation? Is it not perfectly possible for you, Evangelical Christians, without one whit abandoning your conception of conversion as the visible and sensible change of the heart to God, to admit that there is something long before conversion, which is to the Spiritual birth what Conception is to the Natural, and to the Spiritual death what mortal disease is to the Natural, and that this may be by other Christians, and perhaps even by your Master Himself, held quite of as much consequence as that visible change, which you watch so closely, and that this may be with more accuracy and with more Scriptural authority expressed by the term Regeneration? For, remember, Generation is not Birth. It is carelessly called so in our Church of England articles and services—and here is one of the inaccuracies of language which you will have to amend or forgive—but Genesis is not Birth; the two things are spoken of in Scripture indifferently, because both are equally necessary stages in the Christian being— "Of His own will Begat He us," * "Ye must be Born again," † "Not circumcision but a new creature" ‡ (new creation would be a closer translation), the last and first expression both referring to the new Genesis but not to the new Birth. So, also, one of the only two passages[1] in which the word "regeneration" occurs (Matthew xix. 28) has nothing to do with conversion whatsoever, but speaks of the New World (as the "I make all things new" of Rev. xxi. 5), and in the other (Titus iii. 5) the word regeneration means making the soul new—the new Creation of St. Paul—the Re-Genesis, a thing wholly previous to the new Birth or visible and sensible conversion. Think over this, and consider whether one side of the Church is not disputing with the other in consequence of a most simple, gross, and easily detected confusion of terms.

§ 16. And now let us examine three instances of actual conversion in which there is no chance of our being deceived as to the time or manner of the change, since they are all recorded and described in the Word of God.

The most conspicuous and violent conversion on record is that of St. Paul. But we fall into singular error if we ever permit ourselves to think of that Conversion as in anywise resembling the changes to which the term is now so nearly limited—caused by some sudden impression made on persons of Godless life, or of unalarmed conscience. What was St. Paul's state of mind before his conversion?

He was (first) an upright man, doing his duty as far as he knew it. I *verily* (mark the word) "thought with myself that I *OUGHT* to do many things contrary to the name of Jesus of Nazareth."[2] This, his inspired record of his own truth and desire to do his duty, we may not doubt.

He was (secondly) as touching the Law Blameless, and besides, zealous towards God. Now what do you think that St. Paul, looking back with the keen and purged sight of Christianity to his early life, would have ventured to call *blameless* as touching the Law? He could mean nothing

* James i. 18.
† John iii. 7.
‡ Gal. vi. 15.

---

[1] [See above, § 7, p. 576.]
[2] [Acts xxvi. 9. The following references are—Philippians iii. 6; Numbers xxv. 7-11; Acts vi. 13; 1 Kings xviii. 40.]

less than that he had lived continually to God under the old dispensation. He means that he had lived the life of Enoch, or of Daniel. Would you not be apt to call yourselves converted already if you were living Daniel's life, or Enoch's, ay, even though with something of Phinehas in you, you had consented unto the death of one who you thought had blasphemed God, or, with something of Elijah in you, had said of a sect whom you supposed adverse to Him, "Let not one of them escape"?

§ 17. Take another instance—the conversion of Cornelius. You fix the time of it, I suppose, to his hearing of Peter. Yet he was a man who prayed to God, and whom God heard, long before.[1] He was, moreover, a man of perfect obedience, for he is much more ready to obey his vision of the Angel, than St. Peter to obey his of the Sheet; St. Peter's had to be repeated Thrice, but Cornelius never paused because it was a tanner's house, though it might have seemed a strange place to which he was told to send for Salvation. He was a devout and almsgiving man, and a man of brotherly love, for he had made his soldiers devout also, and he would not hear St. Peter's message alone, though God had not told him to send for his kinsmen. Now if we were all almsgiving people, all praying people, all obedient people, and all loving people, should we need to quarrel about the time of our conversion?

§ 18. If, however, we are able to fix the moment of conversion in this case of St. Paul and of Cornelius, is it as easy to do this in that of St. Peter himself? We know from Luke xxii. 32, that St. Peter was not converted until the close of our Lord's ministry. We may gather therefore from his former history what it is possible for an Unconverted person to do and to be. He may have Faith—"I have prayed for thee that thy faith fail not."[2] "Blessed art thou, Simon Bar-jona, for flesh and blood hath not revealed it unto thee." Peter had faith enough to walk on the sea, Conviction of sin enough to make him cry out in agony under the sense of the presence of his Maker, and Love enough of God to make him leave all for Him; and if we were to reason about his conversion unassisted, when should we place it? When he was called by his brother to Christ, and received his name of Peter—having been previously baptized by John with the baptism of repentance for the Remission of Sins? That must at least have been *one* marked time of his life. He had left his fishing, and come far away down the Jordan to hear the great desert preacher; he had been summoned to Christ as the Messiah; had been received by Him; named by Him, yet not converted; he went back to his Fishing; he went on casting his nets for a while; but Christ came one day walking by the shore, and called him, and he forsook his nets and followed Him[3]—yet not converted. He followed Him but a little time, and went back to his nets: a severer lesson was needed, and given (Luke v. 1–8). This time Peter seems hard struck indeed, and we never hear of his leaving Christ any more. Yet not converted! When will you place his real conversion? When his denied Master turned and looked on him? or over the fire of coals by the old shore of Galilee, or at Pentecost?

[1] [Acts x.]
[2] [Luke xx. 32 ; Matthew xvi. 17, xiv. 29 ; Mark i. iv.]
[3] [Mark i. 18 ; Luke xxii. 61.]

§ 19. Does it not appear from all this—and I do not state it dogmatically, but merely as proposing to you in clear terms, for your acceptance or rejection, what seems to me to follow from the considerations I have laid before you—that the change of heart in Man is brought about progressively, having certain marked places, of which the principal is that which removes him from a state of condemnation to a state of justification, commonly called Conversion or the new Birth.   But that the Beginning of this Change—of which the Man himself and all around him may perhaps be totally unconscious—is *as* important a phase in the sight of God ; and may more properly be termed Regeneration.   Connected with this gradual change of heart is the Giving of the Holy Spirit, which it appears alike rash to confound with Conversion or Regeneration, or to limit to any particular time.   Scripture is especially indefinite in its evidence on this point; for, observe, the Apostles received the Holy Ghost at Three several periods— once by the Breathing of Christ (John xx. 22), again at Pentecost, and again in answer to their first prayer under persecution (Acts iv. 31)—and on none of these occasions in definite connection with Baptism or conversion ; and although on many occasions we find the Holy Ghost given after Baptism by the laying on of hands, yet both faith in God and Good Works are frequently found previously to this special descent of the Spirit (the very Stranger Jews who were baptized at Pentecost having been previously " devout persons " [1]) ; and since faith and good works are supposed by the Evangelical Churchmen only to accompany conversion, and are by all Churchmen acknowledged to be the effect of the influences of the Spirit, it is no presumption to say that contests in the Church must be endless, unless it be admitted that while Regeneration and Conversion only take place once, the Holy Ghost may be given at different times, and for different purposes.

§ 20. If the view of Regeneration which I have above expressed be accepted, it will follow from it that we have no right to deny the fact of Baptismal Regeneration, merely because for some time after Baptism no signs of a change of Heart appear.   But if to the *Begun* work of Christ the Evangelical Churchman insist, as I have supposed he will, upon attributing the same constancy and irrevocability which he attributes to Conversion, then no person who lives and dies unsanctified can possibly have been Regenerate in Baptism ; and since it is admitted that many Baptized persons live godless to their deaths, we are compelled to consider next the Second interpretation of the Church's words which have been above suggested.

§ 21. (II.) " That all persons are regenerate in Baptism, but that regenerated persons are not safe for ever."

I know that many faithful Christians will recoil from this idea, and God forbid I should either doubt or disturb the assurance He has given to many of those who walk with Him that He will be their God even to the end.[2] But if, instead of rejoicing in this as a gracious special mercy, they claim it as an undoubted right ; if they hold that God *cannot* desert them ; and if on the strength of this supposed impossibility they proceed to dishonour his Resisted Spirit, to call the Grieved Spirit of God *no* Spirit of God, and

---

[1] [Acts ii. 5.]
[2] [Matthew xxviii. 20 ; Acts vi. 10 ; Ephesians iv. 30 ; Psalms xix. 13.]

the Holy Ghost which has been sinned against *no* Holy Ghost; and if, further, their doubt of the Reality of all heavenly influence which has not borne visible fruit lead them both into acrimonious schism and into neglect of the right use and honour of God's ordinances (if not into presumptuous sin), then I would pray them to answer the following questions faithfully and thoughtfully, to answer them in writing, and to take pains to support their answers, not by reasonings about God's attributes, not by their own conjectures as to what God must do or cannot but do, but by the plain words of Scripture.

(1.) Whom does Christ mean by the "Salt of the Earth"? What is the "Savour" of Unregenerate persons? Why are they "good for nothing but to be cast out" when they have lost it?[1]

(2.) When Christ says that a man "believes," does He mean that the man half believes, or does not believe at all? When He says "for a while believe, and in time of temptation fall away,"[2] would you desire to interpolate the text and read "for a while pretend to believe"? and does "fall away" mean the same thing as "stay away"?

(3.) What is the meaning of Esau's selling his Birthright? Is the true view of the case that he never had any Birthright to sell?[3]

(4.) In the parable of the wise and foolish virgins, what is the meaning of their taking their lamps, and going forth to meet the bridegroom?[4] Is "going forth" the same thing as staying at home? Is expecting a Bridegroom, being expected by him and desiring to be with him, the same thing as caring for no Bridegroom, and not believing that any will ever come? What were the lamps, and what is the meaning of their going out? What was the Oil, and why did it take time to buy it?

(5.) In Luke xii. 45, does "that servant" mean "another servant," and not the "faithful and wise steward" of verse 42? Is the word "servant" said of Men in general, not of Christ's servants? Does the servant who thinks his Lord is long in coming signify a person who acknowledges no Lord, and expects none? Does "Begin to eat" imply that he had never refrained from eating? and does the phrase "appoint him his portion with the unbelievers," imply that his portion was originally and always among them, and that he was an Unbeliever himself?

(6.) What is the meaning of the Unclean spirit going out of a man— of his house being swept and garnished? and[5]

(7.) What plough is it which unconverted persons put hand to and look back?[6]

(8.) In John xv. 2, what is the meaning of a Branch in Christ, and in the 4th verse is the counsel or command "Abide in Me" wholly superfluous, and the "except ye abide in Me" an impossible supposition? In the 6th verse, what is the meaning of being cast forth *as a branch*?

(9.) The whole XVIIth Chapter of St. John is a most anxious prayer of Christ's that His Father would protect those whom He Himself was now about to leave. From what "evil" is it that He prays they may be kept, in the 15th verse? Then, and in the Lord's prayer, the words being the

---

[1] [Matthew v. 13.]
[3] [Genesis xxv.]
[5] [Matthew xii. 43, 44.]

[2] [Luke viii. 13.]
[4] [Matthew xxv.]
[6] [Luke ix. 62.]

same, does "the Evil" or evil one stand only for the power of Satan to annoy or tempt, but not to destroy?

(10.) How do you understand the "leaving the first love" of Rev. ii. 4, and what punishment is signified by "moving the candlestick out of his place," in the 5th verse; what dread should we, as Christians, feel of having our "candlestick moved out of its place?"

(11.) What may we suppose the Church of Sardis had "received and heard," in Rev. iii. 3, before it stood again in need of repentance? With what judgment is she threatened when Christ says in the same verse He will "come upon her as a thief"?

(12.) Throughout these chapters of Revelations, what is the sense of "overcometh"? Does not the reward promised to him that overcometh imply that some who had entered the combat might be overcome?

(13.) What is the meaning of a man's name being written in the Book of Life, and blotted out of it?[1]

(14.) In John v. 14, and viii. 11, is there no spiritual meaning beneath the literal one? Did Christ mean, in the first of the two passages, to countenance the idea which on other occasions He had expressly reprobated, that temporal misfortune was a punishment for moral delinquency; or if not, what is the "worse thing" which the healed man had to dread?

(15.) Could you spare out of the Bible without missing them the following texts—Matt. xii. 31, 32; Heb. vi. 4, 5, 6; Heb. x. 26, 29, 38; 2 Pet. ii. 20, 21, iii. 17?

I will suppose that after the due weighing of such of the above questions as you may not have considered before, your conclusion is still that the Grace of Regeneration is irrevocable.

Then is there only one more manner of accepting the words of the Church yet to be submitted to you.

§ 22. (III.) May not the efficacy of the Rite of Baptism be dependent on the faith of the Receiver, or, in infant Baptism, of the Sponsor?

This supposition has lately been denounced as heresy.[2] Of those who thus denounce it, I would fain be permitted to ask one or two questions on my own account.

Suppose in Nero's time some Roman spy, desiring to do secret service in the catacombs, had with that intent professed belief in Christ, and obtained baptism of St. Paul, would such a man have received the Grace of Christ, and the Inspiration of His spirit?

Or if with no mischievous intention, but at the persuasion of his relations, some young Pagan Pliable[3]—as ready to believe in Christ as in Jupiter—had asked for baptism as a matter of form, would the rite have been efficacious in this case?

Or if in these days some Heathen, not understanding the English language, but *hoping to get* money or clothes from an English missionary, were to learn the responses of the Baptismal service by rote and ask to

---

[1] [Psalms lxix. 28.]

[2] [In the Gorham affair: see above, Introduction, p. lxxvii.]

[3] [See, again, *The Pilgrim's Progress* for Christian's neighbour, Pliable, who went with him as far as the Slough of Despond and then turned back.]

be baptized, and go through the ceremony decorously, would the Grace of Christ be given here? If not, what is the exact difference in the sight of God between a man's hearing a service without understanding it, or without attending to it? and would not God be quite as likely to give His Grace at the prayer of a Heathen who listened to the service which he did not understand, as of the respectable English Sponsor who understood the service to which he did not listen? Again, if people are forced, against their wills, to ask God in a set form of words for something which they do not care whether He gives them or not—perhaps even without believing that God hears them or that He exists—will God assuredly give it them?

Are not people usually *forced* to baptize their children, because everybody would be shocked if they did not? Would they not sometimes in their own hearts be quite as glad to give the child a name at home, and save the fees? When they do baptize their children, do they know exactly what they are to expect, or care for anything that God is to give them? Is God then likely to give them anything for lying in public, and saying that they renounce the Devil, when they are his sworn servants, and that they "steadfastly believe" what they totally deny.

We have no record in Scripture of an hypocritical or formal prayer offered to Christ. But we find one prayer refused, when they who offered it knew not what they asked; and we are told what is to be the reward of them who "for a pretence make long prayers." Greater Damnation!¹

§ 23. It may be asked, on the other side, how we are to define the exact measure of Faith which will make Baptism Efficacious.

But it is not for us to define exactly the number of tears with which a father ought to ask for his child's salvation, or of prayers which Christ may require before answering, or of knocks which must be repeated before He opens.² But we know that He will open at last, and that a Faithful Parent praying for the regeneration of his child, is as likely to be accepted as if he prayed for his own. Is the Generation of the Upright *not* Blessed, in spite alike of the parent's prayers and of God's promise? Is it objected that in thus supposing the efficacy of Baptism dependent on the Parents' or Sponsors' faith, I suppose the child will be punished for the Parents' want of faith? Well, if a father diligently taught his child to cheat at cards, and the child finally shot himself over the card-table, you would probably have some doubts of his salvation, and might admit that some drops of his blood were to be required of his father's hand. But if the father only mean the lighter sin of lying to Christ, and mocking God in a polite manner at the Baptismal font, for this sin you think it rash to say that the child may suffer, and the parent be made responsible for the suffering.

§ 24. Well, but you still think the salvation of a child too great a boon to be granted to a Parent's prayer. Be it so. High or Low Churchmen, you will at least grant this much, that Christ is as ready *now* to receive and to bless your children, as even when He stood "by the farther side of

---

¹ [Matthew xxiii. 14.]
² [Matthew vii. 7; Psalms cxii. 2.]

Jordan"[1]—that He stands personally beside the Baptismal font, and that you still may, if you will, have His hands laid upon your child, and His blessing given to it. You believe this, at least, unless you think that Christ is no real Person, or does not mean what He says—unless you think that if we ask anything according to His will, He heareth us *Not*, and that when two or three are gathered in His name,[2] He is Not in the midst of them. But you do believe it—if you believe anything. Then, if Christ verily stands by the Font to bless the Child, I ask you, parent or Sponsor, what does Christ's blessing mean, and what is it worth? You have read of the worth of Human blessing before now, you know that it has been sought carefully and with tears (though perhaps it was without tears that you sought Christ's). Isaac's blessing gave the Fatness of Earth and the dew of Heaven.[3] But a greater than Isaac is here. Jacob's blessing prevailed unto the utmost bound of the everlasting hills. But a greater than Jacob is here. Shall Christ's blessing do no more—did you come to Him expecting no more? Was it in the hope of wealth for your child, or of honour, or of length of days that you brought him to be blessed by Christ? Not so. You expected something else than this, or if not, we may learn from Christ's own lips what you ought to have expected, for those whom He calls blessed must be so in the sense which He has Himself attached to the word—

> "Blessed are the pure in Heart, for they shall see God."
> "Blessed are the poor in spirit, for their's is the Kingdom of Heaven."

You came, therefore, that your child might be made Pure in heart and lowly in spirit. Is this anything else than Regeneration, or would Christ call any one blessed whose sins He retained? I press no other argument respecting Baptism than this, for a thousand volumes of arguments—and you may find more, if you will—would probably be of less weight with you than your quiet answering for yourself of the simple question, How much less than the Inheritance of Heaven will make a Child Blessed in the Eyes of its Redeemer?

§ 25. Nay, but—you object incredulously—can Baptism, to which a believing Christian has brought the child, be a full assurance of its final salvation? I dare not answer; but you, if you are an experienced Christian, and know that you are yourself a Child of God, and that your salvation is secure, may answer boldly, and say that the salvation of that new Christian is as secure as your own, on the same conditions. If, therefore, you feel that there is no farther need for you to resist unto death, striving against sin, no farther need to keep under your body and bring it into subjection, no farther occasion for mortifying your members which are upon the earth;[4] if you feel that you can dispense with all the aids with which God has furnished you, and brave all the dangers against which He has warned

---

[1] [Mark x. 1, 14.]
[2] [Matthew xviii. 20.]
[3] [Genesis xxvii. 28 (Isaac), xlix. 26 (Jacob); Proverbs iii. 16; Matthew v. 3, 8.]
[4] [1 Corinthians ix. 27; Colossians iii. 5.]

you, and this without risk to your soul; then, also, from this younger Soldier in Christ's army, from this feebler pilgrim in Christ's way, withdraw the breastplate of Righteousness, the Sword of the Word; let him trust in his assurance of salvation, subject him to no discipline and to no reproof, instruct him not in the will, train him not in the ways of God, and trust still that he will endure to the end, and be saved.[1] But if you dare not do this in your own case, much less dare you do it in his? For a time, you are just as literally the Keeper of that Child's Conscience and Soul as you are of your own; do not meet me with the common escape-truism, that Christ is your soul's keeper—you will not be able to tell Christ at the Judgment, if then you have lost your soul, that you thought He would have taken care of it for you. You are just as much the Keeper of your soul as you are of your Life; and as much of your child's soul as of your own. What you tell him he will believe, until he finds you out in a lie; what you do before him he will imitate; what you suggest to him he will pursue; all his thoughts, affections, and habits are at your mercy; and do you say that with this power, and God to pray to, you cannot keep his Soul? Have you ever heartily tried—have you not left it in a thousand instances to his own keeping or to that of Strangers—or have you cared about his soul at all, or as much as you cared whether he were handsome and well bred?

§ 26. "Yes," perhaps you answer, unhappy parent, "I have done all I could for him, and he is reprobate still; I baptized him in faith, I taught him God's Word, I set good and evil before him and he has chosen the evil."   And fain would we leave this bitter sorrow without even the shadow of reproach. But if ever in your sorrow you are led to doubt the efficacy of the rite which God ordains, or the faithfulness of this promise attached thereto, dare to ask yourself whether your treatment of the lost child was wise as well as religious, consistent as well as holy. Was there common sense, common resolution, in the education, as well as piety and love? Nay, you reply, a child is not a reprobate because its Parent wants common sense! Alas, why not because of this want, as well as for any other? Are not Men's souls lost every day for want of common sense? and why not Children's also? There is no cause, no instrument so small, but God uses it to produce, or prevent, events the most momentous. You see the Ship drift to the Rocks, but you know not how many times God, when He had appointed its destruction, touched the finger of the Steersman months ago, on the calm water of its Path. And perhaps you would know, if you were admitted for an instant into the Counsel of the Most High, that one of those light touches of the steersman's finger was more the cause of the destruction of the Ship than the current which carried her to the Reef, or the white waves that are rending her before your eyes. And when His judgment is set, and the books are opened, you will perhaps discover that while no soul was ever lost but by the determined counsel and Foreknowledge of God, yet a strange account of Secondary Causes has been kept against those who dealt with them upon the Earth, and that many and many a one of those condemned Spirits has been lost for want of a single quiet word spoken at the right time.

---

[1] [Ephesians vi. 14; Matthew x. 22.]

§ 27. And yet you will cast your words and thoughts away while spirits are perishing all around you. Ah, you Churchmen, let your flocks deny Baptismal Regeneration as much as they please so only that they teach their children to love Christ. They will not tell you *that* is contrary to Scriptures. And you Evangelicals, instead of spending all your efforts against this "pestilent" doctrine, would it not be wiser to make as much of Baptism as you can? Let others preach what they choose of it, only do you prove and use it. Put Christ to the fair trial. See if He will not, at your prayer, bless the Child which you baptize in His name, and whether those whom their Lord has blessed, shall not be Blessed for Ever.

PART IV

LETTERS ON POLITICS

(1852)

LETTERS ON POLITICS[1]

I

"TAXATION, AND PRINCIPALLY BREAD TAX"

VENICE, *March 9th*, 1852.

§ 1. THOSE who have neither influence to press nor opportunity to diffuse their opinions, had better in general leave them unexpressed. Neither my circumstances nor my health admit of my entering into public life—and having little sympathy with the present course of English policy, and less power to resist it, I am forced, while my own country is multiplying errors and provoking dangers, to pass my days in deciphering the confessions of one which destroyed itself long ago. But the crisis we have reached in England no longer permits the silence of any one who perceives its peril. By our system of taxation, we have fevered the populace, and palsied the commerce of the country for the last twenty years; by our system of election we have achieved a Parliament which is unoffended at a proposal formally to deny the Christian faith,[2] and which can produce from its ranks no one fitter to manage our exchequer than a witty novelist;[3] and by our system of education we have made half the youth of our upper

---

[1] [For the circumstances in which these Letters were written, and for others explanatory of them, see above, Introduction, pp. lxxviii.–lxxxv.]

[2] [The reference is presumably to the Jewish Disabilities Bill, which passed the House of Commons in 1848, though it was thrown out by the House of Lords.]

[3] [Here, again, see the correspondence between Ruskin and his father, above, pp. lxxxiii., lxxxiv.]

classes, Roman Catholics,[1] and of our lower classes, infidels. Yet the first principles of taxation, election, and education, are, I believe, so clear and simple that he who runs may read them. Give me room for a few words on all three.

§ 2. *Taxation, and primarily Bread Tax.* There is much that is wonderful in the proceedings of the English House of Commons, but nothing more wonderful than the way in which they have blinded each other and the people to the real value of the struggle just past (and unhappily now likely to be revived), by putting forward the Farmers as if they were the persons whom the abolition of bread tax would injure, and for whose protection it was therefore to be retained.[2] The farmers have nothing whatever to do with it. The landlords are the persons who must eventually suffer, if any one suffers, and the whole question is whether landed property in England is to lose part of its value, or whether that value is to be maintained by making the poor pay more for their bread. Let the question be once reduced to these simple terms and we know how to deal with it, but the cunning introduction of the farmers, as a body much to be pitied, has absurdly complicated the inquiry, and rendered the advocacy of Protectionist principles possible for a much longer time than it could otherwise have been. That men now actually engaged in farming operations may be ruined by the change in the laws, is exceedingly probable;—all changes however beneficial to the public, are likely to ruin some innocent persons: but this temporary effect is no more to be considered than the ruin of hotel-keepers in certain towns by the introduction of railroads.

§ 3. The farming interest in the long run will not be in the least affected by the abolition of bread tax, but the rental of landed property will be, if any injury be done at

---

[1] [For the conversions among his own friends or contemporaries, which suggested this generalisation, see Vol. XI. p. 259.]

[2] [The reference is to Disraeli's motion for a Committee of Inquiry into Agricultural Distress in connexion with the abolition of the Corn Laws: see above, p. lxxix.]

all. I introduce this proviso, because no man can say whether different modes of agriculture or various commercial accidents may not, in spite of the change in corn laws, maintain the value of land. But if *any* harm is done, this will be *the* harm, and the whole question at issue is whether the landed proprietor is to run the risk of losing some certain percentage of an income, or whether the lower orders are to maintain that income out of their mouths. What ultimate effect the depreciation of the value of land may have on the disposition of capital, and indirectly on the interests of the lower classes, or how far the lower classes may wisely be listened to, when with threats and tumult they demand the surrender to them of a portion of the property of the higher, are other questions altogether; questions which it was the business of Parliament to have discussed before they altered the law, and of which they avoided the discussion because the greater number of the Protectionists dared not avow the true nature of the question.

§ 4. But I do not care to enter into this intricate inquiry, for I would desire to see the bread tax abolished on a broader principle than any connected either with agricultural or manufacturing interests. The entire system of import and export duties appears to me one of the most amazing and exquisite absurdities which mankind have ever invented or suffered from. I can understand a child's refusing to take medicine unless it is given him in sweetmeat; but I cannot understand a man's refusing to pay necessary taxes unless they are laid upon him in the form of custom-house dues (not, one should have thought, a particularly agreeable mode of concealment). We all know that we *must* pay a certain sum in order to have a government and army; that is to say, to have peace, liberty, or security for a single hour; but we are too cowardly to take this sum simply out of our pockets, and have done with it; we like better to have it cunningly filched from us in duties on tea and sugar, and to have the chance of smuggling a sixpenny-worth on occasion. And the whole nation, and all European nations, are precisely in this respect acting as rationally as an individual would do, who disliking, as it is natural for all men to dislike, to pay his rent on quarter day, should go to his landlord and say, "Sir, it is painful to my feelings to pay my rent in this straightforward and visible manner. If you could conveniently let your steward watch at my house door, and make my cook pay him so much a pound on all the meat that comes into the house, it would be much pleasanter for me, and I would pay the steward for his extra trouble." And thus we must have our taxes, as nervous people have their teeth, extracted under chloroform, and a kind of chloroform too, which is expensive, and infinitely hurts our constitution; for the whole array of customs executive is not only a useless expense, but grievously injurious to the operations of commerce.

§ 5. The minds of nations are confused, on this subject, between the two uses of import duties, for purposes of revenue, and purposes of protection. As far as regards the revenue, I believe that the mass of the people might in time be brought to understand that direct taxation was always the lightest possible taxation; but in parliamentary debate the interests of classes dependent on some particular national produce confuse the plain question, and the selfish cunning of a few, aided by the simplicity of the many, prevents its solution. Let it be clearly understood, that for all purposes of revenue, direct taxation is the best, and then discuss the various questions of protection on their own proper basis, and we should soon begin to perceive that if the genius of the people and nature of the country be adapted to a particular produce, protection of that produce is useless; and if not, ridiculous. It would be useless to protect the manufacture of tea in China, and absurd to protect that of wine in England, and all protection by import duties is in like manner, in degrees more or less marked, either absurd or useless as regards the branch of industry which is protected, and every way injurious, in its effects on other branches of commerce.[1]

§ 6. I say all protection *by import duties*, for there are other means of encouraging the energies and developing the resources of a country, which it may often be in the power, and must then always be the duty, of its Government to adopt. But, still more definitely, excise duties may be made the means of *dis*couragement of injurious and ruinous branches of industry, and at the same time a relief from the pressure of direct taxation. I am no republican, but it does not need republican prejudices to perceive the truth written in fiery letters on the last pages of all histories, that the luxury of the richer classes is, in nine cases out of ten, the cause of the downfall of kingdoms, at once undermining the moral strength of those classes themselves, and provoking the envy and cupidity of the poor. It is therefore the duty of every Government to prevent, as far as possible, the unreasonable luxury of the rich, and if it cannot prevent it, to maintain itself by it. There is justice in this as well as prudence. The man by whom the existing state of things is most enjoyed, may justly be called upon to pay most for its maintenance, and the man who by his luxury increases the perils of a Government, may justly be required to contribute largely to its resources.

§ 7. Abolishing therefore all import and export duties whatsoever, let heavy taxes be laid either on the sale or the possession of all articles which tend to enervate the moral strength of the people, or to minister to its indolent pleasure; considering such taxes rather as educational than fiscal, rather as fines than sources of revenue, and regulating their distribution with a view rather to their effect on the character of the people than on the prosperity of the exchequer. I do not here enter into details, but it is evident

---

[1] [Compare *Stones of Venice*, vol. iii. (Vol. XI. pp. 197–198), where Ruskin gives as an instance of the world being still in its childhood, "that no nation dares abolish its custom-houses," and *Unto this Last*, § 53.]

there are some articles of luxury, jewels, for instance, of which the harmful effect is chiefly in excess, and which within certain limits might by a moderate duty be made a considerable source of revenue, and beyond certain limits might by heavier duty be nearly prohibited, while there are others altogether injurious, cigars,[1] for instance, on which the duty ought at once to be rendered as far as possible prohibitory.

§ 8. Having thus arranged the excise duties, let the revenue of the country be boldly and permanently provided for by both an income and property tax, the latter only on fortunes exceeding £10,000 (for in the case of fortunes less than this a tax on property is a tax on economy).[2] Let the income tax be 10 per cent. on all fortunes exceeding £1000 a year, and let the weight of it die away gradually on the poorer classes. A man whose income was under £100 a year should pay nothing; above 100, 1 per cent.; above 200, 2 per cent., above 300, 3 per cent., and so on, up to 1000—all fortunes above which should pay 10 per cent.; and in addition to this, there should be a tax on property above £10,000, according to the necessities of the revenue. The resistance made by men receiving small salaries to income tax is exceedingly short-sighted. All work for which regular salary is given, is done in the long run for as small a salary as it is possible to do it for

---

[1] [Ruskin was a sworn foe of tobacco—"the worst natural curse of modern civilisation," he called it (Queen of the Air, § 76); "the most accursed of all vegetables" (Proserpina, i. ch. vi.).]

[2] [The income-tax, it should be remembered, was not at this time regarded as a permanent burden; it had been reimposed by Peel in 1842, for a limited term of years (as was proposed and hoped), in connexion with his free-trade measures. As originally imposed (in 1798 and again in 1803), the tax was graduated on incomes below £200 (1798) or £150 (1803); incomes below £60 were in those years exempt. At the time when Ruskin wrote £150 was the limit of exemption, and there was no graduated scale. In 1853 Gladstone lowered the limit to £100, but levied the tax at a lower rate on incomes between £100 and £150. The principle of graduation (by means of exempting a certain amount of income where the total was below a certain amount) was further carried out in 1861, 1871, 1876, 1894, and 1899. But in none of these cases was any graduation admitted on an income of more than £700. The fuller exercise of the principle, for which Ruskin here argues, was to be seen in Sir William Harcourt's "Death Duties" of 1894. Ruskin returned to the subject in Fors Clavigera (1871), Letter 7.]

in respectability and comfort. Persons at present receiving such salaries are of course grievously oppressed by income tax, but all this will soon settle itself, and all salaries will be increased by the amount of the income tax, the weight of which will therefore bear on employers, and on the public who deal with those employers, not on officials. And as to the weight of it, felt by men living by the variable gains of daily labour, I conceive it wiser to tax the incomes of such men than their savings. A property tax would "dull the edge of husbandry";[1] and still less would it be just or desirable that a man should be able to lay claim to any exemption from income tax because he was in the habit of always living up to his income.

I have occupied enough of your valuable space for the present. I will—if you favour me by the insertion of this letter—proceed to the subject of Election in a future one.

[1] [*Hamlet*, i. 3.]

II

ELECTION

Venice, *March* 11, 1852.

§ 9. *Election.* I pass to the second of the subjects named in my former letter, namely, "Election." If by a "member of Parliament" we at present, in England, understand the mouthpiece of a constituency; a person, that is to say, sent into the House of Commons to express by vote * what he believes to be the opinion of the majority of his constituents on any given question, subject to the penalty of the loss of seat if he venture to express any other opinion, I have nothing to say respecting our principles of election; but in that case it is a pity we take the pains and undergo the agitation of elections at all. It would be wiser and cheaper to make wooden members of Parliament and work them by electric telegraph from the constituent towns and counties.

But if a member of Parliament is in any sort supposed to be a man chosen because he is wiser than other people, in order that, with other such chosen men, he may deliberate on questions too hard for the body of the people to decide (they not having, for the most part, time or opportunity to examine all their bearings), and that, having arrived at conclusions on such questions, the chosen body may declare and put them in practice, irrespective of the opinions of those who elected them—as far, I say, as this is the idea of a member of Parliament, so far our modes of election are simply insane (and if this be *not* the idea of a member of Parliament, any election whatever is useless).

---

* I do not say by advocacy. For if each member's vote is predetermined by his constituents—all advocacy is useless.

§ 10. I say our modes of election under such a supposition are simply insane. Consider a moment. If we want a head servant, we may indeed make inquiries respecting him, as we have opportunity, of every one who knows him; but we shall attach little weight to the opinions except of those whom he has served, and among these we shall be guided finally, in all probability, by the advice of some one person, whom we suppose to be the best judge of a servant's qualities. If we want a tutor for our sons, we shall be still more earnest in our investigations, and still more guarded in our acceptance of testimony, giving weight only to the recommendation of men grave and wise. But if we want a man to be at once servant and tutor to the whole nation, and to form, in limited periods, judgment on questions which the most profound human sagacity cannot altogether fathom, and the decision of which is to affect the interests of millions, for millions of years—who *this* man is to be, we ask every twenty-pound householder in the parish, and we attach exactly equal weight to every man's opinion!

§ 11. Nay, but, it is answered, the cases are not parallel. In the one case the man is to be *your* servant; in the other, he is to be the servant of every man in the parish, and every one has therefore a right to a voice in choosing him.

Unquestionably he has a right; but it is a right he will waive if he is wise. For, take another case. Four men go out to California and club their funds to buy land. Grant their resources equal (which in the case of electors they are not) so that they have all a right to a voice in the selection of the ground to be bought. One is a good geologist, the others do not know gold from iron pyrites. Will they be wise in making the choice of the land a matter of vote, or will the three give up their rights to the geologist, and let him choose for all? Exactly in like manner when golden men, the Heads of Gold, are to be sought for, instead of golden rocks, a nation, if it is not

XII. 2 Q

mad, will give authority in the choice chiefly to those who have already given proof of superior sagacity. Observe, the geologist can prove to his three partners that he *does* know gold from firestone. This proof they must require of him before they allow him to act. He cannot impart to them his knowledge or his experience, but he can easily prove to them that he possesses it. He can tell them that in this or that spot they will find treasure, or that this and that appearance of treasure is deceptive. And they can test his assertions before they trust him in the great assertion which they cannot test, the probable productiveness of a large district.

§ 12. In like manner there are tests of men's sagacity which may at once justify a nation in making those men electors of others, though there is no test of sagacity which will enable a nation at once to fix on the men fittest to act for it and think for it in Parliament. I do not say infallible tests; but evidences, assuredly in the long run indicative of the best men. The first and most natural is age. Much of the misery and evil of Continental systems of policy arises from the absurd weight attached to the acts and opinions of young men. I believe the chief error of Continental nations at present is Rehoboam's,[1] and that it is one of the soonest punished, because one of the most ridiculous errors that men can possibly commit. The second most natural test is wealth. Many a foolish man indeed is wealthy, and many a wise one poor, but in the long run, wealth is an important index of three qualities— sagacity, economy, and method—all of them of much importance in electors, and this without taking into account that a rich man has commonly most interest in the prosperity of the country. The third test is position, and the fourth, education. Position, that is to say, of authority, for the attainment of which certain more or less eminent

---

[1] [1 Kings xii. 8 : " But he forsook the counsel of the old men, which they had given him, and consulted with the young men."]

qualities are necessary, as high military and naval commands, judicial and other civil authorities, governorships, presidencies, and such like; and Education, either specially attested, as by University and other degrees, or proved by generally acknowledged eminence in science, art, and literature.[1]

[1] [The MS. here ends, the letter on " Election " not being finished ; for the nature of an intended third letter, on Education, see above, p. lxxx.]

END OF VOLUME XII

Printed by BALLANTYNE, HANSON & Co.
Edinburgh & London